vegetarian
times COMPLETE COOKBOOK

The Editors of *Vegetarian Times*

Wiley Publishing, Inc.

Published by Wiley Publishing, Inc., Hoboken, New Jersey
Published simultaneously in Canada

For general information on our other products and services or for technical support, please contact our Customer Care Department within the United States at 800-762-2974, outside the United States at (317) 572-3993 or fax (317) 572-4002.

Color photography by Renée Comet.
Food styling by Lisa Cherkasky.
Interior text design by Jay Anning, Thumb Print.

Library of Congress Cataloging-in-Publication Data:

Vegetarian times complete cookbook / by the editors of Vegetarian times.—2nd ed.
    p. cm.
    Includes bibliographical references and index.
    ISBN 0-7645-5959-1 (cloth : alk. paper)
  1. Vegetarian cookery. I. Vegetarian times.
    TX837.V427 2005
    641.5'636--dc22

                                2005004381

Printed in the United States of America

10 9 8 7 6 5 4 3 2 1

contents

acknowledgments

The editors of *Vegetarian Times* are indebted to the many talented professionals who contributed to the creation of this cookbook. Our heartfelt thanks go to manuscript editor Susan Derecskey; recipe editor Sarah Belk King; recipe developer Joyce Piotrowski; nutritionist Katherine Tallmadge; photographer Renée Comet; food stylist Lisa Cherkasky; writer Melanie Mayhew; copy editor Robin Cheslock; and design director Bill McKenney.

Thanks also to Anne Ficklen, our editor at John Wiley & Sons, Inc., whose enthusiasm for this project never wavered; and Mary Ann Naples, our literary agent.

Finally, a hearty thank you goes to food editor Alexandra Greeley, whose selfless dedication to collecting, sorting and editing more than 600 recipes made this book possible; and to editorial assistant Lisa Barley, without whose attention to detail and top-notch computer skills we'd have certainly missed a deadline or two.

CARLA DAVIS
Project Manager
2005 Vegetarian Times Complete Cookbook

the vegetarian decision

VEGETARIAN COOKING HAS NEVER BEEN more popular or easier to enjoy. You don't have to drive a hybrid car, shop in a health food store, grow your own bean sprouts—or even be a vegetarian!—to appreciate the flavors and combinations of vegetarian foods available today. Even if your town has only a handful of zip codes, a trip to your local market likely will reveal an array of taste-tempting vegetables, legumes, fruits, grains, seeds and nuts positioned right alongside protein-rich tofu and soymilk products that many vegetarians have enjoyed for centuries.

It's precisely the accessibility of packaged soy foods and the well-publicized health benefits of a soy-based meatless diet that have pushed vegetarianism into the common vernacular—and pushed traditionally vegetarian foods straight onto grocery store shelves from coast to coast.

While only 2.5 percent of Americans are consistent vegetarians, an estimated 25 percent of us replace meat with meat alternatives for at least some meals. Here's why:

- More of us increasingly understand the connection between the food we consume and our health. Four of the top seven causes of death—heart disease, cancer, stroke and diabetes—are related to diet.

- Concerns about cholesterol have spurred many of us to consider making dietary changes, including reducing our meat consumption and increasing the amount of soy and vegetables we eat.

- Food allergies and lactose intolerance are moving many of us from dairy to nondairy beverages, cheeses and other products.

- From mad cow disease to genetically modified foods to bioterrorism, we're becoming more concerned about our food's safety. We want to know where our food is coming from and where it's been.

- Natural and organic foods, once found only in out-of-the-way or ethnic markets, have gone mainstream. About 70 percent of us say our primary supermarket sells natural or organic foods.

- The definition of dieting has changed. People in their midthirties and older are realizing that a diet can be about living a healthier, more balanced life over the long term. The popularity of South Beach–style low-carb diets as lifestyle choices—not quick weight-loss solutions—reflects this.

- The growing ethnic diversity in the United States, our exposure to TV chefs who highlight regional cuisine and the affordability of international travel all are driving an interest in spicier and more flavorful foods.

Fifty percent of all illnesses could be delayed or eliminated by dietary changes.

Given those facts, it's no wonder that people of all ages, income levels and ethnicities are finding a vegetarian diet appealing. If you're not a vegetarian by definition—that is, a person whose diet excludes meat, poultry and fish—you've probably at one time or another thought about going meatless, or you've tried doing so for a period of time. About 5 million people in the United States have gone meatless for good, and they couldn't be a more diverse group: musicians, politicians, actors, athletes, school kids, professors, artists, entrepreneurs, grandmothers, chefs and countless others!

TYPES OF VEGETARIANS

Here's a look at the five main categories of vegetarians.

LACTO-OVO VEGETARIANS

Motivated by a desire for better health, lacto-ovo vegetarians don't consume any animal flesh, but they do include dairy products (lacto) and eggs (ovo) in their diets. Most vegetarians choose this lifestyle: It's easy to follow and restricted only by your imagination. Because this diet allows for so many possibilities, lacto-ovo vegetarians easily can adapt meat-based menus into meatless ones. Ethnic dishes are especially appealing to lacto-ovo vegetarians because of their complex flavors and their use of grains, beans and other staples in the vegetarian pantry. If you're just considering vegetarianism, the lacto-ovo diet is a great first step.

Although a well-balanced vegetarian diet is inherently healthy, many new vegetarians compensate for not eating meat by overindulging in high-fat dairy products and desserts. It's a common mistake that, with a bit of education and menu planning, a novice vegetarian can easily avoid or correct.

About 80 percent of vegetarians are women.

LACTO-VEGETARIANS

Many Americans become lacto-vegetarians to lower their cholesterol. Lacto-vegetarians don't eat any animal flesh or eggs—both high in cholesterol— but they do consume dairy products. By eliminating eggs, lacto-vegetarians avoid the high-cholesterol yolks that may contribute to coronary heart disease. People also avoid eggs because of food allergies or out of concern for laying chickens, whose factory farm conditions are known to be deplorable. Some people don't eat eggs for spiritual reasons: Hindus, for instance, consider an egg a potential life. Because eggs lurk in everything from baked goods to soups, lacto-vegetarians are avid label readers and are skilled at asking restaurant wait staff whether menu items were prepared with eggs.

OVO-VEGETARIANS

Close cousins to lacto-vegetarians, ovo-vegetarians eat eggs but don't eat milk, butter, cheese and other dairy products. According to the American Gastroenterological Association, close to 50 million Americans are lactose intolerant or have trouble digesting the sugar, or lactose, found in milk and dairy products. As a result, they may experience abdominal bloating, flatulence, nausea or diarrhea after consuming milk or dairy products. A vegetarian who says no to dairy products also can take a stand against the milk industry, which engages in controversial practices such as injecting dairy cows with hormones to increase milk production and feeding antibiotics to cows whose udders have become infected, often due to unsanitary conditions.

VEGANS

Entirely plant-based, the vegan diet excludes all animal products, dairy products, eggs and honey. Because vegans (VEE-guns) seek to avoid exploitation of animals for all purposes, including food and clothing, most don't wear leather, wool or silk. They don't want to contribute to the harming or killing of animals for any reason. Still, it's extremely difficult for us to eliminate all traces of animal products from our lives, even if we make a conscious decision to do so. Products and processes that exploit animals can be found in countless foods, including maple syrup, sugar and marshmallows, and in everyday products including automobile tires, shampoos and videotapes.

About 1 percent of vegetarians are vegans; many of them started as lacto-ovo vegetarians. While the lifestyle is indeed strict, committed vegans tend to shrug off any inconveniences. Because dining out is problematic, most vegans cook at home and have perfected a number of tantalizing recipes, many of which we share in these pages.

SEMI-VEGETARIANS/FLEXITARIANS

Can you eat meat and still call yourself a vegetarian? Sure, many of us do it all the time, although it's technically incorrect. People who are vegetarian most of the time but who occasionally eat fish, poultry or meat are best described as semi-vegetarians, or flexitarians. The terms also describe people who eat fish and poultry but skip meat, or who regularly eat lots of vegetables. The Vegetarian Resource Group estimates that flexitarians make up as much as 40 percent of the US population. As we increasingly understand the connection between the food we eat and our health and welfare, this number undoubtedly will rise.

People are drawn to vegetarianism by all sorts of motives. Some of us want to live longer, healthier lives or do our part to reduce pollution. Others of us have made the switch because we want to preserve Earth's natural resources or because we've always loved animals and are ethically opposed to eating them.

Thanks to an abundance of scientific research that demonstrates the health and environmental benefits of a plant-based diet, even the federal government recommends that we consume most of our calories from grain products, vegetables and fruits. And no wonder: An estimated 70 percent of all diseases, including one-third of all cancers, are related to diet. A vegetarian diet reduces the risk for chronic degenerative diseases such as obesity, coronary artery disease, high blood pressure, diabetes and certain types of cancer including colon, breast, prostate, stomach, lung and esophageal cancer.

Why go veg? Chew on these reasons:

- **You'll ward off disease.** Vegetarian diets are more healthful than the average American diet, particularly in preventing, treating or reversing heart disease and reducing the risk of cancer. A low-fat vegetarian diet is the single most effective way to stop the progression of coronary artery disease or prevent it entirely. Cardiovascular disease kills 1 million Americans annually and is the leading cause of death in the United States. But the mortality rate for cardiovascular disease is lower in vegetarians than in nonvegetarians, says Joel Fuhrman, MD, author of *Eat to Live: The Revolutionary Formula for Fast and Sustained Weight Loss.* A vegetarian diet is inherently healthful because vegetarians consume less animal fat and cholesterol and instead consume more fiber and more antioxidant-rich produce—another great reason to listen to Mom and eat your veggies!

- **You'll keep your weight down.** The standard American diet—high in saturated fats and processed foods and low in plant-based foods and complex carbohydrates—is making us fat and killing us slowly. According to the Centers for Disease Control and Prevention (CDC) and a division of the CDC, the National Center for Health Statistics, 64 percent of adults and 15 percent of children aged 6 to 19 are overweight and are at risk of weight-related ailments including heart disease, stroke and diabetes. A study conducted from 1986 to 1992 by Dean Ornish, MD, president and director of the Preventive Medicine Research Institute in Sausalito, California, found that overweight people who followed a low-fat, vegetarian diet lost an average of 24 pounds in the first year and had kept off that weight five years later. They lost the weight without counting calories or carbs, and without measuring portions or feeling hungry.

- **You'll live longer.** If you switch from the standard American diet to a vegetarian diet, you can add about 13 healthy years to your life, says Michael F. Roizen, MD, author of *The RealAge Diet: Make Yourself Younger with What You Eat.* "People who consume saturated, four-legged fat have a shorter life span and more disability at the end of their lives. Animal products clog your arteries, zap your energy and slow down your immune system. Meat eaters also experience accelerated cognitive and sexual dysfunction at a younger age."

Want more proof of longevity? Residents of Okinawa, Japan, have the longest life expectancy of any Japanese and likely the longest life expectancy of anyone in the world, according to a 30-year study of more than 600 Okinawan centenarians. Their secret: a low-calorie diet of unrefined complex carbohydrates, fiber-rich fruits and vegetables, and soy.

- **You'll build strong bones.** When there isn't enough calcium in the bloodstream, our bodies will leach it from existing bone. The metabolic result is that our skeletons will become porous and lose strength over time. Most health practitioners recommend that we increase our intake of calcium the way nature intended—through foods. Foods also supply other nutrients, such as phosphorus, magnesium, vitamin D and lactose, that are necessary for the body to absorb and use calcium. Dairy products—milk, cheese, ice cream and yogurt—are the most concentrated natural sources of calcium.

    People who are mildly lactose intolerant can often enjoy small amounts of dairy products such as yogurt, cheese and lactose-free milk. But if you avoid dairy altogether, you can still get a healthful dose of calcium from dry beans, tofu, soymilk and dark green vegetables such as broccoli, kale, collards and turnip greens.

- **You'll reduce your risk of food-borne illnesses.** The CDC reports that food-borne illnesses of all kinds account for 76 million illnesses a year, resulting in 325,000 hospitalizations and 5,000 deaths in the United States. According to the US Food and Drug Administration (FDA), foods rich in protein, such as meat, poultry, fish and seafood, are frequently involved in food-borne illness outbreaks.

- **You'll ease the symptoms of menopause.** Many foods contain nutrients beneficial to perimenopausal and menopausal women. Certain foods are rich in phytoestrogens, the plant-based chemical compounds that mimic the behavior of estrogen. Since phytoestrogens can increase and decrease estrogen and progesterone levels, maintaining a balance of them in your diet helps ensure a more comfortable passage through perimenopause.

    Soy is by far the most abundant natural source of phytoestrogens, but these compounds also can be found in hundreds of other foods such as apples, beets, cherries, dates, garlic, olives, plums, raspberries, squash and yams. Because menopause is also associated with weight gain and a slowed metabolism, a low-fat, high-fiber vegetarian diet can help ward off extra pounds.

- **You'll have more energy.** Good nutrition generates more usable energy—energy to keep pace with the kids, tackle that home improvement project or have better sex more often, Michael F. Roizen, MD, says in *The RealAge Diet*. Too much fat in your bloodstream means that arteries won't open properly and that your muscles won't get enough oxygen. The result? You feel zapped. Balanced vegetarian diets are nat-

Until 1847, vegetarians were known as Pythagoreans. The name came from the Greek philosopher Pythagoras (580–500 BC), whose writings on beans and cabbage made a case for vegetarianism in his day.

urally free of cholesterol-laden, artery-clogging animal products that physically slow us down and keep us hitting the snooze button morning after morning. And because whole grains, legumes, fruits and vegetables are so high in complex carbohydrates, they supply the body with plenty of energizing fuel.

- **You'll be more "regular."** Eating a lot of vegetables necessarily means consuming more fiber, which pushes waste out of the body. Meat contains no fiber. People who eat lower on the food chain tend to have fewer instances of constipation, hemorrhoids and diverticulitis.

- **You'll help to reduce pollution.** Some people become vegetarians after realizing the devastation that the meat industry is wreaking on the environment. According to the US Environmental Protection Agency (EPA), chemical and animal waste runoff from factory farms is responsible for more than 173,000 miles of polluted rivers and streams. Runoff from farmlands is one of the greatest threats to water quality today. Agricultural activities that cause pollution include confined animal facilities, plowing, pesticide spraying, irrigation, fertilizing and harvesting.

- **You'll avoid toxic chemicals.** The EPA estimates that nearly 95 percent of the pesticide residue in the typical American diet comes from meat, fish and dairy products. Fish, in particular, contain carcinogens (PCBs, DDT) and heavy metals (mercury, arsenic, lead, cadmium) that can't be removed through cooking or freezing. Meat and dairy products can also be laced with steroids and hormones, so be sure to read the labels on the dairy products you purchase.

- **You'll help reduce famine.** About 70 percent of all grain produced in the United States is fed to animals raised for slaughter. The 7 billion livestock animals in the United States consume five times as much grain as is consumed directly by the American population. "If all the grain currently fed to livestock were consumed directly by people, the number of people who could be fed would be nearly 800 million," says David Pimentel, professor of ecology at Cornell University. If the grain were exported, it would boost the US trade balance by $80 billion a year.

- **You'll spare animals.** Many vegetarians give up meat because of their concern for animals. Ten billion animals are slaughtered for human consumption each year. And, unlike farms of yesteryear where animals roamed freely, today most animals are factory farmed— crammed into cages where they can barely move and fed a diet tainted with pesticides and antibiotics. These animals spend their entire lives in crates or stalls so small that they can't even turn around. Farmed

In a lifetime, according to the authors of The Animal Rights Handbook, *the average meat-eating American will consume 1 calf, 3 lambs, 11 cattle, 23 hogs, 45 turkeys, 1,097 chickens, and 15,665 chicken eggs.*

animals are not protected from cruelty under the law—in fact, the majority of state anticruelty laws specifically exempt farm animals from basic humane protection.

- **You'll save money.** Meat accounts for 10 percent of Americans' food spending. Eating vegetables, grains and fruits in place of the 200 pounds of beef, chicken and fish each nonvegetarian eats annually would cut individual food bills by an average of $4,000 a year.

- **Your dinner plate will be full of color.** Disease-fighting phytochemicals give fruits and vegetables their rich, varied hues. They come in two main classes: carotenoids and anthocyanins. All rich yellow and orange fruits and vegetables—carrots, oranges, sweet potatoes, mangoes, pumpkins, corn—owe their color to carotenoids. Leafy green vegetables also are rich in carotenoids but get their green color from chlorophyll. Red, blue and purple fruits and vegetables—plums, cherries, red bell peppers—contain anthocyanins. Cooking by color is a good way to ensure you're eating a variety of naturally occurring substances that boost immunity and prevent a range of illnesses.

- **It's a breeze.** It's almost effortless these days to find great-tasting and good-for-you vegetarian foods, whether you're strolling the aisles of your local supermarket or strolling down the street at lunchtime. If you need inspiration in the kitchen, look no further than the Internet, your favorite bookseller or your local vegetarian society's newsletter for culinary tips and great recipes. And if you're eating out, almost any ethnic restaurant will offer vegetarian selections. In a hurry? Most fast food and fast casual restaurants now include healthful and inventive salads, sandwiches and entrées on their menus. So rather than asking yourself why go vegetarian, the real question is: Why *haven't* you gone vegetarian?

nutrition

MANY OF US REMEMBER THE FOUR FOOD groups—meats, dairy, grains, and fruits and vegetables—from elementary school, where our well-meaning teachers told us that we needed to eat from each group daily to be healthy. The US Department of Agriculture Food Guide Pyramid's suggestion of eating 2 to 3 servings each day of meat, poultry or fish is enough to make any vegetarian cringe. Thankfully, there's plenty of proof that a vegetarian diet is extremely healthful.

THE FOUR FOOD GROUPS
AND THE FOOD GUIDE PYRAMID

With all of the scientific research and studies backing up a vegetarian diet as the healthiest diet, why does the USDA Food Guide Pyramid still recommend so much meat? And although vegetarian sources of protein are much healthier than the steaks and drumsticks pictured in the pyramid, why do beef and poultry get top billing?

Fortunately, many groups and organizations have created vegetarian versions of the pyramid and other food charts. Here is a basic chart that sums up vegetarian dietary recommendations.

vegetarian dietary recommendations

FOOD GROUP	SERVING SIZE	SUGGESTIONS
Whole Grains 6–11 servings daily	1 slice bread ½ cup cooked grains, cereal or pasta ½ cup hot cereal 1 ounce dry cereal	whole-grain bread, brown rice, pasta, seitan, cereal, corn, barley, bulgur, kasha, rice cakes, tortillas
Vegetables 3–5 servings daily	1 cup raw vegetables ½ cup cooked vegetables 1 cup salad ¾ cup vegetable juice colorful	vegetables (carrots, squash, sweet potatoes), green leafy vegetables (broccoli, collards, kale, spinach), mushrooms
Fruits 2–4 servings daily	1 medium whole fruit ½ cup chopped fruit ¾ cup fruit juice ¼ cup dried fruit	apples, bananas, oranges, pears, peaches, grapes, strawberries, cherries, melons, kiwi
Legumes, Protein Sources 2–3 servings daily	1 cup cooked legumes ½ cup tofu or tempeh 1 veggie burger or dog ¼ cup nuts or seeds 2 cups soymilk	beans (soy, black, navy, pinto, lima, kidney), lentils, chickpeas, tofu, tempeh, textured vegetable protein (TVP), nuts (almonds, pine nuts, peanuts, walnuts)
Milk, Calcium Sources 2–3 servings daily	½ cup milk 1 cup yogurt 1½ ounces cheese ½ cup fortified juice 1 cup high-calcium greens	soymilk, ricemilk, soy cheese, soy yogurt, tofu, fortified orange juice, kale, collards, broccoli, okra
Fats, Oils, Sweets use sparingly	2 to 3 teaspoons oils (use the rest sparingly)	oils (flax, canola, olive, safflower, peanut, etc), salad dressing, margarine, butter, candy

BEYOND THE RDAs

Our needs for different nutrients have long been expressed in terms of Recommended Dietary Allowances (RDAs). The guidelines for RDAs were developed in 1941 and represent the quantities of nutrients that you need to get at various life stages to avoid certain deficiency diseases. These recommendations are general, applying to adults and children 4 years of age and older (separate information is available for younger children and pregnant or lactating women), and they often allow for some leeway. Nutrient needs are usually determined by body size, calorie intake and a number of other factors, including age and gender, although every person's nutrient needs are unique. However, to keep things simple and give people one number to work with, RDAs are often higher than most people need for optimal health.

Government organizations revise nutritional information periodically. There is some confusion in thinking that the RDA refers to daily eating, and that people need to get 100 percent of every nutrient, every day. That's simply not true. What is important is meeting your nutrient needs over time so that your *average* intake is close to the RDA.

The Dietary Reference Intakes (DRIs) are the new standard of nutrient reference values. DRIs provide four different types of nutritional reference, including RDAs. The others that you may not be as familiar with are the Estimated Average Requirement (EAR), the Adequate Intake (AI) and the Tolerable Upper Intake Level (UL). These four references have replaced the 1989 RDAs, and they help paint a broader picture of our nutritional needs, from minimum requirements to avoid deficiency diseases to the maximum that can be safely ingested. They are also used as a reference point when RDAs cannot be determined. The EAR, based on scientific research, is the amount of a nutrient that meets the needs of most healthy people. If the EAR for a nutrient cannot be determined, or if current research is inconclusive, the AI is used. The AI is an estimate of the amount of a nutrient needed to meet the needs of most healthy people. The UL adds another dimension to the DRIs, letting people know how much of a nutrient is too much—it shows the highest amount of a nutrient that can be safely consumed.

If this sounds complicated, don't worry. As long as you are eating a healthful, varied vegetarian diet, you are very likely meeting all of your nutritional needs. As you will see, many foods are good sources of multiple nutrients, and nutrients often work together to keep us healthy.

FAT

"Fat" used to be a bad word, the classic shorthand for heart disease, cancer and a host of other health problems. But nutritional experts have learned that some dietary fats are essential to our systems. Fats help maintain body temperature and protect our organs, and they form an important partnership with the fat-soluble vitamins, A, D, E and K.

It is recommended that 20 to 25 percent of the calories we consume daily come from fat, but saturated fats and trans fats—"bad" fats— should account for no more than 10 percent of the total fat intake. Saturated fats, commonly found in meat and dairy products, and trans fats, found in fried foods, cookies, popcorn, pies, frostings, pastries and hydrogenated oils, lurk in vegetarian foods, so read packages carefully. These fats can increase cholesterol levels.

The "good" fats—monounsaturated and polyunsaturated fats—tend to lower LDL ("bad") cholesterol levels in the blood and are found mostly in plant sources, including vegetable oils and nuts.

Vegetarians eat a good deal less fat than nonvegetarians. High-fat diets increase your risk for obesity, diabetes, heart disease and cancer, so continue to make healthful choices.

CHOLESTEROL

Cholesterol intake should not exceed 300 milligrams (mg) per day. Too much cholesterol in the blood will raise your risk for atherosclerosis, a buildup of fatty deposits in arteries and blood vessels, which puts you at risk for a heart attack.

High-density lipoprotein (HDL) and low-density lipoprotein (LDL) are found in the bloodstream and affect cholesterol levels. LDLs deposit cholesterol in the artery walls, while HDLs help to remove cholesterol from the blood. You have probably heard references to "good" and "bad" cholesterol, and that refers to HDL and LDL respectively.

Fortunately for our hearts, lacto-ovo vegetarians consume about 200 mg of cholesterol a day, while vegans consume none. And meat eaters? A worrisome 500 mg each day. It's no wonder heart disease is such a widespread problem.

FIBER

Another category where vegetarians lead the pack! It is recommended that we get between 25 and 30 grams (g) of fiber daily to reduce indigestion, constipation and cholesterol, and to prevent heart disease and some cancers. Meat eaters get only about 12 g of fiber each day. Vegetarians eat two to four times this much!

Fiber-rich foods include whole grains, legumes, raw vegetables and fruits. It's deliciously easy to get all the fiber that you need on a vegetarian diet.

Myth: Vegetarians are food faddists.

Reality: Some vegetarians eat tofu, sprouts and granola regularly; others don't. Some vegetarians shop in natural food stores; the majority shop in supermarkets. Some vegetarians make their meals from scratch; few of us have the time. The upshot: What you eat is a matter of choice.

Rennet is an enzyme in the lining of cows' stomachs and is used in the making of cheese. An animal byproduct, rennet is added to milk to speed up the curdling process. (The thin liquid that remains is known as whey.) After the curds form, they are pressed together and aged to make cheese. Rennetless cheese is available. Look for phrases such as "rennetless," "made with vegetable rennet" or "contains no animal coagulant" on cheese packages if you don't want to eat cheese with rennet.

PROTEIN

Guess what? If you're eating enough calories, you're getting enough protein—unless your diet consists of alcohol, sugar and fats, the only foods lacking this important nutrient. The RDA for protein is 50 g. Protein is crucial to every cell in our bodies in a variety of ways. Bones, muscles, many hormones and antibodies all contain protein, and protein is essential to the structure of red blood cells. Deficiency is rare in Western countries, but too much protein can worsen kidney problems and may increase the risk of osteoporosis. Too much animal protein in particular causes calcium loss from bones.

Before you think that less protein might be better, it's important to note that plant proteins tend to be less digestible than animal proteins, so vegetarians often need to take in more protein than nonvegetarians. A simple solution is to get your protein from a variety of sources: Vegetables, grains, beans, nuts and seeds are all high in protein, so vegetarians have plenty of healthful options.

CALCIUM

Calcium does a body good, and you don't need an ounce of cows' milk to get it. The total calcium in the adult body weighs about three pounds, and nearly all of it is in our teeth and bones; about 1 percent is in the bloodstream. In fact, it is actually more important to have healthy levels of calcium in your blood than in your bones. The reason? If there isn't enough calcium in your bloodstream, you body will take calcium from your bones to make up for it. The RDA for calcium is 1,300 mg for 9–18 year olds, 1,000 mg for 19–50 year olds, and 1,200 mg for adults older than 51, and the UL for calcium is 2,500 mg. Too much calcium can cause kidney problems and inhibit the absorption of iron, zinc and magnesium.

A study at the University of Texas Health Science Center showed that a vegetarian diet may lead to healthier bones, because of the sources of protein and calcium in the diet. The subjects in the study ate the same amounts of protein and calcium. One diet supplied protein from meat and cheese; the second included protein from soy foods, eggs and cheese; and the third included protein from soy foods only. When the subjects got their protein from meat and cheese, they lost 50 percent more bone calcium than when they got their protein from soy foods alone. When they got their protein from soy foods, eggs and cheese, their calcium loss fell between the other two.

Sodium also increases calcium excretion, and some studies have shown that diets containing too much phosphorus may affect bone health as well.

Healthful sources of calcium include broccoli, kale, collard greens, bok choy, beans, tofu prepared with calcium, tempeh, sea vegetables and fortified soymilk.

IRON

Don't worry about being "big and strong" without meat! Healthful vegetarian diets actually contain more iron than diets that include meat. The RDA for both men and postmenopausal women is 10 mg. Since premenopausal women lose more iron during menstruation, their RDA is 15 mg. Iron's most important role is in the production of hemoglobin, which carries oxygen throughout the body. This mineral is important for growth and maintaining a healthy immune system. About 25 percent of the body's iron is found in the liver.

Iron deficiency is a concern in the United States, however. One in six children and 10 to 25 percent of the general US population are affected by iron-deficiency anemia. Very young children, teenagers and premenopausal women are most at risk for iron deficiency.

Iron isn't very well absorbed by the body, especially when a diet includes dairy products, but a healthy intake of vitamin C has been shown to increase iron absorption. This is good news for vegetarians, who tend to have high intakes of vitamin C. Healthful sources of iron include green leafy vegetables, beans and legumes, whole grains, dried fruits, and watermelon. Spinach, broccoli, Swiss chard, and vitamin C–fortified cereals are rich in both iron and vitamin C.

Vegetarian meals are the most commonly requested special meal on airplanes.

VITAMINS

Vitamin B12

Considering that the RDA for vitamin B12 is only 2.4 micrograms (mcg) per day—and 1 mcg is about one thirty-millionth of an ounce—it may seem surprising to hear of so many people worrying about this vitamin. However, B12 is needed for cell division, and a deficiency over the years can lead to permanent nerve damage. Although a B12 deficiency initially manifests itself in the form of anemia, people who eat enough folic acid will not develop anemia and may not discover their B12 deficiency until it has gotten more serious.

This vitamin comes primarily from animal foods, including dairy and eggs. Tempeh and sea vegetables may contain some B12, but whether or not this is a reliable source is up for debate.

The best bets for vegetarians are foods that are fortified with B12, such as nutritional yeast, cereals and soymilks. However, read packaging very carefully to make sure that the product has been fortified. When some cereal manufacturers list nutritional information, they include the milk they assume you are pouring over it. In this case, you would be getting B12, but not from the cereal.

Non-animal-derived supplements are also available. There is no reason to take a 50 mcg supplement—you'll only absorb 1 or 2 mcg from it. Currently, much research is being done about the importance of this vitamin, along with examining its sources, so expect more information.

Vitamin A and the Carotenes

Vitamin A, a group of three compounds (retinol, retinaldehyde, and retinoic acid), is necessary for healthy vision, skin, reproduction, growth and maintaining a healthy immune system. Humans can get vitamin A from animal foods, but we can make our own vitamin A by eating plants containing carotenoids. Carotenoids are what give fruits and vegetables their bright colors; the most common carotenoid is beta-carotene. Beta-carotene (along with some other carotenoids) is an antioxidant, which protects cells against disease. Vitamin A from animal sources has no antioxidant properties.

The RDA for vitamin A is 1,000 retinol equivalents (RE) for men and 800 RE for women. (One RE is equal to 1 mcg of vitamin A, 6 mcg of beta-carotene, or 12 mcg of any of the other carotenoids.) A vitamin A deficiency is rare in Western countries but very serious elsewhere. Vitamin A deficiency is the leading cause of childhood blindness, with a half million children developing vision problems every year. While vitamin A can be toxic in large doses, carotenoids are not toxic. The only side effect for those who ingest large doses of beta-carotene (usually in the form of carrot or tomato juice) is an orangy skin color. However, this is neither harmful nor permanent, and skin returns to normal after they stop ingesting such large amounts of beta-carotene.

Foods rich in carotenoids include carrots, broccoli, peppers, spinach, sweet potatoes, squash, pumpkins, tomatoes, mangoes, apricots and melons.

Vitamin B1 (Thiamin)

This vitamin is used to convert carbohydrates to energy and also to help the nervous system function properly. We need about 0.5 mg of B1 for every 1,000 calories we eat. The RDA for B1 is 1.2 mg for men and 1.1 mg for women. Beriberi is the disease associated with vitamin B1 deficiency, and it involves serious damage to the cardiovascular and nervous systems, which can lead to paralysis.

Vegetarians get plenty of this vitamin by eating whole grains, nuts, legumes, soy foods, nutritional yeast and brewer's yeast.

Vitamin B2 (Riboflavin)

Like the other B vitamins, vitamin B2 works with the enzyme systems in our bodies. The RDA for this vitamin is 1.3 mg per day for men and 1.1 mg for women. Because it has so many functions in the body, deficiency

If Americans abandoned their meat-centered diets, 200 million acres could be reforested.

symptoms can be widespread, from anemia to skin disorders to neurological problems.

Strong sources of B2 include legumes, soybeans, broccoli, asparagus, mushrooms, avocados, whole grains and even enriched refined grains. If you are taking a supplement and notice that your urine has turned bright yellow, that is the excess B2 leaving your body.

Vitamin B6 (Pyridoxine)

Our bodies use vitamin B6 in dozens of enzyme systems, but mostly for protein metabolism and cell growth. Since B6 and protein share an important relationship in this way, the amount of B6 you need is proportional to the amount of protein that you consume. The RDAs for this vitamin are 1.3 mg for men and women. A deficiency of this vitamin is rare and usually occurs when a diet is nutritionally lacking overall. Most studies show that vegetarians have a healthy intake of B6.

Proportionally, plant foods contain more B6 in relation to protein than animal foods. Another plus for vegetarians—the B6 in plant foods is less likely to be destroyed during cooking. You can get healthful amounts of B6 by eating unrefined whole grains, brown rice, oats, soybeans, nuts and bananas. Some studies have shown fiber to inhibit B6 absorption, but high-fiber foods are often high in B6, so things seem to even out.

Vitamin C

No worries here—vegetarians consume much more vitamin C than meat eaters do and much more than the RDA of 90 mg for men and 75 mg for women. Vitamin C is used to maintain the connective tissues in our bodies and to build healthy teeth, gums and blood vessels. A deficiency of this important vitamin can lead to scurvy and a breakdown of tissues that will cause bleeding throughout the body. This antioxidant has also been shown to help maintain a healthy immune system.

Get plenty of vitamin C while enjoying broccoli, spinach, Brussels sprouts, tomatoes, potatoes, peppers, collard greens, citrus fruits and strawberries.

Vitamin D

Vitamin D is unique. Not only is it a vitamin *and* a hormone, but our bodies can only make it when we are exposed to sunlight. Also, it is one of the only hormones that we can get through diet.

Our bodies use vitamin D to maintain normal levels of calcium in the blood and to increase calcium in the bones. Studies have shown a positive relationship between vitamin D and the immune system, the skin, the pancreas and perhaps even the prevention of cancer.

The AI for adults is 5 mcg, but it has been difficult to identify vitamin D needs because the amount we need to get from our diets is related to how

Foods grown organically (without chemicals) are preferred to foods treated with herbicides, fungicides and other "-cides."

much vitamin D our bodies make from sun exposure. While we can get all of the vitamin D that we need from sun exposure, factors that make sunlight less accessible (smog, cloudiness, sunscreen) can make it more difficult to meet our needs this way. Also, people with darker skin need even more sun exposure to synthesize vitamin D.

Vitamin D deficiency in children can lead to rickets, a disease involving stunted growth and deformed bones. In adults, a deficiency results in excessive bone loss. Too much vitamin D can irreversibly harm your kidneys and heart and may be a risk factor for Alzheimer's disease. As little as four times the RDA for vitamin D can be very harmful for children.

Many people inaccurately believe that milk is a natural source of vitamin D. This is not the case; milk is fortified with vitamin D. However, vitamin D is added to very large amounts of milk and may not be dispersed evenly throughout all of the milk. Samples from the US milk supply have shown that some milk contains very little vitamin D while other samples contain several times the amount allowed by the government. Because of similar problems and the fact that too much vitamin D presents serious health risks, Great Britain no longer fortifies its milk supply.

Fortunately, soymilks and other vegan milks are fortified with vitamin D in much smaller batches, making the vitamin D content safer and more reliable. Many cereals are also fortified with vitamin D. If you decide to take a supplement (plant-based formulas are available), make sure that it provides no more than 5 mcg of vitamin D. Fair-skinned adults can synthesize adequate vitamin D with 15 minutes of sun exposure on their faces and hands two or three times a week. It is also worth noting that our bodies can store vitamin D for months, so summer exposure can carry us through the less sunny winter months.

Vitamin E

Like vitamin A, vitamin E is made up of a number of compounds (eight, in this case), so the RDA for this nutrient is expressed in terms of tocopherol equivalents (TE). The RDA for vitamin E is 15 mg of TE for men and women. Vitamin E deficiency is a rare problem, usually only occurring in premature babies or in people who have problems with absorption. Anemia is the most noticeable symptom of this deficiency, but adults with a long-term deficiency can develop neurological problems.

Vitamin E is an antioxidant, protecting red blood cells. It has been linked to the prevention of heart disease and cancer. Because of vitamin E's relationship with polyunsaturated fats, the amount that we need is related to our intake of polyunsaturated fats. Since vegetarians tend to get most of the fat in their diets from polyunsaturated fats, they may need more vitamin E. The good news? Foods that are high in this type of fat are usually high in vitamin E, too.

Vegetable oils are an excellent source of vitamin E, especially soybean, corn, safflower or cottonseed oils, as are margarine, wheat germ, sweet potatoes, greens and nuts.

Vitamin K

Necessary for blood clotting, vitamin K is also involved in the synthesis of the proteins found in the bones and kidneys. The RDA for this nutrient is 120 mcg for men and 90 mcg for women. The average vitamin K intake in the United States is more than four times the RDA. Fortunately, vitamin K (unlike other fat-soluble vitamins) is not toxic, even at high doses. However, it's important to note that synthetic forms of the vitamin can be toxic in very high doses. Vitamin K deficiency is rare, although people with absorption problems may experience prolonged bleeding since their blood will not clot. Newborn babies are also susceptible to this deficiency because this nutrient does not reach the fetus very well and is not abundant in breast milk. However, newborns in the United States receive vitamin K injections at birth.

Vitamin K is found in many foods, but the best sources are leafy green vegetables such as spinach, lettuce, kale and cabbage. Other sources include cauliflower, wheat bran and some fruits.

Folic Acid

Vegetarians often have levels of folic acid that are as high as three times that of nonvegetarians. The RDA for folic acid is 200 mcg for men, 180 mcg for women, and 400 mcg for women who are pregnant or may become pregnant. Folic acid is important for cell division, the metabolism of proteins, digestion and the healthy development of a fetus. Deficiency results in anemia.

Foods rich in folic acid include green leafy vegetables, orange juice, legumes, nuts, brewer's yeast and some fruits.

Niacin

Our bodies actually convert tryptophan, one of the essential amino acids, into niacin. About 60 mg of tryptophan becomes 1 mg of niacin. For this reason, the RDA for this vitamin is conveyed as niacin equivalents (NE). The RDA for men is 16 mg and 14 mg for women.

Niacin is needed for energy metabolism, normal digestion and a healthy nervous system. Dark green, leafy vegetables are a good source of this nutrient.

MINERALS

Zinc

The RDA for this mineral is 11 mg for men and 8 mg for women. Our bodies use zinc for cell growth, blood health, making new proteins in the body

Vegans avoid all animal products; however, vegans should include protein, vitamins B12 and D, omega-3 fats, calcium and iodine in their diets to ensure optimal health.

and maintaining a healthy immune system. Since zinc is not stored in our bodies, a deficiency can manifest quickly. Complete deficiency of zinc is rare in Western countries, but a consistently low zinc intake can result in lack of appetite, growth problems and a longer recovery from injury. Many people, regardless of diet, have zinc intakes lower than the RDA, although their blood levels tend to still be in the normal range. This could be because of the safety cushion that was applied when the RDAs were developed.

Phytate, fiber and calcium can inhibit zinc absorption. Healthful sources of zinc include legumes, oatmeal, brown rice, spinach and nuts.

Potassium

The minimum RDA for potassium is 1,600–2,000 mg. Most people easily surpass this, especially vegetarians—whose diets naturally tend to be high in potassium. Our bodies use potassium to maintain fluid balance, nerve function, and muscle health. Large amounts of potassium in the diet may lower blood pressure and improve bone health. Potassium is found in bananas, potatoes, broccoli, legumes, orange juice, nuts, spinach, and many other fruits and vegetables.

Iodine

Iodine is essential to the formation of the thyroid hormones, which are needed for healthy growth and energy. The RDA for iodine is 150 mcg. Iodine deficiency disappeared in the United States after the addition of iodine to commercial table salt. One teaspoon of iodized salt contains about 400 mcg of iodine, so it's easy to see why most of us don't need to worry about this nutrient. Sea vegetables also are a reliable source of iodine.

Magnesium

This mineral is crucial to bone health. The RDA for magnesium is 420 mg for men and 320 mg for women. Although most of us don't meet the RDA for magnesium, vegans and vegetarians have higher levels of this mineral than nonvegetarians. Whole grains, nuts, legumes and green vegetables are excellent sources of magnesium.

Selenium

This antioxidant protects cells, and some research shows that selenium has a role in the prevention of breast cancer and heart disease. The RDA for this mineral is 55 mg for men and women. Although selenium deficiency is very rare, it can result in heart-damaging diseases.

Sources of selenium vary based on the selenium of the soil in which the food was grown. Good sources of selenium include nuts, vegetables and whole grains. Although soil content may seem unreliable, vegetarians and nonvegetarians have comparable levels of selenium in their bodies.

Sodium

Our bodies need sodium to help maintain blood pressure and the function of nerves and muscles. Although the RDA is to consume less than 2,400 mg per day (about 1 teaspoon of table salt), the average daily intake in the United States is 4,000–5,000 mg. Sodium deficiencies are certainly not common, and many people need to reduce their sodium intake drastically.

Sodium is an essential nutrient, but ingesting more sodium than our bodies need can lead to high blood pressure, which in turn puts us at risk for heart attacks, kidney disease and strokes. Vegetarians aren't exempt from high sodium intakes and, like everyone else, should examine the sodium in their diets. Use less salt during cooking, and let your foods and herbs provide the flavor. Read packaging carefully, because canned beans, soups and meat analogs are among the many foods that can be alarmingly high in sodium. Draining and rinsing canned beans before cooking will help to reduce their sodium content.

Fluoride

Fluoride is important for good dental health, because it protects tooth enamel and reduces decay. Some studies have shown it helps keep bones healthy as well. This mineral is added to the water in most Western countries, so it isn't difficult to get between 1.5 and 5 mg per day. Excessive fluoride intake over several years can result in damage to the kidneys, but most people maintain healthful levels of this mineral.

Copper

This mineral may reduce the risk of heart disease. Although there is no RDA for copper, 1.5–4 mcg daily of this mineral appears adequate for health. Copper deficiency is rare and usually happens only if someone is malnourished. Healthful sources of copper include whole grains, legumes and nuts.

Chromium

This mineral stimulates insulin activity and helps in the metabolism of sugar. Chromium also helps to control the levels of fat and cholesterol in the blood. There is no RDA for chromium, but the safe and adequate range for adults is 20–200 mg. Good sources of this mineral include whole grains and fruit juices.

Manganese

This mineral is crucial to enzyme structure, and manganese deficiencies are rare. Vegetarians take in much more manganese than nonvegetarians do, but the requirements for this mineral seem to be quite low. It is recommended that we get 2 to 5 mg of manganese daily, which isn't difficult, because many vegetarian foods are rich in this mineral, including whole grains and cereals, legumes, nuts, vegetables and fruits.

Casein is found only in dairy products and is integral to cheesemaking. It helps make cheese melt. If you buy a casein-free cheese pizza, expect the cheese to get warm but not gooey.

Molybdenum

Molybdenum is essential for the healthy metabolism of fats, carbohydrates and iron. It is recommended that we get at least 75 mcg of this mineral daily. Dark green, leafy vegetables, legumes and whole grains are good sources of molybdenum.

NUTRITION AND SPECIAL NEEDS

PREGNANCY

Wash all vegetables thoroughly, but avoid soaking them. Nutrients can be lost in the water.

Without question, a vegetarian pregnancy is a healthful choice for both you and your baby, even before he or she is born. The American Academy of Pediatrics, the National Academy of Sciences, the American Medical Association and the American Dietetic Association all recommend having a vegetarian pregnancy and raising a vegetarian infant.

Keep in mind that pregnancy is not the time to quickly change from eating meat to eating legumes and grains. Any radical diet change is not easy for your body, especially on top of being pregnant. Also, suddenly changing from a high-protein, high-fat diet to a vegetarian diet can mean digestive discomforts such as gas and reduced nutrient availability for a while—something you don't want if you're nourishing a baby. A more reasonable approach is to gradually change your diet, ideally before you become pregnant.

If you're already a vegetarian, you're on your way to providing a healthful environment where your baby can develop. During the first eight to ten weeks of pregnancy, the baby uses nutritional stores that are already in the mother's body. Since many women do not realize they are pregnant during the first month, it is important to be well-nourished before conception.

When looking for an obstetrician, try to find a doctor who is either a vegetarian or who is familiar with the vegetarian diet. A supportive, educated doctor will eliminate the frustration of dealing with someone who may think you need to eat meat to have a healthy pregnancy. A nutritionist may also be helpful, especially if you want to avoid taking unnecessary supplements. Having approval of medical professionals can also ease the worries of any friends or relatives who may be concerned that you're not eating meat.

If you're unable to find a doctor who is knowledgeable about the vegetarian diet, take this opportunity to educate him or her about your choice. Many vegetarian Web sites and the Web sites of the previously mentioned health organizations can link you to information about scientific studies you can share with your doctor. Even though your doctor may not have been familiar with this information before, you're doing him or her a great service that will assist future patients who may share your diet!

To nourish a growing baby, pregnant women need to eat about 300 extra calories each day. These extra calories and nutrients will let you and your baby share a healthy pregnancy.

It is recommended that pregnant women gain a total of 25 to 30 pounds gradually during pregnancy. A weight gain of less than 5 pounds in the first 12 weeks, then a gain of a pound or two a week thereafter is best. This number may vary for women who were underweight or overweight before pregnancy.

The key for vegetarians is choosing nutrient-dense foods such as nuts and seeds. One cup of almonds will provide you with 837 calories, 28 g of protein, 378 mg of calcium, 5.2 mg of iron and 83 mcg of folate. Simply eating an additional one-half cup of nuts a day can give you most of the extra nutrients that your body needs. Also choose from these food products to increase your intake of calories, protein, vitamins and minerals: blackstrap molasses, brewer's yeast, dried figs, granola, natto (fermented whole soybeans), nut butters, nuts, soybeans, soy nuts, tempeh, tofu pudding, tortula yeast and toasted wheat germ. Many doctors also recommend that pregnant women take prenatal vitamins. These supplements can be a healthful addition to a wholesome vegetarian diet and should be taken as directed by your physician.

Make sure that your carbohydrate intake is adequate — and that it does not come just from junk foods. Eat nutrient-dense whole grain foods; they are better for you and your baby.

Dieting during pregnancy is a bad idea. Low birth weight has been tied to inadequate weight gain in mothers, and a lower birth weight can result in an increased risk of health problems and learning disabilities for your baby.

As your body grows and changes during pregnancy, you may notice changes in your eating habits. Many women experience some form of nausea or morning sickness early in pregnancy. Don't worry that your baby might not be getting enough nutrients just because you can't always keep down food. During the early stages of pregnancy, your baby will be getting most of its nutrients from what you have stored from before you became pregnant, and the prenatal vitamins will help ensure adequate nutrition for your developing baby. Many women also find that certain types of food contribute to their nausea—even some meat eaters can't stomach the thought of eating meat when they're pregnant! Some women may find that vegetarian foods they once loved—spicy bean dishes or leafy greens, for example—now turn their stomachs. Be patient, listen to your body and experiment with different types of food to satisfy both your hunger and your need for nutrients. Eating low-fat, high-carbohydrate foods, which are digested faster, and avoiding foods with strong smells may help.

Cancers that are most directly caused by diet are sometimes known as "hormonal cancers," because eating certain types of foods increases the number of cancer-causing hormones in our bodies. Breast, prostate and colon cancer are particularly linked to red meat consumption.

Luckily, vegetarian women get the digestive advantage in pregnancy. During pregnancy, the digestion process becomes more efficient, with higher percentages of each nutrient being absorbed. Meat takes much longer to be broken down than vegetarian foods, and if meat sits in the digestive tract, it will begin to rot and putrefy. Therefore, pregnant meat eaters are more likely to experience pain from gas and constipation.

Of course, vegetarians certainly aren't exempt from foods that cause gas. Some foods that are most likely to cause gas during pregnancy are beans, onions, dried fruits, Brussels sprouts, cabbage and broccoli. To help prevent or alleviate gas problems during pregnancy, eat slowly and chew your food thoroughly. Broccoli is extremely nutritious, and eating broccoli soup may not give you as much gas as eating it raw or lightly cooked. To reduce the flatulence-producing effects of beans, presoak them, cook them for a longer time over a lower heat, and/or add some kombu (a sea vegetable) or a bay leaf to the beans before or during cooking. If you do experience pain from digestion, try eating foods that are rich in digestion-enhancing enzymes such as avocados, bananas, mangoes, sprouts, papayas and pineapples.

If you're planning a pregnancy, it's a smart idea to have your iron level checked before pregnancy and a month or two after you become pregnant. Iron is used more rapidly in the body during pregnancy and helps your baby grow. Having strong iron levels before conception will help keep your iron levels from dropping too low during your pregnancy. Vegetarians can keep their iron levels high by eating iron-rich foods such as whole grains, legumes and dark green leafy vegetables. For best results, eat iron-rich foods with foods or juices that are high in vitamin C—this helps your body absorb the iron. Avoid drinking milk, tea or coffee with iron-rich foods, because they can cut your absorption of iron by half.

Grains, vegetables and fruits form the foundation of the US Department of Agriculture's Food Guide Pyramid.

Contrary to what many people believe, you don't need to drink several glasses of cows' milk a day to get the calcium you need to help your baby's bones form. In fact, you don't need to drink any cows' milk at all! Turn to calcium-rich foods such as soymilks and spreads, dark green vegetables (broccoli, spinach, kale, collard greens, mustard greens, chard, etc.), tofu processed with calcium sulfate, and legumes such as pinto beans, black beans and soybeans. It's important to note that spinach and chard contain oxalic acid, which can inhibit the absorption of calcium, so eat those vegetables with rice, which contains an oxalic-acid neutralizing substance.

Other good reasons that you don't need cows' milk during pregnancy? You and your baby will be ingesting the same growth hormones and antibiotics given to many cows.

Also, by avoiding cow's milk, you may avoid painful leg cramps that are common among pregnant women. There is evidence that an imbalance of calcium, phosphorus and magnesium causes this problem. Since milk is a high-phosphorus calcium source, many pregnant women find relief by seeking out sources of calcium that are lower in phosphorus and avoiding processed foods and carbonated drinks.

Vitamin D is important in helping pregnant women properly absorb calcium, so make sure that you have adequate vitamin D in your diet. Look for foods that are vitamin D–enriched, such as soymilk and some cereals. If you aren't getting adequate vitamin D, ask your doctor about taking a supplement.

Worries about proteins are outdated; anyone who thinks vegetarians don't get enough protein doesn't know much about the diet. Vegetarians get lots of protein from legumes, nuts, seeds, root vegetables, whole-grain breads, cereals and pastas. In fact, many vegetarians have higher protein levels than meat eaters and often have enough protein prepregnancy to support a baby. If you're concerned, evaluate the protein sources in your diet to make sure that you're getting enough.

Zinc is another important nutrient in which some pregnant women are deficient. Dairy is a significant source of zinc for many women, but vegan women can get zinc from plant foods such as peas, beans, brown rice, spinach, nuts, tofu and tempeh. Zinc from plant foods is less easily absorbed, so increase your intake of zinc-rich foods.

All pregnant women hear about the importance of folic acid in their diets to prevent birth defects such as spina bifida in their babies. Because folic acid is most important to a baby during its early development (when most women do not even know they are pregnant), women of childbearing age should make sure they are getting adequate folic acid, either from their diets or from supplements. Vegetarians who eat a balanced diet are almost guaranteed to have sufficient amounts of folate. One cup of lentils provides nearly two-thirds of the daily requirement of folate for pregnant women. Other good sources include dark leafy greens, whole grains and orange juice. And folic acid is added to many foods such as cereals. Again, read nutrition labels and examine your diet to see if you may need to take a supplement.

Vitamin B12 is also important during pregnancy and breastfeeding. A B12 deficiency can cause anemia and damage to the nervous system. Although vitamin B12 is found in animal products such as milk and eggs, vegans need not worry. More and more vegan foods are fortified with vitamin B12, such as soymilk, meat analogs, cereals and nutritional yeast. Be sure to read labels carefully, and don't assume that a product contains B12 unless the package clearly states that the product has been fortified with B12. If you are concerned about getting adequate B12 from foods, take a supplement.

Now that you know what to keep an eye on during your pregnancy, enjoy the nutritious, delicious foods that will prepare your baby to enter the world healthy and happy. If you have questions or concerns, be sure to check with your doctor or nutritionist. And, if you're eating healthful, wholesome, nutrient-dense foods overall, don't forget to allow yourself treats now and then!

BREASTFEEDING

From birth to at least six months, the American Pediatric Association says that exclusive breastfeeding is best for babies. Not only does breastfeeding fulfill your baby's dietary requirements, it is naturally structured for easy digestion and emotionally and socially nourishes your baby. Breast milk strengthens a baby's immunity in ways that infant formulas can't, especially in the first few days after birth. It's also the most economical way to feed your baby.

If you breastfeed, you still need to pay attention to what you're eating. In fact, breastfeeding mothers have slightly higher calorie, protein and vitamin B12 needs than pregnant women, although the iron needs diminish a bit. So, continue your healthy diet from pregnancy, paying special attention to the areas where you need to be getting more nutrients. If you're eating a balanced diet, your breast milk (and your baby!) will have all the necessary nutrients.

People who live in industrialized countries are exposed to many contaminants, including pesticides and antibiotics and hormones in meat and dairy products. Because contaminants are fat soluble, it's harder for our bodies to get rid of them. Unfortunately, one of the routes by which they can leave the body is through breast milk. Several states and Canada have recommended that women have their milk tested for safety.

Fortunately, this is another time when eating a vegetarian diet pays off. Studies have shown that the milk of most vegetarian mothers has only 1 to 2 percent of the contaminants found in the milk of meat-eating mothers. For women with high levels of contaminants, breastfeeding might not be a wise choice, but this is far less likely to occur in vegetarian women.

Dairy milk and soymilk are not adequate replacements for breast milk or infant formulas. Regular milks do not provide the complete nutrition that your baby needs, so stick with breast milk or infant formula.

If you are considering not breastfeeding, research your decision carefully. Breast milk is nature's most perfect food for babies, and eating properly will help you provide the best possible milk for your baby. Oh, and you won't be alone—studies show that vegetarian moms are more likely than meat eaters to breastfeed their infants.

CHILDREN

Babies can start experimenting with "real foods" around 6 months of age. Some are ready a month earlier; some aren't ready until later. Start with small amounts of iron-fortified infant rice cereal. Once your baby becomes comfortable eating this food, introduce new foods one at a time. Follow rice cereal with other cereals such as oats, barley and corn. Then begin offering your baby well-mashed or puréed vegetables such as potatoes, carrots or green beans. Next, introduce your baby to the sweet taste of fruits: Well-mashed bananas, peaches or pears are a good place to begin.

Feed small amounts of only one food for several days to watch for an allergic reaction. If your baby shows a sensitivity—gas, diarrhea, vomiting, a rash, crankiness, runny nose—discontinue feeding her that food and try it again in a few weeks or months.

If one parent is not a vegetarian, it's important to agree on dietary guidelines early on. For example, will you raise your child on a certain diet (lacto-ovo or vegan)? How will meals be prepared in the home? Are occasional meat-eating episodes acceptable (i.e., at a restaurant with the non-vegetarian parent)? It is important to discuss your desires in regard to your child's diet, and to support each other in your decisions.

If friends or relatives treat you as if you are harming your child by feeding him a vegetarian or vegan diet, share with them the thought that you have put into your child's nutrition. Explain that your child gets his nutrients (including protein) from a variety of sources and that you are careful to include B12-fortified foods in his diet if necessary. If your doctor has commented on your child's good health, tell that to people who question his diet. Often, seeing how happy and healthy your child really is will be enough to get friends and relatives to at least tone down their criticisms.

If you find yourself fielding a lot of questions about your family's diet, don't automatically be insulted. Most people who become vegetarian have learned about it from a friend or relative. Be proud of your choice when people ask you about your diet, and don't be afraid to share your reasons for it and the benefits you've experienced.

If you choose to introduce dairy milk to your child, watch carefully for signs of allergic reaction or lactose intolerance, especially if you are a member of certain ethnic groups (Hispanics, Asians, people of African descent, Native Americans). Keep in mind that there are plenty of nutritious dairy-free alternatives to cows' milk, including soymilks and ricemilks. A number are fortified with calcium and vitamins A and D to make their nutrients comparable to those of cows' milk—without the hormones or pesticides.

Don't make the mistake of overloading your child's diet with eggs and dairy just because he isn't eating meat. This will result in a diet that is fatty and loaded with cholesterol. However, if your child does not eat any animal foods, make sure to give him B12-fortified foods, or ask your doctor about a supplement.

You've made the decision to go vegetarian. Should you take the gradual approach, cutting back on nonvegetarian foods over time, or rid your home of meat, poultry and fish overnight? Either way is okay. Most important, pick the method that suits you (do you warm up slowly to new ideas or prefer to dive right in?), and experiment in the kitchen with new recipes.

Children under the age of two need fats in their diet for proper growth and development. At this age, they need concentrated calories, and, gram for gram, fat has more than twice the calories as carbohydrates or protein. Breast milk derives about half of its calories from fat. When your child reaches the age of two, he should eat a low-fat diet, getting between 20 and 25 percent of total calories from fat.

If your child goes through a phase where she refuses to eat the food you put before her, don't worry—children will eat when they're hungry. But don't let them have sugary or fatty snacks like candies or chips. Have healthy foods on hand, like fruits and sliced veggies, for snacks.

Some children turn their noses up at cooked vegetables, but they may just prefer the raw version that is more colorful and crunchy. At mealtimes, if you're cooking vegetables, set aside a portion of uncooked vegetables for your child, and serve them with the rest of the meal.

If your child develops a sweet tooth and wants sweet treats all the time, don't forbid sweet-tasting food entirely. Simply offer healthy options, such as fruits, banana bread, oatmeal and raisin cookies, and blueberry muffins. If your family eats good, healthy foods regularly, it's okay to have treats like cupcakes occasionally, but don't let candy or junk foods be the only sweet treats in your house.

To avoid fights with your toddler about his not wanting to eat or try a new food, offer only a small amount of the new food (along with other foods) to allow your child to try it. At this age, toddlers want to assert themselves and may even refuse to eat foods you know they like. Your toddler can try the food and say no, and you won't have wasted food or spent a meal fighting. And if the does like it, he just might ask for more!

As your child gets older, he may notice that his friends or relatives eat foods that he doesn't eat, or that other kids seem to have a lot of fun going to fast food restaurants. Explaining your decisions in simple terms may help your child understand why his diet may be different than that of his friends. In fact, it may instill a sense of pride. Tell your child that being a vegetarian keeps your family healthy and strong, or that you're a vegetarian because you care about animals and don't want to eat them.

Children have a natural fondness for animals, which often are the subject of their storybooks and videos. Now is a good time to talk to them about your values in relation to animals. Teaching your children that living creatures deserve care and respect will instill important values in them, often for the rest of their lives.

Children this age are also extremely curious—you may hear "Why?" fifty times a day! But this is a great time to teach your children about nutrition and healthy choices. They love learning, and involving your children in cooking and gardening is a great way to introduce them to the importance of food choices.

Estimates indicate that 35 to 50 percent of cancers in the United States may be diet related. The two types with the strongest links to fat consumption are breast and colon cancers.

Letting children make some decisions about what they eat can increase their acceptance of different foods. Offer small amounts of a variety of foods for your child to try or introduce one new food at a meal with some of their favorites. But keep mealtimes enjoyable. Don't force your child to eat. If you act unfazed by your child's refusal to try a certain food, he may be more likely to try it the next time it's offered.

If you think your child is at an age where he can understand how meat production hurts animals, start having an open discussion. A good first step is explaining the connection between names for food and names for animals—beef and hamburgers are cows, pork and bacon are pigs, veal is a baby calf. Talk about how these are the same animals that used to be alive. Try to stay neutral as you talk; if you get very emotional, your child may pick up your feelings but tune out the information you're sharing.

Now is also a good time to explain the differences between good food and junk food. Use advertisements on television and in magazines to show your child that each company wants to make their product look as exciting as possible so that you will buy it and give them money. But most companies aren't worried about nutrition. Show him that some foods that look fun actually have lots of yucky things in them that aren't good for people to be eating.

As your child gets older, and you feel confident that he can handle the details, you might explain factory farming. There's no need for gruesome details at this point; simply explain that animals are kept in small cages or stalls and aren't allowed to have the carefree life pictured in children's books.

Once your child begins spending mealtimes away from your home, it will become more difficult to control his diet. If your child is in daycare, talk to the care providers about what kind of meals and snacks are served and if there are healthful vegetarian options available. Sometimes simple alterations can be made—for example, meatballs can be served separately if spaghetti is one of the meals. Suggest healthy snacks be served a few times a week (you could even volunteer to provide them). Another option is packing your child's lunch and snacks daily, but if your child feels left out, she may still try to eat what the other kids are having. It's often best to find a daycare that respects your dietary choices or one that has vegetarian options regularly.

Other challenging situations may arise when your child plays at a friend's home where meat is served, or is invited to a birthday party where hot dogs and cake are on the menu. Will you allow your child to eat meat in these situations because it is not a regular occurrence, ask the party hosts to provide a peanut butter and jelly sandwich for your child, or feed your child beforehand and tell him or her just to eat the cake? Young children are very aware if they are being singled out for any reason, so keep this in mind.

Helping your school-aged child make healthy choices can be difficult when at least one of his meals is spent away from home. Most school lunches are laden with meats, fried foods, fats and sodium and can hardly be called nutritious.

An easy alternative is to pack your child's lunch, but make sure that it is kid friendly and not something his friends will make fun of, or it may end up uneaten. Ask your child about the types of things he'd like to have for lunch. Some kids may enjoy eating tofu and sprouts at lunch, but most kids probably want a lunch that looks similar to what their friends are having.

Vegetarians tend to have lower blood pressure than non-vegetarians.

Try interesting, flavorful options like peanut butter and jelly sandwiches with ricotta cheese, cheese and vegetable sandwiches with a pickle, peanut butter and banana or tahini and banana sandwiches, fresh fruits, air-popped popcorn, low-fat and fat-free cookies, yogurt and baked tortilla chips.

You can always try talking to the school about its lunch program and ask if it would be possible to offer vegetarian options, at least occasionally. Stress that it's unlikely that your child would be the only one to eat this option if it were available. If you know of other vegetarian families at the school, talk to them about what they would like to see on the menu at school and then bring your concerns to the school at the same time.

As your child progresses in school, his friends will play a more important role in his life, and your child may feel he doesn't fit in if he isn't eating pepperoni pizza or hotdogs. Help your child feel more comfortable by letting him choose the meal when he has friends over. If his friends like to hang out at fast-food restaurants, encourage him to suggest places for them to go. Mexican restaurants, even fast-food ones, offer plenty of vegetarian choices, and pizza places easily have options for everyone. Your child doesn't need to force his friends to eat tofu, and they don't need to eat somewhere where a burger is the only option.

If your child needs further help to feel accepted by his peers, look into activities that are not food based, such as sports, music, student government or church youth groups. He'll still find himself in situations where the team stops at a hot dog stand after a game, but it won't be the focus of their gatherings.

If your child becomes overly self-righteous about being vegetarian, perhaps saying rude things to meat-eating classmates or relatives, have a talk with him about respecting differences. After all, if he wants to be accepted and accommodated, why should he say hurtful things to others who are different from him? Praise his commitment to vegetarianism, but remind him that it's better to discuss his choices only occasionally or with people who want to talk about it.

If your vegetarian child is the butt of jokes at school because of her diet, talk to her about teasing and let her know that it is not her fault that she is being teased. Point out examples of famous vegetarians. If a celebrity that your child and her friends admire is a vegetarian, she's less likely to feel that her differences are negative. If your child is comfortable, consider talking to her class about vegetarianism. Bring tasty vegetarian treats and baked goods.

Join a local vegetarian group or spend time with other friends and family who are vegetarian. Your child won't feel alone if he has vegetarian friends who enjoy the same things he does.

In junior high and high school, children are reaching the age where differences are more widely accepted. Your child who was teased in grade school for not eating meat might now find that she is considered cool for it!

Teenagers can find support for their vegetarianism in many places. Check if there are vegetarian or environmental groups in your community. With supervision, allow your teen to look for vegetarian chat groups on the Internet. Your teen could also subscribe to vegetarian periodicals such as *Vegetarian Times.*

However, if your child wants to eat meat when she is with her friends to fit in, it's more difficult to fight it at this age. Studies have shown that most children who are raised vegetarian become vegetarian adults, even if they eat meat for a period in between. So letting your child experiment with meat eating doesn't mean that she's throwing away everything that you've taught her about nutrition. Also, having a big confrontation or guilt trip about a hamburger may make your child more reluctant to talk to you and perhaps even more likely to eat meat out of rebellion. Continue to serve your same nutritious meals at home, and don't cook meat for your child unless you really want to. Your example is important and you have more of an effect than you know!

Even though some vegetarian teens—even those who happily ate healthily as vegetarian children—go through a major junk food phase, don't worry too much. Tossing nutritional facts their way probably won't change their behavior. Teens often care about health only where it might concern their weight or appearance. Encourage your teen to eat healthily, and continue to provide healthy snacks around the house. You can ban junk food in your house, but you won't be able to control his choices outside of the house. Hopefully your concerns will be alleviated by knowing that the diets of vegetarian teens—even in a junk food phase—are healthier than those of their meat-eating peers.

If your child or teenager decides to become a vegetarian, and your family eats meat, you may view his newfound eating habits as rebellious. But remember that he hasn't made a decision that is harmful. In fact, it's healthy! Try to be supportive of his decision, and keep an eye on his nutrition. You may feel like you don't know much about vegetarianism, but that doesn't mean that you should let your child plan out his diet all on his own.

Of the 127 million overweight adults in the United States, 60 million are obese and 9 million are severely obese.

Soda, potato chips, candy bars, doughnuts and french fries are all meatless, but that doesn't make them healthy. Also, your child can't be a vegetarian on peanut-butter-and-jelly sandwiches alone.

Encourage your child to eat a variety of foods, including whole grains, legumes, vegetables and fruits while limiting her consumption of fats and sweets. She may decide to eat dairy products and eggs, or she may avoid those as well.

Decide how household meals will work. Will you allow your child to prepare his own meals every night? Will you have occasional meatless meals as a family? Preparing vegetarian meals together (or helping your child prepare the meatless part of her meal) will not only help you learn more about your child's new diet, but you'll also be spending quality time together.

Talk to your child about his new diet and his reasons for it in a nonaccusatory manner. Approach your child's vegetarianism with an open mind.

If your family decides to become vegetarian, remember that the older your children are, the more difficult the transition may be. Talk to your children about why you are making the decision to go meatless, and encourage them to explore vegetarianism. They might be open to the change right away, or you may need to compromise, at least at the beginning.

Try slowly cutting down on the meat you're eating. Serve meatless meals every other night, and when you do have meat, use smaller portions of meat and larger portions of vegetables, legumes and grains. Use less and less meat in your cooking until you are using none at all.

Be sure to introduce your family to vegetarian meals with tasty, exciting options. Have a burrito night, pizza with veggie toppings, pasta, veggie kabobs with rice, even breakfast for dinner. Also involve family members in dinner preparation. If your family is excited about the food that they're making and eating, the transition will be a lot easier.

Meat analogs made from soy, tempeh and seitan may entice your formerly meat-eating family. Your kids may still enjoy eating burgers or having "meat" crumbles in food. However, serving tofu or tempeh right away before your family learns to enjoy meatless meals may not be a smart idea. Use small amounts of tofu at first, and don't worry if your kids try to pick around it.

As you make the transition, consider allowing your kids to eat meat occasionally. If you don't allow them to eat any meat, they may want it more. At least you know they're eating healthily the rest of the time.

Whether your children have been meatless since day one or are making the transition to vegetarianism, keep in mind that they are taking part in healthy eating habits that can benefit them for the rest of their lives. Vegetarian children eat less fat and more fiber than nonvegetarian children, and they also eat more fruits and vegetables. They are also slimmer and

The number of calories from fat in a typical meal from the US government's school lunch program is a whopping 38 percent.

have lower cholesterol levels than nonvegetarian children. Some studies have even shown vegetarian children to be above average in their mental development—now that's food for thought!

A vegetarian diet is a healthy, delicious adventure in foods, and committing your family to this diet is a wonderful gift that you can give them for the rest of their lives.

OLDER ADULTS

There are many great reasons to continue your vegetarianism into your golden years, not the least of which is that many major studies have found that vegetarians live five years longer than the general population.

Whether you've been a vegetarian for decades or are considering becoming one now, a vegetarian diet can help you get all the nutrients that you need, alleviate symptoms of aging and even prevent some diseases altogether. Aging doesn't have to mean pain, illness and a cabinet full of prescription drugs; a healthy diet can help you stay active and healthy for longer, so take control of your health—today!

For years scientists have assumed that nutrient needs decrease as we age, but after studying older adults, many realized that seniors need more of certain nutrients. As we age, our bodies become less efficient in absorbing nutrients, so we often need to take in more nutrients to make up for it.

Recent studies published in major medical and nutritional journals have shown that nutritional deficiencies can cause symptoms like dementia and memory loss. Their determination? That eating foods rich in folic acid such as lentils, dark leafy greens, whole grains, and orange juice can improve mental functioning. Also try brewer's yeast, or taking a folic acid supplement if necessary.

Other studies point to a vitamin B12 deficiency as responsible for senile dementia. B12 is an important nutrient anyway, and vegetarians and vegans should take care to make sure they get ample amounts of it. For lacto-ovo vegetarians, eggs and milk can provide some B12. Many vegan foods are fortified with B12, so look for soymilks, cereals and nutritional yeast that have been fortified. Another approach is to take a B12 supplement.

Vitamin E is another nutrient to be aware of. Adequate intake of this vitamin significantly lowers the risk of heart attacks and cancer as well as strengthens the immune system. Get vitamin E while enjoying nuts and nut butters, vegetable oils (especially safflower and wheat germ oil), sweet potatoes, cabbage, parsnips, green vegetables and mangoes. Some doctors also recommend a supplement of between 100 IU and 400 IU of vitamin E.

Older adults can't absorb calcium as well as they used to, so it's important to get enough in your diet to keep your bones healthy. A diet that is too high in protein and sodium can speed up the loss of calcium from bones, so meat eaters have a higher risk of suffering from osteoporosis. Still, eat plenty of calcium-rich foods like dark green vegetables, tofu processed with calcium sulfate, legumes and soymilk.

Most seniors can (and should) take part in light exercise. Try walking, using an exercise bike or swimming. Working with light weights can improve muscle mass no matter how old you are. Talk with your doctor to determine the type of exercise that is right for you.

Older adults don't need as many calories as they used to, but since they still need high levels of nutrients, this can pose a challenge for some. The solution is to eat nutrient-rich foods and avoid foods that are "empty calories," with little or no nutritional value.

Many seniors struggle with household tasks like cooking because of joint pain, vision problems or unsteadiness. Some are no longer comfortable with driving, which makes it more difficult to keep cupboards stocked. There are several options for older adults who have trouble in the kitchen.

Family, friends and neighbors can be one of your best resources. Many older adults don't like to ask for help out of fear that they are a burden, but family and friends usually want to help. They can assist with the purchase and preparation of food.

Another option is using a meal delivery service, such as Meals on Wheels. While vegetarian meals through this service are not available in all areas, it is possible to make a special request to have non-vegetarian items left out of a dish. Having at least some foods prepared for you can be a big help. Also, your local vegetarian society can be a great resource to help you with information and to work with you to find vegetarian meals.

Most vegetarian societies meet regularly to share vegetarian meals, either at restaurants or a member's home. Call your local group to find out if transportation to events is available. Even if you haven't been involved before, new members can always add something to a group. Senior centers and churches also often sponsor meal get-togethers for older adults and almost always offer transportation to their events. In this case, you will need to ask if vegetarian options are available. You may be surprised at how accommodating groups can be, and it's likely that others will share your concern.

If you are more mobile, consider putting an ad in your church bulletin or in senior newsletters to see if there is enough support to start your own group of vegetarian adults who can meet for meals. Sharing healthy meals and companionship will nourish both your body and your mind—very important at any age.

All nursing home residents have the right to have vegetarian meals in accordance with the Nursing Home Reform Law. Simply speak to your dietitian or a cafeteria supervisor to let them know about your dietary

Soybeans contain more protein than beef, more calcium than milk, more lecithin than eggs, and more iron than beef.

preferences. If you are not pleased with the meals you are given, contact the Vegetarian Resource Group, the Vegetarian Nutrition Practice Group of the American Dietetic Association or the Physicians Committee for Responsible Medicine. They can work with your institution to educate them about nutritional information and materials for preparing tasty and well-balanced vegetarian dishes.

If you're able to prepare meals in the kitchen, there are many food options that are healthy and easy to make. Utilize tools in your kitchen that will make cooking simpler. A microwave is an excellent time-saver when cooking or reheating foods. A freezer is a great tool. Cook a large amount of food and freeze it in small batches for reheating later. You can also freeze whole-grain breads, muffins and bagels. Use your blender, food processor or grinder to do your chopping, dicing and mixing for you. Slow cookers make nutritious meals with little work on your part.

Here are some easy-to-prepare foods that are also nutritious:

- Potatoes baked in the microwave

- Fruit juice blended with a banana in the blender

- Toasted bagels with fruit spreads

- Cereal with milk

- Instant oatmeal

- Pasta with sauce from a jar and a salad

- Canned vegetable soup with toast

- Steamed frozen vegetables

- Instant brown rice with canned beans

- Vegetable and bean soup in a slow cooker

- Frozen veggie burgers

- Peanut butter and banana sandwiches

Many seniors are on a tight budget, but a healthy diet needn't be expensive. Look for inexpensive foods that will provide a lot of nutrients. Great options include beans, potatoes, rice, oatmeal, peanut butter, and fresh fruits and vegetables.

The government has estimated that by 2030, one out of five Americans will be 65 or older, and 150 million of them will suffer from chronic diseases. Vegetarianism is linked to a lower risk of heart disease, cancer, high blood pressure, diabetes, osteoporosis, and dementia. Seniors in general are at a higher risk for all of these diseases, and it's important to realize that a balanced vegetarian diet can help.

There are approximately 2.1 million farms in the United States. Of those, 0.2 percent are organic.

It's never too late to make a difference in your health. Many arthritis sufferers find that they have less pain when they remove animal products from their diet, diabetics have an easier time keeping their insulin at a healthy level, and most people report that they simply feel better overall. Many older vegetarians are living longer, healthier lives—it's time to join them!

DISEASE PREVENTION AND MANAGEMENT

HEART DISEASE
Research indicates that diets devoid of meat and dairy are responsible for lower rates of cancer, high blood pressure, diabetes, obesity and, notably, heart disease. Heart disease kills 1 million Americans annually. Vegetarians who maintain diets low in fat or saturated fat have much healthier hearts than non-vegetarians and consequently live significantly longer lives than non-vegetarians. One 12-year study says that vegetarians have 20 percent less heart disease compared to the general population.

Studies of Seventh-Day Adventists (members of a Protestant denomination that promotes vegetarianism as a method of caring for one's body) have proven that vegetarians have lower risks of heart attacks, strokes and other types of circulatory illnesses, because vegetarians have lower blood cholesterol levels. Although vegetarians don't necessarily eat low-fat diets, they eat less saturated fat than non-vegetarians. Additionally, the 50 to 100 percent more fiber found in vegetarians' diets assists in lowering blood cholesterol levels, because phytochemicals within plant foods have antioxidant properties that make it difficult for blood cholesterol to stick to artery walls.

In a landmark study published in 1990, Dean Ornish, MD, determined that a low-fat vegetarian diet can actually reverse heart disease. Ornish asserted that eating a low-fat diet, exercising and practicing meditation can unclog arteries and improve the efficiency of the heart. Ornish insisted that heart surgery and drug therapy did not cure patients; instead, they merely delayed the next heart attack.

For his study, Ornish placed an experimental group of 48 patients with severe heart disease on his nearly-vegan diet program, with a fat intake of less than 10 percent of overall calories; the control group followed the usual advice of the American Heart Association to keep fat intake at no more than 30 percent of overall calories. After only one week, the experimental group participants had fewer chest pains, less depression and more energy. Within a month, their blood cholesterol levels were markedly lower, and their blood flow had improved, allowing many in the experiential group to stop using antihypertensive and cardiac medications. In contrast, after a year, the heart conditions of the people in the control group

Rice bran, oat bran and other types of bran add a bit of flavor and a lot of nutrients—most notably, fiber—to your meal. Bran is the outer layer of the grain. In various studies, the intake of bran has been shown to have positive effects, such as lowering blood cholesterol levels and alleviating constipation.

had worsened, with more blockage in their arteries than before they had adopted the American Heart Association's diet for heart-disease patients.

Before heart disease strikes you, here are a few things you can do to help prevent it.

- Eat foods that are rich in vitamin E. Research indicates that a risk factor for dying from heart disease is a low blood level of vitamin E, an antioxidant nutrient. Researchers believe that it protects low-density lipoproteins (so-called "bad cholesterol") from oxidizing in the bloodstream, thereby slowing or preventing the buildup of deposits on artery walls. The richest dietary sources of vitamin E include whole wheat, wheat germ, nuts and oils; however, go easy on the nuts and oily foods because they are high in fat.

- Avoid saturated fat. Saturated fats (found in meat, eggs, dairy products and tropical oils)—not dietary cholesterol—have the strongest influence on blood cholesterol levels, followed by excess of total calories and then dietary cholesterol intake.

- Exercise regularly. People who are routinely physically active reduce their risk of heart disease by half.

- Avoid smoking tobacco.

- If you are overweight, try to lose weight. A 5 or 10 percent reduction in body weight can significantly lessen your risk of heart disease.

- Reduce stress in your life as much as possible and learn stress management skills.

- Teach yourself and your children good eating habits. Forty percent of US coronary heart disease cases are linked to diet.

CANCER

Between 35 and 50 percent of US cancer cases are related to diet. The American Cancer Society suggests that Americans modify their diets to prevent this deadly disease, which kills more than 500,000 people in the United States each year. The National Cancer Institute encourages diets rich in beta-carotene—an antioxidant and the plant form of vitamin A—and vitamins C and E, which may lessen the chance of developing certain cancers. Combined, they turn unstable molecules, which can wreak havoc in the body (possibly leading to cancer growth), into stable molecules by swapping electrons with other molecules).

Reducing the fat in your diet may decrease the risk of cancer, heart attacks and strokes. Worldwide, a population's incidence of breast, colon and prostate cancer reflects total fat intake, including saturated fats such as butter and unsaturated fats such as vegetable oil. Fat intake varies among countries such as Japan, Italy and the United States, and this intake is directly proportional to the breast cancer deaths in each of these countries.

On average, the Japanese take in 40 grams of fat a day and have five annual breast cancer deaths per 100,000 people, says John A. McDougall, MD, a leading author on the benefits of a very low-fat vegetarian diet. Italians, who use a lot of olive oil and eat twice as much fat as the Japanese, have fifteen annual breast cancer deaths per 100,000 people. The average fat intake of Americans is about 100 grams a day, and breast cancer claims twenty lives per 100,000 each year.

For the China Health Project, scientists from Cornell University in New York, Oxford University in England, the Chinese Academy of Preventative Medicine and the Chinese Academy of Medical Sciences gathered detailed lifestyle and dietary habits of 6,500 Chinese (100 Chinese in each of 65 counties). Many epidemiological studies, which analyze statistics of large groups to form links between disease and their causes, sometimes are not exact enough to provide convincing results. China is different. Because the Chinese tend to stay in the same place and eat the same foods for their entire lives, the effect of diet on health is apparent. Conclusions from the research indicated that people living in counties where the diet is refined and high in protein and fat have a higher incidence of cancer than those in areas where a traditional grain-based diet is the norm. Also, fiber seems to protect against cancer, especially colon cancer, which the American Cancer Society estimated would kill 29,089 men and 27,281 women in the United States in 2004. Fiber-rich diets may reduce the risks of colon and rectal cancers, says the National Cancer Institute, and cabbage-family vegetables may decrease the risk of developing colon cancer, the second leading cause of cancer death in the United States.

One twelve-year study says that vegetarians have 40 percent less cancer compared to the general population, and vegetarians have considerably lower rates of prostate and colorectal cancers. Mark and Virginia Messina, authors of The Dietitian's Guide to Vegetarian Diets, say that the lower cancer rates among vegetarians are directly attributable to vegetarians' lifestyle decisions: "Vegetarians are generally more health conscious, smoke less, drink less alcohol, are often more highly educated and are leaner than the general population."

So, what does the next century hold for cancer victims? Keith Block, MD, medical director of the Cancer Treatment Program at Edgewater Medical Center, Chicago, predicts that the medical community will be so well-versed about the impact of nutrition on disease that it will be standard care to advise therapeutic diets for patients suffering from cancer and other medical disorders.

"And way before [twenty years from now], there will be a successful national vegetarian fast-food chain that will serve chickpea burgers and

Corn is used in more than 800 different processed foods.

low-fat sweet potato fries. It may not have golden arches—perhaps a deep broccoli green or carrot orange," he predicts.

Before you become a cancer victim, here are a few things you can do to prevent the deadly disease that took more than 550,000 American lives in 2001:

- Eat more fruits and vegetables.

- Reduce your fat intake.

- Eat more fiber.

- Limit your alcohol intake.

- Stop smoking.

- Limit your consumption of processed foods.

OBESITY

The American Obesity Association estimates that about 127 million adults in the United States are overweight, 60 million are obese and 9 million are severely obese. Being overweight is the most common nutrition-associated health problem in North America, and 60 percent of all adults are overweight. Obesity has been linked to coronary heart disease, high blood pressure, stroke, osteoarthritis, gallstones, lipid disorders, gastrointestinal diseases, fatty infiltration of the liver, restrictive lung disease, obstructive sleep apnea, adult onset diabetes and cancer. Weight gain, for example, proportionally increases women's risk of breast cancer. If a woman gains 45 pounds or more after age 18, her chance of developing breast cancer after menopause doubles. About 300,000 deaths each year are attributable to obesity, says the US Surgeon General, and researchers predict that this number will grow.

Several studies conducted in the past few years have dispelled the popular belief that the number of calories is the only factor in keeping trim. Equally important is the source of the calories—fat, protein or carbohydrate. Fat calories are the most fattening of all. The National Food Consumption Survey and the National Health and Nutrition Survey show that Americans get between 34 and 37 percent of their calories from fat because Americans eat high-calorie, high-fat diets.

Another study compared Chinese to American caloric intake and explained why Americans are fatter than the Chinese. "Our information indicates that the Chinese consume more calories than Americans do, but aren't as fat," says T. Colin Campbell, PhD, author of *The China Study*. On average, the Chinese consume only 15 percent of calories from fat, although they eat about a fifth more calories than Americans. The average American diet contains 34 percent of calories from fat.

Pasta is a good source of protein, vitamin B, iron and other minerals, and it's low in fat and sodium.

When many Americans switched to margarine—either to the low-fat or regular kind—to avoid the saturated fat in butter, they may have done themselves more harm than good. Margarine and solid vegetable shortening contain trans–fatty acids (or trans fat, for short), which are produced when a liquid vegetable oil is turned into a solid vegetable shortening or margarine through a process known as hydrogenation (trans fats do not naturally exist). During the hydrogenation process, the fat undergoes an unusual change, and the trans fat gets twisted out of shape. There's still a lot to be learned about trans fats and their effects, but scientists say these nasty compounds may be two or three times more dangerous than saturated fats. According to the researchers' work, trans fats may not only raise low-density lipoproteins, or "bad" cholesterol, but also lower high-density lipoproteins, or "good" cholesterol.

The good news is that eating low-fat vegetarian foods can help you shed excess pounds. Even if you're 10 or 100 pounds overweight, the vegetarian choice is a great option because you won't lack for food—willpower, maybe, but not food. And studies have shown that in general, vegetarians are much thinner than meat eaters.

Try to avoid thinking of the vegetarian choice as a diet, because people go on and off diets. The vegetarian choice—even if you modify it by including small amounts of meat, poultry or fish—is for keeps. It requires no calorie counting and no need for a food scale to weigh your portions. Just choose your foods wisely—and eat. (Please note that if you have an eating disorder, you may benefit from counseling to discover why you overeat. Also, check with your doctor in case you have a medical condition that may be contributing to your weight problem.)

The following are a few suggestions that could prevent further weight gain and could help you lose a healthy amount of your current weight.

- Limit your calories and substitute low-calorie and low-fat products for high-calorie and high-fat products.

- Avoid items with "empty calories" such as alcohol, sugary desserts and candies, and high-fat, high-salt snack foods.

- Exercise regularly.

- Talk to a counselor or a physician about your eating habits.

- Consider the vegetarian choice!

OSTEOPOROSIS

Osteoporosis, a disease in which bones become less dense or more porous, leads to bone fragility and increased propensity to fractures, especially of the hip, spine and wrist. The disease debilitates more than 10 million

Americans, and, according to the National Osteoporosis Foundation, almost 34 million more have low bone mass, which places them at risk for osteoporosis. It results in more than 1.5 million fractures annually.

If you know even a little bit about osteoporosis, you probably link it to calcium, and you're right to make the connection. But preventing osteoporosis isn't a matter of guzzling several glasses of skim milk each day. The connection is more complex: When your body doesn't have enough calcium in its bloodstream to handle basic metabolic functions, your body leaches calcium from your bones. This is called reabsorption, and it is a normal part of aging. At about age forty, both men and women lose about 0.5 percent of their skeletons each year. When women reach menopause, their rate of bone loss increases to about 1 or 2 percent each year. Postmenopausal women are the most vulnerable to osteoporosis because their ovaries have stopped producing estrogen, which helps maintain bone mass. By age sixty, a woman may have lost 40 percent of her skeleton.

You can have strong bones in your later years by making good food choices—and the earlier you start, the better. Because you will lose bone mass as you age, a sound approach is to have as much bone mass as possible before you reach your middle years. Your bones stop growing at age thirty-five, so it is important to take in a lot of calcium before you begin losing bone mass. After your bones stop growing, you goal should be zero calcium balance—losing no more calcium than you take in.

You've probably heard that milk products are the best sources of calcium. And yes, many of them do contain significant amounts of this mineral, but they are loaded with protein. So what? Well, the more protein in the diet, the more the kidneys work overtime, and the more calcium is leached from the body. So eating high-calcium foods that are high in protein can backfire. What can you do? Eat plant sources of calcium, especially dark green leafy vegetables. Greens such as kale and bok choy are particularly strong contenders, despite pronouncements from some nutritionists that the oxalic acid in the vegetables inhibits calcium absorption.

The body is wonderfully made to absorb a higher percentage of calcium from food when overall calcium intake is relatively low; but eating tons of calcium-rich foods makes little difference, because your body will excrete what it doesn't need. To boost calcium absorption, go for vitamin D by getting a healthy amount of sun exposure and by drinking fortified milk, soy and rice beverages. The skin metabolizes vitamin D from the sunlight, and the body stores the vitamin after exposure to sunlight for use during the cold months, when people tend to stay indoors.

Vitamins K and C are two other minerals that promote increased bone density and reduce fracture rates. Friendly bacteria that live in your intestines help to make a large portion of the vitamin K you need, and the rest can be found in leafy green vegetables, green peas, broccoli, spinach, Brussels sprouts, romaine lettuce, cabbage and kale. Vitamin C is found in fruits and vegetables, and especially citrus fruits.

Another proven method to increase bone mass is through weight-bearing exercise. Though there have been few studies on the long-term effects of exercise on the development of osteoporosis, current evidence indicates that weight-bearing exercise, such as jogging, aerobic dancing, weight lifting and racquet sports, help make your bones denser by putting stress on the skeleton.

What is out of your control is your genetics: Some people are more likely to develop osteoporosis. Women of Mediterranean and African descent, for example, have denser skeletons than Caucasians or Asians, so they are less likely to develop osteoporosis. Because you can't do anything about your genetics, focus on calcium-rich foods and exercise. And wait for more research on this disease, because there's still a lot to learn.

DIABETES

For decades, physicians advised their diabetic patients to eat a high-fat, low-carbohydrate and low-fiber diet. That eating regimen would get loud hisses from doctors and dietitians today, but back then, the common belief was that such a diet would help keep blood-sugar levels constant.

Research indicates that a high-carbohydrate diet improves blood-sugar control by enhancing insulin sensitivity. It can even head off the development of diabetes: In an important study of Seventh-Day Adventists, researchers found that vegetarians had significantly less risk of diabetes than the general population. The long-term studies by noted fiber researcher James Anderson, MD, show that patients on his high-fiber, largely vegetarian diet are able to lower their insulin requirements, and their blood cholesterol and blood pressure levels also are reduced. (High cholesterol and blood pressure levels are typical complications of diabetes.)

Before moving on to particulars about diet, here is some background about diabetes, the sixth leading cause of death in 2001 in the United States. There are two major types of diabetes: Type I, insulin-dependent diabetes, and Type II, in which the body either produces very little insulin or does not use it properly. Type II is by far the more common form of diabetes, plaguing 90 to 95 percent of the 17 million Americans whom doctors diagnose with diabetes. Type II, also known as adult-onset diabetes, often can be treated without drugs by following a proper diet and getting exercise.

The onset of Type II is caused by the eating and exercising habits of aging individuals. Additional risk factors include age (being over forty-five), obesity, physical inactivity, a diet high in fat and cholesterol and a family history of Type II diabetes. Additionally, people with African American, Latino, Asian and Pacific Islander and Native American heritage have an increased risk of developing the disease. But in general, eating too much and the wrong kinds of food—particularly foods high in fat—are usually what cause Type II diabetes. So switching to a low-fat vegetarian diet, exercising and losing weight sometimes are all that is needed to get the disease under control, though some Type II diabetics will need medication. Type I diabetics, who must inject insulin, may also be helped through dietary changes.

Diabetics are familiar with exchange lists developed by the American Diabetes Association; the lists are divided into groups of foods to ensure that diabetics get the right balance of nutrients. Below is a list of some foods commonly eaten by vegetarians that may not show up on the lists.

Whether you, a family member or a friend has diabetes, spread the message: Eating a high-carbohydrate, low-fat, high-fiber vegetarian diet is the best way to prevent and manage this disease.

Diabetic Exchanges for Vegetarians

FOOD	EXCHANGE VALUE
Almond or cashew butter (2 teaspoons)	1 Meat Exchange
Bulgur (½ cup, cooked)	1 Bread Exchange
Brown rice (½ cup, cooked)	1 Bread Exchange
Kefir (1 cup)	1 Milk Exchange
Meatless burger (3 ounces)	3 Meat Exchanges
Meatless hot dog (1 ounce)	1 Meat Exchange
Miso (3 tablespoons)	1 Bread Exchange
Soybeans (⅓ cup, cooked)	1 Meat Exchange
Soymilk (1 cup)	1 Milk Exchange (because soymilk does not contain as many carbohydrates as cows' milk, you will need to consume an extra bread exchange with each cup of soymilk)
Tahini (2 teaspoons)	1 Meat Exchange
Tempeh (2 ounces, cooked)	1 Meat Exchange
Textured vegetable protein (reconstituted, ½ cup)	2 Meat Exchanges
Tofu (4 ounces)	1 Meat Exchange

3 *kitchen wisdom*

ANYONE WHO SETS FOOT IN THE KITCHEN needs a few basic tools to get a delicious meal on the table: quality ingredients, cooking utensils and, most likely, a recipe or two. For the vegetarian cook, the process is altered only by the makeup of the pantry. Of course, a basic understanding of kitchen fundamentals aids cooks of every skill level, and the text that follows will be a useful and convenient guide to creating successful meals.

First things first. Draw up your meal plan for the week, taking into account your family's schedules and activities. You know best how to gauge your needs and to tailor meal planning around them.

Then, before you head to market, take stock of your pantry, and decide which are the essential staples—vegetable stock, seasonings, canned beans, dried pastas, grains, sauces and salsas. Then consider which perishables you will need—from fresh fruits and vegetables to tofu, tempeh, eggs and cheese.

Most well-stocked supermarkets will offer all commonplace and most ethnic ingredients you will need for the recipes in this book. You may find that a few recipes require planning ahead for purchase of the offbeat or unusual items available at ethnic markets or through mail-order concerns. Check the mail-order sources listed on pages 454–455. For a complete rundown on vegetarian ingredients, consult the glossary (page 456).

And finally, when you get out your pots and pans, and you aren't clear about certain cooking instructions, read through the basic how-to primer in this chapter. These handy tips help to demystify the cooking process.

THE VERY BASIC PANTRY

- Whole-grain breads such as sandwich and artisan breads, English muffins and tortillas
- Rice, including conventional or quick-cooking brown rice and white rice such as basmati or jasmine rice
- Whole grains such as barley, bulgur, cornmeal, rolled oats, millet, quinoa and kasha
- Pasta, preferably whole grain
- Whole-grain cold cereals
- Whole-grain flours, including whole wheat flour, whole wheat pastry flour and other favorites
- Unbleached all-purpose flour
- Legumes (dried or canned), including kidney beans, black beans, navy beans, cannellini beans, chickpeas, lentils and other favorites
- Condiments such as soy sauce, vegetarian Worcestershire sauce, mustard (Dijon and American), dark sesame oil, pickles, jellies and other favorites
- Sweeteners such as honey, brown rice syrup, granulated sugarcane juice, molasses, and confectioners' sugar, brown sugar and granulated sugar
- Vanilla, almond and lemon extracts
- Baking powder

- Baking soda

- Arrowroot, cornstarch or other thickener

- Vinegars, such as balsamic, umeboshi and herb

- Vegetable oils, including olive and canola oils

- Salt, including kosher salt, sea salt and seasoning salts

- Peppercorns, whole, for freshly ground black pepper

- Herbs and spices

- Beverages, including fruit and vegetable juices

COOKING METHODS AND KITCHEN TECHNIQUES

BASIC EQUIPMENT

- Pots and pans with lids
- Large skillet, preferably non-stick
- Steamer basket
- Griddle
- Baking pans and cookie sheets
- Wooden cooking spoons and other utensils
- Handheld shredder
- Measuring cups and spoons
- Vegetable peeler
- Large colander
- Small- and medium-size strainers with fine sieves
- Kitchen scissors

Baking: Baking refers to cooking food with dry heat in an oven. If you plan to bake or roast, always preheat the oven before you begin preparing the recipe, otherwise the oven won't be ready when you are.

When you bake more than one thing at a time, stagger the placement of the dishes so the air may circulate, and if a recipe calls for baking a dish on a rack placed in the center of the oven, then follow directions. Also keep in mind that few ovens are calibrated accurately, and they may cook slower or faster than you anticipate. A good way to check your oven's accuracy is to check the cooking time—and to use an oven thermometer.

Blanching: Quickly dipping fruits or vegetables into boiling water, and then putting them into cold water for a few seconds loosens skins, sets color and readies them for freezing or for further cooking using another technique, such as stir-frying. You also may blanch nuts, but skip the cold water dunk. To remove the skins, rub the nuts between your fingertips.

Braising: This traditional French method of cooking vegetables in a little butter or oil and liquid in a covered pot over low heat makes for richly flavored dishes.

Broiling: Simply set your oven on "broil" and place your ovenproof dish or pan on the broiling rack at the height called for in your recipe. In vegetarian cooking, broiling is used primarily for melting cheese on casseroles or for top browning.

Deep-frying: Fill a pot one-third full of vegetable oil—not olive oil or butter, which has a low smoke point—and heat it to 375F. Do not let the oil smoke, as it may burn. Use a deep-fat thermometer to help regulate the temperature. Make sure that the food you are deep-frying is in small enough pieces and is dry—moisture in food, especially raw vegetables, can cause hot oil to splatter. Another option is to coat the food with a batter.

Use a wire basket or slotted spoon to lower and lift your food, and fry only small amounts of food at a time. If you add too much food at once, you will reduce the temperature of the oil too much and end up with soggy, greasy food. For that same reason, do not deep-fry frozen foods or foods that are colder than room temperature. Cook vegetables coated with batter about 3 to 5 minutes, until they are crisp and lightly browned. Drain fried foods on paper towels and serve immediately.

Grilling: Your backyard gas or charcoal barbecue is a handy piece of equipment for anyone who likes to infuse his food with extra flavor—and to cook outdoors. Once you buy a small-meshed basket or screen to fit over the grilling rack, you can barbecue any number of vegetables and fruits—plus veggie burgers—without fear of losing them to the flames below. You may also want to invest in a long-handled spatula, a long-handled brush for basting and appropriate hot pads for lifting the cooking racks off the grill.

Stove-top grilling: Many modern ovens have grilling inserts set into their stove top, and these grills give the cook the chance to approximate outdoor grilling while staying indoors and avoiding the fuss. Follow the manufacturer's directions for your particular unit.

Pan-frying: If you want to fry vegetables, pan-frying is probably the easiest method. Choose a metal pan with sides high enough to hold the food and enough cooking oil or fats to cover about one-half the thickness of the food. This way you can cook the food throughout with only one turning. Because pan-frying involves high temperatures, you cannot pan-fry with butter, margarine or olive oil because they will smoke and burn. Use vegetable oil instead.

Poaching: Cooking vegetables, fruits and eggs in simmering water or vegetable stock can produce flavorful results in a short time without the added calories from fat. Adding vinegar to the poaching water when cooking eggs helps set the whites.

Puréeing: Puréeing means to turn ingredients such as fruits or vegetables into a thick, uniformly smooth paste. You may use a food mill, blender or food processor to purée. If you want to purée hot liquids in a blender, check that you have a heatproof container. Fill the blender no more than half full, and hold the cover in place with a thick towel.

Roasting: Roasting, like baking, uses dry oven heat to cook the food, but the food remains uncovered during cooking. To keep the food from drying out or charring during roasting, you may brush it with oil to keep the surface moist. To prevent the top of the food from becoming too brown, create a loose tent of aluminum foil over the top to protect the surface while still allowing hot air to circulate underneath. Keep in mind that smaller pieces of food can become very dry when roasted and may be better suited for pan-frying or broiling.

HOT!

When grilling, try flavor-enhancing woods, such as mesquite or hickory, or drop some fresh herbs into the flames and cover the grill to jazz up your dinner.

Sautéing: Sautéing means quick-cooking foods in a small amount of butter or oil over medium to medium-high heat. It's similar to the Chinese technique of stir-frying, but generally is used for larger pieces of food.

Simmering: A liquid simmers when heated over low heat, and the liquid's surface shimmers but does not actually bubble or boil.

Steaming: Steaming vegetables makes them tender-crisp. Fill a saucepan with about one inch of water and set a steamer basket in the pan. Bring the water to a boil, and add rinsed vegetables to the basket. Reduce the heat to medium-low, cover the pan and cook until the vegetables reach the desired doneness. Time varies depending on the vegetable, but often just a few minutes will be enough. The big plus: Because the vegetables do not touch the water, they do not lose their vitamin and mineral content in the water.

Stir-frying: Stir-frying is a method of quick-cooking vegetables over high heat while you constantly stir them. You may use a wok, but a skillet or other pan works fine, too. A wok has a rounded bottom, where the heat is the hottest, and sloping sides that remain cooler. The differences in heat allow you to cook the ingredients evenly by rearranging the food. For stirring, you may use a wooden spoon, but a Chinese-style spatula is best.

Before cooking, have your ingredients prepared as directed in your recipe and lined up in order. The oil will sear the vegetables, locking in their juices. This takes a minute or two, and sometimes only seconds, depending on the ingredient. The final product ought to be tender-crisp and taste fresh. It's the healthy answer to fast food.

MORE KITCHEN TECHNIQUES

Preparing food involves more than cooking. Here are some extra tips:

Seeding tomatoes: To peel and seed tomatoes, cut an X on the bottom of each one. Then drop them into a small pot of boiling water for 1 to 2 minutes, until the skins begin to loosen. Drain and rinse under cold water. The skins will easily slip off. Slice the tomatoes in half crosswise, then squeeze to remove the seeds.

Roasting bell peppers: To roast bell peppers, place them under your broiler until the skin is charred, turning frequently, 8 to 12 minutes. Remove the peppers from the broiler, place them in a paper bag and close the top. Let stand for about 10 minutes. Remove the peppers from the bag and peel off the charred skin. Slice the peppers into strips and remove the seeds.

Making bread crumbs: You can make your own bread crumbs by cutting fresh bread into cubes. Then place them on a baking sheet and bake at 350F until crisp, 15 to 20 minutes. Process the cubes in a blender or food processor until finely ground.

Toasting seeds and nuts: To toast nuts, bake at 350F for about 10 minutes on a baking sheet. Alternatively, you may dry-roast them in a large skillet over medium heat, stirring them often to prevent burning.

To toast pumpkin seeds, rinse them thoroughly and remove all strings and pulp. Allow them to dry, then toss with 1½ tablespoons oil and salt to taste. Place them on a baking sheet. Bake at 350F for 20 to 30 minutes, stirring every 5 minutes, until the seeds are golden brown.

For mustard seeds, a dry skillet with a lid over medium-low heat is best. When they heat up, they pop. Lightly shake the contents as they pop. Remove them from the heat when the popping slows down. Other seeds, such as sesame and sunflower seeds, may be toasted in a dry skillet until lightly brown. Stir frequently to prevent burning.

Making yogurt cheese: To make yogurt cheese, line a colander with a large cloth napkin or paper towels. Place the colander over a bowl. Spoon two cups plain yogurt into the colander. Let the yogurt drain in your refrigerator for several hours or overnight. The yogurt will become thicker like cheese. Yields 1 cup.

Handling tofu I: Depending on your recipe, you may want to make your tofu firmer by pressing out some of its water. For instance, if you want cubes that'll hold their shape in your stir-fry, press the block of tofu before cutting it. Otherwise, you might end up with crumbled tofu when you stir-fry. But if you're making scrambled tofu, don't bother with pressing unless your recipe gives that instruction.

To press tofu, wrap it in a cloth towel or several paper towels. Place a breadboard on top of the tofu, and if you wish, set a pot of water or several books on the breadboard. (Be careful not to place too much weight on top; the block of tofu might smoosh down irrevocably.) Let it sit for 25 or 30 minutes. Check the tofu. Still too water-logged? Then replace the breadboard and the weight, and allow the tofu to drain another 15 minutes. Now you're ready to use it in your recipe.

Handling tofu II: When you freeze and then thaw tofu, it transforms into a chewier, more "meaty" food, making it a satisfying meat substitute in many dishes, such as sloppy joes, spaghetti sauce and casseroles.

To freeze tofu, wrap the block in plastic wrap and place it in the freezer until it is frozen solid, at least 24 hours. Thawing takes longer, all day or overnight in the refrigerator. If you didn't leave enough time in your schedule for a complete thaw, you may place the frozen block in a bowl and pour boiling water over it several times until thawed. Or try microwaving the frozen block on high power a minute at a time. When it's thawed, squeeze out excess water by hand.

If you thaw more tofu than you can use, it's fine to refreeze the unused portion. The refrozen tofu will become chewier the next time you thaw it.

BRAN FAN

Rice bran, oat bran and other types of bran add a bit of flavor and a lot of nutrients—most notably, fiber—to your meal. Bran is the outer layer of the grain. In various studies, the intake of bran has been shown to have positive health effects, such as lowering blood cholesterol levels and alleviating constipation.

Freezing: Freezing is an excellent way to preserve food. You may freeze leftovers, of course, or you may plan ahead and freeze food for those busy days when you barely have time to set the table.

Either way, freeze and store food properly. For fresh vegetables, blanch them first. Most vegetables may be frozen, but salad vegetables such as lettuce become mushy when thawed. For fruits, peel and slice them before freezing them in a thick sweet liquid; berries may be flash frozen on baking sheets then transferred to plastic bags and sealed. Breads, cooked legumes and cooked grains may be placed in plastic bags or in tightly covered containers and frozen.

In general, use your frozen foods in about three to six months. And don't forget to label and date your food, or you may be in for a big surprise.

Juicing: From a nutritional standpoint, whole fruits contain more vitamins and minerals than juices. But many juicers are made to extract as much of the fruit as possible. When comparing fresh juice to the store-bought variety, fresh tastes fresher and its nutrients are more potent. Look for and select a juicer with a powerful motor that can do big batches of vegetables or fruit quickly and easily.

COOKING IS A BLEND OF SCIENCE AND ART

The science portion of cooking requires a knowledge of basics; the art builds on the fundamentals, allowing you to tinker with recipes, substituting one ingredient for another or turning a stew into a pot pie crowned with a golden crust.

As your confidence grows, you become an adventuresome culinary artist. Then cooking is pure joy. Let's forge ahead into the specifics of cooking grains and legumes, staples in vegetarian cuisine.

COOKING GRAINS

Rice, barley, quinoa and kasha—these are but four grains common in vegetarian cuisine. As you try out recipes, you'll become accustomed to their flavors and textures: mild, nutty, robust, chewy, tender—you name it. But first, a cooking lesson.

Simmering is by far the most common way to cook grains. The grains swell and absorb moisture as they cook, while a tight-fitting lid traps the steam. Choose the boiling water method or the cold water method. For the boiling water method, bring a pot of water or vegetable broth to a boil and sprinkle in the grain (using the measurements below). Cover the pot and reduce the heat to a simmer. This method causes the grains to swell quickly and stay separate. For the cold water method, rinse the grain through a sieve under cool running water. Place the grain in a pot, add cold water, cover and bring to a boil. Reduce the heat to low.

KEEP FRESH

Whole-grain flours and cracked grains, such as bulgur, are susceptible to rancidity. Keep them covered in your refrigerator or freezer.

Your grains will be fluffier if you don't stir them while they simmer. Also, after the cooking time is up, leave the lid in place a few minutes longer; the grains will continue to cook.

Guidelines for Cooking Grains

GRAIN	WATER PER CUP OF DRY GRAIN	COOKING TIME (COVERED)	YIELD (APPROX.)
Amaranth	3 cups	25–30 min.	2½ cups
Whole barley (presoaked)	3 cups	35–40 min.	4 cups
Brown rice	2½ cups	45 min.	2½ cups
Bulgur	2½ cups	20 min.	2½ cups
Corn/Cornmeal	4 cups	30 min.	4 cups
Farro (presoaked)	3 cups	20–30 min.	2½ cups
Hominy	4 cups	10–15 min.	3 cups
Kamut (presoaked)	3 to 4 cups	15–20 min.	2½ cups
Kasha	2 cups	15 min.	2½ cups
Millet	3 cups	25–30 min.	3 to 4 cups
Oats	3 cups	30–40 min.	3½ cups
Oatmeal	2 cups	10 min.	4 cups
Quinoa	2 cups	15 min.	2½ cups
Rye	4 cups	15–20 min.	2⅔ cups
Spelt	3 to 4 cups	40–50 min.	2½ cups
Teff	4 cups	15–20 min.	3 cups
Triticale (presoaked)	4 cups	15–20 min.	2½ cups
Wild rice	3 cups	45–50 min.	3 to 3½ cups

Note: Some grains—whole barley, millet and brown rice—may be prepared in a pressure cooker. Use a little less water and cut the cooking time by one-third to one-half. Check your pressure cooker manual for specifics.

COOKING LEGUMES

You may cook legumes in a few different ways. Pick the one that suits your time schedule.

Traditional method: After rinsing the beans and picking out any debris, such as tiny stones (usually there isn't anything to pick out), place the beans in a large pot with three to four times their volume of water. Cover them and soak overnight or for about 8 hours. (In warm weather or heated houses, soak beans in your refrigerator to prevent fermentation.) Bring the water and beans to a boil, lower the heat to a gentle simmer and cook until done. Please note that lentils, split peas and mung beans do not require soaking.

Quick-soak method: Here's a way to speed up preparation. Instead of soaking beans overnight, place them in a large pot with three to four times their volume of water. Bring to a boil, remove from heat and let stand, covered, for an hour. Then cook the beans as above.

Pressure-cooker method: Soak the beans by either the traditional or quick-soak method. Follow the equipment manufacturer's instructions, and make sure that the vents on the cooker don't get clogged with foam. One way to reduce foam is to fill your cooker no more than one-third full with water and beans. Adding a tablespoon of oil also helps.

Slow-cooker method: After soaking by either the traditional or quick-soak method, place beans with four times their volume of water in your slow cooker. Cover and cook for 6 to 8 hours. If you wish, you may add onion, garlic and herbs to the beans before cooking to produce a delicious broth.

Cooking Times for Legumes

The times will vary depending on the type of bean, simmering temperature, the soaking time and the age of the beans. You can tell that they are cooked when you bite into one and it is tender but not mushy. You'll end up with 2¼ to 2½ cups of cooked beans for every cup of dry beans.

Many varieties of beans are available canned in supermarkets. Unless a recipe says differently, be sure to rinse the legumes to reduce salt and sugar that may have been added during processing. If a recipe calls for dried beans, but you don't have the time to start cooking from scratch, a good rule of thumb is that for 1 cup of dried beans, you can substitute one 15-ounce can (about 2 cups, drained) of canned beans.

PICKY ABOUT BEANS

When buying dried legumes, look for beans with a vibrant color. Fading is a clear indication of long storage. The longer beans are stored, the less fresh they'll taste. And if their surface looks cloudy, they may also be moldy.

Guidelines for Cooking Legumes

LEGUMES	PRESOAK	COOKING TIME
Adzuki Beans	yes	1 to 1½ hours
Black Beans	yes	1 to 2 hours
Black-Eyed Peas	yes	1 to 1½ hours
Cannellini Beans	yes	1 to 2 hours
Chickpeas	yes	2½ to 3 hours
Cranberry Beans	yes	1 to 2 hours
Fava Beans	yes	1½ to 2 hours
Fava Beans, skins removed	yes	40 to 50 min.
Great Northern Beans	yes	1 to 2 hours
Kidney Beans	yes	1½ to 2 hours
Lentils (brown)	no	30 min. to 1 hour
Lentils (green)	no	30 to 45 min.
Lentils (red)	no	20 to 30 min.
Lima Beans (small)	yes	45 min. to 1½ hours
Lima Beans (large)	yes	1 to 1½ hours
Mung Beans	no	1 hour
Navy Beans	yes	1 to 2 hours
Pink Beans	yes	1 to 2 hours
Pinto Beans	yes	1 to 2 hours
Red Beans	yes	1½ to 2 hours
Soybeans	yes	3 to 4 hours
Split Peas (green)	no	45 min. to 1 hour
Split Peas (yellow)	no	45 min. to 1½ hours

YIELDS

BREADS

1 pound = 12 to 16 slices
1 slice fresh = ½ cup soft crumbs
1 slice dried = ⅓ cup dry crumbs
28 saltine crackers = 1 cup fine
    crumbs
14 square graham crackers = 1 cup
    fine crumbs
24 round crackers = 1 cup fine
    crumbs

CHEESES

**Grating cheeses (i.e.,
    Parmesan)**
    3 ounces = 1 cup grated
**Hard cheeses (i.e., cheddar,
    mozzarella)**
    1 pound = 4 cups shredded
    4 ounces = 1 cup shredded
**Soft cheeses (i.e., cottage,
    cream)**
    1 pound = 2 cups
    8 ounces = 1 cup
    3 ounces = 6 tablespoons

DRY BEANS

Large beans (i.e., kidney)
    1 cup = 2 to 3 cups cooked
    1 pound = 2 cups uncooked =
      5½ to 6 cups cooked

Small beans (i.e., navy)
    1 cup = 2 to 3 cups cooked
    1 pound = 2⅓ cups uncooked
      = 5½ to 6 cups cooked
Lentils
    1 cup = 3 cups cooked
Split peas
    1 cup = 2½ cups cooked

EGGS

Whole
    1 pound = 5 large eggs
    9 medium eggs = 1 cup
Whites
    1 large egg white = 2 table-
      spoons
    8 to 11 egg whites = 1 cup
Yolks
    1 large yolk = 1 tablespoon
    12 to 14 yolks = 1 cup
Replacer
    1 large egg = ¼ cup liquid egg
      replacement

FATS

Butter or margarine
    1 pound = 4 sticks = 2 cups
    1 pound whipped = 3 cups
    4 ounces = 1 stick = ½ cup
    1 ounce = 2 tablespoons
Vegetable oil
    8 ounces = 1 cup

WHAT'S A BOUQUET GARNI?

A *bouquet garni* is indispensable to French cooks. It imparts a subtle herb flavor to stews and other dishes. To make a basic *bouquet garni*, place 3 bay leaves, 12 peppercorns, 10 to 12 parsley stems, 1 sprig of fresh thyme (or 1 teaspoon of dried) and 2 to 3 whole cloves of garlic in the center of a 12-inch square of cheesecloth, then tie the ends together.

FRUITS, VEGETABLES, HERBS

Apples
1 pound = 3 medium = 3 cups sliced
1 medium = 1 cup sliced

Bananas
1 pound = 3 medium = 3 cups sliced = 2½ cups mashed (approx.)

Bell peppers
1 medium to large = 1 cup chopped

Cabbage, raw
1 pound = 4 cups shredded

Carrots
8 ounces = 1¼ cups chopped
2 medium = 1 cup sliced
1½ medium = 1 cup shredded

Cauliflower
1 pound = 3 cups

Celery
2 medium stalks = ¾ to 1 cup sliced

Cherries
4 cups unpitted = 2 cups pitted

Coconut, flaked or shredded
1 pound = 5 cups
4 ounces = 1⅓ cups

Corn
2 medium ears = 1 cup kernels

Cranberries
1 pound = 4 cups
4 cups fresh = 6 to 7 cups sauce

Cucumbers
1 small to medium = 1 cup chopped

Dates, pitted
1 cup = ½ pint = 3 cups chopped

Dates, unpitted
1 pound = 1½ cups chopped

Garlic
1 medium clove = ¾ teaspoon minced

Grapes
1 pound = 2 cups halved

Green beans
1 pound = 3 cups cut

Herbs
1 tablespoon fresh = ½ to 1 teaspoon dried = ½ teaspoon ground

Lemon
Juice of 1 lemon = 3 tablespoons
Grated zest of 1 lemon = 2 to 3 teaspoons

Lettuce
1 pound head = 6¼ cups torn

Lime
Juice of 1 medium lime = 1½ to 2 tablespoons
Grated zest of 1 medium lime = 1½ 1 tsp. teaspoon

Mushrooms, fresh
8 ounces = 3 cups unsliced = 1½ cups sliced

Onion
1 medium = ½ cup chopped
1 medium = 1 teaspoon onion powder = 1 tablespoon dried minced

Orange
Juice of 1 orange = ⅓ cup
Grated zest of 1 orange = 2 tablespoons

Peaches
1 medium = ½ cup sliced

Pears
1 medium = ½ cup sliced

Peas in the pod
1 pound = 1 cup shelled

Potatoes
1 pound = 3 medium
3 medium = 2 cups sliced or cubed
3 medium = 1¾ cups mashed
3 medium = 3 cups grated

Prunes
12 ounces = 2 cups pitted

Raisins, seedless
1 pound = 3 cups

Rhubarb
8 ounces = 2 to 4 stalks = 1 cup cooked

Scallions
9 (with tops) = 1 cup sliced
1 sliced = 1 tablespoon

Strawberries
1 quart = 3 cups sliced

Sweet Potatoes
3 medium = 3 cups sliced

Tomatoes
1 medium = 1 cup chopped
1 cup canned = 1⅓ cups fresh, cut up and simmered for 5 minutes

Zucchini
1 medium = 2 cups sliced

GRAINS

Barley
1 cup uncooked = 3½ cups cooked

Bulgur
1 cup uncooked = 2½ cups cooked

Cereal, flakes
3 cups uncrushed = 1 cup crushed

Cornmeal
1 pound = 3 cups
1 cup uncooked = 4 cups cooked

Flour, all-purpose
1 pound = 4 cups unsifted
1 ounce = ¼ cup

Flour, cake
1 pound = 4¾ to 5 cups sifted

Flour, whole wheat
1 pound = 3½ cups unsifted

Kasha (buckwheat groats)
1 cup uncooked = 2½ to 3 cups cooked

Millet
1 cup uncooked = 3½ cups cooked

Pasta
1 pound macaroni = 5 cups uncooked = 8 to 10 cups cooked
4 ounces macaroni = 1 cup uncooked = 2½ cups cooked
4 ounces spaghetti = 2 cups cooked

Rice
1 pound rice = 2½ cups uncooked = 8 cups cooked
7 ounces white rice (long grain) = 1 cup uncooked = 3 to 4 cups cooked
1 cup uncooked white rice (instant) = 2 cups cooked
1 cup uncooked brown rice = 3 cups cooked

Rolled Oats
1 pound = 5 cups uncooked = 8¾ cups cooked
1 cup uncooked = 1¾ cups cooked

Wild Rice
1 cup uncooked = 3 to 4 cups cooked

NUTS

Almonds
1 pound unshelled = 1 to 1¾ cups nutmeats
1 pound shelled = 3½ cups nutmeats

Peanuts
  1 pound unshelled = 2¼ cups
    nutmeats
  1 pound shelled = 3 cups nut-
    meats

Pecans
  1 pound unshelled = 2¼ cups
    nutmeats
  1 pound shelled = 4 cups nut-
    meats

Walnuts
  1 pound unshelled = 1⅔ cups
    nutmeats
  1 pound shelled = 4 cups nut-
    meats

OTHER
Chocolate, baking
  1 ounce = 1 square
Chocolate chips
  6 ounces = 1 cup
  12 ounces = 2 cups
Cocoa
  1 pound = 4 cups
Coffee
  1 pound = 80 tablespoons = 40
    cups brewed
Cream, whipping
  1 cup = 2 cups whipped
Salt, coarse or kosher
  1 ounce = 2 tablespoons
Salt, table
  1 ounce = 1½ tablespoons
Shortening
  1 pound = 2 cups

Sugar, brown
  1 pound = 2⅔ cups firmly
    packed
Sugar, granulated
  1 pound = 2 cups
**Sugar, powdered
  (confectioners')**
  1 pound = 2½ cups unsifted =
    4 cups sifted
Yeast
  1 cake = 1 package active dry
    yeast
  ¼ ounce = 2½ teaspoons

WEIGHTS AND MEASURES

Pinch = about ¹⁄₁₆ teaspoon
Dash = about ⅛ teaspoon
3 teaspoons = 1 tablespoon
4 tablespoons = ¼ cup
5⅓ tablespoons = ⅓ cup
8 tablespoons = ½ cup
10⅔ tablespoons = ⅔ cup
12 tablespoons = ¾ cup
16 tablespoons = 1 cup
1 ounce = 28.35 grams
1 gram = 0.035 ounces
1 cup = 8 fluid ounces
1 cup = ½ pint
2 cups = 1 pint
4 cups = 1 quart
1 quart = 946.4 milliliters
1 liter = 1.06 quarts
4 quarts = 1 gallon

RICE COOKER

One time-saving device is an electric rice cooker. It still takes about 30 minutes to cook rice, but you can leave your home to run some errands and the appliance will turn itself off when the rice has finished cooking. Many cooks say they can't do without their rice cooker because the cooked rice is perfect every time. There are many manufacturers of rice cookers and various sizes, so shop around.

appetizers

APPETIZERS ARE MINI SNACKS THAT can launch a party or a meal, and they add an extra flourish to any event. They aren't a full meal, but if paired with other appetizers, you can turn snack time into mealtime. You will find that most ethnic cuisines have their version of small bites, which is reflected in the following recipes.

MOCK MEATBALLS

Bulgur, a type of crushed wheat of Middle Eastern origin, is an excellent substitute for meat. Try it in these mini mock meatballs.

2 cups uncooked bulgur, rinsed

1 tablespoon minced onion

1 large egg, beaten

Dried oregano to taste

Freshly ground black pepper to taste

1 to 3 tablespoons olive oil

1 cup tomato juice plus extra if needed

1. Mix together the bulgur, onion and egg. Season with the oregano and pepper. Form into walnut-sized balls.

2. Coat a large skillet lightly with oil, and heat over medium-high heat. Add the balls, and cook until browned. Add the tomato juice, cover, and cook until the bulgur softens, adding extra juice if the skillet becomes dry, for about 5 minutes. Serve the balls in a shallow serving dish with cocktail forks or toothpicks.

PER BALL: 61 CAL; 2G PROT; 1G FAT; 11G CARB; 9MG CHOL; 4MG SOD; 1G FIBER

GRILLED VEGETABLES WITH EGGPLANT TAPENADE

Tapenade is a condiment hailing from Provence in southern France. In its classic form, this thick paste is made from capers, anchovies, ripe olives, olive oil, lemon juice, seasonings and sometimes tuna, but this version omits the fish. This delectable spread can be served on slices of French baguette or whole-grain bread.

Eggplant Tapenade

1½ teaspoons salt

2 tablespoons olive oil

1 cup finely chopped onion

1 cup thinly sliced fennel

1 tablespoon minced garlic

½ teaspoon dried basil

½ teaspoon dried oregano

¼ teaspoon dried thyme

1 tablespoon tomato paste

Grilled Vegetables

8 ounces tempeh

½ cup fresh lemon juice

2 tablespoons tamari or low-sodium soy sauce

2 tablespoons mirin

¼ teaspoon minced garlic

⅛ teaspoon cayenne, or to taste

1 large red or yellow bell pepper

2 tablespoons olive oil

½ teaspoon red wine vinegar

2 medium portobello mushrooms, stemmed

1 French baguette

4 ounces fresh spinach, rinsed and dried

1. Preheat the oven to 400F.

2. To make the Tapenade: Peel and dice the eggplant. Sprinkle with ½ teaspoon of the salt, and place on paper towels to drain. Heat the oil over medium-high heat, add the onion and cook, stirring often, for 1 minute. Add the fennel, garlic, remaining teaspoon salt, basil, oregano and thyme, and cook, stirring often, for 1 minute. Stir in the eggplant and tomato paste. Reduce the heat to medium, and cook, stirring occasionally, until the eggplant begins to soften, for about 3 minutes. Transfer to the oven and bake, uncovered, for 35 minutes, stirring once or twice, until the eggplant is completely softened.

3. Meanwhile, to make the Grilled Vegetables: Prepare a hot charcoal fire or preheat a gas grill to medium-high. Cut the tempeh in half crosswise. Cut again in half lengthwise to yield 4 pieces. Steam the tempeh over simmering water for 20 minutes. Combine the lemon juice, tamari, mirin, garlic and cayenne in a mixing bowl. Add the tempeh, and let stand while you cook the tapenade.

4. Cut the bell pepper in half lengthwise, and remove the seeds and ribs. Mix the oil and vinegar in a bowl. Place the tempeh, pepper and mushrooms on the grill, brush with the oil mixture, and cook until golden brown on both sides. Alternatively, broil the tempeh and vegetables for 5 to 10 minutes per side.

5. Cut the mushrooms into thick slices. Cut the bell pepper into 4 strips. Trim the ends from the baguette. Cut the loaf in half lengthwise. Spread 5 to 6 tablespoons of the tapenade onto the bottom half (reserve the remaining tapenade for another use) and top with the tempeh, mushrooms, bell pepper and spinach. Cover with the top half of the bread, and cut into 4 equal pieces. Serve right away.

PER SERVING: 339 CAL; 16G PROT; 18G FAT; 33G CARB; 0MG CHOL; 1322MG SOD; 6G FIBER

GRILLED ASPARAGUS BRUSCHETTA
WITH CHÈVRE AND TAPENADE

This makes a hearty hors d'oeuvre or a rustic first course, and it's a great way to use extra tapenade from the previous recipe.

2 tablespoons olive oil plus extra for drizzling

1 pound asparagus, tough ends trimmed and spears peeled and blanched

4 slices Italian country bread, cut ½ inch thick

1 large clove garlic, peeled and halved

4 teaspoons Eggplant Tapenade (page 57), or more to taste

4 ounces mild chèvre cheese such as Montrachet cheese

½ cup black olives, pitted and chopped

Freshly ground black pepper to taste

1. Heat 1 tablespoon of the oil in a ridged grill pan or skillet over medium-high heat. Add the asparagus, and cook, turning frequently, until tender and golden brown. Remove from the pan, and set aside.

2. Rub both sides of the bread with the cut side of the garlic. Add the remaining 1 tablespoon of oil to the ridged grill pan or skillet, and heat over medium heat. Place the bread in the pan, and cook for about 4 minutes per side, or until golden and crisp. Remove from the pan, and let stand until cool enough to handle.

3. Spread 1 teaspoon of the tapenade on 1 side of each bread slice. Top the tapenade with 1 ounce of the chèvre cheese, either spreading the cheese or crumbling it. Top the chèvre with the asparagus, cut to fit the bread. Scatter the olives over the top, drizzle with oil and season with black pepper. Cut in half, and serve warm.

PER SERVING: 270 CAL; 9G PROT; 18G FAT; 19G CARB; 15MG CHOL; 430MG SOD; 3G FIBER

WALNUT-STUFFED BABY RED POTATOES

These little red potatoes, topped with sour cream, walnuts and a festive sprig of dill, will dress up any buffet. Potatoes may be boiled and scooped out up to 3 days in advance. Filled potatoes may be prepared up to several hours in advance, but they are best served when freshly assembled. Reserve the remaining pieces of potatoes for use in an omelet or for pan-fried potatoes.

24 small baby red potatoes

24 walnut halves, toasted (see page 47)

¾ cup sour cream

24 sprigs fresh dill

1. Preheat the oven to 350F. Cook the potatoes in boiling water until just tender, 8 to 12 minutes. Drain and let cool.

2. Slice off the bottom end of each potato so it sits upright, and slice off one-third of the top. If the potatoes are medium size, cut them in half horizontally and use both halves. Using a melon baller, scoop out a bit of each potato, and fill the hollow with a dollop of sour cream. Top with a walnut half, and tuck in a sprig of dill.

PER POTATO: 51 CAL; 1G PROT; 3G FAT; 7G CARB; 3MG CHOL; 4MG SOD; 0.3G FIBER

MIXED AUTUMN ROLLS

These refreshing appetizers are perfect for a warm day. Look for Korean red pepper powder at Korean markets.

Bean Paste Sauce

1 tablespoon packed brown sugar

2 tablespoons Korean *toenjang* bean paste or Japanese miso

1 teaspoon sesame seeds

Wrapping

8 pieces leaf lettuce, rinsed and dried

8 sesame leaves or fresh herb leaves such as basil

Salad

1 tablespoon vegetable oil

3 ounces firm tofu, cubed

½ avocado, peeled

¼ red bell pepper

2½ ounces Korean white radish or daikon, julienned

2 teaspoons dark sesame oil

2 teaspoons sesame seeds

2 teaspoons packed brown sugar

1½ teaspoons salt

1 teaspoon Korean red pepper powder or paprika

2 ounces uncooked bean sprouts

2 small cucumbers, preferably Kirby variety, peeled and diced

1. To make the Bean Paste Sauce: Put the sugar in a heavy saucepan, and melt over medium-low heat, taking care not to burn it. Remove from the heat, and stir the bean paste and sesame seeds into the melted sugar.

2. To make the Wrapping: Trim the edges of the lettuce leaves to make them uniformly circular. Stack the sesame leaves alongside.

3. To make the Salad: Heat the oil in a skillet or wok over medium-high heat, and stir-fry the tofu for 2 to 3 minutes, or until tofu begins to turn golden-. Remove from the heat and set aside.

4. Slice the avocado into 1½-inch-long pieces. Slice the bell pepper into 1½-inch-long pieces. Set aside.

5. Combine the radish with 1 teaspoon of the sesame oil, 1 teaspoon of the sesame seeds, the sugar, ½ teaspoon of the salt and the red pepper powder. Set aside.

6. Combine the bean sprouts with the remaining 1 teaspoon sesame oil, 1 teaspoon sesame seeds and 1 teaspoon salt.

7. To assemble the rolls, place 1 lettuce leaf on a flat surface, separate filling ingredients into 8 uniform piles and layer remaining ingredients on top in the following order: 1 sesame leaf, bean sprout mixture, radish mixture, tofu, cucumber, avocado and bell pepper. Spoon about ½ teaspoon of the Bean Paste Sauce over top. Wrap by tucking the ends in, and roll up. Repeat with remaining ingredients and serve with the remaining Bean Paste Sauce

PER SERVING: 190 CAL; 7G PROT; 16G FAT; 13G CARB; 0MG CHOL; 1250MG SOD; 2G FIBER

GOUGÈRES

Gougères is the classic French name for cheese puffs. Gougères can be adapted to include your favorite cheese such as Roquefort or Parmigiano-Reggiano instead of Gruyère cheese, making these the perfect hors d'oeuvres for just about any occasion. You can also add a couple of tablespoons of minced herbs or chives to the mix. If made ahead, these can be reheated in the oven in a matter of minutes.

4 tablespoons (½ stick) unsalted butter

¼ cup plus 2 tablespoons whole milk

1¼ teaspoons sea salt

6 grinds black pepper

¾ cup sifted all-purpose flour

¼ teaspoon baking powder

3 large eggs, at room temperature

1 cup plus 2 tablespoons coarsely grated Gruyère cheese

1. Preheat the oven to 375F. Line 2 baking sheets with parchment paper, and set aside.

2. Combine the butter, ¼ cup of the milk, ½ cup of water, ¼ teaspoon of the salt and the pepper in a 2-quart saucepan, and heat over medium heat. Bring to a boil, remove from the heat and add the flour and baking powder. Stir well with a wooden spoon, and return to the heat. Cook, stirring constantly, until the dough pulls away from the sides of the pan and forms a ball.

3. Transfer the dough to the bowl of an electric mixer fitted with the paddle attachment, and mix on low speed until the dough is just warm, for about 2 minutes.

4. Add the eggs, 1 at a time while mixer is running, and add ½ cup of the cheese. Beat the mixture until uniformly smooth and shiny, about 12 minutes.

5. Transfer the dough into a pastry bag fitted with a #3 tip. Pipe the gougères into small 1-inch mounds on the baking sheets. Space evenly about ½ inch apart, making about 18 gougères per sheet. Brush the tops with the remaining 2 tablespoons of milk, and sprinkle with the remaining cheese and salt.

6. Bake for 20 to 25 minutes, or until the gougères turn golden brown. Remove from the oven, and serve warm.

PER SERVING (3 PIECES): 130 CAL; 6G PROT; 9G FAT; 7G CARB; 75MG CHOL; 300MG SOD; 0G FIBER

SOY MOCK BOURSIN

Keep this recipe in mind for a party spread, or pack it in a crock and serve it with crackers.

6 ounce soy cream cheese

¼ cup (½ stick) soy margarine

1 teaspoon crushed garlic

½ teaspoon freshly ground black pepper

Pinch each of basil, marjoram and thyme

Bring cream cheese and margarine to room temperature, and cream together with remaining ingredients. Taste, and adjust seasonings to your liking.

PER SERVING: 110 CAL; 1G PROT; 12G FAT; 1G CARB; 0MG CHOL; 170MG SOD; 0G FIBER

GARDEN ROLLS

Inspired by the delicious garden, or salad, rolls from Vietnam, this Americanized vegetarian version retains the concept but calls for a different approach, including the use of scallions instead of garlic chives, cellophane noodles instead of rice vermicelli and baked tofu instead of shrimp.

1½ to 2 ounces dried cellophane noodles or bean thread noodles

Boiling water

6 rice paper wrappers

6 leaves red leaf lettuce, rinsed, dried and stem ends trimmed

1 cup shredded carrots

1 bunch cilantro, rinsed and dried

4 ounces Asian-seasoned baked tofu

6 thin scallions, green ends slivered

1. Soak the noodles in the boiling water to cover for about 7 minutes, or until softened. Drain, rinse in cold water and drain again. When cool, divide into 6 equal portions.

2. Assemble the ingredients in separate piles on the work surface, cutting the tofu into 12 thin slices. Starting with the first roll, quickly wet the rice paper wrapper in warm water, and place flat on the work surface. Place 1 piece of lettuce on the wrapper and layer shredded carrots on top, then leafy sprigs of fresh cilantro, 2 strips of tofu and 1 portion of noodles. Begin to wrap up the roll tightly, starting at the nearest rounded edge, making 1 turn. Fold in the left edge over the filling, leaving the right edge open. Continue rolling the wrapper tightly into a neat packet. Insert a scallion into the unwrapped edge of the roll so the green end protrudes like a plume. Repeat the process with the remaining ingredients. Set aside the rolls on a serving platter, and cover with damp paper towels until ready to serve. Serve with the Asian Dipping Sauce (below) or other sauce.

PER SERVING: 314 CAL; 19G PROT; 7G FAT; 45G CARB; 0MG CHOL; 340MG SOD; 6G FIBER

ASIAN DIPPING SAUCE

This delicious condiment resembles the thick, sweet paste served with Vietnamese summer or garden rolls. It's so good, you may want to double the recipe and keep it on hand for other Asian dishes.

½ cup hoisin sauce

1 tablespoon crunchy peanut butter

1 tablespoon Asian chili paste, or to taste

To mix the dipping sauce: Stir together the hoisin sauce, the peanut butter and the chili sauce until well mixed. Place in a serving dish and pass with the rolls.

PER SERVING: 200 CAL; 4G PROT; 6G FAT; 32G CARB; 0MG CHOL; 1,310MG SOD; 2G FIBER

HERB-STUFFED GRAPE LEAVES
WITH MINTY YOGURT SAUCE

Stuff grape leaves with a refreshing combination of rice, dill, mint, parsley and currants, and watch them disappear.

Filling

40 grape leaves (116-ounce jar) plus extra for lining the pan, drained

Boiling water

1 cup uncooked basmati rice

1 14½-ounce can vegetable stock or Vegetable Stock (page 332) plus enough water to make 2 cups

2 onions, minced

4 cloves garlic, pressed or minced

½ cup currants, soaked in water until softened and drained

¼ cup chopped fresh dillweed or 2 tablespoons dried dillweed

¼ cup chopped fresh flat-leaf parsley or 1 tablespoon plus 1 teaspoon dried parsley

2 teaspoons freshly ground black pepper

Sauce

2 cups plain nonfat yogurt

4 scallions, minced

¼ cup chopped fresh mint or 2 tablespoons dried mint

1 clove garlic, minced

1 teaspoon salt

1. To make the Filling: Pour the boiling water over the grape leaves to cover in a mixing bowl, and let them soak for 1 hour.

2. Meanwhile, combine the rice and stock-water mixture in a saucepan. Cover, bring to a boil, reduce the heat to low and cook for 10 minutes. Stir in the onions and garlic, cover and cook until all of the liquid has been absorbed, for about 10 minutes more. Remove the saucepan from the heat. Stir in the currants, dillweed, parsley and pepper with a fork while fluffing the rice.

3. Drain the grape leaves and pat them dry with a paper towel. Remove the stems. Lay a grape leaf vein side up with stem end toward you on a flat surface. Place a heaping tablespoon of the rice filling in the center. Fold in the sides, then roll up the leaf from the bottom to the tip. Repeat with the remaining grape leaves and filling, and set aside, seam sides down to prevent unrolling.

4. Line the bottom of a large saucepan with extra grape leaves to prevent the stuffed grape leaves from sticking to the pan. Place the filled grape leaves in the saucepan, seam sides down, in layers. Pour 2 cups of water over the leaves, cover and simmer until the leaves are tender, for about 45 minutes. Add an additional ⅓ to ½ cup more of water during cooking to keep the leaves from sticking, if needed. Remove from the heat and cool.

5. To make the Sauce: Combine the yogurt, scallions, mint, garlic and salt in a bowl, and stir together. Pass the grape leaves and serve the sauce on the side.

PER SERVING: 80 CAL; 3G PROT; 0.3G FAT; 15G CARB; 0.5MG CHOL; 164MG SOD; 2G FIBER

GRILLED POLENTA WITH MUSHROOM TOPPING

Polenta is cornmeal simmered in water. It can be eaten hot or cooled and sliced. It can be served plain or made fancy with a delicious topping like this one. This makes a particularly appetizing first course.

½ teaspoon salt

½ teaspoon freshly ground black pepper

1 cup cornmeal, preferably coarsely ground

¼ cup olive oil

1 pound white button mushrooms, thinly sliced

½ small onion, minced

4 cloves garlic, minced

1 tablespoon dried basil

1 tablespoon minced fresh parsley

1. Combine 4 cups of water, the salt and pepper in a heavy saucepan, and cook over high heat. When the water boils, add the cornmeal in a steady thin stream, stirring constantly with a wooden spoon. Reduce the heat to low, and continue cooking for 20 minutes, stirring frequently, until the polenta becomes very thick.

2. Spoon the polenta onto a sheet of wax paper. With a wet spatula, spread the polenta until it is ½ inch thick. While the polenta cools, heat the oil in a skillet over high heat, and cook the mushrooms, onion, garlic, basil and parsley, stirring, for about 5 minutes, or until the mushrooms are soft. Set aside, and keep warm.

3. Preheat the broiler. Spray a baking sheet with nonstick cooking spray.

4. Cut the polenta into 6 large or 12 small squares, and place them on the baking sheet. Broil on both sides until golden-brown spots appear. Top with the mushroom sauce, and serve at once.

PER SERVING (1 LARGE OR 2 SMALL PIECES): 195 CAL; 3G PROT; 10G FAT; 23G CARB; 0MG CHOL; 180MG SOD; 4G FIBER

OLIVE-TOMATO CROSTINI

A mild-flavored bulb, the shallot has an onionlike taste. You can find it in the produce section of supermarkets. Feel free to substitute scallions, onions or leeks for shallots in most recipes. The flower buds of a Mediterranean shrub, capers are picked before they blossom, then packed in salt or brine. They are used to flavor a number of dishes. Crunchy and slightly salty, these crostini are perfect with before-dinner drinks.

Olive Paste

1 cup pitted kalamata or niçoise olives

2 tablespoons chopped shallot or onion

2 tablespoons capers, rinsed, optional

2 tablespoons olive oil

¼ teaspoon dried thyme

2 to 3 teaspoons fresh lemon juice or red wine vinegar, or to taste

Crostini

16 thin slices French bread

1 to 2 cloves garlic, halved

16 small ripe, firm tomatoes (red and yellow if possible), sliced

Fresh basil leaves

Freshly ground black pepper to taste

1. To make the Paste: Rinse the olives to remove excess salt. Put the olives, shallot, capers, oil and thyme into a food processor, and purée until it becomes a smooth or textured paste, whichever you prefer. Stir in the lemon juice. Set aside.

2. To make the Crostini: Toast the bread on both sides, and immediately rub with the garlic. Spread a thin layer of Olive Paste on the bread and top with a few slices of the tomato. Put a few basil leaves between the tomatoes. Sprinkle with a generous amount of pepper. Serve at once.

PER CROSTINI: 97 CAL; 3G PROT; 3G FAT; 15G CARB; 0MG CHOL; 166MG SOD; 1G FIBER

GREEN PEA AND ARTICHOKE TERRINE

Artichokes are in season in fall or in spring when fresh peas are also available. Make the terrine with frozen peas in fall. Either way, you'll have a beautiful terrine with two layers of contrasting green shades. If fresh artichokes are unavailable, substitute 2 cups chopped canned artichoke hearts, not packed in oil.

4 fresh artichokes

½ cup Vegetable Stock (page 332)

2 cups fresh or frozen green peas

3 medium-sized baking potatoes, peeled and diced

¼ teaspoon ground nutmeg

Salt and freshly ground black pepper to taste

1. Cut off the tops of the artichokes, using a sharp knife. Remove the thorns on the outer leaves and the tiny inner leaves. Steam the artichokes, upside down, in a steamer basket or in a saucepan with 1 inch of water for 30 to 60 minutes. The artichokes are done when the outer leaves come off easily. Remove from the heat, and cool.

2. Meanwhile, bring the stock to a boil in a saucepan over medium heat. Add the peas and potatoes. Reduce the heat to low, and cook until the potatoes are tender, for about 15 minutes. Remove from the heat, and cool. Add the nutmeg, salt and pepper. Put the mixture into a blender or food processor, and purée. Set aside.

3. Remove the outer artichoke leaves, and scrape off the tender flesh with a spoon when the artichokes are cool enough to handle. The central leaves will come off together. Chop the tender portion. Spoon out the fuzzy choke from the center and discard. Dice the heart, which is directly beneath the choke, for a total of 2 cups of artichoke meat. Put into a blender or food processor with enough liquid to process, and purée. Set aside.

4. Pour the pea-potato purée into a terrine pan or a 5-cup loaf pan. Spread the artichoke purée on top. Cover with plastic wrap, and refrigerate overnight. Just before serving, run a thin knife around the perimeter of the pan to loosen the terrine. Place an inverted serving platter over the pan, carefully turn it over to unmold the terrine and serve.

PER SERVING: 71 CAL; 3G PROT; 0G FAT; 15G CARB; 0MG CHOL; 54MG SOD; 5G FIBER

PITA CRISPS WITH SPINACH, RED PEPPER AND FETA

SERVES 8

The ever-useful pita bread converts into handy "crackers" for appetizers.

4 whole wheat pita breads

2 large cloves garlic, halved

4 cups fresh spinach leaves, well rinsed but not dried

½ cup roasted red bell pepper strips (see page 46)

3 tablespoons crumbled feta cheese

1. Preheat the broiler. Split the pita in half horizontally. Toast the halves under the broiler or in a toaster. Rub each toasted pita half with the garlic. Set aside.

2. Put the spinach in a large saucepan and steam it, covered, over medium-high heat for about 3 minutes, or until the leaves wilt. Remove from the heat, and, using tongs, squeeze out excess liquid.

3. Arrange the toasted pita halves on a heatproof serving platter. Top them evenly with the spinach, bell pepper strips and feta. Broil, rotating the platter once, until the cheese begins to melt, for about 2 minutes. Remove from the oven, and serve.

PER SERVING: 82 CAL; 3G PROT; 2G FAT; 16G CARB; 3MG CHOL; 197MG SOD; 3G FIBER

CRISPY BAKED EGG ROLLS

SERVES 12 (MAKES 24)

Egg rolls are usually fried, but these are baked until golden, one way to cut back on the calorie count. You may want to serve these egg rolls with the Asian Dipping Sauce (page 61).

1 cup diced onion

4 cloves garlic, minced

1 tablespoon minced fresh ginger

3 cups diced green cabbage

2 cups diced celery

1 cup diced drained bamboo shoots

1 cup diced drained water chestnuts

½ cup diced fresh shiitake mushrooms

½ cup diced white button mushrooms

2 tablespoons low-sodium soy sauce

1 tablespoon rice wine or mirin

1 tablespoon honey

24 egg roll wrappers

2 tablespoons dark sesame oil, warmed

1. Preheat the oven to 400F.

2. Heat ¼ cup of water in a wok until simmering. Cook the onion, garlic and ginger until the onion is soft but not browned, about 5 minutes. Add the cabbage, celery, bamboo shoots, water chestnuts and mushrooms and cook until the vegetables soften, for about 8 minutes. Remove from the heat. Add the soy sauce, rice wine and honey, and toss well. Place the mixture in a colander over a bowl, and let stand 10 minutes to drain off any excess moisture.

3. Be sure your work surface is dry for egg roll wrapping. Stack the egg roll wrappers with 1 corner pointing away from you. Have a small bowl of water ready. Spoon ¼ cup of the drained filling into the center of each wrapper. Lightly brush the edges of the wrapper with water. Fold the side corners to the center, covering the filling. Next bring the bottom corner to the center, tuck slightly under the filling, and continue to roll the wrapper into a cylinder, sealing the top corner by moistening it slightly with water and pressing it down. Place the egg rolls, seam sides down, on 2 nonstick baking sheets without crowding. Lightly brush them with some sesame oil.

4. Bake the rolls in the center of the oven, turning once, until golden and crisp, for 15 to 20 minutes. Remove from the oven, and serve at once.

PER EGG ROLL: 80 CAL; 3G PROT; 1G FAT; 14G CARB; 0MG CHOL; 57MG SOD; 1G FIBER

POT STICKERS

The combination of pan-frying and steaming makes these little dumplings both crunchy and juicy. Dip them into small bowls filled with soy sauce, rice vinegar or chili oil. You can use Japanese gyoza or Chinese wonton skins instead of making your own dough.

Filling

5 dried shiitake mushrooms, soaked

1½ cups finely shredded napa or other Chinese cabbage

1 cup finely chopped carrots

2 scallions, finely chopped

1 tablespoon regular or low-sodium soy sauce

1 tablespoon rice wine or dry sherry

1 tablespoon cornstarch

2 teaspoons dark sesame oil

1 teaspoon grated fresh ginger

½ teaspoon granulated sugar

Dough

3 cups all-purpose flour plus extra for rolling

1⅓ cups boiling water

2 tablespoons vegetable oil

⅔ cup Vegetable Stock (page 332)

1. To make the Filling: Soak the dried mushrooms in warm water for 30 minutes. Drain. Cut off, and discard the stems and finely chop the caps. Combine the mushrooms with the remaining filling ingredients in a bowl, mixing well. Set aside.

2. To make the Dough: Measure the flour into a large bowl. Mix in the boiling water, stirring with chopsticks or a fork until the dough is evenly moistened. Cover and let stand for 30 minutes. Knead the dough on a lightly floured surface until smooth and elastic, for about 5 minutes. Divide the dough in half. Roll each half into a 14-inch-long cylinder, and cut crosswise into 1-inch pieces. Shape each piece into a ball, and cover with a damp dishcloth.

3. To shape each pot sticker, flatten 1 ball of dough with a rolling pin on a lightly floured surface to make a 3-inch circle. Keep the remaining dough covered to prevent it from drying. Place 1 heaping teaspoon of the filling in the center of the circle. Lightly moisten the edges of the circle with water. Fold the circle in half to form a semicircle. Starting at one end, pinch the curved edges together to make 4 to 6 pleats along the edge. Press to seal securely. Place the pot sticker, seam sides up, on a baking sheet. Cover with a damp towel while you shape the remaining pot stickers.

4. Preheat the oven to 200F.

5. Heat a large nonstick skillet over high heat until hot. Add 1 tablespoon of oil, swirling to coat the sides. Set half of the pot stickers, seam sides up, in the skillet. Cook until the bottoms are golden brown, for 2 to 3 minutes, gently swirling the skillet occasionally. Drain excess oil, and reduce the heat to medium. Pour in ⅓ cup stock, cover and cook until the liquid has evaporated, for 5 to 6 minutes, swirling the skillet occasionally. Transfer the pot stickers to a serving platter, and keep them warm in the preheated oven. Cook the remaining pot stickers with the remaining oil and remaining stock. Serve hot.

PER POT STICKER: 63 CAL; 2G PROT; 2G FAT; 11G CARB; 0MG CHOL; 39MG SOD; 1G FIBER

CARIBBEAN SPICE POPCORN

SERVES 4

The fiery taste of the islands comes with the cayenne, so use as much or as little cayenne as you like. Look for vegetable seasoning on the spice shelf in a supermarket or natural foods store. The seasoning is used in place of salt or to bolster flavors in a dish.

2 tablespoons vegetable seasoning

1 teaspoon grated lemon zest

1 teaspoon curry powder

Pinch cayenne, or to taste

1 teaspoon salt, optional

8 cups hot air-popped popcorn

1. Combine the vegetable seasoning, lemon zest, curry powder, cayenne and salt, if using, in a bowl.

2. Spray a large serving bowl lightly on all sides with nonstick butter-flavored cooking spray. Add 2 to 3 cups of the hot popcorn, spray lightly and sprinkle evenly with a heaping teaspoon of mixed seasonings. Add another layer of the popcorn, spray and seasoning mixture. Add a final layer of the popcorn and spray, and sprinkle the remaining seasoning all over. Serve at once without tossing.

PER SERVING: 69 CAL; 2G PROT; 2G FAT; 13G CARB; 0MG CHOL; 3MG SOD; 2G FIBER

ATHENIAN MUSHROOMS

SERVES 4

Serve this as an appetizer course, or use it as an accompaniment. Try an assortment of wild mushrooms, taking advantage of the wide array at your local market.

3 tablespoons olive oil

1 large onion, diced

2 cups dry white wine

1 cup tomato juice

2 teaspoons coriander seeds, coarsely crushed

1 teaspoon ground coriander

2 bay leaves

1 pound wild mushrooms, ends trimmed

Salt and freshly ground black pepper to taste

Several paper-thin slices black truffle, for garnish, optional

1. Heat the oil in a large skillet or wok over medium heat. Add the onion, cover and cook until translucent, about 8 minutes, stirring occasionally.

2. Add the wine, tomato juice, coriander seeds, ground coriander and bay leaves. Bring to a boil, and cook until the mixture is reduced to ¾ cup.

3. Add the mushrooms, and continue to cook for 2 minutes, stirring constantly. Cook completely, until the mushrooms are tender, stirring occasionally. Season with salt and pepper to taste.

4. Remove from the heat, cover and refrigerate for 1 day. Remove from the refrigerator about 30 minutes before serving.

5. To serve, drain the mushrooms, and arrange them on a platter or in a bowl. Or use the mushrooms in a salad. Garnish with truffles, if using.

PER SERVING: 245 CAL; 4G PROT; 11G FAT; 15G CARB; 0MG CHOL; 252MG SOD; 5G FIBER

SAVORY FARRO CAKE

This is a traditional recipe from the Garfagnana region of Tuscany. The cake works well as a first or main course with vegetables or a salad.

Pie Crust

6 tablespoons (¾ stick) unsalted butter, at room temperature, divided

1⅓ cups all-purpose flour

Pinch salt

1 large egg, lightly beaten

Filling

2 cups cooked farro (see page 48)

1 cup low-fat or whole milk ricotta

¼ cup grated Parmesan cheese

3 large eggs, lightly beaten

¼ teaspoon freshly grated nutmeg

2 tablespoons chopped fresh flat-leaf parsley

2 tablespoons chopped fresh marjoram

Salt and freshly ground black pepper to taste

1. Preheat the oven to 325F. Butter an 8-inch springform pan with 2 tablespoons of the softened butter.

2. To make the Pie Crust: Combine the flour and salt in a bowl. Cut in the remaining 4 tablespoons of butter, and work into the flour. Add the egg, and mix the dough until it just holds together. Press the dough into the springform pan, bottom crust first, then the sides.

3. To make the Filling: Combine the farro, ricotta, Parmesan cheese, eggs, nutmeg, parsley, marjoram, salt and pepper. Spoon the mixture into the prepared crust.

4. Bake for 40 minutes, or until set. Remove from the oven, cool to lukewarm, cut into wedges and serve.

PER SERVING: 480 CAL; 17G PROT; 25G FAT; 48G CARB; 200MG CHOL; 190MG SOD; 7G FIBER

TOMATO AND HERB BRUSCHETTA

Bruschetta is a simple but superb Italian appetizer of thick slices of toasted bread spread with a garden-fresh topping of ripe red tomatoes, basil, garlic and olive oil. It's a welcome appetizer for pasta or just about any other entrée.

1½ pounds ripe plum tomatoes, seeded and chopped

⅓ cup chopped fresh basil

1 tablespoon extra virgin olive oil

1 tablespoon balsamic vinegar

1 small clove garlic, minced

2 teaspoons chopped fresh oregano or generous ½ teaspoon dried oregano

1 teaspoon fresh lemon juice

Salt and freshly ground black pepper to taste

6½-inch- to ¾-inch-thick slices crusty bread, grilled or toasted

1. Mix the tomatoes, basil, oil, vinegar, garlic, oregano and lemon juice in a bowl. Season with salt and pepper.

2. Cut the grilled bread slices in half to serve. Set the slices on serving plates, and spoon the tomato mixture over them.

PER SERVING (2 HALVES): 99 CAL; 2G PROT; 3G FAT; 14G CARB; 0MG CHOL; 134MG SOD; 1G FIBER

ASIAN "CHICKEN" ROLLS

SERVES 2 (MAKES 6)

These crispy spring rolls make a perfect appetizer for a full-blown Asian dinner of fried rice, sweet-and-sour tofu or crispy noodles. The accompanying dipping sauce offers a satisfying counterpoint to the jasmine tea, which is the ideal beverage. Ginger ice cream complements the meal.

"Chicken" Rolls

1 tablespoon plus 1 cup vegetable oil for frying

6 ounces soy "chicken" strips

1 teaspoon onion powder

1 teaspoon garlic powder

6 rice paper wrappers

1 packed cup shredded carrots

12 stems cilantro, rinsed and trimmed

½ cup fresh mint leaves

Crushed peanuts, for garnish, optional

Dipping Sauce

⅓ cup fresh lime juice

¼ cup shredded carrots

¼ cup granulated sugar, or to taste

1 teaspoon minced garlic

1 teaspoon Asian chili paste, or to taste

1. To make the "Chicken" Rolls: Heat 1 tablespoon of the oil in a large wok or skillet over medium heat. Toss the "chicken" strips with the onion and garlic powders, and stir-fry for about 5 minutes, or until golden. Remove them from the heat, and drain on paper towels.

2. Moisten the rice paper wrappers, 2 sheets at a time, by dipping the sheets in cold water for about 10 seconds. Set them aside on a flat surface until they are soft and pliable, about 1 minute. Assemble the remaining ingredients in separate equal-sized piles on the work surface, making sure that the mint and cilantro stems are trimmed. Starting with the first roll on the edge closest to you, place several pieces of "chicken" on a wrapper, and layer on top shredded carrots, leafy sprigs of cilantro and several mint leaves. Wrap up the roll tightly by starting at the closest rounded end, taking 1 turn. Fold in each side over the filling, and continue rolling up the wrapper tightly into a neat packet. Repeat the process until done, placing the rolls seam sides down to prevent unrolling.

3. Heat the remaining 1 cup of the oil in a large wok or skillet over medium heat. Fry the rolls in batches until they are golden on all sides, for about 3 minutes. Remove them from the heat, and drain them on paper towels.

4. Meanwhile, to make the Dipping Sauce: Combine the ingredients with ¼ cup of water, stirring until the sugar dissolves. Pour into a small serving bowl.

5. To serve, arrange the rolls on a serving plate, garnish them with crushed peanuts, if desired, and pass with the Dipping Sauce.

PER SERVING (3 ROLLS): 310 CAL; 14G PROT; 11G FAT; 45G CARB; 0MG CHOL; 180MG SOD; 5G FIBER

SOUTHWESTERN PINWHEELS

This appetizer can easily be doubled or tripled to serve a crowd, and it needs to be made ahead, so it's perfect for a party. Look for flavored tortillas in large supermarkets or specialty food shops.

4 ounces light cream cheese, softened

¼ cup finely shredded Mexican-style or sharp cheddar cheese

2 tablespoons thinly sliced scallion

2 tablespoons chunky salsa or ½ tablespoon chopped, canned chipotle chiles in adobo sauce

2 tablespoons chopped cilantro

½ teaspoon ground cumin

2 10-inch green chile or spinach-flavored flour tortillas

About 20 small spinach leaves, rinsed and dried

12 small cilantro sprigs, for garnish

Salsa

1. Combine the cream cheese, shredded cheese, scallions, salsa, chopped cilantro and cumin in a bowl; mix well. Spread evenly over the tortillas. Place a layer of the spinach over the cheese on each tortilla. Roll tightly; wrap in plastic. Chill at least 1 hour or up to 8 hours.

2. Cut crosswise into 1-inch pieces. Arrange cut sides up on a serving platter. Garnish each pinwheel with a cilantro sprig. Cover and chill up to 1 hour before serving. Serve with a dollop of salsa on top.

PER SERVING (2 PIECES): 80 CAL; 3G PROT; 3.5G FAT; 9G CARB; 10MG CHOL; 160MG SOD; <1G FIBER

PATACONES WITH SPICY BEAN DIP

Patacones are fried slices of plantain, a typical dish served in Costa Rica. Serve them as an appetizer with the Spicy Bean Dip.

Patacones

2 green plantains

About 3 cups vegetable oil for deep-frying

Salt to taste

Spicy Bean Dip

2 tablespoons vegetable oil

½ large onion, diced

3 cloves garlic, minced

2 red or green chiles, sliced, or to taste

2 cups cooked beans, such as black turtle or pinto beans, drained and rinsed

1 sprig fresh rosemary, chopped

½ teaspoon ground cumin

Salt and freshly ground black pepper to taste

½ cup chopped cilantro

¼ cup sour cream for garnish

1. To make the Patacones: Score the plantains lengthwise, peel, cut into discs about ½ inch thick, and set aside.

2. Heat the oil in a deep saucepan or large skillet. When hot, gently place several plantain slices into the pan, and fry, turning occasionally, about 7 minutes, or until golden. Remove from the oil, and drain on paper towels.

3. Let cool for 5 minutes, and, using the side of a cleaver, press each piece until flat. Reheat the oil in the skillet, and refry all the plantain pieces until slightly browned. Remove from the heat, drain on paper towels and sprinkle with salt before serving. Set aside.

4. To make the Spicy Bean Dip: Heat the oil in a large skillet over medium heat. When very hot, add the onion, and sauté for about 5 minutes, or until translucent. Add the garlic and chiles, and sauté for 2 minutes. Add the beans, rosemary, cumin, salt and pepper. Cook until heated through, for about 5 minutes. Remove from the heat. Spoon the mixture into a food processor, adding water as needed to process. Add the cilantro, and purée until smooth. Spoon into a serving dish, top with the sour cream and serve hot with the patacones.

PER SERVING: 150 CAL; 1G PROT; 5G FAT; 29G CARB; 0MG CHOL; 0MG SOD; 2G FIBER

PER SERVING (SPICY BEAN DIP): 230 CAL; 9G PROT; 11G FAT; 26G CARB; 5MG CHOL; 15MG SOD; 9G FIBER

Late-season tomatoes are perfect for baking. They're firm and sturdy, but more importantly, baking brings out the flavor that hasn't fully matured because the sunshine has diminished in the last month. If you don't like blue cheese, substitute any creamy soft cheese, such as St. Honoré or Explorateur cheese. Be sure to squeeze spinach as dry as possible to avoid a soggy filling.

1 10-ounce package frozen chopped spinach, thawed and squeezed to remove excess liquid

1 cup low-fat small-curd cottage cheese

½ cup thinly sliced scallions

¼ cup crumbled soft blue cheese

½ teaspoon freshly ground black pepper

1 14-ounce can white kidney beans, drained and rinsed

2 large tomatoes

8 cups mixed salad greens, rinsed and dried

8 thin slices Italian bread, toasted

1. Preheat the oven to 400F. Bring a large pot of water to a boil over medium heat.

2. Meanwhile, mix the spinach, cottage cheese, scallions, blue cheese and pepper in a bowl until well blended. Gently stir in the beans. Set aside.

3. Score an "x" in the base of each tomato, using a sharp paring knife. Carefully place the tomatoes into the boiling water, and cook for 20 seconds. Remove from the water with a slotted spoon. When cool enough to handle, peel the tomatoes with a small sharp knife, and cut out the cores. Cut each tomato in half through the center. With a spoon, scoop out and discard the seeds, then remove and discard about half of the flesh from each tomato half.

4. Stuff the tomato halves with the spinach–cheese mixture, and place them in a shallow baking dish just large enough to hold the tomatoes. Bake until soft and beginning to exude juices, for about 20 minutes.

5. Meanwhile, arrange the salad greens in a circle on each of 4 plates. Carefully transfer 1 tomato half to the center of each ring. Serve with the toasted bread slices.

PER SERVING (1 SALAD): 389 CAL; 25G PROT; 7G FAT; 58G CARB; 11MG CHOL; 770MG SOD; 13G FIBER

CURRIED POTATO-STUFFED BREADS

You've probably eaten something like this in Indian restaurants—flatbread stuffed with curried vegetables. We've made these from scratch, with homemade dough, but really they are just as good, and certainly much easier, made with store-bought flour tortillas. The potato mixture doesn't take long to prepare, less than 30 minutes. Serve alongside curries or as an appetizer with a savory yogurt dipping sauce, such as Raita (page 144).

3 cups peeled and coarsely chopped all-purpose potatoes

1 cup finely diced carrot

Salt to taste

1 tablespoon vegetable oil plus extra for cooking breads

1 cup finely chopped onion

2 teaspoons curry powder

4 8-inch flour tortillas

1. Put the potatoes and carrot in a large saucepan with enough water to cover by 1 inch, and add ½ teaspoon of salt. Boil until the potatoes are soft, for about 8 minutes. Drain, reserving the cooking liquid, and transfer the vegetables to a bowl.

2. Heat the oil in a large skillet. Add the onion, and sauté over medium heat, stirring often, until translucent, for 6 to 7 minutes. Stir in the curry powder, and cook, stirring, for 15 seconds. Add ½ cup of the reserved cooking liquid to the pan. Cook briefly over high heat to reduce the liquid by about half, for 30 seconds. Add the onion with liquid to the potatoes, and mash well, adding additional salt if desired.

3. Working with 1 tortilla at a time, spread some of the mashed potato mixture thickly over half of the tortilla. Fold the tortilla over the potato mixture to close. Heat 1 teaspoon of oil in a large skillet. Add the bread, and fry over medium heat until browned, for 45 to 60 seconds. Flip the bread, and cook until browned on the other side. Transfer to a chopping board, and slice in half. Repeat for the remaining breads. Serve immediately, or place in a warm oven until ready to serve.

PER SERVING (1 STUFFED TORTILLA): 311 CAL; 6G PROT; 10G FAT; 50G CARB; 0MG CHOL; 234MG SOD; 5G FIBER

SPICY POTATOES

The combination of crispy potatoes and spicy tomato sauce makes this appetizer simply irresistible. If you prefer less heat, use one jalapeño chile instead of two.

5 tablespoons olive oil

8 large baking potatoes, peeled and cut into 1-inch cubes

1 medium-sized onion, finely chopped

3 cloves garlic, minced

1 16-ounce can peeled plum tomatoes, finely chopped

½ cup Vegetable Stock (page 332)

2 jalapeño chiles, seeded and finely chopped

2 tablespoons chopped fresh flat-leaf parsley

1. Preheat the oven to 425F.

2. Heat 4 tablespoons of the oil in a large skillet over medium-high heat. Add the potatoes, and cook, stirring often, for about 8 minutes, or until browned. Transfer the potatoes and any oil remaining in the skillet to a baking dish, and bake until crisp and tender, for 12 to 15 minutes.

3. Heat the remaining 1 tablespoon of oil in the same skillet. Add the onion and garlic, and cook, stirring often, until the onion is softened, for about 5 minutes. Add the remaining ingredients, and cook, uncovered, for 10 to 12 minutes, or until heated through. Transfer the potatoes to a serving bowl. Add the tomato mixture, and toss to coat. Serve warm.

PER SERVING: 94 CAL; 2G PROT; 4G FAT; 13G CARB; 0MG CHOL; 72MG SOD; 1G FIBER

ARTICHOKES WITH QUINOA FILLING
AND SWEET RED PEPPER COULIS

This colorful appetizer salad calls for combining vegetable flavors and textures in a wholesome quinoa dish. Use the Sweet Red Pepper Coulis as both salad dressing and dipping sauce for the artichoke leaves after you have eaten the quinoa filling.

Sweet Red Pepper Coulis

3 large red bell peppers

1 large onion, unpeeled

2 teaspoons garlic powder

1 tablespoon balsamic vinegar

2 teaspoons garlic powder

Salt and freshly ground black pepper to taste

Artichokes with Quinoa Filling

2 large artichokes

¼ cup uncooked quinoa

½ cup fresh or frozen corn kernels

¼ cup diced red onion

1 tablespoon minced fresh basil

1 teaspoon onion powder, or to taste

1 teaspoon garlic powder, or to taste

1. Preheat the oven to 400F.

2. To make the Sweet Red Pepper Coulis: Wrap the peppers and onion in separate foil packets, place on a baking dish and bake for about 1 hour, or until tender.

3. Meanwhile, to make the Artichokes with Quinoa Filling: Using kitchen shears, snip off the prickly ends of the artichoke leaves and discard. Trim off the bottoms evenly so the artichokes stand upright without tipping. Place a steamer rack in a large saucepan, stand artichokes upright in the steamer, fill the pan with about 2 inches water, cover the pan and bring water to a boil. Steam the artichokes until tender, for about 30 minutes. Using tongs, remove the artichokes from the heat, turn upside down to cool and allow the water to drain.

4. Fill a saucepan with water, and bring to a boil. Stir in the quinoa, cook for 2 to 3 minutes, cover the pan and reduce the heat to medium-low. Continue cooking for about 15 minutes, or until the grains are tender. Remove from the heat, and drain. Set aside.

5. When the peppers and onion are tender, remove from the heat, and set aside until cool enough to handle. Unwrap the foil, and carefully peel off the pepper skins. Open the peppers, catching pepper juices in the blender, and remove seeds. Put the peppers into the blender. Peel off the onion skin, cut the onion into pieces and put in the blender. Add the balsamic vinegar, garlic powder, salt and pepper to taste, and purée until smooth. Set aside.

6. Combine the quinoa, corn and red onion. Stir in the basil, onion and garlic powders and enough Sweet Red Pepper Coulis to moisten the mixture. Set aside.

7. Pry open the artichoke leaves carefully, and scoop out the inner prickly chokes, leaving the artichokes intact. Spoon the quinoa mixture into the artichokes, stand upright on plates, and serve.

8. Pass the remaining Sweet Red Pepper Coulis with the artichokes for dipping the leaves. Save any remaining coulis for another use.

PER SERVING (1 ARTICHOKE WITH FILLING): 320 CAL; 13G PROT; 2.5G FAT; 69G CARB; 0MG CHOL; 170MG SOD; 18G FIBER

VEGETABLE-STUFFED TOFU

Most baked marinated tofu is packaged in four pieces. If not, slice lengthwise into four equal slabs.

Dipping Sauce

1 tablespoon regular or low-sodium soy sauce

1 tablespoon rice vinegar

1 tablespoon mirin

1½ minced teaspoons scallion

1 teaspoon dark sesame oil

Tofu

3 teaspoons olive oil

1 small clove garlic, minced

1 teaspoon minced fresh ginger

6 scallions, thinly sliced

½ red bell pepper, finely chopped

½ green bell pepper, finely chopped

1 teaspoon tamari or low-sodium soy sauce

¼ cup chopped cilantro plus additional for garnish

1½ teaspoons curry powder

10 ounces baked marinated tofu, cut lengthwise into 4 equal pieces

1. To make the Dipping Sauce: In a small bowl, mix all the sauce ingredients. Set aside.

2. To make the Tofu: Heat 1 teaspoon of the olive oil in a large skillet over medium heat. Add the garlic, and cook, stirring, for 30 seconds. Add the ginger, and stir well. Add the scallions, bell peppers, and tamari, and cook until softened, for about 3 minutes. Remove from the heat, and stir in the cilantro. Set aside.

3. Heat the remaining 2 teaspoons of olive oil in a large skillet over medium heat. Add the curry powder, and stir well. Add the tofu slices in single layer, and cook until golden, turning once, for about 2 minutes per side. Remove to paper towels, and drain.

4. Slice each piece of tofu horizontally about three-quarters of the way through, holding a knife parallel to the work surface. Place the tofu on plates. Gently lift the top of 1 piece of tofu, and spoon some of the vegetable mixture over the bottom portion. Replace the top of the tofu, and sprinkle with additional chopped cilantro. Repeat with the remaining tofu, vegetable mixture and cilantro. Serve with the Dipping Sauce.

PER SERVING: 95 CAL; 6G PROT; 7G FAT; 4G CARB; 0MG CHOL; 346MG SOD; 1G FIBER

SPICY CUCUMBER SANDWICHES

Delicate and delicious, these are suitable accompaniments for a tea party or for other social gatherings when you want to keep the food light before dinner.

¼ cup soy mayonnaise or yogurt cheese

¼ to ½ teaspoon prepared horseradish

8 thin slices whole wheat or white bread, crusts removed

1 English cucumber, thinly sliced

½ cup torn arugula or watercress leaves, rinsed and dried

Salt

Ground white pepper

1. Mix together the soy mayonnaise and horseradish. Spread half of the bread slices with the mixture, and cover with the cucumber slices. Top with the sprigs of arugula and season with salt and pepper. Cover with the remaining bread slices, and apply firm but delicate pressure with the palm of your hand.

2. Cut each sandwich into 4 triangles. Pile the triangles neatly on a serving plate, and cover with a lightly dampened cloth until serving.

PER SANDWICH (4 PIECES): 164 CAL; 5G PROT; 5G FAT; 26G CARB; 0MG CHOL; 371MG SOD.; 4G FIBER

SNAPPY TACOS

Use these as appetizers or starters for a Tex-Mex spread.

4 teaspoons vegetable oil

1 medium-sized onion, finely chopped, divided

3 cloves garlic, minced, divided

12 ounces soy "ground meat," plain or taco-flavored

½ cup low-sodium vegetable stock or Vegetable Stock (page 332)

¼ cup dark beer

2 large jalapeño chiles, seeded and finely chopped

2 teaspoons chili powder

1 teaspoon dried oregano

½ cup salsa, drained

½ cup chopped cilantro

Salt and freshly ground black pepper to taste

8 taco shells

Garnishes: shredded lettuce, salsa, shredded Jack or Tex-Mex soy cheese, sliced avocado, soy sour cream, chopped scallions.

1. Heat 2 teaspoons of the oil in a skillet over medium-high heat. Add ¼ cup of the onion and ¼ teaspoon of the garlic and cook, stirring often, until the onion is softened, for 2 to 3 minutes. Reduce the heat to medium, and mix in the "meat," stock and beer. Reduce the heat to low, and cook until the liquid has almost evaporated, for about 8 minutes. Transfer the mixture to a plate, and set aside. Wipe out the skillet.

2. Heat the remaining 2 teaspoons of oil in the skillet over medium-low heat. Add the remaining onion and garlic, and cook, stirring often, until the onion is softened, for about 4 minutes. Add the jalapeños, chili powder and oregano , stirring until the mixture is fragrant, for about 30 seconds. Add the reserved "meat," salsa and cilantro, and stir well. Season to taste with salt and pepper. Cook, stirring occasionally, for 3 to 4 minutes.

3. Spoon ¼ cup of the filling into each taco shell. Top with the garnishes, as desired, and serve hot.

PER SERVING (WITHOUT GARNISHES): 302 CAL; 22G PROT; 11G FAT; 28G CARB; 0MG CHOL; 633MG SOD; 8G FIBER

GREAT GUACAMOLE

Always welcome at the table or at parties, guacamole is a many-splendored dish that works as well as a garnish as it does as a dip with chips or trimmed vegetables. If you want to make this in advance, be sure to store the mashed avocado in an airtight container, otherwise the avocado darkens when exposed to air.

2 ripe avocados

2 tablespoons fresh lemon juice

3 tablespoons chopped tomato

1 shallot, minced

2 cloves garlic, minced

1 tablespoon chopped cilantro

½ teaspoon salt

Several drops hot pepper sauce

Cut the avocados in half, and remove the seeds. Scoop out the pulp, and place in a shallow bowl. Drizzle with the lemon juice, and mash with a fork. Add the remaining ingredients, and mix well. Serve.

PER SERVING (¼ CUP): 86 CAL; 1G PROT; 8G FAT; 5G CARB; 0MG CHOL; 6MG SOD; 2G FIBER

BABA GHANOUSH

This much-revered Middle Eastern eggplant purée gets its name—apocryphally—from the tale of a devoted son who set out to prepare something wonderful that his very old and very toothless father could eat.

When choosing an eggplant, look for one with a firm, glossy skin. When you press the skin, it should give and bounce back. If you want an eggplant with a minimum of seeds, look at the spot opposite the stem end. If it is round, the eggplant is a not-so-seedy "male"; if oval, it is "female" and likely to be seedy. Eggplants soak up the juices or oils with which they are cooked. When cooking eggplant, avoid excess amounts of oil. Before cooking an eggplant, especially if you are frying it and want to remove some of the liquid and bitterness, slice and salt the eggplant, and let it drain for 1 hour, rinse if desired, then cook.

Tahini, or sesame paste, is available in large supermarkets, whole food markets and Middle Eastern groceries. For an authentic smoky taste, grill or broil the eggplant first. Serve baba ghanoush with wedges of pita bread or with crackers.

2 pounds purple eggplant, cut in half lengthwise, flesh side scored deeply in a crosshatch pattern

1 tablespoon olive oil

¼ cup plain low-fat or nonfat yogurt

¼ cup tahini

Juice from 1 to 2 lemons, or to taste

2 small cloves garlic, finely minced

1 teaspoon salt, or more to taste

Minced fresh parsley

Assorted raw vegetables, including at least 3 of the following: red bell pepper strips, green bell pepper strips, carrot sticks, celery sticks, cucumber spears, jícama sticks, fennel slices

1. Prepare a hot charcoal fire, or preheat a gas grill to medium-low heat. Alternatively, preheat the broiler, and turn it down to the lowest possible heat.

2. Brush the eggplant halves with the oil, and place, flesh sides down on the grill, or flesh sides up under the broiler. Cook until charred and very soft, turning once, for about 40 minutes. Set the eggplant in a colander in the sink to drain until it's no longer warm to the touch.

3. Scoop the cooled eggplant flesh into a food processor or food mill, discarding the skin. Process the eggplants with a few pulses, or force them through a food mill into a bowl. Stir in the yogurt, tahini, lemon juice, garlic and salt. Place the mixture in a serving dish, and sprinkle the top with parsley. Chill well. Serve as a dip with raw vegetables.

PER SERVING: 225 CAL; 5G PROT; 9G FAT; 28G CARB; 1MG CHOL; 611MG SOD; 88 FIBER

beverages

INSTEAD OF TURNING TO YOUR supermarket for high-sugar, costly drinks to go with your meals, make your own beverages at home. Not only can you be assured that the nutritional value of your drinks will be higher, but you can create flavorful, delicious refreshments that no market carries. And, you can keep the costs down to fit easily into your budget.

SOUTHERN-STYLE RUSSIAN TEA

When you have company coming, put a pot of this tea on to simmer and fill your home with a spicy, welcoming aroma.

2 quarts boiling water

6 orange pekoe tea bags or any other black tea

4 cinnamon sticks

1 teaspoon whole cloves

1 quart apple cider or apple juice

1 quart pineapple juice

4 oranges

3 lemons

1 cup granulated sugar or sucralose-type sweetener

1. Put the tea bags into the boiling water in a pot with the cinnamon and cloves. Cover, and let steep for 10 minutes. Add the apple cider and pineapple juice. Cut a long spiral of peel from 1 orange and 1 lemon, and add to the pot.

2. Juice all of the oranges and lemons, and strain into the pot. Stir in the sugar, and bring to a boil. Reduce the heat to low, and cook for 30 minutes. Serve hot.

PER SERVING (1 CUP): 80 CAL; 0G PROT; 0G FAT; 21G CARB; 0MG CHOL; 0MG SOD; 0G FIBER

EARL GREY TEA PUNCH

This is a really good nonalcoholic punch for adults. The flavor is not too sweet and tastes a little like Artillery Punch, a nineteenth-century bourbon-based punch that was often served at New Year's receptions, especially on military posts.

5 Earl Grey tea bags

1 quart boiling water

1 quart pineapple juice

1 cup granulated sugar or sucralose-type sweetener

2 quarts ginger ale (regular or diet)

Put the tea bags into the boiling water, and allow them to steep for 15 minutes or longer. Remove the tea bags, and while the tea is still warm, add the pineapple juice and sugar. Stir until dissolved. Put in the refrigerator to chill until serving time. Pour over ice in a large punch bowl, and add the ginger ale.

PER SERVING (1 CUP): 120 CAL; 0G PROT; 0G FAT; 32G CARB; 0MG CHOL; 15MG SOD; 0G FIBER

LAVENDER LEMONADE

This very special lemonade has a delicate perfume, a subtle lavender color and an enchanting flavor. If you don't find infusion bags at your herb store, you can place the lavender flowers in two layers of cheesecloth, gather up the edges and tie it up with a string.

2 ounces dried lavender flowers

2 muslin infusion bags, optional

Juice of 6 lemons

3/4 cup granulated sugar, or to taste

1. Place the lavender in the infusion bags, if using. Bring 1 quart of water to a boil, add the lavender and remove from the heat.

2. Steep for 10 minutes, and remove the bags or strain the lavender. Set aside.

3. Combine the lemon juice and sugar, and dilute with 3 quarts of cold water. Add the lavender infusion. Adjust sugar to taste, and chill.

PER SERVING: 80 CAL; 0G PROT; 0G FAT; 22G CARB; 0MG CHOL; 0MG SOD; 0G FIBER

HIBISCUS AND PINEAPPLE TEA

SERVES 8 (MAKES 2 QUARTS)

With the scent and flavor of the Hawaiian Islands, this tea whispers of summers on the veranda. The hibiscus blossoms are sold in herb and tea shops. After steeping, the tea will be a bright pink color.

2 ounces dry hibiscus blossoms

1 quart boiling water

1 quart pineapple juice

6 fresh hibiscus blossoms for garnish, optional

Drop the dry hibiscus into the boiling water, and cover a 3-quart container. Let steep for 10 minutes. Strain into the pineapple juice in a pitcher, and chill. Serve over ice, decorating each glass with a hibiscus blossom, if using.

PER SERVING (1 CUP): 70 CAL; 0G PROT; 0G FAT; 17G CARB; 0MG CHOL; 0MG SOD; 0G FIBER

HIBISCUS COOLER

SERVES 12 (MAKES 3 QUARTS)

This beverage simulates the rose-colored iced drinks at Caribbean street carnivals in Manhattan. For best results, make the tea the night before serving or the morning of the day you plan to serve it. For variations, add a cinnamon stick to the tea as it brews, or add 1 to 2 teaspoons fresh ginger juice just before serving.

8 tea bags, such as Red Zinger or other tea containing hibiscus flowers

1 quart boiling water

1 quart pineapple juice, chilled

1 quart sparkling water, chilled

1 to 2 cups orange juice, optional

2 sliced limes, lemons or oranges, for garnish

1. Steep the tea bags in the boiling water for 30 minutes. Remove and discard the tea bags. Refrigerate for about 4 hours or overnight.

2. Combine the tea with the pineapple juice, sparkling water and orange juice, if using, and stir. Add more or less juice or water to taste. Garnish with the citrus slices.

PER SERVING (1 CUP): 48 CAL; 0G PROT; 0G FAT; 12G CARB; 0MG CHOL; 3MG SOD; 0G FIBER

EXOTIC ICE TEA

SERVES 6 (MAKES 2 QUARTS)

The lively tang of fresh ginger sparks this green tea drink.

½ cup grated fresh ginger

⅓ cup fresh lemon juice

4 green tea bags

Honey or granulated sugar to taste, optional

1. Combine 2 quarts of water, the ginger and lemon juice in a large saucepan, and bring to a boil over medium heat. Reduce the heat to low, and cook for 5 minutes, stirring occasionally. Remove from the heat.

2. Add the tea bags, and let stand for 5 minutes. Remove the tea bags, and stir in the honey, if using. Let cool. Pour the tea through a fine sieve into a large pitcher, and serve over ice.

PER SERVING (¼ CUP): 57 CAL; 0G PROT; 0G FAT; 19G CARB; 0MG CHOL; 2MG SOD; 0G FIBER

On Taking Teas

On its own or as a base for more complex beverages, tea is an ancient brew that has its fans in almost every country. Enjoyed as a soothing tonic, as a drink to encourage sociability, or as a symbol in elegant rituals, tea also may bestow numerous health benefits, such as relieving headaches and kidney trouble, aiding digestion and mitigating ulcers. Tea is rich in plant chemicals known as flavonoids or polyphenols, and these function as antioxidants that neutralize free radicals in the body. Though tea contains caffeine, most people consider tea a relaxant. A cup of tea, even very strong black tea, contains about half the caffeine of a similar amount of coffee.

Tea drinkers may find the numerous types of tea—black, green, oolong and white—bewildering. To clarify the tea scene:

Black Tea: Of the more than 3,000 varieties of black tea, most are dark brown in color and have a full-bodied flavor. Popular teas such as English Breakfast, Irish Breakfast and Earl Grey are blends of black teas from different regions.

Green Tea: Green tea is known for its light green color and smooth, delicate flavor. Sencha, Gyokuru and Matcha Uji are the most popular varieties. Green tea has high levels of flavonoids and less caffeine than black tea. High in vitamins and minerals, green tea contains as much vitamin C as a whole lemon. Five cups of green tea per day provide 5 to 10 percent of the daily requirement of magnesium, riboflavin, niacin and folic acid, and 25 percent of the daily requirement of potassium.

Oolong Tea: Grown in China, oolong tea has a complex flavor and aroma. Noted for having many of the same cancer-fighting properties as green and black teas, oolong can be any shade of green to black.

White Tea: This rare Chinese tea with its sweet and subtle flavor is the least processed of teas and is also the most expensive.

ALMOND COOLER

SERVES 4

This creamy-white almond milk is a good hot weather drink. It is sweetened with just a little honey and flavored with orange-flower water. Extracted from the blossoms of orange trees, orange-flower water is available in gourmet food shops and Greek and Middle Eastern groceries. You may omit it, or use a drop of orange extract instead.

¾ cup blanched almonds

¼ cup honey

2 drops almond extract

1 to 2 tablespoons orange-flower water, or to taste

4 sprigs fresh mint, for garnish

Additional water or seltzer, optional

1. Pour 1 quart of cold water into a blender. Turning the blender on high speed, gradually add the almonds, processing until well pulverized, for about 5 minutes. Set a strainer lined with cheesecloth over a medium saucepan. Pour the liquid through the strainer and twist the cheesecloth to squeeze out all of the liquid. Stir in the honey. Bring the mixture to a boil, reduce the heat to low and cook for 2 minutes. Let cool.

2. Stir in the almond extract and orange-flower water. Transfer the almond milk to a covered 2-quart container, and refrigerate.

3. To serve, pour the almond milk into glasses with ice, and garnish with mint. If the drink is too thick, dilute it with cold water or seltzer.

PER SERVING: 189 CAL; 5G PROT; 11G FAT; 22G CARB; 0MG CHOL; 3MG SOD; 3G FIBER

POMEGRANATE SPRITZER SERVES 1

Pomegranate molasses is found in Middle Eastern grocery stores. It is pomegranate juice that has been concentrated to a thick syrup. It has a thirst-quenching, sweet-tart flavor. While it may be diluted with plain cold water for a fine drink, club soda makes it special.

2 tablespoons pomegranate
   molasses
1 cup club soda
½ cup ice cubes

Put the pomegranate molasses in a tall 12-ounce glass, and add a few ounces of the club soda. Stir. Add the ice cubes, and fill the glass with club soda. Stir, and serve with a straw.

PER SERVING: 90 CAL; 0G PROT; 0G FAT; 19G CARB; 0MG CHOL; 0MG SOD; 0G FIBER

CRANBERRY SPARKLER SERVES 8

A bright, slightly tart drink that cools as it refreshes.

16 ice cubes
2 cups cranberry juice, chilled
2 quarts sparkling water, chilled

Divide the ice cubes among 8 glasses. Add ¼ cup of the juice to each glass, then fill the glasses with the sparkling water.

PER SERVING: 36 CAL; 0G PROT; 0G FAT; 9G CARB; 0MG CHOL; 4MG SOD; 0G FIBER

FRUITY SPRITZER SERVES 8

This bubbly drink takes on the color and nutritional value of the fruit concentrate you choose.

½ cup frozen fruit juice concentrate,
   thawed
16 ice cubes
3 cups sparkling water, chilled

Put 1 tablespoon of the thawed fruit juice concentrate in each of eight 4- or 5-ounce glasses. Divide the ice cubes among the glasses and stir in the sparkling water.

PER SERVING (ABOUT ½ CUP): 50 CAL; 0G PROT; 0G FAT; 12G CARB; 0MG CHOL; 2MG SOD; 0G FIBER

BETTER THAN CHAMPAGNE

This drink tastes amazingly like the real thing, but lacks the alcoholic buzz. If you prefer pink champagne, add a tablespoon or two of grenadine or cranberry juice.

1 32-ounce bottle club soda

2 6-ounce cans frozen white grape juice concentrate, thawed

Stir together the club soda and the grape juice concentrate. Pour into 2 soda bottles or other container with a lid. Cap tightly, and chill. Serve in champagne glasses.

PER SERVING (5 OUNCES): 30 CAL; 0G PROT; 0G FAT; 7G CARB; 0MG CHOL; 29MG SOD; 0G FIBER

ICY SHERRIED LEMONADE

Your guests will have a hard time guessing what's in this very refreshing drink. You may want to try different kinds of sherry, such as cream, cocktail, dry or tawny, to find which suits your taste. Serve this with straws.

1 12-ounce can frozen lemonade concentrate, thawed

1 quart sherry

Crushed or shaved ice

8 fresh mint sprigs, optional

Mix the lemonade concentrate with the sherry, and, at serving time, pour ½ cup over a tall glass of crushed ice. Stir well, and serve garnished with a mint sprig.

PER SERVING (1/2 CUP): 140 CAL; 0G PROT; 0G FAT; 22G CARB; 0MG CHOL; 10MG SOD; 0G FIBER

MANGO-APRICOT DAIQUIRI

Although you may use a canned mango for this drink, you will achieve the best flavor by waiting until mangoes come into season in spring and summer.

1 large ripe mango, peeled, pitted and diced

1 cup crushed ice

½ cup apricot nectar

1 ounce dark rum

½ ounce apricot liqueur, optional

Juice of ½ lime

2 thin slices lime

Combine the mango, ice, apricot nectar, rum, apricot liqueur, if using, and lime juice in a blender, and purée until smooth. Pour into 2 tall glasses, and garnish each with a slice of lime.

PER SERVING: 135 CAL; 1G PROT; 0G FAT; 27G CARB; 0MG CHOL; 4MG SOD; 2G FIBER

SPICED TOMATO SUNSET

An acceptably delicious substitute for a Bloody Mary, this spicy drink has plenty of kick.

1 can vegetable or tomato juice

1 tablespoon vegetarian
  Worcestershire sauce

2 teaspoons prepared horseradish

1 small lemon, thinly sliced

Hot pepper sauce to taste

Freshly ground black pepper to taste

Stir together all the ingredients in a large pitcher. Cover and chill. Serve cold over ice, or heat the beverage and serve hot in mugs.

PER SERVING: 29 CAL; 0.8G PROT; 0G FAT; 7G CARB; 0MG CHOL; 59MG SOD; 1G FIBER

AVOCADO FRAPPÉ

In the Philippines, this pale green drink is made with condensed milk. Here, soymilk and a dash of fresh lime juice turn it into a lively breakfast smoothie. It's particularly recharging after a morning workout. Asian food stores sell palm sugar, as do some supermarkets in the international foods section. You can also substitute brown sugar.

¾ cup plain soymilk

¼ ripe medium-sized avocado

3 tablespoons palm sugar or firmly
  packed light brown sugar

4 ice cubes

2 teaspoons fresh lime juice

Put all the ingredients into a blender, and purée until smooth and thick. Pour into a tall glass, and serve.

PER SERVING: 313 CAL; 7G PROT; 12G FAT; 48G CARB; 10MG CHOL; 121MG SOD; 2G FIBER

ORANGE COLADA

This is a creamy orange drink. Use the coconut cream product made for tropical drinks, not the unsweetened canned coconut milk.

2 cups orange juice

2 cups ice cubes

1 cup pineapple juice

½ cup canned sweetened coconut
  cream

⅓ cup dry nondairy coffee creamer

Put all the ingredients in a blender, and purée until smooth.

PER SERVING: 130 CAL; 1G PROT; 6G FAT; 19G CARB; 0MG CHOL; 15MG SOD; <1G FIBER

PINEAPPLE GINGER ADE

In the islands, this drink is made with the skin cut from a whole pineapple. It's a surprise to find so much pineapple flavor left there. Just be sure to scrub the skin well under running water before cutting the skin from the pineapple. If you prefer, just use one quarter of a large pineapple instead.

4-inch-long piece fresh ginger, chopped

Peel and core from a large pineapple, chopped, or ¼ large pineapple

1 cup granulated sugar or sugar substitute, or to taste

1 quart pineapple juice

1. Put the ginger in a blender or food processor, and process until finely chopped. Chop the pineapple skin in 1-inch pieces. Add the pineapple skin to the ginger, and process until chopped, using about 1 quart of water to help.

2. Mix with 2 more quarts of water, and set aside at room temperature for 15 minutes. Pour the mixture through a sieve into a large pitcher to remove the coarse fibers. Discard the fibers. Mix the pineapple water with the sugar, and stir until dissolved. Add the pineapple juice. Taste, and adjust the sugar as needed. Refrigerate until serving time.

3. To serve, pour over crushed ice in tall glasses.

PER SERVING (1 CUP): 90 CAL; 0G PROT; 0G FAT; 23G CARB; 0MG CHOL; 0MG SOD; 0G FIBER

BLUEBERRY-CHERRY JUICE

The dominant flavors of fresh blueberries and fresh cherries make this a fruity, seasonal treat.

1 cup blueberries

1 cup pitted cherries

½ cup red seedless grapes

½ cup raspberries

Put all the ingredients into a blender, and purée until smooth. Serve in a tall glass.

PER SERVING: 88 CAL; 1G PROT; 1G FAT; 22G CARB; 0MG CHOL; 5MG SOD; 3G FIBER

MÉLANGE

Costa Rica is deservedly known for its fresh fruit drinks, such as the favorite mélange.

½ ripe cantaloupe, cut in 1-inch pieces plus extra for garnish

2 cups fresh orange juice

Sugar to taste

5 to 6 ice cubes

Put all the ingredients in a blender, and purée until smooth. Serve in tall glasses with a cantaloupe spear decorating the rim of each glass.

PER SERVING: 80 CAL; 1G PROT; 0G FAT; 19G CARB; 0MG CHOL; 15MG SOD; 1G FIBER

SUN JUICE

Store-bought juice is watery compared to the orange juice you squeeze yourself, so roll up your sleeves. This thick, blushing eye-opener is worth it. It's a great way to use even bananas that have turned totally black, since the riper the banana, the creamier your juice will be.

4 medium-sized juice oranges

1-inch wedge very ripe papaya, cut into small chunks

1 overripe large banana, cut into 1-inch pieces

1 teaspoon grated fresh ginger

1 ice cube

Squeeze juice from the oranges, and pour into a blender to make about ¾ cup. Add the papaya, banana, ginger and ice. Blend until the ice is crushed and the mixture is creamy and golden. Pour into a tall glass, and serve.

PER SERVING: 261 CAL; 3G PROT; 1G FAT; 64G CARB; 0MG CHOL; 5MG SOD; 5G FIBER

MANGO-CITRUS COCKTAIL

Although optional, fresh mint adds a certain refreshing flavor.

2 large, ripe mangoes, pitted, peeled and sliced

2 cups fresh orange juice

2 limes, juiced

8 ice cubes plus additional cubes for glasses

1 to 2 tablespoons granulated sugar

2 cups sparkling water, or to taste

Fresh mint sprigs, optional

1. Put the mangoes, orange juice, lime juice, ice cubes and sugar into a blender, and process for 1 minute. Pour the mixture into a pitcher, and refrigerate.

2. To serve, thin the mixture with sparkling water, and stir. Pour into 4 glasses filled with ice cubes. Garnish with mint, if using.

PER SERVING: 138 CAL; 2G PROT; 0.7G FAT; 35G CARB; 0MG CHOL; 3MG SOD; 2G FIBER

MELON-LIME REFRESHER

This beverage is good as a wake-up call in the morning, or any time during the day to quench thirst.

5½ cups chopped seeded cantaloupe or watermelon pieces

½ cup granulated sugar

½ cup fresh lime juice

1. Put all the ingredients into a blender, and purée until smooth. Strain the mixture through a fine sieve into a large bowl, and stir in 4 cups of water. Rub the sieve with the back of a spoon to push through any remaining fruit liquid, and discard the pulp.

2. Put the fruit-water mixture in a gallon jar or 2 large pitchers. Cover and chill. Before serving, mix well, and pour over ice into glasses.

PER SERVING: 88 CAL; 0G PROT; 0.1G FAT; 21G CARB; 0MG CHOL; 10MG SOD; 1G FIBER

PURPLE PASSION

Blueberries, bananas and apples combine for a scintillating violet-colored drink that's a powerhouse of vitamin C, potassium and flavonoids. It also can be made with ripe fresh strawberries, raspberries or blackberries instead of the blueberries.

2 medium-sized ripe bananas

½ cup fresh or frozen and thawed blueberries

½ cup unsweetened applesauce

½ cup plain low-fat or nonfat yogurt or soft tofu, drained

1½ tablespoons honey

2 teaspoons vanilla extract

Put all the ingredients into a blender with 3 cups of water, and purée until smooth. Pour into 4 glasses, and serve.

PER SERVING: 130 CAL; 2G PROT; 1G FAT; 31G CARB; 2MG CHOL; 21MG SOD; 2G FIBER

WATERMELON COCKTAIL

This refreshing drink helps you cool off on very hot summer days.

8 cups seeded, cubed watermelon

Pinch salt

2 limes, halved

1 teaspoon orange-flower water, optional

Ice cubes

Combine the watermelon and salt in a blender, and purée until smooth. Cut a lime half into 4 thin slices, and set aside. Juice the remaining halves and add to the purée. Add the orange-flower water, if using. Stir well. Pour into 4 glasses filled with ice cubes. Garnish with the reserved lime slices.

PER SERVING: 106 CAL; 2G PROT; 1G FAT; 24G CARB; 0MG CHOL; 9MG SOD; 3G FIBER

GREEN DREAM SMOOTHIE

Rich avocado adds a luscious, velvety texture to this drink.

1 ripe avocado, peeled and pitted

½ cup whole milk

½ cup vanilla yogurt

4 tablespoons frozen limeade concentrate

3 tablespoons granulated sugar, or to taste

Put all of the ingredients into a blender, and purée until smooth. Pour into a tall glass, and serve.

PER SERVING: 390 CAL; 7G PROT; 18G FAT; 55G CARB; 10MG CHOL; 80MG SOD; 5G FIBER

BANANA-BERRY SMOOTHIE

What a wonderful duo: bananas and strawberries, with a citrus component. Very refreshing!

1 medium-sized banana, sliced and frozen

6 frozen strawberries

2 tablespoons frozen orange juice concentrate

1 cup vanilla soymilk

Combine the banana, strawberries and orange juice concentrate in a blender. Add the soymilk, and blend until smooth and creamy. Serve right away.

PER SERVING (ABOUT 3/4 CUP): 170 CAL; 5G PROT; 2G FAT; 36G CARB; 0MG CHOL; 45MG SOD; 3G FIBER

B-VITAMIN JUICE

This combination will get you pepped up in the morning!

1 cup fresh pineapple chunks

1 banana, peeled

½ cup pineapple juice

¼ cup almond milk or soymilk

1 teaspoon ground flaxseeds

1 tablespoon wheat germ

1 teaspoon hemp oil

Put all the ingredients into a blender, and purée until smooth. Serve immediately.

PER SERVING: 372 CAL; 7G PROT; 9G FAT; 73G CARB; 0MG CHOL; 40MG SOD; 6G FIBER

CHAI COOLER

Chai, a sweetened Indian-style tea with spices, is sold ready to use, making for a delicious quick smoothie. Chai is readily available at natural food stores and supermarkets.

¾ cup chai, chilled

¾ cup vanilla soymilk, chilled

½ banana, sliced and frozen

2 tablespoons frozen apple juice concentrate

Put all of the ingredients in a blender, and purée until smooth. Serve immediately.

PER SERVING (1 CUP): 109 CAL; 3G PROT; 2G FAT; 22G CARB; 0MG CHOL; 60MG SOD; 1G FIBER

COCONUT-BANANA SMOOTHIE

This tropics-inspired smoothie will have you dreaming of sunny beaches and swaying palm trees.

1 cup vanilla soymilk, chilled
1 banana, sliced and frozen
¼ cup canned light coconut milk
2 tablespoons frozen apple juice
concentrate

Put all of the ingredients into a blender, and puree until smooth. Serve immediately.

PER SERVING (ABOUT 1 CUP): 177 CAL; 5G PROT; 5G FAT; 33G CARB; 0MG CHOL; 68MG SOD; 1G FIBER

KIWI-MELON SMOOTHIE

This pretty, pale green smoothie is our favorite. For extra ease, buy fresh, cubed melon at the salad bar or in packages, already sliced, then cut it into cubes to freeze.

1 kiwi, peeled and cut into 8 pieces
1 cup honeydew melon cubes,
frozen
1 cup vanilla soymilk
6 ounces kiwi-lemon, lemon or Key
lime soy yogurt
1 tablespoon frozen apple juice
concentrate

Combine all the ingredients in a blender, and purée until smooth. Serve immediately.

PER SERVING (1½ CUPS): 205 CAL; 8G PROT; 6G FAT; 32G CARB; 0MG CHOL; 122MG SOD; 1G FIBER

MANGO CREAM SMOOTHIE

A mango makes this drink a rich tropical blend. Different yogurt flavors vary the effect—peach is certainly a favorite, but orange or apricots are good too. Don't worry about mashing the mango flesh when removing it from the pit and the skin, because it's going to be puréed. Adding soy powder boosts the protein content.

1½ cups vanilla soymilk
1 cup frozen, canned or fresh mango
1 cup peach or orange soy yogurt
2 tablespoons frozen orange juice
concentrate
Juice of ½ lime

Combine all the ingredients in a blender, and purée until smooth and creamy. Serve immediately.

PER SERVING (1 CUP): 247 CAL; 8G PROT; 6G FAT; 44G CARB; 0MG CHOL; 111MG SOD; 4G FIBER

PEACH GLOW SMOOTHIE SERVES 1

Here's a complete breakfast packed with vitamins A and C, potassium, protein and more, in one bright drink.

6 ounces peach or orange cream soy yogurt

½ cup carrot juice

2 tablespoons frozen orange juice concentrate

Put all of the ingredients into a blender, and purée until smooth. Serve immediately.

PER SERVING: 210 CAL; 8G PROT; 2G FAT; 41G CARB; 0MG CHOL; 47MG SOD; 1G FIBER

VERY BERRY SHAKE SERVES 1 (MAKES ABOUT 1½ CUPS)

This drink can be made with just about any fruit, not just berries. It's delicious, colorful and hearty enough for breakfast—and big enough to share with a friend.

1 cup chopped strawberries, whole blueberries or mixed berries

½ cup low-fat or nonfat yogurt or ricemilk

2 ice cubes

1 teaspoon granulated sugar, or to taste

¼ teaspoon vanilla extract

Combine all the ingredients in a blender. Process on and off until finely chopped, then blend on high speed until smooth and creamy. Pour into a tall glass, and serve.

PER SERVING: 143 CAL; 5G PROT; 1G FAT; 31G CARB; 0MG CHOL; 59MG SOD; 5G FIBER

WILD ORANGE SHAKE SERVES 1 TO 2 (MAKES ABOUT 2 CUPS)

A refreshing drink charged with citrus flavor, this frothy shake works equally well for breakfast or for a between-meal refresher.

1 cup nonfat milk

½ cup vanilla yogurt

½ cup frozen orange juice concentrate

2 teaspoons grated orange zest

2 teaspoons vanilla extract

Place all the ingredients in a blender, and blend until smooth. Pour into a tall glass or two, and serve.

PER SERVING (1 CUP): 220 CAL; 9G PROT; 1G FAT; 42G CARB; 5MG CHOL; 105MG SOD; <1G FIBER

6 *breakfasts, brunches and lunches*

OUR MOTHERS—AND MEDICAL EXPERTS—HAVE always told us that nutritious breakfasts fortify us for the day, giving us the energy jump start we need to think and do our very best. Busy schedules often interfere with breakfast time, but whether you plan for a sit-down meal, or one on the run, you'll find plenty here to rev up the day. And if you don't even have the time to do more than pause for a second, plan on whipping up and chilling a filling smoothie— see the Beverages chapter (page 77)—the night before, and grab your breakfast as you head out the door. Brunches, on the other hand, offer us a chance to relax over a leisurely meal. And at lunchtime, well, it can be more than sandwiches, and you will find plenty of intriguing wraps and fillings to take on your way.

breakfasts

SWEDISH PANCAKES

This batter needs to rest for at least two hours, so you'll need to plan ahead and rise early enough to make this in time for breakfast or brunch. Or, you can make the batter the night before, cover it tightly and refrigerate it until the next morning. Make the pancakes to order, or keep them warm on a covered platter in a low oven. Serve the pancakes with butter, lingonberries or other tart preserves, and/or sour cream with or without brown sugar. But try them with just butter at first—they are delicate and faintly sweet.

3 large eggs
1½ cups whole milk, divided
1 cup all-purpose flour
6 tablespoons (¾ stick) unsalted butter, melted, plus extra for greasing the pan
1 teaspoon granulated sugar
½ teaspoon salt

1. Beat the eggs with ½ cup of the milk until thoroughly blended. Add the flour, and stir in completely. Stir in the remaining 1 cup of milk, the butter, sugar and salt, blending well. Cover and refrigerate for at least 2 hours or overnight.

2. Remove from the refrigerator, and whisk the batter just to recombine it before cooking the pancakes.

3. Grease a large heavy skillet or electric griddle lightly with butter, and heat to medium-high heat. When hot, drop on 2 tablespoons of the batter per pancake, spreading it into rounds. When the edges of the pancakes begin to brown, turn them over, and cook for 1 to 2 more minutes, or until firm. Remove from the heat, and serve.

PER SERVING: 380 CAL; 11G PROT; 24G FAT; 30G CARB; 215MG CHOL; 380MG SOD; 1G FIBER

TROPICAL PANCAKES

Packed with nutrients, these rich pancakes can supercharge you with energy and provide plenty of flavor at the same time. The batter is thick, so cook the pancakes slowly over medium-low to medium heat to firm the centers. Sweeten the cooked pancakes with maple syrup or a fruit syrup of your choice.

2 large eggs
1 pound low-fat, small-curd cottage cheese
¾ cup pineapple juice
½ cup diced pineapple
1 tablespoon vegetable oil
1½ cups all-purpose flour
2 teaspoons baking powder
½ teaspoon baking soda
Pinch salt
¼ cup wheat germ, optional

1. Beat the eggs well in a mixing bowl. Stir in the cottage cheese, pineapple juice, pineapple and oil, and mix until well blended. Stir in the flour, baking powder, baking soda, salt and wheat germ, if using.

2. Spray a nonstick skillet with nonstick cooking spray, and heat over medium-low to medium heat. Drop ¼ cup of the batter onto the skillet for each pancake, using a spatula to pat the batter down, and cook until the bottoms turn golden. Flip and cook the other sides, spraying the skillet as needed. Remove from the skillet when both sides are golden and the centers are firm. Repeat with the remaining batter until used up, and serve.

PER SERVING: 340 CAL; 20G PROT; 7G FAT; 49G CARB; 115MG CHOL; 840MG SOD; 2G FIBER

GOOD GRAINS PANCAKE MIX

For a high-fiber meal in minutes, keep a supply of this pancake mix in your freezer. You can also use it to make waffles.

1 ½ cups all-purpose flour
1 cup rye flour
1 cup whole wheat flour
½ cup wheat germ
½ cup cornmeal
⅓ cup granulated sugar
2 tablespoons baking powder
1 teaspoon baking soda
1 tablespoon salt

1. Combine all the ingredients in a bowl, and stir to mix.

2. Divide the mixture into thirds, about 2 cups each. Place each portion in a separate plastic food storage bag, seal tightly and store in the freezer up to 6 months. Use to make Good Grains Pancakes (below).

GOOD GRAINS PANCAKES

To make waffles instead, use the same batter, but follow manufacturer's directions for using your waffle iron.

1 ¼ cups skim milk or soymilk
½ cup egg substitute or 2 large eggs
2 tablespoons vegetable oil
1 batch (about 2 cups) Good Grains Pancake Mix (above)

1. Combine the milk, egg substitute and oil in a bowl, and whisk to mix. Add the pancake mix until moistened. Do not overmix. The batter will be somewhat lumpy.

2. Heat a griddle or large skillet over medium-high heat until a drop of water bounces off the surface. Pour ¼ cup of batter per pancake onto the hot griddle. Cook until bubbles form. When the bottom of each pancake is golden brown, flip and cook the other side until browned. Repeat with the remaining batter until it is used up. Serve warm.

PER SERVING (2 PANCAKES): 460 CAL; 16G PROT; 16G FAT; 60G CARB; 4MG CHOL; 1416MG SOD; 8G FIBER

BLUEBERRY SAUCE

A perfect topping for pancakes and waffles or a filling for crêpes.

2 cups apple or mixed berry juice
1 10-ounce jar blueberry preserves
2 to 3 teaspoons arrowroot, dissolved in ½ cup cold water
1 pint blueberries, fresh or frozen
1 to 2 teaspoons fresh lemon juice, optional
1 teaspoon vanilla extract
Pinch salt
Pinch ground cinnamon or nutmeg

Heat the apple juice in a saucepan over medium heat. Add the preserves, reduce the heat to low and cook for about 7 minutes, until the preserves have dissolved. Add the dissolved arrowroot, and stir until the sauce thickens and becomes shiny. Stir in the blueberries, lemon juice, vanilla, salt and cinnamon. Reduce the heat to very low, and keep warm until ready to serve. Or cover, refrigerate and reheat over low heat in a small saucepan.

PER SERVING: 140 CAL; 0G PROT; 0G FAT; 34G CARB; 0MG CHOL; 37MG SOD; 1G FIBER

GOLDEN GLAZE

Try this lightly sweetened topping on crêpes or pancakes.

½ cup instant soymilk powder
¼ cup soya-lecithin spread or
   margarine
¼ cup light honey or maple syrup
1 teaspoon vanilla extract or grated
   orange or lemon zest
Pinch salt
Soymilk for thinning, optional

Put all the ingredients in a food processor or blender, and purée until smooth. Thin the mixture with a little soymilk if it is too thick to spread.

PER CUP: 860 CAL; 12G PROT; 55G FAT; 87G CARB; 0MG CHOL; 216MG SOD; 0G FIBER

BERRY TOPPING

This fruity topping is a tasty accompaniment to pancakes, crêpes and angel food cake.

1½ tablespoons cornstarch
2 tablespoons honey
2 cups unsweetened berries of your
   choice

Blend the cornstarch, honey and 2 tablespoons of water in a small saucepan. Add ½ cup of the berries, and heat until the mixture thickens slightly, about 5 minutes. Add the remaining berries, and stir to mix. Serve warm.

PER SERVING: 33 CAL; 0G PROT; 0G FAT; 8G CARB; 0MG CHOL; 1MG SOD; 1G FIBER

BLUE PLATE PANCAKES

A hearty pancake dish, this would go well with crumbled soy "sausage" and hot coffee.

1 cup buckwheat flour
½ cup amaranth flour
½ cup finely ground cornmeal
   (yellow or blue)
1 tablespoon baking powder
½ teaspoon salt
2 cups soymilk or skim milk
3 tablespoons maple syrup
2 tablespoons vegetable oil plus
   extra for frying
1 large egg
Blueberry Sauce (page 92)

1. Combine the buckwheat flour, amaranth flour, cornmeal, baking powder and salt in a large bowl.

2. Whisk together the soymilk, maple syrup, oil and egg in a separate bowl. Add the soymilk mixture to the flour mixture, and stir until smooth. Be sure to dissolve any lumps, but do not overmix. Let sit 10 minutes.

3. Oil lightly a well-seasoned skillet over medium heat. Pour ⅓ cup of batter per pancake into the skillet, and cook until bubbles begin to form on the surface of the pancakes. Flip the pancakes, and cook the other sides until lightly browned, for about 3 minutes. Repeat with the remaining batter until it is used. Serve warm with Blueberry Sauce or any other topping.

PER SERVING (2 PANCAKES, WITHOUT SAUCE): 302 CAL; 11G PROT; 11G FAT; 40G CARB; 33MG CHOL; 493MG SOD; 6G FIBER

BASIC CRÊPES

Crêpes are the fashion plate of the brunch and breakfast crowd, ready for elegant fillings, such as the Soy Mock Boursin (page 60) or Blueberry Sauce (page 92). But the crêpe is eminently versatile, and takes well to savory fillings such as Raita (page 144) for the dinner table.

2 cups whole wheat pastry flour or unbleached white flour (or a combination of the two) 1 cup low-fat milk or soymilk

4 large eggs

2 tablespoons vegetable oil plus extra for brushing pan

½ teaspoon salt

1. Put all the ingredients and 1¼ cups of water in a blender or food processor, and process at high speed for 1 minute. Pour into a bowl, cover and refrigerate for 2 hours before cooking. The batter should be the consistency of heavy cream. If necessary, thin with more water, milk or soymilk.

2. Use either a well-seasoned omelet or crêpe pan or a nonstick 8-inch skillet. Brush the pan with oil, and heat over low heat for 3 minutes. Remove from the heat, pour in 3 or 4 tablespoons of the batter and tilt the pan all around so the batter lightly coats the bottom of the pan.

3. Return the pan to medium-low heat, and cook for 1 to 3 minutes or until the crêpe is lightly browned or begins to bubble. Using a spatula, flip the crêpe, and cook for 30 seconds more. Gently remove the crêpe from the pan, and place on a plate. Repeat the process with the remaining batter, stacking crêpes when cooked layered with wax paper to prevent sticking. Use right away, or cool, cover with plastic wrap and refrigerate up to 1 week or freeze up to 1 month.

PER CRÊPE: 124 CAL; 5G PROT; 5G FAT; 16G CARB; 73MG CHOL; 123MG SOD; 0.5G FIBER

NO-CHOLESTEROL CRÊPES

Watching your cholesterol has never been so delicious!

2 tablespoons egg substitute

2 cups whole wheat pastry flour or all-purpose white flour (or a combination of the two)

1 cup soymilk

½ cup chickpea flour

2 tablespoons vegetable oil

½ teaspoon salt

Put the egg substitute and ½ cup of water in a food processor or blender, and purée until smooth. Add the flour, soymilk, chickpea flour, oil and salt. Add 1 more cup of water, and blend 1 minute at high speed. Cook the crêpes according to the directions for Basic Crêpes (above).

PER CRÊPE: 115 CAL; 4G PROT; 3G FAT; 19G CARB; 0MG CHOL; 90MG SOD; 0.8G FIBER

BUCKWHEAT PANCAKES

Buckwheat flour lends pancakes a rich, nutty flavor. Because these use yeast as a leavener, the batter needs to be started about 1½ hours before you want to cook it.

1½ cups milk

2 tablespoons molasses

2 tablespoons soy margarine or unsalted butter, melted, or canola oil

½ cup warm (105F to115F) water

1 package active dry yeast

1 large egg or ¼ cup egg substitute

1 cup all-purpose flour

½ cup buckwheat flour

½ teaspoon salt

Unsalted butter or margarine and maple syrup to taste

1. Heat the milk in a 2-quart saucepan just until bubbles form around the sides of the pan. Remove from the heat. Stir in the molasses and margarine. Allow to cool until just warm.

2. Put the warm water into a bowl, and sprinkle in the yeast. Stir. Allow to rest in a warm place for 10 minutes, or until it becomes foamy. Add the yeast to the milk. Beat the egg into the yeast-milk mixture, and transfer to a medium-sized bowl.

3. Sift together the flours and salt. Stir into the wet ingredients. Allow to rest in a warm spot for 1 hour, or until doubled in bulk.

4. Heat a griddle over medium-high heat, and coat with nonstick cooking spray. Use a ¼ cup measure to pick up the frothy batter on the top of the bowl, and pour onto the griddle. Repeat to make as many pancakes as will easily fit on the griddle, always taking the batter off the top. When the pancakes are well browned on the bottom, flip and cook the other sides. Keep in a 200F oven until all the batter is used. Serve with butter or margarine and maple syrup.

PER SERVING: 210 CAL; 7G PROT; 6G FAT; 32G CARB; 40MG CHOL; 280MG SOD; 2G FIBER

SAVORY OVEN-BAKED PANCAKE

This showy, oven-baked pancake, often referred to as a Dutch Baby, makes a complete meal-in-one. This is a filling and generous dish, good served with fruit to start and other breakfast-brunch items to round out the meal.

3 tablespoons unsalted butter, divided

2 large eggs

¼ cup low-fat milk

¼ cup all-purpose flour

Salt and freshly ground black pepper to taste

¼ cup diced onion

½ cup fresh or frozen green peas

¼ cup diced red bell pepper

2 large white button mushrooms, rinsed and grit removed

¼ cup dry white wine

½ cup grated Jarlsberg or other low-fat Swiss-style cheese

Sprigs fresh thyme or chives, for garnish

1. Preheat the oven to 400F. Preheat a 5- or 6-inch round baking dish. Melt 2 tablespoons of the butter in the baking dish.

2. Meanwhile, beat together the eggs, milk and flour until smooth. Season with salt and pepper. When the butter is melted, pour the egg mixture into the baking dish, and place in the oven.

3. Heat 1 teaspoon of the remaining butter in a skillet over medium heat. When hot, sauté the onion until translucent, for about 5 minutes. Add the peas and bell pepper, and cook for 2 minutes more. Scrape into a bowl, and set aside.

4. Slice the mushroom caps and stems thinly. Heat the remaining 2 teaspoons of the butter in the skillet over medium heat. When hot, sauté the mushrooms for 5 minutes, or until browned. Add the wine and cheese, return the onion mixture to the skillet, season with salt and pepper and cook 2 to 3 minutes more, until the mushrooms are cooked through.

5. Bake the pancake for 15 minutes, or until puffed and golden. Remove from the oven, heap the mushroom mixture into the center, garnish with fresh thyme and serve. The pancake may deflate slightly as it cools.

PER SERVING: 495 CAL; 21G PROT; 32.5G FAT; 24.5G CARB; 290MG CHOL; 205MG SOD; 3.5G FIBER

OATMEAL-APPLE WAFFLES

A delightful way to launch the day, these waffles bring together the comforting fall flavor of apples under-scored by the zing of lemon.

1 large apple, halved and unpeeled

2 large eggs, separated

1 cup apple juice

½ cup low-fat milk

3 tablespoons vegetable oil

1 teaspoon lemon extract

Grated zest of 1 lemon

1½ cups all-purpose flour

2 teaspoons baking powder

½ teaspoon salt

⅓ cup rolled oats

⅓ cup oat bran

2 teaspoons granulated sugar

1 teaspoon ground cinnamon, or to taste

2 to 2½ cups warm applesauce, for garnish

1. Heat a waffle iron. Core and dice half of the apple, keeping the skin on. Set aside the diced apple and the half apple.

2. Beat the egg yolks in a mixing bowl until frothy. Add the apple juice, milk, oil, lemon extract and lemon zest, and beat until smooth. Sift the flour together with the baking powder and salt, and fold into the egg mixture. Stir in the oats, oat bran, sugar, cinnamon and diced apple. Beat the egg whites until stiff, and fold into the batter.

3. Spray the hot waffle iron with nonstick cooking spray. Ladle some of the batter onto the iron, and cook according to the manufacturer's directions and desired doneness. Place the cooked waffle on a serving plate, and repeat until all the batter is used up.

4. To serve, garnish each waffle with ½ cup of applesauce in the center. Slice the remaining half apple very thinly, and garnish the applesauce and waffles with several apple slices.

PER SERVING: 440 CAL; 9G PROT; 12G FAT; 77G CARB; 85MG CHOL; 470MG SOD; 5G FIBER

RAISIN-CHEESE BLINTZES

Blintzes are rolled crêpes traditionally filled with cheese, fruit or potatoes. Instead of eggs and butter, this low-cholesterol version is made with bananas and cornstarch. Go easy on the oil, or the blintzes will be greasy. For a potato-filled version, finely chop 1 small onion, and sauté it in 1 to 2 tablespoons of butter or vegetable oil until softened, for about 5 minutes. Combine the onion with 3 medium-sized cooked, mashed potatoes, and stir until blended. Use the potato mixture in place of the cottage cheese-raisin mixture. If the crêpes fall apart, they are undercooked. If they are crisp, they are overcooked.

Crêpe Batter

¾ cup whole wheat pastry flour

1 cup skim milk or soymilk

4 tablespoons cornstarch

1 small banana, peeled and mashed

Vegetable oil for greasing dish

Filling

1 cup low-fat cottage cheese

¼ cup raisins

¼ teaspoon ground cinnamon

1. To make the Batter: Combine the flour, milk, cornstarch and banana in a bowl, and mix to blend.

2. Spray a crêpe pan or skillet with nonstick cooking spray, and heat over medium heat. Pour about 6 tablespoons of the batter into the skillet, and lift and tilt the pan gently to spread the batter evenly and thinly. Cook until the top is slightly dry. Remove with a spatula, and place on a napkin. Repeat with the remaining batter.

3. Preheat the oven to 350F. Lightly oil a baking dish, and set aside.

4. To make the Filling: Combine all the ingredients in a bowl, and mix to blend. Place a few tablespoons of the filling in the center of each crêpe. Roll up, and fold the ends under to make rectangular "packages." Place the blintzes seam sides down in the baking dish.

5. Bake for about 30 minutes, or until golden.

PER SERVING: 147 CAL; 9G PROT; 2G FAT; 26G CARB; 2MG CHOL; 176MG SOD; 3G FIBER

NUTTY BLINTZES

These unusual blintzes are dairy free and delicious.

Vegetable oil for greasing pan

12 ounces firm tofu

⅓ cup raisins or currants

⅓ cup lightly toasted walnuts (see page 47), chopped

¼ cup lightly toasted slivered almonds (see page 47), optional

3 tablespoons honey or maple syrup

¼ teaspoon ground nutmeg

Pinch ground cinnamon

4 to 6 No-Cholesterol Crêpes (page 94)

1. Preheat the oven to 350F. Lightly grease a baking sheet, and set aside.

2. Mash the tofu with a fork in a bowl until almost smooth. Add the raisins, nuts, honey, nutmeg and cinnamon, and mix well.

3. Fill the crêpes with the tofu mixture, and fold by rolling up the crêpes or folding them into packages. Place the blintzes seam sides down on the baking sheet, and cover with aluminum foil.

4. Bake for 10 to 15 minutes, or until golden. Or place the blintzes in a serving dish, cover with plastic wrap, and heat the blintzes in a microwave on high power for 2 to 4 minutes. Serve at once.

PER SERVING: 352 CAL; 11G PROT; 10G FAT; 58G CARB; 0MG CHOL; 222MG SOD; 4G FIBER

SUMMERTIME BERRY FRENCH TOAST

Although food historians disagree about the origins of this popular breakfast and brunch dish, Americans have made French toast their own, creating hundreds of variations. Scented with vanilla and ground cinnamon, this particular version draws on summer's berries, but the fruit can be changed to suit the season. Plan for a leisurely meal when you can enjoy the toast with hot coffee or tea, chilled fruit juices—and the morning paper.

¾ cup vanilla soymilk

⅓ cup plus 2 tablespoons granulated sugar

4 large eggs

3 tablespoons vanilla extract, or to taste

1 tablespoon baking powder

8 slices whole-grain bread

2 tablespoons ground cinnamon, or to taste

1½ cups fresh raspberries

2 cups sliced strawberries

2 tablespoons unsalted butter or as needed for frying

Strawberry or maple syrup to taste

Confectioners' sugar, for garnish

1. Combine the soymilk, ⅓ cup sugar, eggs, vanilla and baking powder in a bowl, and beat until thick and foamy. Pour into a large baking pan, and place the bread in the egg mixture. Allow the bread to soak up the egg mixture, 7 to 10 minutes, and sprinkle the slices evenly with 1½ tablespoons of the cinnamon. Turn the bread over to soak the second sides, and sprinkle evenly with the remaining ½ tablespoon of the cinnamon.

2. Meanwhile, sprinkle the berries with the remaining 2 tablespoons of sugar, or more to taste, and set aside.

3. Heat the butter in a large skillet over medium heat and, when bubbling, start frying the bread, several slices at a time. Pour any extra egg batter over the slices. Cook 3 to 5 minutes, or until the bottoms are golden. Carefully turn over to brown the second sides. Remove from the skillet, and cook the remaining bread slices, pouring any remaining egg mixture over the uncooked tops of slices.

4. To serve, place 1 slice of toast on a plate, top with some berries, and place a second cooked slice on top, making a berry sandwich. Add more berries, syrup and confectioners' sugar as desired. Repeat with the remaining toast and berries until used up.

PER SERVING (2 PIECES, PLUS BERRIES): 490 CAL; 15G PROT; 15G FAT; 73G CARB; 225MG CHOL; 820MG SOD; 11G FIBER

APPLE-LEMON FRITTERS

SERVES 4 TO 6

These puffy, fruit-filled gems turn breakfast or brunch into a festive meal. Serve them with warmed applesauce, maple syrup or a dusting of confectioners' sugar. Offer plenty of hot coffee and hot cider.

½ cup whole milk or soymilk

3 large eggs

2 tablespoons unsalted butter or soy margarine, melted

1½ cups all-purpose flour

¼ cup cornmeal

1 teaspoon baking powder

½ teaspoon salt

2 cups diced apples

1 tablespoon grated lemon zest

1 tablespoon granulated sugar

1 teaspoon ground cinnamon

2 cups vegetable oil or more as needed

Warmed applesauce, maple syrup or confectioners' sugar, for topping

1. Combine the milk, eggs and butter in a mixing bowl, and beat until well combined. Fold in the flour, cornmeal, baking powder and salt, and stir until well combined. Fold in the apples, lemon zest, sugar and cinnamon.

2. Heat the oil in a large skillet or deep saucepan over medium heat. When hot, spoon about ¼ cup portions of the fritter batter into the oil and fry until golden brown on both sides, for 3 to 4 minutes. Remove from the oil, and place on several layers of paper towels to blot the excess oil. Repeat until the batter is used up.

3. To serve, place the fritters on individual plates, and pass with a selection of toppings.

PER SERVING: 280 CAL; 7G PROT; 12G FAT; 35G CARB; 120MG CHOL; 350MG SOD; 2G FIBER

BREAKFAST PITA

SERVES 1

Start your day right with this portable breakfast sandwich, which can also be the centerpiece of a more leisurely sit-down breakfast when you can relax with the morning coffee.

1 7-inch pita bread

2 teaspoons unsalted butter or soy margarine

2 ounces soy "sausage"

2 scallions, thinly sliced

2 ounces white button mushrooms, thinly sliced

2 large eggs

2 tablespoons heavy cream, optional

1 ounce shredded soy cheese

Salt and freshly ground black pepper to taste

1 tablespoon ranch salad dressing

Avocado slices, for garnish, optional

Leafy watercress stems, for garnish

1. Warm the pita in the oven or toaster, and set aside. Meanwhile, melt the butter in a large skillet over medium heat. Crumble in the soy "sausage." Add the scallions and mushrooms, and sauté for 5 minutes.

2. Combine the eggs, heavy cream, if using, cheese, and salt and pepper, stirring well. Reduce the heat to medium-low, and stir in the egg mixture. Continue stirring slowly until the eggs set, for about 5 minutes. Remove from the heat.

3. Slit the warmed pita in half. Spoon in equal portions of the egg mixture, and top with the ranch salad dressing, avocado, if using, and watercress.

PER SERVING: 590 CAL; 33G PROT; 30G FAT; 45G CARB; 445MG CHOL; 1,260MG SOD; 4G FIBER

BREAKFAST HASH

Look for chipotle chile flakes in specialty food stores, in well-stocked supermarkets or Hispanic groceries (see also pages 454–455). If you prefer, the eggs can be omitted from this dish. If you do not have a large skillet, use two 10-inch skillets. Cook the onions and potatoes in one skillet and the garlic, peppers, rosemary and "sausages" in the other. Add the sausage mixture to the potatoes just before adding the eggs.

2 pounds small white or red-skinned potatoes, unpeeled and cut into 1-inch cubes

2 tablespoons olive oil

1 medium-sized onion, finely chopped

2 bell peppers, preferably red or yellow, chopped

8 small soy "sausages," thinly sliced

1½ tablespoons finely chopped fresh rosemary

3 cloves garlic, minced

4 ounces fresh baby spinach, well rinsed and coarsely chopped

4 large eggs

Salt and freshly ground black pepper to taste

Chipotle chile flakes, optional

1. Put the potatoes in a large pot, and add enough cold water to cover. Bring to a boil over medium heat, reduce the heat to medium-low, and cook until the potatoes are almost tender, for 10 to 12 minutes. Drain and cool.

2. Heat the oil in a very large heavy skillet (see head note, above) over medium-high heat. Add the onion, and cook, stirring often, until it is beginning to soften, for 5 minutes. Add the potatoes, and cook, stirring occasionally, until crisp and brown, for about 10 minutes. Add the bell peppers, "sausages," rosemary and garlic. Cook, stirring occasionally, until the peppers soften, for about 10 minutes. Stir in the spinach, and cook, stirring often, just until the spinach wilts.

3. Break the eggs over the hash, and cook until the eggs are set. Quickly flip the eggs over to briefly cook on the other side, for about 1 minute. Add salt and pepper to taste, and garnish with a dash of chipotle flakes, if desired. Serve hot.

PER SERVING: 359 CAL; 25G PROT; 11G FAT; 49G CARB; 142MG CHOL; 550MG SOD; 6G FIBER

SLOW-SCRAMBLED EGGS OVER ASPARAGUS

Scrambled eggs as smooth and creamy as a well-crafted custard are easy to produce if you do it the French way—using room temperature eggs cooked very slowly over low heat.

2 bagels, sliced horizontally into thirds or quarters

1 pound asparagus, tough ends trimmed and spears peeled

4 tablespoons (½ stick) unsalted butter

8 large eggs, lightly beaten

Salt and freshly ground black pepper to taste

1 tablespoon minced red onion

1. Preheat the broiler.

2. Toast the bagel slices lightly, remove from the oven and set aside. Steam or blanch the asparagus until just tender, drain thoroughly and set aside.

3. Sliver 3 tablespoons of the butter. Beat the eggs in a bowl. Melt several butter slivers in a large nonstick saucepan over very low heat. Add the eggs, and stir constantly with a wooden spoon for 15 to 20 minutes, adding slivers of butter occasionally, . Season with salt and pepper.

4. Meanwhile, heat a large skillet over medium heat. Add the remaining 1 tablespoon of butter, and when it melts, add the asparagus. Cook for 5 minutes, tossing occasionally.

5. To serve, arrange the asparagus spears on 4 warm plates, top with the eggs, sprinkle with onion and serve with bagel crisps.

PER SERVING: 350 CAL; 17G PROT; 23G FAT; 19G CARB; 455MG CHOL; 280MG SOD; 2G FIBER

OMELET WITH CHOPPED GREENS

This is a basic, simple breakfast, brunch dish or lunch dish. As with any omelet, you can vary the filling to suit the occasion, substituting fried potato cubes for the mushrooms and a generous sprinkling of minced parsley for the greens. Or you can give this dish an Asian flavor by using fresh cilantro in the eggs and stir-fried bean sprouts accented by soy sauce for the filling.

12 ounces portobello mushrooms

3 tablespoons olive oil

1 bunch (7 ounces) greens, such as watercress, dandelion or arugula

6 large eggs

Salt and freshly ground black pepper to taste

¼ teaspoon crushed red pepper, optional

½ cup grated Fontina cheese

1. Wipe the mushroom caps with a damp towel, and scrape off and discard the black gills from underneath the caps. Slice the caps. Heat a large skillet, and when hot, add 2 tablespoons of the oil. Sauté the portobello slices, cooking until slightly soft but not browned, for 5 to 7 minutes. Remove from the heat, and set aside.

2. Rinse the greens well, shake off the excess water and chop into small, uniform pieces.

3. Beat the eggs in a large bowl, and season with salt and pepper and crushed red pepper, if using. Fold in the cheese and chopped greens.

4. Heat the remaining 1 tablespoon of oil in a skillet. When hot, pour in the eggs, cooking until the bottom sets, tipping the skillet so the uncooked eggs run underneath. When the egg mixture is firm and the bottom golden, about 2 minutes, heap the portobello slices on one side of the omelet, and flip the other side over the top to cover. Slide onto a serving plate or slice in the skillet, and serve.

PER SERVING: 580 CAL; 33G PROT; 45G FAT; 12G CARB; 665MG CHOL; 460MG SOD; 4G FIBER

PINEAPPLE-COCONUT PORRIDGE

Eat this for breakfast, or make it and set it aside for lunch or an afternoon snack. Top with maple syrup or fruit syrup, if you wish, but it will be equally good moistened with soymilk, nonfat milk or eaten solo. Dried pineapple pieces are very sweet, so adjust other sweeteners to taste.

2 cups pineapple juice

½ cup quick-cooking grits

2 tablespoons packed brown sugar, or to taste

1 cup silken soft tofu

1 cup crushed pineapple, well drained

1 cup dried pineapple pieces

¼ cup toasted shredded coconut, optional

1. Heat 1¾ cups of the pineapple juice in a saucepan over medium heat until boiling. Slowly stir in the grits and brown sugar, reduce the heat to low, cover the pan and cook for 5 minutes, stirring occasionally.

2. Meanwhile, put the remaining ¼ cup of juice, the tofu and crushed pineapple into a blender, and process until smooth. Stir into the grits mixture, and continue cooking and stirring over low heat for 8 to 10 minutes more, or until almost firm. Remove from the heat, stir in the pineapple pieces, garnish with the toasted coconut, if using, and serve.

PER SERVING: 310 CAL; 4G PROT; .5G FAT; 72G CARB; 0MG CHOL; 55MG SOD; 2G FIBER

COUSCOUS PORRIDGE

This porridge tastes similar to a cinnamon bun—really!

4 cups ricemilk
1⅓ cups couscous
½ cup raisins
1 teaspoon ground cinnamon
2 tablespoons honey, optional

1. Bring the ricemilk to a boil in a 2-quart saucepan over medium heat. Stir in the couscous, raisins, cinnamon and honey, if using, and bring back to a boil.

2. Cook over medium heat for 10 minutes. The porridge should be a bit soupy, so add more milk if needed.

PER SERVING: 420 CAL; 11G PROT; 2.5G FAT; 87G CARB; 0MG CHOL; 95MG SOD; 6G FIBER

CREAMY LOW-FAT BAGEL SPREAD

Try this for an unusual "schmear" for bagels. This may be kept for 1 week in the refrigerator.

1 cup low-fat ricotta
2 tablespoons plain yogurt
1 teaspoon fresh lemon juice

Combine all the ingredients in a food processor and blend until very smooth. Scrape down the sides several times and continue processing. Place in an airtight refrigerator bowl, and refrigerate until use.

PER SERVING (2 TABLESPOONS): 25 CAL; 2G PROT; 1.5G FAT; 1G CARB; 5MG CHOL; 20MG SOD; 0G FIBER

OVERNIGHT WHOLE-GRAIN CEREAL

This breakfast cereal requires just a few minutes of advance preparation the night before serving. You can find the grains in the bulk-food section of a well-stocked supermarket, at a natural food store or through a mail-order supplier. You may double or triple the amount of grains to be ground for use on other days. Keep the ground grains in an airtight container in your refrigerator to ensure freshness.

1 tablespoon uncooked wheat berries
1 tablespoon uncooked rye berries
1 tablespoon uncooked barley
1 tablespoon uncooked millet
1 tablespoon uncooked rolled oats
1½ cups apple juice or water
2 tablespoons uncooked oat bran
2 tablespoons raisins

1. Put the wheat berries, rye berries, barley, millet and oats in a grain mill or blender and process on high speed until coarsely ground.

2. Put the mixture in a saucepan with the apple juice, bran and raisins. Bring to a boil over medium-high heat. Cook the cereal for 10 minutes, stirring occasionally, until thickened, and remove from the heat.

3. Cover the pot, and let sit overnight on the stove. The next morning, reheat over medium heat before serving.

PER SERVING: 103 CAL; 3G PROT; 1G FAT; 21G CARB; 0MG CHOL; 4MG SOD; 2G FIBER

BLUEBERRY-PECAN OATMEAL SUNDAE

Fancy oatmeal that looks like a sundae! For a special weekend breakfast, try the super-smooth slow cooker oatmeal (see below) instead with this recipe. You might also want to offer an "oatmeal buffet," with plenty of already cooked oatmeal and different choices of toppings on hand.

2 cups fresh or frozen blueberries

2 tablespoons honey

½ cup orange juice

2 teaspoons cornstarch

½ teaspoon salt

2 cups rolled oats or steel-cut oats

¼ cup toasted chopped pecans (see page 47)

1. Wash the blueberries, and put them in a 2-quart saucepan with the honey. Mix together the orange juice and cornstarch, and add to the pan. Place over medium heat, and bring to a boil. Stir several times as the mixture boils. When the liquid is thick, after about 2 minutes, remove from the heat. This part may be done up to 2 days ahead and refrigerated.

2. Bring 4 cups of water to a rapid boil over medium-high heat, and add the salt. Shake in the oats while stirring. Reduce the heat to medium, and cook for about 5 minutes over medium heat, until the oatmeal is thickened.

3. Divide the oats among 4 large bowls. Top each with ½ cup of the warm blueberry mixture and a heaping tablespoon of pecans.

PER SERVING (WITH TOPPINGS): 410 CAL; 9G PROT; 15G FAT; 64G CARB; 0MG CHOL; 290MG SOD; 9G FIBER

Cooking Oatmeal

In the days when homes had wood-burning stoves, the oatmeal for breakfast was put on the stove at bedtime so that it cooked over low heat all night. The long, slow cooking produced a cereal that was thick, creamy and smooth. No instant cereal can give you that taste. You can experience it, however, if you cook your rolled oats overnight in a slow cooker. Just put 8 cups of water and a little salt in the cooker with 2 cups of oats and set on medium. Seven to 8 hours later you can serve old-time, slow-cooked oatmeal to 6 hungry people.

If you want to cook your oatmeal more quickly, put 1½ cups of water in a small saucepan with a pinch of salt, and when it comes to a boil, shake in 1 cup of oats, reduce the heat to low, and cook until thick and creamy. If you want a richer flavor, cook the oatmeal in skim milk or ricemilk. Try adding honey, cinnamon or ¼ cup dried fruit to the water before adding the oats for variety. Add maple sugar, dried apples, dried bananas and such to shake up your breakfast routine.

What Kind of Oats?

Oats cook more easily when they are rolled flat or steel-cut. You will find both Irish and Scottish oats in your co-op or fine food store. If you like oats, enjoy a taste treat by buying one of the different varieties. Instant oatmeal is an American invention that shortens the cooking time but takes away some of the taste. Save it for desperation mornings.

In Scotland, oats are eaten at meals other than breakfast. They are often cooked in the water left from boiling turnips, cabbage and other strong vegetables. Oats are cooked into thin gruels and served as soup. And for the real oats lover, a Scottish cook will make oats for dessert by soaking the uncooked oats overnight in cream and layering them with fresh fruit or stirring some honey and Scotch whiskey into the oats.

STRAWBERRY CHEESECAKE OATMEAL SUNDAE

Here's a quick breakfast sundae.

1 cup nonfat vanilla yogurt
2 tablespoons honey
2 teaspoons vanilla extract
1 teaspoon grated lemon zest
½ teaspoon salt
2 cups rolled oats or steel-cut oats
2 cups sliced strawberries

1. Mix the yogurt with the honey vanilla and lemon zest, and set aside.

2. Bring 4 cups of water to a rapid boil, and add the salt. Shake the oats into the water while stirring. Cook for about 5 minutes over medium heat, or until the oatmeal is cooked through.

3. Divide the oatmeal evenly among 4 bowls. Top with strawberries and a dollop of the yogurt mix.

PER SERVING: 330 CAL; 11G PROT; 4G FAT; 62G CARB; 0MG CHOL; 340MG SOD; 8G FIBER

MANGO-APRICOT OATMEAL SUNDAE

SERVES 4

A fruit-filled oatmeal sundae topped with almonds hits the spot.

1 cup chopped dried apricots
1 cup pineapple juice
1 ripe mango, peeled and finely diced
2 cups rolled oats or steel-cut oats
½ cup sliced almonds
Salt to taste

1. Place the apricots in a 1-quart saucepan with the pineapple juice and 1 cup of water, and bring to a boil over medium heat. Cook for 10 minutes, until the apricots are plumped. Remove from the heat, and let cool. Remove half of the apricots, put in a blender or food mill, and purée. Return the purée to the remaining apricots. Add the mango, and stir. Set aside.

2. Bring 4 cups of water to a rapid boil, and stir in the salt. Shake the oats into the water as you stir. Cook over medium heat for about 5 minutes, until the oatmeal is cooked through.

3. Divide the oatmeal evenly among 4 bowls, and top with the mango mixture. Sprinkle with sliced almonds, and serve.

PER SERVING. 440 CAL, 12G PROT; 10G FAT, 77G CARB, 0MG CHOL, 5MG SOD, 10G FIBER

TUTTI-FRUTTI OATMEAL

SERVES 6

This recipe can be made with any combination of fresh and dried fruit that appeals to you.

2 large apples, peeled and chopped
¼ cup golden raisins
¼ cup sweetened dried cranberries
¼ cup chopped dried apricots
1 teaspoon grated orange zest, optional
1 teaspoon ground cinnamon
2 cups apple cider
2 cups rolled or steel-cut oats

1. Put the chopped apples in a 2-quart saucepan with the raisins, dried cranberries, apricots, orange zest and cinnamon. Add the cider and 2 cups of water, and bring to a rapid boil. Shake in the oats as you stir. Cook over medium heat for about 5 minutes, until the oatmeal is thickened.

2. To serve, remove from the heat, and spoon into individual bowls.

PER SERVING: 330 CAL; 8G PROT; 4G FAT; 70G CARB; 0MG CHOL; 10MG SOD; 8G FIBER

brunches and lunches

CURRIED MANGO OMELET
SERVES 1

This extravagant omelet calls for special accompaniments such as chilled mango juice, a basket of hot muffins and a spicy chai tea or a champagne cocktail.

1 tablespoon unsalted butter

2 extra-large eggs, beaten

1 teaspoon curry powder, or to taste

Salt and freshly ground black pepper to taste

1 large mango, peeled, seeded and diced

2 tablespoons plain yogurt

1 tablespoon mango chutney

¼ cup crushed macadamia nuts

Cilantro leaves

1 teaspoon fresh lime juice

1. Heat the butter in a medium nonstick skillet or omelet pan over medium heat. Season the eggs with the curry powder, salt and pepper. When the butter is hot, add the eggs and swirl around to cover the bottom of the skillet. Lift up the edges of the omelet, and tip the skillet so the uncooked egg runs underneath. Cook until the omelet firms, about 30 seconds.

2. Place the diced mango on half of the omelet. Fold the omelet over the filling, and slide from the skillet onto a plate. Top with the yogurt, chutney, macadamia nuts, cilantro and lime juice. Serve hot.

PER SERVING: 610 CAL; 21G PROT; 50G FAT; 24G CARB; 525MG CHOL; 180MG SOD; 7G FIBER

APPLE-CHARD QUICHE
SERVES 6

Pairing cheese with apples is a gastronomic pleasure. Adding ruby chard embellishes the combination and amplifies the texture of this homey quiche.

1 tablespoon olive oil

1 tablespoon unsalted butter

1 large Vidalia or other sweet onion, thinly sliced

1 cup shredded ruby Swiss chard

1 cup thinly sliced mushrooms

Salt and freshly ground black pepper to taste

½ cup chopped apple

2 tablespoons all-purpose flour

½ teaspoon ground nutmeg

2 large eggs

1 cup shredded Jarlsberg cheese

½ cup skim milk

1 premade 9-inch deep-dish piecrust, unbaked

1. Preheat the oven to 375F.

2. Heat the oil and butter in a large skillet over medium heat. Reduce the heat to medium-low, and sauté the onion until caramelized, for about 15 minutes. Add the Swiss chard, mushrooms, salt and pepper. Increase the heat to medium, and cook, stirring often, for about 7 minutes, or until the mushrooms and chard are soft.

3. Combine the apple, flour and nutmeg in a bowl, and toss to coat the apples. Combine the eggs, cheese and milk in a separate bowl, and beat until the ingredients are well blended. Fold in the apple mixture. Spoon the chard mixture into the piecrust. Pour the egg mixture over the top.

4. Bake for 35 to 45 minutes, or until the eggs are set and the top is browned. Cool slightly before slicing into wedges, and serve.

PER SERVING (1 WEDGE): 300 CAL; 11G PROT; 19G FAT; 23G CARB; 105MG CHOL; 200MG SOD; 1G FIBER

BROCCOLI-POLENTA QUICHE

Here's a way to make a great-tasting quiche with fewer eggs. The filling is bound with a quick-cooked version of polenta, which firms things up nicely and adds much in the way of flavor and texture. Broccoli and onions make a delicious filling, but any steamed vegetable works well.

1 9-inch whole wheat piecrust

2½ cups broccoli florets

1 tablespoon olive oil

1 large onion, halved and thinly sliced

2 cups whole or low-fat milk

⅓ cup fine yellow cornmeal

1½ cups shredded sharp cheddar cheese

2 large eggs, 1 separated

2 teaspoons Dijon mustard

1 teaspoon dried basil

½ teaspoon salt

1. Preheat the oven to 375F.

2. Prepare, bake and cool the piecrust. Keep the oven on.

3. Meanwhile, bring 2 inches of water to a boil in a large saucepan fitted with a steamer basket. Add the broccoli, cover and cook until just tender, for about 4 minutes. Set aside to cool.

4. Heat the oil in a medium skillet over medium heat. Add the onion, and cook, stirring often, until softened, about 5 minutes. Remove from the heat, and set aside.

5. Whisk together the milk and cornmeal in a saucepan. Bring to a very slow boil over medium heat, whisking often. When the mixture starts to thicken, reduce the heat to very low, and cook, whisking constantly, for about 5 minutes, or until medium-thick. Remove from the heat, and whisk in the cheese, half at a time. Cool briefly, and whisk in the whole egg, egg white, mustard, basil and salt. Add the sautéed onion, and mix well.

6. Arrange the broccoli in the cooled piecrust. Scrape the cornmeal mixture over the broccoli, and smooth with a spoon, wiggling the spoon so the mixture settles.

7. Bake until the quiche is golden brown, for about 40 minutes. Transfer to a wire rack, and cool for at least 20 minutes before cutting into wedges. Serve warm.

PER SERVING (1 WEDGE): 393 CAL; 14G PROT; 24G FAT; 31G CARB; 115MG CHOL; 395MG SOD; 3G FIBER

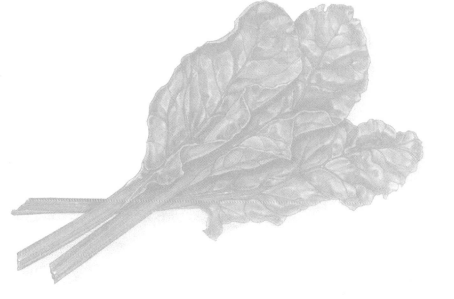

SPANISH TORTILLA

An excellent dish for a festive brunch, this recipe may be doubled if you have a very large skillet. For 1 pound of potatoes, you will need a well-seasoned cast-iron 10-inch skillet or a similar nonstick one. For 2 pounds of potatoes, you will need the same skillet in a 14-inch size. It can be hard to handle the heavier one when the pan is fully loaded. If you prefer to make 2 tortillas, keep the first one warm in a 200F oven. You may peel the potatoes if you prefer, but remember, unpeeled potatoes will give you more fiber. If you like, add ½ cup of shredded cheese sprinkled on top after the tortilla is flipped–Cheddar, Emmentaler, manchego or Asiago cheeses are all good choices.

5 tablespoons olive oil, divided

1 pound baby red-skinned potatoes, sliced very thinly

1 teaspoon salt

½ teaspoon freshly ground black pepper

1 red onion, sliced very thinly

2 extra-large eggs

3 large egg whites

½ cup shredded cheese, optional

1. Heat the skillet over medium heat, and add 3 tablespoons of the oil. Add the potatoes and sauté, stirring frequently, until some slices are golden and the remaining potatoes are transparent and soft, for 15 to 20 minutes. Season the potatoes with salt and pepper. Transfer the potatoes to a bowl.

2. Add the onion to the skillet, and sauté until soft and transparent, for about 6 minutes. Transfer to the bowl with the potatoes.

3. Beat the eggs and egg whites together until there are no streaks. Add the eggs to the bowl with the potatoes.

4. Use a clean cloth to wipe out the skillet used to cook the onions, scraping out any crusty bits. Reheat the skillet. Add the remaining 2 tablespoons of oil. When the oil is sizzling hot, spoon the potato mixture into the skillet, and push down on the potatoes lightly to spread them evenly in the skillet. Cook over low heat for about 10 minutes, or until the bottom is golden.

5. Wearing 2 oven mitts, place a large plate or a pizza pan on top of the skillet, and quickly invert it. Return the skillet to the stove, and slide the tortilla back in. Cook until the bottom is golden and set, for about 4 minutes. Allow the tortilla to rest in a warm place for 2 or 3 minutes. Cut in wedges, and serve.

PER SERVING: 300 CAL; 9G PROT; 20G FAT; 21G CARB; 125MG CHOL; 670MG SOD; 2G FIBER

ITALIAN OMELET

Handsome yet hearty, this dish works well for a casual supper or for a brunch entrée, especially accompanied by crusty Italian bread, sparkling white wine and plenty of fresh fruit with cheese.

1 tablespoon pesto

1½ tablespoons olive oil

½ bell pepper, diced

6 ounces sliced mushrooms

1½ cups canned quartered artichoke hearts, well drained

6 large eggs, beaten

Salt and freshly ground black pepper to taste

2 tablespoons grated Parmesan cheese, for garnish

1. Preheat the broiler.

2. Heat the pesto and oil in a large skillet over medium heat. Add the pepper and mushrooms, and sauté for 5 minutes, or until the mushrooms soften. Stir in the artichoke hearts, and sauté for about 1 minute more.

3. Pour the eggs over the vegetables, tilting the skillet so the eggs uniformly cover the vegetables. Cook the eggs, lifting up the edges and tilting the pan so uncooked eggs run underneath. When the bottom and edges look firm, after about 5 minutes, broil the top of the omelet until the eggs brown and puff up. Remove from the oven.

4. To serve, sprinkle the omelet with the Parmesan cheese, and slice.

PER SERVING (ONE-SIXTH): 160 CAL; 9G PROT; 10G FAT; 7G CARB; 215MG CHOL; 150MG SOD; 3G FIBER

FRESH FAVA BEAN AND DILL KUKU

Kuku is an Iranian egg dish, similar to an Italian frittata. It is usually filled with vegetables and herbs. This one calls for fava beans and dill. Fresh or frozen fava beans, Thai basil, flatbreads and drained yogurt are available at Iranian markets. Labneh is the Arab word for drained yogurt. You can buy it in a Middle Eastern grocery store or make it yourself by salting yogurt, putting it in a cheesecloth-lined sieve over a bowl and leaving it in the refrigerator overnight. Note: The recipe analysis does not include the bread.

¼ cup vegetable oil, unsalted butter or ghee

1 large onion, thinly sliced

2 pounds fresh or 1 pound frozen and thawed fava beans, waxy skins removed

2 cups chopped fresh dillweed

6 cloves garlic, crushed and chopped

6 large eggs

½ cup milk or soymilk

½ cup grated Parmesan cheese or shredded fresh mozzarella cheese

1 tablespoon all-purpose flour

2 teaspoons salt

1 teaspoon ground cumin

1 teaspoon freshly ground black pepper

1 green Thai chili, chopped, or ½ teaspoon crushed red pepper

½ teaspoon baking powder

¼ teaspoon paprika

¼ teaspoon turmeric

1 cup drained yogurt or *labneh*

1 package flatbread, such as pita or lavash, toasted, if desired

1 cup fresh Thai basil leaves

1. Heat the oil in a 10- or 11-inch ovenproof nonstick skillet over medium heat. Add the onion, and fry for 5 minutes, or until translucent. Add the beans, dill-weed and garlic. Cover and cook over medium heat for 5 minutes, or until the fava beans are soft.

2. Meanwhile, break the eggs into a bowl, add the milk, Parmesan, flour, salt, cumin, pepper, chili, baking powder, paprika and turmeric and whisk lightly.

3. Preheat the broiler.

4. Pour the egg mixture over the fava beans in the skillet. Cover, reduce the heat to low and cook for 15 to 20 minutes.

5. Place the skillet under the broiler for 1 to 5 minutes, or until the eggs are golden brown. Serve warm or at room temperature with yogurt, flatbread and Thai basil leaves.

PER SERVING: 360 CAL; 6G PROT; 30G FAT; 18G CARB; 90MG CHOL; 873MG SOD; 2G FIBER

EGGPLANT AND POTATO HASH

This sturdy offering fits well into a brunch menu plan. Why not serve this with the Bald Eagle Valley Tomato Salad (page 142)?

2½ cups peeled and cubed baking potatoes

¾ cup Vegetable Stock (page 332) plus additional if needed

Salt to taste

1 tablespoon unsalted butter

1 medium-sized onion, finely chopped

4 cups peeled and diced eggplant

1 tablespoon olive oil

1 clove garlic, minced

1 tablespoon all-purpose flour

¾ cup whole milk

¼ cup grated Parmesan cheese or ½ cup shredded sharp cheddar cheese, optional

Sprigs fresh parsley for garnish

1. Combine the potatoes and Vegetable Stock in a large nonstick skillet, and add salt. Bring to a boil over medium-high heat, cover partially, reduce the heat to medium and cook until the potatoes are almost tender and most of the liquid has evaporated, for about 6 minutes. Transfer to a bowl, and set aside.

2. Melt the butter in the same skillet over medium heat. Add the onion and cook, stirring often, until softened, for about 5 minutes. Stir in the eggplant, oil, about 3 tablespoons of water, and season lightly with salt to taste. Cover, reduce the heat to medium-low and cook, stirring occasionally for about 5 minutes, or until the eggplant is tender.

3. Add the garlic and flour, and cook, stirring, for 1 minute. Reduce the heat to low, stir in the milk and cook, uncovered, stirring, for 2 minutes. Stir in the potato mixture. Cover and cook, stirring occasionally, until the hash is thick and saucy, for 5 to 7 minutes. (If the hash sticks to the pan, stir in additional Vegetable Stock or water by the tablespoonful.) During the last minute of cooking, sprinkle the cheese over the hash, if using. Garnish with parsley, and serve hot.

PER SERVING: 170 CAL; 5G PROT; 8G FAT; 15G CARB; 14MG CHOL; 99MG SOD; 4G FIBER

BUTTERNUT SQUASH PANCAKES

These savory pancakes are easy to make and are good for you, too: Butternut squash is high in vitamin A. For entertaining, you may want to bake and mash the squash a day in advance (steps 1 and 2) to save time the day of the brunch.

1 small butternut squash, halved and seeded

½ cup skim milk or water

1 large egg

1 large egg white

2 cups whole wheat pastry flour

2 teaspoons baking powder

1 teaspoon salt

½ teaspoon ground cinnamon

¼ teaspoon ground cloves

1 tablespoon vegetable oil

1. Preheat the oven to 350F. Place the squash in a baking dish, and bake for about 40 minutes, or until tender when pierced with a fork.

2. Discard the skin. Put the squash pulp in a bowl, and mash with a fork or potato masher until smooth. Let cool to room temperature.

3. Add the milk, egg and egg white, stir to blend and set aside.

4. Combine the flour, baking powder, salt, cinnamon and cloves in a separate bowl, and stir to mix. Add the flour mixture to the squash mixture, and mix well.

5. Heat the oil in a nonstick skillet over medium-high heat. Pour in about ¼ cup of batter per pancake. Cook for about 3 minutes, turn and cook for 3 minutes more, or until lightly browned. Remove from the skillet, and keep warm. Repeat with the remaining batter until it is used up.

PER PANCAKE: 101 CAL; 4G PROT; 2G FAT; 18G CARB; 17MG CHOL; 227MG SOD; 3G FIBER

CHEESE AND SPINACH QUICHE

This makes a satisfying lunch or light supper dish, and is complemented by a tossed green salad and a lemon sorbet. This quiche is so simple that you will get it ready for the oven in just minutes.

2 bunches (about 1 pound) spinach, trimmed and well rinsed

3 large eggs, beaten

1 bunch scallions, trimmed and thinly sliced

1 cup shredded cheddar cheese

1 cup low-fat ricotta cheese

1 teaspoon dried oregano

Salt and freshly ground black pepper to taste

1 premade unbaked 9-inch deep-dish piecrust

1. Preheat the oven to 400F.

2. Steam the spinach in a pot with the water clinging to it until it wilts, for about 5 minutes, and set aside.

3. Meanwhile, combine the eggs, scallions, cheddar cheese, ricotta cheese, oregano, salt and pepper in a mixing bowl, stirring to mix well. Using tongs, press out all the liquid from the spinach, and chop it finely. Stir into the egg mixture. Spoon the mixture into the piecrust.

4. Bake for about 25 minutes, or until the center is firm and the top turns golden. Remove from the oven, cool slightly and eat warm.

PER SERVING (ONE-SIXTH): 400 CAL; 15G PROT; 26G FAT; 27G CARB; 135MG CHOL; 440MG SOD; 2G FIBER

CHEDDAR CORNMEAL WAFFLES

SERVES 4 TO 5

Inspired by the Southwest, these wholesome waffles can turn fiery with plenty of hot pepper sauce and a salsa containing smoky chipotle chiles. Although you may serve these at breakfast, their savory flavor suits a midday meal better.

Cheddar Cornmeal Waffles

3 large eggs

1¾ cups buttermilk or soymilk

2 tablespoons vegetable oil

1 cup all-purpose flour

1 tablespoon granulated sugar

2½ teaspoons baking powder

1 teaspoon salt

¼ teaspoon baking soda

1 cup fine cornmeal

½ cup shredded cheddar cheese or soy cheese plus extra for garnish

½ cup fresh, frozen or canned corn kernels, rinsed

Hot pepper sauce to taste

½ cup chopped cilantro, for garnish

1 ripe avocado, diced, for garnish

Salsa

1 cup thinly sliced pitted black olives

1 cup salsa

1 cup canned black beans, drained and rinsed

½ cup corn kernels

1. Preheat a waffle iron, and spray with nonstick cooking spray.

2. To make the Cheddar Cornmeal Waffles: Beat the eggs well in a bowl, and stir in the buttermilk and oil. In a separate bowl, sift together the flour, sugar, baking powder, salt and baking soda. Stir into the egg mixture, and stir in the cornmeal, cheese, corn and hot pepper sauce.

3. To make the Salsa: Stir together the olives, salsa, black beans and corn in a saucepan, and bring to a boil over medium heat. Cook for 5 minutes, or until the mixture reduces slightly.

4. Bake the waffles according to the manufacturer's instructions for the iron. To serve, place a waffle on a plate, top with the salsa mixture and garnish with the cheese, cilantro and avocado.

PER SERVING: 570 CAL; 20G PROT; 23G FAT; 72G CARB; 145MG CHOL; 1,490MG SOD; 10G FIBER

VEGGIE PANCAKES

A complete meal in one, these pancakes partner well with a tossed salad and a simple fruit dessert. If you want a sweet, dessert-like dish, use maple syrup, honey or even a fruit butter such as apple butter as a topping.

1 cup buttermilk

2 large eggs

3 tablespoons olive oil, or more as needed

1 cup all-purpose flour

½ cup nonfat cottage cheese

1 cup shredded uncooked sweet potato

1 cup shredded onion

¼ cup minced fresh parsley

Salt and freshly ground black pepper to taste

2 cups applesauce, warm

1. Combine the buttermilk, eggs and 1 tablespoon of the oil in a bowl, and beat. Stir in the flour and cottage cheese, mixing together well. Stir in the vegetables, parsley, salt and pepper, and mix well.

2. Heat the remaining 2 tablespoons of the oil in a large skillet over medium heat. Using a ¼-cup measure, spoon the batter into the skillet, making 2 cakes at a time, patting the batter down with a spatula. When the bottom of each pancake is golden brown, flip and cook the other side. Add more oil as needed.

3. When both sides are golden, remove the cakes to a dish lined with paper towels. Repeat with the remaining batter until used up. Serve the pancakes, passing with the applesauce.

PER SERVING: 440 CAL; 13G PROT; 14G FAT; 66G CARB; 110MG CHOL; 230MG SOD; 4G FIBER

APPLE–WILD RICE PANCAKES

This makes an ideal breakfast or brunch for a leisurely fall or winter morning. The pancakes are sturdy enough for a chilly day, but fit for a dressy meal. Offer them with maple syrup or other fruit syrup or honey.

2 large eggs, beaten

3 tablespoons vegetable oil

1 cup evaporated skim milk

1½ cups all-purpose flour

2 teaspoons baking powder

1 teaspoon salt

2 tablespoons granulated sugar

1 cup cooked wild rice (see page 48)

1 apple, cored and chopped

1. Beat the eggs with the oil and whisk in the milk. Sift together the flour, baking powder, salt and sugar, and fold into the egg mixture. Stir in the wild rice and apple.

2. Heat a griddle or large skillet over medium heat, and spray with nonstick cooking spray. Ladle about ¼ cup of the batter at a time onto the hot skillet. When the bottom of each pancake is golden brown, flip and cook the other side. Remove from the skillet, and repeat with the remaining batter until it is used up. Serve hot.

PER SERVING: 280 CAL; 10G PROT; 9G FAT; 39G CARB; 70MG CHOL; 620MG SOD; 1G FIBER

GALLO PINTO

Natives of Costa Rica say there are as many recipes for Gallo Pinto as there are Costa Ricans. This rice and beans dish, which translates as "spotted rooster," is eaten with gusto by the majority of the population every single day—often for breakfast—and there are those who eat it at every meal. Many Costa Ricans add several generous dashes of Salsa Lizano, a condiment native to their country, although vegetarian Worcestershire sauce is a reasonable facsimile. There is a famous saying, "Wherever there is a Costa Rican, there is peace," but in Costa Rica, billboards proclaim, "Wherever there is a Costa Rican, there is Salsa Lizano."

2 to 3 tablespoons canola or soybean oil

1 medium onion, finely chopped

2 cloves garlic, minced

3 cups cooked white rice (see page 48)

2 cups cooked black beans, strained to reserve liquid and rinsed

2 to 3 tablespoons Salsa Lizano or vegetarian Worcestershire sauce

1 teaspoon ground cumin

1 teaspoon ground coriander

½ teaspoon ground ginger

Salt and freshly ground black pepper to taste

1. Heat the oil in a large skillet over medium heat, and add the onion. When it starts to turn color, add the garlic, and sauté for about 5 minutes, or until the onion is golden.

2. Stir in the rice, beans, Salsa Lizano, cumin, coriander and ginger, combining well. Add ¼ to ½ cup of liquid from the beans, if desired, to make the rice "dirty." Cook until heated through, and add salt and pepper to taste. Serve hot.

PER SERVING: 260 CAL; 8G PROT; 5G FAT; 44G CARB; 0MG CHOL; 2MG SOD; 6G FIBER

CURRIED MANGO IN AVOCADO

For a dramatic serving presentation, select the largest avocado you can find. This is a substantial luncheon entrée or elegant first course for dinner.

1 jumbo avocado

1 large ripe mango, peeled and cubed

½ cup crushed banana chips or plantain chips

¼ cup chopped cilantro

2 tablespoons mayonnaise

Juice of ½ lime

1 to 2 teaspoons curry powder, or to taste

3 tablespoons sliced pickled ginger, for garnish

1. Slice the avocado in half, cutting lengthwise. Carefully pull or twist the halves apart, and remove the seed. Using a sharp paring knife, cut a crosshatch pattern into the flesh, almost to the skin, and spoon out the cubes, leaving a ⅛-inch layer of avocado flesh. This keeps the avocado shell stable.

2. Combine the avocado cubes, mango, banana chips, cilantro, mayonnaise, lime juice and curry powder in a bowl, stirring together gently.

3. Mound the mixture in the avocado halves. Sprinkle each with pickled ginger slices, and serve.

PER SERVING (½ FILLED AVOCADO): 760 CAL; 7G PROT; 66G FAT; 46G CARB; 10MG CHOL; 620MG SOD; 19G FIBER

GNOCCHI WITH SOY "BACON" ON CHARD

Gnocchi is Italian for dumplings, and the little balls are generally made of potatoes or flour. The flavors of blue cheese and "bacon" enliven this otherwise bland pasta dish.

Salt

1 pound fresh gnocchi

1 bunch (about 8 ounces) chard, ends trimmed

2 tablespoons vegetable oil

1 tablespoon minced garlic

⅓ cup white wine or more as needed

4 ounces crumbled blue cheese

⅓ cup soy "bacon" bits, or more to taste

1 tablespoon unsalted margarine or butter

1. Bring a large pot of lightly salted water to a boil over medium-high heat. Add the gnocchi, and cook according to the package directions, or until all the gnocchi float to the surface. Drain and set aside.

2. Meanwhile, stack the chard leaves one on top of the other, roll them up into a loose bundle and thinly slice. Heat the oil in a large skillet over medium heat, and sauté the garlic for 2 to 3 minutes. Add the chard, and sauté 2 minutes. Add the wine, cover the skillet and steam for 3 to 4 minutes, or until the chard is tender but not limp. Remove the chard from the skillet with tongs, and place in a serving dish.

3. Spoon the gnocchi onto the chard, and sprinkle with the cheese and "bacon" bits. Add the margarine to the skillet, and heat over high heat. When melted, spoon the margarine and any remaining pan juices over the gnocchi, and serve.

PER SERVING: 480 CAL; 18G PROT; 24G FAT; 47G CARB; 30MG CHOL; 1,290MG SOD; 5G FIBER

NOODLES DIABLO

This slurpy, spicy, fusion stir-fry showcases big flavors, generous portions and lots of heat. If you prefer a milder flavor, use less chili sauce. Look for preserved black beans in Asian markets. You can ready the bean sprouts, broccoli and udon noodles up to 8 hours ahead. If so, store each of them separately, tightly covered, in the refrigerator.

2 cups bean sprouts

2 cups broccoli florets

4 ounces dried udon noodles

2 tablespoons olive oil

½ teaspoon dark sesame oil

1 onion, finely chopped

2 tablespoons preserved black beans

4 cloves garlic, minced

2 tablespoons finely chopped fresh ginger

2 teaspoons Asian chili sauce

4 plum tomatoes, seeded and chopped

1 teaspoon salt

¾ cup dry white wine

½ cup Vegetable Stock (page 332)

8 ounces baked tofu, diced

2 teaspoons black sesame seeds

1. Bring a large pot of water to a boil over medium heat. Place the bean sprouts in a colander or heatproof strainer, and plunge them into the boiling water for 10 seconds. Run cold water over them until chilled so they remain crisp, and set aside. Add the broccoli to the same pot, and cook for 3 minutes. Transfer with a slotted spoon to a bowl of cold water.

2. Cook the udon in the boiling water according to the package instructions, for about 8 minutes. Rinse the noodles under cold water, and set aside.

3. Heat the olive oil and the sesame oil in a large, nonstick skillet over medium-high heat. Stir-fry the onion, beans, garlic, ginger and chili sauce until the onion softens, for 3 minutes. Add the tomatoes and salt, and cook until the tomatoes soften, stirring often, for about 3 minutes. Pour in the wine and broth. Boil vigorously until the liquid reduces by one-third, for 2 to 3 minutes. Add the tofu, udon and broccoli, stir-frying for about 2 minutes, or until just heated through. Divide the noodles among 2 or 3 large shallow bowls. Top each with bean sprouts and sesame seeds, and serve.

PER SERVING: 641 CAL; 26G PROT; 25G FAT; 70G CARB; 0MG CHOL; 238MG SOD; 9G FIBER

PITA POCKETS STUFFED WITH VEGETABLES AND CHICKPEAS

The protein-rich filling for these sandwiches can be made a day in advance. It's delicious spread on crackers, too!

2 teaspoons vegetable oil

2 cloves garlic, minced

½ cup finely chopped scallions

⅓ cup chopped green bell pepper

3 tablespoons chopped fresh parsley

1 tablespoon sesame seeds

½ teaspoon dried oregano or 1½ teaspoons chopped fresh oregano

½ teaspoon dried mint or 1½ teaspoons chopped fresh mint

1 15-ounce can chickpeas, drained and rinsed

Pinch salt, or to taste

Hot pepper sauce to taste, optional

2 large whole wheat pita breads, halved

2 small tomatoes, sliced about ½ inch thick

1 small onion, thinly sliced

4 leaves romaine or other crisp lettuce, rinsed and dried

1 cup alfalfa sprouts or other sprouts

1 cup (4 ounces) shredded low-fat Monterey Jack or soy cheese, optional

1. Heat the oil in a skillet over medium heat. Add the garlic and scallions and cook, stirring frequently, until the scallions are soft, for about 5 minutes. Add the bell pepper, parsley and sesame seeds and cook, stirring frequently, until the pepper is soft, for about 5 minutes. Add the oregano and mint, and cook, stirring, for 1 minute more.

2. Put the vegetable mixture and chickpeas in a food processor, and purée until smooth. Add the salt and hot pepper sauce to taste. Stuff the mixture into pita pockets. Add the tomatoes, onion, lettuce, sprouts and cheese. Serve.

PER SERVING: 276 CAL; 13G PROT; 7G FAT; 42G CARB; 0MG CHOL; 220MG SOD; 8G FIBER

SLOPPY FALAFEL SANDWICHES

This variation on Sloppy Joes is terrific for a comforting lunch or a quick supper. A side of coleslaw and a tall glass of iced herbal tea are nice accompaniments. To make Sloppy Falafel Chili, add 1 can of pinto or kidney beans, and heat through before serving.

1 6-ounce package falafel mix

1 teaspoon vegetable oil

1 28-ounce can tomatoes with juice, chopped

½ teaspoon salt

Chili powder to taste

4 whole wheat burger buns

1. Prepare the falafel according to the package directions.

2. Heat the oil in a large skillet over medium heat, and add the falafel mix. Cook, stirring frequently, until the falafel is crumbly and beginning to dry out. Add the tomatoes with juice, salt and chili powder. Stir, reduce heat to low, and cook until thickened. Spoon the mixture over the buns, and serve immediately.

PER SERVING: 236 CAL; 11G PROT; 4G FAT; 30G CARB; 0MG CHOL; 1,129MG SOD; 12G FIBER

PITA WITH HUMMUS, TOMATO, RED ONION, CUCUMBER AND BLACK OLIVES

SERVES 6

This is a great sandwich when you have leftover hummus in the refrigerator. If you eat cheese, you can add crumbled feta. The escarole gives this sandwich a tang that makes it special, but if it's not available, just use the lettuce of your choice.

2 tomatoes, diced

1 large red onion, chopped

1 large cucumber, diced

1 cup pitted kalamata olives

2 tablepoons olive oil

1 tablespoon fresh lemon juice

1 teaspoon crushed garlic

1 teaspoon chopped fresh oregano

1 teaspoon freshly ground black pepper

1½ teaspoons minced fresh basil leaves or ½ teaspoon dried basil

6 whole wheat pita breads

1½ cups prepared hummus

2 cups chopped escarole

1. Mix the tomatoes, onion, cucumber and olives in a bowl. In another bowl, mix the oil, lemon juice, garlic, oregano, pepper and basil, and pour over the vegetables. Toss well. Set aside.

2. Cut the pitas in half. Fill each half with 2 tablespoons of hummus, ¾ cup of vegetables and as much escarole as will fit. Serve 2 halves per person. If more hummus is available, place a bowl of it on the table so those who want it can add extra to their sandwiches.

PER SERVING: 360 CAL; 9G PROT; 20G FAT; 38G CARB; 0MG CHOL; 1,010MG SOD; 9G FIBER

PITA SANDWICHES WITH MEDITERRANEAN-STYLE EGGPLANT FILLING

SERVES 4

This hearty sandwich filling is delicious accompanied by a romaine and cucumber salad. To make Eggplant Pasta Sauce, omit the rice and proceed as the recipe directs.

1 cup uncooked quick-cooking brown rice

1 tablespoon olive oil

1 eggplant, peeled and diced

1 onion, chopped

2 cloves garlic, minced

1 16-ounce can whole tomatoes with juice, chopped

Salt and freshly ground black pepper to taste

¼ teaspoon cayenne pepper

4 large pita breads, halved

1. Cook the rice according to the package directions, and set aside. Heat the oil in a wok or large skillet over medium-high heat. Add the eggplant, and stir-fry for 5 to 10 minutes or until the eggplant is golden brown. Add the onion and garlic, and stir-fry for 2 to 3 minutes or until the onion has wilted slightly. Add the tomatoes and their juices, salt, pepper and cayenne. Cover, and cook for 5 to 15 minutes, or until the eggplant reaches desired tenderness. Add the cooked rice, and stir to mix.

2. Fill the pita pockets with the eggplant mixture, and serve warm.

PER SERVING: 430 CAL; 12G PROT; 6G FAT; 83G CARB; 0MG CHOL; 805MG SOD; 8G FIBER

This Middle Eastern classic gets the skinny treatment in this remake. Note: For a dairy-free Yogurt Sauce, substitute half of a 10½-ounce package of firm tofu plus ¼ cup fresh lemon juice for the yogurt. Reserve any leftover sauces for another use.

Yogurt Sauce

1 cup nonfat plain yogurt

1 tablespoon chopped fresh mint or 1 teaspoon dried mint

2 cloves garlic

¼ teaspoon salt

Pinch sugar

Freshly ground black pepper to taste

Hot Sauce

1 cup Vegetable Stock (page 332)

6 tablespoons tomato paste

1 tablespoon fresh lemon juice

1 tablespoon minced fresh parsley or 1½ teaspoons dried parsley

1 tablespoon minced fresh cilantro l or 1½ teaspoons dried cilantro

2 teaspoons Asian red chili paste

½ teaspoon ground cumin

Falafel

½ onion, chopped

½ cup minced fresh parsley

3 cloves garlic

1½ cups cooked chickpeas

1 tablespoon fresh lemon juice

1 teaspoon ground cumin

½ teaspoon dried basil or 1½ teaspoons chopped fresh basil

½ teaspoon ground coriander

½ teaspoon dried thyme or 1½ teaspoons chopped fresh thyme

½ teaspoon salt

½ teaspoon hot pepper sauce

Freshly ground black pepper to taste

2 slices French bread, torn into large pieces and soaked in cold water to cover

½ cup whole wheat flour

1 tablespoon olive oil

4 large whole wheat pita breads

Lettuce, sliced tomatoes, sliced cucumbers and chopped onions, for garnish

1. To make the Yogurt Sauce: Put all the ingredients into a blender or food processor, and purée until smooth. Set aside.

2. To make the Hot Sauce: Combine all the ingredients in a saucepan. Heat over medium heat until the mixture has thickened slightly, for about 5 minutes. Set aside.

3. Preheat the oven to 375F. Lightly grease a baking sheet.

4. To make the Falafel: Put the onion, parsley and garlic in a food processor or blender, and purée until smooth. Add the chickpeas, and process until finely chopped and somewhat pasty. Add the lemon juice, cumin, basil, coriander, thyme, salt, hot pepper sauce and pepper. Squeeze the bread to extract the water. Add the bread to the food processor, and process until well mixed.

5. Form the falafel mixture into 16 balls. Flatten each ball to form ½-inch-thick patties. Dredge the patties in the flour, and place on the baking sheet. Bake for 10 minutes, turn over and bake for 10 minutes more, or until crisp.

6. Heat ½ tablespoon of the oil over medium-high heat in a large skillet. Add the falafel patties, and pan-fry until golden brown and crispy on the bottom. Turn patties over, and add the remaining oil, swirling the oil so that it comes into contact with all the patties. Pan-fry until golden brown and crispy, drain on paper towels and keep warm.

7. To serve, cut off about one-third of each pita, and open the larger section to form a pocket, reserving the scraps to make stuffing or breadcrumbs. Fill each pita pocket with 4 hot falafel patties. Top with the lettuce, tomatoes, cucumbers, onions, Yogurt Sauce and Hot Sauce, and serve warm.

PER SERVING (WITH 1 TABLESPOON OF EACH SAUCE): 386 CAL; 15G PROT; 7G FAT; 68G CARB; 0.1MG CHOL; 774MG SOD; 10G FIBER

BRAIN POWER PITA POCKETS

Packed with antioxidants (from the tahini, tomatoes, spinach, and avocado), B vitamins (from the pitas and spinach) and protein (from the yogurt and tofu), these pitas will give your brain a midday boost.

Tahini Sauce

1 cup low-fat or nonfat plain yogurt

2 tablespoons tahini

1 clove garlic, minced

1 teaspoon fresh lemon juice

Salt to taste

Pita Pockets

4 large whole wheat pita breads

8 ounces soft tofu, well drained and cubed

4 ripe plum tomatoes, diced

1 cup fresh spinach leaves, torn into bite-size pieces

1 cup sprouts, such as alfalfa, sunflower or mung bean

1 large ripe avocado, halved, pitted, peeled and cut into thin wedges

1. To make the Tahini Sauce: Mix all the sauce ingredients in a bowl until blended.

2. To make the Pita Pockets: Slice an edge from each pita bread, and carefully open the pockets. Combine the tofu, tomatoes and spinach. Add ¼ cup of the Tahini Sauce, and toss gently to mix. Spoon the mixture into each pocket. Divide the sprouts and avocado among the sandwiches. Drizzle each with 1 more tablespoon of the Tahini Sauce. Serve immediately.

PER SERVING: 385 CAL; 19G PROT; 15G FAT; 51G CARB; 1MG CHOL; 390MG SOD; 15G FIBER

MEGA VEGGIE BURRITO

These veggie-filled burritos make a hearty lunch entrée, and they pair nicely with sliced melon and strawberries. For a complementary starter, whip up a tomato-rich gazpacho or the Souper Salad (page 304) in summer, or offer a thick cheddar cheese soup or the Chipotle Black Bean Soup (page 317) in cold weather.

1 tablespoon olive oil

8 ounces seitan, thinly sliced

1 cup salsa

¾ cup fresh or frozen corn kernels

½ cup diced mushrooms

1 large green bell pepper, seeded and diced

4 tomatillos, diced, optional

1 tablespoon taco seasoning or chili powder

1 teaspoon ground cumin

Salt and freshly ground black pepper to taste

½ cup chopped cilantro leaves

2 cups (8 ounces) shredded cheddar cheese

1 jalapeño chile, minced, optional

1 10-inch flour tortillas

1 avocado, peeled and diced

1. Preheat the broiler.

2. Heat a large skillet over medium heat, and add the oil. When hot, place the seitan slices in the oil, and sauté for 2 to 3 minutes. Add the salsa, corn, mushrooms, bell pepper, tomatillos, if using, salsa, taco seasoning, cumin, salt and pepper. Reduce the heat to medium-low, and cook for 10 minutes, stirring occasionally, until heated through. Stir in the cilantro, and remove from the heat.

3. Meanwhile, sprinkle ½ cup of the cheese and ¼ jalapeño, if using, on a tortilla, and broil until the cheese melts and bubbles. Remove from the broiler, spoon on some of the seitan mixture, sprinkle with ¼ avocado and wrap. Repeat with the remaining ingredients until used up. Serve while hot.

PER SERVING (1 BURRITO): 620 CAL; 39G PROT; 34G FAT; 44G CARB; 50MG CHOL; 1,440MG SOD; 6G FIBER

GRILLED EGGPLANT IN PITA WITH
POMEGRANATE-WALNUT SAUCE

Look for small Italian eggplants for these sandwiches so that the eggplant slices fit into the pita pocket. Otherwise, cut larger slices in quarters after grilling. These sandwiches are best when dressed with the Pomegranate-Walnut Sauce—look for pomegranate syrup in Middle Eastern markets. It's sometimes labeled pomegranate molasses. A satisfactory substitute is frozen cranberry juice concentrate. If you want a less time-consuming sauce, bottled ranch salad dressing makes a fine option. Select a good-quality pita because some brands are not sturdy, and they fall apart after filling.

Grilled Eggplant Pitas

1½ pounds Italian eggplant
2 teaspoons salt
2 medium zucchini
2 large red bell peppers
2 large red onions
⅓ cup olive oil
¼ cup fresh lemon juice
2 cloves garlic, mashed
1 teaspoon freshly ground black
    pepper
8 whole wheat pita breads

Pomegranate-Walnut Sauce

1 tablespoon canola oil
1 cup diced onion
1 clove garlic, minced
1 cup ground walnuts
¼ teaspoon ground cinnamon
⅓ cup pomegranate syrup
1½ tablespoons honey
½ teaspoon salt

1. To make the Pitas: Slice the eggplants crosswise into ⅓-inch-thick pieces, and sprinkle with 1 teaspoon of the salt. Slice the zucchini in half lengthwise and then crosswise into ⅓-inch-thick pieces. Sprinkle with the remaining salt. Place both vegetables on paper towels for 1 hour or longer to extract some of their moisture. Press dry using fresh paper towels, and set aside.

2. Cut the bell peppers into ½-inch-wide strips. Slice the onions into ¼-inch-thick slices, breaking apart the circles. Place all the vegetables in a large container, and set aside.

3. Whisk together the oil, lemon juice, garlic and pepper, and pour over the vegetables. Toss well, and refrigerate. Cut the pita breads in half, and open them for stuffing. Set aside.

4. To make the Pomegranate-Walnut Sauce: Heat the oil in a skillet over medium heat, and sauté the onion and garlic until soft and transparent. Remove from the heat. Put the walnuts, cinnamon and cooked onion in a blender, and purée until smooth. Add the remaining ingredients, along with 1 cup of water, and blend for 2 minutes, scraping down the sides of the container several times. Taste and adjust the flavors with honey and salt, as needed. If mixture is thicker than mayonnaise, add water, 1 tablespoon at a time, to the desired consistency. Chill until serving time, and store in a container in the refrigerator.

5. Prepare a hot charcoal fire about 30 minutes before serving. Otherwise, heat a gas grill to medium-high at serving time. Grill the vegetables using a basket for the onions and peppers and turning at least once.

6. When the vegetables are soft and browned, remove from the heat, and fill the pitas with vegetables. Drizzle each sandwich with the Pomegranate-Walnut Sauce, and serve 2 halves per person.

PER SERVING: 330 CAL; 8G PROT; 15G FAT; 45G CARB; 0MG CHOL; 840MG SOD; 9G FIBER

BEST BURRITOS

You can assemble these healthful burritos as directed, wrap airtight in foil, skip the baking step and freeze for up to three months. Thaw overnight in the refrigerator before heating as directed.

2 cups fat-free vegetarian refried beans

1¾ cups medium to hot salsa, divided

5 teaspoons vegetable oil, divided

14 ounces ground soy "sausage"

3 large onions, chopped

2 large potatoes, diced

⅛ teaspoon paprika

Freshly ground pepper to taste

6 8-inch flour tortillas

1. Preheat the oven to 425F.

2. Stir together the beans and ¾ cup of the salsa in a small saucepan. Cook, stirring occasionally, over very low heat just until warmed through. Meanwhile, heat 2½ teaspoons of the oil in a large nonstick skillet over medium heat. Add the "sausage," and cook, stirring occasionally and breaking up large pieces with a fork, for about 5 minutes, or until browned. Transfer to a bowl, and set aside.

3. Add the remaining 2½ teaspoons of the oil to the skillet, and heat over medium heat. Add the onions, and cook, stirring often, until softened, for about 4 minutes. Stir in the potatoes, paprika and pepper. Cook, stirring often, until the potatoes are almost tender, for 17 to 20 minutes. Return the "sausage" to the skillet, and mix well. Cook for about 3 minutes more, or until the potatoes are tender. Remove from the heat.

4. Tear 6 large pieces of foil. Place a tortilla flat on each piece of foil, and thinly spread with about ¼ cup of the bean mixture. Spoon a heaping ½ cup of the potato mixture down the center of each tortilla. Top the potato mixture with the remaining salsa, about 2½ tablespoons of salsa for each tortilla. Fold the bottom of each tortilla up to cover the filling. Fold the sides toward the center, then roll up from the bottom. Wrap in the foil and bake until hot, for about 10 minutes. Remove from the oven, unwrap and serve.

PER SERVING (1 BURRITO): 358 CAL; 17G PROT; 10G FAT; 51G CARB; 0MG CHOL; 978MG SOD; 7G FIBER

MUSHROOM "BURGERS"

These hearty, healthy burgers get an unexpected crunchiness from oat bran. Offer these with sliced tomatoes and cucumbers in a salad, and end the meal with Almost Traditional Chocolate Mousse (page 410). Instead of wine, you might pair these with a flavorful stout ale.

2 cups (8 ounces) shredded low-fat Swiss cheese plus extra, for garnish

1½ cups cubed portobello mushrooms

½ cup oat bran

½ cup chopped fresh parsley plus extra leaves, for garnish

3 extra-large eggs, beaten

Salt and freshly ground black pepper to taste

3 tablespoons vegetable oil

1. Combine the cheese, mushrooms, oat bran, parsley, eggs, salt and pepper in a bowl. Shape the mixture by hand, pressing the ingredients together into 4 burgers.

2. Heat a skillet over medium heat. When hot, add 2 tablespoons of the oil. Place 2 burgers at a time in the skillet, and pan-fry for 3 to 4 minutes, or until golden. Turn over, and pan-fry the second sides until golden. Remove from the heat, and drain on paper towels. Repeat, adding the remaining oil, until the mixture is used up.

3. To serve, arrange the burgers on plates, and garnish with parsley and cheese, if desired.

PER SERVING (1 BURGER): 230 CAL; 23G PROT; 12G FAT; 11G CARB; 195MG CHOL; 410MG SOD; 2G FIBER

SAVORY BURRITOS WITH CHUNKY AVOCADO SALSA SERVES 6

Try these veggie-filled burritos with an avocado salsa for lunch or for a light supper. For a dessert, try out the Chocolate Cupcakes (page 402). Their vegetable filling differs from the Mega Veggie Burritos (page 116).

Chunky Avocado Salsa

1 large, ripe Haas avocado
3 medium scallions, thinly sliced
1 stalk celery, chopped
½ cup chopped red bell pepper
⅓ cup diced jicama
2 cloves garlic, minced
Juice of 1 lime
1 14 ½-ounce can Mexican-style
 stewed tomatoes, sliced
⅓ cup chopped cilantro
Hot pepper sauce to taste

Savory Burritos

1 teaspoon olive oil
¼ teaspoon crushed red pepper
4 cloves garlic, minced
1 cup sliced scallions
2 bell peppers, 1 red and 1 yellow,
 seeded and cut into 2-inch strips
12 ounces soy "chicken" strips
6 ounces sliced cremini mushrooms
3 medium zucchini, sliced in half
 lengthwise and crosswise
1 15-ounce can cannellini beans,
 drained and rinsed
6 6—inch nonfat whole wheat
 tortillas
Sliced jalapeño chiles, optional

1. To make the Salsa: Peel and dice the avocado, and set aside. Combine the scallions, celery, bell pepper, jicama, avocado, garlic and lime juice in a nonreactive bowl. Add the tomatoes and cilantro. Season with hot pepper sauce to taste. Cover, and refrigerate until ready to serve.

2. To make the Burritos: Heat the oil and crushed red pepper over medium-high heat in a electric frying pan, a 5-quart saucepan or a wok for about 1 minute. Add the garlic, scallions and bell peppers, and sauté for 3 minutes. Add the "chicken" strips and mushrooms. Cook for 5 minutes, stirring frequently. Add the zucchini and beans, reduce the heat to low, and cook for 8 minutes, or until tender. Heat the tortillas for 5 minutes in a tortilla warmer or wrapped in foil in a 325F oven.

3. Spoon some filling onto a warmed tortilla, and add the jalapeños, if using. Fold the tortilla sides over the filling, and secure with a toothpick. Serve with the Avocado Salsa.

PER SERVING (1 BURRITO, WITH SALSA): 322 CAL; 18G PROT; 7G FAT; 51G CARB; 0MG CHOL; 798MG SOD; 15G FIBER

"TOFUNA" SANDWICHES SERVES 4 TO 6

A great filling for lunchtime or picnic sandwiches, this mixture is easy to whip together. Try spreading it on whole-grain breads for a more traditional sandwich.

8 ounces baked marinated tofu
⅓ to ½ cup soy mayonnaise
1 large stalk celery, finely chopped
1 scallion, finely chopped, optional
4 regular or 6 mini pita breads,
 warmed and cut crosswise in half

Crumble the tofu in a bowl. Add the mayonnaise, celery and scallion, if using, and stir until well combined. Stuff the mixture into warmed pita bread halves, and serve.

PER SERVING: 187 CAL; 10G PROT; 7G FAT; 19G CARB; 0MG CHOL; 315MG SOD; 2G FIBER

TOFU SALAD SANDWICH

Enjoy this tofu spread as is, or add a personal touch—capers, chopped onion, fresh herbs of your choice, bell pepper or olives.

1 pound firm low-fat tofu, well drained

½ cup soy mayonnaise

1 tablespoon chopped fresh parsley

2 teaspoons Dijon mustard

1 teaspoon chopped fresh tarragon or ¼ teaspoon dried tarragon

¼ teaspoon minced garlic

⅛ teaspoon turmeric

Salt and freshly ground black pepper to taste

½ cup diced celery

2 tablespoons finely chopped scallions

8 slices whole wheat bread

2 large carrots, grated

1 cup sprouts, such as clover or alfalfa

1. Put the tofu in a mixing bowl. Using clean hands or a fork, crumble until the texture resembles mashed hard-boiled eggs. Add the mayonnaise, and stir to blend. Stir in the parsley, mustard, tarragon, garlic, turmeric, salt and pepper. Stir in the celery and scallions until blended.

2. Place 4 slices of the bread on a work surface. On each slice, layer the tofu salad, carrots and sprouts. Top with the remaining bread, cut the sandwiches in half and serve.

PER SERVING (1 SANDWICH): 333 CAL; 16G PROT; 10G FAT; 48G CARB; 0MG CHOL; 788MG SOD; 8G FIBER

BLACK BEAN AND GRILLED VEGETABLE TACOS

This recipe may be made with leftover black beans or canned black beans (drained very well and mashed), but the instant black beans available in bulk or packages are fast, easy and have just the right taste and texture. The easiest way to grill the vegetables on an outdoor grill is to use a grill basket. It looks like a square metal bowl with lots of holes in it.

1½ cups instant black beans or about 1¾ cup leftover or canned black beans, drained and rinsed

2 zucchini

4 large carrots

2 green bell peppers

2 large onions

1 teaspoon salt

1 teaspoon freshly ground black pepper

16 corn tortillas

2 cups salsa

1. Prepare the black beans according to the package directions, or drain canned or leftover beans and mash them lightly. Set aside, and keep them warm.

2. Prepare a charcoal fire or preheat a gas grill to medium.

3. Slice the zucchini and carrots thinly on a 3-inch-long diagonal. Cut the peppers and onions into strips. Grill all the vegetables, spraying with nonstick cooking spray if needed to prevent burning, for about 5 minutes, or until they are soft and moderately charred, turning at least once. Season with salt and pepper. Keep warm.

4. To serve, heat a griddle or skillet over high heat, and warm the tortillas until they soften. Place a large dollop of black beans in the center of each tortilla, and top with ½ cup of the vegetables. Fold in half, and serve 2 per person, offering salsa on the side.

PER SERVING (2 TACOS, WITH SALSA): 250 CAL; 10G PROT; 2.5G FAT; 51G CARB; 0MG CHOL; 550MG SOD; 9G FIBER

BLACK BEAN AND VEGETABLE HASH

SERVES 2

Made with dehydrated flavorings and instant beans, this dish is perfect for day hikes and camping trips, though it's also nice for a casual meal for two. Look for dehydrated vegetables in camping supply stores. Serve it as is or spoon it into pita bread.

¼ cup dehydrated onion

2 tablespoons dehydrated garlic

2 tablespoons dehydrated mixed vegetables

1 7-ounce package instant black beans or instant pinto beans

Cooked instant brown rice, optional

½ teaspoon chili powder

Pinch cayenne pepper

1 tablespoon grated Parmesan cheese

1. Heat the onion, garlic, vegetables and 2½ cups of water in a saucepan over medium-high heat, and bring to a boil.

2. Reduce the heat to low, and cook for 2 to 3 minutes, or until rehydrated. Remove from the heat. Add the beans, rice, if using, chili powder and cayenne. Mix well, cover and let sit for 5 minutes. Sprinkle with the Parmesan cheese before serving.

PER SERVING (WITHOUT RICE): 365 CAL; 24G PROT; 3G FAT; 64G CARB; 2MG CHOL; 56MG SOD; 13G FIBER

CARROT AND CASHEW SANDWICHES WITH TARTAR SAUCE

SERVES 6

These cakes can be made very quickly with frozen sliced carrots or leftover cooked carrots. The flavor is indescribably delicious. If you like them, consider making walnut-sized balls for your next cocktail party. If you like a little crunch, press panko (Japanese breadcrumbs) into the cakes before frying. Although the Tartar Sauce goes well with this filling, you might keep some on hand to use with other sandwiches or as a dip with raw vegetables. It stores well in the refrigerator for a week.

Tartar Sauce

½ cup soy mayonnaise

2 tablespoons minced onion

2 tablespoons pickle relish

1 teaspoon dried dillweed

Carrot and Cashew Sandwiches

2 cups sliced frozen carrots, thawed, or cooked carrots

½ cup extra-firm silken tofu, drained and squeezed dry

1 cup ground unsalted cashews

2 scallions, minced

1 teaspoon ground coriander

1 teaspoon salt

1 tablespoon canola oil

6 whole wheat buns or bread of your choice

1. To make the Tartar Sauce: Combine all the ingredients in a bowl, and refrigerate until ready to use. Makes ¾ cup.

2. To make the Carrot and Cashew Sandwiches: Put very soft, well-drained and patted-dry carrots in a food processor, and process until finely chopped. Scrape into a bowl.

3. Mash the tofu with a fork, and add to the bowl. Add the cashews, scallions, coriander and salt, and mix with a fork until combined. Shape the carrot mixture into 6 cakes.

4. Heat a skillet, and add the oil. Fry the cakes until golden brown, about 3 minutes per side. Place a cake on each bun and top with 1 tablespoon of the Tartar Sauce.

PER SERVING (WITH 1 TABLESPOON TARTAR SAUCE): 360 CAL; 10G PROT; 21G FAT; 35G CARB; 0MG CHOL; 750MG SOD; 5G FIBER

GARDEN PO' BOY

New Orleans folks take crisp French bread, cut it in half, remove some of the soft bread center and fill that hollow with anything good to eat. This recipe fits that bill, and has the added benefit of calling your grill into play. You can change the flavor of the baste by adding a tablespoon of pesto to the marinade. The easiest way to grill the vegetables on an outdoor grill is to use a grill basket. It looks like a square metal bowl with lots of holes in it. This allows you to toss the vegetables freely without having them fall in the fire. Grilled vegetables have an entirely different taste and texture than fried or boiled.

18 jumbo asparagus stems or smaller asparagus

4 large carrots, peeled and sliced lengthwise

6 scallions

3 large red onions, sliced ¼ inch thick

3 red bell peppers, quartered

4 tablespoons olive oil

2 teaspoons mashed garlic

1 teaspoon salt

1 teaspoon freshly ground black pepper

2 18-inch French baguettes or 6 submarine rolls

8 ounces Boursin cheese or goat cheese (or Soy Mock Boursin, page 000)

1. Prepare a medium charcoal fire or preheat a gas grill to medium.

2. Snap off the bottom ends of the asparagus. Using a vegetable basket, grill the asparagus over on all sides until done. Set aside.

3. Grill the carrot slices and scallions in the basket until done. When finished, grill the onion slices and bell peppers. All of the vegetables should be cooked through and lightly charred.

4. Meanwhile, mix the oil, garlic, salt and pepper in a bowl. Pour over the grilled vegetables while they are still hot. Toss gently.

5. Cut the bread in half lengthwise. Tear out about one-third of the interior soft bread to hollow it slightly. Spread both the bottom and top of each loaf with cheese. Divide the vegetables evenly on the bottom parts of the bread, and drizzle with any olive oil marinade that remains in the bowl.

6. Place the tops on the loaves, and press lightly. Cut each loaf in 3 equal sections.

PER SERVING: 410 CAL; 7G PROT; 26G FAT; 40G CARB; 0MG CHOL; 850MG SOD; 4G FIBER

HOT AND SPICY HUMMUS

For a quick lunch, serve this hearty bean spread on toasted whole-grain bagels. It also makes a luscious, low-fat dip alongside carrots and broccoli florets.

3 cups cooked chickpeas, drained and rinsed

¼ cup tahini, olive oil or light sesame oil

¼ cup fresh lemon juice

3 cloves garlic, crushed

1 teaspoon ground cumin

½ teaspoon cayenne pepper

¼ cup minced jalapeño or other chile

¼ cup diced red bell pepper plus slices, for garnish

Salt and freshly ground black pepper to taste

1. Put the chickpeas, tahini and lemon juice in a food processor or blender, and purée until smooth, adding water as needed to make a creamy mixture. Transfer to a bowl.

2. Add the garlic, cumin, cayenne, jalapeño and diced bell pepper to the chickpeas mixture, and mix well. Season with salt and pepper to taste. Cover and chill 2 to 4 hours to allow the flavors to blend.

3. To serve, garnish with the red pepper slices.

PER SERVING (¼ CUP): 80 CAL; 4G PROT; 3G FAT; 10G CARB; 0MG CHOL; 4MG SOD; 3G FIBER

CARROT, RAISIN AND CHOPPED PEANUT SPREAD   SERVES 8

This is a colorful and flavorful spread that may be used as a stuffing for celery sticks or simply spread on crackers or bread. Other dried fruits and many other nuts may be used for totally different taste treats.

1 cup grated carrots
½ cup raisins
½ cup chopped dry-roasted peanuts
⅓ cup soy mayonnaise
2 tablespoons honey or rice syrup

Put all the ingredients in a bowl, and mix well. Place in an airtight container, and store in the refrigerator until ready to serve.

PER SERVING: 130 CAL; 3G PROT; 1G FAT; 15G CARB; 0MG CHOL; 160MG SOD; 1G FIBER

PEANUT-RICOTTA SPREAD   MAKES ABOUT 2 CUPS

Combining peanut butter and ricotta cheese produces a spread that's far lower in fat than straight peanut butter but just as delicious. Try it with your favorite jam on bread as a sandwich or as a spread for low-fat crackers. For a slightly different flavor, use cottage cheese instead of ricotta cheese.

1 15-ounce carton low-fat or nonfat
  ricotta cheese
¼ cup peanut butter
1 tablespoon honey
¼ teaspoon almond extract
¼ teaspoon vanilla extract
¼ teaspoon ground cinnamon

Put all the ingredients in a food processor or blender, and purée until smooth. Store in a tightly covered container in the refrigerator for up to 1 week.

PER SERVING (2 TABLESPOONS): 70 CAL; 5G PROT; 4G FAT; 4G CARB; 10MG CHOL; 56MG SOD, 0G FIBER

HERBED COTTAGE CHEESE–BELL PEPPER SPREAD   MAKES 3 CUPS

This spread is a great warm-weather filling for pita bread or whole-grain bread. It's also good spread on crackers.

2 cups low-fat cottage cheese
⅔ cup finely chopped green bell
  pepper
⅔ cup finely chopped red bell
  pepper
2 scallions, thinly sliced
1 tablespoon minced fresh basil
1 tablespoon minced jalapeño chile
1 tablespoon salt, or to taste
2 teaspoons rice vinegar
1 teaspoon dried dillweed or 1
  tablespoon minced fresh dillweed
1 teaspoon curry powder
1 teaspoon minced garlic
Freshly ground black pepper to taste

Combine all the ingredients in a bowl, and mix well. Store in an airtight container in the refrigerator up to 5 days.

PER SERVING (½ CUP): 152 CAL; 14G PROT; 2G FAT; 18G CARB; 6MG CHOL; 511MG SOD; 2G FIBER

7 *baked goods*

Baked goods—from breads and muffins to tortillas and sweet crisps—are the treats that home cooks store up for special moments of celebration, of relaxation, of indulgence. Perhaps more than any other product from the kitchen, it's these home-made gems that truly speak of comfort, and all the nostalgia of childhood.

SAVORY EGGPLANT-DILL MUFFINS

These are savory—not sweet—muffins that can make a grand entrance at brunch or a light supper and partner well with a vegetable-filled Western omelet, a green salad or a hearty soup. Serve them with or without butter.

2 cups all-purpose flour

1 tablespoon granulated sugar

1 tablespoon baking powder

1½ teaspoons baking soda

1½ teaspoons dried dillweed

½ teaspoon salt

½ teaspoon freshly ground black pepper

1 cup buttermilk

2 large eggs, beaten

2 tablespoons unsalted butter, melted

12 ounces eggplant, peeled and coarsely grated (about 2 cups)

2 tablespoons minced yellow onion

Zest of 1 lemon, grated

1. Preheat the oven to 400F. Line a 12-cup muffin tin with baking liners, and set aside.

2. Stir together the flour, sugar, baking powder, baking soda, dillweed, salt and pepper in a bowl, and mix thoroughly.

3. Combine the buttermilk, eggs and butter, mixing well. Add the eggplant, onion and lemon zest, and stir together, using as few strokes as possible, just until the dry ingredients are moist. Spoon the batter into the baking cups, filling each about two-thirds full.

4. Bake for 20 to 25 minutes, or until beginning to brown. Remove from the oven, and cool completely before serving.

PER SERVING: 150 CAL; 5G PROT; 3G FAT; 26G CARB; 40MG CHOL; 430MG SOD; 4G FIBER

LOW-FAT APRICOT-PECAN MUFFINS

Apricots and pecans combined make positively yummy muffins, especially when served right out of the oven, because the pecans taste best hot. These muffins keep well for up to three days and also freeze well. For an unusual nutty flavor, use grapeseed oil instead of almond or canola oil.

1 cup boiling water

1½ cups dried apricots, chopped

2 cups unbleached all-purpose flour

1 cup whole wheat flour

1 cup granulated sugar

1 tablespoon baking powder

1 teaspoon baking soda

½ teaspoon salt

1 cup chopped pecans

1 cup orange juice

2 large eggs, beaten, or ½ cup egg substitute

¼ cup almond oil or canola oil

1. Preheat the oven to 375F. Line two 12-cup muffin tins with baking liners, or spray them with nonstick cooking spray.

2. Pour the water over the apricots, and set aside to soften. When soft, remove from the water.

3. Sift the flours, sugar, baking powder, baking soda and salt into a bowl. Add the pecans. Stir the juice, eggs and oil into the softened apricots. Add to the dry ingredients, and mix just enough to moisten. Do not overmix. Fill the muffin cups two-thirds full.

4. Bake for 20 to 25 minutes, or until beginning to brown. Remove from the oven, and serve hot.

PER MUFFIN: 180 CAL; 3G PROT; 6G FAT; 28G CARB; 20MG CHOL; 170MG SOD; 2G FIBER

PUMPKIN-CORN MUFFINS

Although you may enjoy these muffins any day of the year, these seem the most appropriate in the fall when both corn and pumpkins make their seasonal appearance.

½ cup (1 stick) margarine or unsalted butter, at room temperature

¼ cup granulated sugar

1 cup pumpkin purée

½ cup whole milk or soymilk

2 large eggs or ½ cup egg substitute

¾ cup all-purpose flour

¾ cup fine-ground cornmeal

1 tablespoon baking powder

½ teaspoon ground cinnamon

½ teaspoon ground coriander

½ teaspoon ground cardamom

½ teaspoon salt

½ cup canned, fresh or frozen corn kernels

½ cup canned diced mild green chiles, optional

1. Preheat the oven to 350F. Line a 12-cup muffin tin with baking liners, or spray it with nonstick cooking spray.

2. Combine the margarine and sugar in a bowl, and using an electric beater, mix until fluffy. Add the pumpkin, milk and eggs.

3. Sift the flour, cornmeal, baking powder, cinnamon, coriander, cardamom and salt together, and fold them into the pumpkin mixture. Fold in the corn and green chiles, if using. Spoon the batter into the tins, filling them about three-quarters full.

4. Bake for about 18 minutes, or until the centers are firm when tested with a toothpick?. Remove from the oven, and serve.

PER MUFFIN: 180 CAL; 3G PROT; 2G FAT; 21G CARB; 35MG CHOL; 240MG SOD; 2G FIBER

SWEET-TART CRANBERRY MUFFINS

Serve these with your Thanksgiving Day dinner, or celebrate leisurely fall breakfasts with these sweet treats.

1¼ cups unbleached all-purpose flour

1 teaspoon baking powder

½ teaspoon ground cinnamon

½ teaspoon ground cardamom

½ teaspoon ground nutmeg

½ teaspoon baking soda

½ teaspoon salt

½ cup finely chopped pitted prunes

½ cup rolled oats

¾ cup buttermilk or soymilk

½ cup fresh or frozen cranberries

6 tablespoons maple syrup

3 tablespoons canola oil

3 large egg whites, lightly beaten

1. Preheat the oven to 400F. Line a 12-cup muffin tin with baking liners, or spray it with nonstick cooking spray.

2. Sift together the flour, baking powder, cinnamon, cardamom, nutmeg, baking soda and salt in a bowl. Add the prunes and oats, and toss to coat. In another bowl, whisk together the buttermilk, cranberries, maple syrup and oil. In a third bowl, beat the egg whites to soft peaks. Set aside.

3. Combine the dry and wet ingredients, and fold in the egg whites until just incorporated. Spoon the batter into the muffin tins, filling them three-quarters full.

4. Bake until the muffins are light and springy to the touch, for 12 to 15 minutes. Remove from the oven, and serve.

PER SERVING: 140 CAL; 4G PROT; 4G FAT; 17G CARB; 1MG CHOL; 212MG SOD; 2G FIBER

BANANA-APPLESAUCE MUFFINS

Unlike most muffins, these nutritious treats are blessedly low in fat. If you prefer, substitute 1 cup fresh blueberries or 1 cup chopped fresh cranberries mixed with 3 tablespoons granulated sugar for the bananas.

1¼ cups whole wheat flour

½ cup oat bran

¼ cup wheat bran

2 teaspoons baking powder

1 tablespoon vegetable oil

¼ cup honey

⅔ cup skim milk or soymilk

½ cup unsweetened applesauce

1 large egg or 2 large egg whites, beaten

½ teaspoon vanilla extract

2 ripe bananas, mashed

1. Preheat the oven to 350F. Line a 12-cup muffin tin with baking liners, or spray it with nonstick cooking spray.

2. Combine the flour, oat bran, wheat bran and baking powder in a bowl, and set aside.

3. Combine the oil and honey in a separate bowl, and mix well. Add the milk, applesauce, egg and vanilla, and whisk to blend. Add the applesauce mixture to the flour mixture, and mix until just blended. Do not overmix. Gently fold the bananas into the batter. Spoon the batter into the muffin tins, filling them two-thirds full.

4. Bake for 20 to 30 minutes, or until the muffins just begin to brown. Remove from the oven, and serve warm.

PER MUFFIN: 120 CAL; 3G PROT; 2G FAT; 23G CARB; 18MG CHOL; 71MG SOD; 3G FIBER

CHEESE MUFFINS

Make these savory muffins when you want to accent a brunch or supper main course.

2 tablespoons chopped yellow onion

2 tablespoons butter or vegetable oil

1¼ cups buttermilk

½ cup grated Swiss or cheddar cheese

1 large egg, beaten

¾ teaspoon dried dillweed or parsley flakes or ½ teaspoon dry mustard

2 teaspoons baking powder

½ cup whole wheat pastry flour

½ teaspoon salt

½ teaspoon baking soda

2¼ cups rolled oats,

1. Preheat the oven to 375F. Line a 12-cup muffin tin with baking liners, or spray it with nonstick cooking spray.

2. Heat the butter in a skillet over medium heat. Add the onion, and cook, stirring frequently, until softened, for about 5 minutes. Cool slightly.

3. Transfer the onion to a bowl, and stir in the buttermilk, cheese, egg and seasoning. Choose the dillweed or parsley if using the Swiss cheese, or the mustard if using the cheddar cheese.

4. Sift together the flour, baking powder, salt and baking soda in a bowl. Put the oats into a food processor or blender, and process them to a coarse powder. Add the ground oats to the flour mixture, and stir to blend.

5. Add the flour mixture to the cheese mixture, and stir until just blended. Do not overmix. Spoon the batter into the muffin tins, filling them two-thirds full.

6. Bake for about 15 minutes, or until the muffins are golden brown. Remove from the oven, and serve warm.

PER SERVING: 111 CAL; 6G PROT; 6G FAT; 10G CARB; 33MG CHOL; 230MG SOD; 0.5G FIBER

GINGER-PEACH MUFFINS

The hint of ginger enlivens these lush warm-weather muffins. Serve just out of the oven with peach jam and plenty of butter.

1 cup all-purpose flour

¾ cup cake flour

1 cup granulated sugar

2 teaspoons baking powder

1 teaspoon baking soda

½ teaspoon salt

2 large eggs, beaten

¾ cup buttermilk

½ cup (1 stick) unsalted butter, melted

1 peach, diced

1½ tablespoons grated peeled fresh ginger

1 teaspoon vanilla extract

1. Preheat the oven to 400F. Spray a 12-cup muffin tin with nonstick cooking spray, or line with baking liners.

2. Sift the flours together into a bowl. Add the sugar, baking powder, baking soda and salt, and stir to combine.

3. Beat the eggs and buttermilk together in a separate bowl. Add the butter, peach, ginger and vanilla, stirring well to combine. Pour into the dry mixture, and stir together quickly, taking care not to overbeat. Spoon the batter into the muffin tin, filling each cup about two-thirds full.

4. Bake the muffins for 8 to 10 minutes, or until the tops brown. Remove from the oven, cool in the tin for 5 minutes and remove to finish cooling on a cake rack.

PER SERVING: 190 CAL; 3G PROT; 8G FAT; 27G CARB; 50MG CHOL; 330MG SOD; 0G FIBER

CRANBERRY-CASHEW QUICK BREAD

Two complementary ingredients—cranberries and cashews—make this seasonal bread a real treat. This bread tastes best the second day, so maybe you should bake two loaves and keep one hidden away!

2 cups unbleached pastry flour

½ cup granulated sugar

1 tablespoon baking powder

½ teaspoon salt

¾ cup fresh orange juice

2 large eggs, beaten, or ½ cup egg substitute

3 tablespoons vegetable oil plus extra for greasing pan

1½ cups fresh cranberries

½ cup chopped cashews

Zest of 1 lemon

1. Preheat the oven to 375F. Grease an 8½ x 4½-inch loaf pan, and set aside.

2. Combine the flour, sugar, baking powder and salt in a bowl, and stir with a whisk. In a separate bowl, combine the juice, eggs and oil. Pour the liquid ingredients into the flour mixture, and stir gently until just combined. Add the cranberries, cashews and lemon zest, and fold them together. Scoop into the loaf pan.

3. Bake for 45 to 50 minutes, or until a toothpick inserted into the center comes out clean. Remove from the oven, and cool slightly before serving.

PER SERVING (1-INCH SLICE): 290 CAL; 6G PROT; 11G FAT; 44G CARB; 55MG CHOL; 350MG SOD; 5G FIBER

APPLE-PECAN TEA LOAF

SERVES 8

Borrowing a technique from the Shakers, you can line the bread pan with scented unsprayed geranium leaves—preferably the apple-scented variety—to underscore the apple flavors in this luscious bread, and discard them before eating.

3 tablespoons margarine or unsalted butter, at room temperature

1 cup plus 6 tablespoons granulated sugar, divided

2 large eggs

1 teaspoon lemon extract

1 tablespoon grated lemon zest

1½ cups all-purpose flour

1½ teaspoons baking powder

1 teaspoon salt

½ apple, cored and diced

½ cup plus 1 tablespoon apple juice, divided

½ cup pecan pieces

1. Preheat the oven to 350F. Grease and flour a 9-inch loaf pan, and set aside.

2. Beat the margarine and 1 cup of the sugar until well combined. Add the eggs, lemon extract and zest, and beat until very thick and creamy. Sift together the flour, baking powder and salt, and add alternately with the apple pieces and the ½ cup apple juice, continuing until all the ingredients are used up. Spoon the batter into the loaf pan, and sprinkle the top with the pecans.

3. Bake for 45 to 50 minutes, or until the top is golden and the center is firm. Remove from the oven, and allow to cool in the pan for 2 or 3 minutes. Remove from the pan, and cool on a rack.

4. Meanwhile, combine the remaining 1 tablespoon of apple juice and 6 tablespoons of sugar, and after 10 minutes, drizzle over the top of the loaf. Cool completely before slicing and serving.

PER SERVING: 270 CAL; 4G PROT; 9G FAT; 46G CARB; 40MG CHOL; 360MG SOD; 1G FIBER

HOT CORN STICKS

SERVES 14 (MAKES 14)

Plan to serve these with any Southern- or Southwestern-oriented meal. You can substitute a standard 12-cup muffin tin if you don't have "ear of corn" cast-iron pans.

1 cup unbleached all-purpose flour

¾ cup cornmeal

¼ cup granulated sugar

2 teaspoons baking powder

¼ teaspoon salt

¾ cup skim milk or soymilk

¼ cup canola oil

1 large egg, lightly beaten

1. Preheat the oven to 450F. Generously spray 2 cast-iron "ear of corn" pans or one 12-cup muffin tin with nonstick cooking spray, and set aside.

2. Sift the flour with the cornmeal, sugar, baking powder and salt. Add the milk, oil and egg. Stir with a fork until just blended. Do not overmix. Fill the pans three-quarters full or the muffin tins one-third full.

3. Bake for about 20 minutes, or until golden brown. Remove from the oven, and serve at once. Alternatively, remove the cornbread from the pans, let cool and wrap them tightly in foil. Reheat before serving.

PER STICK: 111 CAL; 3G PROT; 4G FAT; 15G CARB; 20MG CHOL; 114MG SOD; 1G FIBER

BLUEBERRY UPSIDE-DOWN CAKE

You can use many different fruits and berries in this recipe, so create your own upside-down world.

Topping

2 cups fresh or frozen blueberries

2 tablespoons cornstarch or arrowroot

½ cup packed brown sugar

⅓ cup soy margarine, melted

Cake

1¼ cups unbleached all-purpose flour

2 teaspoons baking powder

1 teaspoon salt

⅓ cup soy margarine

¾ cup granulated sugar

2 large eggs or ½ cup egg substitute

½ cup almond milk or soymilk

1 teaspoon vanilla extract

2 teaspoons almond extract

1. Preheat the oven to 375F. Grease a 9-inch square pan, and line it with baking parchment. Spray the parchment with nonstick cooking spray.

2. To make the Topping: Toss the blueberries with the cornstarch, and mix them in a bowl with the sugar and margarine. Pour into the baking pan, and set aside.

3. To make the Cake: Whisk together the flour, baking powder and salt. Cream together the margarine and sugar in a bowl. Beat in the eggs. Stir the vanilla and almond extracts into the milk.

4. Stir one-third of the dry ingredients into the egg mixture. Stir in half of the milk mixture. Add another one-third of the flour, and stir until smooth. Add the remaining milk mixture, and finally the remaining flour. Beat well. Pour the cake batter over the blueberries.

5. Bake for 50 to 60 minutes, or until a toothpick inserted in the center comes out clean. Remove from the oven, and cool on a rack for 5 minutes. Invert the cake pan on a large platter, and carefully lift the pan off. While still warm, peel away the parchment. Cut the cake into 9 pieces, and serve.

PER SERVING: 340 CAL; 4G PROT; 15G FAT; 48G CARB; 45MG CHOL; 550MG SOD; 1G FIBER

BLUEBERRY BUTTERMILK COFFEE CAKE

Start the day right with a slice of warm, homemade coffee cake and your favorite breakfast beverage.

1 cup whole wheat flour

1 cup unbleached all-purpose flour

2 teaspoons baking powder

2 teaspoons baking soda

¼ teaspoon salt

2 cups fresh or frozen blueberries

¾ cup honey or maple syrup

¾ cup buttermilk or soymilk

½ cup mashed banana

⅓ cup puréed pitted prunes (such as Lekvar)

1 large egg plus 3 large egg whites or ¼ cup egg substitute

¼ cup vegetable oil

1 tablespoon chopped walnuts

⅓ cup packed light brown sugar

1. Preheat the oven to 350F. Lightly oil a 13 x 9–inch baking dish, or spray with nonstick cooking spray.

2. Sift together the flours, baking powder, baking soda and salt in a bowl. Fold in blueberries, and set aside.

3. Whisk together the honey, buttermilk, banana, prunes, egg and egg whites and oil in a separate bowl.

4. Add the honey mixture to the flour mixture, and mix until just combined. Do not overmix. Pour the batter into the prepared baking dish, and smooth the top with a spatula. Sprinkle with the walnuts and sugar.

5. Bake for 40 to 50 minutes, or until a toothpick inserted in the center comes out clean. Remove from the oven, let cool and cut into 3 x 3¼–inch pieces.

PER SERVING (1 PIECE): 245 CAL; 5G PROT; 5G FAT; 22G CARB; 14MG CHOL; 292MG SOD; 3G FIBER

FEATHER-BED BISCUITS

These light, airy biscuits can be served for breakfast, lunch or dinner. Heart-shaped biscuits are fun, but round or fluted cutters could also be used. Be sure to enjoy biscuits warm, right from the oven.

2 cups unbleached all-purpose flour plus extra for kneading

1 tablespoon granulated sugar

1 tablespoon baking powder

½ to 1 teaspoon salt, optional

¼ cup vegetable shortening

1 package active dry yeast

¾ cup warm (105F to 115F) skim milk

Melted butter, optional

1. Sift together the flour, sugar, baking powder and salt, if using, in a bowl. Cut in the shortening just until the mixture resembles coarse meal. Set aside.

2. Sprinkle the yeast over ⅓ cup of warm water in a bowl. Stir to mix. Let sit until bubbly, about 10 minutes. Add the milk, and mix well. Add the yeast mixture to the dry ingredients, and stir with a fork until moistened. The dough will be sticky.

3. Turn out the dough onto a heavily floured breadboard, and knead gently until smooth and elastic, about 30 seconds. Cover the dough with a tea towel, and let rise in a warm place for 20 minutes.

4. Sprinkle a work surface lightly with flour, and gently roll out the dough to a ½-inch to ¾-thick round. Cut with floured cutters, and reroll and cut out any scraps. Place 2 inches apart on ungreased baking sheets, and let rise while the oven preheats, for about 15 minutes.

5. Preheat the oven to 400F.

6. Bake the biscuits for 12 to 15 minutes, or until golden brown. Brush with melted butter, if using, and serve warm.

PER BISCUIT: 116 CAL; 3G PROT; 4G FAT; 16G CARB; 1MG CHOL; 204MG SOD; 1G FIBER

ONE-RISE BREADSTICKS

These are perfect partners for a bowl of hot soup.

1 package active dry yeast

1 teaspoon plus 1½ tablespoons honey

½ cup boiling water

⅓ cup canola oil

½ cup egg substitute, divided

3½ to 4 cups whole-wheat pastry flour plus extra for rolling

Sesame seeds, for garnish

1. Combine the yeast, ½ cup warm (105F to 115F) water and 1 teaspoon honey in a bowl, and set aside for 5 minutes. In another bowl, mix the boiling water, oil and remaining 1½ tablespoons of honey. Let cool to lukewarm. Add ¼ cup of the egg substitute and the yeast mixture, and mix well.

2. Stir in 3½ cups of the flour. Mix well, but do not knead. If the dough is too soft and sticky to handle, add a small amount of additional flour. Cover with a towel, and refrigerate to chill until firm.

3. Preheat the oven to 425F. Spray a baking sheet with nonstick cooking spray, and set aside.

4. Flour a work surface lightly, and divide the dough into 12 equal parts. With floured hands, roll each part into a stick about 12 inches long. Place the sticks 1½ inches apart on the baking sheet. Brush with the remaining ¼ cup egg substitute, and sprinkle with the sesame seeds. Let rise in a warm place for 30 minutes.

5. Bake for 15 minutes, until the sticks are golden brown. Remove from the oven, and serve warm.

PER BREADSTICK: 199 CAL; 6G PROT; 8G FAT; 24G CARB; 0MG CHOL; 22MG SOD; 5G FIBER

BASIC SWEETENED BREAD DOUGH

SERVES 16

This dough may be used to make lots of sweetened bread recipes, including some wonderful holiday breads.

2 cups soymilk

½ cup plus 1 teaspoon honey

½ cup vegetable oil

2 tablespoons fresh lemon juice

2 teaspoons salt

2 tablespoons active dry yeast

2 tablespoons potato flour or starch

7 cups all-purpose flour, whole wheat bread flour or half of each

1. Heat the soymilk in a saucepan over medium heat just until bubbles form around the edges. Remove from the heat. Stir in ½ cup of the honey, the oil, lemon juice and salt. Let cool.

2. Put ¾ cup of warm (105F to 115F) water in a bowl, and stir in the remaining 1 teaspoon of honey. Sprinkle in the yeast and potato flour, and stir to dissolve. Pour in the soymilk mixture. Stir in 3 cups of the flour. Beat for 2 minutes with a wooden spoon or an electric mixer. Add 1 more cup of flour, and beat for 2 minutes more. Knead in the remaining 3 cups of flour, and knead on a lightly floured surface for 10 minutes, adding a little more flour if necessary. The dough should feel velvety smooth, but not sticky.

3. Put the dough in a lightly oiled bowl, cover with a towel and let rise in a warm place until doubled, for about 1½ hours. Punch the dough down. To finish making the bread, see the specific recipe you are using for instructions.

PER SERVING: 281 CAL; 6G PROT; 8G FAT; 48G CARB; 0MG CHOL; 269MG SOD; 2G FIBER

LOW-CALORIE BLACK AND WHITE BROWNIES

SERVES 16

This brownie bakes up very moist and very rich tasting. It may be the best brownie you've ever had—especially since it's low calorie!

⅔ cup all-purpose flour

½ cup granulated sucralose-type sweetener

1 teaspoon baking powder

¼ cup (½ stick) butter or soy margarine, at room temperature

2 large eggs or ½ cup egg substitute

2 teaspoons vanilla extract

½ cup unsweetened applesauce

½ cup white chocolate chips or chunks

½ cup Dutch-process cocoa powder

½ cup mini chocolate chips

1. Preheat the oven to 350F. Butter an 8- or 9-inch square cake pan.

2. Stir together the flour, sweetener and baking powder in a bowl. Beat together the butter, eggs and vanilla in a separate bowl until the butter is broken into little pieces. Add the applesauce, and stir until blended. Fold in the flour mixture until moistened. Fold in the white chocolate. Measure out ½ cup of this mixture and drop by the spoonful into the prepared pan.

3. Fold the cocoa powder and chocolate chips into the remaining batter. Gently spoon the chocolate batter over the white batter. The batter is thick, so you must smooth out the surface.

4. Bake for 20 minutes, or until a toothpick inserted into the center comes out clean. Cool before cutting into 1½-inch squares.

PER SERVING (1 SQUARE): 120 CAL; 2G PROT; 7G FAT; 14G CARB; 35MG CHOL; 65MG SOD; 1G FIBER

VERY BERRY GOOD TREATS

These fruit-sweet, slightly sticky cookie bars have less than 1 gram of fat per bar.

1¾ cups rolled oats

4 cups fresh or frozen unsweetened boysenberries or other berries plus 16 whole berries, for garnish

¼ cup arrowroot

¼ cup apple juice concentrate

2 teaspoons ground cinnamon or to taste

1 teaspoon ground cloves

1. Preheat the oven to 350F. Lightly oil an 8-inch-square baking pan or spray with nonstick cooking spray, and set aside.

2. Put the oats into a food processor or blender, and process them to a coarse powder. Combine the oats, 4 cups berries, arrowroot, apple juice, cinnamon and cloves in a bowl and mix well. Spread the batter into the pan. Scatter the 16 whole berries evenly over the surface.

3. Bake for 35 to 45 minutes, or until firm. Remove from the oven, cool and cut into 16 squares.

PER SERVING (1 SQUARE): 54 CAL; 1G PROT; 0.7G FAT; 12G CARB; 0MG CHOL; 4MG SOD; 3G FIBER

CRAN-RASPBERRY CRISP

Because it's made with frozen fruit, this sweet-tart, old-fashioned dessert can be enjoyed any time of year.

4 cups fresh or frozen cranberries

1 10-ounce package frozen sweetened raspberries, thawed

¾ cup quick-cooking rolled oats

½ cup packed brown sugar

½ cup all-purpose flour

1 teaspoon ground cinnamon

¼ cup (½ stick) unsalted butter, cold, plus extra for greasing pan

Frozen vanilla yogurt, optional

1. Preheat the oven to 375F. Lightly grease a 9-inch round or square baking dish, and set aside.

2. Wash fresh cranberries, if using, in cold water. If using frozen cranberries, place them in a colander, and run warm water over them to thaw slightly. Drain. Place the cranberries in the prepared baking dish, and spoon the raspberries over them.

3. Combine the oats, sugar, flour and cinnamon in a bowl. With your fingertips, rub the cold butter into the mixture until it resembles cornmeal. Sprinkle the mixture evenly over the berries.

4. Bake until the crumb topping is crisp and brown, about 30 minutes. Serve warm with scoops of frozen yogurt, if desired.

PER SERVING: 290 CAL; 3G PROT; 8G FAT; 26G CARB; 20MG CHOL; 86MG SOD; 6G FIBER

BANANA-BLUEBERRY CRISP

This dish makes a great dessert, breakfast or snack. Serve it with yogurt or ice cream.

2 cups cooked rice or bulgur (see page 48)

⅔ cup skim milk

¼ cup packed brown sugar

1 tablespoon butter or margarine, melted, optional

1 teaspoon ground cinnamon

2 bananas, sliced

2 cups fresh or frozen blueberries

1. Preheat the oven to 350F. Lightly grease an 8-inch square baking dish or spray with nonstick cooking spray, and set aside.

2. Combine the rice, milk, brown sugar, butter, if using, and cinnamon in a bowl. Add the bananas and blueberries, and mix gently. Transfer the mixture to the prepared baking dish, and cover with foil.

3. Bake for 30 minutes, or until golden brown on top. Remove from the oven, and let cool slightly before serving.

PER SERVING: 277 CAL; 5G PROT; 0.9G FAT; 49G CARB; 1MG CHOL; 35MG SOD; 4G FIBER

LOW-FAT SPICE COOKIES WITH SWEET POTATOES AND YOGURT

These are soft, cakelike little cookies that aren't overly sweet. Although perfect in fall, these are delicious all year long.

⅔ cup packed dark brown sugar

4 tablespoons (1 stick) soy margarine

½ cup nonfat plain yogurt

2 teaspoons vanilla extract

1¾ cups unbleached all-purpose flour

1 teaspoon baking soda

2 teaspoons ground cinnamon

1 teaspoon ground ginger

½ teaspoon ground nutmeg

½ teaspoon ground allspice

1 large uncooked sweet potato, peeled and grated

1 cup raisins

½ cup chopped pecans

1. Preheat the oven to 350F. Line 2 baking sheets with baking parchment or spray them with nonstick cooking spray, and set aside.

2. Beat the sugar and margarine together until well mixed. Add the yogurt, and beat until creamy. Stir in the vanilla.

3. Sift together the flour, baking soda and spices, and stir into the yogurt mixture. Do not overmix. Fold in the sweet potato, raisins and pecans gently. Drop the dough by rounded teaspoons onto the baking sheets, about 2 inches apart.

4. Bake for 25 minutes, or until firm and browned on the bottoms but not dry. Remove from the oven, and cool on wire racks.

PER SERVING: 50 CAL; 1G PROT; 2.5G FAT; 8G CARB; 0MG CHOL; 40MG SOD; 0G FIBER

LOW-FAT OATMEAL COOKIES

These are old-fashioned cookies with plenty of flavor and without the fat. You might add some chopped walnuts, if you like. Remember, if you like crisp cookies, the browner they are, the crispier they are.

1 cup unbleached all-purpose flour
1 teaspoon baking powder
½ teaspoon baking soda
½ teaspoon salt
2 tablespoons soy margarine, at room temperature
1 cup packed brown sugar
¼ cup applesauce
1 large egg or ¼ cup egg substitute
2 teaspoons vanilla extract
1⅓ cups rolled oats
½ cup raisins

1. Preheat the oven to 375F. Line 2 baking sheets with baking parchment or spray them with nonstick cooking spray, and set aside.

2. Whisk together the flour, baking powder, baking soda and salt in a bowl.

3. Put the margarine in another bowl, and beat until fluffy. Add the sugar, and cream together. Add the applesauce, egg and vanilla, and beat for 1 minute. Fold the dry ingredients into the applesauce mixture until well blended. Fold in the oats and raisins. Drop the dough by rounded teaspoons onto the baking sheets, about 2 inches apart.

4. Bake for 15 minutes, or until the cookies are well browned on the bottoms. Remove from the oven, and cool on wire racks.

PER SERVING: 40 CAL; 1G PROT; 0.5G FAT; 8G CARB; 5MG CHOL; 55MG SOD; 0G FIBER

LOWER-CALORIE PEANUT BUTTER COOKIES

These are very tender cookies, and they break easily, so handle carefully.

1 cup creamy, well-stirred peanut butter, preferably all natural
1 cup apple juice concentrate, thawed and undiluted
½ cup sucralose-type sweetener
2 teaspoons vanilla extract
1 cup whole wheat flour
1½ teaspoons baking soda

1. Preheat the oven to 350F. Lightly spray 2 baking sheets with nonstick cooking spray or line them with baking parchment, and set aside.

2. Mix the peanut butter, apple juice, sweetener and extract until blended but not smooth. In a second bowl, whisk together the flour and baking soda, and fold into the peanut butter mixture. Stir until the batter is thick. Drop the dough by rounded teaspoons onto the baking sheets, about 2 inches apart. Use a fork dipped in flour to make crisscross marks on top of each cookie.

3. Bake for 12 minutes, or until lightly browned. Remove from the oven, and cool on the sheets. .

PER SERVING: 40 CAL; 1G PROT; 2G FAT; 5G CARB; 0MG CHOL; 35MG SOD; <1G FIBER

LOW-FAT CHOCOLATE CHIP–WALNUT COOKIES   MAKES ABOUT 60 COOKIES

Nuts plus chocolate chips add up to a very delicious cookie.

1¾ cups unbleached all-purpose
  flour
½ teaspoon baking soda
½ cup (1 stick) soy margarine
⅓ cup granulated sugar
⅓ cup packed brown sugar
½ cup nonfat plain yogurt
2 teaspoons vanilla extract
1 cup chocolate chips
1 cup chopped walnuts

1. Preheat the oven to 375F. Line 2 baking sheets with baking parchment or spray with nonstick cooking spray, and set aside.

2. Sift together the flour and baking soda; put in a mixing bowl. In a second bowl, cream together the margarine and sugars until fluffy. Stir in the yogurt and vanilla, and beat well. Stir the flour mixture into the margarine mixture. Stir in the chocolate chips and nuts. Drop the dough by rounded teaspoons onto the baking sheets, about 2 inches apart.

3. Bake for 10 to 13 minutes, or until golden. Remove from the oven, and cool on the sheets.

PER SERVING: 60 CAL; 1G PROT; 3.5G FAT; 7G CARB; 0MG CHOL; 30MG SOD; 0G FIBER

NAN WITH CUMIN   SERVES 6

This East Indian flatbread—also spelled naan—*is traditionally baked in a tandoori oven, but a gas or charcoal grill works fine, too.*

Dough
2 cups unbleached all-purpose flour
⅓ cup potato flakes
3 cloves garlic, minced
1 tablespoon vegetable oil
1 tablespoon granulated sugar
1 teaspoon salt, optional
1 teaspoon active dry yeast
1 teaspoon cumin seeds, toasted

Glaze
1 to 2 tablespoons vegetable oil
2 cloves garlic, minced

1. To make the Dough: Put all the ingredients into a food processor, and process for 30 seconds.

2. Add 1 cup of warm (105F to 115F) water gradually in a thin stream through the feed tube with the machine running. Pulse on and off until the dough forms a soft ball.

3. Transfer the dough to a lightly floured work surface, and knead for 5 minutes by hand, sprinkling with flour as needed to prevent sticking. The dough should be very soft and pliable.

4. Dust the inside of a plastic bag with flour. Place the dough in the bag, seal it and let it sit for 15 to 20 minutes in a warm place.

5. Prepare a hot charcoal fire or preheat a gas grill to high.

6. Meanwhile, to make the Glaze: Combine the oil and garlic in a bowl, and set aside.

7. To form the nan, remove the dough from the bag, and cut it into 6 equal pieces. On a lightly floured work surface, roll each piece into a circle as thin as a flour tortilla and about 8 inches in diameter. The circle need not be perfect and a few holes are fine. As each piece is rolled, brush it lightly with the glaze, and place it glazed-side down onto the grill.

8. To cook the nan, cover the grill, and bake the nan for 5 minutes. Brush the tops with the glaze, flip the nan over and brown the other sides. There should be bubbles and brown patches on both sides when the bread is done. Serve warm.

PER SERVING (1 NAN): 227 CAL; 5G PROT; 5G FAT; 41G CARB; 0MG CHOL; 17MG SOD; 3G FIBER

EASY CORN TORTILLAS

You don't need a tortilla press to make tortillas—a rolling pin works just as well. Look for masa harina in the Mexican food sections of most supermarkets. You can also use these later as the base for making tacos or tortilla baskets or cups to hold salads and other ingredients.

2 cups masa harina

1. Mix the masa harina with 1 cup of warm (105F to 115F) water in a bowl to form a ball. If the dough is too dry to hold together, add a few more tablespoons of water. Knead the dough lightly for a few minutes, cover with a tea towel and let sit for 1 hour.

2. Form the dough into 2-inch balls. Preheat a heavy skillet or griddle over medium-high heat, and place a cloth napkin in a shallow basket. Place a ball of dough between 2 plastic bags, and roll it into a 6-inch circle.

3. Remove the tortilla from the plastic bags, and place it on the hot griddle. Cook until bubbles begin to form on the surface. Turn the tortilla, and cook the other side for a few seconds only. As each tortilla is cooked, place it in the napkin-lined basket, and cover it completely. Repeat the procedure with the remaining dough.

PER TORTILLA: 72 CAL; 2G PROT; 0.5G FAT; 15G CARB; 0MG CHOL; 0MG SOD; 3G FIBER

FLAME-TOASTED WHOLE WHEAT TORTILLA

6 whole wheat tortillas
Flavored oil or melted butter,
    optional

1. Place 1 tortilla directly over a medium-high gas flame or on a metal cooling rack set over an electric burner.

2. Toast until the surface becomes lightly flecked with char, about 10 to 20 seconds, and the tortilla begins to puff up and fill with steam. Turn over and toast the other side.

3. Brush the tortilla with oil or butter if desired. Place it in a towel-lined basket while toasting the remaining tortillas. Serve hot.

PER TORTILLA: 130 CAL; 4G PROT; 1G FAT; 26G CARB; 0MG CHOL; 250MG SOD; 3G FIBER

India's everyday flatbread is called a chapati. *Made with wheat flour and water, the bread is very thin, soft and pliable.*

1 cup whole wheat flour
1 cup whole wheat pastry flour
½ cup unbleached all-purpose flour
½ teaspoon salt

1. Mix together the flours and salt in a bowl. Add 1 scant cup of warm or cold water slowly, while tossing the flour mixture.

2. Turn the dough out onto a lightly floured work surface when it comes together in a ball. Knead for 5 to 8 minutes, or until the dough is smooth and elastic. Let sit at room temperature for 30 minutes.

3. Form the dough into 12 balls the size of large walnuts. Working with 1 ball at a time, roll each ball on a lightly floured surface into a very thin, flat circle, about 7 inches in diameter.

4. Preheat the oven to 200F.

5. Heat a skillet, preferably cast iron, until a drop of water bounces off the surface. Cook 1 chapati at a time as follows: Cook on 1 side until a large bubble of steam forms in the center, then turn the chapati over and cook on the other side. There should be golden brown spots on each side. Keep the chapatis warm by stacking them in a towel-lined basket and placing the basket in the oven. Serve warm.

PER CHAPATI: 83 CAL; 3G PROT; 0.4G FAT; 18G CARB; 0MG CHOL; 90MG SOD; 1G FIBER

FOCACCIA WITH COARSE SALT AND FENNEL

This Italian flatbread is delicious as a snack or for making sandwiches. The dough can be made up to 1 day in advance. Cover and refrigerate it up to 24 hours, then let the chilled dough sit at room temperature for about 30 minutes before baking.

1 teaspoon active dry yeast

1 teaspoon granulated sugar

5 to 6 cups all-purpose flour

1½ teaspoons salt

¼ cup olive oil plus extra for brushing dough

2 to 4 teaspoons coarse sea salt or kosher salt

1 to 2 teaspoons fennel seeds

1. Dissolve the yeast and sugar in ½ cup of warm (105F to 115F) water in a bowl. Let sit until bubbly, for about 10 minutes. Combine 5 cups of the flour and the salt in a separate bowl. Make a well in the center, and pour in the yeast mixture and the oil. Stir until combined, adding up to 1 cup of additional warm water to make a soft but not sticky dough.

2. Turn the dough out onto a floured surface, and knead until smooth, about 10 minutes. Knead in just enough of the remaining 1 cup of flour to make the dough easy to handle. Place the dough in an oiled bowl, and cover with a damp tea towel. Let rise in a warm spot until doubled in bulk, about 1 hour.

3. Divide the dough into 2 equal pieces, and knead each piece briefly. Shape each piece into a ball, and let rest for about 10 minutes.

4. Preheat the oven to 425F.

5. Roll out each ball into a 5- to 6-inch circle or oval about ½ inch thick. Place the dough on a baking sheet. Use a sharp knife to score the dough, making ½-inch deep slits every 2 or 3 inches on the dough. Brush the dough with oil, and sprinkle with the coarse salt and fennel seeds.

6. Bake on the middle rack for about 10 minutes. Reduce the heat to 400F, and bake for 10 to 20 minutes more, or until golden brown on top.

PER SERVING: 444 CAL; 10G PROT; 12G FAT; 63G CARB; 0MG CHOL; 1,246MG SOD; 3G FIBER

8

salads, sauces and dips

A universal favorite, the versatile salad is an everyday food that is welcome hot or cold, sweet or tart, dressed with fancy toppings or served plain and simple. Salads can be composed of fruits, vegetables, grains, nuts, pasta and/or legumes in almost infinite combinations. Best of all, the salad can become the mainstay of breakfast, lunch or dinner . . . no questions asked.

As for salad dressings and accompanying sauces and dips, these are the elements that add that last bit of flavor for a truly great dish.

DANDELION GREENS WITH SPICY VINAIGRETTE

SERVES 4

Green salads were not usually part of the African-American culinary lexicon, but because they could be foraged, dandelion greens became an exception. Select the smallest, most tender leaves for this salad.

1 pound young dandelion greens, rinsed and dried

1 Vidalia onion, thinly sliced

3 tablespoons vegetable oil

1 tablespoon red wine vinegar

Pinch granulated sugar

4 dashes hot pepper sauce, or to taste

Salt and freshly ground black pepper to taste

1. Discard any discolored or fibrous dandelion leaves, and tear into bite-sized pieces. Place with the onion in a nonreactive salad bowl.

2. Combine the oil, vinegar, sugar, pepper sauce, salt and pepper in a small jar, cover and shake well to mix thoroughly. Adjust the seasonings, pour over the greens, toss and serve immediately.

PER SERVING: 100 CAL; 2G PROT; 8G FAT; 8G CARB; 0MG CHOL; 60MG SOD; 3G FIBER

EMERALD SEA SALAD

SERVES 4

Calcium-dense sea vegetables make a novel, attractive first course salad. Serve as a starter or with a bowl of miso soup for a light lunch or dinner. Arame is a type of seaweed sold in Japanese markets, but if it is unavailable, use hijiki instead.

2 cups dried wakame (see page 474)

1 cup dried arame

¼ cup rice vinegar

2 tablespoons dark sesame oil

2 tablespoons brown rice syrup

1 tablespoon tamari or low-sodium soy sauce

½ teaspoon ground white pepper

¼ cup sesame seeds

1. Soak the wakame in warm water to cover until soft, for about 5 minutes. Drain well, and cut into strips, removing the tough center stem.

2. Soak the arame in warm water to cover until soft, for about 5 minutes. Drain well. Combine the wakame and arame.

3. Mix the vinegar, sesame oil, rice syrup, tamari and pepper. Add to the sea vegetables, and toss to coat. Stir in the sesame seeds. Cover, and refrigerate. Serve chilled.

PER SERVING: 211 CAL; 4G PROT; 11G FAT; 24G CARB; 0MG CHOL; 11MG SOD; 8G FIBER

MINTED FIG AND ORANGE SALAD

SERVES 4

Figs deserve a culinary spotlight and, as here, adapt well to other assertive flavors, such as mint and oranges.

2 navel oranges

8 fresh figs, sliced

1 cup raspberries

1 cup plain yogurt

2 to 3 tablespoons chopped fresh mint leaves plus sprigs for garnish

1 tablespoon honey

½ teaspoon ground cinnamon

1. Peel the oranges, removing as much of the white pith as possible. Separate the oranges into sections, and cut each section into 1-inch pieces. Place the oranges and any juice that has accumulated on the cutting board into a salad bowl.

2. Add the remaining ingredients to the bowl, and toss to mix. Chill until ready to serve. Garnish with sprigs of mint.

PER SERVING: 173 CAL; 4G PROT; 3G FAT; 38G CARB; 8MG CHOL; 30MG SOD; 6G FIBER

BALD EAGLE VALLEY TOMATO SALAD

This delightful 1920s church-picnic salad from central Pennsylvania depends on vine-ripe summer tomatoes for much of its flavor. Choose plump, sweet-tasting beefsteak tomatoes. For added zest, sprinkle freshly chopped mint over the salad just before serving.

3 pounds large sun-ripened tomatoes

1 cup diced celery

½ cup apple cider vinegar

1 tablespoon granulated sugar or honey

1 tablespoon finely minced onion

Salt and freshly ground black pepper to taste

1 tablespoon minced fresh parsley

1. Cut the tomatoes into large, irregular chunks, and place with the celery in a salad bowl.

2. Combine the vinegar, ¼ cup of water, the sugar and onion. Stir to dissolve the sugar, and set aside for about 5 minutes, or until the flavors blend. Pour over the tomatoes, and add the salt and pepper. Stir to coat all pieces of the tomato with the vinegar mixture. Scatter the parsley over the top, and serve immediately.

PER SERVING: 60 CAL; 2G PROT; 1G FAT; 14G CARB; 0MG CHOL; 45MG SOD; 3G FIBER

AVOCADO SALAD WITH CITRUS VINAIGRETTE

Mild-tasting avocados offset the tartness of citrus fruit and the slight bitterness of the chicory, and the avocados also make a textured counterpoint to both.

6 tablespoons olive oil

2 tablespoons fresh lime juice

1 clove garlic, minced

Salt and freshly ground black pepper to taste

1 medium-sized navel orange, peeled and sectioned

1 small head chicory or frisée, rinsed and dried

2 large avocados, peeled, pitted and sliced

1 small red onion, thinly sliced

2 tablespoons chopped cilantro

1. Whisk together the oil, lime juice, garlic, salt and pepper in a bowl. Add the orange sections, and toss to mix.

2. Arrange the lettuce leaves on 4 plates. Spoon the oranges over the lettuce, reserving the dressing. Top with the avocado and onion. Drizzle each salad with one-quarter of the remaining dressing, and garnish with the cilantro. Serve immediately, or chill briefly.

PER SERVING: 270 CAL; 5G PROT; 21G FAT; 19G CARB; 0MG CHOL; 87MG SOD; 2G FIBER

ARUGULA AND ROASTED RED PEPPER SALAD

SERVES 4

You can use other garnishing elements such as mushrooms, olives and cheese in addition to or instead of the roasted red peppers in this simple salad.

2 canned roasted red bell peppers, rinsed, patted dry and julienned

3 tablespoons balsamic vinegar, divided

2 tablespoons olive oil, or up to ⅓ cup as needed for salad

Salt and freshly ground black pepper to taste

1 clove garlic, halved

2 bunches arugula, trimmed, rinsed, dried and torn into d pieces

1. Combine the peppers with 1 tablespoon of the vinegar, 2 tablespoons of the oil and a pinch each of salt and pepper. Let the peppers marinate at room temperature for 15 minutes.

2. To serve, rub the inside of a bowl well with cut sides of the garlic. Add the arugula to the bowl. Add the remaining 2 tablespoons of the vinegar, ½ teaspoon salt, the peppers and marinade, and toss again.

PER SERVING: 133 CAL; 2G PROT; 10G FAT; 9G CARB; 0MG CHOL; 15MG SOD; 1G FIBER

AUTUMN PEAR SALAD

SERVES 6

This simple salad graces any mealtime with its contrasting sweet and salty flavors. Consider this dish for a holiday meal accompaniment.

9 cups mixed greens

2 Anjou or Bosc pears, cored and thinly sliced lengthwise

3 ounces crumbled blue or Gorgonzola cheese

3 tablespoons chopped walnuts

3 tablespoons dried cranberries

⅓ cup rice vinegar

2 teaspoons cranberry juice concentrate

1 teaspoon Dijon mustard

⅓ cup olive oil

Salt and freshly ground black pepper to taste

1. Divide the greens among 6 individual serving plates. Top each with the pears, cheese, walnuts and cranberries.

2. Whisk together the vinegar, cranberry juice and mustard. Slowly add the oil, whisking until blended and thickened. Season with salt and pepper. Drizzle each salad with dressing, and serve.

PER SERVING: 260 CAL; 6G PROT; 19G FAT; 19G CARB; 10MG CHOL; 240MG SOD; 4G FIBER

RAITA

Fresh yogurt is made and eaten daily in many Indian homes, and variations of this refreshing Indian yogurt salad provide a great way to enjoy yogurt as a mealtime staple.

4 cups plain low-fat yogurt

1 cup sliced almonds, toasted (see page 47)

1 cup fresh mint leaves

1 cup raisins

1 cucumber, unpeeled and grated

2 teaspoons ground cumin

1 teaspoon salt

Freshly ground black pepper to taste

1. Drain the yogurt in a cheesecloth-lined strainer for about 30 minutes. Beat the drained yogurt with an eggbeater until smooth.

2. Add the remaining ingredients. Serve the salad chilled.

PER SERVING: 320 CAL; 14G PROT; 14G FAT; 36G CARB; 10MG CHOL; 510MG SOD; 4G FIBER

PEA AND SUNFLOWER SEED SALAD

A retro salad from the '70s, this recipe is adaptable to what's freshest and most appealing at the market. Layer to suit your whim. For a vegan version, use soy mayonnaise and omit the honey.

Salad

1 tablespoon vegetable oil or more as needed

5 ounces soy "bacon"

2 cups fresh or frozen peas

8 ounces mesclun, rinsed and dried

2 cups sunflower seeds, toasted (see page 47)

2 cups cubed pineapple, preferably fresh

1 pint grape tomatoes

Chopped fresh parsley, for garnish

Dressing

1 cup low-fat mayonnaise

¼ cup apple cider vinegar

¼ cup granulated sugar or honey

Salt and freshly ground black pepper to taste

1. To make the Salad: Heat the oil in a large skillet over medium heat, and cook the soy "bacon," several strips at a time, according to the package directions. Drain the strips on paper towels. When cool enough to handle, crumble or chop, and set aside.

2. Put the peas in a saucepan with water to cover, and bring to a boil. Cook for 1 minute, remove from the heat, rinse under cold water, drain and set aside.

3. To make the Dressing: Whisk together the mayonnaise, vinegar, sugar, salt and pepper. Set aside.

4. To assemble the salad, layer the ingredients into the serving bowl, starting with the mesclun, then the seeds, peas, pineapple, tomatoes and crumbled bacon. Dress as desired, garnish with the parsley and toss before serving.

PER SERVING: 540 CAL; 18G PROT; 37G FAT; 39G CARB; 15MG CHOL; 640MG SOD; 9G FIBER

CAESAR SALAD

This very popular salad can often become a calorie trap to the unwary. This version, however, strips away unwanted calories and fat, yet retains a full flavor. Another plus? No eggs are used in this salad. Reserve leftover salad dressing for another day, another salad.

½ day-old baguette, preferably whole wheat, diced

½ cup soft tofu

2 tablespoons grated Parmesan-style soy cheese

1 tablespoon fresh lemon juice

1 tablespoon red wine vinegar

2 teaspoons Dijon mustard

1 clove garlic, minced

1 teaspoon chopped capers

¼ teaspoon honey

Salt to taste

⅛ teaspoon freshly ground black pepper

1 large head romaine lettuce, rinsed, dried and chopped into bite-size pieces

1. Preheat the oven to 375F.

2. Place the diced baguette on a baking sheet, and bake until golden brown, for about 10 minutes. Remove from the oven.

3. Put the tofu, soy cheese, lemon juice, vinegar, mustard, garlic, capers and honey in a blender or food processor, and process until smooth. Season with salt and pepper.

4. To assemble the salad, put the lettuce in a salad bowl. Add ¼ cup of the croutons and half of the dressing. Toss well to coat the leaves evenly with the dressing. Garnish with another ¼ cup of croutons. Serve immediately.

PER SERVING: 110 CAL; 9G PROT; 4G FAT; 12G CARB; 0MG CHOL; 210MG SOD; 3G FIBER

PAPAYA AND WATERCRESS SALAD WITH LIME

This selection of ingredients provides a light counterpoint to a heavy meal.

Salad

½ cup watercress leaves

1 cup peeled, seeded and thinly sliced papaya

½ cup canned hearts of palm, drained and sliced

½ cup thinly sliced tomato

Dressing

1 tablespoon fresh lime juice

1 tablespoon chopped cilantro leaves

¼ teaspoon salt

Pinch ground coriander

Pinch allspice

1. To make the Salad: Arrange the watercress on 2 salad plates. Top with the papaya, hearts of palm and tomato.

2. To make the Dressing: Combine all the ingredients in a bowl, and whisk together well. To serve, drizzle dressing over the salads, and let stand for 30 minutes before serving.

PER SERVING: 90 CAL; 3G PROT; 0.1G FAT; 19G CARB; 0MG CHOL; 354MG SOD; 5G FIBER

ROASTED RED PEPPER AND POTATO SALAD

SERVES 8

Two well-liked ingredients pair up well for this lusty salad. If you really enjoy the tang of feta and the meatiness of roasted peppers, select the larger amount of both.

Salad

2 pounds new potatoes (about 20), cut into 1-inch cubes

6 to 8 red bell peppers, roasted, peeled and sliced (see page 46)

2 to 4 ounces feta cheese

Dressing

½ cup olive oil

¼ cup raspberry vinegar or red wine vinegar

1½ teaspoons Dijon mustard

Salt and ground white pepper to taste

1. To make the Salad: Steam the cubes for 15 to 20 minutes, or until tender. Put the potatoes and pepper slices in a salad bowl

2. To make the Dressing: Combine the oil and vinegar in a jar, seal tightly and shake to mix. Add the mustard, salt and pepper, and shake again. Add the dressing to the potatoes. Stir gently to blend, cover and refrigerate until serving time.

3. To serve, remove the peppers with a slotted spoon, and arrange on a large platter like the spokes of a wheel. Remove the potatoes with a slotted spoon and place between the peppers. Crumble the feta cheese, and drizzle the dressing over the salad.

PER SERVING: 262 CAL; 6G PROT; 7G FAT; 44G CARB; 6MG CHOL; 159MG SOD; 3G FIBER

STAR FRUIT SALAD

SERVES 4

Star fruit—also known as carambola—has a juicy, citrus flavor, and when sliced crosswise looks like a star.

4 large leaves red leaf or Boston lettuce, rinsed and dried

1 star fruit, sliced ¼ inch thick

1 14-ounce can artichoke hearts, drained

½ red bell pepper, cut into thin strips

¼ cup fresh lime juice

2 teaspoons honey

⅛ teaspoon salt

Fresh parsley sprigs, for garnish

1. Arrange the lettuce on 4 plates. Divide the star fruit among the plates, overlapping the slices slightly. Divide the artichoke hearts among the plates, next to the star fruit. Place the bell pepper strips over each plate in a crisscross pattern.

2. Whisk together the lime juice, honey and salt in a bowl, and drizzle over the salads. Garnish each plate with a parsley sprig.

PER SERVING: 73 CAL; 2G PROT; 0.1G FAT; 13G CARB; 0MG CHOL; 134MG SOD; 4G FIBER

GOAT CHEESE–STUFFED ZUCCHINI BLOSSOMS
ON TOMATO SALAD

Zucchini blossoms—squash flowers—are either male, which have stems, or female, which are attached to baby squash. Either will work for this recipe. If possible, use zucchini blossoms picked the same day you plan to use them. Store them in a tightly sealed plastic bag in the refrigerator until you are ready to cook them.

4 ounces fresh, mild, soft goat cheese, at room temperature

2 tablespoons coarsely chopped fresh basil

2 tablespoons coarsely chopped fresh marjoram

8 large fresh zucchini blossoms

3 tablespoons olive oil

Salt to taste

2 cups vine-ripened cherry or other small tomatoes, halved or quartered, or 2 large vine-ripened tomatoes, cut into bite-sized pieces

1. Preheat the oven to 350F. Lightly oil a baking sheet, or line it with parchment paper and set aside.

2. Mix the cheese with half of the basil and half of the marjoram. Form into 8 balls of equal size.

3. Inspect the blossoms for insects, and, using your fingertips, snap off the pistils inside the flowers. Cut the stems to about 1 inch. Put a ball of cheese inside each blossom, and arrange them on the baking sheet. Brush the blossoms with half of the oil, and season lightly with salt.

4. Bake the stuffed blossoms for 7 to 10 minutes, or until the petals collapse onto the cheese and sizzle slightly around the edges.

5. Meanwhile, toss the tomatoes with the remaining oil, marjoram and basil, and season with salt.

6. To serve, arrange the tomatoes on 4 plates, and top each with 2 warm blossoms.

PER SERVING: 190 CAL; 6G PROT; 17G FAT; 4G CARB; 15MG CHOL; 110MG SOD; 1G FIBER

KAZUN YWEK THOKE (WATERCRESS SALAD)

This is a tart and refreshing Burmese salad. Burmese cooks would use Chinese watercress, but Western watercress works fine.

3 tablespoons vegetable oil

1 onion, sliced

2 cloves garlic, sliced

1½ tablespoons sesame seeds, toasted (see page 47)

2 scallions, thinly sliced

2 tablespoons white vinegar

2 tablespoons low-sodium soy sauce

1½ tablespoons granulated sugar

1 teaspoon crushed red pepper, or to taste

½ teaspoon freshly ground black pepper

Salt to taste

2 bunches watercress, rinsed and trimmed into 1-inch lengths

1. Heat the oil in a skillet over medium heat. Sauté the onion and garlic until golden, for about 5 minutes. Remove from the heat, and set aside.

2. Combine the onion and garlic with the scallions, vinegar, soy sauce, sugar, crushed red pepper, pepper and salt, stirring to mix well. Add the watercress, and toss again to coat the leaves. Garnish with the sesame seeds, and serve.

PER SERVING: 130 CAL; 2G PROT; 8G FAT; 11G CARB; 0MG CHOL; 150MG SOD; 1G FIBER

HOT POTATO SALAD

The addition of rich spices such as cumin and coriander instead of the traditional bacon transforms this dish into a lively salad.

1 pound Yukon gold potatoes,
   unpeeled and cubed

¼ cup olive oil

¼ cup finely minced onion

2 cloves garlic, minced

¼ cup finely minced celery

Cumin seeds to taste

Coriander seeds to taste

Celery seeds to taste

Salt and freshly ground black pepper
   to taste

2 tablespoons balsamic vinegar

Pinch granulated sugar

1. Cook the potatoes in water to cover until tender, for 20 to 40 minutes. Timing will depend on the size and freshness of the potatoes. Drain, dry with paper towels, and put the potatoes in a nonreactive bowl.

2. Heat the oil in a skillet over medium heat, and sauté the onion and garlic for about 5 minutes, or until lightly browned. Add the celery and seasonings, and cook for 1 minute. Add the vinegar, sugar and 1 tablespoon of water, and cook for 1 minute more, stirring constantly. Pour over the potatoes, and serve immediately.

PER SERVING: 170 CAL; 2G PROT; 9G FAT; 20G CARB; 0MG CHOL; 10MG SOD; 2G FIBER

NEW POTATOES WITH LEEKS AND FENNEL

This salad with its tricolored potato mixture lends itself to an unusual presentation. Try placing portions in cup-shaped red cabbage or radicchio leaves, or select unusual serving bowls.

8 ounces new potatoes, mixture of
   white, Yukon gold and Peruvian
   purple

1¾ cups cooked or canned
   chickpeas, drained and rinsed

1 cup sliced leeks

1 cup diced fennel bulb

2 tablespoons raisins

⅓ cup soy mayonnaise

1 tablespoon fresh lime juice

1 teaspoon minced garlic

1 teaspoon fresh thyme leaves

Salt and freshly ground black pepper
   to taste

1. Cook the potatoes in water to cover until tender, for 20 to 40 minutes. Timing will depend on the size and freshness of the potatoes. Drain, and when cool enough to handle, cut into eighths.

2. Put the chickpeas, leeks and fennel in a bowl. Add the potatoes and raisins. Combine the mayonnaise, lime juice, garlic and thyme, and stir until well combined. Pour over the vegetables, and toss to cover well. Season with salt and pepper, and serve.

PER SERVING: 210 CAL; 10G PROT; 4G FAT; 34G CARB; 0MG CHOL; 95MG SOD; 7G FIBER

CURRIED POTATO AND RED LENTIL SALAD

In this clever combination of tastes, red lentils brighten up potatoes spiced with curry powder. Offer this salad with wedges of warmed pita bread and as a side to heartier Indian dishes.

¾ cup uncooked red lentils, rinsed

6 large red-skinned potatoes

4 firm, ripe tomatoes, diced

½ cup soy mayonnaise

½ cup plain soy yogurt or low-fat yogurt

¼ cup chopped cilantro, or more to taste

1 scallion, thinly sliced

1 to 2 teaspoons curry powder, or to taste

Salt and freshly ground black pepper to taste

1. Combine the lentils with 2 cups of water in a saucepan. Bring to a boil, reduce the heat to medium and cook for about 25 minutes, or until the water is absorbed and the lentils are tender but still firm. Drain off any excess cooking liquid, and let the lentils cool to room temperature.

2. Meanwhile, cook the potatoes in water to cover until tender, for 20 to 40 minutes. (Timing will depend on size and freshness of the potatoes.) Drain, and set aside. When cool enough to handle, cut into 1-inch pieces.

3. Combine the lentils and potatoes in a serving bowl. Add the remaining ingredients, and toss gently to mix and coat. Serve at room temperature.

PER SERVING: 235 CAL; 10G PROT; 5G FAT; 38G CARB; 1MG CHOL; 168MG SOD; 10G FIBER

MEXICAN POTATO SALAD

Sparked with lime juice and mustard, the salad becomes a natural for such accompaniments as hot corn tortillas and chilled Mexican beer.

2½ pounds new red-skinned potatoes, unpeeled, quartered lengthwise

1 cup canned, fresh or frozen white corn kernels

1 small onion, chopped

1 plum tomato, diced

½ cup canned whole fire-roasted chiles, diced and seeded

2 cloves garlic, minced

½ cup soy mayonnaise

1 tablespoon Dijon mustard

Juice of 1 lime

¼ cup chopped cilantro

½ teaspoon sea salt

1 teaspoon dried cilantro

1. Cook the potatoes in water to cover until tender, for 20 to 40 minutes. (Timing will depend on size and freshness of the potatoes.) Drain, and cool.

2. Put the potatoes in a large bowl, and add the corn, onion, tomato, chiles and garlic. Stir with a large, slotted spoon.

3. Make a shallow well in the center of the potato mixture, and add the soy mayonnaise, mustard and lime juice. Mix thoroughly, and add the cilantro and salt. Sprinkle with the dried cilantro, cover, and chill for 1 hour, or until ready to serve.

PER SERVING: 231 CAL; 4G PROT; 5G FAT; 45G CARB; 0MG CHOL, 418MG SOD, 5G FIBER

AÏOLI POTATO SALAD

Aïoli is garlic mayonnaise from the south of France; this recipe offers a convenient shortcut. You can use an egg-free soy-based mayonnaise or any other mayonnaise.

2 pounds small red-skinned
  potatoes

1 cup chopped scallions

1½ cups soy mayonnaise or regular
  mayonnaise

2 tablespoons fresh lemon juice

1½ tablespoons mashed garlic

2 teaspoons salt

1 teaspoon freshly ground black
  pepper

1. Cook the potatoes in water to cover for 20 to 40 minutes, or until tender. Timing will depend on the size and freshness of the potatoes. Remove from the heat, and while still warm, cut the potatoes into quarters. Put the potatoes in a mixing bowl. Toss the scallions with the potatoes.

2. Mix the remaining ingredients in a separate bowl, and toss with the warm potatoes. Cover, and chill overnight. Serve cold.

PER SERVING: 270 CAL; 3G PROT; 14G FAT; 35G CARB; 0MG CHOL; 1,050MG SOD; 3G FIBER

SPINACH SALAD WITH CRISPED TEMPEH

Crunchy sautéed tempeh replaces bacon in this satisfying salad with its traditional sharp, warm dressing. Refrigerate the leftover flavored oil, and use it in green salads or drizzled over boiled potatoes or other vegetables.

½ cup vegetable oil

3 cloves garlic, halved lengthwise

1 teaspoon dried oregano

8 ounces fresh spinach, stemmed,
  rinsed well, dried and coarsely
  torn

4 thin slices red onion, separated
  into rings

2 large button mushrooms, thinly
  sliced

1 large scallion, thinly sliced

1 tablespoon peanut oil

4 ounces tempeh, chopped

3 tablespoons red wine vinegar

1 teaspoon fresh lemon juice

¼ teaspoon salt

¼ teaspoon freshly ground pepper

1. Combine the vegetable oil and garlic in a small saucepan. Bring to a boil over medium heat (the oil should bubble gently), and cook for 8 to 10 minutes, or until the garlic is tender but not browned. Remove from the heat. Stir in the oregano, and let stand for 30 minutes to blend the flavors.

2. Meanwhile, combine the spinach, onion, mushrooms and scallion in a salad bowl. Set aside.

3. Heat the peanut oil in a skillet over medium-high heat. Add the tempeh, and cook, stirring often and shaking the pan, until lightly browned and crisp, for 7 to 10 minutes.

4. Meanwhile, strain the garlic-flavored oil through a fine sieve, and set aside. Transfer the cooked garlic to a cutting board. Holding the blade of a large, heavy knife parallel to the board, smear the garlic over the board, and grind it into a paste.

5. Transfer the cooked tempeh to a bowl. In the same skillet, combine 2 tablespoons of the reserved garlic oil, the garlic paste, vinegar, lemon juice, salt and pepper. Bring to a simmer, and pour over the salad. Add the crisped tempeh, toss well, and serve.

PER SERVING: 170 CAL; 7G PROT; 12G FAT; 9G CARB; 0MG CHOL; 181MG SOD; 2G FIBER

CHARRED EGGPLANT SALAD

You can char the eggplants—and the peppers and garlic—on the grill over hot coals or under the broiler.

8 (about 3 pounds) Japanese
  eggplants

1 large red bell pepper

1 head garlic

½ cup kalamata olives, pitted and
  chopped

3 tablespoons olive oil

2 tablespoons capers, rinsed and
  coarsely chopped

2 tablespoons chopped cilantro

2 tablespoons chopped fresh mint

2 tablespoons balsamic vinegar

1 to 2 tablespoons fresh lime juice

1 teaspoon cumin seeds, toasted
  and ground

Salt and freshly ground black pepper
  to taste

1. Prepare a hot charcoal fire, or preheat a gas grill to medium-high. Place a vegetable grilling rack on the grill. Alternatively, preheat the broiler.

2. Char the eggplants and pepper over direct heat on all sides. Roast the garlic over indirect heat until soft. Place the eggplants and pepper in a bowl, and cover with plastic wrap. Let stand for 10 minutes. Carefully peel off the charred skins. Chop the eggplants and pepper. Peel and mash the roasted garlic. Put the eggplant, pepper and garlic in a glass bowl with the remaining ingredients. Season to taste with salt and pepper, and serve.

PER SERVING: 130 CAL; 3G PROT; 6G FAT; 19G CARB; 0MG CHOL; 190MG SOD; 7G FIBER

GREEN SALAD WITH MANGO AND TOMATO

Good, ripe sweet mangoes have a definite springtime season, so you may wish to wait to enjoy this salad when these fruits are at their best.

4 cups mixed baby salad greens,
  rinsed and dried

1 large ripe tomato

1 ripe mango, peeled and sliced

2 tablespoons fresh lemon juice

½ teaspoon salt

Freshly ground black pepper to taste

2 tablespoons olive oil

1. Arrange the greens evenly among 4 serving plates. Slice off the top and bottom of the tomato, and discard. Slice the tomato into four ½-inch slices. Place 1 slice in the center of each plate of greens. Arrange the mango slices over the tomato slices.

2. Whisk together the lemon juice, salt and pepper in a bowl. Whisk in the oil. Drizzle the dressing over the salad, and serve.

PER SERVING: 111 CAL; 1G PROT; 7G FAT; 12G CARB; 0MG CHOL; 275MG SOD; 2G FIBER

CUCUMBER, WALNUT AND YOGURT SALAD

This refreshing Persian salad calls for using drained yogurt, a popular ingredient in Persian cooking and one that is easy to make at home. To make, line a fine-mesh strainer with two layers of cheesecloth, and spoon 3⅓ to 4 cups undrained the yogurt into the strainer, depending on how thick you want the yogurt. Set the strainer in a bowl or sink. Alternatively, you can cover the yogurt with several layers of paper towels, which absorb the excess liquid in the yogurt, and place the bowl in a larger container or sink to catch the drips. For a thicker yogurt, change the towels often, and repeat for several hours. When ready, the drained yogurt will have the consistency of cream cheese. Persian cucumbers and edible organic rose petals are sold at Middle Eastern markets. Use only fresh, unsprayed rose petals. Combining the raisins with the rose petals imparts a rose fragrance to the raisins. **Note:** *The recipe analysis does not include the bread.*

½ cup raisins

¼ cup fresh, organic rose petals

2½ cups drained plain whole yogurt or labneh

1 seedless English cucumber or 3 Persian cucumbers, peeled and very thinly sliced

½ cup sour cream, optional

2 scallions, chopped

¼ cup fresh mint leaves

¼ cup fresh Thai basil leaves

¼ cup fresh dillweed

¼ cup fresh tarragon

2 red radishes, thinly sliced

1 clove garlic, crushed and finely minced

2 teaspoons salt

1 teaspoon freshly ground black pepper

½ cup toasted walnuts (see page 47)

1 package toasted flatbread, such as pita, lavash, *sangak* or *barbary*

1. Combine the raisins and rose petals in a small container, cover and freeze for at least 30 minutes, or until ready to serve.

2. Combine the yogurt, cucumbers, sour cream, if using, scallions, mint, basil, dillweed, tarragon, radishes, garlic, salt and pepper in a serving bowl. Mix thoroughly, and adjust the seasonings to taste. Refrigerate for at least 30 minutes before serving.

3. To serve, add the walnuts, raisins and rose petals, stir well and serve with flatbread.

PER SERVING: 320 CAL; 13G PROT; 16G FAT; 34G CARB; 30MG CHOL; 1,290MG SOD; 3G FIBER

GARDEN COUSCOUS AND BLACK BEAN SALAD

SERVES 6

Loads of fresh vegetables are offered with the couscous and beans for a hearty and healthful salad.

1 cup uncooked couscous

2 cups cooked or canned black beans, drained and rinsed

1 large stalk celery, diced

1 small red bell pepper, seeded and diced

2 medium-sized tomatoes, diced

½ cup chopped green olives

½ cup chopped fresh parsley

2 scallions, thinly sliced

2 tablespoons chopped fresh dillweed

Juice of ½ to 1 lemon, or to taste

2 tablespoons olive oil

Salt and freshly ground black pepper to taste

1. Bring 2 cups of water to a boil in a saucepan, and stir in the couscous. Bring back to a boil, cover and turn the heat off. Let stand until all the water is absorbed, for 5 to 10 minutes. Fluff with a fork, and allow to cool to room temperature.

2. Transfer the couscous to a large bowl. Add the remaining ingredients, and toss to mix. Serve at room temperature, or cover, refrigerate, and serve chilled.

PER SERVING: 219 CAL; 8G PROT; 6G FAT; 39G CARB; 0MG CHOL; 658MG SOD; 7G FIBER

TROPICAL FRUIT SALAD

SERVES 4

A very soft, sweet cream cheese, the fromage blanc *pairs well with fresh fruit.*

2 large ripe mangoes, peeled and chopped

2 ripe papayas, peeled and chopped

3 ripe guavas, fresh or canned, halved and scooped into chunks

8 red grapes, preferably seedless, halved

8 white grapes, preferably seedless, halved

1 small pineapple, peeled and cut into chunks

2 bananas, peeled and sliced

1 red apple, peeled and cut into chunks

2 fresh figs, quartered

2 kiwifruits, peeled and sliced

1 tablespoon confectioners' sugar

½ cup slivered almonds, toasted (see page 47)

1 cup low-fat *fromage blanc* or plain low-fat yogurt, optional

Combine all the fruit in a large bowl, and toss gently to mix. Sprinkle the salad with the confectioners' sugar and almonds. Serve topped with a scoop of *fromage blanc*, if desired.

PER SERVING: 480 CAL; 7G PROT; 6G FAT; 112G CARB; 0MG CHOL; 40MG SOD; 17G FIBER

TUSCAN BREAD SALAD

Thrifty Italian cooks have developed a subcuisine based on leftovers. Day-old bread in particular has inspired a number of excellent solutions.

Dressing

4½ teaspoons red wine vinegar

3 tablespoons olive oil

3 tablespoons vegetable stock or Vegetable Stock (page 332)

1 teaspoon Dijon mustard

Salt and freshly ground black pepper to taste

Salad

4 slices sourdough bread, cut ½ inch thick

1 clove garlic, halved

2 ripe medium-sized tomatoes, diced

1 15-ounce can cannellini beans, drained and rinsed

1 medium-sized green bell pepper, roasted (see page 46) and cut into thin strips

¼ cup chopped fresh basil

1. Preheat the broiler.

2. To make the Dressing: Whisk together the vinegar, oil, stock and mustard in a bowl until well blended. Season with salt and pepper.

3. To make the Salad: Rub the bread slices with the garlic. Toast the bread under the broiler, turning once, for about 4 minutes on each side. Cut the bread into small cubes, and put into a bowl. Add the tomatoes, beans, bell pepper and basil. Pour the dressing over the salad, and toss to mix and coat. Let rest for 5 to 10 minutes before serving.

PER SERVING: 202 CAL; 8G PROT; 8G FAT; 30G CARB; 0MG CHOL; 145MG SOD; 5G FIBER

WINTER FIG AND PEAR SALAD

You can prepare the salad plates a few hours ahead and hold at room temperature, covered with plastic wrap. Make the vinaigrette a day or two ahead. Shake well, and drizzle over the salads just before serving.

Winter Fig and Pear Salad

6 cups mesclun, rinsed and dried

2 Bosc pears, cored and thinly sliced

6 fresh figs, cut into eighths

1 cup shaved Parmesan cheese (see page 160)

1 cup chopped walnuts, toasted (see page 47)

½ cup chopped fresh flat-leaf parsley

Vinaigrette

¼ cup olive oil

2 tablespoons white wine vinegar

¼ teaspoon coarse salt

¼ teaspoon freshly ground black pepper

1. To make the Winter Fig and Pear Salad: Line 4 plates with the mesclun. Arrange the pear slices on top in a fan shape. Scatter the figs and cheese over the pears. Sprinkle the walnuts and parsley over the salads.

2. To make the Vinaigrette: Combine all the ingredients in a glass jar with a tight-fitting lid, and shake well. Just before serving, drizzle the vinaigrette over the salads, and serve.

PER SERVING: 352 CAL; 10G PROT; 26G FAT; 22G CARB; 13MG CHOL; 396MG SOD; 4G FIBER

SWEET-AND-SPICY LAYERED FRUIT SALAD

The triad of jalapeño, ginger and lime juice give this dish backbone and personality.

Honey-Lime Dressing

½ cup honey

1 or 2 jalapeño chiles, seeded and quartered, or to taste

3-inch piece fresh ginger, unpeeled and sliced

½ cup fresh lime juice

Salad

2 cups fresh pineapple cubes

4 kiwifruits, peeled and cubed

3 cups trimmed and halved strawberries

3 cups unpeeled, diced English cucumber

2 mangoes, peeled and cubed

⅓ cup pine nuts, toasted (see page 47)

1. To make the Honey-Lime Dressing: Starting at least 1 hour before serving, combine the honey, ½ cup of water, the jalapeños and ginger in a small saucepan. Bring to a boil over high heat, reduce the heat to medium-low and cook for 2 minutes. Remove from the heat, cool to room temperature and chill completely. Strain the jalapeño and ginger from the syrup.

2. To make the Salad: Layer the fruit in a 2½-quart straight-sided glass dish, starting with the pineapple and continuing with the kiwifruits, strawberries, cucumber and mangoes. Sprinkle the pine nuts on top.

3. To serve, add the lime juice to the dressing, and whisk until well blended. Drizzle the dressing over the salad, and serve immediately.

PER SERVING: 180 CAL; 3G PROT; 3G FAT; 39G CARB; 0MG CHOL; 5MG SOD; 5G FIBER

NORWEGIAN WINTER FRUIT SALAD

When fresh fruits are not plentiful, you can rely on dried fruits to compose a cold-weather salad.

1 cup orange juice

1 lemon, scrubbed, thinly sliced and seeded

⅓ cup honey

1 teaspoon grated orange zest

1 cinnamon stick

12 dried apricots, diced

½ cup dried cherries

1 tart apple, peeled, cored and chopped

1½ cups pineapple chunks, fresh or canned

Splash brandy

1. Stir together the juice, lemon, honey, zest and cinnamon in a nonreactive saucepan. Stir in the apricots and cherries, and heat over medium-low heat. When the mixture simmers, remove it from the heat, and set it aside to cool to room temperature, for about 30 minutes.

2. Place the fruit mixture in a large bowl, and stir in the apple, pineapple and brandy. Serve immediately, or chill before serving.

PER SERVING: 270 CAL; 2G PROT; 0G FAT; 63G CARB; 0MG CHOL; 0MG SOD; 4G FIBER

GREENS AND CHEESE LAYERED SALAD

Watercress, curly endive and escarole all have the spine to stand up to onion, fennel and oil-cured olives.

Salad

1¾ cups canned chickpeas, drained and rinsed

4 cups chopped dandelion greens, watercress or arugula

1 cup pitted, coarsely chopped oil-cured olives

1 cup thinly sliced red onion

4 navel oranges, peeled, halved and thinly sliced

1 cup diced low-fat Swiss-style cheese or goat Gouda cheese

1 cup coarsely chopped toasted pecans (see page 47)

2 cups diced fennel

Dressing

6 tablespoons chopped fresh mint

⅓ cup sherry vinegar

5 tablespoons extra-virgin olive oil

Salt and freshly ground black pepper to taste

1. To make the Salad: Layer the ingredients in a 3-quart, straight-sided glass bowl, starting with the chickpeas, then in order spread one-third of the dandelion greens followed by all of the olives and onions. Top with another one-third of the greens and half of the orange slices. Sprinkle the cheese over the oranges, and top with nuts and fennel. Cover the salad with the remaining greens and oranges.

2. To make the Dressing: Whisk all the ingredients together until well blended. Drizzle over the salad, and serve.

PER SERVING: 460 CAL; 14G PROT; 31G FAT; 35G CARB; 5MG CHOL; 380MG SOD; 11G FIBER

PRIMAVERA SALAD

This luncheon salad celebrates spring's arrival with a splash of early-season ingredients, such as fresh straw-
berries. Use already-cooked eggs, or hard-boil and cool eggs as you ready the salad. For the seasoning salt,
select a lemon-pepper or a Greek-style salt, or one that best suits your palate.

Salad

1 cup dried small quinoa or wheat shell pasta

4 ounces sugar snap peas or snow peas

4 ounces slender asparagus, trimmed and cut on the diagonal

1 large English cucumber

3 cups mesclun, rinsed and dried

2 cups fresh strawberries, hulled and thinly sliced

4 large hard-boiled eggs, quartered

Dressing

½ cup vegan sour cream

1½ tablespoons fresh lemon juice

1 tablespoon olive oil or more if needed

1 tablespoon granulated sugar, or to taste

Grated zest of 1 lemon

Seasoning salt to taste

1. To make the Salad: Bring a large pot of lightly salted water to a boil. Cook the pasta according to the package directions, drain, rinse under cold water, drain again, and set aside.

2. Bring another large pot of lightly salted water to a boil, and blanch the peas for 1 minute. Remove from the water, and put in cold water. Blanch the asparagus for 2 minutes. Remove from the heat, put asparagus in cold water with the peas, drain and set aside.

3. Slice the cucumber, and put the slices in a salad bowl. Put the greens in the bowl. Add the strawberries, cooled pasta, asparagus and peas.

4. To make the Dressing: Beat together all the ingredients with 1 tablespoon of water. Spoon the dressing over the salad, and toss. Arrange the quartered eggs over the top, and serve.

PER SERVING: 300 CAL; 12G PROT; 13G FAT; 36G CARB; 210MG CHOL; 130MG SOD; 6G FIBER

Simple hard-boiled eggs, always a happy companion to the flavor of truffles, are elevated in this elegant salad.

Croutons

2 tablespoons olive oil

2 cups French or sourdough bread cubes

Dressing

½ cup snipped fresh dillweed

½ cup low-fat or regular mayonnaise

¼ cup fresh lemon juice

2 tablespoons olive oil

2 to 3 teaspoons truffle oil, optional

Salt and freshly ground black pepper to taste

Salad

1 pound asparagus, trimmed and cut into 2-inch lengths

2 cups halved grape or cherry tomatoes

5 large hard-boiled eggs, sliced

3 tablespoons capers

4 scallions, sliced

1 cup cubed low-fat Swiss-style cheese or regular Havarti cheese

1. To make the Croutons: Warm the oil in a nonstick skillet over medium-high heat. Add the bread cubes, and toast them, tossing often, until crisp and nicely browned, for about 6 minutes. Set aside to cool.

2. To make the Dressing: Put all the ingredients in a blender or food processor, and process until the dillweed is finely chopped. Set aside.

3. To make the Salad: Steam or blanch the asparagus until tender, for 30 seconds to 2 minutes, depending on thickness. Drain, and refresh under cold water. Set aside.

4. Layer the salad ingredients in a 2-quart glass bowl. Start with 1 cup of the tomatoes, then, in order, add the eggs, capers, scallions and cheese. Top with the remaining tomatoes, and add the asparagus.

5. To serve, drizzle with the Dressing, and sprinkle the top with the croutons.

PER SERVING: 420 CAL; 20G PROT; 26G FAT; 29G CARB; 270MG CHOL; 890MG SOD; 3G FIBER

CHINESE NOODLE SALAD WITH
PORTOBELLOS AND BROCCOLI

Chinese wheat noodles have a delightful springy texture, making them a perfect candidate for a salad. Grilled portobello mushrooms make this dish especially satisfying. The dressing can be made up to 2 days ahead and refrigerated.

Chinese Noodle Salad

3 tablespoons vegetable oil, divided

8 to 10 ounces dried Chinese wheat noodles

2 teaspoons dark sesame oil

12 ounces broccoli, cut into 1-inch florets; stems peeled and sliced (4 cups)

2 large portobello mushrooms (12 to 16 ounces), gills removed, stem ends trimmed and cut into ½-inch-thick slices

1 tablespoon low-sodium soy sauce

1 cup grated carrots

2 tablespoons toasted sesame seeds (see page 47)

Dressing

1/3 cup soy mayonnaise or low-fat regular mayonnaise

¼ cup low-sodium soy sauce

1½ tablespoons rice vinegar

1 tablespoon dark sesame oil

1 tablespoon packed brown sugar

1 tablespoon minced fresh ginger

2 cloves garlic, minced

1½ teaspoons Asian chili paste with garlic

1. Prepare a hot charcoal fire or preheat a gas grill to medium-high. Place a vegetable grilling rack on the grill. Alternatively, preheat the broiler.

2. To make the Chinese Noodle Salad: Heat a pot of lightly salted water and 2 tablespoons of the vegetable oil over medium heat, and when it is boiling, cook the pasta according to the package directions. Drain, rinse under cold water briefly and set aside. Transfer the noodles to a mixing bowl, and drizzle with the sesame oil. Toss to coat, and set aside.

3. Steam the broccoli for 2½ to 3 minutes, or until just tender. Rinse with cold water, and drain well. Arrange the portobello slices on a baking sheet. Mix the soy sauce and remaining 1 tablespoon of the vegetable oil together, and brush over both sides of the portobellos. Place them on the grilling rack or under the broiler, cover and grill until browned and tender, for 3 to 4 minutes per side. Let cool slightly, then dice.

4. To make the Dressing: Put the mayonnaise into a bowl, and gradually whisk in the soy sauce until smooth. Add the remaining dressing ingredients, and whisk until blended. Cover, and set aside.

5. Add the broccoli, portobellos and carrots to the noodles. Add the reserved dressing, and toss to coat. Transfer to a large shallow serving bowl. Sprinkle with the sesame seeds, and serve.

PER SERVING: 202 CAL; 6G PROT; 11G FAT; 24G CARB; 0MG CHOL; 467MG SOD; 5G FIBER

GRILLED VEGETABLES WITH GREENS AND CROUTONS

Grilled vegetables add a smoky taste to the salad bowl. To make Parmesan cheese shavings, start with a chunk of cheese that's at least 4 ounces. Use a swivel-edged vegetable peeler to shave off attractive curls, letting them fall onto a piece of parchment or wax paper.

8 cups mesclun, rinsed and dried

4 portobello mushrooms (about 1 pound total), stemmed and cut into ½-inch-thick slices

2 sweet onions, such as Vidalia or Walla Walla (about 1½ pounds total), cut into ½-inch-thick rings

1 large red bell pepper, cut into ½-inch-wide strips

16 cherry and/or yellow pear tomatoes

3 tablespoons olive oil plus extra for brushing

Salt and freshly ground black pepper to taste

8 ¾-inch-thick slices Italian bread

1 clove garlic, halved

2 tablespoons balsamic vinegar

½ teaspoon Dijon mustard

½ cup Parmesan cheese shavings or ¼ cup grated Parmesan-flavored soy cheese

1. Prepare a charcoal fire or preheat a gas grill to medium-high. Place a vegetable grilling rack on the grill. Alternatively, preheat the broiler.

2. Put the greens in a salad bowl, and set aside. Spread the mushrooms, onions, bell pepper and tomatoes on 2 baking sheets. Brush the vegetables all over with oil, and season with salt and pepper. Grill or broil the vegetables in batches until browned and tender, for 2 to 4 minutes per side. Grill or broil the bread with the vegetables for the last 4 minutes of grilling. Remove the vegetables, and set aside. Immediately rub the grilled bread with the cut sides of the garlic, and set aside.

3. Whisk together the 3 tablespoons of oil, the vinegar, mustard and 1 tablespoon of water in a bowl until well blended.

4. Put the grilled vegetables into the bowl with the greens, and toss with the vinaigrette. Divide the salad evenly among individual plates, and sprinkle the Parmesan cheese shavings on top. Serve with the garlic bread.

PER SERVING: 420 CAL; 15G PROT; 15G FAT; 60G CARB; 5MG CHOL; 498MG SOD; 10G FIBER

PESTO GARDEN VEGGIE WRAPS

Practically the whole garden goes into these fresh-tasting wraps, which are like salads you eat out of hand. Feel free to substitute or add other favorite vegetables. Both the flavor and texture are improved by making the salad ahead and chilling it thoroughly before serving.

6 dry-packed sun-dried tomatoes

Boiling water

1 cup low-fat cottage cheese

½ cup part-skim ricotta cheese

½ medium-sized green or red bell pepper, finely diced

3 radishes, finely diced

1 stalk celery, finely diced

3 tablespoons prepared pesto

2 tablespoons chopped fresh parsley

1½ tablespoons minced red onion

1½ teaspoons fresh lemon juice

¼ teaspoon salt

⅛ teaspoon freshly ground black pepper

6 9- to 10-inch flour tortillas

4 cups loosely packed mesclun or other greens, rinsed and dried

2 medium-sized tomatoes, thinly sliced

1. Combine the sun-dried tomatoes with enough boiling water to cover in a small bowl. Let stand for 30 minutes. Drain well, and coarsely chop.

2. Combine the chopped sun-dried tomatoes, cottage cheese, ricotta, bell pepper, radishes, celery, pesto, parsley, onion, lemon juice, salt and pepper in a bowl. Mix well. Cover, and refrigerate at least 2 hours or up to 24 hours.

3. Warm each tortilla in a large skillet over medium heat just until soft and flexible, for about 1 minute on each side. Place a row of greens down the center of each tortilla. Top with the tomato slices, overlapping slightly, and season lightly with salt and pepper. Dividing it equally, spoon the pesto-cheese mixture over the tomatoes. Fold the bottom end of each tortilla partially over the filling, then roll into a bundle, and serve.

PER SERVING (1 WRAP): 361 CAL; 19G PROT; 13G FAT; 42G CARB; 15MG CHOL; 864MG SOD; 4G FIBER

AVOCADO AND FETA CHEESE SALAD WRAPS

Here is a salad to go: As wrappers for a savory mixture, this dish borrows flour tortillas from Mexico as the way to take your salad along, or to enjoy seated with family and friends. Present the tortillas open, and let people do the wrapping themselves.

1 ripe avocado, seeded and diced

½ cup crumbled feta cheese

2 teaspoons fresh lime juice

Freshly ground black pepper to taste

½ cup sliced scallions

¼ cup sunflower seeds, preferably toasted (see page 47)

2 tablespoons soy "bacon" bits

2 tablespoons fat-free soy mayonnaise

16 grape tomatoes

1 cup shredded leaf lettuce plus 4 whole leaves

4 8-inch low-fat plain or flavored flour tortillas

1. Preheat the broiler.

2. Put the avocado into a bowl, and stir in the cheese, lime juice and pepper. Add the scallions, sunflower seeds, "bacon" bits and mayonnaise, stirring gently to combine. Stir in the tomatoes and lettuce.

3. Spray the tortillas lightly with nonstick cooking spray, and heat under the broiler until softened, for about 30 seconds. Remove from the oven, and place each tortilla on an individual plate.

4. To serve, line each tortilla with a whole lettuce leaf, and mound the salad mixture on top.

PER SERVING: 350 CAL; 12G PROT; 17G FAT; 40G CARB; 10MG CHOL; 540MG SOD; 9G FIBER

SUMMER GARDEN PASTA SALAD

This elegant pasta salad stars ultra-fresh, just-picked vegetables—all of which are accented by Gorgonzola cheese and lemon juice. If possible, select the vegetables from a farmers' market or farm stand.

2 tablespoons plus ¼ cup olive oil

9 ounces fresh angel hair pasta

¼ cup fresh lemon juice

1 tablespoon Dijon mustard

1 teaspoon grated lemon zest

1 teaspoon minced garlic

1 teaspoon granulated sugar, or to taste

Salt and freshly ground black pepper to taste

3 medium-sized tomatoes, cut into eighths

1 zucchini, thinly sliced

1 yellow summer squash, diced

1 bunch scallions, thinly sliced

2 tablespoons julienned ounce fresh basil, julienned

½ cup chopped fresh parsley

4 ounces crumbled Gorgonzola cheese

3 tablespoons capers, drained

1. Heat a pot of lightly salted water and the 2 tablespoons oil over medium heat, and when it is boiling, cook the pasta according to the package directions. Drain, rinse under cold water briefly and set aside.

2. Combine the remaining ¼ cup of oil, the juice, mustard, zest, garlic, sugar, salt and pepper in a bowl, beating well. Add the pasta to the oil mixture while still warm, and toss to combine well. Set aside.

3. Put the tomatoes, zucchini, squash, scallions, basil, parsley, cheese and capers in a bowl, and toss. Add to the dressed pasta, and toss again before serving, making sure the vegetables are well distributed.

PER SERVING: 350 CAL; 11G PROT; 21G FAT; 33G CARB; 50MG CHOL; 480MG SOD; 4G FIBER

CONFETTI COUSCOUS

This salad is perfect for a summer dinner, served over a bed of radicchio or watercress. Garnish the salad with sliced avocados and cherry tomatoes, or dice ½ cup of each and toss right into the salad.

1 teaspoon salt

½ teaspoon ground cumin

1 cup uncooked couscous

1¾ cups (about 1 15-ounce can) cooked black beans, drained and rinsed

1 cup fresh or frozen corn kernels

½ cup diced red onion

½ cup diced yellow bell pepper, optional

½ cup diced red bell pepper, optional

¼ cup finely chopped cilantro

1 small jalapeño chile, seeded and diced

2 tablespoons olive oil

3 to 4 tablespoons fresh lime juice (2 limes)

1. Bring 2 cups of water, the salt and cumin to a boil in a saucepan, and stir in the couscous. Bring back to a boil, cover and turn the heat off. Let stand until all the water is absorbed, for 5 to 10 minutes. Fluff with a fork.

2. Add the beans, corn, onion, bell peppers, if using, cilantro and jalapeño. Stir in the oil and enough lime juice to give the salad a puckery edge. Serve warm or at room temperature.

PER SERVING: 300 CAL; 11G PROT; 5G FAT; 52G CARB; 0MG CHOL; 368MG SOD; 7G FIBER

FRUITED GRAIN SALAD

What a delightful combination: tart and sweet fruits with wholesome, nutty-flavored grains.

1 cup uncooked wheat berries, rinsed

1 cup uncooked pearl barley, rinsed

1 cup uncooked millet seeds, toasted (see page 47)

6 scallions, chopped

½ cup chopped fresh parsley

⅓ cup chopped fresh mint

⅓ cup dried tart cherries

2 teaspoons grated orange zest

¼ cup fresh lemon juice

½ cup olive oil

Salt and freshly ground black pepper to taste

2 cups sliced fresh fruit and/or berries such as peaches, raspberries or blueberries

1. Bring 4 cups of lightly salted water in a large saucepan to a boil over medium heat. Add the wheat berries. Reduce the heat to low, cover and cook for 30 minutes. Add the barley, cover and cook for 20 minutes more.

2. Add the millet to the wheat berry-barley mixture after it has cooked for 50 minutes, cover and cook until all the grains are tender and the water is absorbed, for about 15 minutes more. Remove from the heat, fluff the grains with a fork and set aside to cool.

3. Combine the grains, scallions, parsley, mint, cherries and zest. Toss well.

4. Whisk together the lemon juice and oil in a separate bowl. Season to taste with salt and pepper. Pour over the grain mixture, and toss well. Cover, and refrigerate for at least 1 hour. Before serving, top with the fresh fruit.

PER SERVING: 268 CAL; 6G PROT; 8G FAT; 45G CARB; 0MG CHOL; 4MG SOD; 7G FIBER

BARLEY SALAD WITH CORN AND PEAS

This grain-vegetable salad calls for accompaniments of grilled cheese toasts and spicy iced tea.

¾ cup uncooked pearl barley, rinsed

3 cups cooked fresh corn kernels (about 5 ears)

4 ripe plum tomatoes, diced

½ cup fresh green peas, lightly steamed, or frozen petite peas, thawed

1 large celery stalk, diced

2 scallions, sliced

3 to 4 tablespoons minced fresh dillweed

Juice of ½ to 1 lemon to taste

3 tablespoons olive oil

Salt and freshly ground black pepper to taste

Lettuce leaves, rinsed and dried

Feta cheese for garnish, optional

1. Bring 2½ cups of water to a boil in a large saucepan over medium heat. Add the barley, reduce the heat to low and cook, covered, until the barley is tender and the water is absorbed, for 40 to 45 minutes. Remove from the heat, and let the barley cool to room temperature.

2. Combine the barley with the corn, tomatoes, peas, celery, scallions, dillweed, juice, oil, salt and pepper, and mix well.

3. To serve, line 6 salad plates with several lettuce leaves, and spoon the salad into the center of each. Sprinkle with the feta, if using. Serve at room temperature or chilled.

PER SERVING: 165 CAL; 4G PROT; 8G FAT; 23G CARB; 0MG CHOL; 13MG SOD; 5G FIBER

PARSLEY AND MINT THREE-GRAIN TABBOULEH

SERVES 8

The Lebanese salad tabbouleh is traditionally made with cracked wheat and plenty of parsley. In this version, cracked wheat is accompanied by millet and quinoa for a Westernized spin on the classic dish. As a full meal, this salad would go well with pita bread and Hot and Spicy Hummus (page 122). The recipe makes about 10 cups.

¾ cup uncooked fine-grain cracked wheat, rinsed

4 cups boiling water

½ cup uncooked millet, rinsed

¾ cup uncooked quinoa, rinsed

2 tomatoes, chopped

1 bunch fresh parsley, finely chopped

1 cup finely chopped fresh mint leaves

Salt and freshly ground black pepper to taste

¼ cup olive oil

Juice of 2 lemons, or more to taste

1. Soak the cracked wheat in the boiling water, set aside for about 20 minutes and drain.

2. Meanwhile, bring 6½ cups of water to a boil in a large saucepan over medium heat. Toast the millet and the quinoa together in a dry skillet over medium heat, stirring often to prevent burning. When the grains become fragrant and begin to pop, in about 7 minutes, remove from the heat and spoon them into the boiling water. Cook the grains for about 15 minutes, or until crunchy-tender. Remove from the heat, and drain in a fine-mesh strainer.

3. Combine the grains in a bowl with the drained wheat. Stir in the tomatoes, parsley, mint, salt and pepper.

4. Mix together the oil and lemon juice, and drizzle over the grains, tossing and stirring to mix well.

PER SERVING: 290 CAL; 9G PROT; 9G FAT; 47G CARB; 0MG CHOL; 15MG SOD; 5G FIBER

SPELT SALAD

SERVES 4

Cooked grains are ideal candidates for main-course salads because they're filling and they provide a neutral base for other livelier and more assertive ingredients. Use either spelt or kamut in this salad, and use only the most flavorful tomatoes. For a vegan version, omit the hard-boiled eggs.

1 cup uncooked spelt, rinsed and soaked in cold water for at least 1 hour

¼ cup olive oil or as needed

¼ cup red wine vinegar or as needed

Salt and freshly ground black pepper to taste

2 cups diced seeded tomatoes

1 cup cooked beans or lentils

½ cup chopped red onion, or more to taste

½ cup chopped red bell pepper

½ cup chopped celery or fennel

½ cup diced seeded cucumber

2 tablespoons chopped fresh flat-leaf parsley

4 tablespoons chopped fresh basil or mint

2 large hard-boiled eggs, chopped, for garnish

1. Drain and cook the grain in a large saucepan, covered, in 4 cups of lightly salted water over medium-low heat. Start checking for doneness after 15 minutes. If not all the water has been absorbed once the grains are done, drain the spelt in a strainer, and cool.

2. Season with the oil, vinegar, salt and pepper. Fold in the tomatoes, beans, onion, bell pepper, celery and cucumber. Add the parsley and the basil. Garnish with the hard-boiled eggs.

PER SERVING: 440 CAL; 15G PROT; 18G FAT; 55G CARB; 105MG CHOL; 1,220MG SOD; 15G FIBER

KAMUT AND WILD RICE SALAD

Grains and wild grasses have complementary nutty flavors that are heightened in this salad with the addition of sweet oranges. If you are running short on time, look for already cooked and vacuum-packed wild rice sold at specialty food stores and some supermarkets.

1 cup uncooked kamut, rinsed and soaked in water for at least 1 hour

1 teaspoon coarse salt, divided

½ cup uncooked wild rice,

¾ cup blanched slivered almonds, toasted (see page 47), optional

1 large red bell pepper, quartered

6 scallions, thinly sliced

6 navel oranges, sectioned

5 small stalks celery, thinly sliced on diagonal

Cilantro-Lime Vinaigrette (page 173) to taste

1. Drain the kamut. Bring 2 quarts of water to a boil over medium heat. Add the kamut and ½ teaspoon of the salt, and return to a boil. Reduce the heat to low, and cook until the grains are tender and begin to open, about 45 minutes. Drain, rinse under cold running water and drain well. Set aside.

2. Meanwhile, bring 4 cups of water to a boil in a saucepan over medium heat. Add the wild rice and the remaining ½ teaspoon of salt, and return to a boil. Reduce the heat to low, cover and cook until tender, for 45 to 50 minutes. Drain, rinse under cold running water and drain well. Set aside.

3. Preheat the broiler. Place the pepper quarters on the broiler pan, skin sides up. Watching carefully, broil until the skin is charred. Transfer to a paper bag, seal it, and let stand until cool. Peel the peppers, rinse briefly under cold running water and cut into strips.

4. Combine the kamut, wild rice, almonds, if using, pepper strips, scallions, orange sections and celery in a bowl. Add the vinaigrette, and toss to blend. Cover, and refrigerate for at least 1 hour. Bring to room temperature before serving.

PER SERVING: 266 CAL; 7G PROT; 10G FAT; 43G CARB; 0MG CHOL; 422MG SOD; 6G FIBER

COUNTRY QUINOA SALAD WITH CREAMY MINT DRESSING

When you want to turn a simple salad into a substantial dish, adding quinoa is the answer. Its delicate flavor takes well to leafy greens and light dressings. Toasting the grains in a dry skillet before cooking adds a rich, nutty flavor.

Salad

2½ cups Vegetable Stock (page 332)

1½ cups uncooked quinoa, rinsed

Salt to taste, optional

3 cups shredded romaine lettuce

2 cups halved cherry tomatoes

2 cups peeled and chopped cucumber

½ cup chopped scallions

Creamy Mint Dressing

½ cup crumbled goat cheese or silken tofu

5 tablespoons plain low-fat yogurt

2 tablespoons fresh lemon juice

2 tablespoons chopped fresh mint

1 clove garlic, minced

1 teaspoon Dijon mustard

⅔ cup olive oil

Salt and freshly ground black pepper to taste

1. To make the Salad: Bring the Vegetable Stock to a boil in a saucepan over medium heat. Add the quinoa and salt, if desired. Reduce the heat to low, cover and cook until the quinoa is tender and the liquid is absorbed, for about 15 minutes. Remove from the heat, and set aside to cool.

2. Meanwhile, to make the Creamy Mint Dressing: Combine the cheese, yogurt, juice, mint, garlic and mustard in a food processor or blender, and process until smooth. With the motor running, add the oil in a thin, steady stream until well blended. Season with salt and pepper to taste.

3. Combine the lettuce, tomatoes, cucumber and scallions in a salad bowl. Add the quinoa, and toss to mix. Serve the dressing separately.

PER SERVING (WITH 2 TABLESPOONS DRESSING): 227 CAL; 10G PROT; 6G FAT; 36G CARB; 2MG CHOL; 470MG SOD; 4G FIBER

MEXICALI ROSE TACO SALAD

Enjoy the festive flavors of Mexico in this robust main-course salad. This would also make a great brunch main dish. In either case, offer a basket of hot corn or flour tortillas as wrappers. To underscore the taco flavor, garnish this salad with whole or crushed taco chips, if desired.

Salad

1 head red leaf lettuce, rinsed and dried

About 2 cups black or navy beans, drained and rinsed

About 2 cups canned, fresh or frozen corn kernels

1 6-ounce can pitted black olives, drained

1 bunch scallions, cut into 1-inch lengths

2 medium-sized tomatoes, thinly sliced

1 ripe avocado, peeled and thinly sliced

1 cup (loosely packed) cilantro leaves

1 to 2 jalapeño chiles, seeded and thinly sliced, for garnish

Dressing

½ cup olive oil

Juice of ½ lime

3 tablespoons taco sauce

1 tablespoon granulated sugar, or to taste

1 teaspoon chili powder, or to taste

Salt and freshly ground black pepper to taste

1. To make the Salad: Trim off the tough ends of the lettuce, and line a bowl with the leaves.

2. Combine the beans, corn, olives, scallions and tomatoes in a bowl, and toss to combine. Add the avocado and cilantro, and stir in gently.

3. To make the Dressing: Combine all the ingredients in a bowl, and whisk together to combine. Toss the salad ingredients with the dressing.

4. To serve, scoop the bean mixture into the salad bowl. Garnish with sliced jalapeños.

PER SERVING: 470 CAL; 20G PROT; 30G FAT; 46G CARB; 0MG CHOL; 280MG SOD; 10G FIBER

TWO-RICE SALAD WITH ALMONDS AND GINGER

SERVES 8

If you can't find quick-cooking or already prepared vacuum-packed wild rice, cook up a pot of regular wild rice and measure 1½ to 2 cups for the salad.

Salad

1½ cups uncooked quick-cooking brown rice

1 cup uncooked quick-cooking wild rice

1 10-ounce package frozen green peas, thawed

½ cup thinly sliced scallions

¼ cup chopped red bell pepper

Dressing

¼ to ⅓ cup vegetable oil

¼ cup tarragon vinegar

2 tablespoons Dijon mustard

1 tablespoon grated fresh ginger

½ teaspoon salt, optional

1 teaspoon freshly ground black pepper

⅔ cup sliced almonds, toasted (see page 47)

Lettuce, for garnish, optional

1. To make the Salad: Prepare the brown rice according to the package directions. In a separate pan, prepare the wild rice according to the package directions.

2. Combine the cooked rices in a bowl, and let cool. Add the peas, scallions and bell pepper.

3. To make the Dressing: Whisk together the oil, vinegar, mustard, ginger, salt and pepper in a bowl. Add to the rice mixture. Add the almonds, and toss to blend. Serve in a lettuce-lined bowl or on individual plates.

PER SERVING: 226 CAL; 5G PROT; 10G FAT; 28G CARB; 0MG CHOL; 197MG SOD; 4G FIBER

COUSCOUS SALAD WITH FRESH MANGO

SERVES 6

A paste made from ground sesame seeds, tahini is an essential ingredient in the Middle Eastern pantry.

⅔ cup uncooked whole wheat couscous

2 tablespoons orange juice

1 tablespoon tahini

1 cup plain low-fat yogurt or soft tofu

½ teaspoon ground cumin

Pinch ground ginger

1 large ripe mango, peeled, pitted and diced

½ cup cooked or canned chickpeas, rinsed and drained

¼ cup golden raisins

¼ cup chopped cilantro

1. Bring 2 cups of water to a boil in a saucepan, and stir in the couscous. Bring back to a boil, cover and turn the heat off. Let stand until all the water is absorbed, for 5 to 10 minutes. Fluff with a fork, and allow to cool to room temperature.

2. Meanwhile, mix the orange juice and tahini in a cup until well blended. Whisk the yogurt in a bowl until smooth, and whisk in the tahini mixture, cumin and ginger. Stir in the mango, chickpeas and raisins.

3. Stir the couscous and cilantro into the mango mixture. Serve chilled or at room temperature.

PER SERVING: 242 CAL; 9G PROT; 3G FAT; 47G CARB; 2MG CHOL; 37MG SOD; 6G FIBER

SOUTHWESTERN SALAD

Fans of Tex-Mex food will enjoy this vegetarian taco salad.

1 cup crumbled firm tofu

2 tablespoons chopped cilantro leaves

2 teaspoons ground cumin

1 teaspoon salt

½ teaspoon chili powder, or to taste

¼ teaspoon freshly ground black pepper

1 teaspoon vegetable oil

6 corn tortillas

3 cups torn romaine lettuce

4 large tomatoes, coarsely chopped

1 cup canned, fresh or frozen corn kernels

2 large carrots, coarsely grated

½ cup minced red onion

1 cup seeded and diced cucumber

½ cup salsa

½ cup grated low-fat mozzarella cheese, optional

1. Preheat the oven to 400F.

2. Combine the tofu, cilantro, cumin, salt, chili powder and pepper in a bowl, and toss so that the spices coat the tofu.

3. Lightly spray a nonstick skillet with nonstick cooking spray, and place over medium heat. Add the oil and tofu mixture, and cook for 10 minutes. Let cool.

4. Cut the tortillas into wedges, and place on a nonstick baking sheet. Bake until crisp, for about 15 minutes.

5. Put the lettuce in a large bowl, and spoon the tofu mixture into the center. Arrange the tomatoes, corn, carrots, onion and cucumber on top, and sprinkle with the salsa and cheese, if using. Garnish with the tortilla wedges, and serve.

PER SERVING: 208 CAL; 10G PROT; 5G FAT; 29G CARB; 0MG CHOL; 672MG SOD; 5G FIBER

PROVENÇAL LENTIL SALAD

You can serve this tasty salad right away, but it gets better with time. Make it a day before you plan to serve it.

½ cup uncooked lentils, picked over, rinsed and drained

½ yellow onion, halved

1 clove garlic, crushed

1 bay leaf

1 red bell pepper, finely diced

½ red onion, chopped

2 tablespoons chopped fresh flat-leaf parsley

2 teaspoons olive oil

2 teaspoons white wine vinegar

1 teaspoon chopped fresh sage

1. Bring a large pot of water to a boil over high heat. Add the lentils, yellow onion, garlic and bay leaf. Cook until the lentils are just tender, for 20 to 30 minutes. Drain. Discard the onion, garlic and bay leaf.

2. Transfer the lentils to a bowl, and toss with the remaining ingredients. Cool to room temperature before serving.

PER SERVING: 128 CAL; 8G PROT; 3G FAT; 20G CARB; 0MG CHOL; 125MG SOD; 9G FIBER

SPICY BLACK BEAN AND LENTIL SALAD

Properly seasoned, black beans and red lentils lend tremendous flavor and depth to main-dish salads. Marinate them separately so the colors don't blend.

2 cups cooked black beans (see page 50), drained and rinsed

2 cups cooked red lentils (see page 50), drained and rinsed

½ cup rice wine vinegar

3 tablespoons minced garlic

Juice of 1 lemon

2 to 3 tablespoons olive oil

1 tablespoon minced fresh parsley

1 tablespoon minced cilantro leaves

1 teaspoon dry mustard

1 teaspoon salt, or to taste

1 teaspoon cayenne

1 small head butter leaf or Boston lettuce, rinsed, dried and torn

2 large red bell peppers, cut into 8 rings each

2 large red potatoes, cooked and thinly sliced

½ cup grated carrots or raw beets

1. Put the beans in 1 bowl and the lentils in another. In a third bowl, whisk together the vinegar, garlic, lemon juice, oil, parsley, cilantro, mustard, salt and cayenne. Divide the mixture evenly between the beans and lentils, and cover each bowl with plastic wrap. Marinate for 1 hour in the refrigerator.

2. Line 8 salad plates with the lettuce, and top with the bell pepper rings. Arrange small piles of the potatoes, carrots, beans and lentils on each plate, and drizzle any remaining marinade over all. Serve at once.

PER SERVING: 205 CAL; 8G PROT; 4G FAT; 33G CARB; 0MG CHOL; 277MG SOD; 5G FIBER

QUINOA AND BLACK BEAN SALAD

The grain quinoa is a good source of calcium as well as protein. This dish can be eaten cold or enjoyed warm as a pilaf.

2 cups uncooked quinoa, rinsed

1 canned chipotle chile in adobo sauce

2 oil-packed sun-dried tomatoes

1 tablespoon minced garlic

⅛ teaspoon ground cumin

⅛ teaspoon ground cinnamon

½ teaspoon salt

⅓ cup olive oil

1 15-ounce can black beans, drained and rinsed

¼ cup sunflower seeds, toasted (see page 000)

⅓ cup chopped cilantro

1. Combine the quinoa, 4 cups of water and a pinch of salt in a saucepan. Bring to a boil over medium-high heat. Reduce the heat, cover and cook until most of the water has been absorbed, for 10 minutes. Remove from the heat, and let stand for 5 minutes. Fluff with a fork, and let cool.

2. Combine the chipotle chile with 1 tablespoon of adobo sauce, the sun-dried tomatoes, garlic, cumin, cinnamon and ½ teaspoon of salt in a food processor, and purée until smooth. With the machine running, slowly add the oil through the feed tube, and process until blended.

3. Combine the beans and quinoa, sunflower seeds and cilantro in a salad bowl. Add the dressing, and toss to mix.

PER SERVING: 422 CAL; 14G PROT; 18G FAT; 53G CARB; 0MG CHOL; 614MG SOD; 8G FIBER

CREAMY GREEN DRESSING

Here's a tasty, low-fat alternative to ranch-style dressing. It's good on salads, of course, but can also be enjoyed as a dip for raw or steamed vegetables.

¾ cup low-fat ricotta cheese

¼ cup skim milk

¼ cup minced fresh parsley

2 cloves garlic, minced

1 teaspoon dried basil or 1 tablespoon minced fresh basil

Salt and freshly ground black pepper to taste

Put all the ingredients in a blender or food processor, and purée until smooth.

PER TABLESPOON: 19 CAL; 2G PROT; 1G FAT; 1G CARB; 4MG CHOL; 4MG SOD; 0G FIBER

GARLICKY VEGAN CAESAR DRESSING

Say good-bye to anchovies and egg: An excellent Caesar dressing may be made without them. Pour over romaine lettuce, and top with croutons.

4 to 5 cloves garlic, or to taste

1 teaspoon extra-virgin olive oil

Juice of 1 lemon

2 teaspoons balsamic vinegar

1 teaspoon red wine vinegar

½ teaspoon dry mustard

1 to 2 drops hot pepper sauce

Use a fork to mash the garlic in the oil in the bottom of a salad bowl. Whisk in the remaining ingredients and 1 teaspoon of water. Serve immediately, or store in an airtight container in the refrigerator for a stronger garlic flavor.

PER TABLESPOON: 16 CAL; 0G PROT; 1G FAT; 2G CARB; 0MG CHOL; 27MG SOD; 0G FIBER

GREEN GODDESS DRESSING

This tofu-based salad dressing is a low-fat take on the high-fat original. It's also good over steamed vegetables or as a sandwich spread.

4 ounces soft tofu, crumbled

1 scallion, sliced

2 tablespoons coarsely chopped fresh parsley

1 tablespoon fresh lemon juice

1 tablespoon white wine vinegar

1 clove garlic, minced, optional

1 teaspoon Dijon mustard

½ teaspoon salt

Combine all the ingredients in a blender or food processor, and purée until smooth. Store in an airtight container in the refrigerator for up to 5 days.

PER SERVING (2 TABLESPOONS): 20 CAL; 2G PROT; 1G FAT; 1G CARB; 0MG CHOL; 256MG SOD; 0G FIBER

FRESH ORANGE SALAD DRESSING

MAKES 1¼ CUPS

This lively dressing balances sweet with sour and hot for a pleasing result.

⅓ cup fresh orange juice
¼ cup white wine vinegar
1 tablespoon chopped fresh parsley
1 teaspoon grated orange zest
1 teaspoon granulated sugar
½ teaspoon paprika
¼ teaspoon salt
½ cup vegetable oil

Whisk together the juice, vinegar, parsley, zest, sugar, paprika and salt until well blended. Gradually whisk in the oil until well blended.

PER serving (1 tablespoon): 29 CAL; 0G PROT; 3G FAT; 1G CARB; 0MG CHOL; 29MG SOD; 0G FIBER

ORANGE AND TAHINI DRESSING

MAKES 1 CUP

Orange sweetens this creamy dressing. Try it with grilled vegetables, couscous and tofu.

1 medium orange, peeled, sectioned and seeded
2 tablespoons balsamic vinegar
1 tablespoon fresh lemon juice
2 teaspoons tahini
2 teaspoons honey, or to taste
½ teaspoon dry mustard
Pinch cayenne
Pinch ground cumin

Put all the ingredients in a food processor or blender with ½ cup of water, and purée until smooth.

PER TABLESPOON: 11 CAL; 0.3G PROT; 0.1G FAT; 1G CARB; 0MG CHOL; 1MG SOD; 0G FIBER

SWEET SESAME DRESSING

MAKES ½ CUP

Try this Asian-inspired dressing over steamed or stir-fried vegetables.

⅔ cup pineapple juice
1 tablespoon sesame seeds, lightly toasted (see page 47)
1 teaspoon grated fresh ginger
1 teaspoon minced garlic
1 teaspoon brown sugar
Splash low-sodium soy sauce
Splash brown rice vinegar or cider vinegar

Combine all the ingredients in a small saucepan. Cook over low heat, stirring occasionally, until the liquid has thickened and reduced in volume, for about 7 minutes. Remove from the heat, and let cool.

PER TABLESPOON: 21 CAL; 0.5G PROT; 0.5G FAT; 4G CARB; 0MG CHOL; 31MG SOD; 0G FIBER

CILANTRO-LIME VINAIGRETTE

This zesty dressing is excellent on salads of all kinds or drizzled over steamed new potatoes.

2 small cloves garlic
½ teaspoon coarse salt
¼ cup fresh lime juice (3 to 4 limes)
3 tablespoons dark sesame oil
2 tablespoons vegetable oil
1 tablespoon cider vinegar
¼ teaspoon Dijon mustard
2 tablespoons chopped cilantro
2 teaspoons grated lime zest

1. Mash the garlic and salt into a paste using a mortar and pestle or using the flat side of a chef's knife on a cutting board.

2. Combine the garlic paste, lime juice, both oils, vinegar and mustard in a bowl. Whisk until well blended. Add the cilantro and zest, and mix well.

PER TABLESPOON: 63 CAL; 0G PROT; 7G FAT; 1G CARB; 0MG CHOL; 108MG SOD; 0G FIBER

BUTTERMILK-BLUE CHEESE DRESSING

This creamy dressing tastes great drizzled over sliced tomatoes as well as tossed with salad greens.

½ cup soft tofu
½ cup low-fat buttermilk
3 tablespoons white wine vinegar
1 tablespoon vegetable oil
1 clove garlic, minced
2 tablespoons crumbled sharp blue cheese

Put the tofu, buttermilk, vinegar, oil, garlic and 1 tablespoon of the blue cheese in a blender or food processor, and purée until smooth. Stir in the remaining cheese.

PER TABLESPOON: 17 CAL; 1G PROT; 1G FAT; 0.5G CARB; 1MG CHOL; 9MG SOD; 0G FIBER

CRANBERRY VINAIGRETTE

This dressing is excellent drizzled over green salads. To reconstitute dried cranberries, cover with boiling water and let stand for 15 minutes. Drain, and blot with paper towels before using.

1½ cups fresh or frozen cranberries or reconstituted dried cranberries
1 cup apple cider
⅓ cup pure maple syrup
⅓ cup olive oil
1 tablespoon Dijon mustard
1½ teaspoons cider vinegar
1 teaspoon salt
½ teaspoon freshly ground black pepper

Put all the ingredients in a blender, and purée until smooth.

PER TABLESPOON: 29 CAL; 0G PROT; 2G FAT; 4G CARB; 0MG CHOL; 56MG SOD; 0G FIBER

GOOD FAT DRESSING

This zingy dressing makes enough for several salads. Try it in bean-and-vegetable combos or drizzle it over mixed green salads. Use a glass canning jar marked in 1-ounce increments both to measure ingredients (1 ounce equals 2 tablespoons) and to store leftovers.

½ cup balsamic vinegar

¼ cup olive oil

¼ cup canola oil

2 tablespoons coarse-grained mustard

1 tablespoon pure maple syrup or ½ teaspoon granulated sugar

2 teaspoons dried basil

Combine all the ingredients in a glass jar, and shake to blend. Store in the refrigerator. Bring to room temperature, and shake well before using.

PER TABLESPOON: 53 CAL; 0G PROT; 5G FAT; 1G CARB; 0MG CHOL; 20MG SOD; 0G FIBER

LOW-FAT CHEESE SAUCE

Surprisingly, making low-fat sauces doesn't necessarily mean giving up cheese. A trio of low-fat cheeses gives this sauce a rich flavor. Try it over linguine or other pasta.

⅓ cup white wine

2 large cloves garlic, minced

½ cup sliced scallions

1 large red bell pepper, seeded and finely chopped

2 tablespoons grated Parmigiano-Reggiano cheese

¼ cup grated low-fat mozzarella cheese

¼ cup low-fat or nonfat cottage cheese

2 tablespoons chopped fresh basil leaves

1. Heat the wine in a large skillet over medium-high heat until bubbling. Add the garlic, and cook for 1 minute. Add the scallions and bell pepper, and cook until the pepper is soft, stirring frequently, for 5 to 6 minutes.

2. Put the Parmigiano-Reggiano cheese, mozzarella and cottage cheese in a food processor or blender, and purée until smooth. Add the cheese mixture to the sautéed vegetables, and stir to mix. Remove from the heat, stir in the basil and toss with pasta.

PER SERVING: 76 CAL; 8G PROT; 2G FAT; 3G CARB; 9MG CHOL; 218MG SOD; 0.1G FIBER

TOFU-CILANTRO SAUCE

Try this over steamed or sautéed vegetables.

1 pound firm tofu, drained and cut into 8 pieces

¼ cup plain nonfat yogurt

1 scallion, chopped 3 to 4 tablespoons fresh lemon juice

1 tablespoon coarsely chopped cilantro leaves

1 teaspoon coarse-grained mustard

¼ teaspoon salt

1. Place the tofu in a steamer, and steam for 3 to 5 minutes. Set aside.

2. Put the remaining ingredients in a blender or food processor, and purée until smooth. Add the tofu 1 piece at a time, and blend until smooth. Serve warm.

PER SERVING (2 TABLESPOONs): 19 CAL; 2G PROT; 1G FAT; 1G CARB; 0MG CHOL; 35MG SOD; 0G FIBER

ALMOND SAUCE

Based on a béchamel sauce, this version goes a step further, turning something basic into an especially flavorful sauce with a very fine almond crunch. Spoon this sauce over any dish where you'd like a nutty touch: vegetables, pilafs, croquettes and more.

½ cup whole almonds (skin on)

3 tablespoons margarine or corn oil

¼ cup all-purpose flour

2½ cups soymilk, heated

1 teaspoon low-sodium soy sauce, optional

1. Preheat the oven to 350F.

2. Put the almonds on a baking sheet, and roast them to a golden brown, for about 10 minutes. Put into a food processor or nut grinder, and grind finely. Set aside.

3. Heat the margarine in a saucepan, letting it brown slightly. Add the flour, and cook for 2 or 3 minutes over low heat, stirring so that the flour doesn't burn. Slowly add the hot soymilk, whisking until thickened. Add the ground almonds, and cook for 4 or 5 minutes. Stir in the soy sauce, if using.

PER SERVING (2 TABLESPOONS): 46 CAL; 2G PROT; 4G FAT; 2G CARB; 0MG CHOL; 20MG SOD; 0G FIBER

AVOCADO SALSA

Depending on how hot you like your salsa, remove the seeds (the hottest part) of the chile or leave them in.

1½ cups canned tomatoes, drained and diced

1 small avocado, diced, divided

2 tablespoons fresh lime juice

2 tablespoons fresh lemon juice

2 tablespoons chopped fresh mint

2 tablespoons chopped cilantro

1 jalapeño chile, seeded and minced

1 tablespoon honey or other liquid sweetener

Salt and freshly ground black pepper to taste

Put ¼ cup of the tomatoes and ¼ cup of the avocado in a food processor or blender, and purée until smooth. Transfer to a bowl. Add the juices, mint, cilantro, jalapeño, honey, salt and pepper, and stir to mix. Stir in the remaining tomatoes and avocado. Serve immediately.

PER SERVING: 17 CAL, 0.3G PROT; 0.7G FAT; 1G CARB; 0MG CHOL; 27MG SOD; 0.1G FIBER

PINEAPPLE-CUCUMBER CHUTNEY

This chutney is a delicious accompaniment to Indian fare, such as Samosas (page 419).

½ small pineapple, cored, peeled and finely chopped

2 medium-sized cucumbers, peeled, seeded and finely chopped

1 bunch fresh mint leaves, chopped, plus a few leaves for garnish

¼ to ½ serrano chile, seeded and minced

1 tablespoon packed brown sugar

1 tablespoon minced fresh ginger

Grated zest and juice of 1 lime

Pinch salt, optional

Combine all the ingredients in a nonreactive bowl, and toss to mix. Refrigerate for at least 40 minutes. Place on a serving platter, and garnish with mint leaves.

PER SERVING: 123 CAL; 1G PROT; 0.6G FAT; 28G CARB; 0MG CHOL; 6MG SOD; 4G FIBER

PINEAPPLE-MANGO CHUTNEY

Tangy-sweet with a touch of heat, this chutney keeps several weeks in the refrigerator. Be sure to use plastic gloves when removing seeds from the jalapeño since the seeds can irritate bare skin.

2 cups diced fresh pineapple

1 large mango, peeled, pitted and chopped

1 cup diced onion

1 apple or pear, cored and diced

1 cup red wine vinegar

½ cup packed brown sugar or ⅓ cup maple syrup

½ cup dry white wine or apple juice

3 to 4 cloves garlic, minced

1 jalapeño chile, seeded and minced

1 tablespoon minced fresh ginger

1 teaspoon ground cumin

½ teaspoon ground cloves

¼ teaspoon salt

Combine all the ingredients in a large nonreactive saucepan, and cook over low heat, stirring occasionally, until the mixture has a jam-like consistency, for 15 to 20 minutes. Store in an airtight container in the refrigerator up to 3 weeks.

PER SERVING: 51 CAL; 0G PROT; 0G FAT; 12G CARB; 0MG CHOL; 38MG SOD; 1G FIBER

CILANTRO CHUTNEY

Chutneys are indispensable flavor boosters for most Indian meals. Considered digestive aids as well as appetite stimulants, chutneys come in many different varieties and degrees of sweet, sour and hot. This version—a chutney that should be familiar to many Westerners—is easy to make and delicious with vegetables.

2 cups chopped cilantro leaves

3 tablespoons grated unsweetened coconut

2 green chilies

2 tablespoons fresh lemon juice

1 tablespoon granulated sugar

1 tablespoon white vinegar

1 teaspoon ground cumin

Salt to taste

Put all the ingredients in the container of a food processor or blender, and process until smooth. Spoon into a container, and chill before serving.

PER SERVING: 15 CAL; 0G PROT; 0.5G FAT; 3G CARB; 0MG CHOL; 0MG SOD; 0G FIBER

BANANA CONDIMENT

Here's a sweet complement to savory dishes, such as Gallo Pinto (page 111). Stored in a jar in the refrigerator, it will last two to three weeks.

5 very ripe bananas

Juice of 1 lemon

¼ cup raisins or fresh berries in season

1. At least 1 day before preparation, put the bananas in the refrigerator to blacken.

2. Discard the peels, and put the bananas in a bowl. Mash them with a fork until almost smooth. Add the juice and raisins. Transfer to a saucepan, and bring to a boil, stirring constantly, until the mixture thickens, for about 10 minutes. (The longer it cooks, the thicker it will become.) Cool slightly before serving.

PER SERVING (1 TABLESPOON): 40 CAL; 0G PROT; 0G FAT; 9G CARB; 0MG CHOL; 0MG SOD; 1G FIBER

YOGURT CHEESE SPREAD

This versatile spread can be tailor-made to suit your taste: The following list of ingredients should inspire you to make up your own combination.

¼ cup sherry or Vegetable Stock (page 332)

1 tablespoon minced onion

1 tablespoon minced fresh chives

1 tablespoon minced carrot

½ cup Yogurt Cheese (see page 47)

Heat the sherry in a saucepan over medium-high heat. Stir in the onion, chives and carrot to taste, and cook for about 5 minutes, or until onion is softened. Remove from the heat, cool and combine with the Yogurt Cheese.

PER SERVING (1 TABLESPOON): 30 CAL; 0G PROT; 2.5G FAT; 1G CARB; 10MG CHOL; 10MG SOD; 0G FIBER

side dishes

Although the entrée may be the star of the meal, side dishes are essential supporting cast members that can make or break the performance. Because these help the main course shine, be sure to select complementary colors, flavors and textures. With that as a guideline, be as creative as you wish with your selections.

GOLDEN VEGETABLES

Yellow zucchini is also called "gold bar" squash. It has an intense yellow color and a smooth skin that makes it easy to julienne. This dish looks best if you purchase the really tiny baby carrots. If they aren't available, you may want to julienne large ones. Yellow Holland bell peppers, available at most supermarkets, are essential for flavor as well as color in this dish. Presentation is everything in this recipe—the julienned vegetables must be neat and cut to approximately the same length.

2 large (1 pound) yellow Holland bell peppers
1 pound yellow zucchini
1 pound very small baby carrots
4 tablespoons (½ stick) unsalted butter or soy margarine
Large pinch saffron
Salt to taste
¼ teaspoon white pepper
Pinch nutmeg

1. Put the whole bell peppers upright on a cutting board. Using a sharp knife, cut off 4 or 5 strips from top to bottom. This should leave the top, bottom and seed core in one piece. Save the ends for another use. Remove any white membranes from the strips, and cut the strips into very thin slices that are about 2½ inches long and ⅛ inch wide.

2. Repeat this style of cutting on the squash, julienning only the yellow skin.

3. Peel the carrots, if necessary, and cook them in boiling water until tender, for about 5 minutes. Set aside.

4. To serve, heat the butter in a heavy-bottomed skillet over medium heat. Crush the saffron, and add it to the butter. Add the salt, pepper and nutmeg. Do not let the butter brown. Add the vegetables, and cook for 4 minutes, stirring gently or tossing them in the skillet. Remove from the heat before the peppers and zucchini wilt. Serve hot.

PER SERVING: 90 CAL; 2G PROT; 6G FAT; 10G CARB; 15MG CHOL; 35MG SOD; 3G FIBER

GRILLED PORTOBELLO MUSHROOMS

These versatile mushrooms may be served on a large kaiser roll, on a plate as an appetizer or as a side dish. Use homemade or commercial pesto.

½ cup pesto
½ cup olive oil
8 large portobello mushrooms, stemmed
1 pound crumbled feta cheese
2 cups peeled, seeded and diced fresh tomatoes (see page 46)

1. Stir together the pesto and oil, and set aside. Scrape off the black gills under the mushroom caps, and discard. Spoon 2 tablespoons of the pesto mixture into each mushroom cap.

2. Mix the feta cheese with the tomatoes, and divide the mixture evenly among the mushrooms. Wrap each mushroom in plastic wrap, and chill for at least 30 minutes.

3. Prepare a hot charcoal fire about 30 minutes before cooking, or preheat a gas grill to medium.

4. Remove the plastic wrap from the mushrooms, and cook them on the grill, over medium heat for 10 to 20 minutes, or until soft when pierced with a knife. Remove from the heat, and serve.

PER SERVING: 350 CAL; 12G PROT; 31G FAT; 9G CARB; 50MG CHOL; 680MG SOD; 2G FIBER

SHREDDED CARROT GRATIN

Rich-tasting and unusual, this colorful side dish complements savory entrées.

8 tablespoons (1 stick) unsalted butter, divided

1½ pounds carrots, peeled and shredded

1 cup puréed silken soft tofu

Salt and freshly ground black pepper to taste

8 ounces shredded Colby cheese

⅓ cup unseasoned breadcrumbs (see page 46)

1. Preheat the oven to 375F.

2. Heat 4 tablespoons of the butter in a large skillet, and sauté the carrots for about 10 minutes, or until they become slightly tender. Stir in the tofu, salt and pepper. Pour the mixture into an ovenproof casserole, and top with the cheese.

3. Sauté the breadcrumbs in a large skillet with the remaining 4 tablespoons of the butter over medium heat until well coated and lightly browned. Sprinkle over the cheese.

4. Bake for 30 minutes, or until the cheese turns golden. Serve hot.

PER SERVING: 270 CAL; 9G PROT; 21G FAT; 12G CARB; 55MG CHOL; 260MG SOD; 2G FIBER

AUTUMN RED CABBAGE WITH PEARS

Germans use a special device for slicing their cabbage, but, working carefully, you can use a food processor or a very sharp, long-bladed slicing knife to achieve the fine slices this dish calls for. You may make this up to 4 days in advance and refrigerate before use.

¼ cup vegetable oil

2 red onions, halved and very thinly sliced

2 heads (about 5 pounds total) red cabbage, cored and thinly sliced

4 Anjou pears, cored and diced

1½ cups red wine vinegar

1 cup granulated sugar

2 teaspoons salt

1 teaspoon ground cloves

1 teaspoon freshly ground black pepper

1. Heat a very large skillet or saucepan over medium heat. Add the oil, and sauté the onions until wilted, for about 7 minutes. Add the cabbage and pears, and sauté for 10 minutes more.

2. Meanwhile, mix together the vinegar, sugar, salt, cloves and pepper in a saucepan, and heat over medium heat for 3 minutes. Pour over the cabbage mixture, cover and reduce the heat to low. Cook for about 1 hour, adding water or red wine if mixture is drying out, or until the cabbage is very tender and the onions and ears have taken on the color of the cabbage.

3. Remove from the heat, and serve or store in the refrigerator until ready to use.

PER SERVING: 210 CAL; 3G PROT; 5G FAT; 44G CARB; 0MG CHOL; 430MG SOD; 6G FIBER

AUTUMN VEGETABLES

This recipe makes glorious vegetables look beautiful by combining their bright colors, and it tastes wonderful since the vegetables are just barely cooked and are flavored with garlic, olive oil and herbs. To cook quickly, the vegetables must be sliced very thinly. This may be done in a food processor or by hand. The vegetables may be cooked on a grill if you have a grill basket that will keep them from falling into the fire. For the slender green beans, look for the French haricots vert.

8 ounces zucchini

8 ounces yellow squash

1 large red onion

8 ounces baby carrots

6 ounces very slender green beans or *haricots vert*

1 large red bell pepper

1 large yellow bell pepper

½ cup olive oil, preferably extra virgin

2 large cloves garlic, minced

¼ cup minced fresh parsley

¼ cup mixed chopped fresh herbs such as basil, tarragon, oregano, thyme

1 teaspoon salt

½ teaspoon freshly ground black pepper

1. Cut the zucchini into 2½-inch lengths. Standing the zucchini on a cut edge, use a small sharp knife to slice off the skin less than a ¼ inch thick. This should result in 4 or 5 strips from each section of zucchini. Cut the strips into thin sticks about ¼ inch wide. Place in a bowl. Do the same with the yellow squash.

2. Cut the onion in half, end to end. Remove about 5 center sections of the onion, leaving a hollow. Cut ¼-inch wedges of the onion. Cut the removed sections in similar wedges. Put the onion in the bowl with the squash.

3. Cook the carrots in boiling water until just barely tender. Drain, and rinse in cool water. Place in the bowl with the other vegetables.

4. Remove the stem ends from the green beans. Drop them into boiling water, and cook for 6 minutes, or until barely tender. Drain and chill. Place green beans in the bowl with the other vegetables.

5. Set the whole bell peppers upright on the cutting board. Cut off 4 or 5 strips from top to bottom using a sharp knife. This should leave the top, bottom and seed core in 1 piece. Save the ends for another use. Remove any white membranes from the strips, and cut them in very thin slices that are about 2½ inches long and ¼ inch wide. Add the slices to the bowl of vegetables.

6. Mix the oil with the garlic, parsley, herbs, salt and pepper. Drizzle the oil mixture over the vegetables, and toss gently to coat. Refrigerate until serving time.

7. Prepare a hot charcoal fire 30 minutes before cooking, or preheat a gas grill to medium-high. Place a vegetable grilling basket on the grill.

8. At serving time, grill the vegetables in the basket. Or sauté them in a large, heavy skillet over high heat for about 8 minutes, or until they are tender but still crunchy. Toss constantly as the vegetables cook to prevent softening. Adjust seasonings as needed, and serve.

PER SERVING: 170 CAL; 2G PROT; 14G FAT; 10G CARB; 0MG CHOL; 320MG SOD; 3G FIBER

ASIAN-STYLE ACORN SQUASH

SERVES 2

The mild flavor of acorn squash gets an Asian accent here. If you like things hot, you may want to sprinkle on some crushed red pepper.

1 acorn squash, halved, seeded and scraped to remove fibrous strings

3 tablespoons fresh lemon juice

2 tablespoons honey

1 tablespoon low-sodium soy sauce

1 tablespoon grated fresh ginger

1. Preheat the oven to 400F.

2. Place the squash halves cut sides down in a baking dish, and add enough water to come ½ inch up the sides of the baking dish.

3. Bake for about 30 minutes, or until tender. Remove from the oven, and turn the squash halves cut sides up.

4. Combine the lemon juice, honey, soy sauce and ginger in a bowl. Spoon this mixture into the squash cavities.

5. Bake for 10 minutes more. Remove from the oven, and serve warm.

PER SERVING (½ SQUASH): 162 CAL; 3G PROT; 0.3G FAT; 38G CARB; 0MG CHOL; 523MG SOD; 6G FIBER

WINTER SQUASH WITH CRANBERRIES AND RAISINS

SERVES 4

This recipe calls for delicata squash, an oblong-shaped vegetable about 9 to 9½ inches in length. Its skin is ivory, striped with dark green; the flesh is yellow. Look for delicata squash in autumn.

2 delicata or acorn squashes, halved and seeded

½ cup fresh cranberries or thawed, frozen cranberries

1 small apple, chopped

¼ cup chopped raisins

Juice and grated zest of 1 small orange

1½ tablespoons honey

Pinch salt

1. Preheat the oven to 375F. Place the squash cut sides up in a lightly oiled baking dish, and set aside.

2. Combine the cranberries, apple, raisins, orange juice, zest, honey and salt in a bowl, and mix to blend. Pile the mixture into the squash cavities, and cover.

3. Bake until the squash is tender, for 25 to 45 minutes, depending on the variety. (Acorn squash cooks more quickly than delicata.) Remove from the oven, transfer to a serving dish and serve warm.

PER SERVING (½ SQUASH): 185 CAL; 3G PROT; 1G FAT; 45G CARB; 0MG CHOL; 4MG SOD; 11G FIBER

SUGAR SNAP PEAS WITH MUSHROOMS

SERVES 8

Unlike snow peas, sugar snaps are relatively stringless and need to be trimmed only at the stem ends.

1 ½ teaspoons olive oil

1 tablespoon minced garlic

1 medium-sized sweet onion, such as Vidalia or Maui, chopped

2 large shallots, minced

1 large red bell pepper, cut into 2-inch strips

6 ounces portobello mushrooms, diced

2 pounds fresh sugar snap or snow peas, trimmed

3 tablespoons fresh lemon juice

1 ½ teaspoons dried marjoram

⅓ cup toasted sesame seeds (see page 47)

1. Heat the oil in a wok or 10-inch skillet, add the garlic and sauté over medium-high heat for 1 minute. Add the onion, shallots and bell pepper, and sauté for 3 minutes. Add the mushrooms, and cook for 4 minutes, or until the vegetables begin to soften. Add the peas, and cook for 2 minutes more, stirring frequently.

2. Reduce the heat to medium-low, and add the lemon juice and marjoram. Cook for 1 minute to heat everything through, sprinkle with the sesame seeds and serve immediately.

PER SERVING: 131 CAL; 6G PROT; 3G FAT; 22G CARB; 0MG CHOL; 127MG SOD; 7G FIBER

ARTICHOKES WITH GREEN HERB SAUCE

SERVES 6

You may steam the artichokes and put together the sauce (except for the lemon zest and juice) the morning of your dinner. Always use a nonaluminum pot when cooking artichokes to keep them green. Aluminum causes artichokes to discolor.

6 large artichokes

6 tablespoons pine nuts

1 cup chopped fresh Italian flat-leaf parsley

½ cup chopped fresh basil

¼ cup chopped fresh marjoram or oregano leaves

2 cloves garlic, minced

2 tablespoons capers, rinsed, optional

½ to 1 cup olive oil

Grated zest and juice of 2 lemons

½ teaspoon salt

Freshly ground black pepper to taste

1. Trim the bases of the artichokes so that they stand upright. Use kitchen shears to snip the points from the artichoke leaves.

2. Turn the artichokes upside down in a steamer basket set in a nonaluminum pot of boiling water. Steam until a leaf can be easily plucked from an artichoke, for 25 to 30 minutes. Drain.

3. Toast the pine nuts in a dry skillet over medium heat until golden. (Watch carefully since the nuts burn easily.) Let cool, then chop finely.

4. Combine the pine nuts, parsley, basil, marjoram, garlic and capers in a bowl. Stir in ½ cup of the oil, or more as needed. Just before serving, stir in the lemon zest and juice and add more oil if desired. Season with the salt and pepper.

5. To serve, place each artichoke in the center of a salad plate. Spoon the sauce into its cavity. Pour extra sauce into a serving bowl, and pass at the table.

PER SERVING (WITH 1 TABLESPOON SAUCE): 212 CAL; 4G PROT; 17G FAT; 14G CARB; 0MG CHOL; 262MG SOD; 5G FIBER

ARTICHOKES WITH LIGHT LEMON DIPPING SAUCE

SERVES 2

Artichokes are one of the most sensuous of vegetables, because they are always eaten with the fingers. This dish is not only sensuous but also kind to the waistline.

Sauce

⅔ cup plain nonfat yogurt

⅓ cup fresh lemon juice

2 tablespoons Dijon mustard

1 tablespoon frozen apple juice concentrate, thawed, or apple juice

1 tablespoon minced garlic

1 teaspoon curry powder

Artichokes

2 artichokes

1 lemon, quartered

1. To make the Sauce: Whisk together all the ingredients in a bowl. Let sit at room temperature while you prepare the artichokes.

2. To cook the Artichokes: Trim the bases of the artichokes so that they stand upright. Use kitchen shears to snip the points from the artichoke leaves.

3. Bring a large nonaluminum pot of water to a boil. Add the artichokes and lemon. Boil, uncovered, until tender, for about 25 minutes. Drain well.

4. To serve, place each artichoke in the center of a salad plate. Spoon the sauce into its cavity or into a small bowl for dipping.

PER SERVING: 185 CAL; 8G PROT; 3G FAT; 32G CARB; 1MG CHOL; 332MG SOD; 4G FIBER

BRAISED GREENS WITH VINEGAR AND SESAME SEEDS

SERVES 2

Greens flavored with vinegar are a classic combination in the South; the acidity of the vinegar is a tasty complement to the naturally bitter greens. If beet greens aren't available, you can use collard greens, kale or dandelion greens instead. Try this dish with Black-Eyed Peas with Tomatoes and Herbs (page 199).

¼ cup flavored vinegar such as red wine vinegar

1 clove garlic, minced

1 pound beet greens, chopped coarsely

Pinch cayenne

1 tablespoon sesame seeds

Heat the vinegar and garlic in a nonaluminum saucepan over medium heat. Add the greens and cook until wilted, about 10 minutes. Add ¼ cup of water, cover and cook for 2 minutes, adding more water as necessary to keep from sticking. Uncover, and cook until any remaining liquid evaporates and the greens are tender, adding water as necessary. (Exact timing will depend on the age and freshness of the greens.) Sprinkle with the cayenne and sesame seeds before serving.

PER SERVING: 81 CAL; 4G PROT; 2G FAT; 12G CARB; 0MG CHOL; 456MG SOD; 8G FIBER

BAKED PARSNIPS WITH APPLES AND ORANGES

SERVES 4

Oranges, apples and honey highlight the natural sweetness of this humble root vegetable.

6 small parsnips, peeled and sliced

3 apples, peeled, cored and sliced

1 orange, peeled and sliced

¼ cup apple juice or water

2 tablespoons honey

1. Preheat the oven to 350F.

2. Mix together the parsnips, apples and orange in a baking dish. Stir in the apple juice and honey, and cover.

3. Bake until the parsnips are tender, for about 20 minutes, stirring several times. Uncover, and bake for 10 minutes more, to brown the top slightly. Remove from the oven, and serve warm.

PER SERVING: 193 CAL; 2G PROT; 0.4G FAT; 49G CARB; 0MG CHOL; 11MG SOD; 6G FIBER

BRAISED RED CABBAGE WITH CURRANTS

Vegetables are braised by first sautéing them, and then baking or cooking them in a small amount of liquid. The result? Plenty of flavor. Raisins or diced fresh apple can be substituted for the currants.

2 teaspoons dry red wine
1 red or yellow onion, thinly sliced
¼ to ½ teaspoon salt
1 small red cabbage, thinly sliced
⅔ cup apple juice or water
½ cup currants
2 to 3 tablespoons red wine vinegar, cider vinegar or rice vinegar
1 tablespoon caraway seeds or cumin seeds, toasted (see page 47)

1. Preheat the oven to 375F. Lightly oil a 2-quart baking dish, and set aside.

2. Heat the wine in a large nonaluminum saucepan over medium heat. Add the onion and salt, and cook, stirring frequently, until the onion is soft, for about 5 minutes. Add the cabbage and cook, stirring frequently, over medium-low heat until it wilts slightly, for about 5 minutes. Add water as needed to prevent the vegetables from sticking.

3. Add the apple juice, currants, vinegar and caraway, and mix well. The cabbage should become bright red. Transfer the cabbage mixture into the prepared baking dish, and cover.

4. Bake until very tender, for 45 to 60 minutes. Remove from the oven, and serve warm or at room temperature.

PER SERVING: 43 CAL; 1G PROT; 0.1G FAT; 8G CARB; 0MG CHOL; 98MG SOD; 2G FIBER

GRILLED PLANTAINS

The plantain looks like a large banana, but it tastes more like a winter squash. Unlike bananas, plantains must be cooked before eating. In different stages of ripeness, plantains are a starch, a vegetable or even a dessert—the riper they are, the sweeter they are.

2 large plantains
Cayenne pepper to taste

Cut the plantains into quarters crosswise, then slice lengthwise to form rectangular pieces about ¼ inch thick and about 2 inches long. Sprinkle with cayenne. Grill or broil until just tender, for about 6 minutes. Serve warm.

PER SERVING: 109 CAL; 1G PROT; 0.3G FAT; 26G CARB; 0MG CHOL; 4MG SOD; 2G FIBER

ORANGE-SCENTED ASPARAGUS WITH SWEET RED PEPPER AND KIWI

SERVES 2

Tangy oranges and kiwifruit are a refreshing foil to the naturally herbaceous flavor of asparagus. A bonus: The acid in the orange juice helps keep the grilled asparagus bright green. Lemon juice can be substituted for the orange juice concentrate and lemon slices can be substituted for the kiwifruit.

5 to 6 ounces fresh asparagus, trimmed

½ teaspoon olive oil

½ red bell pepper, seeded and julienned

1 teaspoon frozen orange juice concentrate, thawed

Freshly ground black pepper to taste

1 kiwifruit, peeled and thinly sliced

1 teaspoon packed brown sugar, optional

1. Preheat the broiler. Lightly oil a gratin or other baking dish, and set aside.

2. Cook the asparagus in a steamer or large pot of water until barely tender, for about 7 minutes, and drain.

3. Meanwhile, heat the oil and 1 teaspoon of warm water in a skillet over medium-high heat. Add the bell pepper, and cook, stirring frequently, until slightly softened, for about 5 minutes. Remove from the heat, and gently stir in the orange juice and pepper. Arrange the asparagus spears and kiwifruit in the gratin dish. Spoon the bell pepper and sauce on top. Sprinkle with the sugar.

4. Broil until lightly browned, for 2 to 3 minutes. Remove from the oven, and serve hot.

PER SERVING: 61 CAL; 2G PROT; 1G FAT; 10G CARB; 0MG CHOL; 6MG SOD; 3G FIBER

ROASTED ASPARAGUS WITH SESAME SEEDS

SERVES 8

Roasting brings out extra flavor in this springtime vegetable. Serve warm or at room temperature.

2 pounds fresh asparagus, trimmed

1 tablespoon olive oil

1 teaspoon coarse salt (sea salt or kosher salt)

3 to 4 tablespoons sesame seeds, toasted (see page 47)

1. Preheat the oven to 425F.

2. Spread the asparagus spears in a single layer in a shallow baking dish and lightly brush with the oil, rolling them to distribute the oil evenly. Sprinkle with the salt.

3. Roast, uncovered, until the spears are just tender when pierced with the tip of a knife, for about 10 minutes. Remove from the oven, arrange the asparagus on a serving plate and sprinkle with the sesame seeds.

PER SERVING: 63 CAL; 2G PROT; 4G FAT; 5G CARB; 0MG CHOL; 273MG SOD; 2G FIBER

SAUTÉED PEPPERS AND SQUASH WITH CAPERS AND CAYENNE

SERVES 1

This quick dish tastes best at room temperature, so make it first and let it cool while you prepare the rest of the meal. This would be easy enough to double or triple when serving a group of family or friends.

1 to 2 teaspoons olive oil

4 scallions, thinly sliced

½ red, yellow or green bell pepper, halved and sliced into strips

4 ounces zucchini or yellow squash, sliced on the diagonal

2 teaspoons capers, drained, optional

¼ teaspoon salt

¼ teaspoon freshly ground black pepper

⅛ teaspoon cayenne

Heat the oil in a medium skillet over medium heat. Add the scallions and bell pepper, and cook, stirring frequently, for 3 minutes. Add the squash, and cook for about 5 minutes, or until softened. Add the remaining ingredients, and heat through. Serve warm or at room temperature.

PER SERVING: 75 CAL; 1G PROT; 4G FAT; 7G CARB; 0MG CHOL; 538MG SOD; 3G FIBER

STEAMED BROCCOLI WITH GARLIC

SERVES 1

This simple side dish is quick to prepare, and can be easily doubled for two. Serve warm or at room temperature as a side dish or toss with cooked pasta and a little olive oil for a main dish.

2 cups broccoli florets

1 to 2 teaspoons vegetable oil

1 clove garlic, minced

½ red or yellow bell pepper, diced

Salt and freshly ground black pepper to taste

1. Cook the broccoli in a steamer set over a saucepan of simmering water for 2 minutes. Set aside.

2. Heat the oil in a medium skillet over medium heat. Add the garlic and bell pepper, and cook, stirring frequently, for 2 minutes. Add the broccoli, and cook for 2 minutes more, until all the vegetables are heated through. Season with salt and pepper, and serve.

PER SERVING: 91 CAL; 3G PROT; 4G FAT; 9G CARB; 0MG CHOL; 569MG SOD; 6G FIBER

ZUCCHINI PANCAKES WITH DILL

When your garden is overproducing zucchini, try shredding them and freezing the shreds in plastic bags. Then you can use them in these pancakes or in zucchini bread all winter long. These are more a vegetable dish than a pancake—the batter just holds it all together. Select a commercial biscuit mix from your market for this recipe.

4 cups shredded zucchini

1 teaspoon salt

1 cup minced scallions

1 cup biscuit mix

1 tablespoon dried dillweed

1 teaspoon coarsely ground black pepper

2 large eggs, beaten, or ½ cup egg substitute

¼ cup canola oil or more for frying

1. Put the zucchini in a mixing bowl, and toss with the salt. Let sit for 30 minutes, if possible, to remove some of the moisture. Add the scallions, biscuit mix, dillweed and pepper. Toss well. Add the eggs, and stir until the biscuit mix is wet.

2. Preheat the oven to 200F.

3. Heat a well-seasoned griddle or large flat skillet over medium heat, and brush with a thin coat of oil. Use a ¼-cup measure to scoop up the zucchini mix, and drop the mix onto the griddle. Use a fork to spread into a 3-inch pancake. Leaving 1 inch or more between pancakes, repeat until the griddle is filled. When the bottom of each pancake is golden brown, flip and cook the other side. Remove from the griddle when both sides are done, and stack the cakes on a heatproof dish.

4. Keep the pancakes warm in the preheated oven. Oil the griddle again, and cook the remaining mixture until it is used up.

PER SERVING: 140 CAL; 4G PROT; 8G FAT; 13G CARB; 55MG CHOL; 510MG SOD; 2G FIBER

STIR-FRIED KALE WITH GINGER

Fresh ginger and soy sauce give this dish an Asian flair. You can substitute spinach or bok choy for the kale, if desired, and you can double the ingredients to serve two.

½ tablespoon vegetable oil

1 tablespoon minced fresh ginger

4 ounces kale, chopped coarsely

1 teaspoon low-sodium soy sauce

1 teaspoon sesame seeds, toasted (see page 47)

1. Heat the oil in a medium skillet over medium heat. Add the ginger, and stir-fry for 1 minute.

2. Add the kale, and increase the heat to medium-high. Add the soy sauce and ¼ cup of water, and stir-fry until the kale is wilted but still slightly crunchy, for about 3 minutes. Sprinkle with the sesame seeds. Serve warm or cold.

PER SERVING: 124 CAL; 3G PROT; 7G FAT; 11G CARB; 0MG CHOL; 396MG SOD; 7G FIBER

CELERY ROOT AND POTATO PURÉE

Here are sophisticated mashed potatoes with a hint of celery flavor and a wonderfully creamy texture. The purée is ethereal on its own, but it also makes a perfect companion for vegetable stews.

1 tablespoon plus ¼ teaspoon salt

12 ounces celery root, peeled and cubed

1½ pounds red-skinned potatoes, peeled and cubed

2 cloves garlic

2 tablespoons unsalted butter

Freshly ground white pepper to taste

1. Bring 10 cups of water to a boil with the 1 tablespoon salt in a large saucepan over medium heat. Add the celery root, and cook for 15 minutes. Add the potatoes and garlic. Continue to cook for 15 minutes more, or until the celery root and potatoes are tender.

2. Drain the vegetables in a colander, reserving about ¼ cup of the cooking liquid. Transfer the vegetables to a bowl, and mash with the butter, the remaining ¼ teaspoon of salt and pepper to taste. Add 2 to 3 tablespoons of the reserved water to make the mixture creamy. Serve immediately.

PER SERVING: 160 CAL; 3G PROT; 4G FAT; 30G CARB; 10MG CHOL; 550SOD; 3G FIBER

FIREHOUSE POTATOES

This is a spiffed up, Tex-Mex version of home fries, complete with jalapeño chiles, your favorite salsa, sour cream and pepper Jack cheese. If you don't care for the heat of pickled jalapeños, substitute any kind of finely chopped pepper you like. Bake the potatoes the evening before you need them.

4 medium-sized baking potatoes, baked and cooled

3 tablespoons vegetable oil, divided

1 cup finely chopped onion

Salt to taste

½ teaspoon paprika or mild chili powder

½ cup prepared salsa

⅓ cup low-fat sour cream

¼ to ⅓ cup sliced pickled jalapeño chiles, drained

1 to 1½ cups grated pepper Jack cheese

1. Preheat the oven to 400F.

2. Cut the potatoes into large, bite-size pieces, and set aside. Heat 2 tablespoons of the oil in a large, ovenproof skillet over medium heat. Add the onion, and cook, stirring often, until softened, for about 5 minutes. Add the remaining 1 tablespoon of oil and the potatoes, and cook, stirring often, until heated through, for about 5 minutes. Season with salt. Sprinkle with the paprika, and cook, stirring often, for 1 minute. Remove the pan from the heat.

3. Spoon the salsa and the sour cream over the potatoes. Sprinkle with the jalapeños and cheese. Bake the potatoes in the skillet for 5 to 7 minutes, or until the cheese is melted. Serve right from the skillet.

PER SERVING: 315 CAL; 9G PROT; 15G FAT; 39G CARB; 30MG CHOL; 371MG SOD; 5G FIBER

CANARY ISLANDS POTATOES WITH MOJO SAUCE

SERVES 6

In the Canary Islands, off the northwest coast of Africa, potatoes are cooked in seawater and liberally splashed with mojo sauce, a tart and fiery concoction.

12 medium-sized red-skinned potatoes, scrubbed and halved

½ cup red wine vinegar

2 tablespoons olive oil

2 cloves garlic, pressed or minced

2 teaspoons minced fresh parsley

¾ teaspoon paprika

¾ teaspoon cumin seeds, toasted (see page 47) and crushed slightly

½ teaspoon salt, or to taste

⅛ teaspoon cayenne pepper, or to taste

1. Cook the potatoes in water to cover until tender, for 20 to 40 minutes. (Timing will depend on size and freshness of the potatoes.) Drain, and set aside.

2. Meanwhile, combine the vinegar, oil, garlic, parsley, paprika, cumin, salt and cayenne pepper in a bowl, and whisk to blend.

3. Transfer the potatoes to a serving dish, and top with the oil and vinegar sauce. Serve warm or at room temperature.

PER SERVING: 203 CAL; 4G PROT; 5G FAT; 36G CARB; 0MG CHOL; 184MG SOD; 6G FIBER

FLUFFY MASHED SWEET POTATOES

SERVES 6

Instead of white potatoes, why not use sweet potatoes? Bananas, prune juice, honey and spices add a hint of sweetness to this vitamin A–rich side dish.

About 1 pound sweet potatoes

3 ripe bananas, mashed

1½ cups soymilk or milk

½ cup prune juice

3 tablespoons honey

1 teaspoon ground allspice

2 teaspoons chopped candied ginger

1. Preheat the oven to 375F. Lightly oil a baking dish, and set aside.

2. Cook the sweet potatoes in water to cover for 20 to 40 minutes, or until tender. (Timing will depend on size and freshness of the potatoes.) Under cool running water, pull off the peels, and discard. Drain, and mash for 2 cups cooked. Combine the potatoes, bananas, soymilk, prune juice, honey and allspice in a bowl, and beat until light and fluffy. Spoon into the baking dish.

3. Bake for 50 to 60 minutes, or until golden brown. Remove from the oven, sprinkle with the candied ginger and serve warm.

PER SERVING: 236 CAL; 3G PROT; 1G FAT; 52G CARB; 0MG CHOL; 24MG SOD; 6G FIBER

MASHED POTATOES AND RUTABAGAS

SERVES 6

If you haven't tried rutabaga yet, here's a delicious opportunity to discover its mellow flavor. Rutabaga is heavily waxed for shipping, and a vegetable peeler sometimes doesn't work well, so try using a sharp paring knife instead.

1½ pounds baking or boiling potatoes

1½ pounds rutabaga

½ cup evaporated skim milk

2 tablespoons unsalted butter or margarine

1 teaspoon salt

¼ teaspoon ground white pepper, or to taste

Pinch ground nutmeg

1. Cook the potatoes in water to cover for 20 to 40 minutes, or until tender. (Timing will depend on size and freshness of the potatoes.) Drain. Under cool running water, pull off the peels, and discard.

2. Cut the rutabaga into quarters, and peel each section with a paring knife. Cut the rutabaga into 2-inch chunks, and cover with cold water in a heavy pan. Add a pinch of salt, cover, bring to a boil and cook for 10 to 15 minutes, or until fork-tender. Drain, reserving the cooking water.

3. Force the potatoes and rutabaga through a ricer into a mixing bowl, or mash them with a potato masher. Add the milk, butter, 1 teaspoon of salt and pepper, and beat vigorously with a potato masher. Slowly add the reserved cooking water while beating constantly, until the mixture is light and fluffy but still holds stiff peaks. Transfer to a serving bowl, sprinkle with the nutmeg and serve warm.

PER SERVING: 160 CAL; 5G PROT; 4G FAT; 27G CARB; 17MG CHOL; 455MG SOD; 6G FIBER

PAPRIKA MASHED POTATOES

SERVES 6

These mashed potatoes have an old-fashioned flavor, but more color and less fat than your mother's mashed. Instead of paprika, you can add ½ tablespoon of dried thyme, oregano or basil.

6 medium-sized russet potatoes, peeled and cubed

¾ cup plain nonfat yogurt

¼ cup evaporated skim milk or low-fat soymilk

½ tablespoon paprika

Salt to taste

½ teaspoon freshly ground black pepper

1 teaspoon unsalted butter or margarine, melted

1. Cook the potatoes in water to cover until tender, for 20 to 40 minutes. (Timing will depend on size and freshness of the potatoes.) Drain.

2. Combine the potatoes with the yogurt, milk, paprika, salt and pepper in a bowl. Mash with a potato masher, or beat with an electric mixer until smooth. Drizzle the potatoes with the butter, and serve.

PER SERVING: 142 CAL; 3G PROT; 1G FAT; 30G CARB; 4MG CHOL; 412MG SOD; 3G FIBER

BROILED POTATO "CROQUETTES" WITH ORANGE AND NUTMEG

SERVES 6

This low-fat dish is also good made with sweet potatoes: Use 1½ pounds sweet potatoes and 1½ pounds boiling potatoes instead of just the boiling potatoes.

3 pounds boiling potatoes, peeled and quartered

½ cup egg substitute or 2 large eggs

2 tablespoons margarine

2 teaspoons grated orange zest

2 teaspoons salt, or to taste

¼ teaspoon ground white pepper

⅛ teaspoon ground nutmeg

1. Cook the potatoes in water to cover for 20 to 40 minutes, or until tender. (Timing will depend on size and freshness of the potatoes.) Drain, and set aside.

2. Put the potatoes through a food mill or potato ricer to make a smooth paste. Transfer to a bowl. Add the egg substitute, margarine, zest, salt, pepper and nutmeg. Beat with an electric mixer or by hand until light and fluffy. Let cool.

3. Preheat the broiler. Spray a baking sheet with nonstick cooking spray, and set aside.

4. Fit a pastry bag with a large star-shaped tip, and fill it about three-quarters full with the potato mixture. Or cut the corner off a quart-size sturdy food storage plastic bag, and fit with a star-shaped tip. Fill the bag with the potato mixture.

5. Squeeze out rows of 3-inch-long logs onto the baking sheet, refilling the bag as needed until all of the potato mixture is used up. Spray the surface of the logs with cooking spray to keep a crust from forming.

6. Broil just until the ridges on the logs turn deep brown. Remove from the oven, and serve warm.

PER SERVING: 292 CAL; 6G PROT; 4G FAT; 58G CARB; 0MG CHOL; 789MG SOD; 6G FIBER

BAKED POTATO AND APPLES "ANNA"

SERVES 6

This layered dish is a simple, satisfying mixture of apples, potatoes and onions.

2 pounds red-skinned or white boiling potatoes, sliced ¼ inch thick

Salt and freshly ground black pepper to taste

1 red onion, chopped

2 large crisp, sweet apples, cored and sliced ¼ inch thick

Freshly grated nutmeg

1. Preheat the oven to 350F. Oil the bottom and sides of a large, cast-iron skillet or baking dish.

2. Arrange a layer of potatoes in the skillet. Sprinkle with the salt, pepper and half of the onions. Place a layer of apples on top, using half of the apples. Repeat the layers, ending with a layer of apple slices. Sprinkle with the nutmeg, and press down the mixture with a plate. Remove the plate.

3. Bake for 35 to 40 minutes, or until the apples are tender and the potatoes are crispy and brown. Let cool for 10 minutes before cutting into wedges. Serve warm.

PER SERVING: 208 CAL; 3G PROT; 2G FAT; 45G CARB; 0MG CHOL; 190MG SOD; 5G FIBER

POTATO KNISHES

Knishes are savory pastries traditionally filled with mashed potatoes and onions. Enjoy them as an appetizer, snack or side dish. Do not whip the potatoes—you want them to be somewhat lumpy.

2 tablespoons oil, unsalted butter, margarine or a combination

2 large onions, chopped

4 large russet potatoes, baked

1 large egg or ¼ cup egg substitute

Pinch ground nutmeg

Salt and ground white pepper to taste

12 sheets thawed phyllo dough

4 tablespoons (½ stick) unsalted butter or margarine, melted

½ cup fresh breadcrumbs (see page 46), toasted

1. Heat the oil in a skillet over medium heat, and add the onions. Reduce the heat to medium-low, and cook, stirring frequently, for about 10 minutes, or until the onions are browned. Remove from the heat, and let cool slightly.

2. Meanwhile, peel the potatoes, and mash them with a fork or put them through a ricer.

3. Combine the potatoes and onions in a bowl, and stir in the egg, nutmeg, salt and pepper.

4. Preheat the oven to 375F. Spray a baking sheet with nonstick cooking spray, and set aside.

5. Unroll the phyllo, and carefully peel apart 12 sheets. Freeze the remaining phyllo for another use. Cover 6 sheets with a damp tea towel to prevent drying. Working with 1 sheet at a time, brush the sheet of phyllo lightly with the melted butter. Quickly lay the second sheet on top, and brush it with butter. Continue this process with the remaining 4 sheets.

6. Sprinkle half of the breadcrumbs over the phyllo, and spoon half of the potato-onion mixture in a ribbon across the width, about 4 inches in from the edge. Fold this 4-inch edge over to cover the filling, and roll into a cylinder. Carefully transfer the filled roll to the baking sheet. Repeat the procedure with the remaining 6 sheets of phyllo, breadcrumbs and potato-onion mixture.

7. Use a very sharp knife to cut partially through the rolls at 2-inch intervals, leaving the rolls intact and being careful not to separate the slices. Brush the tops very lightly with melted butter.

8. Bake until golden brown, for 30 to 40 minutes. Remove from the oven, and serve.

PER KNISH: 182 CAL; 3G PROT; 6G FAT; 28G CARB; 24MG CHOL; 175MG SOD; 2G FIBER

GRATIN OF YAMS AND PINEAPPLE

A gratin can be a dish cooked with lots of cheese or one cooked in a gratin *dish. In France, alternating slices of several vegetables such as tomatoes, peppers and squash are arranged in an oval gratin, drizzled with olive oil, seasoned with garlic and herbs and baked. This recipe is based on that idea. In North America, yams and sweet potatoes are the same vegetable—the name "yam" comes from mistakenly calling the New World sweet potatoes yams because they resemble the South African yam. Red Garnet sweet potatoes make this a colorful and delicious dish.*

1½ pounds red sweet potatoes or yams

½ large fresh pineapple

5 tablespoons margarine, melted

1 teaspoon salt

1 teaspoon ground cinnamon

½ teaspoon freshly ground black pepper

1. Preheat the oven to 350F.

2. Peel the sweet potatoes, and cut them into ½-inch-thick slices. Peel and core the pineapple, cut it in half lengthwise and slice it very thinly.

3. Brush an oval gratin or other shallow baking dish with 1 tablespoon of the margarine. Alternate slices of sweet potatoes and pineapple to fill the dish. Mix the remaining 4 tablespoons of margarine with the salt, cinnamon and pepper, and drizzle it evenly over the sweet potatoes and pineapple.

4. Bake until very tender, for about 1 hour. Remove from the oven, and serve hot.

PER SERVING: 170 CAL; 2G PROT; 10G FAT; 20G CARB; 0MG CHOL; 520MG SOD; 3G FIBER

MEMPHIS-STYLE SWEET POTATO PUDDING

Boiling the sweet potatoes rather than baking them is important—this makes them very soft and puddinglike. If you do bake or microwave them, the texture won't be as good, but the flavor will still be great.

2 pounds sweet potatoes, peeled and cut into 1-inch cubes

1 cup ground pecans

½ cup (1 stick) unsalted butter, at room temperature

⅓ cup packed brown sugar or maple sugar

¼ teaspoon grated nutmeg

1. Preheat the oven to 350F.

2. Boil the sweet potatoes in water to cover for 20 minutes, or until they are very tender when pierced with a fork. Drain. Place in a 2-quart casserole.

3. Meanwhile, mix together the pecans, butter and sugar. Spoon the mixture onto the potatoes.

4. Bake for 20 minutes, or until heated through and lightly browned on top. Serve hot.

PER SERVING: 510 CAL; 5G PROT; 43G FAT; 32G CARB; 40MG CHOL; 140MG SOD; 7G FIBER

SPICED SWEET POTATO AND RUTABAGA GRATIN

Offer this hearty mixture as an accompaniment for an autumnal meal. The lemon juice adds a welcome tartness.

½ medium-sized rutabaga, peeled and cut into ¼-inch slices

2 medium-sized carrots, diagonally sliced

2 large sweet potatoes, peeled, cut into ¼-inch slices and put in cold water until ready to use

3 tablespoons vegetable oil

1 medium-sized onion, chopped

3 cloves garlic, minced

1-inch piece fresh ginger, chopped or grated

1 teaspoon ground turmeric

1 teaspoon coriander seeds, lightly crushed

3 teaspoons cumin seeds, lightly crushed

2 teaspoons fresh lemon juice

⅓ cup sunflower seeds

1. Preheat the oven to 400F.

2. Bring a large pot of lightly salted water to a boil. When the water boils, add the rutabaga, carrots and sweet potatoes, and cook for 5 minutes. Drain, reserving about ½ cup of the cooking liquid.

3. Heat the oil in a Dutch oven over medium heat. Add the onion, garlic, ginger and turmeric, and cook, stirring often, for 3 to 4 minutes. Add the coriander and cumin seeds to the mixture, and add the drained vegetables. Toss gently for 5 minutes, or until heated through. Pour the ½ cup of reserved cooking liquid over the vegetables, and sprinkle the lemon juice over the top. Cover.

4. Bake for 1 hour. Remove the cover. Scatter the sunflower seeds over the top, and bake, uncovered, 10 minutes more, or until the top is browned. Serve warm.

PER SERVING: 186 CAL; 4G PROT; 11G FAT; 20G CARB; 0MG CHOL; 25MG SOD; 4G FIBER

SWEET POTATO STIR-FRY

The natural sweetness of sweet potatoes is a foil for the mild bitterness of the bok choy. Serve as an accompaniment to jasmine rice or whole wheat noodles.

1 pound extra-firm tofu

2 medium sweet potatoes, peeled

1 pound baby bok choy, rinsed and drained

12 ounces broccolini, ends trimmed

6 scallions

5 tablespoons vegetable oil, divided

2 tablespoons dark sesame oil, divided

¼ cup mirin

⅓ cup low-sodium soy sauce

3 tablespoons rice wine vinegar

1 ½ teaspoons cornstarch

3 ¼-inch slices peeled fresh ginger, minced

1 large clove garlic, minced

¼ teaspoon crushed red pepper, optional

1. Slice the tofu in half horizontally, and place on several layers of paper towels. Lay several more sheets of paper towels on top of the tofu, and press out any excess moisture. Cut the tofu into ½-inch-long slices. Set aside.

2. Cut the sweet potatoes lengthwise into ¼-inch-thick slices. Stack the slices, and cut into ½-inch-long slices on the diagonal. Set aside. Trim the ends of the bok choy, and discard. Cut the stalks and leaves into 1-inch-wide slices on the diagonal. Set aside. Cut the broccolini into 1-inch-long slices on the diagonal. Set aside. Cut the scallions, white parts and about 4 inches of the green, into 1-inch-long slices on the diagonal. Set aside

3. Heat 3 tablespoons of the vegetable oil and 1 tablespoon of the sesame oil in a very large skillet or wok over medium heat. Add the sweet potatoes, and cook, stirring occasionally, for 6 to 10 minutes, or until almost cooked through. Remove from the pan.

4. Meanwhile, mix the mirin, soy sauce, vinegar and cornstarch, and set aside. Heat the remaining 2 tablespoons of vegetable oil and the remaining 1 table-spoon of sesame oil in the skillet or wok, and add the tofu. Cook for about 3 minutes on each side, or until light golden brown. Set aside, and keep warm.

5. Combine the bok choy, broccolini, scallions, sweet potatoes and tofu in the skillet, and stir-fry for 2 minutes more, or until crisp-tender. Add the ginger and garlic, and cook for 1 minute more, or until just fragrant. Add the mirin mixture, and cook for about 30 seconds, or until slightly thickened. Sprinkle with crushed red pepper, if using. Serve hot.

PER SERVING: 450 CAL; 16G PROT; 26G FAT; 37G CARB; 0MG CHOL; 900MG SOD; 5G FIBER

BARLEY CROQUETTES

This side dish calls for barley flakes, a quick-cooking form of barley. Herbes de Provence is a mixture of seasonings that usually includes basil, sage, rosemary, and other herbs (see page 462).

1 tablespoon vegetable shortening

⅔ cup chopped onion

1 clove garlic, chopped

1 pinch herbes de Provence

1 teaspoon low-sodium tamari soy sauce

Salt and freshly ground black pepper to taste

3 slices whole wheat bread, cubed

¼ cup plus 1 tablespoon breadcrumbs (see page 46)

¼ cup cubed firm tofu

1 ounce nutritional yeast

¼ cup grated Swiss cheese

3 ounces barley flakes

1 large egg, beaten

2 tablespoons vegetable oil

1. Heat the shortening in a large saucepan over low heat. Add the onion, garlic, herbes de Provence, tamari soy sauce, salt and pepper. Mix, and cook for 8 minutes, or until the onions are soft.

2. Put the mixture into a mixing bowl, and add the bread, breadcrumbs, tofu, yeast and cheese. Using an electric mixer, beat until well blended. Stir in the barley flakes, then stir in the egg until well blended.

3. Shape the mixture into 3-inch rounds. Heat the oil in a large skillet over medium heat. When hot, pan-fry the patties until browned on both sides. Remove from the heat, drain on paper towels and serve.

PER SERVING: 300 CAL; 12G PROT; 15G FAT; 33G CARB; 60MG CHOL; 260MG SOD; 7G FIBER

CORN CUSTARD

A sturdy side dish, this complements Southwestern entrées and is especially welcome at holiday meals.

8 cups canned, fresh or frozen corn kernels

4 cups minced zucchini

1 cup canned diced mild green chiles

2 cloves garlic, minced

3 cups crushed tortilla chips

1 pound shredded cheddar cheese

4 large eggs, beaten

2 cups soymilk or whole milk

Salt to taste

1 cup finely ground unsalted pumpkin seeds

1. Preheat the oven to 350F.

2. Put the corn, zucchini, chiles, garlic and 2 cups of the crushed tortilla chips in a 6-quart ovenproof casserole. Stir in the cheese.

3. Beat the eggs and the milk together, pour over the corn mixture and stir together. Mix together the remaining 1 cup of crushed tortilla chips and the pumpkin seeds. Spread over the top of the corn mixture.

4. Bake for 1 hour, or until the custard is set. Remove from the oven, and serve.

PER SERVING: 510 CAL; 25G PROT; 29G FAT; 45G CARB; 110MG CHOL; 390MG SOD; 6G FIBER

KABOCHA-CORN CUSTARD

This very homey dish may be made with any of the winter squash, though the Japanese kabocha squash, with its fine texture and sweet flavor, is especially good.

1 kabocha squash, halved and seeded

1 tablespoon unsalted butter or vegetable oil

1½ cups diced onion

1 cup diced green bell pepper

2 teaspoons minced garlic

1½ cups canned, fresh or frozen corn kernels

1 cup crushed corn tortilla chips

1 cup shredded pepper Jack cheese

2 cups whole milk

4 large eggs, beaten

1 teaspoon salt

1 teaspoon freshly ground black pepper

½ teaspoon ground cumin

1. Preheat the oven to 350F. Butter a 9 x 13–inch baking dish, and set aside.

2. Place the squash halves, cut sides down, on a baking sheet. Bake for about 35 minutes, or until the squash pierces easily with a knife. Remove from the oven, and cool. When cool enough to handle, use a spoon to scoop out the squash in small pieces, and put the pieces in a bowl.

3. Heat the butter in a large skillet over medium heat, and sauté the onion, bell pepper and garlic until the onion is translucent and the vegetables are soft, for about 7 minutes. Remove from the heat, and combine with the squash. Add the corn, tortilla chips and cheese, and toss well. Put the mixture in the baking dish. Beat together the milk, eggs, salt, pepper and cumin. Pour the milk mixture over the squash mixture.

4. Bake for 1 hour, or until browned on the top and the custard is set. Remove from the oven, cool for 10 minutes and cut into squares to serve.

PER SERVING: 380 CAL; 16G PROT; 18G FAT; 41G CARB; 170MG CHOL; 720MG SOD; 5G FIBER

CLASSIC BAKED BEANS

Homemade baked beans take a bit of effort to make, but the payoff is grand. They're delicious at summer barbecues, of course, but yummy in cooler weather, too. Baked beans will keep up to 5 days in the refrigerator, and they reheat beautifully in the microwave oven.

1½ cups dried Great Northern beans, rinsed and picked over, or 3 cups canned beans

1 large onion, thinly sliced

2 tablespoons molasses or maple syrup

1 tablespoon cider vinegar

1 tablespoon tomato paste

1 teaspoon dry mustard

Pinch cayenne or white pepper

Salt to taste

1. If using dried beans, put them in a large saucepan and add enough water to cover by 3 inches. Soak for 8 hours or overnight in the refrigerator. Drain, and discard the soaking water.

2. Return the beans to the pot and add 3½ cups of fresh water. Bring to a boil, reduce the heat to low and cook for 2 to 2½ hours, or until tender. Drain, reserving ½ cup of the bean-cooking liquid. If using canned beans, let them drain in a colander set over a bowl, and reserve the bean liquid. Rinse the beans.

3. Preheat the oven to 350F.

4. Combine all the ingredients in a baking dish, and stir well. Cover, and bake for 30 minutes. Uncover, and bake for 30 minutes more, or until bubbly and browned.

PER SERVING: 136 CAL; 8G PROT; 0.8G FAT; 26 CARB; 0MG CHOL; 145MG SOD; 8G FIBER

BLACK-EYED PEAS WITH TOMATOES AND HERBS

SERVES 6

Black-eyed peas are a favorite in the South, but just about everyone else likes them, too. Seasoned with herbs and spices, these black-eyed peas are delicious with warm brown or white rice.

3 cups dried black-eyed peas

1 large onion, chopped

1 cup chopped green bell pepper

2 small bay leaves

1 teaspoon ground cumin

2 cups chopped fresh tomatoes or crushed canned tomatoes

1 tablespoon olive oil

1 teaspoon salt

Pinch cayenne pepper

1. Put the beans in a pot, and add enough water to cover by 3 inches. Soak for 8 hours or overnight in the refrigerator. Drain.

2. Return the beans to the pot, and add 6 cups of fresh water. Cover, and bring to a boil. Reduce the heat to low, and add the onion, bell pepper, bay leaves and cumin. Return to a boil, and cook for 45 minutes to 1 hour, or until the beans are tender.

3. Remove and discard the bay leaves. Stir in the tomatoes, oil, salt and cayenne pepper. Cook until heated through. Serve warm over cooked rice.

PER SERVING: 223 CAL; 14G PROT; 4G FAT; 35G CARB; 0MG CHOL; 67MG SOD; 22G FIBER

FETA-PUMPKIN CASSEROLE

SERVES 4

Low in fat and high in vitamin A, this side dish is delicious in fall when pumpkins are at their peak.

¼ cup dry sherry or apple juice

1 cup chopped onion

2 cups peeled and cubed fresh pumpkin

1 medium-sized tomato, diced

1 small zucchini, sliced

3 cloves garlic, minced

½ cup low-fat buttermilk

½ cup nonfat plain yogurt

1 large egg plus 2 large egg whites, lightly beaten

½ cup toasted soft breadcrumbs (see page 46)

¼ cup (1 ounce) crumbled feta cheese

½ teaspoon ground coriander

⅛ teaspoon cayenne

1. Preheat the oven to 375F. Lightly oil a 2-quart baking dish, and set aside.

2. Heat the sherry in a nonstick skillet over medium-high heat. Add the onion and cook, stirring frequently, until the onion is soft, for 2 to 5 minutes. Add the pumpkin, tomato, zucchini and garlic. Cook, stirring, for 2 minutes more. Set aside.

3. Whisk together the buttermilk, yogurt, egg and egg whites in a bowl. Add the breadcrumbs, feta, coriander, cayenne and the sautéed vegetables. Mix well, and spoon into the baking dish.

4. Bake until firm, for about 25 minutes. Remove from the oven, and serve hot.

PER SERVING: 198 CAL; 12G PROT; 4G FAT; 26G CARB; 52MG CHOL; 300MG SOD; 2G FIBER

BASIC POLENTA

These are the basic proportions for making polenta, which can change character according to the kind of cornmeal used and the ratio of cornmeal to water. Polenta should be stirred almost continuously, though you can be somewhat more relaxed about it if you use a nonstick saucepan. As polenta starts to thicken, it tends to splatter, so wear an oven mitt. Once it is quite thick, it is less likely to jump out of the pan.

1 ¼ teaspoons salt

1 ½ cups yellow cornmeal

1 tablespoon olive oil or unsalted
   butter

1. Bring 4½ cups of cold water and the salt to a boil in a nonstick saucepan over medium heat. Gradually add the cornmeal, stirring almost continuously with a wire whisk. When the mixture starts to thicken, stir in the oil with a wooden spoon.

2. Reduce the heat to low. Continue to stir for about 30 minutes, or until the polenta is quite thick and creamy, taking care to scrape the entire bottom and sides of the pan, for about 30 minutes.

SOFT VERSION: Serve at once, use in recipes as directed, or hold over a pan of simmering water for up to 1 hour.

FIRM VERSION: Immediately scrape the warm mixture into a lightly oiled 9 x 5–inch loaf pan. Cool to room temperature, about 30 minutes. Cover with plastic wrap, and refrigerate overnight.

PER SERVING: 150 CAL; 3G PROT; 3G FAT; 27G CARB; 0MG CHOL; 490MG SOD; 3G FIBER

SOFT POLENTA WITH RED PEPPER SAUCE

Polenta can be a meal by itself but it is also a hearty side dish. Try serving this version with grilled portobello mushrooms (page 179).

Sauce

2 tablespoons olive oil

1 cup chopped onion

3 tablespoons crushed garlic

1 large tomato, seeded and chopped

1 teaspoon salt

1 teaspoon cayenne

1 teaspoon granulated sugar

2 cups roasted and seeded red bell
   pepper (see page 46)

Polenta

1 ½ cups coarse stone-ground yellow
   cornmeal

2 teaspoons salt

2 tablespoons unsalted butter

1. To make the Sauce: Heat a 2-quart saucepan over medium heat. Add the oil, onion and garlic, and sauté until the onion is golden and transparent. Add the tomato, salt, cayenne and sugar, and bring to a boil. Cook for 15 minutes.

2. Put the tomato mixture and the bell peppers into a food processor, and purée until smooth. Taste, and adjust the seasoning. The recipe may be done to this point a day ahead.

3. To make the Polenta: Mix the cornmeal with 5 cups of cold water in a 3-quart saucepan. Add the salt. Bring to a boil over medium-high heat. Reduce the heat to medium-low, and cook, stirring constantly using a long-handled wooden spoon, for 20 to 30 minutes. If the polenta becomes too stiff before 20 minutes, add boiling water in small amounts. When the polenta is done, it will be thick and creamy. Add the butter, and, if necessary, some hot water to thin. The perfect soft polenta will mound up slightly when spooned into a bowl.

4. Reheat the sauce. Spoon about 1 cup of polenta into a large soup bowl or onto a plate. Spoon some sauce over each serving.

PER SERVING: 220 CAL; 4G PROT; 10G FAT; 32G CARB; 0MG CHOL; 1,220MG SOD; 4G FIBER

APACHE POLENTA

Every cuisine that uses cornmeal makes cornmeal mush or polenta. To stretch it or to season it, other ingredients are often added. Polenta is a great side dish for a dinner of greens or vegetable stews. For special presentations, cooled and sliced polenta may be cut into fancy shapes, such as diamonds or triangles, before grilling or frying.

2 large onions

4 poblano chiles or 2 cups canned roasted chiles

2 cups coarse stone-ground yellow cornmeal

2 teaspoons salt

4 fresh sage leaves, chopped, or 2 teaspoons dried sage

4 tablespoons olive oil or unsalted butter

1. Prepare a hot charcoal fire, or preheat a gas grill to medium-high. Alternatively, preheat the broiler. Line a large loaf pan with wax paper or plastic wrap. Slice the onions ½ inch thick. Grill the slices until the onions are charred on the outside and soft throughout. Cool, and coarsely chop.

2. Place the poblanos on the grill or under the broiler, and char the skin on all sides. Place the chiles in a paper bag, and let sit until cool. Peel or rub off the skin, and remove the stem and seeds. Chop.

3. Mix the cornmeal with 6 cups of cold water in a 3-quart saucepan. Add the salt. Bring to a boil. Reduce the heat to medium-low, and cook, stirring constantly with a long-handled wooden spoon, for 20 to 30 minutes. If the polenta becomes too stiff before 20 minutes, add boiling water in small amounts. When the polenta is done, it will be thick enough to hold the spoon upright.

4. When the polenta has finished cooking, add the sage, and stir together. Pour the polenta into the loaf pan. Cover, and chill.

5. Just before serving, cut the polenta into ½-inch-thick slices. Heat the oil in a large skillet over medium heat, and fry the polenta slices on both sides until crisp and golden.

PER SERVING: 200 CAL; 4G PROT; 8G FAT; 31G CARB; 0MG CHOL; 660MG SOD; 5G FIBER

CHIPOTLE POLENTA

This soft polenta is a great side dish for black beans or pinto beans. Dried chipotle chile flakes are offered by several spice companies. If you can't find them locally, try locating them on the Internet. If the polenta splashes and burns your hand as you stir, wrap your hand with a dishtowel.

2 cups coarse stone-ground yellow cornmeal

2 teaspoons salt

1 tablespoon dried chipotle chile flakes

3 tablespoons unsalted butter

1. Mix the cornmeal with 6 cups of cold water in a 3-quart saucepan. Add the salt and chipotle. Bring to a boil. Reduce the heat to medium-low, and cook, stirring constantly with a long-handled wooden spoon, for 20 to 30 minutes. If the polenta becomes too stiff before 20 minutes, add boiling water in small amounts. When the polenta is done it will be thick enough to hold the spoon upright.

2. Just before serving, thin as needed with hot water, and stir in the butter.

PER SERVING: 200 CAL; 4G PROT; 7G FAT; 32G CARB; 15MGCHOL; 860MG SOD; 4G FIBER

BAKED BEANS WITH MUSTARD AND TOMATOES

This tangy-sweet dish takes advantage of two veteran convenience foods: canned beans and canned stewed tomatoes.

2 medium-sized onions, chopped

3 16-ounce cans vegetarian baked beans, rinsed and drained

1 16-ounce can stewed tomatoes

1 16-ounce can red kidney beans, rinsed and drained

1 cup packed brown sugar

2 tablespoons prepared mustard

1 tablespoon cider vinegar

1. Spray a skillet with nonstick cooking spray. Add the onions and 2 tablespoons of water, and cook, stirring frequently, over medium-high heat until the water has evaporated and the onions are softened, about 5 minutes.

2. Stir in the remaining ingredients. Cover, and cook for 20 minutes, or until heated through. Serve warm.

PER SERVING: 345 CAL; 11G PROT; 0.8G FAT; 36G CARB; 0MG CHOL; 1,127MG SOD; 17G FIBER

GREEN RICE ·

You can fire this up by adding more jalapeño chiles, if you wish. This would be good with black beans baked with cheese and a side of hot tortillas.

1½ cups packed minced fresh parsley

1 bunch watercress

2 jalapeño chiles, seeded and minced

2 teaspoons minced garlic

2 teaspoons salt

1 teaspoon freshly ground black pepper

½ teaspoon white pepper

3 tablespoons vegetable oil

3 cups uncooked long-grain rice

6 cups Vegetable Stock (page 332)

1. Put the parsley, watercress, jalapeños and garlic in a food processor, and chop very finely. Add the salt and both peppers.

2. Preheat the oven to 350F.

3. Heat the oil in a 4-quart Dutch oven or other ovenproof baking dish, and sauté the rice, stirring well, until it is coated with oil and beginning to brown. Add the greens mixture and Vegetable Stock, stirring well.

4. Bake for 45 minutes, or until the liquid is absorbed and the rice is tender. Remove from the oven, and serve.

PER SERVING: 290 CAL; 6G PROT; 4.5G FAT; 54G CARB; 0MG CHOL; 880MG SOD; 2G FIBER

Grilled Asparagus Bruschetta, page 58

▲ Lavender Lemonade, page 78
◄ Savory Farro Cake, page 68

▲ Banana-Applesauce Muffins, page 127
▶ Norwegian Winter Fruit Salad, page 155

▲ Afghani Squash Casserole, page 213
◀ Springtime Layered Egg and Asparagus Salad, page 158

Wild Mushroom Ragu, page 218

vegetable main courses

SALADS AND SOUPS MAY PLAY A SUPPORTING role at mealtimes, but it is the entrée, the main dish, that really takes center stage. Whatever you, the cook, select as the meal's focus automatically sets the tone for what precedes and what follows during the meal. In this selection of recipes, you'll find luscious vegetable-based dishes that range from the very basic to the more sophisticated, with a collection of flavors and ingredients from around the world—showing off the versatility of the earth's amazing bounty.

COLCANNON

The Irish have made an art of cooking the potato. This recipe may be the epitome of that art. It can be made very rich with lots of cream and butter, but the truth is that there is a richness in the combination of cabbage, leeks and potatoes that needs little help. Russet potatoes are good for this recipe, though any all-purpose potato will do. Serve as a complete meal with a salad and Irish soda bread.

1 pound young green cabbage, halved, cored and diced

4 pounds russet potatoes, peeled and quartered

8 ounces leeks white parts only

2 cups evaporated skim milk, undiluted

2 teaspoons salt

1 teaspoon pepper

¼ teaspoon grated nutmeg

4 tablespoons (½ stick) soy margarine

1. Put the cabbage in a 3-quart saucepan, and cover with water. Bring to a boil, and cook until very tender, for 45 minutes.

2. Put the potatoes in a 4-quart saucepan with water to cover. Bring to a boil, and cook for 20 to 40 minutes, or until the potatoes are very tender. (Timing will depend on size and freshness of the potatoes.)

3. Meanwhile, cut the white parts of the leeks in half lengthwise, and slice thinly. Place the leeks in a bowl of water, and swish to remove any sand or dirt. Remove the leeks from the water, empty the bowl, rinse and refill. Place the leeks in the water again, and repeat. Drain.

4. Put the leeks in a 2-quart saucepan, and add the evaporated milk, salt, pepper and nutmeg. Boil for about 10 minutes, or until the leeks are tender.

5. Preheat the oven to 350F. Butter a 3-quart baking dish.

6. Drain the potatoes, and mash them with an electric mixer. Add the leeks and milk, and stir with a spoon. Drain the cabbage, and fold it into the potatoes. Taste, and adjust the seasonings as needed.

7. Put the mixture into the baking dish, and use a fork to draw a pattern across the top. Dot with bits of the margarine. The Colcannon may be made to this point and refrigerated, covered, for several days until needed, if desired.

8. Bake for about 1 hour, or until heated through and golden on top. Remove from the oven, and serve hot.

PER SERVING: 240 CAL; 8G PROT; 5G FAT; 41G CARB; 0MG CHOL; 600MG SOD; 4G FIBER

MOUNTAIN STEW

Serve this hearty dish with plenty of crusty bread. If you plan to be sledding or skiing all day, use a slow cooker instead of the stovetop. To use the slow cooker, proceed as the recipe directs until you are ready to add the rice, then transfer the mixture to the slow cooker, and add rice, beans and Vegetable Stock. Cover, and cook for 6 hours.

1 cup dried kidney beans or about 3 cups cooked, rinsed and drained

2 tablespoons olive oil

1 large onion, thinly sliced

4 large cloves garlic, minced

1 16-ounce can tomatoes with juice

1 green bell pepper, seeded and coarsely chopped

1 cup coarsely chopped green cabbage

½ cup diced russet potatoes

1 tablespoon chili powder, or more to taste

½ teaspoon ground cumin

4 cups Vegetable Stock (page 332) or water

⅓ cup uncooked brown rice

Salt and freshly ground black pepper to taste

¼ cup grated jalapeño-flavored Monterey Jack cheese or pepper Jack cheese, optional

1. Put the beans in a bowl with enough cold water to cover beans by 3 inches. Soak 8 hours or overnight in the refrigerator, and drain. Rinse, and set aside.

2. Heat the oil in a large pot over medium-high heat. Add the onion and garlic, and cook, stirring frequently, for 3 to 5 minutes, or until the onion is soft. Add the tomatoes with juices, bell pepper, cabbage, potatoes, chili powder and cumin. Continue cooking, stirring frequently, for 3 minutes.

3. Add the Vegetable Stock, rice and beans. Cover, and cook over low heat about 2 hours, or until the stew is thick and the beans and rice are tender. Season with salt and pepper. Top with the cheese, if using, and serve hot.

PER SERVING: 356 CAL; 17G PROT; 7G FAT; 59G CARB; 0MG CHOL; 155MG SOD; 15G FIBER

NUTTY LENTIL LOAF

This one-dish meal is perfect for a nutritious supper at the table, or wrap it up and take it on a hike. On the trail, slice and serve the loaf as is, or use the slices in sandwiches.

1 cup uncooked lentils, rinsed

1 tablespoon vegetable oil

½ cup chopped onion

2 cloves garlic, minced

⅔ cup chopped carrot

⅓ cup chopped celery

¾ cup unsalted raw cashews, chopped

¼ cup raisins

2 large eggs, lightly beaten

2 tablespoons whole wheat flour

1 teaspoon dried thyme

1. Put the lentils in a saucepan, and add enough water to cover by 3 inches. Cook over medium-low heat until the lentils are tender, for about 45 minutes. Drain, and set aside.

2. Heat the oil in a saucepan or skillet over medium heat. Add the onion and garlic, and cook, stirring frequently, for about 10 minutes, or until the onion is translucent. Add the carrot and celery. Cook, covered, until the carrots are tender, for 10 to 15 minutes. Remove from the heat, and let cool.

3. Preheat the oven to 350F. Oil a 9 x 5–inch loaf pan.

4. Mix the lentils, sautéed vegetables, cashews, raisins, eggs, flour and thyme in a bowl until blended. Spoon into the loaf pan.

5. Bake until firm, for about 45 minutes. Slice, and serve warm

PER SERVING (1 SLICE): 338 CAL; 18G PROT; 11G FAT; 45G CARB; 107MG CHOL; 70MG SOD; 9G FIBER

CURRIED RED LENTILS AND POTATOES

Using commercially packaged, precut, blanched potatoes and split red lentils speeds up the cooking of this typical Indian curry. Otherwise, plan your meal to include a lengthier cooking time if you start with uncooked and uncubed potatoes. Start the meal with Curried Potato-Stuffed Breads (page 72) and end with Rice Pudding with Dates (page 407).

1 cup uncooked red lentils, rinsed

1 teaspoon packed brown sugar

1 teaspoon ground turmeric

3 tablespoons vegetable oil

1 teaspoon mustard seeds

1 dried red chile

1 teaspoon cumin seeds

2 teaspoons minced fresh ginger

1 teaspoon minced garlic

1 ½ pounds precooked, precut baby potatoes

1 teaspoon curry powder, or more to taste

1 cup frozen or fresh peas

Salt to taste

2 cups plain low-fat yogurt, for garnish

3 tablespoons cilantro leaves for garnish

1. Bring 3 cups of water to a boil in a covered saucepan over high heat. Pick over the lentils. When the water begins to boil, stir in the lentils, brown sugar and turmeric, reduce the heat to medium, and cook, stirring occasionally, for 20 to 25 minutes, or until tender.

2. Heat the oil in a large skillet over medium heat. Add the mustard seeds, chile and cumin seeds, and stir-fry for about 1 minute, letting the seeds crackle. Stir in the ginger and garlic, and cook for 1 minute more. Add the potatoes, and stir-fry for 10 minutes, or until the potatoes brown. Add ½ cup of water blended with the curry powder and stir thoroughly. Continue cooking and stirring over medium heat until the water evaporates. Slowly add ½ cup of water, a bit at a time, just until the potatoes are tender.

3. When the lentils are tender, stir them with the peas and potatoes. Add salt to taste, and cook just until the peas are heated through. Serve, garnishing each portion with the yogurt and cilantro.

PER SERVING: 380 CAL; 16G PROT; 9G FAT; 59G CARB; 5MG CHOL; 100MG SOD; 9G FIBER

INDIAN-SPICED YELLOW SPLIT PEAS WITH BRUSSELS SPROUTS

We used the microwave oven to make this dish super fast. Serve with your favorite chutney and cooked rice for a tasty feast.

¾ cup dried yellow split peas, rinsed

1 large tomato, finely chopped

1 teaspoon fresh lemon juice

1 tablespoon vegetable oil

1 teaspoon black mustard seeds

¼ teaspoon fenugreek seeds

2 teaspoons chopped garlic

3 to 4 cups trimmed Brussels sprouts

4 ounces fresh green beans, cut into 1-inch pieces

2 tablespoons chopped cilantro leaves

1. Put the peas in a 2-quart saucepan, and cook according to the package directions. Remove from the heat when tender, and set aside, covered, for 5 minutes.

2. Put the tomato and lemon juice in a food processor or blender, and purée until smooth. Set aside.

3. Combine the oil, mustard seeds and fenugreek seeds in a microwave-proof baking dish and cook, uncovered, at high power for 1 minute. Add the garlic, and cook for 1 minute more. Add the Brussels sprouts and beans, and stir to coat with the oil and spices. Add the tomato purée, cover and cook at high power until the vegetables are just tender, for 6 to 8 minutes, stirring once. Add the peas, cover and cook for 2 minutes more. Let sit, covered, for 2 minutes. Stir in the cilantro, and serve.

PER SERVING: 153 CAL; 8G PROT; 4G FAT; 26G CARB; 0MG CHOL; 30MG SOD; 9G FIBER

CABBAGE LEAVES STUFFED WITH CHICKPEAS, RAISINS AND SPICES

Filling cabbage leaves with something that is both sweet and spicy makes for an appealing entrée that will win admirers from all age groups.

1 medium-sized head red cabbage

5 teaspoons fresh lemon juice, divided

1 tablespoon unsalted butter

1 large red onion, chopped

4 carrots, chopped

1 tablespoon apple cider vinegar

1½ cups cottage cheese

1 cup cooked chickpeas, drained and rinsed

1 small Granny Smith apple, peeled, cored and diced

¼ cup diced dried apples or raisins

2 teaspoons honey

1 teaspoon low-sodium soy sauce

Plain yogurt for topping, optional

1. Bring a large pot of water to a boil. Meanwhile, discard the tough outer cabbage leaves. Remove 2 more leaves, chop and set aside.

2. When the water is boiling, add 3 teaspoons of the lemon juice and the head of cabbage. Reduce the heat to low, and cook for 10 minutes, or until the cabbage is tender. Drain in a colander, and set aside until cool enough to handle.

3. Heat the butter in a large skillet over medium heat until bubbling. Add the onion and carrots, reduce the heat to low, and cook, stirring frequently, until the onion is soft, for about 5 minutes. Add the reserved chopped cabbage, and stir until it starts to wilt, for about 1 minute. Add the vinegar, and stir well. Continue to cook, stirring often, until the carrots are cooked and the onion is softened, for about 10 minutes. (If the mixture sticks, add water 1 tablespoon at a time, being careful not to let water accumulate in the pan.)

4. Combine the onion mixture, cottage cheese, chickpeas, apple, dried fruit, remaining 2 teaspoons of lemon juice, the honey and soy sauce in a bowl. Mix well.

5. Preheat the oven to 425F.

6. Peel off 1 cabbage leaf, and place it on a flat work surface. Place one-quarter of the filling in the center of the leaf. Using your fingers, bend the sides of the leaf over the filling, fold down the top and fold up the bottom to make a package. Place the cabbage roll seam side down in a 9 x 13–inch baking dish. Repeat the procedure until all of the filling is used. Pour ¼ cup water in the baking dish, and cover with foil.

7. Bake for about 20 minutes, or until heated through. Remove the pan from the oven, and let sit, covered, for 10 minutes. Serve warm topped with plain yogurt, if desired.

PER SERVING: 269 CAL; 16G PROT; 7G FAT; 34G CARB; 21MG CHOL; 432MG SOD; 6G FIBER

MUSHROOM BOURGUIGNON IN A WHOLE PUMPKIN

If you've used uncarved pumpkins to decorate the table for Halloween, here's a delicious way to use them after All Souls' Day.

5- to 6-pounds pumpkin or equal weight of kabocha squash

2 large yellow or red onions, chopped

1 pound white button mushrooms, halved

¼ cup unbleached all-purpose flour or whole wheat pastry flour

2 to 2½ cups dry red wine

¼ cup low-sodium soy sauce

3 tablespoons dry sherry

2 tablespoons balsamic vinegar

1 tablespoon honey

4 cloves garlic

½ teaspoon dried rosemary

Freshly ground black pepper to taste

2 to 3 vegetable bouillon cubes, optional

1. Preheat the oven to 350F.

2. Use a very sharp knife to carve a 3- to 4-inch zigzagged circle in the top of the pumpkin, and remove the top. If the peel is too thick to cut easily, bake for 15 to 20 minutes to soften it. Remove the top, discard the seeds and use a large spoon to scrape out the strings.

3. Cook the onions in 2 tablespoons of water in a large skillet for 4 to 5 minutes, or until the onions are soft. Add the mushrooms, cover and cook until they have begun to release their juices, for 3 to 4 minutes. Stir in the flour, and cook for 1 minute. Add 2 cups of the red wine and the remaining ingredients, and cook for 15 minutes, stirring frequently. Pour the stew into the pumpkin, place in a large, shallow dish such as a pie plate and cover with the top of the pumpkin.

4. Bake for about 1 hour, or until the pumpkin is very soft. While baking, stir the stew several times, adding the remaining ½ cup of wine if too much liquid has evaporated or has been absorbed.

5. To serve, spoon out some stew, and scrape out some of the pumpkin onto each plate. Serve hot.

PER SERVING: 157 CAL; 3G PROT; 0.1G FAT; 19G CARB; 0MG CHOL; 696MG SOD; 6G FIBER

ITALIAN STUFFED SQUASH

Hubbard or banana squash is the vessel for a filling of eggplant and other southern Italian ingredients. Add a filling squash-based soup, such as the Butternut Cream Soup (page 300), to start.

1 medium-sized eggplant, peeled and cubed

2 large tomatoes, diced

2 green bell peppers, diced

1 onion, diced

4 cloves garlic, minced

2 tablespoons olive oil

1 tablespoon dried basil

1 large hubbard or banana squash, halved and seeded

½ cup grated Parmesan cheese, optional

1. Preheat the oven to 375F.

2. Mix together the eggplant, tomatoes, bell peppers, onion, garlic, oil and basil. Spoon this mixture into the squash halves, and arrange the squash in a baking pan.

3. Bake for about 1 hour, or until the squash is tender when pierced with a fork. Stir the filling ingredients once with a fork during baking. Sprinkle the cheese, if using, on the squash halves for the last 10 minutes of baking.

4. To serve, scoop out pieces of the squash and filling with a spoon, and put into bowls. Serve hot.

PER SERVING (¼ FILLED SQUASH): 242 CAL; 6G PROT; 12G FAT; 40G CARB; 0MG CHOL; 12MG SOD; 12G FIBER

SOUTHERN INDIAN VEGETABLE CURRY (AVIAL)

This South Indian curry is packed with vegetables. Other vegetables—potatoes, green beans, sweet potatoes, broccoli, eggplant, green plantain and white pumpkin—can be substituted for those listed here. Our recipe calls for tamarind juice and curry leaves, which are available at most Asian and Indian markets as well as some natural foods stores. Be sure to accompany this with steamy-hot Indian basmati rice.

2 large carrots, cut into ¼-inch rounds

2 medium-sized all-purpose potatoes, peeled and cut into 1-inch pieces

½ cup green beans, cut into 1-inch pieces

2 green chiles, split down the middle, optional

1 teaspoon tamarind juice, fresh lemon juice or fresh lime juice

3 tablespoons grated unsweetened coconut

¼ teaspoon ground turmeric

4 curry leaves, optional

¼ teaspoon ground cumin, optional

¼ teaspoon chili powder, optional

½ cup plain yogurt, at room temperature

Salt to taste

1. Combine the vegetables and chiles, if using, in a saucepan, and add ½ cup of water. Cover, and cook over medium heat for about 15 minutes, or until the vegetables are tender but not soft.

2. Add the tamarind juice. Stir in the coconut and turmeric, and the curry leaves, cumin and chili powder, if using. Gradually stir the yogurt into the vegetable mixture. Add salt. If using the curry leaves, remove them before serving. Ladle the mixture over rice, and serve warm.

PER SERVING: 112 CAL; 2G PROT; 4G FAT; 14G CARB; 3MG CHOL; 201MG SOD; 2G FIBER

CURRIED SWEET POTATOES WITH SPINACH AND CHICKPEAS

Always rinse canned chickpeas (and other beans) before using to reduce the sodium content and improve their flavor.

About 2 pounds sweet potatoes, peeled and diced

1 16- to 20-ounce can chickpeas, drained and rinsed

1 14½-ounce can diced tomatoes

10 to 12 ounces fresh spinach, stemmed and coarsely chopped

¼ cup chopped cilantro

2 scallions, thinly sliced

1 to 2 teaspoons curry powder, or to taste

½ teaspoon ground cumin

¼ teaspoon ground cinnamon

Salt to taste

1. Cook the sweet potatoes over boiling water in a large saucepan fitted with a steamer basket. Cover, and cook until just tender, for about 15 minutes.

2. Meanwhile, in another large saucepan, combine the chickpeas, tomatoes and ½ cup of water. Bring to a boil over medium heat. Add the spinach, cover and cook just until wilted, for about 3 minutes.

3. Stir in the sweet potatoes, cilantro, scallions, curry powder, cumin, cinnamon and salt until well combined. Reduce the heat to low and cook, uncovered, until the flavors have blended, for about 5 minutes. Serve hot.

PER SERVING: 278 CAL; 8G PROT; 2G FAT; 59G CARB; 0MG CHOL; 392MG SOD; 9G FIBER

CASHEW, TEMPEH AND CARROT CURRY

Shop carefully for the Thai red curry paste because some contain fish sauce. Most health food stores and supermarkets and some Asian markets sell the same spicy mixture without animal products. You may substitute firm tofu or marinated tofu for the tempeh if you like. This is a spicy dish, so serve it with plenty of Thai jasmine rice.

3 tablespoons canola oil, divided

1 pound five-grain tempeh, cubed

2 tablespoons vegetarian red curry paste

1 tablespoon packed brown sugar

2 cups unsweetened light coconut milk, divided, or 2 cups canned skim milk

1 large onion, coarsely chopped

8 thin slices fresh ginger

3 cloves garlic, thinly sliced

3 serrano chiles, minced, optional

2 cups baby carrots, cooked

5 scallions, cut into 1-inch pieces

1 cup dry-roasted cashews

1. Heat 1½ teaspoons of the oil in a wok over medium-high heat. Sauté the tempeh until golden on all sides, for about 6 minutes. Set aside.

2. Reheat the wok with the remaining 1½ teaspoons of oil over medium heat. Add the curry paste, and stir to combine. Add the brown sugar and 1 cup of the coconut milk. When the oil separates, add the onion, ginger and garlic, and cook until soft, about 5 minutes.

3. Add the tempeh and chiles, if using, and stir-fry for 3 minutes. Add the carrots and the remaining 1 cup of coconut milk, and cook for 10 minutes. Add the scallions and cashews, cook for 5 minutes to heat through, and serve.

PER SERVING: 660 CAL; 26G PROT; 40G FAT; 54G CARB; 0MG CHOL; 210MG SOD; 10G FIBER

CURRIED CHICKPEAS AND SWEET POTATOES

Balance the flavors by keeping an eye on the curry you add. If you don't like the heat, select a mild curry powder, and go easy.

1½ pounds sweet potatoes, peeled and diced to make 5 cups

1 tablespoon olive oil

2 large red bell peppers, diced

1 large onion, diced

2 scallions, chopped

3 cloves garlic, minced

1 tablespoon minced fresh ginger

2 tablespoons curry powder, or to taste

1 teaspoon salt, divided

2 15-ounce cans chickpeas, drained and rinsed

1 tablespoon cider vinegar

⅓ cup chopped cilantro

1. Bring 2 inches of water to a boil in a large saucepan fitted with a steamer basket over high heat. Add the sweet potatoes, cover, and steam until tender, for about 10 minutes. Set aside, and keep warm until needed.

2. Heat the oil in a large, heavy pot over medium heat. Add the bell peppers, onion, scallions, garlic, ginger, curry powder and ½ teaspoon of the salt. Stir, cover and cook for 3 to 5 minutes. Stir in the chickpeas, and cook, uncovered, for 5 minutes. Add the vinegar and the remaining ½ teaspoon of salt. Stir in the sweet potatoes. Reduce the heat to low, and cook, gently stirring the mixture, for about 2 minutes to allow the sweet potatoes to release some of their starch. Be careful not to break them up completely. Add the cilantro, and stir to blend. Serve hot.

PER SERVING: 357 CAL; 11G PROT; 5G FAT; 70G CARB; 0MG CHOL; 802MG SOD; 11G FIBER

Roti is an Indian flat bread, usually baked in the Indian tandoori oven. Pita bread can be substituted for the roti, if desired.

Dough

4 cups all-purpose flour

2 teaspoons baking powder

1 teaspoon salt

¼ cup vegetable oil

Filling

4 cups peeled, seeded and diced butternut squash, pumpkin or calabaza

1 to 2 tablespoons vegetable oil

1 red onion, diced

2 to 3 cloves garlic, minced

1 green chile, seeded and minced, optional

2 tablespoons curry powder

½ tablespoon ground cumin

1 teaspoon dried thyme

1 teaspoon ground cloves

½ teaspoon freshly ground black pepper

¼ teaspoon salt

1¾ cups cooked chickpeas, drained and rinsed

1 tablespoon unsalted butter or vegetable oil, or more if needed

1. To make the Dough: Combine the flour, baking powder and salt in a mixing bowl. Gradually mix in the oil and 1 cup of water. Turn out the dough onto a lightly floured work surface, and knead until smooth and elastic, for about 5 minutes. Form into a ball, cover with a tea towel and let sit for 15 minutes.

2. To make the Filling: Heat the oil in a deep skillet over medium heat. Add the onion, garlic and chile, if using, and cook, stirring frequently, until softened, for about 4 minutes. Add the squash, 2 cups of water, the curry powder, cumin, thyme, cloves, pepper and salt, and cook, stirring occasionally, for about 20 minutes, or until the squash is soft. Add the chickpeas, and cook for 5 to 10 minutes more, stirring occasionally. Set aside.

3. To fill the roti, divide the dough into 4 equal portions. Working with 1 portion at a time, flatten each ball on a lightly floured work surface, and roll out each into a circle 6 to 8 inches in diameter. Place about 1 cup of the filling on 1 side of each circle. Fold the dough over the filling, and pinch the edges to seal.

4. Heat the butter in a skillet over high heat until it sizzles. Reduce the heat to medium, and place a filled roti in the skillet. Cook, uncovered, until the crust is golden, for about 3 minutes. Turn over the roti with a wide spatula, and cook on the other side until golden. Transfer to a platter, and keep warm. Repeat with the remaining rotis, adding more oil or butter as needed. Serve warm.

PER SERVING (1 FILLED ROTI): 783 CAL; 21G PROT; 24G FAT; 123G CARB; 0MG CHOL; 835MG SOD; 8G FIBER

CURRIED BEANS AND GREENS

Here's a hearty one-dish meal that's high in calcium to help prevent cold-weather muscle cramps and rich with warming spices to boost circulation. Small, reddish-brown adzuki beans have a sweet flavor and are popular in Japanese cooking. They have a higher protein content than other beans and are easier to digest.

1 cup adzuki beans, rinsed

1 tablespoon olive oil

½ cup diced onion

2 cloves garlic, minced

2 pounds fresh kale or Swiss chard, stemmed and torn into large pieces

2 teaspoons curry powder

Salt and freshly ground black pepper to taste

1. Soak the beans overnight in enough cold water to cover by at least 2 inches; refrigerate. Drain, rinse the beans well and combine in a large soup pot with 4 cups of water. Bring to a boil, reduce the heat to low and cook, covered, until the beans are tender, for about 1 hour.

2. Meanwhile, heat the oil over medium heat in a large, deep skillet. Add the onion and garlic, and cook, stirring often, until the onion is soft, for about 5 minutes. Add the greens to the skillet. Sprinkle with 2 tablespoons of water. Cook, tossing often, until the greens are bright green and wilted slightly, for about 3 minutes. Remove from the heat.

3. Drain the beans, and transfer them to a serving dish. Add the curry powder, and stir well. Reheat the greens if necessary, add to the beans and toss to mix. Season with salt and pepper, and serve.

PER SERVING: 185 CAL; 10G PROT; 3G FAT; 31G CARB; 0MG CHOL; 37MG SOD; 8G FIBER

MASALA VEGETABLE STEW

Creamy coconut milk makes a delectable base for this delicately curried vegetable melange. For a simple and savory feast, serve with a side dish of bulgur studded with dried fruit bits, a salad of cucumbers and tomatoes in yogurt and warm flatbread.

1 tablespoon vegetable oil

2 medium-sized onions, chopped

2 to 3 cloves garlic, minced

4 medium-sized all-purpose potatoes, peeled and diced

4 carrots, sliced

½ medium-sized head cauliflower, cut into bite-sized pieces

2 cups frozen cut green beans

1 to 2 teaspoons grated fresh ginger

2 fresh mild chiles, seeded and minced

2 teaspoons garam masala (see page 461) or good-quality curry powder, or to taste

1 teaspoon ground coriander

½ teaspoon ground turmeric

1 15-ounce can light coconut milk

Salt to taste

1 cup frozen green peas

¼ teaspoon chopped cilantro

1. Heat the oil in a large soup pot over medium heat. Add the onions and garlic, and cook, stirring often, until the onions are golden. Add the potatoes, carrots and 2 cups of water and bring to a boil. Cover, and cook gently until the potatoes are partially tender, for 10 to 15 minutes. Add the cauliflower, green beans, ginger, chiles, garam masala, coriander and turmeric. Continue to cook gently, covered, until the vegetables are tender, for 20 minutes.

2. Mash some potatoes against the side of the pot with a wooden spoon to help thicken the stew. Stir in the coconut milk, and season to taste with salt. If time allows, let the stew stand for an hour or so before serving.

3. Just before serving, heat the stew, and taste and correct the seasonings. Stir in the peas and cilantro, cook just until the peas are heated through, and serve in shallow bowls.

PER SERVING: 275 CAL; 8G PROT; 11G FAT; 45G CARB; 0MG CHOL; 119MG SOD; 7G FIBER

AFGHANI SQUASH CASSEROLE

Make this very colorful main dish with any one of the winter squashes. The sweet taste of the squash is enhanced by the richness of the tomato sauce and the tartness of the yogurt. Use any plain yogurt, but whole milk yogurt imparts a richer flavor and creamier texture.

2 pounds winter squash, peeled and cut into 2½-inch cubes

4 cups spaghetti sauce

2 teaspoons ground cinnamon

1 teaspoon freshly ground black pepper

¼ teaspoon ground cloves

1½ cups plain yogurt

¼ cup minced scallions

1 tablespoon minced fresh mint or 1 teaspoon dried mint plus extra for garnish

1 teaspoon salt

1. Bring 4 quarts of water to a rapid boil over high heat, add the squash and cook for about 25 minutes, or until tender but not mushy. Remove from the heat, drain and set aside.

2. Meanwhile, heat the spaghetti sauce over medium heat, and add the cinnamon, pepper and cloves. Cook for 10 minutes, or until the sauce reduces to about 3 cups. Mix the yogurt with the scallions, mint and salt, and set aside. Place the squash in a serving dish, and pour the spaghetti sauce over the top, leaving some squash uncovered. Drizzle with the yogurt sauce, and garnish with mint leaves.

PER SERVING: 290 CAL; 10G PROT; 7G FAT; 51G CARB; 5MG CHOL; 1,690MG SOD; 12G FIBER

MEXICAN LASAGNA

If you like Mexican fare, you'll love this Hispanic-inspired dish!

½ to 1 tablespoon olive oil

1 onion, chopped

1 green bell pepper, coarsely chopped

1 to 2 cloves garlic, minced

1 tablespoon chili powder, or to taste

1 teaspoon ground cumin

Pinch cayenne, optional

1 16-ounce can pinto or kidney beans, rinsed and drained

1 cup canned, fresh or frozen corn kernels

1 cup tomato sauce

6 7-inch corn tortillas

1 cup low-fat cottage cheese

½ to 1 cup grated cheddar cheese

1. Heat the oil in a large skillet over medium-high heat. Add the onion, bell pepper and garlic, and cook, stirring frequently, until softened, for about 5 minutes. Stir in the chili powder, cumin and cayenne, and sauté for 1 minute more.

2. Remove from the heat. Add the beans, corn and tomato sauce.

3. Preheat the oven to 350F.

4. Place 3 tortillas in the bottom of a lightly greased 2-quart casserole dish. Add half of the corn-bean mixture, and spread ½ cup of the cottage cheese on top. Sprinkle on half of the cheddar. Repeat the layers until all the ingredients are used up.

5. Bake, uncovered, for 45 minutes, or until heated through. Let sit for 5 minutes before serving.

PER SERVING: 424 CAL; 24G PROT; 10G FAT; 62G CARB; 20MG CHOL; 700MG SOD; 13G FIBER

SPICY STUFFED SWEET POTATOES

SERVES 4

These potatoes can be entrées or side dishes. When you are serving the sweet potatoes as the main course for dinner, leave them whole and pair them with a tart salad, such as the Arugula and Roasted Red Pepper Salad (page 143).

4 medium-sized sweet potatoes

2 large bell peppers, preferably 1 red and 1 yellow or orange

4 tablespoons (½ stick) unsalted butter or margarine

⅛ teaspoon ground cumin, or more to taste

Salt to taste

1½ cups shredded pepper Jack cheese

1 cup sour cream

2 tablespoons fresh lime juice, or more to taste

2 tablespoons minced onion

2 tablespoons minced cilantro

1. Preheat the oven to 350F. Line a large baking pan with aluminum foil.

2. Prick the sweet potatoes, and place them in the prepared pan. Bake for about 1½ hours, or until soft in the center. Remove from the oven, but leave the oven on.

3. Meanwhile, seed and dice the peppers, and set aside. Cut the potatoes in half lengthwise, or leave them whole, and make a slit down the center but not through the bottom. Leaving a thin wall of flesh to retain the shape, scoop out the flesh from the potatoes. Halve the halves or the whole potatoes. Place the jackets back on the baking sheet.

4. Mash the potato flesh using a fork, leaving it chunky, with the butter, cumin and salt to taste. Scoop the mixture back into the potato jackets, distributing the mixture evenly. Sprinkle the stuffed potatoes with the cheese and peppers, reserving some peppers for a final garnish. Bake about 10 minutes, or until the cheese melts.

5. Meanwhile, mix the sour cream with the lime juice, and set aside. Garnish the potatoes with the remaining peppers, the onions, cilantro and lime-flavored sour cream. Serve hot.

PER SERVING (1 FILLED POTATO WITH GARNISHES): 550 CAL; 15G PROT; 37G FAT; 42G CARB; 100MG CHOL; 350MG SOD; 6G FIBER

BLACK BEAN AND CORN ENCHILADAS

SERVES 6

Here's a fresh-tasting Mexican dish that is as satisfying to eat as it is simple to make—a real family pleaser.

1 20-ounce can low-sodium enchilada sauce

2 15-ounce cans black beans, drained and rinsed

2 cups frozen corn kernels

⅓ cup sliced scallions

1 large tomato, chopped

⅓ cup plus 2 tablespoons chopped cilantro

1 teaspoon dried oregano

½ teaspoon ground cumin

Dash ground chipotle, optional

12 6-inch corn tortillas

½ cup shredded cheddar cheese or soy cheese

1. Preheat the oven to 375F. Coat a medium baking dish with a thin layer of enchilada sauce.

2. Combine the beans, corn, scallions and tomato in a large nonstick skillet. Heat over medium-high heat. Add the ⅓ cup cilantro, the oregano, cumin and chipotle, if using. Cook, stirring occasionally, until the mixture is slightly thickened, for 4 to 5 minutes. Remove from the heat.

3. Heat the tortillas on a hot griddle or skillet for about 1 minute, or until soft. Dip the tortillas in the enchilada sauce to lightly coat, and spread with about ¼ cup of the bean mixture. Roll the tortillas and place them seam sides down in the baking dish. Spoon any remaining filling over the enchiladas, and cover with the remaining enchilada sauce. Sprinkle with the cheese.

4. Bake, uncovered, until bubbling, for about 15 minutes. Remove from the oven, sprinkle the enchiladas with the remaining 2 tablespoons of cilantro and serve.

PER ENCHILADA: 235 CAL; 9G PROT; 8G FAT; 34G CARB; 20MG CHOL; 138MG SOD; 7G FIBER

This robust and colorful entrée captures Southwestern flavors in a fall main course that calls for warm fresh flour or corn tortillas, a light tossed salad with avocados and a dessert of cinnamon or caramel ice cream. Baked taco chips are healthy options, because they do not require fat for deep-frying. Plan to use one or all of the topping choices to bolster the pudding's subtle flavors.

Pumpkin-Corn Pudding

3¾ cups crushed, baked blue cornmeal tortilla chips

3 large eggs

2 cups pumpkin purée

4 ounces canned chopped mild green chiles

1 cup canned, fresh or frozen corn kernels

1 teaspoon chili powder, or to taste

½ teaspoon ground cumin

Salt and freshly ground black pepper to taste

Hot pepper sauce to taste, optional

Toppings

1 cup salsa

1 cup cilantro

1 avocado, peeled and sliced

1 ripe tomato, thinly sliced

1. Preheat the oven to 400F. Spray a 2-quart baking dish with nonstick cooking spray.

2. To make the Pumpkin-Corn Pudding: Layer the crushed corn chips in the bottom of the baking dish. Beat the eggs in a bowl until foamy. Fold in the pumpkin purée, chiles and corn. Stir in the chili powder, cumin, salt, pepper and hot pepper sauce, if using. Spoon into the baking dish, and smooth it over the chips.

3. Bake for 20 minutes. Remove from the oven, garnish with toppings as desired and serve while hot.

PER SERVING: 390 CAL; 12G PROT; 20G FAT; 49G CARB; 160MG CHOL; 580MG SOD; 11G FIBER

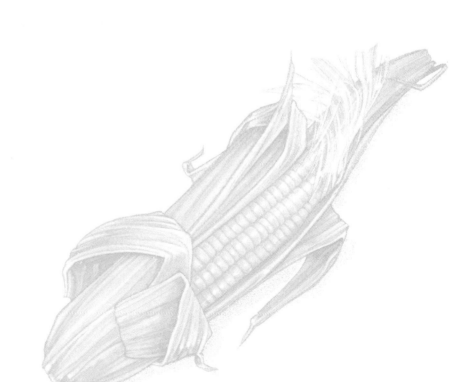

MUSHROOM CHILI STEW

Here's a delicious twist on the classic with a medium-spicy kick. If you like your chili extra picante, *drizzle in a few drops of hot sauce at the end. Feel free to substitute your favorite combination of mushrooms.*

1 tablespoon olive oil

1 medium-sized onion, chopped

4 cloves garlic, minced

8 ounces cremini mushrooms

1 medium-sized portobello mushroom, stemmed

8 ounces shiitake mushrooms, stemmed

2 teaspoons chili powder

1 teaspoon ground cumin

½ teaspoon dried oregano

1 15-ounce can navy beans, drained and rinsed

1 15-ounce can pinto beans, drained and rinsed

1 14½-ounce can diced tomatoes with green chiles

1 tablespoon tomato paste

1 tablespoon balsamic vinegar

1 scallion, cut into ½-inch pieces

Salt to taste

Cilantro for garnish

1. Heat the oil in a saucepan over medium heat. Add the onion and garlic, and cook, stirring often, until the onion has softened, for about 5 minutes.

2. Put all the mushrooms into a food processor, and process until coarsely chopped, to get about 5 cups. Add the mushrooms, chili powder, cumin and oregano to the saucepan, and cook, stirring occasionally, until the mushrooms have released their juices, for about 5 minutes.

3. Add the beans, tomatoes, tomato paste, vinegar and 1 cup of water to the mushrooms. Bring to a boil. Reduce the heat to low, and cook, uncovered, until the mixture has reached the desired thickness, for about 10 minutes. Stir in the scallion, and add salt. Sprinkle with cilantro, and serve.

PER SERVING: 313 CAL; 15G PROT; 5G FAT; 57G CARB; 0MG CHOL; 627MG SOD; 14G FIBER

POLENTA WITH WINTER SQUASH, GORGONZOLA AND WALNUTS

While you may buy Italian polenta at a specialty store, you may also use any finely ground cornmeal—and stone-ground, organic cornmeal is a good choice. If you don't like the assertive flavor of blue cheese, try Asiago cheese or feta cheese instead. Do not overstir after adding the cheese—you want to leave bits of squash and pools of cheese in the polenta. Serve this with grilled asparagus or mixed vegetables.

2 tablespoons olive oil

1 cup minced onion

3 cups diced or shredded winter squash

1 cup cornmeal

1 teaspoon salt

½ teaspoon cayenne pepper

½ cup crumbled Gorgonzola cheese or other blue cheese

1 cup chopped, toasted walnuts (see page 47)

1. Put a 2-quart saucepan over medium heat, and add the oil. Add the onion and squash, and sauté until the onion is soft but not browned. Mix 1 cup of water with the cornmeal, salt and cayenne.

2. Bring 3 cups of water to a boil, and stir in the moist cornmeal as it boils. Add the squash and onion. Reduce the heat to medium, and cook, stirring occasionally, for 20 to 25 minutes.

3. Add the Gorgonzola when the polenta is thick and pulls away from the sides of the pan. Stir in the walnuts, and stir the mixture again. Serve hot.

PER SERVING: 320 CAL; 10G PROT; 19G FAT; 29G CARB; 10MG CHOL; 520MG SOD; 5G FIBER

RATATOUILLE AND POLENTA POT PIE

When you pour a thick layer of polenta over ratatouille and bake it, you end up with a delicious pot pie. Covering the dish during baking helps keep the polenta soft rather than crusting over.

2½ tablespoons olive oil, divided

1 large onion, quartered and thinly sliced

1 large eggplant, peeled and cut into ¾-inch cubes

1 teaspoon salt

1 large green bell pepper, sliced

2 medium-sized cloves garlic, minced

2 cups canned crushed tomatoes or 2 large ripe tomatoes, seeded and chopped

1 medium-sized zucchini, diced

2 tablespoons chopped fresh parsley

2 to 3 teaspoons tomato paste

2 teaspoons red wine vinegar

1 teaspoon dried basil or 1 tablespoon chopped fresh basil

Freshly ground black pepper to taste

1 recipe Basic Polenta, soft version (page 200)

1. Heat 1 tablespoon of the oil in a large ovenproof Dutch oven over medium heat. Add the onion, and cook, stirring often, until softened, for about 6 minutes. Add the remaining 1½ tablespoons of oil, the eggplant and ½ teaspoon of the salt, and cook, stirring often, for 3 minutes. Add the bell pepper and garlic, and cook, stirring often, until the eggplant begins to soften, for 6 to 7 minutes. Stir in the tomatoes and zucchini.

2. Cover partially, reduce the heat to low, and simmer, stirring often to prevent sticking, 10 minutes. Add the parsley, tomato paste, vinegar, basil, the remaining ½ teaspoon of salt and pepper to taste. Cook, uncovered, for 3 minutes. Remove from the heat, smooth the top with a spoon and cool for 1 hour at room temperature.

3. Meanwhile, make the soft polenta. As soon as it is quite thick but still pourable, immediately scrape the warm polenta over the ratatouille, spreading evenly with a spoon. Let cool for 30 minutes.

4. Preheat the oven to 375F.

5. Cover the Dutch oven with a lid or foil, and bake until heated through, for 35 to 40 minutes. Remove from the oven, and let stand, covered, for 10 minutes before serving.

PER SERVING (WITH POLENTA): 250 CAL; 5G PROT; 9G FAT; 39G CARB; 0MG CHOL; 930MG SOD; 5G FIBER

Three mushroom varieties—dried porcini, cremini and shiitake—give this ragu its deep, earthy flavor. The green olives add a lively counterpoint. Despite being low in fat, the sauce is rich, so a little goes a long way, especially when paired with Golden Polenta. The method for cooking the cornmeal, which results in a beautifully textured polenta without the need for constant stirring, is adapted from a recipe by the grande dame of Italian cuisine, Marcella Hazan.

Golden Polenta

1 tablespoon sea salt

2 cups coarse-ground polenta or stone-ground cornmeal

Olive oil, for brushing

Wild Mushroom Ragu

2 ounces dried porcini mushrooms

3 tablespoons olive oil, divided

2 large onions, diced

3 cloves garlic, minced

2 teaspoons minced fresh rosemary, or 1 teaspoon dried rosemary

1 cup dry red wine, preferably Chianti

1½ pounds cremini mushrooms, cleaned, stemmed and sliced

Sea salt and freshly ground black pepper to taste

8 ounces shiitake mushrooms, cleaned, stemmed and coarsely chopped

1 28-ounce can whole Italian roasted tomatoes

1 cup Vegetable Stock (page 332)

¾ cup roughly chopped green olives

½ cup chopped fresh parsley

3 tablespoons tomato paste

1. To make the Golden Polenta: Heat 7 cups of water to a boil in a large stockpot over medium heat, and add the salt. Whisking constantly, slowly sprinkle the polenta into the pot by the handful, letting it trickle through your fingers. Reduce the heat to medium-low, cook and whisk constantly for 10 minutes. Cover the pot, and cook for 10 minutes more. Uncover, and stir vigorously with a wooden spoon. Cover again, and cook for 10 minutes more. Repeat 2 more times for a total cooking time of 40 extra minutes. Uncover, and continue stirring for 10 minutes. Pour the polenta into a 10 x 14–inch baking pan, spreading it out to about ½ inch thick. Set aside to cool. Once cooled, cover and refrigerate for several hours or overnight.

2. To make the Wild Mushroom Ragu: Put the porcini and 2 cups of lukewarm water in a bowl to soak for at least 30 minutes. Remove the mushrooms from the bowl, squeezing gently and letting the liquid drain back into the bowl. Coarsely chop the mushrooms, and set aside. Strain the mushroom liquid through a coffee filter or dampened paper towel to remove grit, and set the liquid aside.

3. Heat 1 tablespoon of the oil in a large skillet over medium-high heat. Add the onions, and sauté until softened, for about 10 minutes. Add the garlic and rosemary, and cook, stirring often, until lightly browned, for 5 to 8 minutes. Transfer the mixture to a large cast-iron casserole. Deglaze the skillet with ½ cup of the red wine, scraping up all the browned bits. Cook over medium-low heat for about 10 minutes, or until the liquid is reduced by half. Add to the onion mixture.

4. Wipe the skillet clean with paper towels. Heat 2 teaspoons of the oil in a skillet over medium-high heat. Add half of the cremini mushrooms and a pinch of salt and pepper. Sauté for about 5 minutes, or until the excess liquid cooks away and the mushrooms begin to brown. Transfer the mushrooms to the casserole, and without cleaning the pan, repeat the process with the remaining cremini, followed by the shiitakes. Transfer each batch to the casserole. Deglaze the skillet with the remaining ½ cup of red wine, scraping up the browned bits. Add the reconstituted porcini and the strained mushroom liquid, and cook over medium heat for about 10 minutes, or until the liquid is reduced by half. Transfer the mixture to the casserole.

5. Squeeze the tomatoes to break them up, and add with the juices to the casserole. Stir in the Vegetable Stock, olives, parsley and tomato paste. Cook over medium-low heat for 15 minutes to blend the flavors, and adjust the seasonings.

6. Preheat the broiler. Cut the polenta into 16 wedges, brush them lightly with oil and place on a baking sheet under the broiler, cooking for about 6 minutes, or until golden brown. Turn the pieces over, and broil for 5 minutes more. Remove from the oven, place 2 wedges of polenta on each plate and top with hot mushroom ragu.

PER SERVING: 340 CAL; 10G PROT; 11G FAT; 44G CARB; 0MG CHOL; 1,180MG SOD; 5G FIBER

SOUTHWESTERN STEW ON SOFT POLENTA

This cumin-spiced stew is good alone but even better served over a bed of soft polenta. And the color scheme—the earthy tan and gold of the stew against the yellow of the polenta—couldn't be more fetching. For best results, make the stew a few hours ahead, and let it sit so that the flavors combine well. Taste and see if it needs a pinch of sugar, a squeeze of lemon juice or both.

1 tablespoon plus 1 teaspoon olive oil

1 large onion, chopped

2 medium-sized cloves garlic, minced

1½ tablespoons all-purpose flour

1 teaspoon ground cumin

½ teaspoon chili powder

½ teaspoon ground coriander

3 cups vegetable broth or Vegetable Stock (page 332)

2½ cups peeled and cubed winter squash, such as butternut or delicata

1 large potato, peeled and cubed

1 cup canned, fresh or frozen corn kernels

1 bay leaf

½ teaspoon salt, or more to taste

1 tablespoon tomato paste

½ teaspoon dried basil

Large pinch ground cinnamon

Freshly ground black pepper or cayenne pepper, to taste

1 recipe Basic Polenta, soft version (page 200)

Finely chopped red bell pepper, for garnish

1. Heat the oil in a large saucepan or Dutch oven over medium heat. Add the onion, and cook, stirring often, until softened, for about 8 minutes. Stir in the garlic, flour, cumin, chili powder and coriander, and cook, stirring often, for 1 minute. Stir in the broth, squash, potato, corn, bay leaf and salt. Increase the heat to high, and bring to a boil. Reduce the heat to low, cover partially and cook for 15 minutes. Stir in the tomato paste, basil, cinnamon and pepper; cover partially, and cook gently until the flavors have blended, for about 10 minutes. Remove from the heat.

2. About 35 minutes before you plan to eat, make the soft polenta. When it is almost done, rewarm the stew over low heat.

3. Spoon portions of polenta into large, shallow soup bowls, making a wide depression in the center. Spoon some stew into each depression, garnish with chopped bell pepper and serve.

PER SERVING: 325 CAL; 7G PROT; 6G FAT; 53G CARB; 0MG CHOL; 284MG SOD; 7G FIBER

ROASTED ACORN SQUASH WITH WHITE POLENTA

SERVES 8

Acorn squash halves are perfect for stuffing. In this preparation, white cornmeal, another important Native American foodstuff, makes a quick, intensely flavorful polenta to place inside the squash. And the pine nut–herb topping provides a crisp, crunchy finish.

4 acorn squash

1½ tablespoons olive oil

1¼ teaspoons salt

2 teaspoons freshly ground black pepper

4 cups vegetable broth, Vegetable Stock (page 332) or water

⅓ cup minced onion

2 small cloves garlic, minced

1⅔ cups white cornmeal or grits

⅔ cup pine nuts

½ teaspoon minced fresh thyme

½ teaspoon minced fresh sage

½ teaspoon minced fresh rosemary

1. Preheat the oven to 400F. Line a baking pan with parchment paper, and set aside.

2. Cut each squash in half lengthwise from tip to stem, and scoop out the seeds and strings. Slice off a small part of the rounded bottom of each half so it sits flat. With a pastry brush, coat the squash cavities with oil. Sprinkle with ½ teaspoon of salt and ½ teaspoon of pepper. Place the halves, cut sides down, in the prepared pan, and roast until tender but still firm, for about 30 minutes.

3. Meanwhile, combine the broth, onion, garlic, ¼ teaspoon of salt and ½ teaspoon of pepper in a large, heavy saucepan, and heat over low heat. Whisk in the cornmeal gradually. Whisking constantly, cook until the mixture is thick, smooth and pulls away from the side of saucepan, for about 15 minutes. Remove the polenta from the heat, cover and set aside.

4. Put the pine nuts in a food processor, and process until coarsely ground. Stir in the thyme, sage, rosemary, the remaining ½ teaspoon of salt and 1 teaspoon of pepper.

5. Remove the squash from the oven, and reduce the heat to 300F. Carefully turn over the squash, fill each cavity with about ½ cup of polenta and sprinkle with about 2 tablespoons of the pine nut mixture, lightly pressing it into the polenta. Return the squash to the oven, and bake until the topping begins to brown, for about 25 minutes. Serve hot.

PER SERVING: 307 CAL; 8G PROT; 10G FAT; 44G CARB; 0MG CHOL; 442MG SOD; 9G FIBER

EGGPLANT PATTIES

SERVES 4 TO 5

These patties are known as melitzanokephtethes *in Greek. In place of grated Parmesan cheese, consider using the Greek cheese Kefalotyri, a natural partner for the patties. Serve these as is or, if you prefer, sliced on pasta with a tomato sauce.*

1½ pounds medium-sized eggplant

1½ cups plain breadcrumbs (see page 46) plus extra for rolling

1 small onion, finely chopped

½ cup grated Parmesan cheese

2 large eggs

2 tablespoons chopped fresh parsley

1 teaspoon baking powder

Salt and freshly ground black pepper to taste

½ cup vegetable oil, or more as needed, for frying

1. Slit the eggplants lengthwise in 2 places. Place in boiling salted water, and cook for about 15 minutes, or until soft. Drain well. When cool enough to handle, remove the skins, and mash the pulp.

2. Combine the pulp with the breadcrumbs, onion, cheese, eggs, parsley, baking powder, salt and pepper. Shape into patties or croquettes, and roll in extra breadcrumbs for a crisp coating.

3. Heat about ¼ cup of the oil in a skillet over medium heat, and fry the patties until golden on both sides. Using a slotted spatula, remove the patties from the oil, and drain on paper towels. Repeat with the remaining mixture until used up, adding more oil if needed.

PER SERVING: 180 CAL; 8G PROT; 10G FAT; 17G CARB; 90MG CHOL; 350MG SOD; 4G FIBER

POLENTA TORTA WITH ROASTED SQUASH

Wedges of torta may be served plain or with leftover Gypsy Sauce (page 262) or marinara. The torta may be made ahead and refrigerated. In that case, the final baking will take longer. Instant and ready-cooked varieties of polenta are sold in many stores, and may be used to save time. The easiest way to cube butternut squash is to cut the squash into 1-inch-thick rings, then use a small, sharp knife to cut the peel from the rings. Cut each ring into 1-inch cubes. Bags of cubed butternut squash are available in some supermarkets.

2 cups coarse stone-ground cornmeal

1 teaspoon salt

½ cup minced oil-packed sun-dried tomatoes

2 pounds butternut squash, peeled and cubed

2 red bell peppers, diced

1 onion, coarsely chopped

½ teaspoon garlic salt

½ teaspoon onion salt

1 teaspoon freshly ground black pepper

1 teaspoon dried thyme

½ teaspoon dried basil

½ teaspoon cayenne pepper

2 tablespoons olive oil

1 cup shredded soy mozzarella cheese or mozzarella cheese

1. Preheat the oven to 350F.

2. Bring 4 cups of water to a boil. Mix the cornmeal with 3 cups of cold water and the salt. Add the cornmeal to the boiling water, bring back to a boil and cook for 35 minutes. Stir frequently for the first 20 minutes, and then stir constantly for the remaining time. Add the sun dried tomatoes, and stir well.

3. Meanwhile, toss the squash, peppers and onion with the garlic salt, onion salt, pepper, thyme, basil and cayenne, and place on a baking sheet.

4. Roast for 20 minutes, or until the squash is tender. Remove from the oven, and set aside.

5. Use the oil to coat a 9-inch springform pan or deep quiche pan. Pack the cooked polenta into the pan in an even layer. Top with the roasted vegetables, and sprinkle with the cheese.

6. Bake for 45 minutes, or until heated through and the cheese is melted and golden. Remove from the oven, and serve.

PER SERVING: 360 CAL; 11G PROT; 5G FAT; 32G CARB; 0MG CHOL; 334MG SOD; 10G FIBER

LIGHT EGGPLANT PARMESAN

Containing only one-fourth of the calories and one-ninth of the fat of traditional eggplant Parmesan, this dish won't make you feel heavy—or guilty.

2 tablespoons dry red wine

1 medium-sized onion, chopped

3 large cloves garlic, pressed or minced

1 medium-sized green bell pepper, chopped

Freshly ground black pepper to taste

4 cups peeled and chopped tomatoes (see page 46)

1 teaspoon dried basil or 1 tablespoon minced fresh basil

1/3 teaspoon dried oregano or 1 teaspoon minced fresh oregano

Pinch dried thyme or 1/2 teaspoon minced fresh thyme

1 teaspoon dried parsley or 1 tablespoon minced fresh parsley

Salt to taste

1 large eggplant

1/4 to 1/2 cup water Vegetable Stock (page 332)

1/2 to 1 cup dry whole wheat breadcrumbs

3/4 cup coarsely grated low-fat mozzarella cheese

1/4 to 1/2 cup grated Parmesan cheese

1. Heat the wine in a large saucepan over medium heat. Add the onion, and cook, stirring frequently, until softened, for 3 to 4 minutes.

2. Add the garlic and bell pepper, and cook, stirring frequently, until tender, for about 5 minutes. Add the black pepper and tomatoes. If using dried herbs, add them at this point, cover, reduce the heat to low, and cook for 5 to 10 minutes. (If using fresh herbs, do not add until step 3.)

3. Add 1/2 teaspoon of salt, increase the heat to medium-low and cook, uncovered, until the sauce thickens, for about 1 hour. If using fresh herbs, add them at this point, and cook for 5 minutes more. Season with additional salt, if desired. Remove from the heat.

4. Peel the eggplant, and cut crosswise into 1/2-inch-thick slices. Layer the slices in a colander, lightly sprinkling them with salt between the layers. Cover with a plate, and set a weight, such as a large can of tomatoes or a pot of water, on top. Let sit for at least 30 minutes to drain excess moisture. Rinse the eggplant, and pat dry.

5. Preheat the oven to 350F. Spray a large baking sheet with nonstick cooking spray.

6. Dip the eggplant slices in the Vegetables Stock and breadcrumbs to coat. Place on the baking sheet.

7. Bake until the eggplant is tender and the crumbs are crisp, for about 30 minutes.

8. Spray the bottom and sides of an 8-inch square baking dish with nonstick cooking spray. Spread a thin layer of sauce on the bottom, and arrange half the eggplant slices on top. Sprinkle about one-third of the mozzarella over the eggplant. Spread on a thicker layer of sauce than the first one, and sprinkle on half the Parmesan cheese. Repeat layers, beginning with the eggplant and ending with the Parmesan cheese. Cover.

9. Bake until heated through, for about 30 minutes. Uncover, scatter the remaining mozzarella on top and bake until the cheese is melted and bubbly, for about 10 minutes. Remove from the oven, and let sit for 5 to 10 minutes before serving.

PER SERVING (ONE 4-INCH SQUARE): 225 CAL; 13G PROT; 7G FAT; 28G CARB; 17G CHOL; 608MG SOD; 5G FIBER

EGGPLANT BOATS

The orange zest transforms this dish from humble to exotic. The boats may be served hot or at room temperature, and make for a sturdy entrée.

3 pounds medium-sized eggplant

½ cup salt

6 tablespoons olive oil

2 medium-sized onions, chopped

2 teaspoons garlic granules

4 ounces mushrooms, fresh or canned

1 28-ounce can Italian Roma tomatoes, drained but reserving ½ cup juice

1 cup pitted black olives

Grated zest from 2 large oranges

1 teaspoon freshly ground black pepper

7½ cups plain breadcrumbs

1 tablespoon chopped fresh rosemary, or to taste

2 tablespoons chopped fresh parsley, or to taste

2 teaspoons chopped fresh dillweed, or to taste

1 teaspoon dill seed

1 clove garlic, slivered

1. Halve the eggplants lengthwise, cutting through the stem ends. Cut crosswise slits about ½ inch apart, and carefully slice around inside the perimeter without cutting through the shell. Salt the eggplant halves, pressing open the slits so the salt can enter. Set aside in a colander to drain for 30 minutes.

2. Rinse the eggplants thoroughly. Using a spoon, scoop out the eggplant flesh, and squeeze out the excess liquid. Set aside.

3. Preheat the oven to 375F.

4. Heat 4 tablespoons of the oil in a skillet over medium-high heat, and sauté the onions, garlic, mushrooms and eggplant pieces. Cook until the juices begin to evaporate and the vegetables brown. Add the tomatoes and juice, olives, orange zest and pepper. Reduce the heat to medium, and cook for 8 to 10 minutes more, stirring often. Stir in the breadcrumbs, rosemary, parsley, dillweed and dill seed.

5. Pour 1 inch of water into a large roasting pan. Place the eggplant "boats" in the pan. Spoon the filling mixture into each boat. Place the garlic slivers on top of the filling. Brush the tops and edges of the boats with the remaining oil. Cover each loosely with aluminum foil.

6. Bake for 5 minutes, and remove the foil. Bake for 15 minutes more, and remove from the oven. To serve, slice each boat into 3 segments and arrange on a serving platter.

PER SERVING: 267 CAL; 5G PROT; 16G FAT; 32G CARB; 0MG CHOL; 400MG SOD; 8G FIBER

EGGPLANT STEAK WITH CHICKPEAS, ROASTED RED PEPPERS, FETA CHEESE AND BLACK OLIVES SERVES 4

This inventive recipe with its bold flavors evokes images of the Mediterranean.

Balsamic Marinade

1 tablespoon balsamic vinegar

1 tablespoon tamari or low-sodium soy sauce

2 cloves garlic, minced

¼ teaspoon freshly ground black pepper

2 tablespoons olive oil

Eggplant Steaks

1 large eggplant (about 1 pound)

1½ cups cooked or canned chickpeas, drained

2 medium-sized red bell peppers, roasted (see page 46), peeled, seeded and cubed

4 ounces feta cheese, cubed or crumbled

½ cup pitted black olives, preferably Greek or Moroccan

2 tablespoons chopped fresh oregano or Italian parsley

Sea salt and freshly ground black pepper to taste

4 6½-inch pita bread

4 teaspoons balsamic vinegar

1 bunch fresh oregano, for garnish

1. To make the Balsamic Marinade: Combine all the ingredients, slowly adding the oil and stirring briskly to combine well. Set aside.

2. Prepare a hot charcoal fire or preheat a gas grill to medium-high. Place a vegetable grilling rack on the grill. Or preheat the broiler.

3. To make the Eggplant Steaks: Cut the eggplant lengthwise into four ½-inch-thick slices to resemble steaks. Brush the "steaks" with the marinade.

4. Grill or broil the eggplant for 2 minutes on each side, or until tender but not soft. Remove from the heat, and place 1 steak on each serving plate.

5. Put the chickpeas, bell peppers, feta, olives and oregano in a bowl. Season to taste with salt and pepper, and stir to combine well. Add some marinade, and stir again. Toast or grill the pita bread, cut into pie-shaped wedges, and set aside.

6. Spoon 1 or 2 scoops of the pepper-olive mixture onto each eggplant steak with some mixture pooling onto the plate. Sprinkle with vinegar, place several pita wedges on the plate, and garnish the eggplant with several sprigs of fresh oregano. Serve immediately.

PER SERVING: 460 CAL; 18G PROT; 16G FAT; 65G CARB; 10MG CHOL; 1,060MG SOD; 10G FIBER

EGGPLANT WITH CARAMELIZED ONIONS, TOMATOES AND MINT

This dish dresses up nicely for company and is also easy to serve. Offer this with crusty sourdough bread.

1½ to 2 pounds Italian eggplants, about 8 inches long and 3 inches round

½ cup olive oil, divided

3 large Vidalia or other sweet onions, halved lengthwise and thinly sliced

½ cup anisette liqueur

1½ cups chopped Roma or other firm tomatoes plus juices

1 cup chopped fresh mint leaves

1 tablespoon dried oregano or 3 tablespoons minced fresh oregano

1 cup pine nuts

Coarse sea salt to taste

Freshly ground white pepper to taste

1. Preheat the oven to 350F.

2. Slice the eggplants in half lengthwise, removing the tough stem ends. Spray the cut sides with nonstick cooking spray, and place, sprayed sides down, on a baking sheet.

3. Bake for 25 to 30 minutes, or until the skin and insides are very tender. Remove from the oven, and set aside.

4. Heat 1 tablespoon of the oil in a large cast-iron or stainless steel skillet over medium-low heat. Sauté the onions until soft and caramelized, for about 12 minutes. Add the anisette, increase the heat to medium-high and cook for about 30 seconds. Remove from the heat, and increase the oven temperature to broil.

5. Using tongs or a spatula, remove the onions from the skillet, and set aside. Arrange the eggplants in the skillet, face up, and cover the eggplants evenly with the onions. Arrange the tomatoes and any juice, the mint, oregano and pine nuts over the onions, in that order. Drizzle the remaining oil over the top.

6. Place the skillet under the broiler for 3 to 4 minutes, or until the mint and onions brown slightly. Remove from the oven, and season with salt and pepper to taste. Serve.

PER SERVING: 470 CAL; 8G PROT; 31G FAT; 32G CARB; 0MG CHOL; 15MG SOD; 6G FIBER

EGGPLANT PIE

This is a lovely entrée, especially when served with a tossed green salad—it also makes a hearty side dish.

1 cup cooked grits or polenta (see page 48)

3 tablespoons olive oil

1½ to 2 pounds eggplant

1 clove garlic, minced

1 small onion, chopped

3 tablespoons cornstarch

1 7-ounce can mushrooms plus liquid

1 teaspoon baking soda

1 teaspoon seasoning salt

½ cup breadcrumbs or cracker crumbs

2 cups shredded soy or regular mozzarella cheese

1. Grease a 9-inch deep-dish pie plate with 1 tablespoon of the oil. Press the grits into the pan and up the sides. Set aside to cool.

2. Peel the eggplant, and slice into chunks. Place the chunks in a saucepan, and add just enough water to cover. Cook over low heat until soft, for 15 to 20 minutes.

3. Meanwhile, heat the remaining 2 tablespoons of oil in a skillet over medium heat, and sauté the garlic and onion until golden, for about 7 minutes.

4. Preheat the oven to 350F.

5. Remove the softened eggplant from the heat, drain and mash lightly with a handheld masher. Mix the cornstarch and mushroom liquid, stirring until smooth. Stir in the baking soda, and add the mixture to the eggplant. Stir in the onion, garlic, seasoning salt, mushrooms and breadcrumbs. Spoon into a pie pan, and top with the cheese.

6. Bake for about 25 minutes, or until the cheese is melted and bubbly. Remove from the oven, and cool slightly before slicing and serving.

PER SERVING: 240 CAL; 8G PROT; 9G FAT; 32G CARB; 0MG CHOL; 960MG SOD; 4G FIBER

STUFFED BABY EGGPLANTS (IMAM BAYILDI)

For a buffet menu, the baby eggplants are a perfect choice as the portion size is smaller.

6 baby eggplants

3 tablespoons olive oil

1 large onion, quartered and thinly sliced

2 cloves garlic, crushed

1 14½-ounce can diced tomatoes in juice, drained and juice reserved

½ cup chopped fresh parsley plus extra for garnish, optional

1 bay leaf

½ teaspoon ground cinnamon

Salt and freshly ground black pepper to taste

¼ cup fresh lemon juice

½ teaspoon granulated sugar

1. Cut the eggplants in half lengthwise. Using a melon baller or small spoon, carefully scoop out the flesh, leaving about ⅛ inch and keeping the skin of the eggplant intact.

2. Chop the flesh finely, and set aside. Arrange the eggplant shells in a large skillet that will hold them snugly. Heat 1 tablespoon of the oil in a saucepan over medium heat. Add the onion, and cook, stirring often, until softened and beginning to brown, for about 10 minutes. Add the garlic and cook, stirring, for 1 minute more. Add the tomatoes, reserved eggplant flesh, parsley, bay leaf and cinnamon. Season with salt and pepper. Cook, stirring occasionally, until the eggplant is soft and most of the liquid has been absorbed, for about 10 minutes. Remove the pan from the heat, discard the bay leaf and fill the eggplant shells with the mixture—they will be very full.

3. Mix the remaining 2 tablespoons of oil, the lemon juice, reserved tomato juice and sugar. Pour over the stuffed eggplants. Cover, and cook over low heat until the eggplants are tender, for about 30 minutes. Remove the pan from the heat, and allow to cool in the skillet.

4. Carefully transfer the eggplants to a serving platter, reshaping if necessary. Spoon the pan juices over and around the eggplants. Serve warm, at room temperature, or cover and chill to serve cold. Sprinkle with chopped parsley, if using.

PER SERVING (2 STUFFED HALVES): 136 CAL; 2G PROT; 8G FAT; 16G CARB; 0MG CHOL; 352MG SOD; 2G FIBER

ARTICHOKE-ASPARAGUS TORTE

Delicious for a light supper, this torte is simplicity itself because it comes together so quickly. Perfect partners would be hot biscuits and a fruit punch, followed by lemon sorbet.

12 plump spears asparagus, trimmed

2 tablespoons olive oil

1 tablespoon minced garlic

1½ cups artichoke hearts, halved and well-drained

6 large eggs, beaten

1 cup low-fat shredded mozzarella cheese

Salt and freshly ground black pepper

1. Preheat the broiler.

2. Blanch the asparagus in boiling water for about 2 minutes. Remove from the heat, dunk into cold water and set aside. When cool enough to handle, cut the asparagus into 3-inch pieces.

3. Heat the oil in a large skillet over medium heat, and sauté the garlic for 1 to 2 minutes. Add the asparagus and the artichoke hearts, and sauté for 3 minutes. Stir the eggs with the cheese, salt and pepper, and pour over the vegetables. Cook the eggs, lifting up the edges and tilting the pan so the uncooked eggs run underneath. When the bottom and edges look firm, after about 5 minutes, broil the top of the omelet until the eggs brown and puff up. Remove from the oven, and serve.

PER SERVING: 300 CAL; 21G PROT; 19G FAT; 11G CARB; 330MG CHOL; 360MG SOD; 4G FIBER

TOMATO-MUSHROOM GALETTE

This savory tart, somewhere between a pizza and a pie, with its free-form crust makes a satisfying casual meal; serve it warm.

2 tablespoons olive oil, preferably extra virgin

1 large onion, thinly sliced

Salt and freshly ground black pepper to taste

8 ounces sliced cremini mushrooms

1 homemade or prepared 9-inch piecrust (see page 402)

4 ounces crumbled chèvre cheese

2 teaspoons coarsely chopped fresh thyme or rosemary or ⅔ teaspoon dried thyme or rosemary

2 to 3 medium-sized tomatoes, cut into ¼-inch-thick slices, then halved

1. Preheat the oven to 450F.

2. Heat 1 tablespoon of the oil in a skillet over medium-high heat. Add the onion, and cook, stirring often, until softened and golden brown, for 8 to 10 minutes. Season with salt and pepper.

3. Transfer the onions to a bowl. Heat the remaining 1 tablespoon of oil in the skillet. Add the mushrooms, and cook, stirring often, until softened and the juices have evaporated, for about 6 minutes. Season with salt and pepper.

4. Add the mushrooms to the bowl with the onions and mix gently.

5. Lay the piecrust flat on a baking sheet. Distribute the onion-mushroom mixture evenly on top, leaving a 1-inch border. Dot with the chèvre cheese, and sprinkle with the thyme and pepper to taste.

6. Starting from the outer edge of the onion mixture, arrange the tomato slices on top. Sprinkle with a pinch of salt and pepper. Fold the pastry over the topping, crimping the dough every inch or two.

7. Bake until the crust is golden, for 18 to 20 minutes. Transfer to a wire rack to cool slightly. Cut into 4 wedges and serve warm.

PER SERVING: 260 CAL; 4G PROT; 6G FAT; 48G CARB; 15MG CHOL; 190MG SOD; 3G FIBER

BRAISED ARTICHOKES AND NEW POTATOES
WITH LEMON-DILL SAUCE

Trimming artichokes is a labor of love, but it's worth the trouble because they contribute a wonderful earthy flavor to any vegetable stew. Taking a cue from Greek cuisine, here they are accented with a lemon- and dill-infused sauce.

1 lemon, halved

8 baby artichokes or 4 large artichokes

2 teaspoons olive oil

1 cup chopped onion

2 medium-sized cloves garlic, minced

1 pound baby carrots, scraped and cut into 1¾ x ½–inch sticks

1 pound new potatoes, quartered or halved

2¼ cups low-sodium vegetable stock or Vegetable Stock (page 332)

1 large egg

3 to 4 tablespoons fresh lemon juice

⅓ cup chopped fresh dillweed, plus sprigs for garnish

Salt and freshly ground black pepper to taste

1. Fill a large bowl with cold water. Squeeze juice from 1 lemon half into the water, then drop in the lemon shell. Snap off the dark green outer leaves from 1 artichoke. With a paring knife, trim all but 1 inch of the stem. Pare away the fibrous green portion of the stem and bottom of the artichoke. Rub the cut surfaces with the other lemon half. Cut the remaining inner leaves off at the ridge just above the heart, exposing the purple choke. With a melon baller or spoon, scoop out the fuzzy choke. Rub the cut surfaces with the lemon. Drop the trimmed artichoke into the lemon water. Repeat with the remaining artichokes.

2. Heat the oil in a Dutch oven or deep sauté pan over medium heat. Add the onion, and cook, stirring often, until softened, for 2 to 3 minutes. Add the garlic, and cook, stirring, for 30 seconds. Add the carrots and potatoes, and cook, stirring, for 2 minutes.

3. Drain the artichokes. If using large artichokes, cut in quarters or eighths. Add the artichokes and broth to the carrot mixture, and bring to a simmer. Reduce the heat to low, cover, and simmer until the vegetables are tender, for 12 to 18 minutes. With a slotted spoon, transfer the vegetables to a large serving bowl or deep platter, and cover to keep warm.

4. Whisk together the egg and 3 tablespoons of the lemon juice in a bowl. Whisk in the dillweed. Gradually whisk a little of the hot vegetable cooking liquid into the egg mixture, then add this mixture to the liquid remaining in the Dutch oven or sauté pan. Cook over medium heat, stirring, until steaming and slightly thickened, for 2 to 3 minutes. Do not let the sauce boil. Season with salt, pepper and additional lemon juice to taste. Spoon the sauce over the vegetables, garnish with dill sprigs and serve immediately.

PER SERVING: 278 CAL; 11G PROT; 3G FAT; 50G CARB; 36MG CHOL; 301MG SOD; 14G FIBER

BRAISED SEITAN WITH FRAGRANT TOMATO GRAVY SERVES 8

If the seitan is packaged in a tub of broth, you will need two tubs for this recipe. After discarding the broth, you will have about 1 pound of seitan.

2 teaspoons olive oil

1 red onion, chopped

5 cloves garlic, minced

1 serrano chile, seeded and chopped

1 pound seitan

1 large zucchini, diced

1 pound sliced cremini mushrooms

1 15-ounce can chickpeas, drained and rinsed

1 cinnamon stick

1 28-ounce can tomato sauce with roasted red peppers

½ cup chopped cilantro

1 tablespoon garam masala (see page 461)

1 teaspoon ground turmeric

3 tablespoons plain soy yogurt

1. Heat the oil, onion, garlic and chile in a 5-quart saucepan over high heat for 2 minutes to soften. Cut the seitan into bite-size pieces, and add to the pan. Add the zucchini, mushrooms, chickpeas and cinnamon stick. Cook the mixture for 6 minutes, stirring frequently.

2. Reduce the heat to low, and add the tomato sauce, cilantro, garam masala and turmeric. Cook for 10 minutes, and stir in the yogurt. Remove from the heat, and keep warm until ready to serve.

PER SERVING: 179 CAL; 13G PROT; 4G FAT; 21G CARB; 0MG CHOL; 126MG SOD; 7G FIBER

BROCCOLI RABE WITH WHITE BEANS AND POTATOES SERVES 6

In this deliciously different stew, the mildly bitter taste of the broccoli rabe is a nice complement to the starchy white beans and potatoes. Serve it in large, shallow soup bowls with hard-crusted Italian bread to soak up all the sauce. With all the greens, you won't need a side salad, but a dessert such as the Total Eclipse Chocolate Cake (page 392) makes a luscious conclusion to the meal.

3 medium-sized potatoes, peeled, quartered and sliced

Salt to taste

2 tablespoons olive oil

5 large cloves garlic, minced

1 teaspoon crushed red pepper, or more to taste

2 large bunches broccoli rabe, bottom 3 inches of stems trimmed, remainder cut crosswise in half

¼ teaspoon freshly ground black pepper

2 cups cooked or canned Great Northern or other white beans, drained and rinsed

About 4 cups Vegetable Stock (page 332)

1. Combine the potatoes with lightly salted water to cover in a medium saucepan, and bring to a boil over high heat. Reduce the heat to medium-low, partially cover, and cook until the potatoes are fork-tender, about 10 minutes. Drain well, and set aside.

2. Meanwhile, heat the oil in a large pot over medium heat. Add the garlic and crushed red pepper, and cook, stirring occasionally, for 2 minutes. Stir in the broccoli rabe, salt, pepper and ¼ cup of water. Cover, and cook until the broccoli rabe is tender, stirring occasionally, for 5 to 8 minutes. Add the potatoes, beans and Vegetable Stock, and mix well. Increase the heat to medium-high, and bring to a boil. Cook, uncovered, stirring occasionally, until the flavors have blended and the mixture is heated through, for about 5 minutes. Adjust the seasonings to taste, and serve hot.

PER SERVING: 267 CAL; 11G PROT; 5G FAT; 42G CARB; 0MG CHOL; 185MG SOD; 8G FIBER

BAKED POTATOES TOPPED WITH SPICY VEGETABLE STEW

The vegetable stew also makes a great topping for baked sweet potatoes.

4 large russet potatoes, scrubbed
1 tablespoon vegetable oil
1 cup chopped onion
½ cup chopped green bell pepper
½ cup diced carrot
1 clove garlic, minced
1 14½-ounce can diced tomatoes
1 15-ounce can black beans, drained and rinsed
½ cup vegetable broth, Vegetable Stock (page 332) or water
1 tablespoon chili powder
1 teaspoon ground cumin
1 cup diced yellow squash
1 cup diced zucchini
2 tablespoons chopped cilantro
Salt and freshly ground black pepper to taste

1. Preheat the oven to 400F.

2. Pierce the potatoes with the tines of a fork, and bake until tender, for about 1 hour.

3. Meanwhile, heat the oil in a large nonstick skillet over medium heat. Add the onion, bell pepper, carrot and garlic, and cook, stirring often, until the vegetables begin to soften, for about 10 minutes. Add the tomatoes, beans, broth, chili powder and cumin. Reduce the heat to low, and cook, covered, for 20 minutes.

4. Add the yellow squash and zucchini. Cover, and cook until the vegetables are crisp-tender, for about 5 minutes more. Stir in the cilantro, and season with salt and pepper.

5. To serve, split the baked potatoes, and mash their pulp slightly. Spoon the vegetable stew into the centers.

PER SERVING: 392 CAL; 12G PROT; 6G FAT; 80G CARB; 0MG CHOL; 225MG SOD; 7G FIBER

CREAMY MUSHROOM RAGU

Browning flour in a dry skillet is the classic way to prepare a roux base—be sure to use a heavy pan and to stir constantly to prevent scorching. For a dairy-free version, replace the milk with an unflavored soy beverage.

½ cup all-purpose flour
3 whole cloves
3 large shallots, peeled
1 tablespoon vegetable oil
1 pound mixed mushrooms, such as shiitake, chanterelle and portobello, sliced
1 teaspoon salt
4 cups low-fat milk
1 small bay leaf
Pinch ground nutmeg

1. Cook the flour in a heavy saucepan over medium heat, whisking constantly, until light tan all over (the color of an almond shell), for about 5 minutes. Immediately remove from the heat, and continue whisking until the flour cools slightly, for 2 to 3 minutes. Set aside to cool completely.

2. Meanwhile, stick the cloves in 1 shallot, and set aside. Thinly slice the remaining 2 shallots. Heat the oil in a large skillet over high heat. Add the sliced shallots, and cook, stirring, until golden brown, for about 3 minutes. Add the mushrooms and ½ teaspoon of the salt, and cook, stirring, until tender and they begin to release their juices, for 3 to 4 minutes. Remove from the heat, and set aside.

3. Whisk ¾ cup of the milk, gradually, into the cooled flour in the saucepan until a smooth paste forms. Gradually whisk in the remaining 1¼ cups of milk until no lumps remain. Add the remaining ½ teaspoon of salt, the whole shallot with cloves, the bay leaf and nutmeg. Place over medium-high heat, and bring to a boil, whisking constantly. Boil until thickened, whisking constantly, for about 5 minutes.

4. Reduce the heat to low, and cook, whisking occasionally, until the flavors have blended, for about 15 minutes. Discard the whole shallot and bay leaf. Stir the mushroom mixture into the milk mixture, and heat through. Serve hot.

PER CUP: 323 CAL; 16G PROT; 8G FAT; 47G CARB; 10MG CHOL; 669MG SOD; 7G FIBER

WILD MUSHROOM AND TOMATO CASSEROLE

This warm-weather, one-pot meal is surprisingly light when fresh from the oven. An earthenware casserole is best because the slow radiant heat creates a crust along the edges that is one of the tastiest parts of the dish. Best eaten when just made, this dish will reheat well in a microwave oven. Kids love it.

1½ ounces mixed dried wild mushrooms, such as oyster mushrooms and porcini

1 quart boiling water

2 large onions, sliced

3 tablespoons unsalted butter or olive oil

3 tablespoons packed brown sugar

1 teaspoon salt

3 tablespoons flour

About 1½ pounds stale, crusty country-style bread, preferably sourdough, cut into thick slices

3 cups chopped tomatoes

2½ cups coarsely grated Gruyère-style cheese

2 tablespoons minced fresh sage

½ cup grated Parmesan cheese

½ teaspoon caraway seeds, optional

1. Put the mushrooms in a large heatproof container, and add the boiling water. Cover, and infuse for 1 to 2 hours, or until the mushrooms are tender. Strain the infusion, reserving the liquid. Coarsely chop the mushrooms, and set aside in a large bowl.

2. Put the onions, butter and sugar in a large skillet, cover and cook over medium heat for 10 minutes, or until the onions are soft and beginning to caramelize on the bottom. Add the salt, and stir in the flour to thicken. Place the onions in a bowl, and deglaze the skillet with about 1 cup of the mushroom infusion, whisking well. Pour the deglazing liquid into the mushroom infusion.

3. Preheat the oven to 375F. Spray a 3-quart casserole with nonstick cooking spray.

4. Layer the bread in the casserole. Chop any remaining bread into small irregular pieces, and set aside. Combine the mushrooms and tomatoes, and cover the bread layer with the mixture. Combine the Gruyère and sage, and scatter evenly over the mushroom-tomato mixture. Cover with the chopped bread. Spread the onions over the bread, and pour on the mushroom infusion. Pat smooth with the back of a wooden spoon. Sprinkle the Parmesan cheese and caraway seeds, if using, over the top.

5. Bake, uncovered, for 45 to 55 minutes, or until set and crispy on top. Serve hot directly from the oven.

PER SERVING: 710 CAL; 32G PROT; 28G FAT; 83G CARB; 75MG CHOL; 1,470MG SOD; 6G FIBER

CLASSIC CHEESE FONDUE

For best results, make this fondue in a heavy saucepan on top of the stove and then transfer it to your fondue pot or slow cooker. The kirsch—a Swiss brandy made from cherry pits—is optional, but it does add a level of flavor.

Classic Cheese Fondue

1 clove garlic, crushed

2½ cups Chardonnay or other dry white wine

2 tablespoons cornstarch

1 pound Gruyère cheese shredded

1 pound Emmentaler cheese shredded

2 tablespoons kirsch, optional

Accompaniments

1 to 2 loaves French bread, cubed

1 loaf unsliced pumpernickel, cubed

2 dozen bread sticks

1. To make the Classic Cheese Fondue: Rub the inside of a saucepan with the garlic. If using a fondue pot or slow cooker, rub them as well. Pour in the wine, and heat over low heat until it simmers.

2. Mix the cornstarch with ¼ cup of water, stirring to make a paste, and stir into the wine. Increase the heat to medium, and cook until the wine mixture boils and begins to thicken, stirring often. Reduce the heat to low.

3. Combine the cheeses, and, using a generous handful at a time, stir into the wine until the cheese melts. Repeat, adding the cheese and stirring until the cheese is used up and the mixture becomes smooth, for about 10 minutes.

4. Stir in the kirsch, if using, and transfer the melted cheese to the fondue pot or slow cooker, and serve. Keep the fondue warm over an alcohol burner or in the slow cooker on the lowest setting. Serve with the accompaniments.

PER SERVING (WITHOUT ACCOMPANIMENTS): 510 CAL; 33G PROT; 34G FAT; 5G CARB; 115MG CHOL; 340MG SOD; 0G FIBER

ITALIAN FONDUE

Supermarkets offer busy fondue cooks many shortcuts: a variety of bagged, preshredded cheeses, prepped vegetables and packaged bread sticks, so dinner can be on the table in fifteen minutes. If you have time to spare, shred your own cheeses—a mixture of mozzarella, fontina, provolone, Romano, Parmesan or Asiago cheeses for a total of 2 pounds, or 8 cups.

Italian Fondue

2½ cups dry white wine

1 clove garlic, crushed

2 teaspoons dried basil

½ teaspoon dried oregano

¼ teaspoon crushed red pepper

2 tablespoons cornstarch

2 pounds shredded Italian cheeses

2 tablespoons minced sun-dried tomatoes, optional

Accompaniments

1 loaf crisp Italian bread

2 dozen bread sticks

3- to 4-quarts combination raw and steamed vegetables, such as baby carrots, bell pepper strips, asparagus, broccoli and cherry tomatoes, cut into serving sizes

1. To make the Italian Fondue: Pour the wine into a saucepan, and heat over low heat until simmering. Add the garlic, basil, oregano and crushed red pepper, and cook for 2 minutes more.

2. Mix the cornstarch with ¼ cup of water, stirring to make a paste, and stir into the wine. Increase the heat to medium, and cook until the mixture boils and thickens. Reduce the heat to low.

3. Combine the cheeses, and, using a generous handful at a time, stir into the wine until the cheese melts. Repeat, adding the cheese and stirring until the cheese is used up and the mixture becomes smooth, for about 3 minutes. Stir in the sun-dried tomatoes, if using.

4. Transfer the cheese mixture to a fondue pot or slow cooker, and serve. Keep the fondue warm over an alcohol burner or in a slow cooker on the lowest setting. Serve with the accompaniments.

PER SERVING (WITHOUT ACCOMPANIMENTS): 430 CAL; 26G PROT; 29G FAT; 10G CARB; 90MG CHOL; 850MG SOD; 0G FIBER

SOUTHWESTERN CHILI-CHEESE FONDUE

Flavorful pepper Jack cheese needs little help to make it taste wonderful. With the cheese melted in Mexican beer and bolstered with ground pumpkin seeds and green chiles, the fondue becomes particularly memorable if accompanied by fresh corn tortillas. The pickled jalapeño chiles (jalapeños en escabeche) *may be eaten as a relish or dipped in the fondue, and are especially suited to those who like fiery foods.*

Southwestern Chile-Cheese Fondue

1 clove garlic, mashed

2½ cups Dos Equis or other Mexican beer

2 tablespoons cornstarch

½ cup raw, hulled pumpkin seeds, finely ground

1½ pounds Pepper Jack cheese, shredded

½ cup canned diced roasted green chiles

Accompaniments

24 corn or flour tortillas, cut into wedges

1 pound tortilla chips, preferably baked

3- to 4-quart combination raw and steamed vegetables for dipping, such as carrot sticks, bell peppers, celery, radishes, baby carrots, broccoli pieces and sugar snap peas, cut into serving sizes

2 cups whole pickled jalapeño chiles

1. To make the Chile-Cheese Fondue: Put the garlic and beer in a saucepan, and heat over low heat until simmering.

2. Mix the cornstarch with ¼ cup of water, stirring to make a paste, and stir into the beer. Increase the heat, and cook the beer until it boils and begins to thicken. Reduce the heat to low. Add the pumpkin seeds, and cook for 2 minutes. Add the cheese and, using a generous handful at a time, stir into the beer until the cheese melts, for 2 to 3 minutes. Repeat until the cheese is used up. Stir in the green chiles.

3. Transfer the cheese mixture to a fondue pot or slow cooker. Keep the fondue warm over an alcohol burner or in the slow cooker over the lowest setting. At serving time, place the tortilla wedges in baskets lined with a damp napkin or dishtowel. Warm each basket in a microwave for 20 seconds; place smaller baskets filled with tortilla chips at each place setting. Put out baskets of crisp vegetables and small bowls of pickled jalapeños. Serve with the accompaniments.

PER SERVING (WITHOUT ACCOMPANIMENTS): 560 CAL; 31G PROT; 41G FAT; 13G CARB; 120MG CHOL; 690MG SOD; 0G FIBER

pizza and pastas

PERHAPS THE MOST BELOVED OF CASUAL fare, pastas and pizzas satisfy the inner hunger for flavor-packed foods that don't sink weekly budgets. But even better, both pastas and pizzas are extremely versatile foods. Because of their agreeably mild flavors, they provide the backdrop for a range of assertive ingredients, from temperate tomato sauces and bland mozzarella cheese to feisty red chiles and tart greens such as rapini. All that limits you from creating fabulous dishes is your imagination, and sometimes, the wilder the better!

GRILLED VEGETABLE PIZZA

Ready-made pizza crusts are a great base for any number of tempting vegetable combinations. This recipe can be varied many ways. For example, sprinkle the pizza with grated mozzarella or cheddar cheese before adding the Parmesan. Use pita bread instead of pizza crust, and drizzle with creamy Italian dressing mixed with a little tahini.

1 small rutabaga, peeled

1 red onion, sliced

4 plum tomatoes

2 small zucchini, halved lengthwise

2 small Japanese eggplants

1 large (about 1 pound) prebaked
pizza crust

2 cloves garlic, minced

2 tablespoons grated Parmesan
cheese, optional

1 tablespoon minced fresh sage or 1
teaspoon dried sage, or to taste

Salt and freshly ground black pepper
to taste

1. Preheat the broiler. Spray a baking sheet with nonstick cooking spray.

2. Cut the rutabaga into ¼-inch-thick slices, and place in a steamer set in a saucepan of water. Cover, and steam for 5 minutes.

3. Place the rutabaga and other vegetables on the baking sheet, and broil, turning frequently, until fork-tender and golden brown. Remove from the heat, and let stand until cool enough to handle. Reduce the oven temperature to 500F.

4. Cut the rutabaga into ¼-inch-thick strips. Cut the zucchini and eggplants into ¼-inch-thick slices.

5. Mash the tomatoes in a bowl with a fork. Spread the tomatoes evenly over the pizza crust. Scatter the garlic on top of the tomatoes, then scatter the broiled vegetables on top. Sprinkle with the Parmesan.

6. Bake until the crust is crisp and the vegetables are hot, for about 12 minutes. Season with sage, salt and pepper, and serve.

PER SERVING: 332 CAL; 11G PROT; 2G FAT; 60G CARB; 0MG CHOL; 934MG SOD; 8G FIBER

PIZZA MARGHERITA

This versatile pie originated in Naples in the 1800s. Tradition has it that a local pizza baker was commissioned to create a special pizza to honor visiting Italian royalty, King Umberto and his queen, Margherita. Hence, the name of the pie. This pizza has probably become the standard by which all others are judged. It welcomes additional cheeses, toppings or sauce, depending on your taste.

1 12- to 14-inch pizza crust, freshly
made or commercial

1 tablespoon olive oil, optional

1 teaspoon minced garlic

1 cup basil-flavored tomato sauce or
pizza sauce

4 plum tomatoes, cored, seeded and
diced (see page 46)

¼ cup julienned fresh basil plus
extra leaves for garnish

2 cups shredded low-fat, regular or
soy mozzarella cheese

¾ cup grated Parmesan cheese

1. Preheat the oven to 450F.

2. Prebake the fresh pizza crust if using, for 3 to 4 minutes. Remove from the oven, and set aside to cool slightly. Brush the crust with the oil, if using. Sprinkle with the garlic, and spread the sauce evenly over the top. Top with the tomatoes, basil and mozzarella. Sprinkle with ½ cup of the Parmesan.

3. Bake for 12 to 15 minutes, or until the cheese melts. Remove from the oven, garnish with the reserved basil leaves and the remaining Parmesan, and serve.

PER SERVING: 340 CAL; 20G PROT; 14G FAT; 34G CARB; 30MG CHOL; 770MG SOD; 4G FIBER

CALZONES WITH SUN-DRIED TOMATOES AND GARLIC SERVES 6

Calzones are like pizza "suitcases": circles of dough folded over a filling, baked and ready to go. You can freeze these before you finish making them. To bake frozen calzones, let them thaw at room temperature almost completely, then proceed as directed in steps 11 and 12.

Crust

1 package active dry yeast

Pinch granulated sugar

3 cups all-purpose flour plus extra for kneading

½ teaspoon salt

2 to 3 tablespoons olive oil

1 tablespoon cornmeal for sprinkling

Filling

2 or 3 large whole heads garlic

12 sun-dried tomatoes, drained if oil-packed (reserve oil)

⅓ cup roughly chopped fresh parsley leaves

1 scallion, minced

1 teaspoon olive oil or oil from sun-dried tomatoes

8 large fresh basil leaves, julienned

2 to 4 ounces fontina or Bel Paese cheese, rind removed and chopped coarsely

2 to 4 ounces mozzarella cheese, diced

1 tablespoon cornmeal

1. To make the Crust: Sprinkle the yeast over 1 cup of warm (105F to 115F) water in a bowl. Add the sugar, and stir to mix. Let sit until foamy, for about 10 minutes.

2. Combine the flour and salt in a nonreactive bowl. Stir in the yeast mixture and the oil, adding more flour if needed to form a ball. Turn out the dough onto a lightly floured surface, and knead until smooth and elastic, for about 5 minutes.

3. Place the dough in a lightly oiled bowl, and turn to coat. Cover with a tea towel, and let rise in a warm spot until doubled in bulk, for about 45 minutes.

4. Punch down the dough, and divide into 6 equal portions. Cover, and let sit for 30 minutes.

5. Preheat the oven to 350F.

6. Meanwhile, to make the Filling: Slice off, and discard the tops of the garlic heads. Place the garlic on a sheet of aluminum foil, drizzle with a few drops of oil if desired, wrap tightly and bake until very soft, for about 1 hour. Remove the garlic from the oven, and when cool enough to handle, squeeze the garlic out of the skins into a small dish. Set aside.

7. Put the tomatoes in a bowl of warm water for 15 minutes, then drain. Thinly slice the tomatoes, and put the slices into a mixing bowl. Combine the parsley, scallion and oil in a separate bowl. Set aside.

8. Working with 1 dough portion at a time, roll it out to a circle about ⅛ inch thick on a lightly floured surface. Spread one-sixth of the scallion mixture on top of the dough, leaving a 1-inch border around the edge. Spread one-sixth of the garlic on top, and add one-sixth of the basil, one-sixth of the fontina cheese, one-sixth of the mozzarella cheese and one-sixth of the tomatoes.

9. Use a pastry brush or your fingertips to moisten the edge of the dough (the unoiled part) with a bit of water. Fold the circle in half to enclose the filling; press tightly to seal and to thin the edges. Using your fingers, fold ½ inch of the thinned-out edge back onto itself, and crimp. Repeat with the remaining dough and filling to make 6 calzones. Refrigerate for 1 hour before baking. (At this point, the calzones may be wrapped in plastic and frozen for up to 8 weeks.)

10. Preheat the oven to 450F. Place the oven rack on the lowest level in the oven. Sprinkle the cornmeal over a large baking sheet.

11. Place the calzones on the baking sheet, and spray them with a fine mist of water to make the dough crisp. Bake, spraying with water again about halfway through cooking time, until lightly browned, for about 30 minutes.

PER CALZONE: 370 CAL; 13G PROT; 9G FAT; 57G CARB; 17MG CHOL; 317MG SOD; 4G FIBER

GREEK PIZZA

This pie offers classic Greek flavors.

1 12- to 14-inch pizza crust, freshly made or commercial

1 cup pizza sauce

1 teaspoon minced fresh oregano or ½ teaspoon dried oregano

10 to 15 thinly sliced red onion rings, or to taste

1½ cups shredded low-fat, regular or soy mozzarella cheese

½ cup crumbled feta cheese

2 plum tomatoes, cored, seeded and diced (see page 46)

⅓ cup chopped or sliced pitted black Greek kalamata olives

1. Preheat the oven to 450F.

2. Prebake the fresh pizza crust if using, for 3 to 4 minutes. Remove from the oven, and set aside to cool slightly. Spread the sauce on the crust. Sprinkle the pizza with the oregano, arrange the onion rings on the sauce and top with the mozzarella cheese. Sprinkle the feta cheese, tomatoes and olives over the mozzarella cheese.

3. Bake for 10 to 12 minutes, or until the cheese melts. Remove from the oven, and serve.

PER SERVING: 300 CAL; 15G PROT; 12G FAT; 35G CARB; 25MG CHOL; 910MG SOD; 4G FIBER

HERB GARDEN PIZZA

If you use dried herbs, simply cut in third the measurements in the recipe. You can also try different variations of herbs based on what you have on hand

1 12- to 14-inch pizza crust, freshly made or commercial

3 tablespoons olive oil

2 to 4 cloves garlic, crushed, or to taste

3 to 4 tablespoons julienned fresh basil

2 tablespoons chopped fresh parsley

1 teaspoon fresh thyme

1 teaspoon minced fresh marjoram

1 teaspoon minced fresh oregano

1 cup (4 ounces) shredded low-fat, regular or soy mozzarella cheese

1. Preheat the oven to 450F.

2. Prebake the fresh pizza crust if using, for 3 to 4 minutes. Remove from the oven, and set aside to cool slightly. Brush the crust liberally with the oil. Sprinkle the garlic and herbs on top of the pizza, and add the cheese.

3. Bake for 6 to 8 minutes. Remove from the oven, and serve.

PER SERVING: 260 CAL; 10G PROT; 13G FAT; 28G CARB; 10MG CHOL; 380MG SOD; 3G FIBER

Making Your Own Crust

Homemade pizzas are a taste treat, and making your own crust at home only adds to the pleasure of eating your pie. You can control what goes into the dough— such as dried herbs and other seasonings—and you can enhance its nutritional value by using whole wheat flour. Best of all, pizza dough and pie making can be a solitary pleasure or together-time for the family. Running out of time? Use premade fresh or frozen pizza dough. If you can't find prepared fresh pizza dough, frozen bread dough is available at most supermarkets. Be sure to purchase frozen dough that comes in packages of 3 loaves, not in prebake or brown-and-serve loaves. Let the dough defrost at room temperature for several hours, and allow 1 loaf for 2 to 3 medium-sized pizzas, depending on how thick you like your crust.

Since frozen bread dough is sweeter than traditional pizza dough, kneading in ¼ cup of oat bran, toasted wheat germ or cornmeal to the dough will add flavor and texture to the finished crust. You may need a small amount of olive oil—up to 1 tablespoon—to soften the bread dough. Other time-saver crusts come premade and prebaked available in most supermarkets. Whole-grain crusts are also sold at specialty food stores.

PUSH-BUTTON DOUGH FOR PIZZAS

MAKES 1 LARGE OR 2 SMALL PIZZAS

Use unbleached all-purpose flour rather than bleached—it makes a better, more resilient food-processor dough. And don't be tempted to process the dough longer than specified in hopes of eliminating the little bit of kneading called for. The results won't be the same.

1½ teaspoons active dry yeast

2 teaspoons salt

2 teaspoons olive oil plus extra for greasing bowl

½ teaspoon granulated sugar

1¾ cups plus 1 tablespoon unbleached all-purpose flour plus extra for kneading

1. Put ¾ cup of warm (105F to 115F) water in a food processor bowl. Sprinkle the yeast over it, and add the salt, oil and sugar. Process briefly to mix. Let rest for 1 minute. Add 1¾ cups of the flour, and process in two 4-second bursts, waiting several seconds between each. Process for one more 4-second burst, adding the remaining 1 tablespoon of flour with the machine running. Let the dough rest for 1 minute.

2. Lightly oil a bowl. Turn the dough out onto a lightly floured surface—the dough will be somewhat sticky. Using floured hands, knead gently for 30 to 45 seconds. Place the dough in the oiled bowl, rotating to coat the entire surface. Cover with plastic wrap, and set aside in a warm spot to rise until doubled in bulk, for 1 to 1½ hours. Proceed as directed in individual recipes.

PER ⅛ OF DOUGH: 112 CAL; 3G PROT; 1G FAT; 21G CARB; 0MG CHOL; 538MG SOD; 1G FIBER

WHOLE WHEAT PIZZA CRUST

MAKES 2 LARGE OR 4 SMALL PIZZAS

1 tablespoon active dry yeast
2 tablespoons olive oil
1½ teaspoons salt
2 cups whole wheat flour
1½ to 2 cups bread flour

1. Mix the yeast with ½ cup warm (105F to 115F) water in a bowl, and set aside for 5 to 10 minutes, or until the yeast begins to foam.

2. Add another 1 cup of warm water, the oil and salt and stir to combine. Using a portable or standing mixer, add the flour by the cupful until a sticky dough comes together. Knead in the machine or by hand for 5 minutes, or until the dough is smooth and elastic. Cover, and set to rise in a warm place for 1 to 1½ hours, or until doubled in size.

3. Punch the dough down, and form into equal-sized balls for 2 large or 4 small pizzas. Spray pizza pans or baking sheets with nonstick cooking spray or rub with oil. Let the dough rest for 30 minutes, shape into pizza crusts and place in the pans or on the sheets.

PER SERVING: 150 CAL; 5G PROT; 3G FAT; 27G CARB; 0MG CHOL; 290MG SOD; 3G FIBER

"MEAT" LOVERS' PIZZA

SERVES 6

For a shortcut on the tomato sauce, use a can of preseasoned Italian crushed tomatoes or tomato sauce instead of making your own.

1 12- to 14-inch pizza crust, freshly made or commercial

Simple Seasoned Tomato Sauce

1 cup canned tomato sauce
¼ cup chopped onion
1 tablespoon olive oil
1 tablespoon Italian seasoning
Salt and freshly ground black pepper to taste

"Meat" Topping

1 tablespoon olive oil, divided
4 ounces soy "ground meat"
2 soy "sausage" links, sliced into ½-inch rounds
¼ cup chopped onion
2 cups shredded low-fat mozzarella or soy mozzarella
12 slices soy "pepperoni"
6 slices soy "Canadian bacon"

1. Preheat the oven to 450F.

2. Prebake the fresh pizza crust if using, for 3 to 4 minutes. Remove from the oven, and set aside to cool slightly.

3. To make the Simple Seasoned Tomato Sauce: Combine the tomato sauce, onion, oil, Italian seasoning, salt and pepper. Set aside.

4. To make the "Meat" Topping: Heat 1 teaspoon of the oil in a large skillet over medium-high heat, and sauté the "ground meat" and "sausage" links for about 3 minutes, or until hot and slightly crispy. Using a spatula, remove the "meat" from the pan, add the remaining 2 teaspoons of oil to the skillet, and sauté the onions for 3 minutes, or until translucent. Add the Tomato Sauce, and stir. Remove from the heat.

5. Spread the Simply Seasoned Tomato Sauce over the crust. Top with the "ground meat," "sausage," cheese, "pepperoni" and "Canadian bacon" slices.

6. Bake for 13 to 15 minutes, or until the cheese melts. Remove from the oven, and serve.

PER SERVING: 360 CAL; 27G PROT; 13G FAT; 36G CARB; 20MG CHOL; 1,040MG SOD; 6G FIBER

SUN-DRIED TOMATO, GOAT CHEESE AND ARTICHOKE PIZZA

If you are not using oil-packed tomatoes, reconstitute them with water before you start making the pie. The goat cheese does not melt completely, but will flatten and brown slightly.

1 12- to 14-inch pizza crust, freshly made or commercial

1 tablespoon olive oil

1 cup tomato sauce

1 cup chopped baby artichokes or artichoke hearts, frozen or water-packed and drained

2 cups shredded low-fat or regular soy mozzarella cheese

4 ounces goat cheese, cut into small pieces

1 cup sun-dried tomatoes, reconstituted, or ⅓ to ½ cup oil-packed sun-dried tomatoes, drained

1. Preheat the oven to 450F.

2. Prebake the fresh pizza crust if using, for 3 to 4 minutes. Remove from the oven, and set aside to cool slightly. Brush the oil on the crust. Top the crust with the sauce and artichokes. Sprinkle with the mozzarella, goat cheese and tomatoes.

3. Bake for 12 to 15 minutes, or until the cheese melts. Remove from the oven, and serve.

PER SERVING: 350 CAL; 20G PROT; 16G FAT; 36G CARB; 30MG CHOL; 830MG SOD; 5G FIBER

PIZZA PROVENÇAL

This pie brings together the robust and sunny flavors of the south of France. For an injection of gusto, add garlic to taste.

1 12- to 14-inch pizza crust, freshly made or commercial

2 tablespoons olive oil

½ cup chopped onion

1 small Italian eggplant, peeled and sliced into ½-inch-thick slices

2 tomatoes, cored and chopped

½ cup green beans, cut into 1- to 2-inch pieces

10 to 15 pitted black olives

2 tablespoons capers, drained

1 tablespoon balsamic vinegar

1 tablespoon julienned fresh basil

1 teaspoon fresh thyme or ½ teaspoon dried thyme

2 cups shredded low-fat, regular or soy mozzarella cheese

1. Preheat the oven to 450F.

2. Prebake the fresh pizza crust if using, for 3 to 4 minutes. Remove from the oven, and set aside to cool slightly. Heat the oil in a large skillet over medium heat, and sauté the onions for 3 to 4 minutes, until translucent. Add the eggplant, cover, and cook for 3 to 4 minutes, turning occasionally. Add the tomatoes and green beans, cover, and stir occasionally for another 3 to 4 minutes. Add the olives, capers, vinegar, basil and thyme. Stir, and remove from the heat. Spread the vegetable mixture over the crust, and top with the cheese.

3. Bake for 12 to 15 minutes, or until the cheese melts. Remove from the oven, and serve.

PER SERVING: 340 CAL; 16G PROT; 15G FAT; 36G CARB; 20MG CHOL; 620MG SOD; 4G FIBER

This pizza sounds unusual, but mashed potatoes add a pleasing taste and texture. If you are using leftover mashed potatoes, reheat them so that they'll spread more easily.

1 12- to 14-inch pizza crust, freshly made or commercial

1 tablespoon olive oil for brushing, optional

1 head roasted garlic (see below)

1 to 2 cups warm mashed potatoes

1 15-ounce container nonfat ricotta cheese, optional

2 cups (8 ounces) grated soy mozzarella cheese or fresh mozzarella, thinly sliced

1. Preheat the oven to 450F.

2. Prebake the fresh pizza crust if using, for 3 to 4 minutes. Remove from the oven, and set aside to cool slightly. Brush the crust with oil, if using, and spread the garlic on the crust. Top with spoonfuls of potatoes, spreading the potatoes evenly over the garlic, ½ to 1 inch thick. Spoon the ricotta, if using, over the potatoes, and top with the mozzarella.

3. Bake for 12 to 14 minutes, or until the cheese melts and the pizza is hot all the way through.

PER SERVING: 340 CAL; 21G PROT; 9G FAT; 42G CARB; 35MG CHOL; 650MG SOD; 4G FIBER

Roasted Garlic

To make roasted garlic, cut ½ to 1 inch off the top of a full head of garlic, drizzle the garlic with 1 tablespoon or more of olive oil, wrap the head in aluminum foil, and roast for 30 minutes or 1 hour at 400F, or until the garlic feels tender when pierced with a knife. Cool the garlic, then squeeze the roasted garlic out of the skins and onto the pizza crust. For garlic lovers, double the amount of garlic. Save unused roasted garlic in a covered container in the refrigerator.

ULTIMATE GREEN PIZZA

Using all of the green vegetables listed will produce a luscious and unusual pie.

1 12- to 14-inch pizza crust, freshly made or commercial

2 tablespoons olive oil

¼ cup chopped onion

1 cup chopped broccoli

½ cup chopped frozen artichoke hearts or canned and drained artichoke hearts

1 small zucchini, sliced into ½-inch-thick slices

½ cup 1-inch-long asparagus tips

1 cup julienned fresh spinach

½ cup pesto sauce

2 cups shredded low-fat, regular or soy mozzarella cheese

¼ cup grated Parmesan cheese

1. Preheat the oven to 450F.

2. Prebake the fresh pizza crust if using, for 3 to 4 minutes. Remove from the oven, and set aside to cool slightly.

3. Heat the oil in a large skillet over medium heat, and sauté the onions for 3 to 4 minutes, until translucent. Add the broccoli, artichokes, zucchini and asparagus. Cover, and cook for 4 to 5 minutes more, stirring occasionally until the vegetables begin to soften. Remove from the heat, and add the spinach. Stir the mixture until the spinach has just begun to wilt, for about 1 minute. Spoon the pesto sauce onto the crust, spreading it evenly. Top with the cooked vegetables, and sprinkle with the mozzarella and Parmesan cheeses.

4. Bake for 10 to 12 minutes, or until the cheese melts. Remove from the oven, and serve.

PER SERVING: 430 CAL; 21G PROT; 24G FAT; 34G CARB; 30MG CHOL; 700MG SOD; 5G FIBER

CARAMELIZED SQUASH PIZZA

The filling is equally good on any kind of sturdy bread or on prebaked pizza crusts. You may roast the vegetables up to 2 days ahead.

1½ pounds winter squash, peeled and sliced very thinly

1 large sweet onion, such as Maui, Bermuda or Vidalia, sliced very thinly

2 teaspoons minced fresh rosemary or 1 teaspoon dried rosemary

1 teaspoon dried sage

1½ teaspoons salt

1½ teaspoons coarsely ground black pepper

6 tablespoons olive oil

1 teaspoon mashed garlic

2 prebaked medium-sized pizza crusts

¼ cup grated Parmesan cheese

1½ cups crumbled feta cheese

1. Preheat the oven to 325F.

2. Place the sliced squash and onion in a baking dish, and toss with the rosemary, sage, 1 teaspoon of the salt, 1 teaspoon of the pepper and 3 tablespoons of the oil to coat. Cover with foil or a tight-fitting lid.

3. Bake for about 1 hour, or until the squash is tender and the onions begin to caramelize. Remove from the oven, and increase the temperature to 375F.

4. Mix the remaining 3 tablespoons of oil with the remaining ½ teaspoon of salt, ½ teaspoon of pepper and the garlic. Brush each pizza with the mixture. Sprinkle on the Parmesan cheese, and top with the squash, onion and feta cheese.

5. Bake for 15 minutes to heat through. Remove from the oven, and serve.

PER SERVING: 240 CAL; 11G PROT; 10G FAT; 31G CARB; 35MG CHOL; 1,220MG SOD; 6G FIBER

MEXICAN PIZZA

This zesty pie captures the beloved flavors of the Southwest.

1 12- to 14-inch pizza crust, freshly made or commercial

2 tablespoons vegetable oil

6 ounces taco-seasoned soy "ground meat"

5 fresh tomatillos, thinly sliced

1 cup salsa, or more as desired

1 2¼-ounce can sliced black olives, drained

2 cups shredded cheddar cheese

1 avocado, peeled and sliced, for garnish

¼ cup cilantro leaves for garnish

¼ cup crumbled tortilla chips for garnish

1. Preheat the oven to 450F.

2. Prebake the fresh pizza crust if using, for 3 to 4 minutes. Remove from the oven, and set aside to cool slightly.

3. Heat 1 tablespoon of the oil in a large skillet over medium heat, and sauté the "ground meat" for about 1 minute. Set aside.

4. Layer the tomatillos on the crust, and top with the "ground meat." Add the salsa, olives and cheddar cheese, spreading evenly.

5. Bake for 12 to 15 minutes, or until the cheese melts. Remove from the oven, garnish with the avocado, cilantro and chips and serve.

PER SERVING: 470 CAL; 22G PROT; 26G FAT; 42G CARB; 40MG CHOL; 940MG SOD; 9G FIBER

POLENTA "PIZZA"

A popular dish in Italy, polenta refers to both a specific type of cornmeal and the dish the cornmeal is used to make. Find granulated garlic in your local health food store.

2 18-ounce packages precooked polenta

2 tablespoons cornstarch

2 tablespoons unbleached all-purpose flour

1 tablespoon granulated garlic

½ cup plus ⅓ cup soy Parmesan or regular Parmesan cheese

2 cups tomato sauce

4 slices soy "Canadian bacon," cut into 2-inch strips

½ medium-sized red bell pepper, sliced into 2-inch strips

3 scallions, thinly sliced

1. Preheat the oven to 450F. Spray a pizza pan with nonstick cooking spray.

2. Slice the polenta, and place in a food processor. Process the polenta, and add 2 tablespoons of water, the cornstarch, flour, garlic and ½ cup of the Parmesan. Blend until smooth. Spread the polenta evenly on the pizza pan.

3. Bake for 15 minutes. Remove the polenta from the oven, and spread the sauce evenly over the crust. Top with the soy "bacon," bell pepper, scallions and remaining ⅓ cup of Parmesan.

4. Bake for 25 minutes more, until heated through. Remove from the oven, and let stand for 5 minutes before serving.

PER SERVING: 179 CAL; 11G PROT; 1G FAT; 31G CARB; 0MG CHOL; 694MG SOD; 3G FIBER

When sweet onions like Vidalia or Maui are in season, by all means use them. Always keep phyllo sheets covered with plastic wrap to prevent them from becoming dry, brittle and difficult to work with.

1½ tablespoons extra-virgin olive oil

3 pounds onions, thinly sliced (10½ cups)

1 large clove garlic, minced

1 tablespoon herbes de Provence

¾ teaspoon salt

½ teaspoon freshly ground black pepper

1 bay leaf

8 18 x 14–inch frozen phyllo sheets, thawed

24 Greek black olives, pitted and halved

1. Heat 1½ teaspoons of the oil in a large, deep nonstick skillet over medium heat. Add one-third of the onions, and cook, stirring, until slightly wilted, for 4 to 5 minutes. Remove to a plate.

2. Repeat twice with the remaining oil and onions, removing each batch of onions to a plate when slightly wilted.

3. Return all of the onions to the skillet. Add the garlic, herbes de Provence, salt, pepper and bay leaf. Cook, stirring occasionally, until the onions are tender and the consistency of a thick, chunky sauce, for about 25 minutes.

4. Remove from the heat and cool slightly, stirring occasionally. Discard the bay leaf.

5. Preheat the oven to 400F. Spray an 11 x 17–inch baking pan with nonstick cooking spray.

6. Unwrap the phyllo, discard any torn sheets and immediately cover with plastic wrap to prevent them from drying. Remove the wrap, and lightly coat the top sheet with nonstick cooking spray, starting from the outside edge. Lift carefully, and center on the prepared pan.

7. Repeat with the remaining phyllo and more cooking spray, stacking the sheets in the pan. Gently ease the phyllo into the corners of the pan, and fold or crimp the edges to form a ½-inch raised crust. Spread the onion mixture evenly over the phyllo, and sprinkle with the olives.

8. Bake until the phyllo is golden brown and shrinks from the edges of the pan, for about 20 minutes. For easy cutting, carefully slide the pizza out of the pan onto the back of another baking pan. Using kitchen scissors, cut into rectangular slices. Serve warm.

PER SERVING: 212 CAL; 5G PROT; 7G FAT; 34G CARB; 0MG CHOL; 552MG SOD; 5G FIBER

SPAGHETTI PIE

If you like pasta, you'll be happy to eat it in a new way. This pie combines cheese and pasta in a hearty main course dish. Serve with a tart green salad and sorbet for dessert.

9 ounces fresh linguini

3 large eggs

1 bunch scallions, thinly sliced

8 ounces goat cheese, crumbled

8 ounces low-fat ricotta cheese

Salt and freshly ground black pepper to taste

1 unbaked 9-inch deep-dish piecrust (page 285)

⅓ cup grated Parmesan cheese

1. Preheat the oven to 375F.

2. Heat a pot of lightly salted water over medium heat, and when it is boiling, cook the linguini according to the package directions. Drain, and set aside.

3. Mix together the eggs, half of the scallions, the goat cheese, ricotta, salt and pepper. Stir in the linguini, and scoop the mixture into the piecrust. Sprinkle the top with the remaining scallions and the Parmesan.

4. Bake for 40 minutes, or until the top turns golden. Remove from the oven, and serve hot.

PER SERVING: 480 CAL; 22G PROT; 25G FAT; 43G CARB; 155MG CHOL; 520MG SOD; 2G FIBER

EASY MANICOTTI ALLA ROMANA

Manicotti noodles are also called "stove-pipe pasta." They are cooked until soft but still slightly firm so that they are tough enough to be handled easily. These tube-shaped noodles will continue to soften up when they are baked in a covered pan.

2 tablespoons olive oil

2 cups diced onion

1 tablespoon minced garlic

1 cup sliced fresh mushrooms, optional

4 12-ounce packages frozen chopped spinach, well thawed and squeezed dry

10½ ounces firm tofu

½ cup grated Parmesan cheese or soy Parmesan cheese

1 teaspoon salt

1 teaspoon freshly ground black pepper

¼ teaspoon ground nutmeg

8 ounces dried manicotti shells

2 cups prepared marinara sauce

1. Preheat the oven to 350F.

2. Heat a 3-quart saucepan over medium heat, and add the oil. Sauté the onion and garlic until golden. Add the mushrooms, and cook until browned, for about 5 minutes.

3. Add the spinach to the pan, and heat through.

4. Put the tofu in a food processor, and purée. Add the Parmesan cheese, salt, pepper and nutmeg. Process again to mix, and pour the mixture into the spinach. Mix well, and heat through.

5. Bring 4 quarts of salted water to a boil, and slide the manicotti into the water. Remove after 1 minute, and drop the manicotti into a bowl of cold water. Remove from the water carefully, and place on a dry kitchen towel. Using a spoon, fill each manicotti with about ½ cup of the spinach filling. Repeat for the remaining manicotti. Place them in a glass baking dish or lasagna pan. Pour the marinara over the top, and cover the dish with foil.

6. Bake for 45 minutes, or until heated through. Remove from the oven, and serve hot.

PER SERVING: 340 CAL; 20G PROT; 9G FAT; 50G CARB; 5MG CHOL; 890MG SOD; 10G FIBER

MOROCCAN TOFU TAGINE WITH JEWELED COUSCOUS

A North African stew, a tagine is one in which vegetables and spices are usually simmered with meat or seafood. This one keeps the spice flavoring and substitutes tofu for the meat. The jeweled couscous adds sparkle to the dish.

Moroccan Tofu Tagine

2 tablespoons olive oil

1 pound extra-firm tofu, drained and cut into ¾-inch cubes

1 large Vidalia or other sweet onion, chopped

3 large cloves garlic, minced

1½ teaspoons ground ginger

1¼ teaspoons ground cinnamon

¾ teaspoon ground cumin

¼ teaspoon paprika

1 cup low-sodium vegetable stock or Vegetable Stock (page 332)

2 tablespoons honey

Juice and grated zest of 1 lemon

Salt and freshly ground black pepper to taste

½ cup sliced almonds, toasted (see page 47)

Jeweled Couscous

2¼ cups low-sodium vegetable stock or Vegetable Stock (page 332)

1¼ cups uncooked couscous

¼ cup chopped dried cranberries

¼ cup chopped dried apricots

3 tablespoons minced fresh flat-leaf parsley

3 tablespoons minced fresh mint

Juice and grated zest of 1 lemon

Salt and freshly ground black pepper to taste

1. To make the Moroccan Tofu Tagine: Heat 1 tablespoon of the oil in a large skillet over medium-high heat. Add the tofu, and stir-fry until lightly browned, for about 7 minutes. Remove to another plate.

2. Heat the remaining 1 tablespoon of oil in the same large skillet over medium-high heat. Add the onion and garlic, and stir-fry for 5 minutes. Add the ginger, cinnamon, cumin and paprika, and stir-fry for 1 minute. Return the tofu to the skillet. Stir in the broth, honey, lemon juice and zest, and bring to a boil. Reduce the heat to medium, cover and cook until the tofu has absorbed the flavors, for about 15 minutes. Using a slotted spoon, remove the tofu to a plate, and cover with foil to keep warm.

3. Add the almonds to the liquid remaining in the skillet, and bring to a boil over high heat. Cook until the liquid is slightly syrupy, for about 5 minutes. Remove from the heat, and season to taste. Set aside.

4. To make the Jeweled Couscous: Bring the stock to a boil in a saucepan over high heat and stir in the couscous, cranberries and apricots. Bring back to a boil, cover and turn the heat off. Let stand until all the water is absorbed, for 5 to 10 minutes.

5. Fluff the couscous mixture with a fork, stirring in the parsley, mint, lemon juice and zest. Remove from the heat, and let stand, covered, for 5 minutes. Season with salt and pepper.

6. Divide the couscous mixture among 6 plates, and top with the tofu. Drizzle with the honey-almond sauce, and serve at once.

PER SERVING: 365 CAL; 12G PROT; 11G FAT; 44G CARB; 0MG CHOL; 137MG SOD; 4G FIBER

SEASHELLS WITH BUTTERNUT SQUASH

Italian cooks love to fill pasta with pumpkin, and butternut squash is a member of the pumpkin family. You may substitute frozen winter squash or canned solid-pack pumpkin for the butternut squash. You will need four 12-ounce packages of frozen squash and 2½ one-pound cans of pumpkin purée. Freezing tofu changes the texture of it, which makes it a better complement to the soft sweetness of the squash.

3 pounds butternut squash

2 tablespoons olive oil

2 cups diced onion

2 10½-ounce packages silken firm tofu, frozen and thawed

1 cup chopped pecans

2 teaspoons salt

½ teaspoon ground white pepper

½ teaspoon freshly ground black pepper

12 ounces jumbo dried pasta shells

4 cups prepared marinara sauce

1 tablespoon ground cinnamon

1. Preheat the oven to 350F.

2. Cut the squash in half lengthwise, and remove the seeds and fibers. Place the squash cut sides down on a baking sheet, and bake until tender when pierced with a thin knife, for about 45 minutes. Remove from the oven, and set aside to cool.

3. Use a tablespoon to scoop out chunks of the squash when cool enough to handle. Use a potato masher or electric mixer to break the squash into smaller pieces, and set aside. This may be done a day ahead.

4. Heat the oil in a 4-quart saucepan over medium heat. Sauté the onion until soft, for 5 to 7 minutes. Crumble the tofu, add it to the pan, and sauté it until lightly browned. Add the pecans, salt, both peppers and the prepared squash. Cook together for 30 minutes over medium heat, stirring often.

5. Bring 8 quarts of salted water to a boil, and drop the shells into the water. Cook for 15 minutes, or until al dente. Drain, and spread on dry kitchen towels.

6. Meanwhile, heat the marinara and add the cinnamon. Bring to a boil, and cook for 10 minutes. Pour 1 cup of the marinara in the bottom of a large baking dish. Fill each shell with a heaping tablespoon of squash filling, and place the shells in rows in the baking dish. Cover the shells with the remaining marinara. Cover with a sheet of aluminum foil.

7. Bake for 25 to 30 minutes, or until heated through, remove from the oven and serve.

PER SERVING: 440 CAL; 15G PROT; 15G FAT; 65G CARB; 0MG CHOL; 970MG SOD; 9G FIBER

PASTA SHELLS WITH
BLACK-EYED PEAS AND ARTICHOKES

This may not be your Italian grandmother's traditional recipe, but the combination of artichokes and black-eyed peas seasoned with caraway seeds and smoked tofu (or smoky cheese) is irresistible.

12 ounces medium-sized dried pasta shells

1 15-ounce can black-eyed peas, rinsed and drained, or 1½ cups cooked black-eyed peas

1 tablespoon olive oil

1 medium-sized red onion, chopped

4 cloves garlic, minced

1½ teaspoons caraway seeds, lightly crushed

⅛ teaspoon crushed red pepper

1 14-ounce can artichoke hearts, drained, rinsed and coarsely chopped

2 cups low-sodium vegetable broth or Vegetable Stock (page 332)

¼ teaspoon salt

⅓ cup chopped fresh parsley

1 to 2 teaspoons cider vinegar

¼ teaspoon freshly ground black pepper

1 cup diced smoked tofu or grated smoked mozzarella cheese

1. Heat a pot of lightly salted water over medium heat, and when it is boiling, cook the pasta according to the package directions. Drain, rinse, drain again and set aside in a serving bowl.

2. Meanwhile, measure out ¼ cup of the black-eyed peas, and mash them with fork in a bowl. Set aside.

3. Heat the oil in a large nonstick skillet over medium-high heat. Add the onion, and cook, stirring often, until softened, for 3 to 5 minutes. Add the garlic, caraway and crushed red pepper, and cook, stirring, for 30 to 60 seconds. Add the artichoke hearts and mashed and whole black-eyed peas, and stir well. Add the broth and salt, and bring to a simmer. Reduce the heat to medium-low, and cook, stirring occasionally, until the flavors have blended, for about 10 minutes. Stir in the parsley, vinegar and pepper. Add the pasta and tofu, and toss to coat. Serve immediately.

PER SERVING: 313 CAL; 10G PROT; 5G FAT; 51G CARB; 0MG CHOL; 299MG SOD; 11G FIBER

FRESH PASTA DOUGH

Making pasta dough may seem complicated, but with a little practice, it's a breeze. Besides, store-bought pasta can't compare in taste or texture. You may make fresh pasta dough by hand or with the help of a food processor—both techniques are described below. The amount of flour you will need can vary greatly, depending on the size of your eggs, the batch your flour comes from and even the weather. If the dough is wet or sticks to your hands rather than forming a soft ball, add 1 teaspoon of flour at a time, kneading between additions, until the dough reaches the right consistency. If the dough is dry and crumbly, add 1 teaspoon of water at a time, kneading between additions, until it reaches the right consistency.

If you use water instead of eggs or egg substitute, the water should be hot from the tap, not boiling. This version is somewhat stickier than the egg or egg-substitute methods, so be extra attentive to flouring the rolling pin, work surface and your hands.

About 3 cups unbleached all-purpose flour

4 large eggs, 1 cup egg substitute or 1 cup hot water

To make Pasta by Hand: Pour the flour onto a flat surface, making a mound. Make a well in the center. Crack the eggs into the well, and break up the yolks with a fork, or pour in the egg substitute or hot water. With your fingers, begin drawing in a little bit of flour at a time and mixing it with the eggs or water. When the mixture forms a paste, draw in all the flour. Mix well, and begin kneading. Knead until the dough forms a soft, firm ball, for about 8 minutes. Wrap the dough in a damp dishcloth.

To make Pasta in a Food Processor: Insert the metal blade in the processor, pour in 1½ cups of the flour and crack 2 eggs on top, or start the processor and pour in half of the egg substitute or hot water through the feeding tube. Process until the dough forms a ball on top of the blades and cleans the sides of the bowl, about 1 minute. Then process for 2 more minutes to knead it. Remove the dough and wrap it in a damp dishcloth. Repeat with the remaining ingredients.

1. To shape the Pasta: Remove a piece of dough appropriate for the recipe you are making—an egg-sized piece for ravioli or cappelletti; a larger piece for tortellini, cannelloni, agnolotti or shells. Keep the remaining dough covered with a towel. Roll out the dough with a pasta machine or a rolling pin until it is almost translucent. When using a pasta machine, pass a floured piece of dough through the first setting, flour again and pass through the second setting, and continue this process ending with the thinnest setting. Cut into shapes needed for the dish you are making and add the filling if necessary. Try to use up as much of the rolled-out pasta as possible the first time. You may collect the trimmings and roll them again, but rolling too many times toughens the dough. Repeat with the remaining dough.

2. To cook the Pasta: Bring a large pot of water to a rolling boil, and add a pinch of salt. Add the fresh pasta, and stir gently. It will begin bobbing to the surface after 1 to 2 minutes, indicating that it's almost ready. Stir and cook for another 30 seconds or until it tastes done. Pasta should be served *al dente*, or slightly firm to the tooth. Do not let fresh pasta overcook.

PER SERVING: 248 CAL; 10G PROT; 4G FAT; 43G CARB; 110MG CHOL; 36MG SOD; 2G FIBER

PASTA WITH PORTOBELLO MUSHROOMS IN MUSTARD SAUCE

SERVES 6

Talk about fusion! This recipe combines Italian pasta and a French-style pan sauce flavored with Japanese mirin, all cooked in a Chinese wok. It also proves you can use a wok for just about anything. For best results, choose a short pasta shape that will hold the sauce.

2½ cups small dried pasta shapes, such as orecchiette or gnocchi

2½ tablespoons olive oill

8 ounces portobello mushrooms, stemmed and thinly sliced

1½ teaspoons salt

6 cloves garlic, minced

1 large red onion, thinly sliced

1½ tablespoons minced fresh rosemary

½ to 1 teaspoon crushed red pepper

¼ cup Vegetable Stock (page 332)

½ cup mirin or dry white wine

½ cup Dijon mustard

¼ cup pine nuts, toasted (see page 47)

1. Bring 2½ quarts of lightly salted water to a boil in a wok over high heat. Add the pasta, and stir to prevent sticking. Cook, stirring occasionally, until just tender, for 10 to 12 minutes. Drain well, and set aside. Dry the wok.

2. Set the wok over high heat, and add 1½ tablespoons of the oil. Add the mushrooms and 1 teaspoon of the salt, and stir-fry until tender, for about 2 minutes. Transfer to a mixing bowl, and set aside.

3. Return the wok to high heat, and add the remaining 1 tablespoon of oil. Add the garlic and onion, and stir-fry for 1½ minutes. Add the remaining ½ teaspoon of salt, the rosemary and crushed red pepper, and stir-fry for 1½ minutes. Add the Vegetable Stock and bring to a boil. Reduce the heat to low, and cook for 2 minutes, scraping up the brown bits from the bottom of the wok. Add to the bowl with the mushrooms.

4. Return the wok to high heat. Add the mirin and mustard, and stir with a wire whisk to blend. Bring to a boil, add the reserved pasta and mushroom mixture and cook, stirring, for 2 minutes. Toss in the pine nuts, and serve.

PER SERVING: 212 CAL; 8G PROT; 5G FAT; 32G CARB; 0MG CHOL; 659MG SOD; 3G FIBER

MACARONI AND CHEESE

SERVES 6

This pasta offering has become a popular comfort food on many American tables. The addition of Parmesan and Roquefort cheeses injects a bold accent and brings it new sophistication.

1½ cups medium-sized dried elbow macaroni

2 tablespoons unsalted butter

2 tablespoons all-purpose flour

1 cup whole milk

1 cup grated extra-sharp cheddar cheese

½ cup grated Parmesan cheese

¼ cup crumbled Roquefort cheese

Salt and freshly ground black pepper to taste

¼ cup fine dry bread crumbs

1. Preheat the oven to 350F. Lightly grease a 1½-quart ovenproof baking dish.

2. Heat a pot of lightly salted water over medium heat, and when it is boiling, cook the pasta according to the package directions. Drain, rinse, drain again and set aside in the baking dish.

3. Meanwhile, melt the butter in a saucepan, and whisk in the flour. Cook for about 2 minutes, or until the mixture thickens. Gradually add the milk, whisking constantly, and cook for 6 to 7 minutes, or until the sauce thickens. Remove from the heat, and set aside.

4. Combine 1 tablespoon of each cheese in a bowl, and set aside. Add the remaining cheese to the white sauce, and stir until smooth. If needed, reheat the cheeses over low heat to melt, and season to taste. Pour the sauce over the macaroni in the casserole, and stir to mix well. Add the bread crumbs to the remaining cheese, and sprinkle over the top.

5. Bake for 35 to 40 minutes, or until hot, bubbly and lightly browned on top. Serve hot from the oven.

PER SERVING: 300 CAL; 14G PROT; 15G FAT; 28G CARB; 45MG CHOL; 500MG SOD; 1G FIBER

PENNE WITH ASPARAGUS AND SPRING HERBS

The sauce for this light spring pasta is made with poached garlic and tofu, blended until velvety smooth and brightened with fresh herbs. You can top the pasta with freshly grated Parmesan cheese, if desired. The sauce can be prepared ahead. Cover, and refrigerate for up to 2 days. Reheat the sauce before continuing with the recipe.

12 ounces dried penne pasta

1¼ cups vegetable stock or Vegetable Stock (page 332)

8 cloves garlic, peeled

¾ cup low-fat silken firm tofu

4 teaspoons olive oil

2 teaspoons fresh lemon juice

½ teaspoon Dijon mustard

Salt and freshly ground black pepper to taste

2 tablespoons chopped fresh chives

2 tablespoons chopped fresh tarragon

2 tablespoons chopped fresh parsley

1½ teaspoons grated lemon zest

1 pound asparagus, trimmed

8 ounces carrots, peeled

Lemon wedges, optional

1. Heat a pot of lightly salted water over medium heat, and when it is boiling, cook the pasta according to the package directions. Drain, rinse, drain again and set aside in a serving bowl.

2. Meanwhile, combine the stock and garlic in a small saucepan, and bring to a boil over medium-high heat. Reduce the heat to low. Cover, and cook until the garlic is very tender, for 15 to 20 minutes. Put the stock, garlic, tofu, oil, lemon juice, mustard, salt and pepper into a blender or food processor, and purée until smooth and creamy. Return to the saucepan. Heat over low heat, but do not boil. Stir in the chives, tarragon, parsley and lemon zest. Cover, and keep warm.

3. Peel the asparagus stalks, if desired, and cut into 1½-inch lengths. Cut the carrots into 1¾ x ¼–inch sticks. Put the carrots in a steamer basket over boiling water, and put the asparagus on top. Cover, and steam until tender, for 4 to 5 minutes.

4. Add the vegetables and reserved herb sauce to the pasta, and toss to coat. Serve hot with lemon wedges for squeezing, if using.

PER SERVING: 400 CAL; 16G PROT; 7G FAT; 71G CARB; 0MG CHOL; 310MG SOD; 7G FIBER

ANGEL HAIR PASTA WITH FENNEL AND SAFFRON SERVES 6

Rich with the flavors of southern Italy—fennel and saffron, pine nuts and currants—this delicate pasta dish is sure to please.

2 medium-sized bulbs fennel with fronds

1 pound dried angel hair pasta

2 tablespoons olive oil

2 small red onions, chopped

½ teaspoon fennel seeds

½ teaspoon saffron threads

3 tablespoons currants or raisins, plumped in warm water and drained

2 tablespoons pine nuts

Salt to taste

1. Bring a large pot of lightly salted water to a boil. Meanwhile, rinse and trim the fennel, discarding the stems but reserving the fronds and bulbs. Set aside half the fronds. Chop the remaining fronds, and set aside. Add the fennel bulbs to the boiling water, and cook for 10 minutes. Using a slotted spoon, remove the fennel bulbs. Dice the bulbs, and set aside.

2. Return the water to a boil, and add the pasta, stirring to prevent sticking. Cook until tender, for about 6 minutes. Drain the pasta, reserving ½ cup of the cooking water.

3. Meanwhile, heat 1 tablespoon of the oil in a large skillet over low heat. Add the onions, fennel seeds and chopped fronds, and cook, stirring, until the onions are tender, for about 10 minutes.

4. Combine the saffron and 1½ tablespoons of warm water in a cup. Stir to blend, and add to the skillet. Stir in the diced fennel, and cook, stirring, for about 15 minutes, or until the fennel is very tender. Add the currants and pine nuts. If the mixture seems dry, add the reserved pasta water by the spoonful to moisten.

5. Add the cooked pasta and the remaining fronds. Increase the heat to medium, and cook, stirring, for 1 minute. Drizzle with the remaining 1 tablespoon of oil, add salt and serve.

PER SERVING: 211 CAL; 6G PROT; 6G FAT; 34G CARB; 0MG CHOL; 43MG SOD; 6G FIBER

INDONESIAN FRIED NOODLES SERVES 6

Tofu and eggs add protein to this robust noodle dish. Keçap manis *and* sambal *are available at Asian markets and some well-stocked supermarkets.*

1 pound dried soba noodles or any other Asian noodles

2 to 4 tablespoons peanut oil

1 onion, finely chopped

3 cloves garlic, minced

1½-inch piece fresh ginger, grated

2 leeks or 6 scallions, chopped

1 to 2 cups snow peas

1 to 2 cups mung bean sprouts

3 tablespoons *keçap manis* or 3 tablespoons low-sodium soy sauce plus 1½ tablespoons brown sugar

1 to 3 teaspoons *sambal* or cayenne

2 large eggs, scrambled, optional

1 pound firm tofu, drained and cubed, optional

1. Heat a pot of lightly salted water over medium heat, and when it is boiling, cook the pasta according to the package directions. Drain, rinse, drain again and set aside in a mixing bowl.

2. Heat the oil in a wok or large skillet over medium heat. Add the onion, garlic and ginger, and stir-fry for about 5 minutes, or until the onion is softened.

3. Add the leeks, snow peas and bean sprouts, and cook until crisp-tender. Stir in the noodles, *keçap manis* and *sambal* to taste. Add the eggs and tofu, if using. Mix thoroughly until heated through, for about 5 minutes.

PER SERVING: 270 CAL; 24G PROT; 15G FAT; 58G CARB; 70MG CHOL; 280MG SOD; 5G FIBER

CAPELLINI-TOMATO PIE

Pasta pies baked in crusts can be heavy, but this recipe, using cabbage leaves, not only cuts carbohydrates, it enhances the flavor of the tomatoes. The flavor improves overnight, so the pie is best served the following day at room temperature. Look for the largest cabbage, and select intact leaves.

1 tablespoon bread crumbs (see page 46)

8 ounces dried capellini or other thin, spaghetti-like pasta

6 large outer leaves of savoy cabbage or more if needed

2 cups chopped tomatoes plus 1 large tomato

20 kalamata olives, chopped

2 tablespoons minced fresh basil

1 tablespoon large capers

1 tablespoon olive oil

1 teaspoon minced garlic

Freshly ground black pepper to taste

⅓ cup grated Parmesan cheese

Minced fresh parsley for garnish

1. Preheat the oven to 350F. Spray a deep 10-inch pie plate with nonstick cooking spray, and dust with the breadcrumbs. Trim off any tough ribs at the base of each cabbage leaf.

2. Heat a pot of lightly salted water over medium heat, and when it is boiling, cook the pasta according to the package directions. Drain, rinse, drain again and set aside in a bowl.

3. Trim off any tough ribs at the base of each cabbage leaf, and cook the leaves in boiling water for about 5 minutes, or until tender. Drain, and pat dry with paper towels.

4. Line the pie plate with the cabbage leaves, using scissors to trim the leaves evenly along the rim of the dish. Make sure to overlap the leaves so they completely cover the bottom.

5. Add the chopped tomatoes, olives, basil, capers, oil, garlic and pepper to the pasta bowl, and toss together. Place the pasta mixture in the lined pie plate, and pat down firmly with a wooden spoon or spatula. Cut the tomato into thin slices, and arrange evenly over the top of the filling. Scatter the Parmesan cheese evenly over the tomatoes.

6. Bake for 30 minutes, until heated through. Remove from the oven, and cool on a rack. Garnish with the parsley, and serve at room temperature.

PER SERVING: 150 CAL; 5G PROT; 6G FAT; 21G CARB; 0MG CHOL; 270MG SOD; 2G FIBER

PESTO PRIMAVERA

Basil lovers, rejoice: This twist on pasta primavera is packed with flavor. The dish is on the table in minutes, too.

Pasta

2 cups fresh broccoli florets

½ medium-sized red bell pepper, seeded and cut into thin strips

1 cup sliced white button mushrooms

½ cup thin (2 x ¼-inch) carrot strips

1 cup sliced zucchini

8 ounces dried fettuccine

Pesto

1 cup packed fresh basil leaves

¼ cup oil-free Italian dressing

1 to 2 cloves garlic, halved

2 tablespoons olive oil

1 tablespoon grated Parmesan cheese

¼ teaspoon grated lemon zest, optional

1. To make the Pasta: Combine the broccoli, bell pepper, mushrooms, carrots and zucchini in a steamer basket fitted into a large saucepan filled with about 2 inches of water. Cook, covered, over medium heat until the vegetables are tender, for about 10 minutes or until done to desired texture. Remove from the heat, and set aside.

2. Heat a pot of lightly salted water over medium heat, and when it is boiling, cook the pasta according to the package directions. Drain, rinse, drain again and set aside in a bowl.

3. Meanwhile, to make the Pesto: Put the basil, dressing, garlic, oil, Parmesan cheese and lemon zest, if using, in a food processor or blender, and purée until smooth. Spoon the pesto over the fettuccine, and toss to coat.

4. To serve, mound the fettuccine on a serving platter. Top it with the vegetable mixture, and serve at once.

PER SERVING: 310 CAL; 10G PROT; 7G FAT; 50G CARB; 1MG CHOL; 84MG SOD; 5G FIBER

BOWTIES WITH POTATOES, CAPERS AND OLIVES

Instead of pan-frying the potatoes, you can slice them, toss lightly with olive oil and roast in the oven until crispy.

1 tablespoon olive oil

⅓ cup chopped onion

2 slices tempeh "bacon," diced

2 cups thinly sliced small red-skinned potatoes

½ cup white wine

¼ cup julienned fresh basil

1 cup low-sodium vegetable stock or Vegetable Stock (page 332)

½ cup halved and pitted Greek or Italian olives

1 tablespoon drained capers

1 tablespoon salt

8 ounces large dried bowtie pasta (farfalle)

¼ cup chopped fresh flat-leaf parsley

Salt and freshly ground pepper to taste

1. Bring a large pot of water to a boil. Meanwhile, heat the oil in a saucepan over medium heat. Add the onion and tempeh "bacon," and cook, stirring occasionally, until lightly browned, for 2 minutes. Add the potatoes, and cook, stirring occasionally, until lightly browned, for 5 to 7 minutes.

2. Add the wine and basil to the pan, and cook until thickened slightly, about 2 minutes. Add the stock, olives and capers, and cook, stirring occasionally, until reduced by half, for 8 to 10 minutes.

3. Add 1 tablespoon of salt and the pasta to the boiling water, stirring to prevent sticking. Cook the pasta until just tender or according to the package directions, for about 10 minutes. Remove from the heat, drain, rinse in cold water and drain well.

4. Add the parsley, and salt and pepper to the sauce, and stir well. Add the pasta, and toss to coat. Serve hot.

PER SERVING: 219 CAL; 5G PROT; 6G FAT; 28G CARB; 0MG CHOL; 250MG SOD; 2G FIBER

PASTA WITH CILANTRO PESTO AND SWEET ONIONS

For a change of pace, try this pasta dish with a Southwestern sensibility. You can also use the cilantro pesto as a condiment for grilled vegetables or thin it with yogurt and serve it with baked tortilla crisps.

Pasta

12 ounces dried orecchiette, gnocchi or medium-sized shell pasta

Cilantro Pesto

1½ cups cilantro

¼ cup slivered almonds, toasted (see page 47)

1 jalapeño chile, seeded and coarsely chopped

3 cloves garlic, crushed

½ teaspoon salt

2 tablespoons vegetable oil

1 tablespoon fresh lime juice

¼ teaspoon freshly ground black pepper

Sweet Onion Mixture

2 teaspoons vegetable oil

1 cup chopped sweet onion, such as Vidalia

1 cup diced red bell pepper

1 4½-ounce can mild green chiles

1 cup grated Pepper Jack cheese

1. To make the Pasta: Heat a pot of lightly salted water over medium heat, and when it is boiling, cook the pasta according to the package directions. Drain, reserving ⅓ cup of the pasta cooking water. Rinse the pasta, drain again and set aside in a mixing bowl.

2. Meanwhile, to make the Cilantro Pesto: Put the cilantro, almonds, jalapeño, garlic, salt and pepper into a food processor or blender, and process until finely chopped. With the motor running, add the oil and lime juice through the feed tube, processing until the mixture forms a paste and stopping to scrape down the sides of the work bowl as necessary. Transfer the mixture to a bowl, stirring in the reserved pasta cooking water. Stir well.

3. To make the Sweet Onion Mixture: Heat the oil over medium-high heat. Add the onion and bell pepper, and cook, stirring often, until tender, for 5 to 6 minutes. Add the chiles, and cook, stirring, for 1 minute. Combine the Sweet Onion Mixture, Pepper Jack cheese and Cilantro Pesto with the pasta, and toss to coat well. Serve immediately.

PER SERVING: 580 CAL; 20G PROT; 22G FAT; 77G CARB; 25MG CHOL; 550MG SOD; 7G FIBER

Tips on Cooking Pasta

It seems that anyone who cooks pasta has his own ideas about the best way to handle this ingredient. Add oil to the water? Drizzle oil on the pasta after cooking? Add salt to the water? Cook salt free? Rinse cooked pasta in cold water? Just drain the pasta in a colander? We suggest that you follow the instructions that come with your pasta, then taste the pasta after several minutes of cooking. When you find its texture appealing, remove the pasta from the heat and drain it. Remember: Fresh pasta cooks in an instant, so keep an eye on that boiling pot!

PASTA WITH GREENS

SERVES 4 TO 6

Want to make this ahead? Just wash and cook the greens a few hours earlier. The cottage cheese mixture can be made ahead and will keep for three days in the refrigerator.

2 pounds greens, alone or in combination, such as Swiss chard, broccoli rabe, beet greens, kale, escarole, dandelion greens, collard greens

1 tablespoon salt plus salt to taste

½ cup nonfat or low-fat cottage cheese

2 tablespoons low-fat milk

1 tablespoon olive oil

2 large cloves garlic, minced

¼ teaspoon crushed red pepper or more to taste

1 pound dried spaghetti

¼ cup grated pecorino cheese

1. Bring a large pot of water to a boil. Fill a large bowl with cold water, and set aside.

2. Meanwhile, stem the greens, and wash thoroughly. When the water comes to a boil, add 1 tablespoon of salt and the greens. Cook until tender, for 2 to 5 minutes. Using a slotted spoon, remove from the water. Transfer to the bowl of cold water, then drain. Reserve the cooking water for the pasta. Gently squeeze most of the water out of the greens, and coarsely chop. Set aside.

3. Blend the cottage cheese in a food processor or blender until fairly smooth. Scrape down the sides of the bowl, and blend again. Add the milk, and blend until creamy.

4. Heat the oil in a large nonstick skillet over medium heat. Add the garlic and crushed red pepper. Cook, stirring, for about 30 seconds, or until the garlic begins to color. Add the greens, stirring for 1 minute. Stir in ½ cup of the cooking liquid reserved from the greens. Add salt, and remove from the heat but keep warm.

5. Bring the pot of water back to a rolling boil, and add the pasta. Cook until just tender, for about 10 minutes or according to the package directions. Drain well. Transfer the pasta to the pan with the greens. Add the cottage cheese mixture and pecorino, toss and serve.

PER SERVING: 189 CAL; 10G PROT; 4G FAT; 28G CARB; 6MG CHOL; 453MG SOD; 4G FIBER

COUSCOUS PILAF WITH SAFFRON CREAM

SERVES 4

Pilaf is traditionally made with rice or bulgur, but it's a delicious method for preparing couscous, too.

Pilaf

1 tablespoon olive oil

½ teaspoon coriander seeds

⅔ cup diced red bell pepper

¼ teaspoon cayenne

¼ teaspoon ground cinnamon

3 cups Vegetable Stock (page 332) or water

1½ cups uncooked couscous

Salt and freshly ground black pepper to taste

¼ cup chopped fresh mint or 1 tablespoon chopped fresh thyme

Saffron Cream

½ cup light cream cheese

⅓ cup low-fat yogurt

Pinch saffron threads, crushed

1. To make the Pilaf: Heat the oil in a saucepan over medium heat. Add the coriander, and fry until toasted. Stir in the bell pepper, cayenne and cinnamon, and cook, stirring frequently, until barely tender, for about 4 minutes.

2. Add the Vegetable Stock, and bring to a boil. Stir in the couscous. Bring back to a boil, cover and turn the heat off. Let stand until all the water is absorbed, for 5 to 10 minutes. Fluff with a fork, and season with salt, pepper and mint.

3. To make the Saffron Cream: Put the cheese, yogurt and saffron in a blender or food processor, and purée until creamy. Serve on the side.

PER SERVING (WITH 1 TABLESPOON SAFFRON CREAM): 141 CAL; 5G PROT; 5G FAT; 21G CARB; 8MG CHOL; 219MG SOD; 3G FIBER

BEAN COUSCOUS WITH POMEGRANATES

The most delicate beans for this dish are the tiny white rice beans or the Italian heirloom variety known as fagioli del Purgatorio. *Unfortunately, these are not available in all parts of the country. The best substitute is the Italian cannellini bean, which can be found in most supermarkets. For the eggplant, choose Thai long green or other long, slender eggplants. They cook quickly and absorb less oil than the larger globe eggplants. You can buy pomegranate vinegar in a Middle Eastern grocery or natural foods store.*

1 cup dried small white beans, rinsed

7 tablespoons olive oil

2 cups diced Asian eggplant

2 tablespoons sesame seeds

1 tablespoon minced garlic

12 ounces uncooked couscous

2 tablespoons pomegranate vinegar

1 cup pomegranate seeds

2 tablespoons minced cilantro leaves

Salt to taste

1. Pour boiling water over the beans, and soak overnight in the refrigerator. The next day, drain the beans, and cook in water to cover for about 25 minutes, or until tender. Drain, and reserve.

2. Pour 2 tablespoons of the oil in a large skillet or wok, and heat until it begins to smoke. Stir-fry the eggplant for about 5 minutes, or until tender. Add the sesame seeds. Continue to stir-fry until the sesame seeds begin to turn color. Add the garlic. Stir, and continue cooking for 1 minute. Remove from the heat, and set aside.

3. To cook the couscous, bring 2 cups of water to a boil in a saucepan, and stir in the couscous. Bring back to a boil, cover and turn the heat off. Let stand until all the water is absorbed, for 5 to 10 minutes. Fluff with a fork, and then pour into a serving bowl.

4. To make the vinaigrette, whisk together the remaining 5 tablespoons of oil and the vinegar, and pour over the hot couscous. Stir well. Add the beans and eggplant. Add the pomegranate seeds and cilantro, adjust the seasonings and serve.

PER SERVING: 530 CAL; 16G PROT; 19G FAT; 76G CARB; 0MG CHOL; 10MG SOD; 13G FIBER

MOROCCAN SAUTÉ

This Moroccan-inspired dinner is delicious served with chopped tomatoes, drizzled with a fruity olive oil, balsamic vinegar and salt and freshly ground pepper. Serve Poached Orange Cake (page 391) for dessert.

1 box quick-cooking couscous

½ teaspoon olive oil

1 medium-sized onion, chopped

1 teaspoon curry powder, or to taste

½ teaspoon plus ⅛ teaspoon ground cinnamon

2 cloves garlic, pressed

2 15-ounce cans chickpeas, drained and rinsed

2 medium-sized zucchini, cut into large chunks

2 cups chopped tomatoes or 1 14½-ounce can diced tomatoes, drained

2 cups frozen sweet corn

Salt and freshly ground black pepper to taste

½ cup chopped cilantro

1. Bring 2 cups of water to a boil in a saucepan, and stir in the couscous. Bring back to a boil, cover and turn the heat off. Let stand until all the water is absorbed, for 5 to 10 minutes. Fluff with a fork, and set aside.

2. Meanwhile, in a large nonstick skillet, heat the oil over medium heat. Add the onion and cook, stirring often, for 4 minutes. Stir in the curry powder, cinnamon and garlic, and cook for 1 minute. Add the zucchini, beans, tomatoes, corn and 1 cup of water, and cook, stirring occasionally, for 10 minutes. If the mixture is too dry, add more water as needed.

3. Season with salt, pepper and cilantro.

4. Fluff the couscous with a fork, and spoon into a serving dish. Top with the vegetable mixture, and serve hot.

PER SERVING: 452 CAL; 18G PROT; 3G FAT; 92G CARB; 0MG CHOL; 271MG SOD; 12G FIBER

12

grains and legumes

THE PROTEIN- AND NUTRIENT-RICH UNDER-pinnings for the vegetarian diet, both grains and legumes make ideal meat substitutes that are easy on the palate and on the pocketbook. Because their flavors tend to be subtle, grains and legumes provide the ideal framework onto which cooks can build complex layers of flavors. And they taste just as tempting when left almost unadorned except for the simplest of seasonings. Thanks to today's curious consumers looking for new and interest-ing ingredients, markets now offer an increasingly expanding array of heritage grains and legumes such as farro and amaranth, which complement such old standbys as barley and oats, lentils and kidney beans.

QUINOA PILAF WITH DRIED FRUIT AND PECANS

SERVES 6

Quinoa is very high in protein, and nutritionally, we consider this to be a main dish. It's great with a curried vegetable, so try it with the Steamed Broccoli with Garlic (page 187). Be sure to rinse the quinoa well unless you purchase saponin-free quinoa. The saponin on the surface of the quinoa grain is very bitter.

3 cups uncooked quinoa, rinsed

2 tablespoons olive oil

1 cup minced onion

2 cups vegetable stock or Vegetable Stock (page 332)

½ cup golden raisins

½ cup chopped dried apricots

½ cup dried cranberries

1 teaspoon salt, or to taste

1 teaspoon ground coriander

½ teaspoon freshly ground black pepper

1 tablespoon grated lemon zest, optional

½ cup chopped pecans

1. Bring 2 quarts of water to a boil, and stir in the quinoa. Reduce the heat to low, and cook, covered, for 10 to 15 minutes, or until tender. Remove from the heat, and drain well.

2. Heat the oil in a 2-quart saucepan over medium heat. Sauté the onion until golden. Add the stock, raisins, apricots, cranberries, salt, coriander, pepper and lemon zest, if using. Bring to a boil, and cook for 3 minutes. Add the quinoa, and stir. Cover the pan, and reduce the heat to very low, cooking for 5 minutes more. Stir in the pecans, fluff and serve.

PER SERVING: 560 CAL; 16G PROT; 17G FAT; 92G CARB; 0MG CHOL; 460MG SOD; 9G FIBER

DELICATA SQUASH STUFFED WITH CURRIED WILD RICE

SERVES 6

You can substitute cooked couscous for the wild rice.

3 delicata squash, halved and seeded

2 tablespoons unsalted butter or margarine

½ cup minced onion

2 teaspoons curry powder

1 teaspoon ground cinnamon

½ teaspoon freshly ground black pepper

¼ teaspoon cayenne pepper

2 Granny Smith apples, peeled, cored and minced

½ cup raisins

½ cup chopped cashews

1 cup cooked wild rice (see page 48)

⅓ cup plain yogurt

⅓ cup mango chutney

1. Preheat the oven to 350F.

2. Place the squash halves, cut sides down, on a baking sheet. Bake for about 20 minutes, or just until the squash is not quite cooked through. Remove from the oven, and set aside until the second baking.

3. Heat the butter in a large saucepan over medium heat, and add the onions. Sauté the onions for about 5 minutes, or until translucent. Add the curry, cinnamon, pepper and cayenne, and toss well. Add the apples, raisins and cashews, and continue cooking until the apples are soft. Add the rice, yogurt and chutney, and toss well. Divide the curried vegetables equally between the squash halves.

4. Bake the squash for 25 minutes, or until they are tender and the stuffing is heated through.

PER SERVING (1 FILLED SQUASH HALF): 260 CAL; 6G PROT; 10G FAT; 43G CARB; 10MG CHOL; 55MG SOD; 5G FIBER

QUINOA AND PUMPKIN SEED PILAF IN ACORN SQUASH

This dish is a beautiful presentation for a main course. The highly nutritious grain, quinoa, makes it a one-dish meal. The green pumpkin seeds and red bell pepper feed the eye as well as the body. Raw hulled pumpkin seeds are available in most health food stores. When the quinoa is perfectly cooked, you will notice small white spirals around the edge of each seed. If you eat dairy products, consider adding the Mexican cheese queso blanco *or a spicy pepper Jack cheese to the pilaf. Or you may want to offer a bowl of sour cream seasoned with salt and minced jalapeños.*

4 small acorn squash
2 cups quinoa, rinsed
4 cups boiling water
2 tablespoons olive oil
2 cups finely diced onion
1 tablespoon minced garlic
1 cup raw hulled pumpkin seeds
1 large red bell pepper, finely diced
2 tablespoons minced fresh parsley
2 teaspoons salt
1 teaspoon ground cumin
1 teaspoon freshly ground black pepper

1. Preheat the oven to 350F.

2. Cut the squash in half, and scrape out the seeds and fibers. Place the squash halves cut sides down on a baking sheet. Bake for 30 minutes, or until the squash are almost tender when pierced with a small knife.

3. Meanwhile, cook the quinoa by stirring it into 4 cups of boiling water. Reduce the heat to low, cover and cook. After 15 minutes, remove from the heat, and set aside for 5 minutes covered.

4. Heat the oil in a 4-quart saucepan over medium heat, and sauté the onion and garlic for about 3 minutes, or until the onion is transparent. Add the remaining ingredients, and sauté until the bell peppers are soft, for about 3 minutes more. Add the quinoa to the pan, and toss gently. Taste, and adjust seasoning.

5. Fill the center of each squash half with a mound of pilaf. Place the filled squash halves in a baking dish with ½ inch of water in the bottom of the dish. Cover with foil or a lid.

6. Bake for 30 minutes, or until squash are tender throughout. Remove from the oven, and serve hot.

PER SERVING (ONE FILLED SQUASH HALF): 510 CAL; 16G PROT; 16G FAT; 85G CARB; 0MG CHOL; 600MG SOD; 18G FIBER

AMARANTH, QUINOA AND BLACK SESAME SEEDS WITH SPICY GROUND PEANUT SEASONING

SERVES 4

Amaranth is an ancient grain that was an important source of protein for the Aztecs. Due to a cultural misunderstanding, the Spanish conquerors abolished its use and possession by the Mexican people, so it vanished from kitchens for nearly 500 years. But now the tiny seed with its interesting flavor is back! One drawback—amaranth becomes sticky if it sits after cooking. To solve that problem, just rinse it after cooking. Serve this luscious Thai-inspired entrée with grilled or sautéed shiitake mushrooms.

½ cup amaranth seeds, rinsed

½ cup quinoa, rinsed

2 tablespoons canola oil

¼ cup black sesame seeds

1 cup thinly sliced scallions

1 teaspoon curry powder

½ cup dry-roasted peanuts

½ cup shredded unsweetenedcoconut

½ teaspoon cayenne

1 tablespoon granulated sugar or Sucanat

1. Put the amaranth and quinoa in a 2-quart saucepan with 3 cups of cold water, and bring to a boil. Reduce the heat to low, cover and cook for 20 minutes.

2. Meanwhile, heat a 2-quart saucepan over medium heat, and add the oil. Sauté the sesame seeds for 1 minute. Add the scallions and curry powder, and remove from the heat.

3. Place the peanuts and coconut in a blender or food processor, and pulverize them. Add the cayenne and sugar, and mix.

4. When the amaranth and quinoa have finished cooking, put them in a strainer, and rinse them well with hot water. Transfer the grains to the saucepan with the sesame seeds, and reheat. Just before serving, add the peanut mixture, and toss well.

PER SERVING: 480 CAL; 14G PROT; 28G FAT; 44G CARB; 0MG CHOL; 160MG SOD; 8G FIBER

SHIITAKE-BARLEY BAKE

SERVES 4

Barley and shiitake mushrooms give this casserole an earthy flavor. Seitan, carrots and Brussels sprouts are interspersed throughout the casserole, providing enough substance and variety to make the dish a meal in itself. Serve with warm rye bread.

3 cups cooked barley (see page 48)

1 cup stemmed, sliced shiitake mushrooms

1 cup diagonally sliced carrots

1 cup quartered Brussels sprouts

2 shallots, minced

1 cup cubed seitan

½ cup finely chopped fresh basil plus several sprigs for garnish

1 tablespoon arrowroot

1 cup Vegetable Stock (page 332)

Salt and freshly ground black pepper to taste

1. Preheat the oven to 375F. Spray a 3-quart baking dish with nonstick cooking spray, and set aside.

2. Combine the barley, mushrooms, carrots, Brussels sprouts, shallots, seitan and basil in a bowl. Combine the arrowroot with the Vegetable Stock, and stir until smooth. Stir into the vegetable mixture, and season with salt and pepper. Put the mixture into the baking dish, and cover.

3. Bake until the vegetables are tender, for about 20 minutes. Garnish with fresh basil, and serve hot.

PER SERVING: 306 CAL; 14G PROT; 8G FAT; 50G CARB; 0MG CHOL; 350MG SOD; 8G FIBER

QUINOA AND MUSHROOM PATTIES WITH GYPSY SAUCE

Quinoa has a great flavor with a hint of malt. The mushrooms add their own flavor and body, and the tofu holds it all together. The Gypsy Sauce is most likely a Romanian recipe that was handed down in a gypsy family living in America. It was originally made by pounding the ingredients in a mortar and pestle. This sauce keeps well in the refrigerator. Remember to rinse the quinoa well to remove any bitter-tasting saponin on the grain's surface. When the quinoa is cooked, you will see a white spiral inside each quinoa grain. These patties would partner well with a side of steamed carrots with dill.

Gypsy Sauce

¼ cup blanched almonds, toasted (see page 47)

⅓ cup dry breadcrumbs (see page 47)

1 tablespoon crushed garlic

½ teaspoon cayenne pepper

1 cup seeded and diced tomato

1 roasted red bell pepper (see page 46) or ¾ cup pimento

½ teaspoon salt

¼ teaspoon freshly ground black pepper, or to taste

2 tablespoons sherry vinegar or cider vinegar

⅓ cup olive oil

Patties

1 cup quinoa, rinsed

2 tablespoons soy margarine

2 cups finely diced onions

4 cups minced fresh mushrooms

2 cups puréed extra-firm silken tofu

1 teaspoon salt

1 teaspoon freshly ground black pepper

2 tablespoons canola oil

1. Preheat the oven to 350F.

2. To make the Gypsy Sauce: Put the almonds, breadcrumbs, garlic and cayenne into a food processor or blender, and process until the almonds are finely ground. Add the tomato, bell pepper, salt and pepper. Process until very smooth. Add the vinegar, and process again. Scrape down the work bowl. Slowly add the oil in a thin stream. Taste, and adjust the seasoning. Add more cayenne for spice or more vinegar for tang.

3. To make the Patties: Bring 2 cups of water to a boil, stir in the quinoa, and reduce the heat to low. Cover, and continue cooking for about 15 minutes, or until the water is absorbed. Set aside.

4. Heat the margarine in a large skillet, and sauté the onions until soft, for about 3 minutes. Add the mushrooms, and sauté over medium heat until the mushrooms are dark brown and crumbly. Remove to a bowl.

5. Add the tofu, quinoa, salt and pepper. Mix well, and form into 8 large cakes of about 1 cup of the mixture each.

6. Heat a large skillet or griddle over medium heat, and brush with some of the oil. Fry the patties until toasted on each side, for about 8 minutes per side. Top each patty with a dollop of Gypsy Sauce, and serve.

PER SERVING: 180 CAL; 7G PROT; 8G FAT; 20G CARB; 0MG CHOL; 350MG SOD; 2G FIBER

WILD RICE CRÊPES

Wild rice adds a nutty flavor and chewy texture to these savory crêpes. For a faster dish, use quick-cooking wild rice available in supermarkets and natural food stores, and follow package directions. The fastest of all is to search for the precooked wild rice available in vacuum packs at many markets. For a delicious change, offer the crêpes with the Almond Sauce (page 175).

¾ cup uncooked wild rice

2¾ cups Vegetable Stock (page 332)

¼ onion, finely chopped plus ¾ onion, coarsely chopped

2 tablespoons vegetable oil

2 stalks celery, thinly sliced

1¼ cups sliced white button mushrooms

½ cup oyster mushrooms, separated into small clumps or an additional ½ cup white button mushrooms

5 to 6 shiitake mushrooms or dried shiitakes reconstituted in warm water, cut into quarters or eighths

1 large tomato, chopped

1 tablespoon low-sodium soy sauce

½ teaspoon dried sage

Salt and freshly ground black pepper to taste

8 to 12 No-Cholesterol Crêpes (page 94)

1. Put the rice, Vegetable Stock and finely chopped onion in a saucepan, and bring to a boil over high heat. Reduce the heat to medium-low, cover and cook until the rice is tender and all the liquid is absorbed, for about 1 hour. (If using quick-cooking wild rice, follow the package directions for cooking time. If using precooked wild rice, go to step 2 and omit the Vegetable Stock; add the onion with the celery in step 3.)

2. Preheat the oven to 350F.

3. Heat the oil in a skillet over medium heat, and add the celery. Cook, stirring frequently, until tender, for about 5 minutes. Add the coarsely chopped onion and all the mushrooms, and cook, stirring frequently, until the vegetables are soft, for about 10 minutes. Add the cooked rice, tomato, soy sauce, sage, salt and pepper, and cook for 10 to 15 minutes more.

4. Fill the crêpes with the rice mixture. Roll up, and place in a single layer, seam-sides down, in a baking dish. Heat for 10 minutes, and serve.

PER SERVING: 468 CAL; 16G PROT; 17G FAT; 65G CARB; 146MG CHOL; 666MG SOD; 9G FIBER

KASHA PILAF WITH VEGETABLES

Kasha, or toasted buckwheat, is a Russian favorite. Here it is combined with three colorful vegetables: sweet potatoes, corn and peas.

1½ tablespoons vegetable oil

½ medium-sized onion, finely chopped

1½ cups uncooked kasha, rinsed

1 large egg, beaten lightly

2½ cups boiling water

1 medium-sized sweet potato, peeled and cubed

½ cup frozen corn kernels

½ cup frozen peas

1. Heat the oil in a skillet over medium heat. Add the onion, and cook, stirring frequently, until golden brown, for 5 to 8 minutes. Remove from the heat, and set aside.

2. Heat the kasha in a dry skillet over medium-low heat. Toast, stirring often, until the kasha becomes slightly darker, for 3 to 5 minutes. Add the egg, and stir quickly to coat the grains. Add the boiling water all at once but do not stir.

3. Add the sweet potato, corn and peas. Reduce the heat to low, and cook, covered, until the water is absorbed, the kasha is puffy and the sweet potato is tender, for 20 to 25 minutes. Top with the cooked onions, and serve warm.

PER SERVING: 330 CAL; 10G PROT; 8G FAT; 58G CARB; 53MG CHOL; 38MG SOD; 7G FIBER

JOLOF RICE

This rice dish comes from West Africa, and has a potent richness and spiciness. You can easily adjust it to suit your taste, however. This is delicious with the Banana Condiment (page 177) on the side.

1 cup dried black-eyed peas or about 3 cups cooked

2 medium-sized eggplants

1 teaspoon salt

1½ tablespoons vegetable oil

2 large onions, chopped

3 tablespoons chopped fresh ginger

2 jalapeño chiles, roasted, stemmed, seeded and chopped

2 cloves garlic, minced

1 green bell pepper, chopped

4 large tomatoes, chopped

1½ tablespoons tomato paste

2 teaspoons cayenne

2 teaspoons curry powder

Hot pepper sauce to taste, optional

1 pound carrots, chopped

1½ cups uncooked long-grain brown rice

8 ounces green beans, cut into thirds

1. Put the peas in a large pot, and add 1 quart of water. Soak for 8 hours or overnight in the refrigerator. Drain. Add 2 quarts of fresh water to the peas, and cook over medium heat for 15 minutes, or until tender. Drain, and reserve the cooking water.

2. Slice the eggplants into rounds about ½ inch thick, and place in a colander. Sprinkle with the salt, and let drain for 5 minutes.

3. Heat the oil in an ovenproof saucepan or casserole over medium heat. Add the eggplants, 1 tablespoon of the onion, 1 tablespoon of the ginger, 1 jalapeño, 1 clove of garlic and the bell pepper. Cook, stirring frequently, for about 5 minutes, or until the eggplants are browned. Remove the eggplants, and set aside.

4. Add the remaining onion, ginger, jalapeño, garlic, the reserved bean liquid, tomatoes, tomato paste, cayenne, curry powder and hot pepper sauce, if using. Cook for 10 minutes.

5. Preheat the oven to 400F.

6. Add the peas, carrots and rice to the onion mixture. Cook for 5 minutes more. Add the green beans and eggplants. Cook for 15 minutes, and cover.

7. Bake for 25 to 30 minutes, or until heated through. Remove from the oven, and serve hot.

PER SERVING: 308 CAL; 8G PROT; 3G FAT; 60G CARB; 0MG CHOL; 311MG SOD; 13G FIBER

ASPARAGUS RISOTTO WITH MUSHROOMS AND SUN-DRIED TOMATOES

SERVES 6

This dish is as comforting as it is elegant. The textures and flavors of asparagus, mushrooms and basil are a tasty foil to the rich creaminess of Arborio rice.

1 tablespoon olive oil

1 large onion, diced

1 large leek, halved, cleaned and thinly sliced

1 tablespoon finely minced garlic

2 cups uncooked Arborio rice

¼ teaspoon freshly ground black pepper

8 cups Vegetable Stock (page 332)

12 sun-dried tomatoes, thinly sliced on the diagonal

1 cup thinly sliced asparagus, sliced on the diagonal

1½ cups sliced white button mushrooms

½ cup coarsely chopped fresh basil

¼ cup grated Parmesan cheese, optional

1. Heat the oil in a large saucepan over medium-high heat. Add the onion, leek and garlic, and cook, stirring frequently, until the onion is beginning to soften, for about 3 minutes. Add the rice and pepper, and cook for 5 minutes more.

2. Heat the Vegetable Stock in a separate pan over medium heat to nearly boiling, and remove from the heat. Add 7 cups of the Vegetable Stock and the sun-dried tomatoes to the mixture. Bring the rice mixture to a boil, reduce the heat to low and cook for 12 minutes, stirring often.

3. Meanwhile, after the rice mixture has cooked for 5 minutes, steam the asparagus, mushrooms and basil until the asparagus is crisp-tender, for about 5 minutes. Add to the rice mixture along with the remaining 1 cup of Vegetable Stock. Mix well, and cook until the mixture is creamy and the rice is just done, for about 5 minutes more. Stir in the Parmesan, if using, just before serving.

PER SERVING: 344 CAL; 9G PROT; 3G FAT; 68G CARB; 0MG CHOL; 94MG SOD; 3G FIBER

RISOTTO WITH ZUCCHINI PETALS AND BASIL

SERVES 4

For this lively dish, select Italy's famed starchy, short-grained Arborio white rice.

5 to 5½ cups unsalted Vegetable Stock (page 332)

4 tablespoons (½ stick) unsalted butter, divided

1 cup finely chopped onion

1½ cups uncooked Arborio rice

½ cup dry white wine

1 teaspoon salt

2 cups diced small, tender zucchini

½ cup grated Parmesan cheese

1 cup coarsely chopped fresh basil

18 zucchini blossoms (see page 147), petals only, cleaned and torn into large pieces, optional

Freshly ground black pepper to taste

1. Heat the Stock in a small saucepan over very low heat, and continue cooking.

2. Melt 2 tablespoons of the butter in a large saucepan over medium heat. Add the onion, and cook, stirring often, for 5 minutes, or until soft but not brown. Add the rice, reduce the heat to medium-low, and stir for 1 minute. Add the wine and salt.

3. Stir the rice constantly with a large wooden spoon until all the liquid is absorbed. Ladle in 1 cup of hot stock, and stir often while the rice cooks gently. When the rice absorbs the first cup of stock, add the second. Continue stirring and adding stock by the cupful, always waiting until the rice absorbs the liquid before adding more, allowing about 30 minutes to cook each time. When done, the rice should be creamy and tender but with a firm center.

4. Stir in the zucchini, and cook for 1 minute. Stir in the cheese, the remaining 2 tablespoons of butter and the basil. If necessary, add more stock to keep the risotto moist and creamy—it should form a spreading mound if spooned onto a plate. Stir in the blossoms, if using. Season to taste with pepper, and serve.

PER SERVING: 470 CAL; 10G PROT; 13G FAT; 76G CARB; 30MG CHOL; 770MG SOD; 2G FIBER

BASMATI RICE–STUFFED CABBAGE

These stuffed cabbage leaves are nestled in a layer of sauerkraut and tomato sauce. Try to find a large cabbage so you will end up with large leaves, and then you can add plenty of filling to each. This dish can be entirely assembled up to 24 hours ahead. Cover and refrigerate, then bring to room temperature before baking. Reserve the remaining cabbage for soup.

1 tablespoon plus 1 teaspoon olive oil

1 cup chopped onion

½ cup chopped celery

½ cup diced red or green bell pepper

Salt to taste

3 cups thinly sliced mushrooms

1 clove garlic, minced

3 cups Vegetable Stock (page 332) or water

1½ cups uncooked basmati rice

Freshly ground black pepper to taste

2 tablespoons chopped fresh parsley

1 large green cabbage, cored

2 pounds fresh sauerkraut

3½ cups prepared tomato sauce

1. Heat the oil in a large saucepan over medium-low heat. Add the onion, celery and bell pepper. Season with salt. Cover, and cook for 5 minutes. Stir in the mushrooms and garlic. Cover, and cook for 5 minutes.

2. Stir in the Stock and rice; season with pepper. Increase the heat and bring to a boil. Cover, reduce the heat to medium-low, and cook for 15 minutes, until the rice is tender. Remove from the heat, and fluff the rice with a fork. Stir in the parsley, and set aside.

3. Bring 1 inch of water to a boil in a large pot. Place the cabbage in the water, cored side down. Cover, and cook for 5 minutes. Remove the cabbage from the pot. As soon as possible—using a fork if necessary to grab the leaves—peel off the first 4 leaves. Return the cabbage to the pot, cover and cook for 5 minutes; peel off 4 more leaves for a total of 8 leaves. Cover the leaves with plastic wrap. When the leaves are cool enough to handle, carve off as much of the tough ridge as you can from the center of the leaves, cutting flush with the leaf.

4. Preheat the oven to 375F. Drain the sauerkraut in a colander. Rinse briefly, then squeeze out most of the liquid. Place the sauerkraut in even layers in a 13 x 9–inch shallow casserole. Top with 2 cups of the tomato sauce.

5. Place about ¾ cup of the rice in the center of each leaf. Fold up the sides and place the stuffed leaves, seam sides down, in the casserole. Spoon the remaining 1½ cups of tomato sauce over the cabbage. Cover with foil.

6. Bake until bubbly and heated through, for about 45 minutes. Check after 30 minutes and, if it seems too liquidy, remove the foil during the last 10 to 15 minutes of baking. Serve hot.

PER SERVING (2 STUFFED LEAVES WITH SAUCE): 504 CAL; 14G PROT; 6G FAT; 90G CARB; 0MG CHOL; 158MG SOD; 12G FIBER

WHEAT BERRIES WITH ORZO AND DRIED CRANBERRIES   SERVES 8

This savory mixture is excellent made with either hard or soft wheat berries. They take a while to cook, but overnight soaking shortens the simmering time. We prefer this dish hot, but you can also serve it at room temperature.

1 cup uncooked wheat berries, rinsed

1 14-ounce can vegetable broth or about 1¾ cups Vegetable Stock (page 332)

1½ cups dried orzo

⅔ cup dried cranberries

¼ cup olive oil

1 large onion, chopped

1 medium-sized Bartlett pear, cored and diced

1 cup (4 ounces) chopped toasted (see page 47) almonds or Brazil nuts

1 bunch fresh chives, thinly sliced (scant ⅓ cup)

¼ cup chopped fresh parsley

3 tablespoons fresh lemon juice

2 teaspoons coarse-grained mustard

1 teaspoon salt

¼ teaspoon freshly ground black pepper

1. Combine the wheat berries and cold water to cover in a shallow bowl. Let stand for at least 12 hours in the refrigerator.

2. Drain the wheat berries. Combine them with the broth and 1½ cups of fresh cold water in a medium saucepan. Bring to a boil, reduce the heat to low, cover, and cook gently for 1 hour, until tender. Drain off any excess liquid, and set aside to cool.

3. Bring a saucepan of lightly salted water to a boil over medium heat. Add the orzo, and stir to prevent sticking. Cook according to the package directions, or until tender, for 5 to 8 minutes. Drain, rinse under cold running water and drain well. Combine the wheat berries, orzo and cranberries in bowl. Set aside.

4. Heat the oil in a large, deep skillet or Dutch oven over medium heat. Add the onion, and cook, stirring occasionally, until softened, for about 10 minutes. Add the wheat berry mixture, and stir until heated through. Stir in the remaining ingredients until well blended. Transfer to a shallow serving dish, and serve hot.

PER SERVING: 321 CAL; 5G PROT; 9G FAT; 54G CARB; 0MG CHOL; 310MG SOD; 7G FIBER

THREE-MUSHROOM MEDLEY

Preserved lemons in jars are available at Middle Eastern grocery stores, as is the super hot red pepper purée known as harissa—*just a few dabs will do.*

2 tablespoons olive oil

1 large green bell pepper, diced

1 large onion, diced

3 medium-sized cloves garlic, minced

1 tablespoon sweet Hungarian paprika or 1½ teaspoons hot Hungarian paprika

1 large ripe tomato, diced

½ to 1 teaspoon salt

¼ teaspoon freshly ground black pepper

½ preserved lemon half, seeded and julienned, optional

1½ pounds mixed mushrooms, such as portobello, oyster and shiitake, chopped

3 stems fresh flat-leaf parsley, chopped

3 stems cilantro, chopped

1 12-ounce package whole wheat or regular couscous

10 pitted green Spanish olives

Harissa, for serving, optional

1. Heat the oil in a large nonstick skillet over medium-high heat. Add the bell pepper and onion, and cook, stirring, until the vegetables are just tender, for about 5 minutes. Add the garlic and paprika, and cook, stirring, for 1 minute. Add the tomato, salt, pepper and half of the julienned lemon, if using. Cook for 1 minute, stirring. Add one-third of the mushrooms, and cook, stirring, until they begin to release their juices, for 2 to 3 minutes. Add another third of the mushrooms, and cook, stirring, for 2 to 3 minutes. Add the remaining mushrooms, and cook until all the mushrooms are tender, for 3 to 5 minutes. Stir in the parsley and cilantro, and cook for 1 minute more. Remove from the heat.

2. Meanwhile, bring 2 cups of water to a boil in a saucepan, and stir in the couscous. Bring back to a boil, cover and turn the heat off. Let stand until all the water is absorbed, for 5 to 10 minutes. Fluff with a fork, mound the couscous on a large platter, surround it with the mushroom mixture and garnish with the olives and the remaining julienned lemon, if using. Serve with a small dish of *harissa*, if using.

PER SERVING: 305 CAL; 10G PROT; 6G FAT; 54G CARB; 0MG CHOL; 349MG SOD; 6G FIBER

Flaxseeds, valued as a plant source of essential omega-3 fatty acids, replace the usual eggs to bind the loaf. If you prefer, you can substitute two large eggs for the flaxseeds and water. For ease, you can use a disposable aluminum loaf pan if you like. Bake the loaf up to two days ahead, and refrigerate in the pan. Reheat, covered with foil, in a 350F oven for about 30 minutes. Make the garlic mayonnaise up to two days ahead, and refrigerate in a covered bowl or plastic food storage container.

Lentil-Bulgur Loaf

2 tablespoons flaxseeds

½ cup uncooked bulgur, rinsed

1 cup boiling water

2 teaspoons salt

1¼ cups lentils, rinsed

2 teaspoons olive oil

2 medium-sized onions, chopped

3 medium-sized carrots, grated

4 medium-sized cloves garlic, minced

1½ teaspoons ground cumin

½ teaspoon ground coriander

⅛ to ¼ teaspoon cayenne pepper

2 cups fresh flat-leaf parsley leaves, rinsed and dried

2 slices whole wheat bread, crusts trimmed and bread torn into large pieces

6 ounces low-fat silken soft or firm tofu

¼ cup fresh lemon juice

⅛ teaspoon freshly ground black pepper

Fresh flat-leaf parsley or mint sprigs for garnish

Garlic Mayonnaise

1 cup soy mayonnaise

½ cup chopped fresh herbs, such as basil, tarragon or chervil

2 small cloves garlic, minced

1 teaspoon freshly ground black pepper

¼ teaspoon salt

1. Preheat the oven to 375F. Coat a 9 x 5–inch loaf pan with nonstick cooking spray. Line the bottom of the pan with a sheet of parchment or wax paper, and lightly coat the paper with the cooking spray.

2. To make the Lentil-Bulgur Loaf: Put the flaxseeds into a food processor or blender, and process to a coarse powder. Add ⅓ cup of cold water, and process until the mixture is blended, stopping once or twice to scrape down the sides of the work bowl with a rubber spatula. Pour into a bowl, cover and set aside in the refrigerator.

3. Combine the bulgur, boiling water and ½ teaspoon of the salt in a bowl. Let stand until the bulgur is tender and most of the liquid is absorbed, for about 25 minutes. Drain the mixture in a sieve, pressing out the excess moisture. Set aside.

4. Meanwhile, bring a large saucepan of water to a boil. Add the lentils and ½ teaspoon of salt, and cook until just tender, for about 20 minutes. Drain, and rinse under cold running water. Set aside.

5. Heat the oil in a large nonstick skillet over medium heat. Add the onions, and cook, stirring often, until softened, for 3 to 5 minutes. Add the carrots, garlic, cumin, coriander and cayenne, and cook, stirring, until fragrant, for 1 to 2 minutes. Transfer to a bowl.

6. Put the parsley in a food processor, and pulse until chopped. Add the bread, and process until coarse crumbs form. Add to the onion mixture. Add the tofu to the food processor, and purée until smooth. Add the reserved flaxseed mixture, 1 cup of the cooked lentils, the lemon juice, pepper and remaining 1 teaspoon of salt, and process until smooth. Transfer to the bowl with the onion mixture. Using a rubber spatula, stir in the remaining cooked lentils and the soaked bulgur until well combined. Scrape the mixture into the prepared pan, spreading evenly and pressing down.

7. Bake for 50 to 60 minutes, or until the top is lightly browned and firm to the touch.

8. Meanwhile, make the Garlic Mayonnaise: Mix all the ingredients in a bowl. Cover and chill at least 1 hour. Whisk well before serving.

9. Transfer the loaf to a wire rack, and let cool in the pan for 5 minutes. Run a knife around the edges to loosen, then invert a serving platter over the loaf. Protecting your hands with oven mitts, firmly grasp the pan and platter together, and turn over. Remove the pan, and peel off the paper. Garnish with parsley, and serve hot or at room temperature with the Garlic Mayonnaise.

PER SERVING (1-INCH SLICE WITH 1 TABLESPOON GARLIC MAYONNAISE): 245 CAL; 13G PROT; 6G FAT; 39G CARB; 0MG CHOL; 683MG SOD; 9G FIBER

GINGERED GRAINS

Here brown rice and vegetables form the foundation of a hearty meal. Serve the dish on its own or as a side dish with marinated and baked tempeh.

Grains

½ cup fresh or frozen peas

½ cup diced carrots

½ cup fresh or frozen corn kernels

3 cups cooked brown rice or other grain (see page 48)

½ cup diced plum tomatoes

¼ cup thinly sliced scallions

Ginger Dressing

2 to 3 tablespoons grated fresh ginger

1 tablespoon tamari or low-sodium soy sauce

1 tablespoon toasted sesame seeds (see page 47)

2 teaspoons red or brown miso

1 teaspoon toasted sesame oil

1. To make the Grains: Steam the peas, carrots and corn just until tender. Combine the rice, tomatoes and scallions in a bowl. Add the steamed vegetables, and mix well.

2. To make the Ginger Dressing: Mix all the ingredients and ¼ cup of water in a bowl until well blended. Add to the rice mixture, and toss to coat. Serve warm or at room temperature.

PER SERVING: 244 CAL; 7G PROT; 4G FAT; 46G CARB; 0MG CHOL; 328MG SOD; 6G FIBER

MOROCCAN GRIDDLED PEPPERS

Tired of traditional stuffed peppers? Try this quick and easy version instead. The spiced couscous filling can also be served on its own, either warm or at room temperature. Try serving with prepackaged baked, marinated tofu slices and have fresh strawberries with yogurt for dessert.

1 cup uncooked couscous

2½ to 3 teaspoons olive oil

4 medium-sized bell peppers, sliced in half lengthwise

1 medium-sized red onion, finely chopped

3 cloves garlic, minced

½ cup golden raisins

1½ teaspoon ground cumin

½ teaspoon ground cinnamon

1 15-ounce can chickpeas, drained and rinsed

½ cup chopped fresh flat-leaf parsley

2 tablespoons fresh lemon juice

Salt and freshly ground black pepper to taste

2 tablespoons chopped cilantro or sprigs of cilantro

1. Bring 1½ cups of water to a boil in a saucepan, and stir in the couscous. Bring back to a boil, cover and turn the heat off. Let stand until all the water is absorbed, for 5 to 10 minutes. Fluff with a fork.

2. Meanwhile, in a large nonstick skillet, heat 1 teaspoon of the oil over medium-high heat. Add the bell pepper halves, and cook, turning once, until starting to soften, for about 6 minutes. Remove the peppers and set aside. Heat another ½ teaspoon of oil in the skillet. Add the onion and cook, stirring often, until softened, about 6 to 7 minutes. If the pan is dry, add ½ teaspoon more oil. Add the garlic, raisins, cumin and cinnamon, and cook, stirring often, for 2 minutes.

3. Transfer the onion mixture to a bowl. Add the couscous, beans, parsley, lemon juice and salt and pepper to taste. Spoon about ⅔ cup of the mixture into each bell pepper half, pressing gently to pack.

4. Heat the remaining 1 teaspoon of oil in a skillet. Add the stuffed peppers skin sides down, and cook until the skins start to blister and brown, for about 5 minutes. Gently turn the peppers over to brown the couscous mixture, for about 2 minutes.

5. Transfer the peppers to individual plates, sprinkle with the chopped cilantro and serve.

PER SERVING (2 FILLED PEPPER HALVES): 357 CAL; 14G PROT; 5G FAT; 91G CARB; 0MG CHOL; 333MG SOD; 9G FIBER

This recipe is related to those famous Middle Eastern pilafs in which lentils are combined with a cooked grain and caramelized onions. Green lentils are best because they hold their shape, as will black "beluga" lentils. The onions must be caramelized but not burned—red onions work best because they have more sugar.

1 cup green or black "beluga" lentils, rinsed

3 tablespoons unsalted butter

3 tablespoons olive oil

3 large red onions, thinly sliced

2 teaspoons granulated sugar, optional

½ teaspoons ground cinnamon

¼ teaspoons ground cumin

Salt and freshly ground black pepper to taste

1½ cups uncooked kamut or spelt, rinsed

Chopped fresh parsley for garnish, optional

1. Put the lentils in a saucepan, and cover by 2 inches with salted water. Bring to a boil. Cover the pan, reduce the heat to low, and cook until the lentils are tender but not soft, for about 20 minutes.

2. Heat the butter and oil in a large sauté pan or skillet over medium heat, and sauté the onions and sugar, if using, stirring often, for about 30 minutes, or until deep golden brown. When almost done, season with the cinnamon, cumin, salt and pepper. Stir well. Drain on paper towels to crisp.

3. Meanwhile, cook the kamut in 4 cups of salted water over medium heat until al dente, for about 45 minutes. Drain well. Add to the lentils, and toss to combine. Heat through, making certain that all the liquids have been absorbed. Stir in half the onions. Season to taste. Top with the remaining onions. Serve warm or at room temperature. Garnish with chopped parsley, if desired.

PER SERVING: 410 CAL; 14G PROT; 14G FAT; 59G CARB; 15MG CHOL; 65MG SOD; 17G FIBER

Amaranth's nutty, earthy flavor is perfect for these cakes.

Amaranth Cakes

2 cups boiling water

½ ounce dried porcini mushrooms

1 cup amaranth seeds, rinsed

2 tablespoons minced shallot

¾ teaspoon salt

1 large egg

2 tablespoons all-purpose flour

1 tablespoon finely chopped fresh marjoram

Olive oil for frying

1 cup shaved (see page 160) Parmigiano-Reggiano cheese

Mushroom Mixture

2 tablespoons olive oil

1 pound wild mushrooms, such as chanterelles or morels, cleaned and cut into bite-size pieces

Salt and freshly ground black pepper to taste

2 tablespoons minced shallot

1 clove garlic, minced

½ cup dry white wine

2 tablespoons unsalted butter

1 tablespoon coarsely chopped fresh marjoram

1. To make the Amaranth Cakes: Pour the boiling water over the porcini, and soak for 15 minutes. Using a slotted spoon, lift the mushrooms from the water. Carefully pour the mushroom water through a fine sieve into another container, discarding any sediment. Rinse the mushrooms again, and chop very finely. Set aside.

2. Place the amaranth, shallots, salt, mushrooms and 1½ cups of the mushroom liquid in a saucepan, and heat over medium heat. Cover, and reduce the heat to very low. Cook for 25 minutes, or until the amaranth absorbs all the liquid. Transfer to a bowl, and cool. Stir in the egg, flour and marjoram.

3. To make the Mushroom Mixture: Heat the oil in a large skillet over medium-high heat. Add the mushrooms, season with salt and cook, tossing from time to time, until the mushrooms release moisture and begin to brown. Add the shallots and garlic, cook for 1 minute more and add the wine. Continue to cook until only a few tablespoons of liquid remain. Stir in the butter and marjoram, and transfer to a bowl or saucepan. Keep warm while making the cakes.

4. Pour a ⅛-inch layer of oil into a large skillet, and heat over medium heat. When the oil is hot, drop in 2 tablespoon–portions of amaranth batter, and flatten with a fork into a pancake shape. Cook until browned on the bottom, about 1 minute, flip and brown the top. Repeat with the remaining batter until used up.

5. To serve, alternate layers of amaranth cakes and mushrooms on individual serving plates or a large platter. Top with the Parmigiano-Reggiano cheese, and serve immediately.

PER SERVING: 280 CAL; 11G PROT; 16G FAT; 22G CARB; 40MG CHOL; 400MG SOD; 5G FIBER

CHICKPEAS IN EGGPLANT-TAHINI SAUCE

Make this with dried chickpeas, not canned, for full, rich flavor.

Chickpeas

2 cups dried chickpeas, rinsed

1 tablespoon olive oil

1 cup coarsely chopped onion

1/3 cup uncooked coarse bulgur, rinsed

1 teaspoon caraway seeds

1/2 teaspoon crushed red pepper plus more to taste

2 pounds eggplant, peeled and cut into 1-inch chunks

3 tablespoons tomato paste

2 tablespoons tahini

2 to 3 cloves garlic, crushed

2 teaspoons ground coriander, or more as needed

1 1/4 teaspoons salt, or to taste

Tomato-Cucumber Salad

3 cups diced plum tomatoes

2 cups peeled, seeded, and diced cucumbers

1/2 cup chopped cilantro or parsley

1/4 cup fresh lemon juice

1 teaspoon salt

1. Soak the chickpeas overnight in the refrigerator in water to cover. Drain, and set aside. Heat the oil in a large skillet over medium-high heat. Add the onion, and cook for 2 minutes, stirring frequently. Add the chickpeas, bulgur, caraway seeds, crushed red pepper and water to cover. Set the eggplant on top. Bring to a boil over high heat, reduce the heat to medium-low and cook until done, for 1 to 2 hours.

2. Meanwhile, blend the tomato paste and tahini into 1/2 cup of hot water. Set aside. When the stew is done, stir in the tomato paste mixture, garlic, coriander and salt to taste. Stir well. If necessary, mash the eggplant pieces against the sides of the pot, and blend them in to create a thick, creamy sauce. Add more red pepper and additional coriander seeds, if needed. Cook over medium heat until the garlic loses its raw edge, for about 3 minutes.

3. To make the Tomato-Cucumber Salad: Mix all the ingredients in a bowl. Set aside.

4. Ladle the stew into large, shallow bowls, and sprinkle on a liberal portion of the salad. Pass the remaining salad at the table.

PER SERVING: 400 CAL; 18G PROT; 10G FAT; 66G CARB; 0MG CHOL; 896MG SOD; 16G FIBER

THREE-BEAN SUPER STEW

This sturdy main course will ward off the deepest chill on winter days. This goes well served over hot rice.

1 tablespoon olive oil

1 small red onion, diced

1 small green bell pepper, diced

1 large tomato, cored and diced

1 tablespoon minced fresh ginger

1 teaspoon cumin seeds

1 teaspoon ground coriander

2 cups vegetable stock or Vegetable Stock (page 332)

1 cup cooked lentils (see page 50)

1 cup cooked black beans (see page 50)

1 cup cooked chickpeas (see page 50)

¼ cup chopped cilantro leaves plus sprigs for garnish

Salt and freshly ground white pepper to taste

1. Heat the oil in a saucepan over medium heat. Add the onion and bell pepper, and sauté until soft. Add the tomato, and cook, stirring occasionally, until soft and juicy, for about 2 minutes. Stir in the ginger, cumin and coriander, and mix well.

2. Add the stock, lentils, black beans, chickpeas and cilantro, and cook, covered, for 5 to 10 minutes to heat through. Season with salt and pepper. Remove from the heat, garnish with cilantro and serve.

PER SERVING: 307 CAL; 15G PROT; 7G FAT; 48G CARB; 0MG CHOL; 757MG SOD; 11G FIBER

BLACK BEAN CHILI POT PIE

The cornbread topping on this spicy bean chili gives it just the right touch.

Chili

2 tablespoons vegetable oil

1 large onion, chopped

1 large green bell pepper, diced

2 cloves garlic, minced

1 tablespoon ground cumin

1 tablespoon chili powder

1½ teaspoons ground coriander

1 teaspoon cocoa powder

Salt to taste

2 19-ounce cans black beans, drained and rinsed

1½ cups canned, fresh or frozen corn kernels

1¼ cups vegetable stock or Vegetable Stock (page 332)

1 cup canned crushed tomatoes

1 tablespoon tomato paste

1 teaspoon dried oregano

1 teaspoon granulated sugar

Cornbread Topping

⅔ cup unbleached all-purpose flour

½ cup fine yellow cornmeal

1½ tablespoons granulated sugar

2 teaspoons baking powder

½ teaspoon salt

2 tablespoons vegetable oil

1. To make the Chili: Heat 1½ tablespoons of the oil in a 4-quart Dutch oven or ovenproof casserole over medium heat. Add the onion and pepper, and cook, stirring often, for about 8 minutes, or until softened. Add the garlic, and cook, stirring, for 1 minute. Mix the cumin, chili powder, coriander, cocoa and salt to taste in a bowl.

2. Add the remaining ½ tablespoon of oil and the spice mixture to the pot, and stir for 1 minute over medium heat. Add the beans, corn, broth, tomatoes, tomato paste, oregano and sugar, and gradually bring the mixture to a boil, stirring occasionally. Reduce the heat to low, and cook for 7 to 8 minutes, stirring occasionally, adding more salt if necessary. Remove the pan from the heat.

3. Preheat the oven to 400F.

4. To make the Cornbread Topping: Mix the flour, cornmeal, sugar, baking powder and salt in a bowl. Make a well in the center of the dry ingredients. Add ¾ cup of water and the oil to the well, and stir until blended. Let the batter stand for 2 minutes. Pour the batter over the chili, and spread evenly (it will be thin).

5. Bake for 25 to 30 minutes, or until the topping is cooked through and the chili is bubbly. Remove from the oven, and let stand at least 10 minutes before serving.

PER SERVING: 383 CAL; 16G PROT; 8G FAT; 62G CARB; 0MG CHOL; 366MG SOD; 15G FIBER

NAVY BEANS IN GYPSY SAUCE

This hot, garlicky sauce will remind you of gypsy music.

Navy Beans

1 pound dried navy beans or other white beans, rinsed

2 cups diced onion

2 teaspoons dried sage

Salt to taste

Gypsy Sauce

See page 62

1. To prepare the Navy Beans: Soak the beans in water to cover for 4 hours or overnight in the refrigerator. Drain, and rinse well. Put in a 4-quart saucepan with the onion, sage and fresh water to cover by 3 inches. Bring to a boil. After 30 minutes of boiling, skim off any foam. Boil for another hour. Taste the beans for tenderness, and remove from the heat. Add salt.

2. Preheat the oven to 350F.

3. Meanwhile, to make the Gypsy Sauce: Brush the bread slices with some of the oil, and bake for 15 minutes, or until they are golden and crisp. Let cool. Break into small pieces, and put into a food processor with the almonds, garlic and cayenne; process until the almonds and bread are ground. Add the tomato, bell pepper, salt and pepper. Process until very smooth. Add the vinegar. Process again. Slowly add the remaining oil in a thin stream. Taste and adjust the seasoning. Add more cayenne for spice or more vinegar for tang. This sauce keeps well in the refrigerator.

4. To serve, stir the sauce into the beans just before serving. Or serve the beans in a bowl, each topped with about 2 tablespoons of the sauce, and allow your guests to stir it into their beans.

PER SERVING: 330 CAL; 14G PROT; 12G FAT; 44G CARB; 0MG CHOL; 180MG SOD; 10G FIBER

SPICY BLACK BEAN CAKES

Using instant black beans in this dish makes the preparation as quick and easy as can be. They are available in natural foods stores and well-stocked supermarkets.

1 small onion, chopped

3 cloves garlic, minced

3 large scallions, sliced

4 ounces canned diced green chiles, undrained

4 plum tomatoes, peeled, seeded and diced (see page 46)

2 tablespoons chunky salsa

7 ounces instant black beans

1 cup boiling water

1 to 3 tablespoons vegetable oil

Optional garnishes: shredded lettuce, diced tomatoes, shredded cheddar cheese, low-fat sour cream or yogurt, and sliced black olives

1. Spray a heavy skillet lightly with nonstick cooking spray. Add the onion, garlic and 1 tablespoon of water, and cook over medium-high heat, stirring frequently, until the water evaporates and the vegetables begin to brown. Add the scallions, chiles with liquid, tomatoes and salsa. Mix well, and remove from the heat.

2. Add the beans and boiling water to the skillet. Mix well, scraping the mixture up from the bottom of the skillet. Let sit until the beans have absorbed the liquid and become smooth like refried beans, about 10 minutes. Form into 6 patties.

3. Heat 1 tablespoon of the oil over high heat in a separate skillet. Add the patties, reduce the heat to medium and cook until crisp on 1 side. Turn, and cook on the other side until crisp. Repeat with the remaining batter, and add oil, if needed. Place the patties on individual plates, and serve with lettuce, tomatoes, cheese, sour cream and olives, if desired.

PER SERVING (1 PATTY): 109 CAL; 4G PROT; 2G FAT; 17G CARB; 0MG CHOL; 66MG SOD; 5G FIBER

BARBADOS BLACK BEAN CAKES WITH MANGO SALSA SERVES 4

Tangy-sweet mango salsa is a tasty accompaniment to these Caribbean-inspired black bean cakes.

Mango Salsa

2 cups peeled, diced mango

½ cup diced red bell pepper

¼ cup finely diced red onion

1 serrano chile, seeded and minced

2 tablespoons coarsely chopped cilantro

1 tablespoon fresh lime juice

2 teaspoons minced fresh ginger

Black Bean Cakes

2 15-ounce cans black beans, drained and rinsed

¼ cup chopped cilantro plus extra for garnish, optional

¼ cup finely chopped red onion

1 large egg white, lightly beaten

1 teaspoon ground cumin

1 teaspoon minced garlic

½ teaspoon ground allspice

⅛ teaspoon cayenne

⅓ cup dry whole wheat breadcrumbs (see page 46)

1 tablespoon olive oil

Lime wedges for garnish, optional

1. To make the Salsa: Combine all the ingredients in a bowl. Set aside.

2. To make the Black Bean Cakes: Put the beans in a bowl, and mash with a fork or potato masher until they stick together. Add the cilantro, onion, egg white, cumin, garlic, allspice and cayenne. Mix until well blended.

3. Divide the bean mixture into 8 equal portions. Shape each portion into a ½-inch-thick patty, and coat the patties with the breadcrumbs. Spray both sides of the patties with nonstick cooking spray.

4. Heat the oil in a skillet over medium-high heat. Add the bean cakes, and fry until golden brown on both sides, turning once, about 8 minutes total. Serve warm with the Mango Salsa. Garnish with the cilantro and lime wedges, if using.

PER SERVING (2 PATTIES WITH SALSA): 424 CAL; 19G PROT; 5G FAT; 75G CARB; 0.1MG CHOL; 81MG SOD; 13G FIBER .

13

soy-centered meals

FLAGGED BY THE EXPERTS AS A PROTEIN-packed food, soy is the only vegetable source of complete protein—but with a major health bene-fit. Soy has no cholesterol or the artery-clogging saturated fat that kills so many Americans each year. For everyone, that makes great soy headlines.

And for vegetarians, soy has several major culinary advantages. Modern researchers have taken the lowly soybean and transformed it into delicious beverages, tempting meat analogs, versatile dairylike products, flours, cereals, condiments and a range of protein-packed tofu and tempeh goods that can enhance any vege-tarian's—or any nonvegetarian's—cookpot.

SEARED TOFU WITH ORANGE GLAZE

Because this dish is ready just minutes after you sauté the tofu, have the watercress prepped and everything at your fingertips before you start to cook. The reduced orange juice in the glaze makes the flavor sing. Offer this with stir-fried brown rice accented with toasted pecans.

1 pound firm tofu, rinsed and drained

½ cup fresh orange juice, strained

2 tablespoons shoyu or low-sodium soy sauce

2 tablespoons sake

1 scallion, thinly sliced

¼ cup unbleached all-purpose flour

1½ tablespoons plus 1 teaspoon vegetable oil

2 medium-sized cloves garlic, thinly sliced

2 bunches watercress, rinsed well, thick stems removed

1 tablespoon sesame seeds

Few drops toasted sesame oil

Salt to taste

Freshly ground black pepper to taste

1. Lay the tofu block on its side. Cut lengthwise into 4 equal slices, then cut through the block diagonally to make 8 triangles. Keeping the block intact, place the tofu on a plate. Place another plate on top, and weight with a heavy object to press out excess moisture. Let stand for 15 minutes.

2. Meanwhile, bring the orange juice to a boil in a saucepan over medium-high heat. Cook until reduced to 2 tablespoons, for about 8 minutes. Transfer to a bowl, and stir in the shoyu, sake, scallion and 2 tablespoons of water. Set aside.

3. Spread the flour on a plate. Press each tofu triangle into the flour, making sure both sides are well coated. Heat a large, heavy skillet over high heat, and add the 1½ tablespoons of vegetable oil. Immediately add the tofu in one layer, cooking in batches if necessary, and cook until lightly golden, turning once, for 2 to 3 minutes on each side. Divide the tofu among 4 plates, and set aside.

4. Heat the remaining 1 teaspoon of vegetable oil in the same skillet over high heat. Add the garlic, and stir for 10 seconds. Add the orange juice mixture (be careful, it will steam), and cook for 30 seconds. Pour the orange glaze over the tofu triangles.

5. Add the watercress to the skillet, and stir-fry over high heat until just wilted, for about 30 seconds. Remove from the heat. Stir in the sesame seeds, drizzle with the sesame oil and season with salt and pepper to taste. Mound the watercress alongside the tofu. Serve hot.

Per serving: 184 CAL; 8G PROT; 10G FAT; 14G CARB; 0MG CHOL; 570MG SOD; 2G FIBER

GRILLED TOFU WITH WASABI-HONEY GLAZE

Tofu gets a boost from wasabi, the green Japanese horseradish.

¼ cup tamari

¼ cup minced fresh ginger

¼ cup rice vinegar

2 tablespoons minced shallots

2 tablespoons dark sesame oil

1 pound extra-firm tofu, drained and sliced into ½-inch-thick slabs

2 tablespoons wasabi

¼ cup honey

4 cups cooked rice (see page 48), such as brown rice, wild rice or japonica, hot

2 tablespoons toasted sesame seeds (see page 47), optional

1. Combine the tamari, ginger, vinegar, shallots and sesame oil in a bowl. Place the tofu cutlets on a platter, and coat both sides with the mixture. Cover, and refrigerate for several hours.

2. Prepare a hot charcoal fire, or preheat a gas grill to medium-high.

3. Arrange the tofu cutlets on the grill or in a grill pan, and cook until lightly browned and the center is warmed through, for about 3 minutes per side. Carefully remove to a platter.

4. Meanwhile, mix together the wasabi and honey in a small bowl. Add water as needed to form a thick glaze.

5. Arrange the grilled tofu steaks on a bed of hot rice. Brush with the wasabi-honey glaze, and sprinkle with the sesame seeds, if desired. Serve hot.

PER SERVING (WITH 1 CUP RICE): 486 CAL; 25G PROT; 15G FAT; 69G CARB; 0MG CHOL; 837MG SOD; 4G FIBER

MEXICAN GRILLED TOFU WITH JÍCAMA SLAW

A little dash of hot sauce and the complementary flavors of cumin and lime juice brighten the grilled tofu. Serve these with refried beans or Mexican-style rice studded with diced chiles.

Grilled Tofu

1 pound extra-firm tofu, well drained

4 medium-sized cloves garlic, crushed

1 tablespoon cumin seeds

1 teaspoon dried oregano

¾ teaspoon salt

3 tablespoons fresh lime juice

1 tablespoon fresh orange juice

1 tablespoon light olive oil or vegetable oil

Freshly ground black pepper to taste

Jícama Slaw

3 tablespoons fresh lime juice

1 tablespoon light olive oil or vegetable oil

2 teaspoons honey or pure maple syrup

¼ teaspoon hot pepper sauce

1 small (1¼ pounds) jícama, peeled and grated

3 carrots (8 ounces total), peeled and grated

¼ cup chopped cilantro

Lime wedges and cilantro sprigs for garnish

1. To make the Grilled Tofu: Cut the tofu in half vertically, and split each piece in half horizontally. Place the tofu pieces in a baking dish, and cover with plastic wrap and a plate. Weight down the tofu with cans. Refrigerate the tofu for 30 to 45 minutes.

2. Meanwhile, using a mortar and pestle or the side of a chef's knife, mash the garlic, cumin, oregano and salt into paste, and put into a bowl. Whisk in the lime and orange juices, oil and pepper.

3. Remove the tofu from the baking dish, and pat dry with paper towels, discarding any remaining liquid. Put the tofu back in the dish, and spoon half of the lime juice mixture over the top, spreading the spices evenly and turning the tofu to coat. Cover, and refrigerate for at least 2 hours or up to 1 day, turning occasionally.

4. Prepare a hot charcoal fire, or preheat a gas grill to medium-high.

5. Meanwhile, to make the Jícama Slaw: Whisk together the lime juice, oil, honey and hot sauce. Stir in the jícama, carrots and cilantro, and toss well. Season with salt and pepper.

6. Lightly oil the grill rack. Remove the tofu from the marinade, reserving the marinade for basting. Grill the tofu, basting occasionally, until lightly browned, for 3 to 4 minutes per side. Divide the slaw among individual plates. Top each with a piece of grilled tofu. Garnish with the lime wedges and cilantro sprigs, and serve.

PER SERVING: 239 CAL; 11G PROT; 11G FAT; 28G CARB; 0MG CHOL; 473MG SOD; 7G FIBER

MARINATED TOFU WITH SHIITAKE STUFFING

Layers of flavors heighten the appeal of this Asian-inspired entrée.

2 pounds soft, firm or silken tofu

2 teaspoons canola oil

1 teaspoon dark sesame oil

1 teaspoon chopped garlic

2 teaspoons chopped fresh ginger

8 ounces fresh shiitake mushrooms, finely chopped

2 scallions, chopped

1 tablespoon sherry

1 tablespoon tamari soy sauce or low-sodium soy sauce plus extra for garnish

1 tablespoon chopped cilantro

½ teaspoon salt, or to taste

¼ teaspoon freshly ground black pepper

Pinch crushed red pepper or dash hot pepper sauce

1. Drain the soft tofu, if using, for 2 to 3 hours by weighting it down with a plate. Cut each piece of tofu in half vertically to form 4 smaller blocks.

2. Use a melon baller or soup spoon, and scoop out the middle of each block, about 1½ inches deep by 1½ inches wide. Mince the scooped-out tofu, and set aside.

3. Heat the canola and sesame oils in a skillet over medium heat, and sauté the garlic and ginger until soft. Add the shiitakes, scallions, sherry and reserved chopped tofu. Cook until dry and dark brown, for about 5 minutes. Add the tamari, cilantro, salt, pepper and crushed red pepper. Cook for another 2 to 3 minutes, remove from the heat and set aside.

4. Put the mushroom mixture into a pastry bag, and pipe it into the hollow of each tofu block. Or use a spoon to scoop the mixture into the hollows.

5. Steam the stuffed tofu on a rack in a vegetable steamer for 5 minutes until hot. Serve with tamari or low-sodium soy sauce.

PER SERVING: 190 CAL; 13G PROT; 10G FAT; 11G CARB; 0MG CHOL; 550MG SOD; 1G FIBER

BARBECUED TOFU AND APPLES

This dish can turn any meal into a walloping country-style bash. It makes a perfect companion for a tossed green salad and a dessert favorite—we like lemon meringue pie.

2 tablespoons vegetable oil

6 ounces barbecue-flavored baked tofu, cubed

1 cup diced celery

1 cup diced onion

1 Anaheim or other chile, seeded and thinly sliced, or more to taste

½ head regular or savoy cabbage, shredded

2 cups vegetarian-style baked beans

½ cup barbecue sauce, or to taste

1 apple, cored and cubed

2 cups cubed cornbread plus extra for garnish

2 tablespoons unsalted butter, cubed

1. Preheat the oven to 350F. Spray a 2-quart ovenproof baking dish with non-stick cooking spray, and set aside.

2. Heat the oil in a large skillet over medium heat, and sauté the tofu, celery, onion, chile and cabbage. Cook for about 8 minutes, and add the beans, ¼ cup of the barbecue sauce and the apples. Continue cooking for about 5 minutes more.

3. Line the baking dish with some of the cornbread cubes, going up the sides of the dish. Spoon the bean mixture into the baking dish, and top with more cornbread cubes, making a top crust. Drizzle the remaining ¼ cup of sauce over the top, and dot with the butter.

4. Bake for 15 minutes, or until the cornbread starts to turn golden. Serve hot.

PER SERVING: 310 CAL; 10G PROT; 13G FAT; 38G CARB; 10MG CHOL; 450MG SOD; 6G FIBER

BREADED OVEN-BAKED TOFU
WITH PORTOBELLO MUSHROOM GRAVY

Chinese-style tofu—with its firm, spongy texture—is packaged in tubs filled with water, or it is vacuum-packed in clear plastic and must be refrigerated. Because most marinades contain an acid ingredient such as vinegar, citrus juice or wine, marinating should always be done in a nonreactive bowl made of glass or ceramic. Look for breadcrumbs that do not contain partially hydrogenated oil. The mushroom gravy recipe follows.

Cabernet Marinade

1 1/3 cups hot Vegetable Stock (page 332)

3/4 cup Cabernet wine

1/4 cup tamari or low-sodium soy sauce

1/4 cup tomato paste

2 scallions, thinly sliced

2 teaspoons granulated garlic

2 teaspoons dried oregano

2 pounds firm tofu, drained and cubed

Cornmeal Breading

1/3 cup yellow cornmeal

3 tablespoons whole wheat flour

3 tablespoons breadcrumbs (see page 46)

1 tablespoon granulated garlic

2 teaspoons dried oregano

3 dashes cayenne pepper

1. To make the Cabernet Marinade: Combine the Vegetable Stock, wine, tamari, tomato paste, scallions, garlic and oregano, and pour into a large baking dish. Put the tofu into the dish, and marinate for several hours or overnight. Remove the tofu from the marinade, and place in a microwave-safe colander suspended over a bowl. Cover loosely with wax paper, and microwave on high for 5 minutes. Set aside.

2. Preheat the oven to 400F. Spray a baking sheet with nonstick cooking spray, and set aside.

3. To make the Cornmeal Breading: Combine all the ingredients in a bowl, and thoroughly coat the tofu pieces. Place the breaded tofu on the prepared pan in a single layer.

4. Bake on the middle rack for 1 hour, turning over after 30 minutes. Cook until golden brown, remove from the oven and serve with Portobello Mushroom Gravy (below).

PER SERVING: 228 CAL; 16G PROT; 4G FAT; 20G CARB; 0MG CHOL; 593MG SOD; 4G FIBER

PORTOBELLO MUSHROOM GRAVY

1 1/2 ounces dried portobello mushrooms

2 cups boiling water

3 tablespoons olive oil

3 tablespoons whole wheat flour

1 1/2 cups boiling vegetarian beef stock, boiling

2/3 cup nutritional yeast

1/2 teaspoon freeze-dried chives

1 tablespoon tamari soy sauce

1. Combine dried mushrooms and boiling water in a saucepan. Cook mushrooms over low heat for 15 minutes. Remove from the heat, and set aside.

2. Heat the oil in a saucepan over medium heat for 2 minutes. Add the flour, stirring to form a roux. Remove the mushrooms from the soaking liquid, chop them coarsely and add to the roux. Cook the mixture for 2 minutes, stirring constantly. Add the hot stock, and, stirring frequently, cook for 3 minutes. Reduce the heat to low, add the yeast and stir or whisk until blended. Add the chives and tamari soy sauce, and cook 5 minutes, stirring occasionally.

PER 1/2 CUP SERVING: 74CAL; 3G PROT; 5G FAT; 4G CARB; 0MG CHOL; 157MG SOD; 1G FIBER

BAKED ZITI

Here, soy fans, get a treat with seitan paired with tofu in one substantial dish. It's easy to assemble and filled with lively flavors.

12 ounces dried ziti

8 ounces seitan

2 cups button or cremini mushrooms

1 25-ounce jar tomato sauce

1 pound extra-firm tofu, drained, or low-fat ricotta

⅓ cup chopped fresh basil or 5½ teaspoons dried basil

2 tablespoons fresh lemon juice

4 teaspoons olive oil

Salt to taste

½ teaspoon coarsely ground black pepper

½ cup chopped flat-leaf parsley

1. Preheat the oven to 400F.

2. Heat a pot of lightly salted water over medium heat, and when it is boiling, cook the pasta according to the package directions. Drain, rinse, drain again and set aside.

3. Chop the seitan and mushrooms until coarse and crumbly. Put the mixture in a large saucepan, stir in the tomato sauce and cook over medium-low heat, stirring occasionally, for 10 minutes. Remove from the heat, and cover to keep warm.

4. Put the tofu, basil, lemon juice, 2 teaspoons of the oil, pepper and salt into a food processor or blender, and process until the consistency resembles ricotta cheese. If using ricotta, mix by hand.

5. Spread several tablespoons of the tomato seitan mixture in a 13 x 9 inch baking dish, making sure to evenly coat the bottom and sides to prevent sticking. Combine the pasta, tofu mixture, the remaining tomato-seitan mixture and the parsley. Fold gently to combine all the ingredients. Spread evenly into the baking dish.

6. Bake for 15 minutes, or until heated through. Remove from the oven, and serve hot.

PER SERVING: 382 CAL; 22G PROT; 7G FAT; 58G CARB; 0MG CHOL; 854MG SOD; 5G FIBER

BABAGHANZA FONDUE

The flavor here captures the essence of the Middle Eastern eggplant classic, Baba Ghanoush (page 76). Consider the traditional accompaniments that go so well with eggplant, such as olives and cucumbers. The perfect dessert? Poached Orange Cake (page 391).

Babaghanza Fondue

1 large (about 1 pound), firm eggplant

12 ounces silken soft tofu

¼ cup tahini

¼ cup fresh lemon juice

¼ cup olive oil

2 large cloves garlic, crushed

1 teaspoon salt, or to taste

½ teaspoon freshly ground black pepper

½ teaspoon cayenne pepper

3 tablespoons minced cilantro leaves

Accompaniments

24 pita breads, quartered

12 to 16 cups combination raw and cooked vegetables for dipping, such as cucumber sticks, carrot sticks, bell pepper strips, celery, radishes, baby carrots, broccoli florets and sugar snap peas, cut into serving sizes

1. Preheat the oven to 350F. Spray a baking sheet with nonstick cooking spray, and set aside.

2. To make the Babaghanza Fondue: Cut the eggplant in half, and place, cut sides down, on the baking sheet. Bake until soft, for about 45 minutes. Scrape the softened eggplant flesh into a blender, and process until smooth. Add the tofu, tahini, lemon juice, oil, garlic, salt, pepper and cayenne, and process until smooth.

3. To serve, stir in the cilantro, and heat the eggplant mixture to boiling. Transfer to a fondue pot or crock-pot. Keep the fondue warm over an alcohol burner or in the crock-pot on the lowest setting. Serve with pita bread and accompaniments.

PER SERVING (WITHOUT ACCOMPANIMENTS): 150 CAL; 4G PROT; 12G FAT; 7G CARB; 0MG CHOL; 300MG SOD; 2G FIBER

DEEP-DISH SUN-DRIED TOMATO QUICHE

When making the pastry, set aside the remainder of the silken tofu to use in the quiche filling. You may make the pastry a day in advance, and store it, covered, in the refrigerator. Remove the dough an hour before proceeding with the recipe.

Pastry

2 cups whole wheat pastry flour plus extra for rolling

⅓ cup rolled oats

¼ teaspoon sea salt

⅓ cup low-fat silken tofu

1 tablespoon olive oil

1 tablespoon brown rice syrup

⅓ cup plus 1 tablespoon ice water

Filling

1 3-ounce package dry-packed sun-dried tomatoes

1 cup boiling water

½ cup soymilk

2 tablespoons fresh lemon juice

2 teaspoons olive oil

¼ teaspoon crushed red pepper

½ cup sliced scallions

4 cloves garlic, minced

1 large shallot, minced

1 13¾-ounce can artichoke hearts, cubed

2 tablespoons capers, rinsed

2 tablespoons chopped fresh basil

1 12.3-ounce package low-fat silken tofu

3 tablespoons mild white miso

¼ cup dry sherry or apple cider

⅓ cup potato flakes

⅓ cup nutritional yeast

¼ teaspoon ground turmeric

1 teaspoon dried basil

1. To make the Pastry: Lightly spray a 9½-inch deep-dish pie plate with olive oil spray. Put the flour, oats and salt in a food processor, and pulse to mix. Add the tofu, oil and rice syrup, and blend. With the motor running, pour the ice water through the feed tube, and process until the mixture comes together in a ball. Turn onto a lightly floured work surface. Sprinkle the dough lightly with flour, and roll out ⅛- to ¼-inch thick. Press into the prepared pan, and trim the edges, leaving a 1-inch overlap. Using your thumb and forefinger, press a decorative edge along the side, around the top edge. Set the dough aside in the refrigerator.

2. Preheat the oven to 375F.

3. To make the Filling: Combine the tomatoes and water in a bowl, and set aside. Combine the soymilk and lemon juice in a nonreactive bowl, and set aside. Heat the oil and crushed red pepper in a 10-inch skillet over medium-high heat for about 1 minute. Add the scallions, garlic and shallots, and sauté for 3 minutes. Drain the tomatoes, reserving the soaking liquid. Add the tomatoes, artichokes, capers and fresh basil to the pan. Reduce the heat to medium-low, and cook the mixture for 5 minutes, stirring occasionally.

4. Put the tofu into a food processor, and blend until smooth. Put the miso in a bowl, add the sherry and blend with a fork until smooth. Add the miso mixture, soymilk mixture and reserved tomato soaking liquid to the tofu, and process. Add the potato flakes, yeast and turmeric, and process. Fold the tofu mixture into the artichokes, and mix thoroughly. Spoon the mixture into the pie shell, and sprinkle with the dried basil. Place on the middle rack in the oven.

5. Bake for 35 minutes, or until lightly browned. Remove from the oven, and let stand for 15 minutes. Serve lukewarm.

PER SERVING: 215 CAL; 14G PROT; 3G FAT; 35G CARB; 0MG CHOL; 800MG SOD; 6G FIBER

ASIAN TOFU CAKES

These tofu cakes are particularly delicious served with rice and sautéed sliced bok choy.

Cakes

15 ounces firm tofu, rinsed and drained

5 large egg whites

⅓ cup all-purpose whole wheat flour

⅓ cup frozen peas

3 scallions, thinly sliced,

1 tablespoon grated fresh ginger

1 tablespoon low-sodium soy sauce

Salt and ground white pepper to taste

2 teaspoons toasted sesame oil, or more if needed

1 tablespoon sesame seeds, toasted (see page 47)

1 medium-sized carrot, shredded

Sauce

3 tablespoons low-sodium soy sauce

½ teaspoon toasted sesame oil or chili oil

½ teaspoon rice vinegar

1. Pat the tofu dry with paper towels, and place in a bowl. Mash the tofu with a fork until it resembles chopped eggs. Mix in the egg whites, flour, peas, all but 1 teaspoon of the scallions, ginger, soy sauce, salt and pepper to taste until well blended.

2. Heat the oil in a large nonstick skillet. Add about ¼ cup of the tofu mixture per cake to the skillet, flattening with the back of a spoon to form small cakes. Cook until golden brown, for about 2 minutes on each side.

3. Meanwhile, to make the Sauce: Mix the soy sauce, oil, vinegar and reserved 1 teaspoon of scallion in a bowl.

4. To serve the tofu cakes, sprinkle with the sesame seeds and shredded carrot, and accompany with the sesame-soy sauce on the side.

PER SERVING: 110 CAL; 10G PROT; 3.5G FAT; 10G CARB; 0MG CHOL; 380MG SOD; 2G FIBER

BARBECUED TOFU

For this recipe, you will need extra-firm or firm tofu that has been frozen. To freeze, drain the tofu, cut into slabs, wrap in plastic and freeze until firm (also see page 47).

2 pounds extra-firm or firm tofu, cut into 3 x 1–inch slabs, frozen, thawed and squeezed dry

Marinade

⅓ cup peanut butter

⅓ cup vegetable oil

1 ½ teaspoons paprika

1 teaspoon salt

½ teaspoon garlic powder

Barbecue Sauce

1 cup canned tomato sauce

½ medium-sized onion, chopped

½ cup packed brown sugar or honey

1 tablespoon chopped fresh parsley

1 ½ teaspoons molasses

½ teaspoon salt

½ teaspoon ground allspice

⅛ teaspoon cayenne

¼ cup fresh lemon juice

1 tablespoon Bragg Liquid Aminos

1. Preheat the oven to 350F. Lightly coat a baking sheet with nonstick cooking spray. Place the tofu slabs on the sheet.

2. To make the Marinade: Put all the ingredients into a blender, and purée until smooth. Spoon over the tofu slabs, turn to coat and marinate in the refrigerator for 1 hour.

3. Meanwhile, to make the Barbecue Sauce: Mix the tomato sauce, onion, sugar, parsley, molasses, salt, allspice and cayenne in a saucepan. Bring to a boil, reduce the heat to low and cook, stirring occasionally, for 1 hour. Stir in the lemon juice and Bragg Liquid Aminos.

4. Bake the tofu for 25 minutes per side. Brush the barbecue sauce over both sides of the baked tofu, and bake until hot, for 15 to 20 minutes more.

PER SERVING: 188 CAL; 10G PROT; 10G FAT; 16G CARB; 0MG CHOL; 453MG SOD; 2G FIBER

Meet the New "Meat"

Versatile, adaptable soy now turns up in countless forms, and especially abundant in the supermarket are the meat look-alikes from "chicken" strips to "meatballs." For those people making the transition to a meatless diet, these products are boons because they help persuade skeptical omnivores that they are not leaving behind familiar beef-, poultry- and seafood-based meals for bland tofu.

Known as "meat analogs," these products are prepared from soy protein and are available fresh, canned, frozen and dried. Soy meat products may be used in much the same way as their real-meat counterparts, but generally they cook up and are ready for the table faster.

Consider the following soy-based products:

- "Ground meat": Plain and taco seasoned; works well in sauces, chilis and as filling for tacos, burritos or crêpes.

- "Sausage": Crumbles or links are lean and may need extra oil for pan-frying.

- "Pepperoni": Good in sandwiches and on pizzas.

- "Chicken" and "beef" strips: Good in stews and stir-fries.

- "Meatballs": Use on heroes or pizzas, in stews and over spaghetti.

GRILLED TOFU KABOBS CHIPOTLE
WITH CORN ON THE COB AND ASPARAGUS

Chipotle chiles in adobo sauce are actually smoked dried jalapeño chiles blended with herbs and vinegar. Sold at Latino markets, specialty foods stores and some supermarkets, these spicy chiles add a unique flavor to many dishes. The tofu kabobs can be grilled, with or without the skewers, on a lightly oiled vegetable grill rack to keep the kabobs intact and prevent the tofu or vegetables from falling through the grill onto the coals.

Chipotle Marinade

1 cup heated vegetarian "chicken"-flavored stock or Vegetable Stock (page 332)

¼ cup tamari or low-sodium soy sauce

1 canned chipotle in adobo, minced

1½ tablespoons adobo sauce

1 large clove garlic, minced

1 tablespoon Dijon mustard

1½ teaspoons granulated onion

1½ teaspoons dried cilantro

Tofu Kabobs

2 pounds extra-firm tofu

3 zucchini, cut into 1-inch circles

1 medium-sized red bell pepper, cut into vertical strips, 1 inch wide

1 medium-sized red onion, cut into 1-inch wedges

12 cherry tomatoes

1 cup pineapple cubes

6 ears corn on the cob, shucked

1 pound fresh asparagus, trimmed

1. To make the Chipotle Marinade: Combine the stock, tamari, chipotle, adobo sauce and garlic in a measuring cup. Add the mustard, onion and cilantro.

2. To make the Tofu Kabobs: Slice each block of tofu in half horizontally, and, in a cross-hatch pattern, make 2 slices vertically and 2 slices horizontally for a total of 36 tofu cubes. Place the tofu in a nonreactive 9 x 13–inch baking dish. Pour the marinade over the tofu, cover and refrigerate for 1 to 24 hours.

3. Prepare a hot charcoal fire, or preheat a gas grill to medium-high. Soak 8 large bamboo skewers in hot water for at least 30 minutes.

4. Thread the tofu, zucchini, bell pepper, onion, tomatoes and pineapple alternately on the skewers, and set aside.

5. Blanch the corn, and set aside. Place the kabobs over the fire, and set the corn and asparagus on the grill. Turning carefully and basting the vegetables and tofu often with the marinade, cook for about 15 minutes, or until done, taking care that the vegetables don't burn. Serve.

PER SERVING: 279 CAL; 20G PROT; 5G FAT; 32G CARB; 0MG CHOL; 334MG SOD; 10G FIBER

BREADED TOFU CUTLETS WITH TARTAR SAUCE

If you are serving more than four, the first part of the recipe doubles easily, and the quantity of sauce given below will suffice.

Tofu Cutlets

1 pound firm or extra-firm tofu, drained

⅓ cup wheat germ

1 teaspoon salt-free herb-and-spice seasoning mix

½ teaspoon salt

Tartar Sauce

¾ cup plain low-fat soy yogurt

1 to 1½ tablespoons pickle relish, or to taste

1 tablespoon reduced-fat mayonnaise or soy mayonnaise

2 teaspoons Dijon mustard, or to taste

1. Preheat the oven to 450F. Lightly oil a nonstick baking sheet, and set aside.

2. Cut the tofu into ½-inch-thick slices. Blot the tofu well between several layers of paper towels, then cut lengthwise into ½-inch-wide strips. Mix the wheat germ, seasoning mix and salt in a shallow bowl. Add the tofu sticks, and coat with the mixture. Arrange the breaded tofu on the baking sheet. Bake for 15 to 20 minutes, or until the cutlets are golden and firm.

3. Meanwhile, to make the Tartar Sauce: Combine all the ingredients in a bowl, and mix well. Set aside.

4. Serve the cutlets warm with the Tartar Sauce as a topping or on the side.

PER SERVING: 269 CAL; 12G PROT; 9G FAT; 36G CARB; 17MG CHOL; 501MG SOD; 5G FIBER

CRISP BLACK SESAME TOFU

This recipe produces tofu with a crisp, flavorful coating. For the best texture, be sure to use extra-firm tofu and drain it well. Regular sesame seeds work fine, but for a striking presentation, use black sesame seeds. Another plus? This recipe doubles easily.

1 cup thinly sliced yellow bell pepper

1 cup mung bean sprouts

⅔ cup chopped scallions

⅓ cup sesame seeds

1 pound extra-firm tofu, cut into ½-inch-thick slices, drained well and patted dry (about 8 slices)

4 tablespoons roasted garlic oil or olive oil,

1½ tablespoons minced fresh ginger

¼ cup rice vinegar

1. Mix the bell pepper, bean sprouts and scallions in a bowl. Divide the vegetables evenly between 2 plates.

2. Place the sesame seeds on a small plate. Dredge the tofu slices in the sesame seeds to coat on all sides. Heat 2 tablespoons of the oil in a heavy skillet over medium heat. Add the tofu, and cook until golden brown, for about 3 minutes on each side. Divide the tofu evenly between the 2 plates, leaning the tofu against the vegetable mounds.

3. Add the remaining 2 tablespoons of oil to the skillet. Add the ginger, and cook over medium heat, stirring often, for 1 minute. Stir in the vinegar, bring to a boil and remove from the heat. Drizzle the tofu and vegetables with the pan sauce. Serve hot.

PER SERVING (8 OUNCES TOFU): 334 CAL; 15G PROT; 24G FAT; 10G CARB; 0MG CHOL; 18MG SOD; 3G FIBER

COCONUT CURRY TOFU AND SNOW PEAS

To cube the tofu, divide the block in half horizontally. Slice through both layers, making three cuts lengthwise and crosswise. To keep the Asian theme intact, serve this curry with jasmine rice or rice noodles.

1 ounce whole dried shiitake mushrooms

18 ounces very firm tofu, pressed (see page 47)

1½ teaspoons olive oil

1 medium-sized red onion, chopped

1 medium-sized red bell pepper, chopped

4 cloves garlic, minced

1 tablespoon grated fresh ginger

¼ teaspoon crushed red pepper

8 ounces white button mushrooms, sliced

¼ cup chopped fresh basil

½ cup fruity white wine, such as Chenin Blanc, or Vegetable Stock (page 332)

1 14½-ounce can diced tomatoes

1 14-ounce can light coconut milk

1 to 2 teaspoons spicy Thai chili sauce

1 teaspoon ground turmeric

Juice of 1 lime

1 teaspoon Bragg Liquid Aminos

12 ounces fresh snow peas, rinsed and trimmed

1. Rinse the shiitakes, place them in a saucepan with water to cover and cook them over medium-high heat. Bring to a boil, reduce the heat to medium and cook for 5 minutes. Remove from the heat, and set aside for 20 minutes.

2. Spray an electric skillet or a Dutch oven with nonstick cooking spray, and set over medium-high heat for 1 minute. Press, and blot the tofu well between several layers of paper towels. Pat the tofu dry, and brown the cubes in the hot pan, spraying with additional oil as needed. Turn frequently, until the cubes are brown on all sides. Remove from the pan, and set aside on a clean, dry plate.

3. Add the oil to the skillet, heat for a few seconds and add the onion, bell pepper, garlic, ginger and crushed red pepper, sautéing for 4 minutes. Drain the shiitakes and add them, the button mushrooms and basil to the mixture. Cook for 5 minutes, stirring frequently.

4. Add the tofu and wine to the pan. Cook for 1 minute, and add the tomatoes and coconut milk. Reduce the heat to low, and stir in the chili sauce, turmeric, lime juice and Bragg Liquid Aminos. Cook for 5 minutes more, and add the snow peas. Cook the mixture just until the snow peas are heated through, for about 2 minutes. Serve immediately.

PER SERVING: 206 CAL; 11G PROT; 8G FAT; 17G CARB; 0MG CHOL; 221MG SOD; 4G FIBER

TOFU GUMBO

Gumbo may be made with a number of main ingredients, so why not tofu? Marinated tofu is a modern addition to this old Cajun favorite—along with the distinctive texture of okra. It's served over Basic Polenta (page 200), which is fluffed with eggs and served golden brown and piping hot right out of the oven.

Marinade

½ onion, diced

¼ cup Dijon mustard

¼ teaspoon cayenne

¼ cup peanut oil

¼ cup cider vinegar

1 tablespoon minced garlic

1 tablespoon packed brown sugar

1 pound extra-firm tofu, cut in ½-inch cubes

Gumbo

3 tablespoons plus ¼ cup canola oil

½ onion, diced

2 ribs celery, diced

1 green bell pepper, diced

½ red bell pepper, diced

1 tablespoon minced garlic

2 cups Vegetable Stock (page 332)

1 cup diced canned tomatoes

1 teaspoon dried thyme

1 teaspoon dried oregano

1 teaspoon dried basil

2 bay leaves

Salt and freshly ground black pepper to taste

4 ounces okra, cut in ½-inch pieces

½ cup all-purpose flour

1. To make the Marinade: Combine the onion, mustard, cayenne, oil, vinegar, garlic and sugar in a bowl. Put the tofu cubes in the mixture, and marinate in the refrigerator for 2 to 24 hours.

2. To make the Gumbo: Heat 1 tablespoon of the oil in a large pot over medium heat. Sauté the onion, celery, bell peppers and garlic for about 10 minutes, or until the onions are translucent and the vegetables are soft. Add the Vegetable Stock, tomatoes, thyme, oregano, basil, bay leaves, salt and pepper. Reduce the heat to medium-low, and cook for 15 to 20 minutes.

3. Heat 2 tablespoons of oil in a large skillet, and sauté the okra until it is light brown. Remove from the skillet, and add to the tomato mixture.

4. Drain the tofu, discarding the marinade, keeping the diced onion. Reheat the skillet, and sauté the tofu and onion until lightly browned. Remove from the skillet, and add to the tomato mixture.

5. Heat the remaining ¼ cup of oil in the skillet, and whisk in the flour. Continue whisking the mixture, or roux, until it is light brown and smells slightly nutty, for 3 to 4 minutes.

6. Reheat the tomato mixture over medium heat, and stir in the roux 1 tablespoon at a time. Continue to stir until the gumbo is the consistency of gravy. Remove from the heat, and serve over Basic Polenta.

PER SERVING: 360 CAL; 8G PROT; 30G FAT; 16G CARB; 0MG CHOL; 240MG SOD; 3G FIBER

A delicious Creole dish in which the meat and seafood are replaced by tofu, this requires frozen and thawed tofu, so plan ahead to make this recipe.

1 pound firm tofu

1 14½-ounce can diced tomatoes

1 tablespoon vegetable oil

1 large onion, coarsely chopped

4 medium-sized cloves garlic, minced

2 medium-sized green bell peppers, seeded and diced

2 stalks celery, thinly sliced

⅔ cup minced fresh parsley

2 bay leaves

1 teaspoon liquid smoke, or more to taste

2 teaspoons dried or ground thyme

2 teaspoons salt

¼ teaspoon cayenne pepper, or more to taste

1½ cups uncooked long-grain brown rice

Freshly ground black pepper to taste

Hot pepper sauce to taste, optional

1. Drain the tofu, and cut into 1-inch-thick slabs. Place in a plastic bag, and freeze for 1 to 2 days (see page 47).

2. Thaw the tofu in the microwave for 2 to 3 minutes or at room temperature for about 4 hours. Drain, and squeeze out excess moisture with your hands. Cut into ½-inch cubes, and set aside.

3. Drain the tomatoes, reserving the juice. In a large measuring cup, combine the reserved juice with enough water to equal 2½ cups. Set the tomatoes and juice mixture aside.

4. Heat the oil in a large, heavy pot over medium-high heat. Add the onion and garlic, and cook, stirring often, until lightly browned, for about 3 minutes. Add the reserved tomatoes and juice mixture, bell peppers, celery, half of the parsley, the bay leaves, liquid smoke, thyme, salt and cayenne. Mix well, and bring to a boil. Stir in the tofu cubes and rice. Cover, reduce the heat to low and cook until the rice is tender, for about 45 minutes.

5. Remove from the heat, and let stand, covered, for 10 minutes. Discard the bay leaves, and stir in the remaining ⅓ cup of parsley. Season with pepper and hot sauce to taste, if using. Serve hot.

PER SERVING: 276 CAL; 9G PROT; 6G FAT; 46G CARB; 0MG CHOL; 866MG SOD; 4G FIBER

SPICY TEMPEH AND CORN SALSA

This hearty entrée is ideal served on its own with rice and beans or as a filling for quesadillas, tacos or burritos. Its Mexican accent comes from cilantro, cumin and jalapeño chiles, and sunflower seeds lend crunch. The dulse (seaweed) flakes lend a nice smoky flavor to the dish.

2 tablespoons olive oil

8 ounces tempeh, crumbled

1½ tablespoons cumin seeds

2 teaspoons salt

½ cup Vegetable Stock (page 332) or water

2 large red onions, diced

2 red bell peppers, diced

2 stalks celery, diced

4 cloves garlic, minced

2 tablespoons seeded, minced jalapeño chiles

2 tablespoons smoked dulse flakes (see Glossary, page 461)

3 cups fresh or frozen corn kernels

2 cups diced tomatoes

2 cups coarsely chopped cilantro

½ cup raw sunflower seeds, toasted (see page 47)

1. Heat a wok over high heat, and add 1 tablespoon of the oil. Add the tempeh, and stir-fry for 1 minute. Add the cumin and 1 teaspoon of the salt, and stir-fry for 2 minutes. Add the Vegetable Stock, and bring to a boil. Reduce the heat to low, and cook for 2 minutes. Remove from the heat, and set aside.

2. Heat the wok over high heat, and add the remaining 1 tablespoon of oil. Add the onions, bell peppers, celery, garlic, jalapeño and remaining 1 teaspoon of salt, and stir-fry for 2 minutes.

3. Reduce the heat to medium, and stir in the dulse and corn. Cover, and cook for 2 minutes.

4. Add the tomatoes and cilantro, and stir-fry for 1 minute. Add the reserved tempeh mixture, and cook, stirring, for 1 minute. Toss in the sunflower seeds, stir well and serve hot.

PER SERVING: 309 CAL; 14G PROT; 15G FAT; 35G CARB; 0MG CHOL; 768MG SOD; 5G FIBER

BARBECUED TEMPEH WITH BELL PEPPERS

Marinated tempeh simmered with sweet bell peppers in a barbecue sauce makes a delicious weekday meal. Serve it over rice or as a sandwich on toasted multigrain rolls.

½ cup tamari soy sauce or low-sodium soy sauce

2 tablespoons rice wine vinegar

4 teaspoons fresh lemon juice

2 teaspoons honey

8 ounces tempeh

1 cup sliced onion

2 red or green bell peppers, cut into strips

¼ cup tomato paste

1 to 2 tablespoons molasses

1 to 2 tablespoons packed dark brown sugar

2 teaspoons prepared yellow mustard

2 teaspoons apple cider vinegar

1 teaspoon minced garlic

1 teaspoon chili powder

Salt and freshly ground black pepper to taste

1. Combine the tamari soy sauce, vinegar, lemon juice and honey in a mixing bowl.

2. Put the tempeh into the bowl, covering it with the marinade. Cover, and refrigerate for several hours or overnight, turning occasionally. Drain the tempeh, and reserve the marinade. Cube the tempeh.

3. Spray a large nonstick skillet with nonstick cooking spray, and heat over medium heat until hot. Add the onion and bell peppers, and cook, stirring often, until just tender, for about 5 minutes.

4. Add the marinade, tomato paste, molasses, sugar, mustard, vinegar, garlic, chili powder and ¾ cup of water to the skillet. Bring the mixture to a boil. Reduce the heat to low, and cook, uncovered, until the mixture thickens, mashing the tempeh slightly with a fork. Season with salt and pepper, and serve.

PER SERVING: 222 CAL; 18G PROT; 5G FAT; 30G CARB; 0MG CHOL; 215MG SOD; 7G FIBER

BLACK BEAN BURGERS WITH TEMPEH CRISPS

These vegan burgers offer complete protein, and the unusual tempeh crisps provide an additional protein-filled treat. As an alternate garnish, use thinly sliced onions for a jolt of color.

Black Bean Burgers

3 cups cooked black beans (see page 50)

2 cups cooked brown rice (see page 48)

1 cup breadcrumbs (see page 46)

1/4 cup chopped scallions

1 tablespoon chili powder

1 tablespoon ketchup

1/2 teaspoon salt

1/2 teaspoon freshly ground black pepper

6 whole wheat buns

Tempeh Crisps

12 ounces tempeh, sliced into thin strips

2 tablespoons chili powder

1/2 teaspoon salt

1/2 teaspoon pepper

1. Preheat the oven to 375F. Spray a sheet pan with nonstick cooking spray.

2. To make the Black Bean Burgers: Combine the beans, rice, breadcrumbs, scallions, chili powder, ketchup, salt and pepper in a food processor, and process, adding just enough water to blend, until smooth. Form into 6 equal-sized patties, and chill for 1 hour.

3. Meanwhile, to make the Tempeh Crisps: Toss the tempeh with the chili powder, salt and pepper. Spread the strips evenly on a baking sheet, and bake for about 15 minutes, or until browned and crisp. Remove from the oven, and set aside.

4. Heat a skillet over medium heat, and spray with nonstick cooking spray. Add the patties, cooking for 5 minutes on each side, or until heated through. Place each burger on a whole wheat bun. Garnish with the Tempeh Crisps and favorite condiments.

PER SERVING: 490 CAL; 26G PROT; 8G FAT; 81G CARB; 0MG CHOL; 820MG SOD; 16G FIBER

SAVORY POTATO PIE

Stumped about how to use up leftover mashed potatoes? Or you can't wait for leftovers? Most supermarkets sell ready-to-go mashed potatoes. Turn the potatoes into a savory pie that goes well with the Spinach Salad with Crisped Tempeh (page 150) and fresh fruit for dessert.

2 tablespoons vegetable oil

1 1/2 cups mashed potatoes (page 296)

1 1/2 cup fresh or frozen peas

6 ounces soy "ground meat"

4 ounces grated low-fat Swiss cheese

2 large eggs, beaten

1/4 cup minced fresh parsley, for garnish

1 1/2 cups (3 1/2 ounces) french-fried onion rings

1. Preheat the oven to 375F. Spray a 10-inch pie pan or cake pan with nonstick cooking spray, and set aside.

2. Heat the oil in a large skillet over medium heat, and stir in the potatoes, peas and "ground meat." Cook, stirring often, for about 5 minutes.

3. Meanwhile, combine the cheese and eggs. Stir in the "meat" mixture, and mix well. Spoon into the pie pan.

4. Bake for 20 to 25 minutes, or until the top turns slightly golden and the center is firm. Remove from the oven, and garnish with the parsley and onion rings.

PER SERVING: 280 CAL; 18G PROT; 13G FAT; 23G CARB; 80MG CHOL; 460MG SOD; 3G FIBER

"SAUSAGE" AND MASH

Inspired by the British favorite Bangers and Mash, or sausages and mashed potatoes, this recipe swaps out the meat for soy "sausage" links. Serve these accompanied with some steamed spinach sparked by a squeeze of lemon juice and a drizzle of olive oil.

2½ pounds small Yukon gold potatoes, rinsed and peeled, if desired

Salt and freshly ground black pepper to taste

1 teaspoon olive oil

1 large onion, halved lengthwise and sliced

1 teaspoon granulated sugar

½ teaspoon dried thyme

2 tablespoons all-purpose flour

1½ cups vegetable or mushroom stock or Vegetable Stock (page 332)

⅓ cup red wine

1 tablespoon low-sodium soy sauce

8 ounces soy "sausage" links, thawed if frozen, cut into bite-size pieces

1 cup low-fat milk or soymilk, heated

1 teaspoon unsalted butter or margarine

1. Cook the potatoes and salt in water to cover until tender, for 20 to 40 minutes. (Timing will depend on size and freshness of the potatoes.) Drain, and set aside.

2. Meanwhile, heat the oil in a large saucepan over medium-high heat. Add the onion, sugar and thyme, and cook, stirring often, until the onion slices are golden. Stir in the flour, and cook, stirring, for 2 minutes. Stir in the broth, wine and soy sauce. Cook until thickened, stirring constantly. Add the "sausage" to the gravy, and cook until heated through.

3. Rinse the potatoes, and mash with a potato masher. Add the warm milk and butter, and whip the potatoes with a hand mixer until fluffy. Add salt and pepper to taste. Serve the mashed potatoes topped with gravy and "sausages."

PER SERVING: 387 CAL; 15G PROT; 9G FAT; 63G CARB; 3MG CHOL; 949MG SOD; 7G FIBER

"BEEF" TAMALE PIE

The combination of chili powder, assorted cheeses and jalapeño chiles makes a bold statement about Tex-Mex flavors. This sturdy main-course dish, however, is a relative of authentic Mexican tamales, with cornmeal as the main starch.

1 tablespoon vegetable oil

1 cup chopped onions

2 jalapeño chiles, minced

2 cloves garlic, minced

2 pounds soy "steak" strips

1 32-ounce can pinto beans, drained and rinsed

1 32-ounce can tomatoes, including juice

2 cups fresh or frozen corn kernels

3 tablespoons chili powder 1 tablespoon ground cumin

1 teaspoon minced cilantro leaves

Salt and freshly ground black pepper to taste

4 cups Vegetable Stock (page 332)

1 cup yellow cornmeal

1 cup grated Monterey Jack and/or cheddar cheese

1. Heat the oil in a large skillet over medium heat. Sauté the onions and jalapeños for about 3 minutes. Add the garlic, and sauté for 30 seconds, or until golden.

2. Add the "steak" strips to the skillet. Stir in the beans, tomatoes, corn, chili powder, cumin, cilantro, salt and pepper, and cook for 10 minutes.

3. Meanwhile, bring 3 cups of the Vegetable Stock to a boil in a large saucepan. Combine the remaining 1 cup of Stock with the cornmeal in a bowl. Blend into the boiling stock, stirring constantly to avoid lumps, and stir until smooth. Reduce the heat to low, and cook until the mixture thickens, for about 30 minutes. Remove from the heat. Spoon the cornmeal mixture into a 9 x 13–inch baking dish.

4. Preheat the oven to 350F.

5. Bake the cornmeal mixture for 20 minutes. Remove from the oven, layer the "steak" mixture on the cornmeal and sprinkle the cheese on top. Bake for 10 minutes more, or until the cheese melts. Remove from the oven, and serve.

PER SERVING: 400 CAL; 28G PROT; 7G FAT; 60G CARB; 15MG CHOL; 1,330MG SOD; 15G FIBER

"CHICKEN" TARRAGON PIZZA

These flavorful pizzas partner well with an arugula salad, and to keep up the Italian theme, try spumoni, tiramisù or gelato for dessert.

3 7-inch prebaked pizza crusts

1 tablespoon olive oil

6 ounces soy "chicken" strips

1 teaspoon garlic powder

1 roasted red bell pepper (see page 46), cut into strips

2 cups quartered artichoke hearts

¼ cup oil-packed, sun-dried tomatoes, well drained

3 sprigs fresh tarragon, leaves removed

2 cups grated low-fat mozzarella cheese

¼ cup grated Parmesan cheese

1. Preheat the oven to 450F. Spray each pizza crust with nonstick cooking spray, and put on a baking sheet.

2. Heat the oil in a large skillet over medium heat. Sauté the "chicken" strips for 2 minutes, and season with the garlic. Add the bell pepper and artichoke hearts to the skillet, and sauté for 2 minutes more.

3. Divide the tomatoes and "chicken" mixture evenly among the pizza crusts, and sprinkle with the tarragon, mozzarella and Parmesan.

4. Bake for 10 minutes, or until the cheese melts. Remove from the oven, and serve hot.

PER SERVING (ONE-HALF PIZZA): 400 CAL; 25G PROT; 16G FAT; 42G CARB; 25MG CHOL; 870MG SOD; 3G FIBER

Greek Pizza, page 237

▲ Frog in the Well, page 335
◀ Farmer's Market Chilled Salsa Soup, page 306

▲ Sloppy Janes, page 371
▶ Fava Bean Cakes, page 345

▲ Noodle Kugel, page 446

◀ Angel Berry Parfait, page 415

Winter Jewel Fruitcake, page 448

14

soups and stews

If you're looking for an ideal way to simplify mealtimes, pare down cooking time or economize on food costs, then the humble—or elegant—bowl of soup or steaming stew is just the answer. What distinguishes a soup from a stew may be blurred as stews are really just more robust soups. In either case, soups and stews are kind to the budget and can easily be stretched to feed a family or a crowd—and let's not forget how delicious they can be! As a reminder, the recipes in this chapter and elsewhere in the book calling for vegetable stock may use store-bought vegetable stock rather than home-made.

BUTTERNUT CREAM SOUP

Use any kind of winter squash to make this soup—each will produce a slightly different taste. In a hurry? Use canned pumpkin solids instead. To reduce calories, use canned evaporated whole milk instead of cream.

1 butternut squash, halved and seeded

2 tablespoons butter

1 cup minced onion

1 teaspoon ground coriander

1 teaspoon ground cardamom

½ teaspoon ground nutmeg

2 cups chicken-flavored vegetable stock

1 teaspoon salt

½ teaspoon white pepper

1½ cups heavy cream

1. Preheat the oven to 350F.

2. Place the butternut squash cut side down on a baking sheet. Bake at 350F for about 25 minutes, or until tender and a knife inserted in the flesh comes out easily. Remove from the oven, and set aside to cool. When cool enough to handle, scrape out the flesh, and purée. Measure 3 cups, and save the remainder for another use.

3. Heat the butter in a saucepan over medium heat, and add the onion. Reduce the heat to low, and cook until the onion is transparent but not browned. Add 3 cups butternut purée, coriander, cardamom, nutmeg, stock, salt and pepper. Cook for 15 minutes. (Soup may be made ahead to this point, and finished just before serving.)

4. Add the heavy cream, and bring the mixture back to a simmer. Adjust the seasonings, remove from heat and serve.

PER SERVING: 210 CAL; 2G PROT; 20G FAT; 8G CARB; 70MG CHOL; 1,170MG SOD; 2G FIBER

BUTTERNUT SQUASH–PEANUT SOUP

Strange but true! This combination of squash and peanuts is unique and delicious.

2 tablespoons vegetable oil

2 teaspoons cumin seeds or 1 teaspoon ground cumin

2 cups unsalted peanuts, preferably raw

2 medium-sized onions, diced

2 cloves garlic, minced

3 carrots, peeled and diced

4 stalks celery, diced

2 teaspoons grated fresh ginger or 1 teaspoon ground ginger

⅛ teaspoon freshly ground black pepper

⅛ teaspoon cayenne, optional

⅛ teaspoon dried thyme

6 cups Vegetable Stock (page 332) or water

1 large butternut squash, peeled and cut into 1-inch chunks

¼ cup fresh lemon juice

Sea salt and freshly ground black pepper to taste

1. Heat the oil in a large pot over medium heat. When hot, add the cumin and peanuts, and sauté until the peanuts begin to brown and the cumin is fragrant. Increase the heat to medium-high, and add the onions, garlic, carrots, celery and seasonings. Cook until the vegetables are soft. Add the stock and squash, and cook until the squash is very soft.

2. Put the mixture in a blender or food processor, and purée until smooth. Return to the pot. Add the lemon juice, and season with salt and pepper. Serve hot.

PER SERVING: 210 CAL; 8G PROT; 15G FAT; 16G CARB; 0MG CHOL; 170MG SOD; 5G FIBER

The traditional version of onion soup calls for beef stock, but here the full-bodied flavor is imparted by herbs. Serve the soup with croutons or garlic toast. A bouquet garni is a traditional French seasoning, which includes parsley, bay leaf and thyme, tied together for cooking and then discarded after cooking.

1 bouquet garni, with additional herbs of choice, fresh or dried, such as rosemary, marjoram, dill, coriander seeds, celery seeds (see below)

2 teaspoons olive oil

4 to 6 cups thinly sliced onions

Pinch salt

6 cups water or Vegetable Stock (page 332)

Salt, low-sodium soy sauce, or light miso to taste, optional

Sliced scallions or minced fresh parsley for garnish

1. Select the herbs for the bouquet garni, and tie. Set aside.

2. Heat the oil in a large pot over medium-low heat, and cook the onions. Add the salt to help prevent sticking, and stir frequently. Cover the pot, leaving the lid slightly ajar. Cook the onions for 30 minutes to 1 hour, or until golden and reduced to about one-third of their original volume.

3. Add the water with the bouquet garni. Cook for at least 30 minutes. Remove the bouquet garni. Season with salt, soy sauce or miso. Garnish with scallions or fresh parsley, and serve.

PER SERVING: 71 CAL; 1G PROT; 3G FAT; 10G CARB; 0MG CHOL; 69 SOD; 2G FIBER

Bouquet Garni

To make a bouquet garni, place 1 bay leaf, 4 sprigs parsley and 2 sprigs thyme in a small square of cheesecloth, and tie securely. Drop it into the soup or stew pot. Discard the bundle before serving.

GINGERED GREEN SOUP

The green vegetables in this soup are enlivened with a shot of fresh ginger, an inspired touch.

1 cup chopped onion
1 cup chopped celery or fennel
1 cup peeled and cubed potatoes
1 small zucchini, chopped
⅓ cup uncooked basmati or other white rice
⅛ teaspoon white pepper
1 bay leaf
Pinch dried thyme
Pinch dried basil
4 cups chopped string beans
¼ cup chopped fresh parsley
1 3-inch piece fresh ginger
½ teaspoon salt, or to taste
¼ teaspoon freshly ground black pepper, or to taste
2 to 3 tablespoons garnish of choice, such as chopped fresh chives, mint, cilantro, scallions or basil leaves

1. Combine the onion, celery or fennel, potatoes, zucchini, rice, white pepper, bay leaf, thyme, basil and 7 to 8 cups of water in a large pot. Bring to a boil, reduce the heat to medium-low and cook until the potatoes are tender, for about 15 minutes. Add the string beans, and cook, uncovered, until tender, for about 10 minutes. Add the parsley. Remove, and discard the bay leaf.

2. Put the ingredients in batches into a food processor or blender, and purée until smooth, adding water if necessary. Peel the ginger, grate and press out the ginger juice through a strainer into a small bowl. Add 2 to 3 teaspoons of the juice to the soup. Add the salt, pepper and garnish of choice. Serve hot or cold.

PER SERVING: 98 CAL; 3G PROT; 0.4G FAT; 21G CARB; 0MG CHOL; 200MG SOD; 5G FIBER

KABOCHA SQUASH SOUP

Kabocha is a sweet winter squash of Japanese origin, although it is now quite commonly available in the United States. It's round and dark green. Look for it in a well-stocked supermarket, natural food store or Asian grocery.

3 leeks, thinly sliced
2 tablespoons vegetable oil
3 green apples, peeled, cored and diced
1 kabocha squash, peeled, seeded and diced
4 cups Vegetable Stock (page 332)
1 12-ounce can evaporated milk or evaporated skim milk
3 cups cooked short-grain brown rice
¼ teaspoon ground ginger
Salt to taste

1. Cook the leeks in the oil in a large pot over low heat for 10 minutes, stirring occasionally. Add the apples, squash and stock. Bring to a boil, reduce the heat to low, cover and cook for 10 minutes.

2. Add the milk, rice, ginger and salt. Heat through, and serve.

PER SERVING: 270 CAL; 8G PROT; 5G FAT; 51G CARB; 2MG CHOL; 197MG SOD; 8G FIBER

SAVORY CUSTARD SOUP

Considered a delicacy in Japan, this soup gets an update: Tofu takes the place of eggs. Kombu is a kind of dried seaweed, popular in Japanese cuisine. It is available in natural food stores and Japanese markets. Ginkgo nuts are available in fall and winter in gourmet food stores and Japanese markets. Fresh ginkgos must be shelled, then soaked in hot water and peeled. Nuts canned in brine are also available. Rinse them before using.

1 pound soft tofu

1 cup Vegetable Stock (page 332), preferably made from kombu

2 tablespoons low-sodium soy sauce

3 tablespoons sake, white wine or dry sherry

4 to 8 spears asparagus

4 large white button mushrooms or shiitake mushrooms (either fresh or reconstituted dried), cut in half or quartered

8 to 12 ginkgo nuts, shelled, optional

2 scallions, minced or sliced

1. Put the tofu, stock, soy sauce and sake in a food processor or blender, and purée until well blended. Cut the asparagus into ½-inch lengths, and steam until barely tender, for 2 to 3 minutes.

2. Divide the asparagus, mushrooms and ginkgo nuts equally in the bottom of 4 ovenproof ceramic coffee mugs. Fill the mugs three-quarters full with the tofu mixture. Cover each mug with aluminum foil, and place the mugs in a large pot. Fill the pot with water so the bottom halves of the mugs are covered. Cover the pot, bring to a boil, reduce the heat to low and cook until the custard has risen and set, for about 40 minutes. Top each mug with scallions, and serve at once.

PER SERVING: 98 CAL; 10G PROT; 4G FAT; 6G CARB; 0MG CHOL; 524MG SOD; 2G FIBER

SPINACH AND PEA SOUP

This easy-to-make soup is a vivid green.

½ tablespoon olive oil

½ tablespoon unsalted butter

2 medium-sized leeks, sliced

1 medium-sized onion, sliced

3 medium-sized carrots, sliced

1 stalk celery, chopped

10 sprigs fresh parsley, chopped

¼ teaspoon dried marjoram or 1 teaspoon fresh marjoram

1 teaspoon salt

1 cup fresh or frozen peas

1 bunch spinach, well-rinsed and stemmed

Freshly ground black pepper to taste

1 to 2 teaspoons fresh lemon juice or white wine vinegar

Calendula, borage blossoms or croutons for garnish, optional

1. Heat the oil and butter in a large saucepan over medium-high heat. Add the leeks, onion, carrots, celery, parsley, marjoram, salt and ½ cup water. Stir well and cook for 1 or 2 minutes, and add 5 cups water. Bring to a boil, reduce the heat to low, cover and cook until the vegetables are tender, for about 25 minutes.

2. Stir the peas and spinach leaves into the soup, and cook until they wilt and turn bright green. Remove from the heat. Put the soup mixture in batches into a food processor or blender, and purée until smooth. Return to the pan.

3. Season with pepper, and stir in enough lemon juice or vinegar to enhance the flavor. Garnish with blossoms or croutons, if using, and serve at once.

PER SERVING: 83 CAL; 5G PROT; 2G FAT; 13G CARB; 3MG CHOL; 453MG SOD; 5G FIBER

BLACK BEAN SOUP

A creamy mixture, this rich and nourishing soup comes together in minutes.

2 15½-ounce cans black beans, drained and well rinsed

1 tablespoon minced garlic

1 tablespoon dried onion flakes

1½ cup Vegetable Stock (page 332)

6 ounces silken soft tofu

Salt and freshly ground black pepper to taste

2 cups croutons as garnish, optional

8 tablespoons French fried onion rings as garnish, optional

4 tablespoons low-fat sour cream as garnish, optional

1. Put 1 can of beans into a food processor or blender. Add the garlic, onion flakes, ¾ cup Vegetable Stock, the tofu, salt and pepper, and purée until smooth.

2. Put this mixture into a large saucepan, and add the remaining beans and the remaining Vegetable Stock. Heat over medium heat until hot. Ladle into individual soup bowls, garnish with croutons, onion rings and sour cream, if using, and serve.

PER SERVING: 230 CAL; 17G PROT; 1.5G FAT; 42G CARB; 0MG CHOL; 780MG SOD; 14G FIBER

SOUPER SALAD

This chilled soup contains lots of crunchy vegetables.

1 46-ounce can tomato juice

1 small red onion, chopped finely

1 clove garlic, minced

½ cup corn kernels, fresh or frozen

1 15-ounce can black beans, drained and rinsed

1 cucumber, seeded and diced

1 red bell pepper, seeded and diced

1 green bell pepper, seeded and diced

1 zucchini, diced

1 stalk celery, diced

4 scallions, minced

1 4-ounce can diced green chilies

1 cup finely chopped jícama

¼ cup chopped cilantro or fresh parsley

2 tablespoons red wine vinegar

2 tablespoons fresh lime juice

Hot pepper sauce to taste

1 teaspoon prepared horseradish

Freshly ground black pepper to taste

16 melba rounds, for garnish

1. Pour the tomato juice into a large bowl, and set aside. Place the onion, garlic and ¼ cup water in a saucepan. Cook and stir until the onion softens slightly, for about 2 minutes.

2. Add the onion-garlic mixture and the remaining ingredients, except the melba rounds, to the tomato juice. Stir well. Cover, and refrigerate several hours to allow the flavors to blend. Stir well, and pour into soup bowls. Garnish with the melba rounds.

PER SERVING: 143 CAL; 6G PROT; 0.3G FAT; 28G CARB; 0MG CHOL; 774MG SOD; 6G FIBER

PESTO SOUP

A great starter for any meal, this chilled, savory blend of ripe tomatoes, herbs and vegetables can be on your table in no time.

½ cup chopped tomato

⅓ cup finely chopped onion

1 small clove garlic, chopped

½ cup shredded carrot

½ cup shredded beet

¼ cup pine nuts

¾ cup (loosely packed) fresh basil

2 tablespoons Bragg Liquid Aminos

1 tablespoon apple cider vinegar, optional

Fresh basil leaves, for garnish, optional

1. Combine all the ingredients and 6 cups water, except the basil for garnish, in a blender or food processor, and process until finely chopped but not smooth.

2. Divide among 6 serving bowls. Garnish with basil leaves, if desired, and serve.

PER SERVING: 61 CAL; 3G PROT; 4G FAT; 6G CARB; 0MG CHOL; 124MG SOD; 2G FIBER

SWEET PEA SOUP WITH QUINOA

Translucent quinoa adds a pearly texture to this vibrant green soup. Make sure to pick out any discolored quinoa grains before cooking, as they will show up as dark specks.

½ cup quinoa, rinsed and drained

1 cup cold water

2 teaspoons vegetable oil

1 medium-sized onion, chopped

3 cups Vegetable Stock (page 332)

4 cups fresh or frozen peas

6 ounces plain soy yogurt

½ teaspoon salt

¼ teaspoon white pepper

2 tablespoons shredded fresh mint leaves, optional

1. Combine the quinoa and water in a medium saucepan. Cover, and bring to a boil over medium-high heat. Reduce the heat to low, cover and cook until the water is absorbed, about 15 minutes. Fluff with a fork, and set aside.

2. Meanwhile, heat the oil in a large saucepan over medium-high heat. Add the onion, and cook, stirring often, until softened, for 4 to 5 minutes. Add the Vegetable Stock, cover and bring to a boil. Add the peas, reduce the heat to medium and cook until the peas are tender, for about 5 minutes.

3. Reserve ½ cup peas. Put the remaining peas in a food processor or blender, in batches if necessary, and purée until smooth. Strain through a fine-mesh sieve back into the saucepan, using a rubber spatula to press the mixture through the mesh. Stir in the reserved quinoa and peas, yogurt, salt and pepper.

4. Reheat over low heat, stirring occasionally. Ladle the soup into 6 bowls, and garnish each serving with mint.

PER SERVING: 207 CAL; 9G PROT; 3G FAT; 28G CARB; 0MG CHOL; 281MG SOD; 6G FIBER

FARMERS' MARKET CHILLED SALSA SOUP

SERVES 8

Buy the freshest from-the-farm vegetables you can find for this invigorating cold soup. If ripe tomatoes and hot chiles are available, make your own salsa, or purchase your favorite brand.

4 large cucumbers, peeled

4 green bell peppers, seeded

1 cup cilantro leaves

2 cups sliced scallions (about 2 bunches)

½ cup canned Mexican-style mild green chiles

2 cloves garlic, mashed

1 tablespoon white wine vinegar

1½ teaspoons salt

¼ cup olive oil

1½ cups salsa, for garnish

1. Cut the cucumbers in half lengthwise, and slice into chunks. Dice the green peppers. Put the cucumbers, peppers, cilantro, scallions and green chiles in a blender or food processor, and process until smooth.

2. Add the garlic, vinegar, salt and olive oil, and mix well. Add 2 cups of water, taste and adjust the seasoning with salt and vinegar. Add more water to thin the soup if needed.

3. Fill 2 ice-cube trays with soup, and freeze overnight. Chill the remainder. Pack the frozen cubes with the chilled soup in large insulated containers. At serving time, pour the soup into cups, and top each with a large spoonful of salsa.

PER SERVING: 130 CAL; 3G PROT; 7G FAT; 16G CARB; 0MG CHOL; 690MG SOD; 5G FIBER

BLACK BEAN PISTOU SOUP

SERVES 4

This updated version of the classic Provençal soup has no Parmesan cheese and finishes with a vegetable garnish.

Black Beans

1½ cups dried black beans, picked over and rinsed

1 large onion, diced

6 cloves garlic, minced

Salt and freshly ground black pepper to taste

8 large basil leaves, julienned, for garnish

Vegetable Garnish

6 ounces green beans, sliced diagonally into 1-inch pieces

2 small zucchini, trimmed and diced

½ potato, for croutons, optional

2 cups peanut oil, for deep-frying, optional

Basil Purée

⅓ cup olive oil

4 large cloves garlic

1½ cups fresh basil leaves

Salt and freshly ground black pepper to taste

1. To make the Black Beans: Put them in a large stockpot, and add enough water to cover by 2 inches. Cover the pot, and set aside at room temperature to soak overnight.

2. Drain the beans, and return to the pot. Cover with 12 cups water. Add the onion and garlic, and bring to a boil, skimming off any foam. Reduce the heat to low, and cook until the beans are very tender, for about 1½ hours, stirring occasionally. Add water, if needed, or boil soup down until thickened but not dried out. Season with salt and pepper to taste.

3. To make the Vegetable Garnish: Cover a drying rack with paper towels. Heat a saucepan of water to boil, and cook the green beans for 3 minutes. Add the zucchini, and cook until the green beans are tender, for about 2 minutes more. Drain, rinse the vegetables under cold water, and place on the rack.

4. For the croutons, if using, peel ½ potato, and cut into ⅛-inch dice. Heat the peanut oil to 375F, and deep-fry 2 teaspoons of diced potatoes until golden. Remove from the heat, drain and set aside.

5. To make the Basil Purée: Put the oil, garlic and basil in a blender, and purée until smooth, pulsing on and off and stopping to scrape down the sides of the container. Season with salt and pepper.

6. To serve, bring the soup to a boil. Season the vegetables with salt and pepper. Stir three-quarters of the vegetables and all the basil purée into the soup. Ladle into 4 soup bowls. Divide the remaining vegetables over the top of each serving, and garnish with julienned basil.

PER SERVING: 320 CAL; 10G PROT; 20G FAT; 31G CARB; 0MG CHOL; 8MG SOD; 11G FIBER

PROVENÇAL SOUP WITH PISTOU

This is a slightly lighter version of a traditional Provençal combination: vegetable soup enriched with pistou. Pistou—a pounded, pesto-like sauce of nuts, olive oil, garlic and basil—is unique to the Mediterranean region of France, since tender basil grows well in temperate climates. It adds both body and an intense, herbaceous flavor to soups and stews. Cooking the soup with a selection of herbs known as a bouquet garni intensifies the flavor.

Provençal Soup

1½ tablespoons olive oil

1½ pounds new potatoes, cut into ½-inch cubes

1 pound carrots, cut on the diagonal into ¼-inch-thick slices

1 cup diced celery

1 bouquet garni (see page 301)

Pinch saffron threads, crushed, optional

½ pound green beans, cut into 1-inch pieces

1 pound zucchini, cut into ½-inch cubes

1 cup uncooked macaroni shells

Salt and freshly ground black pepper to taste

¼ cup chopped fresh flat-leaf parsley

Pistou

½ cup hazelnuts, toasted (page 47)

2 cloves garlic

3 cups (lightly packed) fresh basil or flat-leaf parsley

1 small tomato, peeled, seeded and chopped

Salt and freshly ground black pepper to taste

½ tablespoon olive oil

1. To make the Provençal Soup: Heat 1 tablespoon of the oil in a large soup pot over medium heat. Add the potatoes, carrots and celery, and cook, stirring, for about 5 minutes. Add 8 cups of water, the bouquet garni and saffron, if using. Bring to a boil, reduce the heat to medium, and cook for 10 minutes.

2. Add the green beans, and continue to cook until the vegetables are almost tender, for about 25 minutes. Add the zucchini and macaroni, and cook until the pasta is tender, for an additional 10 minutes. Season with salt and pepper to taste, stir in the parsley, and drizzle with the remaining ½ tablespoon oil. Remove from the heat, cover and keep warm.

3. To make the Pistou: Put the nuts into a food processor, add the garlic and process until finely chopped. Add the basil or parsley and tomato, and process, scraping down the work bowl as necessary, until the mixture forms a smooth paste. Add water to thin as necessary. Transfer to a small bowl, add salt and pepper and stir in ½ tablespoon oil.

4. To serve, ladle the soup into 6 shallow soup bowls, or transfer to a serving dish. Stir in the pistou, or pass it separately for guests to stir in the desired amount themselves.

PER SERVING: 336 CAL, 8G PROT; 12G FAT; 52G CARB; 0MG CHOL; 62MG SOD; 9G FIBER

PEANUT AND CARROT SOUP

If you like spicy food, try adding 1 tablespoon of Thai red curry paste when you add the peanut butter.

3 tablespoons olive oil

2 cups diced onion

1 pound carrots, peeled and sliced thin

½ teaspoon cayenne

2 teaspoons salt

4 cups low-sodium vegetarian broth or Vegetable Stock (page 332)

½ cup peanut butter

½ cup chopped dry-roasted peanuts, for garnish, optional

1. Heat the olive oil in a 3-quart saucepan. Sauté the onion until soft and golden. Add the carrots, and sauté for 5 minutes. Add the cayenne, salt and broth, cover, and cook for 20 minutes, or until the carrots are very tender. Purée the carrots and onions in a blender or food processor, and return to the pot.

2. Add the peanut butter, and whisk well. Cook for 5 minutes. Adjust the seasoning to taste. Ladle into 6 bowls, and sprinkle a tablespoon of chopped peanuts on top of each serving.

PER SERVING: 250 CAL; 6G PROT; 18G FAT; 19G CARB; 0MG CHOL; 1,060MG SOD; 4G FIBER

SPICY ICY PLUM SOUP

On a really hot day this soup looks and tastes wonderful with chunks of ice floating in it. The texture is thick enough so that the melting ice will not be a detriment.

3 pounds very ripe purple or red plums, quartered and pitted

Juice and zest of 1 orange

2 cups orange juice

¼ cup honey, or more as needed

1 teaspoon ground cinnamon

¼ teaspoon ground cloves

¼ teaspoon ground coriander

3 cups red wine

1. Cut the plums into quarters, and remove the pits. Put in a 4-quart stockpot. Peel off the orange zest in 1 or 2 long pieces, and add to the pot. Add all of the remaining ingredients, and heat over medium heat. Bring to a boil, reduce the heat to low, and cook, covered, for 30 minutes. Remove the orange zest. Put the fruit mixture into a food processor, and purée until smooth. Chill.

2. Just before serving, taste, and adjust the seasoning with honey or thin with water as needed.

PER SERVING: 230 CAL; 2G PROT; 1.5G FAT; 43G CARB; 0MG CHOL; 5MG SOD; 3G FIBER

GRILLED CORN SOUP

This is the perfect use for corn that is too old for eating from the cob. Just be sure to remove the husk before grilling so that you get all the smoky flavor. Use whichever sweet onion is in season—Vidalia, Maui, Walla Walla or Bermuda.

8 ears sweet corn, husks removed

2 large sweet onions peeled and sliced thick

3 medium-sized tomatoes, cut in half

2 green bell peppers, halved and seeded

3 cups diced potatoes

8 ounces smoked tofu, diced

2 tablespoons nutritional yeast, optional

2 teaspoons crushed garlic

2 teaspoons salt

1 teaspoon freshly ground black pepper

1. Light a charcoal fire, if using, about 30 minutes before serving. Otherwise, heat a gas grill at serving time. Remove any silk clinging to the corn, and place the corn on the grill, along with the onion slices, tomato halves and green peppers. Turn the corn until it has grill marks on all sides and the yellow turns to a deeper shade. Turn the onions, tomatoes and bell peppers, and grill until soft.

2. Using a small sharp knife, cut the kernels from the cob. Use the back of the knife to scrape the cob. There should be about 5 cups. Chop the onion, tomato and pepper into coarse dice.

3. Put all of the grilled vegetables in a 4-quart stockpot, along with the remaining ingredients and 2 quarts of water. Bring to a boil, and cook for 45 minutes, or until the potatoes are falling-apart tender.

4. Put half of the vegetables into a food processor, and purée until smooth. Return to the pot, and taste. Adjust the seasoning. Reheat before serving.

PER SERVING: 240 CAL; 10G PROT; 3.5G FAT; 46G CARB; 5MG CHOL; 660MG SOD; 7G FIBER

CREAM OF SNOW PEA SOUP

The beautiful pale green color of this soup and the subtle flavor make it perfect for serving in spring with an edible flower for garnish. The frozen peas are not cooked before being puréed because they are blanched before freezing. This will make the color of the soup vibrant.

4 cups Vegetable Stock (page 332)

1 pound snow peas, stems removed

4 scallions, minced

1 teaspoon dried mint or 2 fresh mint leaves

2 teaspoons granulated sugar

½ teaspoon white pepper

2 teaspoons salt

½ teaspoon freshly grated nutmeg

1 cup frozen peas, thawed

2 cups evaporated skim milk, undiluted

Mint sprigs and edible flowers, for garnish, optional

1. Bring the stock to a boil, and add the snow peas, scallions, mint, sugar, pepper, salt and nutmeg. Bring back to a boil, reduce the heat to low and cook, uncovered, for 20 minutes.

2. Put the snow peas into a blender or food processor, along with enough liquid to facilitate processing, and purée until completely smooth. Add the thawed peas, and purée again.

3. Just before serving, add the evaporated milk, and bring to a boil. Taste, and adjust the seasoning. Garnish with mint sprigs and an edible flower for a special dinner.

PER SERVING: 150 CAL; 9G PROT; 0G FAT; 27G CARB; 0MG CHOL; 1,360MG SOD; 4G FIBER

CREAM OF ASPARAGUS SOUP

If you have a food mill, this soup may be made with the bottoms of the asparagus spears, which are normally thrown away. Cook the ends until tender, purée in the food mill to remove the tough fibers, and add to the rest of the purée.

1½ pounds green asparagus

2 cups diced white potato

2 cups diced onion

4 cups Vegetable Stock (page 332)

½ teaspoon white pepper

2 teaspoons salt, or to taste

2 cups canned evaporated skim milk, undiluted

1. Snap off the tough bottoms of the asparagus. Cut the tender parts into 1-inch pieces. Put in a 3-quart saucepan, along with the potato, onion, broth, pepper and salt. Bring to a boil over medium heat, and cook for 20 minutes, or until the potatoes are very tender.

2. Put the cooked vegetables into a blender or food processor, with enough liquid to facilitate processing, purée until completely smooth. The mixture may be refrigerated for 1 to 2 days at this point.

3. Just before serving, bring the soup to a boil, and add the milk. Return to a boil. Taste, and adjust the seasoning. If the soup is too thick, thin with more milk or water.

PER SERVING: 200 CAL; 10G PROT; 0G FAT; 39G CARB; 0MG CHOL; 1,340MG SOD; 5G FIBER

CREAMY SPINACH SOUP

Puréed potatoes give this soup a rich taste and texture.

1 large onion, coarsely chopped

3 potatoes, peeled and chopped

3 zucchini, sliced

1 tablespoon low-sodium soy sauce

2 cups tightly packed fresh spinach leaves, well rinsed

Freshly ground black pepper to taste

⅓ cup trimmed enoki mushrooms, optional

1. Put the onion in a large saucepan with ½ cup water. Cook and stir over medium-high heat until the onion softens, for about 3 minutes.

2. Add 5½ cups water, the potatoes, zucchini and soy sauce. Bring to a boil. Reduce the heat to low, cover and cook for 35 minutes. Add the spinach and pepper, and cook for 2 minutes more. Remove from the heat.

3. Put the vegetables in batches into a food processor or blender, and purée until smooth. Return the mixture to the pan, and stir in the mushrooms. Heat over medium-low heat until the soup is heated through, for about 5 minutes. Serve hot.

PER SERVING: 123 CAL; 3G PROT; 0.1G FAT; 27G CARB, 0MG CHOL; 181MG SOD; 5G FIBER

CHILLED GINGER BORSCHT WITH MUSHROOMS

SERVES 6

This cold soup is elegantly offbeat. It has zip and a nice balance of savory and sweet flavors.

2½ pounds beets, trimmed

2 quarts Vegetable Stock (page 332)

½ cup dry red wine

2 to 4 tablespoons low-sodium soy sauce

Juice of 1 lemon

3 to 4 tablespoons finely slivered fresh ginger

8 ounces white button mushrooms, sliced

Freshly ground black pepper to taste

1 vegetable bouillon cube, optional

1. Boil the beets in the Vegetable Stock in a large stockpot until tender, for 30 to 45 minutes. Remove the beets with a slotted spoon, cool them slightly under running water and slip off their skins.

2. Add the remaining ingredients to the beet water. Slice the beets into thin slivers or matchsticks and return them to the soup. Cook over low heat for 30 minutes. Remove from the heat, and chill at least 3 hours before serving.

PER SERVING: 88 CAL; 2G PROT; 0G FAT; 16G CARB; 0MG CHOL; 437MG SOD; 5G FIBER

OVEN-ROASTED SALSIFY SOUP

SERVES 4

This satisfying soup heralds the crisp days of autumn.

1½ pounds salsify, trimmed and peeled

2 tablespoons olive oil

Salt and freshly ground black pepper to taste

3½ cups Vegetable Stock (page 332)

½ teaspoon chopped fresh thyme

¼ cup soymilk or whole milk, optional

1. Preheat the oven to 400F.

2. Toss the salsify with oil, salt and pepper. Spread onto a baking sheet, and roast until tender, for about 30 minutes.

3. Chop the roasted salsify into 1-inch pieces. Reserve ⅓ cup for garnish. Put the remaining salsify into a large saucepan, and add the stock and thyme. Cook over medium heat until heated through and the flavors are blended, for about 15 minutes.

4. Put the mixture into a blender or food processor, and purée until smooth. Return to the pan, add milk, if desired, and heat through. Ladle the soup into bowls, and garnish with the reserved salsify.

PER SERVING: 186 CAL; 6G PROT; 8G FAT; 28G CARB; 0MG CHOL; 117MG SOD; 5G FIBER

TOMATO AND WHITE BEAN SOUP

Fresh herbal overtones boost the flavor of this ready-when-you-are soup. White beans make a wonderfully creamy base for soups as well as sauces and stews.

2 16-ounce cans cannellini beans, rinsed and drained

1 28-ounce can stewed tomatoes, undrained

2 scallions (green parts only), chopped

1 cup Vegetable Stock (page 332)

2 tablespoons minced cilantro or dill, or more to taste

1 to 2 teaspoons salt-free herb-and-spice seasoning mix to taste

Freshly ground black pepper to taste

1. Put half of the beans into a blender or food processor, and purée. Add the tomatoes with their liquid and scallions, and purée the mixture until smooth.

2. Transfer the purée to a large saucepan. Stir in the remaining beans, Vegetable Stock, cilantro, seasoning mix and freshly ground black pepper to taste. Heat over low heat, stirring occasionally. Serve hot.

PER SERVING: 226 CAL; 13G PROT; 1G FAT; 42G CARB; 0MG CHOL; 375MG SOD; 9G FIBER

ROASTED PEPPER AND TOMATO SOUP

Roasting peppers takes a little time, but once it's done, this cool, colorful soup can be made in a snap. If desired, roast the peppers a day or two ahead and keep refrigerated.

Roasted Pepper and Tomato Soup

3 medium-sized red bell peppers or 3 roasted red peppers from jars or cans

2½ cups tomato juice or mixed vegetable juice

2 medium-sized cloves garlic, peeled

2 tablespoons vegetable oil

2 tablespoons cider vinegar

¼ teaspoon salt

¼ teaspoon freshly ground pepper

Lime wedges for serving

Garnish

1 ripe large avocado, diced

1 cucumber, quartered lengthwise, seeded and diced

¼ cup finely chopped red onion

2 tablespoons chopped cilantro

1 tablespoon minced jalapeño chile, optional

¼ teaspoon salt

Lime wedges as garnish

1. Preheat the broiler.

2. To make the Roasted Pepper and Tomato Soup: Put the peppers on the broiler pan and roast, turning often, until charred all over, for about 15 minutes. Transfer to a paper bag, and let cool for 5 minutes. Rub the charred skins off with your fingers. Wipe the last bits of skin off with paper towels. Discard the cores and seeds. Alternatively, use commercially prepared roasted red peppers, and discard the cores and seeds.

3. Meanwhile, to make the Garnish: Put the avocado, cucumber, red onion, cilantro, jalapeño, if using, and salt into a mixing bowl.

4. Put the pepper, tomato juice, garlic, oil, vinegar, salt and pepper into a food processor or blender, and purée until smooth. Refrigerate until ready to serve.

5. Divide the soup among 4 individual bowls. Spoon the garnish on top, and serve with lime wedges.

PER SERVING (NO GARNISH): 120 CAL; 2G PROT; 7G FAT; 12G CARB; 0MG CHOL; 680MG SOD; 2G FIBER

SPRING VEGETABLE SOUP

Adding lettuce to a soup puts an unusual spin on the dish.

1 tablespoon olive oil

1 cup minced onion

1 small clove garlic, minced

¾ cup minced carrots

1 cup shelled fresh or frozen peas

6 cups Vegetable Stock (page 332), heated

2 cups shredded romaine lettuce

½ teaspoon salt

¼ teaspoon freshly ground black pepper

Lemon wedges for garnish

1. Heat the oil in a large saucepan over medium heat. Add the onion, garlic and carrot, and cook, stirring occasionally, until the onion is soft and beginning to brown, for about 10 minutes.

2. Add the peas, and cook, stirring, for 1 minute. Add the hot Vegetable Stock, and bring to a boil. Cook for 1 minute. Stir in the lettuce, salt and pepper. Serve hot with lemon wedges to squeeze into each portion.

PER SERVING: 115 CAL; 6G PROT; 5G FAT; 15G CARB; 0MG CHOL; 550MG SOD; 3G FIBER

MOROCCAN VEGETABLE SOUP

Cumin, coriander and turmeric give this hearty North African soup its unique flavor. Seitan is a wheat gluten product, and comes in cakes and plastic tubs. Seitan is available in natural food stores and Asian markets. Look for it in the refrigerator case.

2 tablespoons canola oil

1 large onion, coarsely chopped

2 teaspoons ground cumin

1 teaspoon ground coriander

1 teaspoon ground turmeric

1 28-ounce can whole tomatoes with juice, coarsely chopped

6 cups Vegetable Stock (page 332)

2 cups cooked or canned chickpeas

2 large red or green bell peppers, chopped

¼ teaspoon freshly ground black pepper

2 small zucchini, diced

4 ounces seitan, diced

8 ounces uncooked vermicelli or thin spaghetti, broken into 1-inch pieces

1 tablespoon nutritional yeast

1. Heat the oil in a large pot over medium heat, and sauté the onion, cumin, coriander and turmeric until the onion is soft, for about 5 minutes. Add the tomatoes with the juice, Vegetable Stock, chickpeas, bell peppers and black pepper and cook, uncovered, for 1 hour.

2. Add the zucchini, seitan and vermicelli or spaghetti. Cook until the pasta is just tender, for about 10 minutes. Stir in the nutritional yeast, and serve.

PER SERVING: 205 CAL; 7G PROT; 4G FAT; 32G CARB; 0MG CHOL; 407MG SOD; 5G FIBER

FRENCH GARLIC PANADE SOUP

Panade *is French for a paste made by combining liquid and bread to form a smooth purée. It is found in many French dishes. Here, the* panade *provides the soup with a satisfying texture. Leeks look like large scallions. They grow underground in sandy soil, so be sure to wash them well. You can eat only the white base and a little bit of the tender greens above the base. First, trim the long green leaves above the base, then, using a sharp knife, cut deeply into the leek, but not all the way through. Fan open the layers, and rinse the leek under running water to remove the sand and any dirt. Finish preparing the leek as the recipe directs. As in most recipes, you may replace the leeks here with onions, scallions or shallots.*

3 tablespoons canola oil

2 medium-sized onions, chopped

6 shallots, chopped

3 leeks, chopped

3 cloves garlic, minced

6½-inch-thick slices stale French bread, crusts removed

⅔ cup milk or skim milk

6 cups Vegetable Stock (page 332) or water

Bouquet garni (see page 52)

1 teaspoon light miso, or to taste

1 cup evaporated skim milk

Salt and white pepper to taste

½ cup chopped watercress or fresh parsley

1 tablespoon chopped fresh chives

1. Heat the oil in a large pot over medium heat, and sauté the onions, shallots, leeks, and garlic until the onions begin to turn golden.

2. Meanwhile, crumble the bread into a medium bowl. Heat the milk to barely boiling, and pour over the bread. Mix well to form the *panade*. Add the *panade* and stock (or water) to the pot, and bring to a boil. Select the herbs for the bouquet garni, and tie. Stir in the miso and bouquet garni, tying the string to the pot handle for easy retrieval. Cook, uncovered, for 30 minutes over low heat. Discard the bouquet garni.

3. Pour enough of the soup into a blender to fill it half full, and blend until smooth. Repeat with the remaining soup. Add the evaporated skim milk, and reheat gently. Do not allow the soup to boil.

4. To serve, season with the salt and white pepper. Stir in the watercress or parsley and chives.

PER SERVING: 348 CAL; 13G PROT; 11G FAT; 46G CARB; 5MG CHOL; 615MG SOD; 5G FIBER

RUSSIAN BEAN-AND-POTATO SOUP

For convenience's sake, you can cook this soup for 3 hours in a slow cooker rather than for 1 hour on the stove.

1 tablespoon vegetable oil

1 large onion, thinly sliced

3 russet potatoes, peeled and cubed

½ pound green beans, cut into 1-inch pieces

5 cups Vegetable Stock (page 332)

2 tablespoons whole-wheat pastry flour

⅓ cup low-fat sour cream

¾ cup prepared sauerkraut with juice

1 tablespoon dried dillweed

Salt and white pepper to taste

1. Heat the oil in a large saucepan over medium-high heat, and sauté the onion until softened, for about 5 minutes. Add the potatoes and green beans, and cook for 3 minutes more, stirring frequently. Add the Vegetable Stock as needed by tablespoonfuls to keep the potatoes from scorching. Slowly add the remaining stock. Reduce the heat to low, cover and cook for 1 hour more.

2. Meanwhile, combine the flour and sour cream in a small bowl. Add to the hot soup by spoonfuls, stirring to blend. Add the sauerkraut and dill, and continue cooking for 15 minutes on the stove or for 30 minutes in the slow cooker. Season with salt and white pepper, and serve.

PER SERVING: 260 CAL; 6G PROT; 6G FAT; 46G CARB; 5MG CHOL; 810MG SOD; 7G FIBER

CALABAZA SOUP WITH LIMA BEANS

SERVES 4

Calabaza is a favorite squash in Central and South America. It's large and round with orange and green coloring on the outside and an orange-yellow, mild-flavored flesh. Another uncommon ingredient—red miso—is an easy find in natural food stores. This condiment, made from soybeans, comes in various flavors, from light and mellow to dark and quite salty. Red miso is among the salty varieties; you may substitute another salty miso if you like.

1 cup dry lima beans, soaked overnight in water to cover

4 to 5 cups peeled and cubed calabaza

2 bay leaves

1 to 2 tablespoons red miso dissolved in ½ cup water, or salt to taste

1. Drain and rinse the beans. Combine the beans and 4 cups water in a large saucepan, and bring to a boil over medium heat. Add the calabaza, bay leaves and remaining 5 cups water. Cook until the beans are soft and the calabaza "melts" into the liquid, for about 1 hour.

2. Remove 1 cup of the soup to a blender, and purée until smooth. Return it to the pan. Add the dissolved miso or salt. Remove, and discard the bay leaves. Serve hot.

PER SERVING: 144 CAL; 6G PROT; 1G FAT; 30G CARB; 0MG CHOL; 364MG SOD; 15G FIBER

RED LENTIL SOUP

SERVES 4 TO 6

This velvety-smooth soup is especially suitable as a light meal with brown rice and vegetables.

3 tablespoons vegetable oil

2 medium-sized onions, chopped

1 cup red lentils

3 medium-sized carrots, peeled and roughly chopped

About 2 cups canned coconut milk

1 teaspoon salt, or more to taste

1 bay leaf

3 cloves garlic, minced

1 1-inch piece fresh ginger, peeled and minced

1 tablespoon curry powder, preferably hot

½ cup chopped cilantro

1. Heat 2 tablespoons of oil in a saucepan over medium heat. Add the onions, and cook, stirring often, until they start to brown, for about 10 minutes. Add 4 cups of water, the lentils, carrots, coconut milk, salt and the bay leaf. Cover, and bring to a boil. Reduce the heat to medium-low, and cook, partially covered, until the lentils are tender, for about 20 minutes.

2. Meanwhile, heat the remaining 1 tablespoon of oil in a small skillet over medium heat. Add the garlic, ginger, curry powder and cilantro. Cook, stirring often, until fragrant, for about 2 minutes. Add to the soup.

3. Remove the bay leaf. Put the soup in batches into a food processor or blender, and purée until velvety smooth. Taste, and add a bit more salt if desired. Serve hot.

PER SERVING: 399 CAL; 14G PROT; 26G FAT; 33G CARB; 0MG CHOL; 33MG SOD; 14G FIBER

EASY TOMATO ORANGE BISQUE

When you need a fast and easy lunch, try this. The better the quality of the marinara, the better the soup will be. A plain marinara is best and one that is smooth rather than chunky. Substitute rice milk or soymilk for the evaporated skim milk, if you prefer.

4 cups marinara sauce, preferably organic

1 orange

¼ cup cornstarch

4 cups canned evaporated skim milk

1. Put the marinara sauce in a 3-quart saucepan, and bring to a boil. Using a small thin knife, remove the orange zest in a long strip. Add it to the marinara. Squeeze the orange, and strain the juice into the marinara sauce. Cook the sauce for 10 minutes, and remove the zest.

2. Meanwhile, whisk the cornstarch into the milk, and bring the milk to a boil, and cook until the mixture thickens. Add the milk to the saucepan, whisk together and return to a boil. Remove from the heat, and serve.

PER SERVING: 230 CAL; 13G PROT; 0G FAT; 42G CARB; 0MG CHOL; 630MG SOD; 4G FIBER

CROCKPOT POTATO AND CABBAGE SOUP

The flavor of this soup is inspired by the Irish dish Colcannon. All of the ingredients may be prepped the night before, placed in the ceramic bowl of the crockpot and stored in the refrigerator. Brewer's yeast, also known as nutritional yeast, is available at health food stores and natural foods markets.

¼ cup unsalted butter or soy margarine

3 cups diced onion

½ medium-sized head cabbage

4 cups diced peeled potatoes

2 teaspoons salt

1 teaspoon freshly ground pepper

2 tablespoons brewer's yeast, optional

2 bay leaves

1. Heat a skillet over medium heat, and add the butter. Sauté the onion and garlic until the onions are soft and golden, for about 5 minutes. Scrape into a 3-quart crockpot.

2. Add the remaining ingredients to the crockpot with water to cover. Set to cook for 8 hours on medium. Cover. Taste and adjust seasoning at the end of the cooking time, and serve.

PER SERVING: 220 CAL; 4G PROT; 8G FAT; 34G CARB; 20MG CHOL; 850MG SOD; 4G FIBER

GREEN POSOLE SANTA FE

Posole is the Native American version of hominy. The dried posole available in Latino grocery stores and whole food stores is much more flavorful and has a chewier texture than canned hominy. It is soaked overnight, and then cooked until tender in the same manner as dried beans. Canned hominy may be used as a substitute when necessary. The chile of choice is actually the New Mexico green chile, but it is rarely available outside of that state. The garnishes are not necessary, but they make this a festive company dish for entertaining.

3 cups dried posole or 6 cups canned hominy

2 quarts boiling water

3 cups coarsely diced onion

3 tablespoons crushed garlic

3 cups diced red potatoes, unpeeled

1 cup sliced carrot

2 red bell peppers, seeded and diced

3 cups white button mushrooms

3 cups diced poblano chiles (about 4 large poblanos)

2 teaspoons salt

1 avocado, diced for garnish

2 limes, cut into very tiny wedges for garnish

Tortilla chips to taste for garnish

1 cup cilantro leaves for garnish

½ cup minced serrano chiles or canned green chiles for garnish

1. Put the dried posole into a large pot, and cover with the 2 quarts boiling water. Let sit for 2 hours or overnight. Drain, and put the posole in a stockpot with 4 quarts of water. Bring to a boil, cover and cook for 1 hour.

2. Add the remaining ingredients, except the garnishes, and cook, covered, for 1 hour. Add more water as necessary. Taste and adjust the seasonings. Place the garnishes in bowls to pass at the table.

PER SERVING: 320 CAL; 6G PROT; 2G FAT; 69G CARB; 0MG CHOL; 620MG SOD; 6G FIBER

CHIPOTLE BLACK BEAN SOUP

This soup may be made with leftover beans or with canned black beans. Chipotle chiles are jalapeño chiles that are smoked and dried. They are often cooked in a spicy sauce. You may purchase them in four-ounce cans, which contain two whole chiles in sauce. Save the remaining chile for other dishes. Because of the combination of smoky and spicy flavors, there is no substitute for chipotle.

2 tablespoons olive oil

2 cups diced onion

1 tablespoon crushed garlic

4 cups cooked black beans

2 teaspoons salt, or to taste

1 teaspoon black pepper

1 teaspoon ground cumin

1 chipotle chile from a can of chipotles in adobo

2 tablespoons of sauce from the can of chipotles in adobo

1. Heat a 3-quart saucepan over medium heat, and add the oil. Sauté the onion and garlic until very soft and golden. Add the remaining ingredients and water to cover. Cook for 30 minutes.

2. Put more than half of the beans in a food processor or food mill, and purée until smooth. Return to the pot, and stir well. Add water if the soup is too thick. Taste, and adjust the seasoning. Reheat the soup before serving.

PER SERVING: 240 CAL; 12G PROT; 6G FAT; 37G CARB; 0MG CHOL; 920MG SOD; 11G FIBER

POTATO-PUMPKIN SOUP

SERVES 6

This picturesque soup comes to the table in a hollowed-out pumpkin—a real conversation stopper.

1 8- to 10-pound pumpkin

2 medium-sized potatoes, peeled and chopped

2 medium-sized white onions, chopped

6 cups water

1 teaspoon salt, or to taste

White pepper to taste

1 teaspoon dried thyme

½ cup condensed skim milk

2 tablespoons minced fresh parsley, for garnish

Toasted pumpkin seeds, for garnish, optional (see page 47)

1. Cut off the top third of the pumpkin, using a heavy-duty chef's knife. Scoop out the seeds and strings, saving the seeds. Using a sturdy spoon, scoop out the pumpkin flesh, leaving a 1-inch wall inside. Refrigerate the shell and top.

2. Combine the potatoes, onions, 2 cups pumpkin flesh and water in a large stockpot. Add the salt, white pepper and thyme. Bring to a boil, cover and cook over medium heat until the vegetables are fork-tender, for about 20 minutes.

3. Meanwhile, preheat the oven to 200F. Put the pumpkin shell and top on a baking tray, and place it in the oven to warm.

4. Remove the vegetables from the cooking water, using a slotted spoon. Put the vegetables into a food processor and purée until smooth, or mash by hand until no lumps remain. Return the purée to the cooking water. Stir in the condensed milk, adding more if necessary for a creamier consistency. Heat over low heat until hot, taking care not to boil the soup.

5. To serve, place the pumpkin shell on a large serving tray. Pour in the hot soup and sprinkle with parsley and toasted pumpkin seeds, if using. Cover with the lid to keep warm.

PER SERVING: 103 CAL; 3G PROT; 0.1G FAT; 22G CARB; 1MG CHOL; 386MG SOD; 4G FIBER

CREAMY VEGETABLE SOUP

SERVES 4

Traditional cream soups are made with a roux consisting of butter, flour and milk. This tasty recipe omits the flour and thickens the soup with oats.

1 teaspoon olive oil

¼ cup apple juice or white wine

2 cups chopped broccoli

1 cup chopped onion

1 teaspoon minced garlic

1 teaspoon dried thyme

½ teaspoon dried basil

3 cups Vegetable Stock (page 332)

1 cup cooked rolled oats

Cayenne to taste

1. Combine the oil, juice or wine, broccoli, onion and garlic in a large saucepan, and heat over medium heat. Cook, stirring frequently, until the vegetables are softened, for about 15 minutes. Add the thyme, basil and Vegetable Stock.

2. Bring to a boil. Reduce the heat to low, and cook, covered, for 10 minutes.

3. Put the vegetable mixture into a food processor or blender, and purée until smooth. Add the oatmeal, and process until thick and creamy. Return to the pot, and add cayenne to taste. Reheat before serving.

PER SERVING (1 CUP): 97 CAL; 5G PROT; 3G FAT; 16G CARB; 0MG CHOL; 764MG SOD; 3G FIBER

BUTTERNUT SQUASH SOUP WITH
TOASTED SAGE AND HERBED CROUTONS

For an extra-special touch, toast the squash seeds to sprinkle over the soup. Rinse the seeds, pat dry with paper towels, spread on a baking sheet and bake at 350F for 30 to 40 minutes, tossing occasionally. This make-ahead soup can be frozen for up to 1 month.

3 medium-sized or 2 large butternut or acorn squash (4 pounds)

1 quart commercial vegetable broth or 4 cups Vegetable Stock (page 332)

1 teaspoon coarse salt

¼ teaspoon ground white pepper

4 tablespoons extra-virgin olive oil or 3 tablespoons vegetable oil and 1 tablespoon walnut oil

24 fresh small sage leaves

4 slices firm-textured white bread

1. Preheat the oven to 400F.

2. Cut the squash in half lengthwise, and scoop out the seeds. Save the seeds for toasting if desired (see above). Place the squash halves cut side down on a large baking sheet with sides. Bake until the skins are browned and the squash is tender, for about 1 hour and 10 minutes. Let cool slightly.

3. Scoop the cooked squash from the skins, and transfer to a large saucepan. Mash well with a potato masher, and stir in the broth and 2 cups water. Bring to a boil over medium-low heat, stirring often. Season with salt and white pepper, and remove from the heat. The soup should be as thick as tomato sauce—if not, add up to 1 cup more water to thin, if necessary. If you prefer a finer texture, cool slightly and put the soup in a food processor or blender, and purée until smooth. Let cool completely, transfer to a covered container and refrigerate for at least 8 hours.

4. Up to 4 hours before serving, heat 3 tablespoons oil in a skillet over medium heat. Add the sage leaves, and cook until lightly browned, turning once, for about 1 minute. Remove the sage from the skillet, and drain on paper towels. Reserve the oil in the skillet.

5. Trim the crusts from the bread, reserving the crusts for another use. Cut each bread slice diagonally into 4 triangles, and cut each triangle in half to make 32 croutons total.

6. Heat the reserved oil in the skillet over medium heat. Add half the croutons, and cook, turning once, until golden on both sides, for about 1 minute. Transfer to paper towels to drain. Heat the remaining 1 tablespoon oil in the skillet, and cook the remaining croutons as before.

7. Reheat the soup over low heat, stirring occasionally. Ladle the soup into bowls, and scatter 3 toasted sage leaves over each portion. Garnish each with 4 croutons, and serve hot.

PER SERVING: 223 CAL; 4G PROT; 7G FAT; 31G CARB; 0MG CHOL; 428MG SOD; 7G FIBER

ROOT VEGETABLE SOUP

This soup will benefit from overnight refrigeration, which allows the flavors to meld. The soup has a nice sweet-sour tang. Serve it with pumpernickel or rye bread.

1 tablespoon olive or canola oil

3 carrots, trimmed, peeled, thinly sliced

2 medium-sized white or yellow onions, peeled, chopped

3 cloves garlic, minced

6 beets (about 1¼ pounds) trimmed, peeled, quartered and thinly sliced

1 small head cabbage, cored, quartered, very thinly sliced

3 tablespoons tomato paste

3 tablespoons brown sugar

2 tablespoons rice vinegar

1 teaspoon caraway seeds

Salt and freshly ground black pepper to taste

Low-fat yogurt or dairy-free soy sour cream for garnish, optional

1. Heat the oil in a large saucepan over medium heat, tilting the pan to spread. Add the carrots, onions and garlic. Cover and cook, stirring occasionally, for 5 minutes. Add the beets and cabbage. Cover and cook for 10 minutes more.

2. Add the remaining ingredients, including 10 cups water, except the yogurt. Bring to a boil. Reduce the heat to low, and cook for 1½ hours. Taste the soup for seasoning, adding salt and pepper as needed.

3. Ladle the soup into individual bowls. Garnish with the yogurt or soy sour cream, if using. Serve.

PER SERVING: 111 CAL; 3G PROT; 2G FAT; 22G CARB; 0MG CHOL; 84MG SOD; 5G FIBER

PRESSURE COOKER WINTER VEGETABLE SOUP WITH BLACK BARLEY

If you haven't yet stocked your cupboard with black barley, you can make this soup with wheat berries. But you can mail order black barley and use it for its gorgeous color, chewy texture and nutty taste. As the soup cooks, the cabbage becomes meltingly tender and thickens the broth. The mustard cream stirred in at the end adds memorable flavor and gives the humble ingredients an aristocratic finish.

Winter Vegetable Soup with Black Barley

½ ounce (½ cup loosely packed) dried porcini mushrooms

2 cups boiling water

2 teaspoons vegetable oil

1 cup coarsely chopped onion

1 cup diced, peeled carrot

5 cups Vegetable Stock (page 332)

½ cup dried black-eyed peas

½ cup black barley or wheat berries, rinsed

1 pound cabbage, shredded

2 large ribs celery, halved lengthwise and cut into ½-inch slices

2 large parsnips, peeled and cut into 1-inch chunks

½ teaspoon salt

Freshly ground black pepper to taste

Dilled Mustard Cream

¾ cup reduced-fat sour cream

2 tablespoons Dijon mustard, preferably coarse grain, plus more to taste

3 tablespoons chopped fresh dill or 1½ teaspoons dried

1½ tablespoons fresh lemon juice, plus more to taste

1. To make the Winter Vegetable Soup with Black Barley: Put the dried mushrooms in a small bowl, and pour the boiling water over top. Cover, and let steep until the mushrooms are soft, for about 10 minutes.

2. Meanwhile, heat the oil in a pressure cooker over medium heat. Add the onion and carrot, and cook, stirring frequently, until the vegetables are soft, for about 5 minutes. Reduce the heat if the vegetables begin to brown during this period.

3. Using a slotted spoon, remove the softened mushrooms, and chop any large pieces. Pour the mushroom broth into the cooker, taking care to leave any sandy residue on the bottom of the bowl. Add the mushrooms, vegetable broth, black-eyed peas, and barley. Lock the lid in place. Over high heat, bring to high pressure. Reduce the heat just enough to maintain high pressure and cook for 12 minutes. Quick-release pressure. Remove the lid, tilting it away from you to allow the excess steam to escape.

4. Stir in the cabbage, celery, parsnips, and salt. Return to high pressure, and cook for 8 minutes.

5. Meanwhile, to make the Dilled Mustard Cream: Mix the sour cream, mustard, dill and lemon juice. Add more mustard or lemon juice to taste. Set aside.

6. After 8 minutes, quick-release pressure. Remove the lid, tilting it away from you to allow the excess steam to escape. Ladle out about ½ cup of broth, and blend in 2 tablespoons of Dilled Mustard Cream. Stir this mixture back into the soup. Taste the soup, and add a generous amount of pepper and more salt, if needed. Ladle the soup into large bowls, and spoon a dollop of Dilled Mustard Cream in the center of each portion.

PER SERVING (WITH 1 TABLESPOON CREAM): 204 CAL; 5G PROT; 4G FAT; 36G CARB; 10MG CHOL; 288MG SOD; 11G FIBER

This full-bodied soup is more like a stew with its multiple ingredients. The perfect accompaniment is a basket filled with hot roti, just from the oven; toasted pita bread also work well.

1⅓ cups dry black beans

7 to 8 cups Vegetable Stock (page 332) or water

½ cup flat beer or nonalcoholic beer

¼ cup dark rum, additional Vegetable Stock or water

4 cloves garlic, minced

2 medium-sized onions, sliced

2 tablespoons unsalted butter or vegetable oil

1 cup finely chopped celery

1 green bell pepper, seeded and diced

1 red bell pepper, seeded and diced

1 chile pepper, seeded and minced

2 large carrots, peeled and diced

½ cup canned crushed tomatoes

1½ tablespoons ground cumin

½ tablespoon chili powder

1 teaspoon red pepper sauce

½ teaspoon freshly ground black pepper

½ teaspoon salt

¼ teaspoon cayenne

1 tablespoon minced cilantro

Yogurt or sour cream, optional

1. Soak the beans overnight in water to cover. Drain the beans, and put them in a large pot with the Vegetable Stock, beer, rum, garlic and half of the onions. Cook, uncovered, for 1 to 2 hours, over medium-low heat, stirring occasionally. (If the stock evaporates too quickly, reduce the heat to low, add up to 2 cups of hot water and continue cooking.)

2. Heat the butter or oil in a saucepan. Sauté the remaining onions, celery, peppers and carrots over medium heat until the vegetables are soft, for 5 to 7 minutes. Set aside.

3. When the beans are soft, put half of the bean mixture in a food processor, and purée until smooth. Return the purée to the pot, and add the sautéed vegetables, crushed tomatoes and seasonings. Bring to a boil, and cook for 15 minutes, stirring occasionally. Add more hot water or rum if the soup is too thick, or continue to cook if it is too thin. Serve with a dollop of yogurt or sour cream, if using.

PER SERVING: 139 CAL; 5G PROT; 4G FAT; 20G CARB; 10MG CHOL; 281MG SOD; 5G FIBER

GREEK STEWED POTATOES, GREEN BEANS AND ZUCCHINI

This zesty stew tastes just as good if made the day before but don't add the herbs or cheese, if using, until you've reheated it. A fresh, crusty bread, such as sourdough, makes an excellent partner. To round out the meal, serve a big spinach salad with some chickpeas tossed in.

1 tablespoon olive oil

1 large onion, chopped

2 large baking potatoes (1¼ pounds), peeled and cut into ½-inch chunks

2 zucchini, halved lengthwise and cut into ½-inch chunks

1 pound frozen cut green beans, thawed

1 28-ounce can diced tomatoes, undrained

½ teaspoon dried oregano

¼ cup chopped fresh parsley

¼ cup chopped fresh dill

½ teaspoon salt

¼ teaspoon freshly ground pepper

4 ounces feta cheese, cut into chunks, optional

1. Heat the oil in a large pot over medium heat. Add the onion, and cook, stirring often, until softened, for 3 to 4 minutes.

2. Stir in the potatoes until well combined. Add ½ cup water. Bring to a slow boil, and cover and cook until the potatoes are partially tender, for about 10 minutes.

3. Stir in the zucchini, green beans, tomatoes with liquid and oregano. Return to a low boil, cover and cook until the vegetables are just tender, for about 15 minutes.

4. Stir in the parsley, dill, salt and pepper. Ladle the stew into shallow bowls, and sprinkle some feta over each serving, if desired.

PER SERVING: 173 CAL; 5G PROT; 3G FAT; 35G CARB; 0MG CHOL; 411MG SOD; 6G FIBER

SQUASH-AND-WHITE BEAN SOUP

Winter squash gives this soup a healthy dose of vitamin A. Serve with crusty Italian bread and a mixed green salad for a tasty lunch or supper.

2 tablespoons vegetable or olive oil

4 cups chopped and peeled calabasa, butternut squash or acorn squash

2 cloves garlic, minced

1 medium-sized onion, sliced

1 cup chopped celery

½ Scotch bonnet pepper or 1 jalapeño chile, seeded and minced

1 tablespoon minced fresh ginger

6 cups Vegetable Stock (page 332) or water

1 tablespoon minced fresh parsley

1 tablespoon fresh thyme leaves, or 1 teaspoon dried

1 tablespoon curry powder

1 teaspoon ground cumin

½ teaspoon salt

½ teaspoon ground allspice

1 cup finely chopped kale

1 cup cooked white cannelini beans

1. Combine the oil, calabasa or squash, garlic, onion, celery, pepper and ginger in a soup pot. Sauté over medium heat until softened, for 7 to 10 minutes.

2. Add the Vegetable Stock or water, parsley, thyme, curry powder, cumin, salt and allspice. Cook for 20 minutes, stirring occasionally. Add the kale and beans, and cook until the kale is tender, for 5 to 10 minutes. Serve at once.

PER SERVING: 126 CAL; 4G PROT; 3G FAT; 20G CARB; 0MG CHOL; 156MG SOD; 6G FIBER

MOROCCAN STEW

The Berber spice mixture used in this recipe may be refrigerated in a sealed jar for up to two weeks or stored in the freezer for up to three months. It is excellent as a spice rub for grilled eggplant, zucchini and tofu.

Berber Spice Mixture

2 tablespoons cumin seeds or 1 teaspoon ground cumin

½ tablespoon fennel seeds

1 tablespoon black peppercorns

1 tablespoon whole allspice berries

3 whole cloves

½ tablespoon coriander seeds

1 tablespoon grated, peeled fresh gingerroot

Stew

2 tablespoons olive oil

1½ cups chopped onions

1 cup chopped green bell pepper

1 cup chopped red bell pepper

3 cups peeled and chopped potatoes

1 small butternut squash, peeled, seeded and chopped

2 cups peeled, chopped carrots

2 cups chopped tomatoes

2 tablespoons sweet paprika

½ teaspoon ground cinnamon

½ teaspoon ground turmeric

1½ tablespoons Berber Spice Mixture

3 cloves garlic, minced

4 cups water or Vegetable Stock (page 332)

Salt to taste

¼ cup chopped fresh parsley

Pinch saffron

1. To make the Berber Spice Mixture: In a small bowl, combine all of the ingredients, and set aside.

2. Heat the oil over medium heat in a large saucepan or Dutch oven. Add the vegetables, spices, Berber Spice Mixture and garlic, and cook, stirring occasionally, for 3 to 5 minutes. Add the water, cover and cook until the vegetables are tender, for 20 to 25 minutes. Salt to taste; garnish with parsley and saffron.

PER SERVING: 181 CAL; 4G PROT; 5G FAT; 33G CARB; 0MG CHOL; 481MG SOD; 7G FIBER

NORTH AFRICAN PEPPER AND TOMATO STEW

This hearty stew will ward off any wintertime chill.

2 teaspoons olive oil

1 cup slivered onion (½ large)

1 large green or red bell pepper, cut into 2-inch-long slivers

4 medium-sized cloves garlic, minced

2 fresh Anaheim chiles, seeded and cut into 2-inch-long slivers

½ teaspoon ground cumin

3 ripe medium-sized tomatoes, halved, seeded and coarsely chopped

1 15- to 19-ounce can chickpeas, rinsed and drained, or 1½ to 1¾ cups cooked chickpeas

Salt and freshly ground black pepper to taste

4 large eggs

Pinch of paprika

1. Heat the oil in a large nonstick skillet over medium-high heat. Add the onion, and cook, stirring often, until light golden, for 2 to 3 minutes. Add the bell pepper, garlic, chiles and cumin and cook, stirring often, until softened, for 3 to 5 minutes. Add the tomatoes and chickpeas, and bring to a boil. Cook, stirring occasionally, until the tomatoes have broken down into a sauce, reducing the heat as needed, for about 10 minutes.

2. Season the stew with salt and pepper to taste. One at a time, crack each egg, and drop into a separate quadrant of stew, taking care not to break the yolks. Cover the skillet, and cook over medium-low heat until the eggs are set, for 5 to 7 minutes.

3. Sprinkle each egg with a little paprika. With a slotted spoon, transfer 1 egg with some stew to each plate. Spoon additional stew around the eggs, and serve immediately.

PER SERVING: 271 CAL; 15G PROT; 10G FAT; 35G CARB; 213MG CHOL; 88MG SOD; 6G FIBER

THAI SWEET POTATO STEW

Basmati or Thai jasmine rice is the ideal accompaniment to this spicy dish and its incredible sauce. Thai chili paste and lemongrass are readily available at Asian markets.

3 medium-sized cloves garlic, minced

1 tablespoon minced fresh lemongrass

1 tablespoon minced fresh ginger

1 teaspoon Thai chili paste

1 tablespoon toasted sesame oil

1 medium-sized onion, chopped

1 pound sweet potatoes, peeled and cubed

1 cup Vegetable Stock (page 332)

1 14-ounce can light coconut milk

1 teaspoon salt

¼ cup dry-roasted peanuts, chopped

1. Mash the garlic, lemongrass, ginger and chili paste together with a mortar and pestle until a paste forms. Alternatively, mince with a knife.

2. Heat the sesame oil in a saucepan over medium heat. Add the onion, and cook until golden, stirring occasionally, for about 7 minutes. Add the paste mixture, and stir until fragrant, for about 30 seconds. Add the sweet potatoes, Vegetable Stock and coconut milk, and bring to a boil. Reduce the heat to low, and cook until the potatoes are very tender, for about 20 minutes. Stir in the salt, and garnish with peanuts. Serve.

PER SERVING: 366 CAL; 8G PROT; 14 G FAT; 59G CARB; 0MG CHOL; 749MG SOD; 4G FIBER

CASHEW STEW

When cashews are soaked overnight and then cooked, they become soft and seem more at home in a stew than they do when crunchy. Though this stew may be done without the soaking, the texture and flavor will not be the same. The cooked onions will thicken the juices, so very little cornstarch may be needed.

2 cups whole raw cashews

2 tablespoons olive oil

3 cups coarsely chopped onion

2 teaspoons crushed garlic

1 pound parsnips

1 pound carrots

2 cups sliced green cabbage

1 cup whole prunes, pitted

4 cups vegetarian broth or Vegetable
Stock (page 332)

½ cup sherry or apple juice

2 teaspoon salt

1 teaspoon coarse ground pepper

2 teaspoon dried thyme

2 bay leaves

2 tablespoons cornstarch mixed with
2 tablespoons water

1. Soak the cashews in water overnight.

2. Heat a 4-quart saucepan over medium heat, and add the olive oil. Sauté the onions for 3 minutes, or until they begin to brown. Add the garlic, cover and reduce heat to low. Cook for about 30 minutes, or until onions are very limp and an amber brown color.

3. Meanwhile, peel the parsnips and carrots, and cut into 1-inch lengths. Add them to the pot when the onions finish browning. Add the cabbage, prunes, broth, sherry, salt, pepper, thyme and bay leaves, and cook over low heat for 45 minutes.

4. Drain the cashews, and add to the pot. Cook for another 15 minutes. Stir in the cornstarch mixture, and add just enough to thicken the stew as needed.

PER SERVING: 400 CAL; 9G PROT; 20G FAT; 46G CARB; 0MG CHOL; 640MG SOD; 8G FIBER

VEGETABLE STEW WITH GINGER AND HOT PEPPERS

This hearty vegetable dish has its roots in Africa. You can moderate the heat by upping the quantity of chilies, if you wish.

6 small boiling potatoes

3 carrots, quartered lengthwise and
cut into 2-inch lengths

1 cup green beans, cut diagonally
into 2-inch lengths

1 tablespoon vegetable oil

2 teaspoons minced garlic

1 teaspoon grated fresh ginger

6 scallions, cut diagonally into 2-inch
lengths

1 bell pepper, cut into ½-inch pieces

1 to 4 chiles, cut into ¼-inch pieces

1 small cabbage, cut into 8 wedges

1 teaspoon ground turmeric

1 teaspoon freshly ground black
pepper

Salt to taste

1. Put the potatoes in a saucepan, and add lightly salted water to cover. Bring to a boil over medium heat, and cook until the potatoes are almost tender. (Timing will depend on size and freshness of the potatoes.) Add the carrots and beans, and cook for 5 minutes. Drain, and set aside.

2. Heat the oil in a skillet over medium heat. Add the garlic, ginger, scallions, bell pepper, chiles and cook, stirring frequently, until the scallions are soft, for about 5 minutes.

3. Add the potatoes, carrots and beans, and mix gently. Top with the cabbage wedges, and sprinkle with the turmeric. Cover, and let steam for a few minutes, being careful not to overcook the vegetables. Stir gently, and transfer to a serving dish. Season with pepper and salt, and serve.

PER SERVING: 201 CAL; 5G PROT; 3G FAT; 40G CARB; 0MG CHOL; 60MG SOD; 5G FIBER

SPICY SANCOCHO

Sancocho, a hearty Caribbean stew, offers a taste of island comfort food. Serve this meatless version with rice. Look for plantains in large supermarkets or Latino food shops.

1 tablespoon canola oil

1 medium-sized onion, diced

1 medium-sized green bell pepper, diced

8 ounces white button mushrooms, sliced

1 or 2 jalapeño chiles, seeded and minced

2 cups Vegetable Stock (page 332), canned vegetable stock or water

1 14-ounce can stewed tomatoes

2 large carrots, peeled and diced

1 large green plantain, peeled and coarsely chopped

1 large boiling potato, peeled and diced

2 tablespoons minced fresh parsley

1 tablespoon chopped fresh oregano or 1 teaspoon dried oregano

½ teaspoon freshly ground black pepper

½ teaspoon salt

1. Heat the oil in a large pot over medium heat. Add the onion, bell pepper, mushrooms and jalapeños and cook, stirring often, until the vegetables begin to soften, about 7 minutes. Stir in the Vegetable Stock, stewed tomatoes, carrots, plantain, potato and seasonings, and cook.

2. Cook over medium-low heat, stirring occasionally, until the potato and carrots are tender, for about 25 minutes. Serve hot.

PER SERVING: 198 CAL; 5G PROT; 4G FAT; 39G CARB; 0MG CHOL; 92MG SOD; 5G FIBER

ASPARAGUS AND MUSHROOM STEW

Serve the asparagus mixture over quinoa or other grains.

⅓ ounce dried porcini mushrooms

1 tablespoon vegetable oil

3 cloves garlic, minced

½ pound fresh portobello or shiitake mushrooms, chopped

½ cup sherry

½ teaspoon salt

1 pound asparagus spears, trimmed and cut diagonally into 1-inch lengths

1 red bell pepper, seeded and julienned

1 teaspoon cornstarch dissolved in 1 tablespoon water

1 teaspoon red wine vinegar

Salt and freshly ground black pepper to taste

1. Put the dried mushrooms in an ovenproof bowl, and cover with boiling water to cover. Let soak for 15 minutes.

2. Meanwhile, heat the oil in a large skillet over medium heat. Add the garlic and fresh mushrooms, and cook, stirring often, until the mushrooms are tender. Add the sherry, salt and mushroom liquid.

3. Add the asparagus, bell pepper and dried mushrooms. Simmer, uncovered, until the asparagus are tender, about 7 minutes. Add the cornstarch and vinegar. Bring the mixture to a boil and cook until it thickens slightly, for about 30 seconds. Season to taste.

PER SERVING: 100 CAL; 3G PROT; 3.5G FAT; 8G CARB; 0MG CHOL; 300MG SOD; 3G FIBER

FALL BEAN STEW

This composition combines several varieties of old-fashioned legumes that make a colorful mix in the cook pot. Several of the varieties may require different cooking times, so be sure that all the beans are cooked through before you assemble the stew. Look for truffle butter at gourmet food stores, or make your own by stirring truffle shavings into softened butter and setting it aside for several hours so the truffle flavor infuses the butter.

1 tablespoon olive oil

1 shallot, chopped

2 cloves garlic, thinly sliced

Leaves from 10 sprigs parsley, chopped

1 pound mixed, dried heirloom beans, such as flageolets, scarlet runner beans, cranberry beans, lima beans and navy beans, cooked and drained

3 heirloom or any fresh tomatoes, chopped, or equivalent of canned organic tomatoes

½ cup Vegetable Stock (page 332) or water

Salt and freshly ground black pepper to taste

1 tablespoon truffle butter

10 basil leaves, torn

1. Heat the oil in a large skillet over medium heat. Add the shallot, garlic and parsley, and cook, stirring, until softened and fragrant, for 3 to 5 minutes.

2. Add the beans and tomatoes. Cook, stirring, until the tomatoes cook down and become fragrant, for 5 to 10 minutes. Add the Vegetable Stock, and season to taste. Stir in the truffle butter and basil, and serve.

PER SERVING: 310 CAL; 18G PROT; 5G FAT; 50G CARB; 5MG CHOL; 35MG SOD; 19G FIBER

VEGETABLE STEW WITH TOFU

A robust stew, this dish makes an impressive and sophisticated main course appropriate at any season.

¼ pound green beans

4 artichoke hearts, fresh, frozen or canned

5 ounces white button mushrooms

1 bell pepper

1 zucchini

2 stalks celery

2 large onions

8 cloves garlic, crushed

Salt and freshly ground black pepper to taste

1 cup white wine

1 cup Vegetable Stock (page 332)

2 tablespoons vegetable oil

9 ounces firm tofu, drained and cubed

1. Preheat the oven to 400F.

2. Clean and rinse the vegetables, and cut into bite-size pieces. Place the vegetables in an ovenproof dish, adding the crushed garlic, salt and pepper. Add the white wine and Vegetable Stock, and cover the dish. Bake for 45 minutes.

3. Meanwhile, heat the oil in a large skillet over medium heat. When hot, sauté the tofu until the cubes turn golden. Remove from the heat, and set aside.

4. When the stew is cooked, remove from the oven, add the tofu cubes and serve.

PER SERVING: 220 CAL; 8G PROT; 9G FAT; 18G CARB; 0MG CHOL; 115MG SOD; 4G FIBER

COUNTRY CAPTAIN STEW

With plenty of complementary flavors, and minus the typical meat additions, this dish becomes a vegetarian feast.

1 pound firm tofu

1 tablespoon vegetable oil

1½ cups chopped onions

3 to 4 medium-sized cloves garlic, minced

3 medium-sized all-purpose potatoes, peeled and cut into ½-inch cubes

3 medium-sized apples, peeled, cored and diced

1 large green bell pepper, cut into strips

1 14- to 16-ounce can diced tomatoes, undrained

1 to 2 teaspoons good-quality curry powder or garam masala

1 teaspoon minced fresh ginger

½ cup raisins

⅓ cup chopped cilantro or parsley

½ teaspoon coarse (kosher) salt

Plain low-fat soy or regular yogurt, for serving, optional

1. Preheat the oven to 350F. Lightly oil a nonstick baking sheet.

2. Drain the tofu, and cut it into ½-inch-thick slices. Blot between clean tea towels or paper towels. Cut into ½-inch cubes, then place on the prepared baking sheet in a single layer.

3. Bake for 15 minutes. Stir carefully, and continue to bake until the tofu is golden on most sides, stirring every 5 minutes, for about 20 minutes.

4. Meanwhile, in a very large, deep saucepan, heat the oil over medium heat. Add the onions and garlic, and cook, stirring occasionally, until golden, for 10 to 12 minutes. Add the potatoes, apples, bell pepper, tomatoes (with liquid), curry powder, ginger and 2 cups of water. Increase the heat to high, and bring to a boil. Reduce the heat to low, and cook, covered, until the potatoes are tender, for about 20 minutes.

5. Stir in the baked tofu, raisins, cilantro and salt, and cook, uncovered, stirring occasionally, until the flavors have blended, for 10 to 15 minutes. Serve hot, topped with yogurt, if desired.

PER SERVING: 290 CAL; 8G PROT; 5G FAT; 60G CARB; 0MG CHOL; 147MG SOD; 6G FIBER

VEGETABLE STOCK

Commercial vegetable stocks are readily available and are handy when you have run out of your own home-made vegetable stock. Make up many batches of this stock when you have some leisure time, and freeze it for later use.

4 large carrots, sliced

1 large onion, thinly sliced

1 large bulb fennel (including leaves), chopped coarsely or 4 large stalks celery, chopped)

4 cloves garlic, crushed

2 medium-sized red potatoes, quartered

1 bay leaf

2 tablespoons minced fresh oregano leaves or 2 teaspoons dried

2 tablespoons minced fresh basil leaves or 2 teaspoons dried

2 tablespoons minced fresh thyme leaves (or 2 teaspoons dried)

Salt and freshly ground black pepper to taste

1. Combine all the ingredients in a large stockpot. Add 10 cups water, and bring to a boil over medium heat. Cover, reduce the heat to low and cook for 1½ hours.

2. Remove and discard the bay leaf. Line a colander with cheesecloth, set it over a large bowl and strain the liquid. Either discard the vegetables, or purée half of them with the liquid for a thicker stock. Store in an airtight container in the refrigerator for up to 3 days or in the freezer for up to 3 months.

PER CUP (STRAINED): 22 CAL; 0.6G PROT; 0G FAT; 5G CARB; 0MG CHOL; 288MG SOD; 1G FIBER

QUICK STOCK

This fast vegetable stock can be refrigerated up to 5 days or frozen up to 6 months. It's great to have on hand for soups, stews and chili. Store in an airtight container in the refrigerator for up to 3 days or in the freezer for up to 3 months. Frozen stock can be thawed in the microwave oven in about 10 minutes.

2 cups chopped leeks, green part only or 1 cup chopped onion

2 carrots, peeled and chopped

1 celery stalk (including leaves), chopped

1 bay leaf

10 large sprigs fresh parsley, chopped

1 large clove garlic, sliced

¼ teaspoon dried marjoram

Pinch dried thyme

1 teaspoon salt

7 cups cold water

Combine all the ingredients in a large soup pot, and add 7 cups cold water. Bring to a boil over medium heat, reduce the heat to low and cook for 25 minutes. Strain in a colander set over a large bowl.

PER CUP (STRAINED): 12 CAL; 0G PROT; 0G FAT; 1G CARB; 0MG CHOL; 406MG SOD; 0G FIBER

15 *fast, fast foods*

IN TODAY'S FAST-PACED WORLD, EVERY-body craves food that can get to the table—without delay. But few want to give up flavor for speed. These recipes help cooks have it both ways, for delicious dishes prepared in 30 minutes or less!

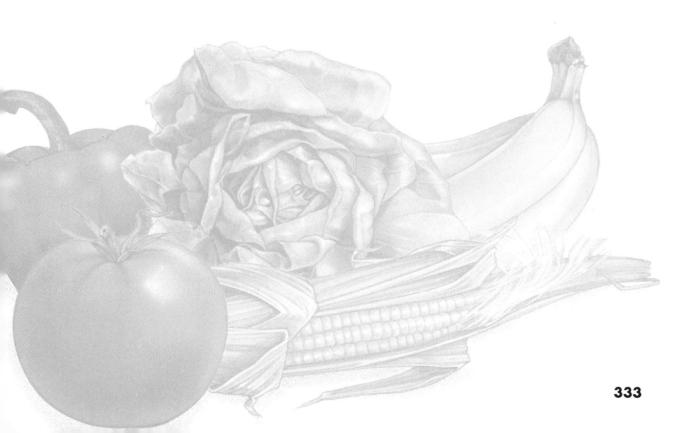

WESTERN OMELET BONANZA

SERVES 4

This variation on the Western omelet calls for a hearty mixture of potatoes, onion, "sausage" and red peppers folded into the eggs for double cooking. Country biscuits, orange juice and hot coffee make perfect partners for this breakfast or brunch entrée.

2 tablespoons unsalted butter or margarine

½ cup diced potato

½ cup diced onion

7 ounces soy "sausage," crumbled

½ cup diced red or green peppers

Salt and freshly ground pepper to taste

6 large eggs, separated

4 tablespoons shredded low-fat cheddar cheese

3 tablespoons minced parsley for garnish

1. Preheat the oven to broil.

2. Heat 1 tablespoon butter in a 10-inch nonstick skillet over medium heat. Add the potatoes, and sauté for 3 to 4 minutes, or until the potatoes begin to turn golden. Reduce heat to medium-low, and add remaining butter, onion, "sausage," peppers, salt and pepper. Sauté until the onion and "sausage" begin to brown, for about 4 minutes. Remove from the heat, and set aside.

3. Beat the yolks until slightly thick. Beat the whites until foamy and slightly stiff. Fold the whites into the yolks, and stir in 2 tablespoons cheese. Pour the eggs over the "sausage" mixture. Cook over medium heat until the eggs begin to firm on the bottom, lifting the edges of the eggs and letting the uncooked eggs run underneath.

4. Put the skillet under the broiler, and cook the egg mixture for 2 to 3 minutes, or until the top begins to brown and the eggs firm up throughout. Remove from the oven, and slide the omelet onto a serving dish. Garnish with the remaining cheese and parsley before serving.

PER SERVING: 390 CAL; 28G PROT; 24G FAT; 15G CARB; 445MG CHOL; 540MG SOD; 3G FIBER

RICOTTA-STRAWBERRY BREAKFAST CAKES

SERVES 4

Almost everyone loves fresh strawberries, and this unusual breakfast offering makes the most of this warm-weather fruit. Accent the cakes with a fruit or maple syrup and a sprinkling of confectioners' sugar, if you want. To accompany them, offer a bowl of strawberries lightly dusted with confectioners' sugar, and to drink, chilled raspberry or other fruit juice and hot green tea.

2 large eggs

1 cup low-fat ricotta cheese

⅓ to ½ cup confectioners' sugar

2 tablespoons cornstarch

1 teaspoon lemon extract

1 cup fresh sliced strawberries plus extra for garnish

1. Preheat the oven to 400F. Spray four ¾-cup glass baking cups with nonstick cooking spray, and set aside.

2. Beat the eggs in a bowl until foamy. Stir in the ricotta cheese, sugar, cornstarch and lemon extract, and blend well. Stir in the strawberries, taking care not to crush. Fill each cup about two-thirds full.

3. Bake for about 20 minutes, or until the tops are lightly browned. Remove from the oven, and serve hot with extra strawberries and the toppings of your choice.

PER SERVING: 210 CAL; 9G PROT; 10G FAT; 19G CARB; 140MG CHOL; 270MG SOD; <1G FIBER

FROG IN THE WELL

This Americanized vegetarian version of the popular British dish "Toad in the Hole"—classically a Yorkshire pudding-and-sausage dish baked in a hot oven—brings together soy "sausages," Gruyère cheese, eggs and sourdough bread in a quick-fix brunch or supper dish. You can double this recipe easily, and soak and bake the 2 pieces of bread in separate baking dishes. Pair this with sliced fresh fruit or a tossed green salad with a tart vinaigrette dressing, plus something sweet for dessert, such as a custard, British trifle or scones spread with lemon curd or strawberry jam.

1 1-inch-thick slice sourdough or other sandwich-sized bread

2 large eggs

⅓ cup low-fat milk

½ cup grated Gruyère cheese

2 links soy "sausage"

Salt and freshly ground black pepper to taste

1. Preheat the oven to 425F. Spray a 4-inch-round ovenproof baking dish with nonstick cooking spray.

2. Cut a hole in the center of the bread slice. Place 1 egg and milk in a large mixing bowl, and beat well. Stir in the grated cheese. Place the bread slice in the mixture, submerging so it absorbs the egg mixture.

3. Spray a large skillet with nonstick cooking spray. Heat over medium heat, and sauté "sausages" until golden, for 5 to 6 minutes.

4. Place the bread slice in the baking dish. Crack the second egg into the hole, place cooked "sausages" around the bread and pour remaining egg mixture over top.

5. Bake for 20 minutes, or until the eggs are set and the cheese is browned. Remove from the oven, and season with salt and pepper.

PER SERVING: 710 CAL; 50G PROT; 37G FAT; 41G CARB; 485MG CHOL; 1,050MG SOD; 4G FIBER

"PIGS" UNDER WRAPS

Inspired by the popular casual dish "pigs in blankets"—frankfurters wrapped in biscuit dough and then baked—this vegetarian version provides a snappy celebration of childhood with an Asian twist. Serve with Hot Potato Salad (page 148) or corn chips. Iced tea or tart lemonade makes the perfect beverage. For dessert? Ice cream pops.

4 soy "frankfurters"

8 egg roll wrappers (6 inches square)

½ cup sauerkraut

4 tablespoons relish

American-style mustard to taste

1 cup shredded low-fat mozzarella cheese

3 tablespoons vegetable oil

1. Cook soy "frankfurters," or "franks," according to the package directions.

2. Meanwhile, separate the 2 egg roll wrappers from the package, and place them flat on the work surface. Arrange ⅛ cup sauerkraut and 1 tablespoon relish on the upper one-third of the wrapper. Using tongs, remove one "frank" from the saucepan, and place it on the wrapper below the sauerkraut. Spread the mustard on the "frank," spread 1 tablespoon relish on the other side, sprinkle ¼ cup cheese on "frank" and wrap, rolling toward you, until the filling is covered. Moisten the long edge with water to seal. Repeat until all ingredients are used up.

3. Heat the vegetable oil in a large skillet over medium heat. Pan-fry "frank" packets until puffy and golden on all sides, for 3 to 4 minutes. Using tongs, remove from heat, and place on several layers of paper towels to blot excess oil. Serve with the mustard in a zigzag line down the center of the egg roll wrapper.

PER SERVING: 410 CAL; 22G PROT; 16G FAT; 72G CARB; 10MG CHOL; 970MG SOD; 2G FIBER

ITALIAN-STYLE "PEPPERONI" HERO

SERVES 4

Inspired by the traditional Italian fire-grilled bruschetta with its brush of olive oil and garlic accent, this hearty open-faced sandwich makes a satisfying luncheon entrée, accompanied by a vinaigrette-dressed salad and custard for dessert.

2 mini baguettes (5 ounces each)

3 teaspoon olive oil

2 teaspoons minced garlic

8 tablespoons marinara sauce

1 4-ounce package soy "pepperoni" slices

1 cup chopped roasted red peppers

2 cups shredded low-fat mozzarella cheese

1. Preheat the broiler to 450F. Split the baguettes in half lengthwise, and place 4 halves side by side on a baking sheet.

2. Combine the oil and garlic in a mixing bowl, and brush on the split baguette halves, dividing equally among each. Place the baguettes in the oven, and heat for 5 minutes, or until the loaves are slightly browned and aromatic. Remove from the oven, and set on a work surface.

3. Spread 2 tablespoons marinara sauce on each half of the baguettes. Carefully arrange pepperoni slices on each half, dividing them into four equal servings. Sprinkle each half with chopped red peppers, and top with the cheese, being sure to cover each half completely.

4. Increase the oven temperature to 475F, and bake the loaves for about 5 minutes, or until the cheese bubbles and browns slightly. Remove from the oven, and serve.

PER SERVING: 540 CAL; 30G PROT; 20G FAT; 62G CARB; 35MG CHOL; 1,030MG SOD; 6G FIBER

PLANTAINS WITH SPICY BLACK BEANS

SERVES 4

These easy-to-fix Caribbean and Latino favorites—fried plantains and beans—will conjure up images of white sand beaches and fun in the sun. The accompanying spiced black beans add a flavor boost, and you can intensify flavors and heat up this dish with a few dashes of hot pepper sauce and some diced jalapeño chiles.

1 tablespoon vegetable oil, plus extra for frying

1 large onion, diced

1 teaspoon minced garlic

3½ cups canned black beans, drained and rinsed

1 cup vegetable stock

2 teaspoons ground cumin

1 teaspoon coriander seeds, toasted and slightly crushed

Salt and freshly ground black pepper

4 large ripe plantains

½ cup salsa, or more as desired

½ cup vegan sour cream

½ cup cilantro for garnish

1. Heat the oil in a large saucepan over medium heat. Sauté the onion and garlic until golden, for about 5 minutes. Add the beans, vegetable stock, cumin, coriander seeds, salt and pepper to taste. Reduce the heat to medium-low, and cook for about 15 minutes, or until aromatic.

2. Meanwhile, slice each plantain in half lengthwise, and peel off the skin. Heat enough oil for frying in a large skillet. Fry the plantain halves until golden on one side, turn over and continue frying until golden. Remove from the heat, and place on paper towels to absorb the extra oil.

3. To serve, place 2 plantain halves on each plate. Spoon the beans over the plantains, or, alternatively, place a scoop on the side. Top each serving with 2 tablespoons salsa, 2 tablespoons sour cream and a sprinkling of cilantro, or pass in serving bowls for individual service.

PER SERVING: 590 CAL; 18G PROT; 16G FAT; 102G CARB; 0MG CHOL; 300MG SOD; 19G FIBER

SWISS RAREBIT

Inspired by the cheese-based Welsh Rarebit, this suppertime offering calls for an accompanying mesclun salad tossed with crunchy croutons and a bowl of fresh whole apples and pears for dessert.

3 whole wheat English muffins, sliced in half crosswise

1 cup sauerkraut, rinsed and drained

1 tablespoon soy margarine

¾ cup beer or ale

1 teaspoon vegetarian Worcestershire sauce

1 teaspoon Dijon mustard, or more to taste

Salt and freshly ground black pepper to taste

¾ pound low-fat Swiss-style cheese, such as Jarlsberg, diced

1 tablespoon cornstarch

1 large egg, lightly beaten

3 tablespoons soy "bacon" bits

½ teaspoon paprika

1. Preheat the oven to 400F. Line a baking pan with foil, and set aside.

2. Place the muffin halves in the baking pan. Toast for 2 to 3 minutes, or until crisp. Place equal portions of the sauerkraut on top of muffin halves, and put pan in the broiler. Cook until the sauerkraut is heated through. Remove from the oven, and set aside.

3. Meanwhile, melt the margarine in the top half of a double boiler over boiling water and medium heat. Stir together the beer, Worcestershire sauce, mustard, salt and pepper, and add to the margarine. Toss the cheese cubes with the cornstarch. As the beer heats, add the cubes a few at a time, and stir often until the cheese melts.

4. Remove ¼ cup of the hot mixture, and beat into the egg to temper it. Cook for 3 to 4 minutes more, stirring constantly. Stir the egg immediately into the melted cheese, and whisk to combine.

5. Spoon equal portions of the hot cheese over the muffin halves, sprinkle with the "bacon" bits and paprika and serve.

PER SERVING: 280 CAL; 24G PROT; 12G FAT; 18G CARB; 55MG CHOL; 710MG SOD; 3G FIBER

FAVA BEAN SALAD WITH FETA

Readily available at most supermarkets, canned fava beans are natural partners for the popular Mediterranean feta cheese. Select your favorite creamy salad dressing, and complement this light, easy-to-assemble dish with a quick bread or toasted English muffins. Serve fruit for dessert.

2 cups canned fava beans, drained and rinsed

4 ounces crumbled feta cheese

½ cup chopped parsley

½ cup seasoned croutons

1 red pepper, diced

4 ounces sliced mushrooms

Combine all ingredients in a large salad bowl. Toss with your favorite dressing, and serve.

PER SERVING. 210 CAL; 12G PROT; 8G FAT; 24G CARB; 25MG CHOL; 560MG SOD; 5G FIBER

PORTOBELLO PIZZAS

SERVES 4

Giant portobello mushroom caps are the foundation for mini pizzas, packed with the same intense flavors as the standard pizza-parlor pie but minus the calories. Use a commercially prepared pesto for quick assembly of these pizzas. Serve with breadsticks or the One-Rise Breadsticks (page 131) and a tossed green salad, and end with an Italian gelato for dessert.

4 giant portobello mushroom caps

2 tablespoons balsamic vinegar, or more as needed

1½ tablespoons basil pesto

1½ cups shredded combination low-fat mozzarella and provolone cheeses

2 ounces soy "pepperoni" slices

6 artichoke bottoms, chopped

2 tablespoons chopped oil-cured olives, optional

Pinch oregano

1. Preheat the oven to 500F. Line a baking sheet with foil, and spray the foil with nonstick cooking spray.

2. Wipe the mushroom caps clean, and remove the stems. Chop the stems, and place them in a mixing bowl. Using a small spoon, gently scoop out the black gills on the underside of the mushroom caps, and discard the gills. Place the mushrooms, cap side down, on a foil-lined sheet.

3. Combine the balsamic vinegar and pesto in a small mixing bowl, and brush the mixture on the mushroom caps. Place in the oven, and cook for 5 to 7 minutes, or until tender.

4. Meanwhile, combine in a bowl 1 cup cheese, soy "pepperoni" slices, artichoke bottoms, chopped mushroom stems, olives, if using, and oregano, tossing to mix well. Remove the mushrooms from the oven, and, dividing mixture evenly, fill each cap. Sprinkle remaining ½ cup cheese over the mushrooms.

5. Bake for 7 to 10 minutes more, remove from the oven and serve.

PER SERVING: 250 CAL; 17G PROT; 13G FAT; 11G CARB; 30MG CHOL; 600MG SOD; 3G FIBER

BAKED TACOS

SERVES 4

To assemble these tacos quickly and efficiently, place all readied ingredients in front of you. That way, the filling and folding can be accomplished in minutes. For a change of taste, use refried pinto beans. Serve the baked tacos with a light salad of watercress, orange sections and nuts, or try the Papaya and Watercress Salad with Lime (page 145).

8 8-inch flour tortillas, plain or flavored

1 15-ounce can nonfat refried black beans

8 ounces Tex-Mex-flavored baked tofu, cut into 16 long pieces

4 ounces chopped mild green chiles

8 ounces shredded low-fat cheddar cheese or soy cheddar cheese

1½ cups salsa

Chopped cilantro for garnish

1 avocado, sliced, for garnish, optional

1. Preheat oven to 450F. Spray a 9 x 13–inch baking dish or larger baking dish with nonstick cooking spray.

2. Starting with 1 tortilla, spread half of the tortilla with 2 heaping tablespoons beans, place 2 slices tofu on the beans, and sprinkle with 1 tablespoon chopped chiles and 1 tablespoon grated cheese. Wrap tightly, and place in the baking dish.

3. Repeat with the remaining ingredients, arranging filled and rolled tortillas snugly into the dish. When complete, pour the salsa over top, spreading it out evenly, and sprinkle with the remaining cheese, covering the tortillas evenly with the cheese. Cover the baking dish completely with foil.

4. Bake for about 20 minutes, or until the cheese melts and the filling is heated through. Garnish as desired, and serve.

PER SERVING: 610 CAL; 40G PROT; 16G FAT; 78G CARB; 10MG CHOL; 1,390MG SOD; 9G FIBER

CHEESE AND BEAN QUESADILLAS

Any time of day you yearn for Tex-Mex flavors, whip up one of these quesadillas for a filling, nutritious meal. These work well with a creamed corn soup to start and a bowl of sweet seasonal berries to end the meal. To drink? Chilled iced mint tea or the Ice Sherried Lemonade (page 82).

1½ cups nonfat vegetarian refried beans

1 cup corn kernels

½ cup salsa

1 teaspoon chili powder, or more as desired

6 8-inch low-fat tortillas, preferably flavored

2 cups grated cheddar-flavored soy cheese

3 tomatoes, stemmed and chopped

1 avocado, peeled and chopped

1 teaspoon ground cumin

Juice of 1 lime

Salt and freshly ground pepper to taste

1. Combine the beans, corn kernels, salsa and chili powder in a saucepan, and cook, stirring, over medium heat until hot.

2. Place a tortilla flat on a work surface. Sprinkle about ⅓ cup cheese over the tortilla. Spread about ½ cup bean mixture on one-half of tortilla, and fold the tortilla over to encase the filling and cheese. Set aside. Repeat with remaining ingredients until 6 quesadillas are ready for cooking.

3. Spray a large nonstick skillet with nonstick cooking spray, and heat over medium heat. Put 3 quesadillas into the skillet, and cook, turning 2 or 3 times, until the tortillas brown slightly on both sides and the cheese melts. Remove from the skillet, and place on individual serving plates. Repeat with the remaining quesadillas. Respray the skillet as needed to prevent any sticking.

4. Toss together the tomatoes, avocado and cumin. Sprinkle mixture with the lime juice, and season with salt and pepper. Spoon equal portions of mixture over the quesadillas, and serve.

PER SERVING: 360 CAL; 18G PROT; 11G FAT; 51G CARB; 0MG CHOL; 870MG SOD; 8G FIBER

TORTILLA TORTE

An eye-catching main dish, this tiered tortilla "cake" will delight brunch or dinner crowds with its robust flavors. Offer a first course bowl of guacamole with chips and, for dessert, chocolate ice cream with chocolate sauce sprinkled with cinnamon.

2 tablespoons vegetable oil

1 12-ounce package taco-seasoned soy "ground meat"

2 cups salsa

1½ cups pinto beans, drained and rinsed

5 8-inch low-fat flour tortillas

8 ounces grated soy cheddar-flavored cheese

1 large tomato, thinly sliced

½ cup cilantro leaves for garnish

½ avocado, diced, for garnish

½ cup soy sour cream for garnish

1. Preheat the oven to 425F. Spray a 10-inch round, deep cake pan with nonstick cooking spray.

2. Heat the oil in a large skillet over medium heat. Sauté the "meat" for 3 to 4 minutes, add the salsa and beans, and cook until heated through, for about 5 minutes, stirring often.

3. Place 1 flour tortilla in the bottom of the cake pan, and place about ½ cup "meat" mixture over top, spreading out to cover the surface. Sprinkle with about ¼ cup cheese. Top with the second tortilla, and repeat with the filling mixture and cheese. Repeat the procedure with the remainder of the tortillas, filling with the mixture and cheese until all the ingredients are used up. Spoon any remaining mixture over top, place the tomato slices on the mixture and sprinkle with the remaining cheese.

4. Bake for about 10 minutes, or until the cheese melts, and remove from the oven. Garnish with the cilantro, diced avocado and soy sour cream. To serve, slice like a cake, including garnishes with each portion.

PER SERVING: 340 CAL; 20G PROT; 12G FAT; 38G CARB; 0MG CHOL; 1,120MG SOD; 7G FIBER

WILD RICE FRITTERS

Nestled on spinach leaves, these savory wild rice fritters get their sweet accent from the fruit-based salsa, which may be made from peach, mango, papaya or other fruit. Buy precooked wild rice, available vacuum-packed at specialty food stores or many well-stocked supermarkets.

3 extra-large eggs

1 cup low-fat ricotta cheese

½ cup seasoned breadcrumbs

3 cups cooked wild rice

1 tablespoon minced garlic

Pinch oregano

Pinch crushed red pepper, optional

Salt and freshly ground black pepper
to taste

4 to 6 tablespoons vegetable oil, for
cooking

5 ounces baby spinach leaves, rinsed

1½ cups fruit-based salsa, or as
desired

1. Beat the eggs in a large mixing bowl until foamy. Fold in the ricotta cheese, breadcrumbs and wild rice, and stir until the rice is evenly distributed. Stir in the garlic, oregano, red pepper, if using, and salt and pepper.

2. Heat 4 tablespoons of the oil in a large skillet over medium heat. When hot, place about ⅓ cup scoop of the rice mixture per fritter into the skillet, cooking 3 to 4 fritters at a time for a total of 12 fritters. Add more oil as needed. Cook the fritters until golden, for 5 to 6 minutes. Using a spatula, turn the fritters over, and brown the second side. Remove from the heat, and drain on paper towels. Continue until the mixture is used up.

3. To serve, arrange equal portions of the spinach leaves on plates, place 2 fritters per serving on the leaves and garnish with salsa, as desired.

PER SERVING: 300 CAL; 13G PROT; 13G FAT; 35G CARB; 14MG CHOL; 480MG SOD; 3G FIBER

OLE FRIJOLE PIE

Chilled beer, guacamole with chips and cinnamon or chocolate ice cream for dessert complement this Southwestern main-course dish.

1 16-ounce can nonfat vegetarian
refried beans

1 teaspoon chili powder, or to taste

½ cup salsa

1 12-ounce package taco seasoned
soy "ground meat"

1 9-inch unbaked deep-dish pie
crust

2 cups shredded low-fat cheddar
cheese

1. Preheat the oven to 400F.

2. Mix together the beans, chili powder, salsa and "ground meat." Spoon the mixture into the pie crust, and top with the cheese.

3. Bake for about 20 minutes, or until the cheese is completely melted and bubbling. Remove from the oven, and serve.

PER SERVING: 340 CAL; 28G PROT; 9G FAT; 36G CARB; 15MG CHOL; 930MG SOD; 8G FIBER

PARMESAN "CHICKEN" ON ENGLISH MUFFINS

Use the popular sandwich-sized English muffins as the base for an Italian-inspired topping. Accompany this dish with a vegetarian minestrone soup, and finish the meal with hot apple pie.

4 thin slices eggplant, about 1½ ounces each

2 tablespoons olive oil

1 tablespoon minced garlic

6 ounces soy "chicken" strips

8 tablespoons spaghetti sauce

2 extra-large English muffins, split in half

2 tablespoons soy margarine

3 ounces oil-packed sun-dried tomatoes

Seasoning salt to taste

4 slices low-fat mozzarella cheese, about 1½ ounces each

4 tablespoons freshly grated Parmesan cheese

1. Preheat the oven to broil. Line a baking sheet with foil, and set aside.

2. Arrange the eggplant slices on the baking sheet, brush with 1 tablespoon olive oil and broil for about 7 minutes, turning once, until the eggplant is tender and just browned. Remove from the oven, and set aside. Reduce the heat to 425F.

3. Heat the remaining 1 tablespoon oil in a large skillet over medium heat. Sauté the garlic and "chicken" strips for 2 to 3 minutes, or until the "chicken" turns golden and is heated through. Stir in 4 tablespoons spaghetti sauce. Remove from the heat, and set aside.

4. Arrange the muffin halves on a baking sheet. Spread 1½ teaspoons margarine on each muffin half. Place the pieces of the sun-dried tomatoes on the muffins, and spread 1 tablespoon spaghetti sauce on each muffin half. Place the eggplant slices on the sauce, top with a portion of the "chicken" strips spread equally among the muffins, and sprinkle with the seasoning salt. Top each muffin with a slice of mozzarella and a sprinkle Parmesan cheese.

5. Arrange the muffins on a baking sheet, and place in the oven. Cook for 7 to 10 minutes, or until the cheese melts and bubbles.

PER SERVING: 440 CAL; 26G PROT; 26G FAT; 29G CARB; 25MG CHOL; 760MG SOD; 5G FIBER

ROBUST TORTILLA SOUP

This colorful dish brings you the lively flavors of the Southwest in a main-course soup. Offer corn or flour tortillas with the soup, and conclude with the Strawberry Cassis Tofu Ice Cream (page 387) and meringues or butter cookies.

4 cups Vegetable Stock (page 332)

1 cup chopped tomatoes with juices

1 tablespoon fresh lime juice

1 tablespoon vegetable oil

12 ounces taco-flavored ground soy "meat"

1 teaspoon taco seasoning, or to taste

1 teaspoon ground cumin, or to taste

1 cup grated soy cheddar cheese

4 ounces chopped green chiles

Salt and freshly ground black pepper to taste

¼ cup cilantro leaves

½ avocado, diced

12 grape tomatoes

¾ cup (about 2 ounces) crushed baked corn chips

1. Heat the Vegetable Stock in a large saucepan, and add the chopped tomatoes and lime juice.

2. Meanwhile, heat the oil in a large skillet, and sauté the ground soy "meat." Stir in the taco seasoning and ground cumin, and continue cooking until browned.

3. When the stock boils, remove from the heat. Stir in the grated cheese, chopped chiles, salt and pepper to taste. Spoon the ground soy "meat" into large soup bowls, and ladle the hot soup on top. Garnish the servings with the cilantro, diced avocado, grape tomatoes and corn chips. Serve hot.

PER SERVING: 550 CAL; 42G PROT; 21G FAT; 49G CARB; 0MG CHOL; 1,850MG SOD; 15G FIBER

RED, RED SALAD

Reminiscent of the '50s favorite chopped salad, this indulges your whim for something red and colorful for spring and summer eating. You can dress this with an oil-and-balsamic vinegar mixture, or any other favorite dressing. Because this is a focal point for lunch or supper, start the meal with a chilled soup such as a gazpacho, accompany the salad with grilled cheese squares and wrap the meal up with a tempting sweet, such as a wedge of berry pie. Toast the meal with icy lemonade.

1 bunch radishes, greens removed, trimmed and quartered

½ head red cabbage, cored and chopped

1 cup grape tomatoes

2½ cups red kidney beans, drained and rinsed

1 large red bell pepper, seeded and diced

½ large red onion, diced

Salt and freshly ground black pepper to taste

Salad dressing to taste

Put all the vegetables and beans in a large salad bowl, and season with salt and pepper. Dress with the salad dressing, toss and serve.

PER SERVING: 100 CAL; 6G PROT; 0.5G FAT; 20G CARB; 0MG CHOL; 200MG SOD; 6G FIBER

KASHA AND PARSLEY BIG BOWL

Cool grain salads are big hits at any time, and this is no exception with its abundant fresh vegetables and crumbles of salty cheese. Fruit muffins offer a flavor counterpoint, while a seasonal fruit pie is an ideal dessert.

2 cups Vegetable Stock (page 332) or water

1 large egg

1 cup uncooked kasha

4 tablespoons olive oil, or more as needed

4 ounces crumbled feta cheese

1 bunch parsley, finely chopped

1 large tomato, cubed

3 ounces diced celery

2 ounces shredded carrots

Juice of 1 large lemon

Salt and freshly ground black pepper to taste

1 head Boston lettuce, leaves separated and rinsed

1. Bring the Vegetable Stock to a boil in a large saucepan over medium-high heat.

2. Meanwhile, beat the egg lightly, and pour over the kasha in a bowl, stirring to coat grains. Heat 1 tablespoon oil in a skillet over medium heat, and sauté the egg-coated kasha for about 2 minutes. Remove from the heat, and, when the Vegetable Stock boils, spoon the kasha into the hot liquid. Reduce the heat to medium-low, cover and cook for 10 minutes, or until the grains are tender. Remove from the heat, spread out in a large baking pan and cool in the refrigerator for 10 minutes, stirring the grains often to cool.

3. Meanwhile, put the cheese and vegetables in a large bowl. Add the cooled kasha, and stir the grains with the vegetables. Combine the remaining oil and lemon juice, beating to mix well. Dress the salad, and season with salt and pepper.

4. To serve, arrange the leaves in a salad bowl or on a serving platter, and spoon the grains and vegetables onto the leaves.

PER SERVING: 270 CAL; 9G PROT; 15G FAT; 29G CARB; 50MG CHOL; 330MG SOD; 5G FIBER

MEDITERRANEAN CHOPPED SALAD

SERVES 6

A retro dish once popular in the 1950s, the chopped salad takes center stage again, featuring an array of ingredients cut to a uniform size. Because it is so versatile, you may adapt it to ingredient combinations of your choice. This particular main-course salad partners well with a crusty garlic-flavored French baguette and a fruit punch. Try something light for dessert such as a fruit sorbet with cookies.

1 cup uncooked orzo

½ head romaine lettuce, rinsed and cored

8 ounces cut-up hearts of palm

1 pint cherry or grape tomatoes

3 ounces oil-cured olives, chopped

1½ cups artichoke hearts, chopped

4 tablespoons capers

8 ounces cubed low-fat mozzarella cheese

1 cup chickpeas, rinsed and drained

¼ cup red wine vinegar

½ cup olive oil

Salt and freshly ground black pepper to taste

1 tablespoon dried oregano

1 teaspoon minced garlic

1. Heat a pot of lightly salted water over medium heat, and when it is boiling, cook the orzo according to package directions. Drain, rinsing the pasta under cold water.

2. Dry the lettuce leaves thoroughly, and cut the leaves into bite-sized pieces. Place in a bowl. Add the orzo, hearts of palm, tomatoes, olives, artichoke hearts, capers, mozzarella and chickpeas.

3. Combine the remaining ingredients. Drizzle over the salad, reserving any left-over dressing, and toss the vegetables. Serve immediately.

PER SERVING: 480 CAL; 20G PROT; 28G FAT; 40G CARB; 20MG CHOL; 790MG SOD; 6G FIBER

WATERMELON, GRAPE AND TOMATO SALAD

SERVES 4

Refreshing and light, this main-course salad graces a hot summer meal with its tangy yet sweet tones. Add or subtract melon, grapes and tomatoes as you please, adjusting the vinegar accordingly. For an attractive variation, use a melon baller to prepare the watermelon. Pizza slices or open-faced grilled cheese squares round out the meal.

3 cups cubed or balled watermelon, seeds removed

2 cups seedless green grapes, rinsed

½ red bell pepper, seeded and cubed

1 bunch Italian parsley, coarsely chopped

1 large yellow tomato

1 large red or orange tomato

4 ounces crumbled Gorgonzola cheese

1 tablespoon balsamic vinegar, or to taste

Combine all the ingredients, toss and serve.

PER SERVING: 230 CAL; 8G PROT; 10G FAT; 29G CARB; 25MG CHOL; 20MG SOD; 3G FIBER

MANGO-CHUTNEY SALAD SERVES 2

A delightful luncheon dish, this light main-course salad calls for a fruit- or vegetable-laden quick bread, muffins or grilled cheese sandwiches. And it allows for a rich dessert such as a lemon or apple tart with vanilla ice cream. Try herbed tea as a beverage.

5 ounces mixed spring greens, rinsed and dried

3 ripe mangoes, peeled and diced

½ cup chopped pecans

1 cup sliced water chestnuts

1 teaspoon curry powder, or more to taste

2 tablespoons vegetable oil

4 tablespoons rice vinegar

¼ cup plain nonfat yogurt

¾ cup mango chutney

Shredded fresh ginger for garnish

1. Arrange greens in a salad bowl, and toss with mangoes, pecans and water chestnuts. Set aside.

2. Stir together curry powder, vegetable oil, vinegar, yogurt and chutney to make a thick, creamy dressing. Pour over the salad mixture, and toss to combine well. Garnish with the shredded ginger, and serve.

PER SERVING: 640 CAL; 10G PROT; 37G FAT; 80G CARB; 0MG CHOL; 80MG SOD; 14G FIBER

"CHICKEN" AND CREAMY GRITS SERVES 4

Grits provide a neutral background for assertive ingredients and seasonings such as those found in this meatless version of a Southern-inspired dish. A delicate, clear soup could introduce this meal, and a fruit cobbler or berry pie or the Berry Chocolate Shortcake (page 401) makes a satisfying dessert.

2 cups plain soymilk

½ cup quick-cooking grits

6½ ounces shredded soy cheese, mixture of Parmesan, mozzarella and Romano flavors, or as desired

1 tablespoon olive oil

1 onion, chopped

1 green bell pepper, chopped

4 ounces sliced mushrooms

6 ounces soy "chicken" strips

2 cups roasted whole tomatoes, crushed and undrained

Salt and freshly ground black pepper to taste

1. Bring the soymilk to a boil in a large saucepan over medium-high heat. Slowly whisk in the grits, stirring to combine well. Sprinkle in the shredded cheese, and stir. Reduce heat to medium-low, cover the pan and cook for about 10 minutes, stirring occasionally, or until grits become thick and creamy. Remove from the heat.

2. Meanwhile, heat the oil in a large skillet over medium heat. Add the chopped onion, green bell pepper and mushrooms, and sauté for 5 minutes. Add "chicken" strips, crushed tomatoes with juice, salt and pepper. Continue cooking, for about 10 minutes more.

3. Spoon grits onto individual plates, top with vegetable mixture and serve.

PER SERVING: 350 CAL; 24G PROT; 11G FAT; 43G CARB; 0MG CHOL; 600MG SOD; 5G FIBER

TOFU TRIANGLES WITH THAI CHILI SAUCE

SERVES 4

Perfect for a quick lunch, these delicious Thai-inspired tofu triangles take well to a splash of Asian seasoning. To keep it Thai, use sweet Thai chili sauce—look for a product that is thickened and textured with pickled shredded red chilies. If unavailable, use Chinese hoisin sauce instead. Round rice stick noodles are sold at Asian markets, natural food markets and some large supermarkets, but you can use spaghetti instead.

1 pound firm or extra-firm tofu

Cornstarch, for dusting

4 ounces dried round rice stick noodles

1 cup vegetable oil, for frying, or more as needed

2 Asian eggplants, rinsed and thinly sliced on diagonal

2 tablespoons tamari soy sauce

8 tablespoons Thai sweet chili sauce or other Asian sweet sauce such as hoisin sauce

½ cup crushed unsalted peanuts, for garnish

4 tablespoons cilantro leaves, for garnish

1 green chili, thinly sliced, for garnish

1. Slice the tofu in half horizontally, and cut each half into triangles for total of 8 triangles. Place the tofu on several layers of paper towels, and press out excess water. Dust each piece of tofu with cornstarch, and set aside.

2. Bring a large saucepan of water to a boil, and cook the noodles for 6 to 7 minutes, or according to package directions. Remove from the heat, drain, and set aside.

3. Heat the oil in a large skillet or wok over medium heat. When hot, carefully place the tofu into the oil, taking care not to crowd the pieces. Fry 3 to 4 minutes on one side until golden, and, using tongs, turn the triangles over to brown the second side. Remove from the heat, and drain on paper towels. Repeat until all the tofu is cooked.

4. Discard all but about 1 tablespoon oil from the skillet or wok. Stir-fry the eggplant slices for 4 to 5 minutes, or until softened and slightly golden. Stir in the soy sauce, cook 30 seconds, or until the eggplant is coated with soy sauce, and remove from the heat.

5. To serve, place a portion of noodles on each individual plate, and top with the tofu triangles and eggplant slices. Garnish each with 2 tablespoons Thai sweet chili sauce, 2 tablespoons crushed peanuts, 1 tablespoon cilantro leaves and green chili slices.

PER SERVING: 520 CAL; 27G PROT; 24G FAT; 54G CARB; 0MG CHOL; 1,100MG SOD; 8G FIBER

FAVA BEAN CAKES WITH DICED RED PEPPERS AND YOGURT

SERVES 4

This simple main course pairs favorite Mediterranean flavors and ingredients. It comes together quickly and plays well with the family, yet looks dramatic enough to impress VIPs.

2 cups canned fava beans, drained and rinsed

1 large egg

1 onion, peeled and diced

1 teaspoon minced garlic

1 tablespoon olive oil plus extra oil for frying

1 tablespoon fresh lemon juice

3 tablespoons all-purpose flour

2 tablespoons chopped Italian parsley

1½ cups plain low-fat or regular yogurt, for garnish

1 red pepper, seeded and diced, for garnish

1. Put the fava beans, egg, onion, garlic, 1 tablespoon olive oil, lemon juice, flour and 1 tablespoon parsley in a food processor or blender, and process until coarsely chopped and well combined.

2. Heat 2 to 3 tablespoons oil in a large skillet over medium heat. When hot, scoop ¼ cup bean mixture into oil, and repeat until the skillet is full. Cook for 2 to 3 minutes on one side, and, when firm and slightly brown, turn over to cook the other side. Carefully remove from the skillet and place on the plates. Repeat with the remaining bean mixture until the mixture is used up.

3. To serve, spoon generous scoops of the yogurt over each serving, and sprinkle with parsley and diced red pepper. Serve immediately.

PER SERVING: 250 CAL; 12G PROT; 11G FAT; 26G CARB; 60MG CHOL; 120MG SOD; 5G FIBER

VEGETARIAN MA PO TOFU

*Stories about the origins of this tofu extravaganza are colorful, and they attribute the dish's creation to a pockmarked old woman (*ma po*) during the Qing Dynasty in Sichuan Province, China. Whatever its true origins, this feisty bean curd dish has countless variations, including this version, which calls for plentiful scallions that add crunch, flavor and color to the dish. If you prefer less ginger, be sure to reduce the amount called for here.*

1 pound firm tofu

2 to 3 tablespoons vegetable oil

1 tablespoon minced fresh ginger, or to taste

1 tablespoon minced garlic, or to taste

8 ounces soy-flavored wheat gluten, cubed

2 cups shredded Chinese broccoli leaves and stems

1 tablespoon Asian chili sauce

2 tablespoons black bean garlic sauce

1 to 2 tablespoons soy sauce

Pinch sugar

2 bunches scallions, cut into 1-inch-long pieces

1 tablespoon cornstarch mixed with 2 tablespoons water

1 cup mushroom or Vegetable Stock (page 332)

1. Drain the tofu, and press out the excess moisture between 2 layers of paper towels. Cut the tofu into cubes, and set aside.

2. Heat a large wok or skillet over medium heat, and add 2 tablespoons oil. Add the ginger and garlic, and stir-fry for 30 seconds. Add the wheat gluten, and continue cooking for 2 to 3 minutes, adding more oil as needed.

3. Add the Chinese broccoli, chili sauce, garlic sauce, soy sauce and pinch sugar, stir-frying for 2 to 3 minutes. Add the scallions. Combine the cornstarch mixture with the mushroom or vegetable stock, and pour into the wok, stir-frying for 2 minutes more. Remove from the heat, adjust seasonings and serve.

PER SERVING: 200 CAL; 36G PROT; 14G FAT; 19G CARB; 0MG CHOL; 1,040MG SOD; 4G FIBER

MOUNDED PORTOBELLO MUSHROOMS

These mushroom caps heaped high with a savory filling are substantial enough for a main course. You may want to begin with a light, vegetable-based soup such as the Spinach and Pea Soup (page 303), and end with an apple dessert such as the Apple-Cinnamon Strudel (page 403) or tart topped with ice cream and a rich caramel sauce.

2 jumbo portobello mushroom caps, about 6 ounces each

1 tablespoon vegetable oil plus extra for brushing

½ cup uncooked orzo

½ zucchini, diced

½ red bell pepper, seeded and diced

4 ounces crumbled feta cheese

2 tablespoons pumpkin seeds, toasted

Flat-leaf parsley leaves, for garnish

1. Preheat the oven to 450F.

2. Wipe the mushroom caps clean, remove the stem ends, and, using a spoon, scrape out the black gills from the underside. Brush the caps lightly with the oil, and place on a baking sheet, cap side down. Roast in the oven for 10 to 15 minutes.

3. Meanwhile, bring a saucepan of lightly salted water to a boil, and add the orzo. Cook for 5 to 6 minutes, or until tender. Drain, and set aside.

4. Heat the oil in a large skillet over medium heat. When hot, sauté the zucchini and red pepper for 4 to 5 minutes, or until softened. Remove the mushroom caps from the oven, and carefully pour the accumulated juices from the centers of the caps into skillet. Set the caps aside.

5. Add the cheese, pumpkin seeds and orzo to the zucchini mixture. Sauté for 2 to 3 minutes. Remove from the heat, and scoop mixture into the caps, dividing evenly. Garnish, and serve while hot.

PER SERVING: 540 CAL; 19G PROT; 31G FAT; 46G CARB; 50MG CHOL; 650MG SOD; 5G FIBER

A robust meal that can become as incendiary as you choose, this chili calls for a trip to your supermarket's salad bar where you can choose a variety of fixings as garnishes, making this dish two meals in one: a salad and a bowl of beans. The chili is delicious served hot, but even cold as a midnight snack, the dish is very pleasing. Because the meal is so substantial, you may want to keep dessert light and with a Tex-Mex flavor, serving, for example, a custard flan. But if calories are not a concern, try sopaipillas or cajeta, or caramelized milk, which are easy to make at home. Of course, the best beverage for this meal is a well-chilled Mexican beer or perhaps a heady, frothy margarita.

1 tablespoon vegetable oil

1 onion, peeled and diced

1 12-ounce package taco-flavored ground soy "meat"

1¾ cups black beans

1¾ cups white beans

1¾ cups kidney beans

2 cups chopped roasted tomatoes with can juice

1 teaspoon canned chipotles in adobo sauce, puréed with sauce, or to taste

1 jalapeño chile, seeded and diced, or to taste

1 teaspoon chili powder, or to taste

Salt and freshly ground black pepper

6 cups salad bar fixings such as sliced radishes, shredded cheese, olives, sliced celery, shredded carrots, sliced scallions, sliced onions, thinly sliced red or green bell peppers, cubed tofu, cauliflower florets, nuts, corn kernels and green peas

1. Heat the oil in a large skillet over medium heat. When hot, sauté the onion and "meat" for about 7 minutes, or until the "meat" browns slightly.

2. Meanwhile, combine the beans and tomatoes in a large saucepan, and heat over medium heat. Stir in the chipotles, jalapeño chile and chili powder to taste. Season with the salt and pepper. Cook until the mixture begins to boil. Stir in the "meat" and onions. Remove from the heat, and set aside.

3. To serve, arrange the salad bar fixings in separate serving dishes, spoon about 1 cup chili into individual bowls and top with 1 cup fixings, as desired.

PER SERVING: 320 CAL; 25G PROT; 3G FAT; 50G CARB; 0MG CHOL; 430MG SOD; 20G FIBER

Become Your Own Fast-Food Cook

It's easy to become a fast-food cook (and we don't mean at a restaurant chain!). To plan fast meals without shorting your nutritional intake or without slighting flavors, take a long, hard look at your pantry. Stock up on the quick-cooking versions of barley, oats, brown rice, cornmeal, couscous and other grains. Select canned goods such as varieties of beans, roasted red peppers, salsas, and vegetables, and choose your favorite brands of dry pasta and canned pasta sauces. Supply your freezer with extra whole grain breads, whole wheat tortillas and cartons of frozen vegetables. Keep your spice shelf and condiments current, and before you head to the market for your weekly trip, check that you have ample eggs, milk and soymilk, soy food products, and cheeses and other dairy products that can become the mainstays of any snappy vegetarian meal. It sounds so effortless, but how many cooks follow these rules? Are you one of them?

HUNAN-STYLE ORANGE "BEEF" AND ASPARAGUS STIR-FRY   SERVES 4

A popular dish at many Chinese restaurants, this sometimes-fiery entrée can easily be replicated at home, minus the beef and, if you like, minus the chiles. This entrée with the "beef" and asparagus makes a complete meal, but you could start with a Chinese-style cream of corn soup and end with a light fruit-based dessert or sorbet served with fortune cookies. What to drink? Try hot jasmine tea or an ice-cold Chinese beer.

8 ounces Asian dried wheat or rice noodles

12 ounces soy "steak" strips

5 tablespoons cornstarch

¼ cup low-sodium soy sauce

2 teaspoons minced garlic

2 tablespoons granulated sugar, or to taste

1½ cups vegetable stock

2 teaspoons sesame oil

2 teaspoons minced ginger

2 tablespoons vegetable oil, or more as needed

1 pound asparagus, trimmed and cut into 2-inch lengths

3 dried red chilies, optional

Grated zest 1 large orange

1 bunch scallions, trimmed and cut into 2-inch lengths

1. Cook the noodles according to package directions, or until tender, for about 8 minutes. Drain, rinse and drain again. Set aside. Toss the "steak" with 3 tablespoons cornstarch. Set aside.

2. Meanwhile, mix together the soy sauce, garlic, sugar, vegetable stock, sesame oil, remaining cornstarch and ginger. Set aside.

3. Heat 2 tablespoons oil in a large skillet or wok over medium-high heat. When hot, stir-fry the "steak" strips for about 2 minutes. Add, and stir-fry the asparagus and chilies, if using, for 30 seconds.

4. Add the soy sauce mixture all at once, and continue cooking until the sauce thickens and the asparagus turns shiny and tender. Return the "steak" to the pan, add the orange zest and stir-fry for 2 to 3 minutes more. Remove from the heat.

5. Arrange the noodles in serving bowl or on platter, and top with the stir-fry. Garnish with the sliced scallions, and serve.

PER SERVING: 370 CAL; 16G PROT; 7G FAT; 62G CARB; 0MG CHOL; 1,010MG SOD; 7G FIBER

CAJUN-STYLE RICE   SERVES 6

Inspired by Louisiana's popular Cajun dish of "dirty" rice, this variation has all the potency and flavor you could expect but omits the pork and the chicken livers, which traditionally give the dish its characteristic color. Perfect accompaniments are hot cornbread and baked pears; minted iced tea or lemonade balances the flavors.

2 cups Vegetable Stock (page 332)

1 cup quick-cooking rice

2 tablespoons olive oil, or more as needed

1 large onion, chopped

2 red bell peppers, seeded and cubed

1 cup cubed celery

5 ounces soy "bacon," diced

9 ounces soy "meatballs"

Cajun or Creole seasoning mixture to taste

Hot pepper sauce to taste

Salt and freshly ground black pepper to taste

1. Pour the Vegetable Stock into a large saucepan, and bring to a boil over medium heat. Add the rice, reduce the heat to low and cook according to the package directions.

2. Meanwhile, heat the oil in a large skillet over medium heat, and sauté the onion, peppers and celery for 7 to 10 minutes, or until wilted, fragrant and slightly golden. Remove from the skillet, and set aside. With the oil remaining in skillet, cook the "bacon" and the "meatballs," adding more oil as needed. Sauté for 5 or 6 minutes, and remove from the heat.

3. When the rice is cooked and all the liquid is absorbed, add the vegetables, "bacon," "meatballs," Cajun seasoning, hot pepper sauce, salt and pepper to the rice, stirring until well combined. Continue to cook for 5 minutes more, and serve.

PER SERVING: 250 CAL; 16G PROT; 8G FAT; 29G CARB; 0MG CHOL; 770MG SOD; 4G FIBER

"BEEF" STROGANOFF

Use either steamed rice or noodles as the base for the stroganoff, and offer steamed asparagus or sautéed green beans as an accompaniment. This recipe doubles easily, making it a natural when company's coming. A fancy dessert such as the Chocolate Ricotta Cream (page 415) makes a fine conclusion.

1 tablespoon vegetable oil

6 ounces sliced mushrooms

6 ounces soy "steak" slices

1 cup nonfat sour cream

¼ cup dry sherry

½ teaspoon onion powder

1 cup Vegetable Stock (page 332)

1 tablespoon cornstarch

1 tablespoon tomato paste

Salt and freshly ground black pepper to taste

1. Heat the oil in a large skillet over medium heat. Sauté the mushrooms and soy "steak" slices until browned, stirring often to prevent sticking. Reduce the heat to medium-low.

2. Combine the sour cream, sherry, onion powder and ¾ cup vegetable stock, and stir into the "beef" mixture. Stir the remaining stock with the cornstarch and tomato paste until smooth, and add to the skillet, stirring to combine. Season with the salt and pepper, and continue cooking until the mixture thickens slightly, for about 5 minutes. Remove from the heat, and serve.

PER SERVING: 150 CAL; 9G PROT; 3.5G FAT; 16G CARB; 10MG CHOL; 480MG SOD; 3G FIBER

CURRIED APPLES AND "CHICKEN"

A hint of India peeks through in this hearty apple-and-"chicken" dish, spiked with lashes of hot—or mild— curry powder. Serve over Indian basmati rice, and pass with yogurt and flat Indian bread.

2 tablespoons vegetable oil

1½ teaspoons ground turmeric

2 teaspoons hot or mild curry powder, or to taste

1 onion, chopped

1 tablespoon grated fresh ginger

¾ cup apple juice or apple cider

2 tablespoons cornstarch

1 6-ounce package "chicken" strips

8 ounces sliced mushrooms

1 apple, cored and diced, skin on

2 cups cooked basmati rice, optional

½ cup dry-roasted peanuts for garnish

1. Heat the oil in a large skillet over medium heat, and stir in the turmeric and curry powder. Sauté for 2 to 3 minutes. Stir in the onions and ginger, and cook for 5 minutes more.

2. Pour ¼ cup apple juice into a small bowl, and whisk in the cornstarch. Pour the mixture and apple juice into the skillet, and add the "chicken" strips, mushrooms and apple. Cook until the mixture thickens slightly, for 7 to 10 minutes.

3. To serve, remove from the heat, and spoon over rice, if using. Sprinkle with the peanuts as garnish.

PER SERVING: 310 CAL; 14G PROT; 18G FAT; 30G CARB; 0MG CHOL; 240MG SOD; 7G FIBER

FRIED CHICKPEAS

A slightly fiery main course, these chickpeas are readied within minutes and are delicious served with Raita, page 144.

About 4½ cups canned chickpeas, ½ cup liquid reserved

2 tablespoons vegetable oil

3 tablespoons grated fresh ginger

2 fresh green chilies or to taste

1 large ripe tomato, cubed

1 teaspoon curry powder or to taste

1 teaspoon ground coriander

4 teaspoons ground cumin

1 teaspoon ground turmeric

1 teaspoon ground cayenne

Salt to taste

Cilantro leaves for garnish, optional

1. Drain the liquid from the chickpeas, and set it aside. Heat the oil in a large skillet over medium heat. Add the chickpeas, ginger and chilies, and stir-fry until the chickpeas start to brown, for about 8 minutes. Add the tomatoes, and continue cooking until the tomato becomes soft, for about 5 minutes more.

2. Meanwhile, combine the curry powder, coriander, cumin, turmeric and cayenne with the reserved chickpea liquid, and stir well. Add to the mixture in the skillet, stirring well. Season with salt, and cook for about 5 minutes more. Serve hot.

PER SERVING: 230 CAL; 10G PROT; 7G FAT; 31G CARB; 0MG CHOL; 580MG SOD; 9G FIBER

MANGO AND SNOW PEA STIR-FRY

Always adaptable, a fresh mango turns up here as a sweet accent in this savory stir-fry main course. If you are a mango fanatic, increase the number of mango cubes to suit your taste—and passion.

1 tablespoon vegetable oil

1 teaspoon garlic

8 ounces teriyaki-seasoned baked tofu, cubed

8 ounces snow peas, trimmed

8 ounces bean sprouts, rinsed

2 mangoes, peeled, seeded and cubed

¾ cup mango juice

1 tablespoon soy sauce, or to taste

1 teaspoon sesame oil

1 tablespoon cornstarch mixed with 1 tablespoon water

3 ounces bean thread noodles, soaked in boiling water for 20 minutes

1. Heat the wok over medium-high heat. When hot, add the oil. Add the garlic, stir-fry for 30 seconds and add the tofu cubes. Stir-fry for 1 minute, and add the snow peas, bean sprouts and flesh from one mango. Continue cooking for 2 to 4 minutes more.

2. Mix the mango juice with the soy sauce, sesame oil and cornstarch mixture, and stir into the wok. Cover the wok, and cook for 3 to 4 minutes more.

3. Drain the noodles. Remove the cover, and stir in the noodles. Cook for 2 to 3 minutes, or until the sauce thickens. Remove from the heat, and place on a serving platter or individual plates. Garnish with the remaining mango cubes, and serve.

PER SERVING: 390 CAL; 20G PROT; 13G FAT; 38G CARB; 0MG CHOL; 520MG SOD; 6G FIBER

NAPA CABBAGE ROLLS

A hearty family dish, these East-Meets-West cabbage rolls come together very quickly and are ideal for cool-weather meals. Offer a piping hot soup to start, and conclude with fresh fruit and cheese.

8 large, unblemished outer leaves Chinese cabbage (napa), rinsed

2 tablespoons vegetable oil

8 ounces thinly sliced mushrooms

1½ cups (about ½ pound) diced eggplant

12 ounces unseasoned ground soy "meat"

2 teaspoons minced garlic

2 teaspoons dried oregano

Salt and freshly ground black pepper to taste

2 cups pasta sauce

1 cup grated low-fat mozzarella cheese

1. Preheat the oven to 425F. Spray a 9 x 12–inch baking dish with nonstick cooking spray.

2. To prepare the cabbage leaves, cut out and discard the triangular wedge at the tough stem end of each leaf, and set aside. Heat a large saucepan of water.

3. Heat the oil in a large skillet over medium heat, and sauté the mushrooms, eggplant, soy "meat," garlic, oregano, salt and pepper for 7 to 10 minutes, or until the mushrooms and eggplant are tender. Stir in 1 cup pasta sauce, and reduce the heat to medium-low.

4. Place the cabbage leaves in boiling water for 2 minutes, or until slightly softened. Using tongs, remove 1 leaf from the water, and place the outer side down in a baking dish. Spoon about ⅓ cup "meat" mixture onto the upper portion of the leaf, and roll the leaf tightly over the filling. Place it seam-side down in the baking dish. Repeat with the remaining ingredients until all the leaves are filled. Spoon the remaining "meat" mixture and pasta sauce over the leaves, and sprinkle with the cheese.

5. Bake for 10 to 12 minutes, or until the cheese has melted. Remove from the oven, and serve.

PER SERVING: 350 CAL; 32G PROT; 13G FAT; 27G CARB; 10MG CHOL; 1,180MG SOD; 9G FIBER

SWEET-AND-SOUR STIR-FRY

This dish combines the classic and much-loved sweet-sour flavors of China. Delicious served on its own, this generously portioned stir-fry also works well as a topping for Asian rice or egg noodles. Accompany this with vegetarian dumplings or the Pot Stickers (page 66) and finish with a delicate fruit sorbet.

½ cup pineapple juice

¼ cup white vinegar

4 tablespoons low-sodium soy sauce

3 tablespoons granulated sugar

2 tablespoons cornstarch

2 tablespoons vegetable oil

1 cup cashews

½ pound extra-firm tofu, cubed

3½ cups fresh pineapple cubes (1 medium-sized pineapple)

½ pound snow peas, trimmed

1 red bell pepper, cut into long, thin strips

2 teaspoons minced garlic

1 tablespoon minced fresh ginger

1. Combine the pineapple juice, vinegar, soy sauce, sugar and cornstarch, and mix well. Heat the mixture in a small saucepan until slightly thick, and set aside.

2. Heat the oil in a large wok over medium heat, and, when hot, add the cashews, and stir-fry for 1 minute. Remove from the heat, and set aside. Add the tofu, pineapple cubes and snow peas, and stir-fry for 1 minute. Add the red bell pepper, garlic and ginger, and stir-fry for 1 minute. Add the sweet-and-sour sauce, stirring to mix well, and stir-fry for 2 minutes more.

3. Remove from the heat, and serve alone or over rice or noodles.

PER SERVING: 620 CAL; 16G PROT; 17G FAT; 106G CARB; 0MG CHOL; 890MG SOD; 8G FIBER

VEGGIE KABOBS ON COUSCOUS

SERVES 2

Warmer days mean outdoor grilling, though this entrée cooks just as well under your broiler or on a stovetop grill. If you want to use charcoal, be sure to light the coals at least half an hour before cooking time. Use metal skewers because bamboo skewers tend to char over hot coals or under the broiler. This recipe provides a guide, but you can vary your grilling selection and the amount of teriyaki marinade to suit your taste— you can also increase the amount of vegetables and quick-cooking couscous to serve more people. Look for a teriyaki marinade in the Asian foods section of your market. Serve the kabobs with a tossed green salad and something light for dessert such as a fruit sorbet.

1 cup quick-cooking couscous
4 ounces teriyaki-flavored baked tofu
8 large white mushrooms, stems on
1 zucchini, cut into wedges
10 cherry tomatoes
4 vegetarian "meatballs"
Teriyaki marinade to taste

Special equipment:
4 10- to 12-inch-long metal skewers

1. Bring a pot with 1½ cups water to a boil over medium heat, and stir in the couscous. Cook according to the package directions. Remove from the heat, and set aside.

2. Preheat the broiler or indoor grill, or, if using an outdoor grill, light a charcoal fire, if using, about 30 minutes before serving.

3. Cut the tofu into 4 large pieces. Start threading the ingredients on the skewers, beginning with a mushroom, cap side first. Alternate the tofu, zucchini wedge and tomato, ending with a mushroom, stem end first. Repeat with the second skewer. For the remaining skewers, use "meatballs" instead of tofu. Place the filled skewers on a baking sheet, and drizzle with teriyaki marinade to taste.

4. Broil or grill the skewers, turning after the first 5 minutes of cooking, and drizzle with additional teriyaki sauce. Cook for about 5 minutes more, or until the mushrooms are tender. Remove from the heat.

5. To serve, spoon the couscous on individual plates, and top with 2 skewers per serving.

PER SERVING: 590 CAL; 39G PROT; 12G FAT; 87G CARB; 0MG CHOL; 500MG SOD; 10G FIBER

POLENTA CAKES WITH ARTICHOKE HEARTS

SERVES 3

Plastic-wrapped tubes of precooked polenta help get this dinner on the table fast. If your salad bar does not offer an antipasto-like salad, look for jars of Italian pickled vegetables. Start with minestrone soup or the Roasted Pepper and Tomato Soup (page 312), and end with scoops of orange sherbet topped with hot fudge.

2 tablespoons olive oil, or more as needed
1 large leek, thinly sliced
About 2 cups water-packed artichoke hearts, squeezed dry
8 ounces antipasto or mixed olive salad
6 2-ounce slices polenta
3 tablespoons grated Parmesan cheese
1 tablespoon capers, drained

1. Heat 1 tablespoon oil in a large skillet over medium heat, and sauté the leek for 5 minutes. Add the artichoke hearts, and continue sautéing for 3 minutes more. Add the antipasto, and sauté until heated through. Remove from the skillet, and set aside.

2. Heat the remaining 1 tablespoon oil over medium heat, and pan-fry the polenta slices until golden on both sides, adding more oil if needed. Remove from the skillet, put on serving plates and top with equal portions of the sautéed vegetables. Sprinkle each serving with the Parmesan cheese and capers, and serve.

PER SERVING: 470 CAL; 13G PROT; 11G FAT; 82G CARB; 5MG CHOL; 1,270MG SOD; 13G FIBER

MUSHROOM-CHARD CRÊPES

Prepackaged, ready-to-use crêpe shells open up vistas for savvy home cooks expanding their repertoires. These crêpe shells are fragile, so plan on eating them right away.

Crêpes

2 tablespoons olive oil

8 ounces mushrooms

2 tomatoes, chopped

1 bunch chard, rinsed and thinly sliced crosswise

¾ cup white wine

8 ounces shredded soy cheese

1 tablespoon dried onion flakes

6 9-inch crêpe shells

3 tablespoons chopped parsley for garnish

Sauce

2 tablespoons unsalted butter or soy margarine

2 tablespoons flour

½ cup white wine

½ cup sliced mushrooms

½ cup soymilk or whole milk, or more as needed

1 cup soy cheese

1. To make the Crêpes: Heat the oil in a large skillet over medium heat. Sauté the mushrooms, 1 chopped tomato and chard for about 1 minute, or until the chard wilts slightly. Add the wine, soy cheese and onion flakes, and continue cooking until the cheese melts throughout, for about 5 minutes. Remove from the heat, and set aside.

2. Place one crêpe shell on a flat work surface, and spoon the filling onto the lower third of the shell. Roll the shell up to enclose the filling, and carefully place the crêpe on an individual serving plate. Repeat the procedure until all the shells and filling are used up.

3. To make the Sauce: Heat the butter or margarine and flour in a saucepan over medium heat, stirring constantly for 2 to 3 minutes. Stir in the wine, mushrooms, soymilk and soy cheese, and cook, stirring often, until the mixture thickens, for about 5 minutes.

4. To serve, spoon the sauce evenly over the crêpes, and garnish with the chopped parsley.

PER SERVING: 690 CAL; 40G PROT; 35G FAT; 40G CARB; 20MG CHOL; 1,870MG SOD; 4G FIBER

WILD RICE HASH

In the food world, a "hash" usually means a dish of chopped-up meat and vegetables often served with a gravy or, less often, a splash of ketchup, and a serving is often topped with a poached egg. This vegetarian version gets its texture and flavor from precooked wild rice—sold vacuum-packed at specialty food stores and some supermarkets—ground soy "meat," grated soy cheese and diced fresh veggies. This makes a substantial meal, so keep dessert light—perhaps just a lime or orange sherbet with vanilla cookies.

2 tablespoons olive oil

1 large onion, diced

12 ounces ground soy "meat"

4 ounces chopped celery

4 ounces mushrooms, diced

1 cup artichoke hearts, well drained and chopped

8 ounces precooked wild rice

Salt and freshly ground black pepper to taste

Dashes hot pepper sauce to taste, optional

8 ounces shredded soy cheese, preferably mozzarella flavor

1. Heat the oil in a large skillet, and sauté the onion for about 5 minutes, or until it turns golden. Add the ground soy "meat," celery, mushrooms and artichoke hearts, and sauté for another 5 minutes.

2. Stir in the wild rice, and cook for 2 to 3 minutes, or until the rice is thoroughly heated. Add the salt and pepper, hot pepper sauce if using, and soy cheese, and cook, stirring, for about 2 minutes, or until the cheese melts. Remove from the heat, and serve.

PER SERVING: 180 CAL; 16G PROT; 6G FAT; 15G CARB; 0MG CHOL; 480MG SOD; 3G FIBER

BAKED BEANS

This hearty meal is pure comfort food, and it comes together in minutes when using canned beans. Best of all, its robust flavors will please every family member, especially when highlighted with a dollop of barbecue sauce or a spicy tomato sauce. Offer a tossed green salad as an accompaniment, and end the meal with chocolate chip cookies and ice cream.

1 cup sliced mushrooms

½ cup seasoned breadcrumbs

About 2 cups cooked navy beans

½ bunch (about ½ pound) spinach, rinsed and julienned

½ red onion, diced

2 cups shredded low-fat cheddar cheese

1 teaspoon Cajun seasoning or similar spicy seasoning, or to taste

5 tablespoons soy "bacon" bits

4 tablespoons grated Parmesan cheese

½ cup chopped flat-leaf parsley for garnish

1. Preheat the oven to 400F. Spray a 2-quart baking dish with nonstick cooking spray, and set aside.

2. Layer the sliced mushrooms on the bottom of the dish, and sprinkle with the breadcrumbs to form a crust. Stir together the beans, spinach, onion, cheddar and seasoning in a large mixing bowl. Spoon into the baking dish. Combine "bacon" bits and Parmesan cheese, and sprinkle over top.

3. Bake the beans for 20 minutes, remove from the oven, garnish with the parsley and serve.

PER SERVING: 400 CAL; 34G PROT; 10G FAT; 46G CARB; 15MG CHOL; 1,850MG SOD; 11G FIBER

SHAPED PASTA WITH GREENS, ARTICHOKE HEARTS, PORTOBELLO MUSHROOMS AND GORGONZOLA CHEESE

SERVES 4

Using an interesting pasta shape enhances the appeal of this robust, cheese-enriched main course.

8 ounces dried shaped pasta, such as campanelle or fusilli

2 tablespoons olive oil, or more as needed

1 to 2 teaspoons minced garlic

8 ounces sliced portobello mushrooms

1 bunch greens, such as broccoli rabe, chard or spinach, rinsed and trimmed

2 tablespoons balsamic vinegar

4 ounces Gorgonzola cheese, or to taste, crumbled

1¾ cups artichoke hearts

Crushed red pepper to taste, optional

1. Heat a pot of lightly salted water over medium heat, and when it is boiling, cook the pasta according to package directions. Drain, rinsing the pasta under cold water.

2. Meanwhile, heat 2 tablespoons oil in a large skillet over medium heat. When hot, sauté the garlic and portobello mushroom slices for 2 to 3 minutes. Turn the slices over, and continue cooking until softened. Add more oil, as needed

3. Slice the trimmed greens crosswise into 1-inch-wide pieces. Add half of the bunch to the skillet. When it cooks down, add the remaining greens and balsamic vinegar, stirring often.

4. Add the pasta, crumbled Gorgonzola cheese and artichoke hearts, and continue stirring until the cheese melts. Remove from the heat, season with the crushed red pepper , if desired, and serve.

PER SERVING: 440 CAL; 18G PROT; 16G FAT; 56G CARB; 30MG CHOL; 620MG SOD; 4G FIBER

CORN AND TOMATOES TART

SERVES 6

This festive main-course tart celebrates summer's bounty by showcasing two summertime favorites: fresh corn and vine-ripened tomatoes. When still hot from the oven, the filling is soft and custardy, but firms slightly after cooling. For extra Mexican-style flair, enrich the filling with sliced black olives and sliced scallions, garnish the tart with avocado slices, and pass heated corn or flour tortillas and a side dish of spiced black beans or frijoles refritos. For a South-of-the-Border beverage, try chilled Mexican beer. Select something light such as meringues or sliced seasonal fresh fruit for dessert.

2 large eggs

2 cups shredded low-fat cheddar cheese, or mixture of cheddar and low-fat mozzarella

1 cup corn kernels, preferably fresh

4 ounces diced mild green chiles

1 teaspoon chili powder

1 teaspoon ground cumin

1 unbaked 9-inch pie shell

2 ripe tomatoes, thinly sliced

¼ cup chopped cilantro for garnish

1 cup salsa for garnish, optional

1. Preheat the oven to 450F.

2. Combine the eggs, cheese, corn kernels, chiles, chili powder and cumin in a mixing bowl, and beat to mix well. Pour into the pie shell, smoothing the top of the filling.

3. Bake for 25 minutes, or until the center is firm. Remove from the oven, place sliced tomatoes on top, sprinkle with cilantro and serve. Pass the portions with salsa of your preference, if desired.

PER SERVING: 250 CAL; 14G PROT; 12G FAT; 23G CARB; 80MG CHOL; 590MG SOD; 3G FIBER

FOUR-BEAN BAKE

An inexpensive way to fuel up on zesty beans with Southwestern flavors, this dish works equally well heated on the stove, with the cheese swirled throughout as it melts. A complete meal, especially when served with tortillas and a side of sliced tomatoes, this dish calls only for herbal tea and a fruit sorbet such as the Apricot Almond Sorbet (page 388) for dessert.

2 tablespoons vegetable oil

1 large onion, diced

1 9-ounce package soy "meatballs"

1 cup kidney beans, drained and rinsed

1 cup navy beans, drained and rinsed

1 cup garbanzo beans, drained and rinsed

1 cup black beans, drained and rinsed

2 cups chunky salsa

1 teaspoon chili powder, or to taste

Salt and freshly ground black pepper to taste

1 8½-ounce package shredded soy cheese

1 cup (about 4 ounces) crushed taco chips

1 large avocado, diced, for garnish

1. Preheat the oven to 425F.

2. Heat the oil in a large skillet over medium heat. Sauté the onion until translucent, for about 5 minutes. Add the "meatballs," and sauté for 2 to 3 minutes more. Remove from the heat, and set aside.

3. Combine the beans in a 2-quart baking dish. Stir in 1 cup salsa, chili powder, salt and pepper. Stir in the onions and "meatballs," and top with the shredded cheese.

4. Bake for 10 to 12 minutes, or until the mixture is heated through. Remove from the oven, spoon the remaining 1 cup salsa over the cheese, sprinkle the crushed taco chips on the salsa and garnish with the diced avocado.

PER SERVING: 520 CAL; 26G PROT; 19G FAT; 62G CARB; 0MG CHOL; 1,160MG SOD; 15G FIBER

CHEESE RAVIOLI WITH GRAPE TOMATOES

A cheerful pasta dish, this entrée builds on several basic ingredients for a quick-cook meal. Serve this with a tossed green salad, the Low-Calorie Black and White Brownies (page 132) or blondies and fruit juice.

9 ounces fresh cheese-filled ravioli

2 tablespoons olive oil

1 bunch spinach, rinsed and stemmed

2 cups grape or cherry tomatoes

1 tablespoon onion powder

Salt and freshly ground black pepper to taste

4 tablespoons grated Parmesan cheese

1. Bring a large pot of lightly salted water to a boil over medium-high heat, and cook the ravioli according to package directions. Remove from the heat, drain and set aside.

2. Heat the oil in a large skillet over medium heat, and add the spinach, grape tomatoes, onion powder, salt and pepper, and sauté until the spinach and grape tomatoes wilt, for 5 to 7 minutes. Stir in the ravioli, and cook for 2 to 3 minutes more. Remove from the heat.

3. To serve, spoon equal portions onto individual plates, and sprinkle with the Parmesan cheese.

PER SERVING: 270 CAL; 12G PROT; 13G FAT; 28G CARB; 30MG CHOL; 260MG SOD; 5G FIBER

SOBA NOODLES WITH ZUCCHINI RIBBONS

Paring zucchini carefully produces a ribbonlike effect that beautifies the dish. This Asian treat is both colorful and flavorful, and it calls for fresh mangoes or papayas for dessert.

4 ounces soba noodles

1 large zucchini

3 tablespoons low-sodium soy sauce, or to taste

3 tablespoons mirin, or to taste

1 teaspoon cornstarch

1 tablespoon vegetable oil

1 tablespoon minced garlic

1 cup fresh shelled edamame

1 cup sliced mushrooms

1 bunch thinly sliced scallions for garnish

1. Heat a pot of lightly salted water over medium heat, and when it is boiling, cook the pasta according to package directions. Drain, rinsing the pasta under cold water.

2. Use a sharp vegetable peeler, and carefully slice the zucchini into long, thin strips. Set aside. Combine the soy sauce, mirin and cornstarch in a bowl, and set aside.

3. Heat the oil in a large skillet or wok over medium-high heat. Stir-fry the garlic for 30 seconds, and add the edamame, mushrooms, zucchini and soy mixture, and stir-fry for about 30 seconds more, or until the vegetables are heated through. Remove from the heat.

4. To serve, put equal portions of the noodles in individual bowls or on plates, and spoon the vegetables and sauce over top. Garnish with scallions, and serve.

PER SERVING: 330 CAL; 20G PROT; 12G FAT; 64G CARB; 0MG CHOL; 680MG SOD; 9G FIBER

PEPPERS GALORE

This colorful sauté is so versatile that it works well as a light main course or as a side dish, depending on your menu. And depending on your tolerance for heat, you can fire this up with the addition of sliced jalapeño chiles, cherry peppers and Hungarian wax peppers—or even a few incendiary habañero chiles. Be sure to vary the color of the sweet peppers, substituting purple or white for one of the other sweet peppers, if you wish. Serve this dish with plenty of beer, and end the meal with cut-up fresh fruit.

1 1-pound package baked tofu, preferably Italian-flavored

2 red bell peppers, stemmed, halved and seeded

1 green bell pepper, stemmed, halved and seeded

1 yellow bell pepper, stemmed, halved and seeded

1 orange bell pepper, stemmed, halved and seeded

3 tablespoons olive oil

1 teaspoon dried oregano

Jalapeños, cherry peppers and Hungarian wax peppers, thinly sliced, optional

Salt and freshly ground black pepper to taste

4 ounces crumbled Gorgonzola cheese

1. Slice the baked tofu lengthwise into 24 thin strips, and set aside. Slice the peppers lengthwise from stem to rounded end into thin strips about ½-inch wide, and set aside.

2. Heat 2 tablespoons oil in a large skillet over medium heat, and add the tofu strips and oregano and, carefully stirring, cook until the strips begin to brown, for about 5 minutes. Remove from the heat, and set aside.

3. Add about half the peppers to the skillet and, using tongs to prevent breaking strips, sauté over medium heat for about 5 minutes, or until the peppers begin to soften and the edges brown slightly. Remove from the skillet. Add the remaining oil, and add the remaining pepper strips. Cook for about 5 minutes, remove from the skillet and place on top of the tofu strips. Season with the salt and pepper, sprinkle with the Gorgonzola cheese and serve.

PER SERVING: 410 CAL; 28G PROT; 29G FAT; 14G CARB; 25MG CHOL; 720MG SOD; 4G FIBER

WARM CURRIED CHICKPEAS

Lush and redolent of the flavors of India, this quick-to-assemble dish suits a warm-weather mealtime. Offer with warmed pita or crunchy, peppery Indian pappadam bread. You may also want to make an order of the Nan with Cumin (page 136).

¾ cup light coconut milk

2 tablespoons grated or minced fresh ginger

1 teaspoon ground cumin

3 teaspoons curry powder, or to taste

1¾ cups cooked or canned chickpeas, drained and rinsed

½ cup raisins

Salt to taste

3 tablespoons chutney, or to taste

2½ to 3 ounces baby spinach

3 large hard-boiled eggs

3 scallions, thinly sliced, for garnish

1. Heat ¼ cup of the coconut milk in a large skillet, and stir in the ginger, cumin and 2 teaspoons of the curry powder, frying the paste mixture for about 5 minutes, or until very fragrant. Add the chickpeas, and sauté for 5 minutes. Add another ¼ cup of the coconut milk, the raisins and salt to taste, and cook for 5 minutes. Remove from the heat, and set aside.

2. Stir the remaining ¼ cup coconut milk with 1 tablespoon of the chutney and the remaining 1 teaspoon of curry powder. Set aside.

3. Arrange the spinach leaves on a platter or individual plates. Peel and halve the eggs. Scoop the chickpea mixture onto the spinach leaves, place the egg halves on the chickpeas and place a portion of chutney on top. Garnish with the sliced scallions, and pour the coconut milk mixture over the salad before serving.

PER SERVING: 400 CAL; 18G PROT; 13G FAT; 59G CARB; 210MG CHOL, 115MG SOD; 11G FIBER

POLENTA WITH FENNEL AND RAPINI

The ever-popular polenta gets a new twist with this easy-to-prepare dish.

1 tablespoon olive oil

6 cloves garlic, coarsely chopped

1 fennel bulb, leafy fronds trimmed and thinly sliced

2 tablespoons chopped oil-packed sun-dried tomatoes, drained

½ bunch rapini (2 cups), stem ends trimmed and leafy part thinly sliced

1½ cups Vegetable Stock (page 332)

½ cup quick-cooking yellow cornmeal

¾ cup shredded low-fat mozzarella cheese

Salt and freshly ground black pepper to taste

1. Heat the oil in a large skillet over medium heat, and sauté the garlic for 2 to 3 minutes, or until it turns golden. Add the fennel bulb and sun-dried tomatoes, and sauté mixture for 2 to 3 minutes, or until fennel softens slightly. Add the rapini, and continue sautéing for 3 minutes more.

2. Add the Vegetable Stock, and stir in the cornmeal, continuing to cook for 5 minutes more. Stir in cheese, salt and pepper, and reduce heat to low. Cook for 5 minutes more, or until the cornmeal becomes tender. Serve while hot.

PER SERVING. 200 CAL; 9G PROT; 7G FAT; 25G CARB; 10MG CHOL; 150MG SOD; 3G FIBER

CORN FOUR WAYS

Imagine the best, fresh-picked crops from a farmstand paired with polenta—and all ready for the table in minutes. This dish puts summer on the dinner plate; bolster it with a creamy tomato soup to start and a berry cobbler for dessert. That's a sure way to beat the heat.

2 tablespoons vegetable oil

1 pound tube polenta

1¾ cups hominy, drained

1¾ cups corn kernels, drained

1½ cups whole baby corn, drained

1½ tablespoons chili powder, or to taste

½ cup shredded soy cheese or low-fat mozzarella cheese

Juice of 1 lime

½ bunch cilantro, chopped, for garnish

1. Heat the oil in a large skillet over medium heat. Slice the polenta into 8 circles, and when the oil is hot, pan-fry the circles on 1 side for 3 to 4 minutes, or until browned. Turn over, and pan-fry on the second side for another 3 to 4 minutes, or until browned. Remove from the skillet, and arrange the circles side by side on individual plates.

2. Add the hominy, corn kernels and whole baby corn to the skillet. Sprinkle with the chili powder and cheese, and sauté for 2 to 3 minutes, or until heated through and the cheese has melted. Remove from the heat.

3. To serve, spoon equal amounts of the corn mixture on plates over or between the polenta circles. Sprinkle each serving with the lime juice, and garnish with the cilantro.

PER SERVING: 560 CAL; 16G PROT; 11G FAT; 106G CARB; 0MG CHOL; 670MG SOD; 14G FIBER

TEXAS TOFU

Pretend you are hunching over a campfire on the Texas plains after a hard day's ride. This robust meal will set you up for the next day with plenty of rib-sticking beans, sourdough bread and picante tofu. You can kick up the heat by garnishing the beans and tofu with sliced jalapeño chiles. And you can intensify flavors by using more chile powder and a few dashes of hot pepper sauce. Dinner is complete with apple turnovers and hot apple cider.

4 1-inch-thick slices sourdough bread

3 cups vegetarian-style baked beans

4 tablespoons vegetable oil for frying

1 onion, diced

2 teaspoons ground cumin

2 teaspoons chili powder

½ teaspoon onion powder

2 tablespoons cornstarch

1 pound firm or extra-firm tofu, cut into large cubes

4 tablespoons soy "bacon" bits

8 ounces shredded soy cheese, preferably mixture of cheddar and Monterey Jack

½ cup cilantro leaves for garnish

1. Preheat the oven to 450F. Arrange the thick slices of bread in a large baking dish, and set them aside.

2. Put the beans in a large saucepan, and heat them over medium heat, warming them through completely. When they are hot, remove them from the heat, and set them aside.

3. Heat 1 tablespoon of oil in a large skillet over medium heat, and sauté the onion until golden, for about 5 minutes. Remove the onion from the heat, and set aside.

4. Meanwhile, combine the cumin, chili powder, onion powder and cornstarch in a large bowl, mixing to combine well. Place the cubed tofu in a bowl, and dust each side with the mixture. Add the remaining oil to the skillet, and heat over medium heat. Sauté the tofu cubes on all sides until crispy, for 3 to 5 minutes. Remove them from the heat, and place them in a bowl with the onion.

5. Spoon the beans over the bread slices in equal portions, and sprinkle the "bacon" bits onto the beans. Top with the tofu and onions, and sprinkle each portion with the grated cheese.

6. Bake for about 5 minutes, or until the cheese melts. Remove them from the oven, and garnish them with cilantro leaves before serving.

PER SERVING: 710 CAL; 39G PROT; 27G FAT; 86G CARB; 0MG CHOL; 1,910MG SOD; 14G FIBER

GREEK-STYLE RICE PILAF

Using up leftover rice may ordinarily pose problems, but not when you can assemble this tasty, extra-fast, Greek-inspired dish. Start off your meal with a vegetarian version of the Greek Egg and Lemon Soup, or Avgolemono, or an appetizer of grilled Italian bread spread with a paste of sun-dried tomatoes, and conclude dinner with a serving of Greek baklava. Offer hot lemon tea with dessert.

1 tablespoon olive oil

1 onion, diced

1 teaspoon minced garlic

3 cups cold cooked rice

¼ cup water or vegetarian "chicken" stock, or more as needed

Juice of 1 lemon

2 cups fresh or frozen green peas

About 2 cups canned quartered artichoke hearts, well drained

2 teaspoons dried oregano

Salt and freshly ground black pepper to taste

2 7-inch-round pita breads, cut into sixths

4 ounces pitted kalamata olives

4 ounces crumbled feta cheese as garnish

1. Preheat the oven to broil.

2. Heat the oil in a large skillet over medium heat. Add the onion and garlic, and sauté for 2 minutes, or until the onion turns golden. Add the rice, breaking up clumps, the water and lemon juice. Stir until the grains are coated with oil. Reduce the heat to medium-low. Stir in the peas, artichoke hearts, oregano, salt and pepper, and continue cooking until the mixture is heated through.

3. Meanwhile, toast the pita pieces in the oven until crisp, for 1 to 1½ minutes, taking care not to burn them. Remove the pita from oven, and set them aside.

4. To serve, stir the olives into the rice mixture, scoop the mixture onto a serving platter or individual plates and garnish with the feta cheese. Stand 2 pita pieces, pointed ends down, in the rice just before serving.

PER SERVING: 350 CAL; 12G PROT; 12G FAT; 49G CARB; 15MG CHOL; 1,040MG SOD; 7G FIBER

BROILED EGGPLANT STEAKS WITH GORGONZOLA CHEESE   SERVES 4

Feature luscious summertime eggplants as a light main course, and dress them up with sprinkles of Gorgonzola cheese. This calls for a clear soup to start, slices of focaccia with the eggplant and a more complex fruit dessert, such as a berry compote with scoops of vanilla yogurt.

1½-pound eggplant, cut into 8 slices
4 tablespoons pesto
2 large tomatoes, chopped
4 ounces crumbled Gorgonzola cheese
4 tablespoons capers, drained
Freshly ground black pepper to taste

1. Preheat oven to broil. Line a baking dish with foil, and set aside.

2. Arrange the eggplant slices on a dish, and brush the tops with 2 tablespoons pesto. Cook until the tops begin to brown and the eggplant begins to soften. Turn over, using a spatula, and spread the remaining pesto on the second sides. Cook again for about 5 minutes more. Remove from the oven.

3. To serve, arrange the eggplant steaks on individual plates, and top each serving with equal amounts of tomatoes, Gorgonzola cheese and capers. Sprinkle with pepper.

PER SERVING: 230 CAL; 11G PROT; 16G FAT; 14G CARB; 30MG CHOL; 770MG SOD; 3G FIBER

GNOCCHI WITH ZUCCHINI SAUCE   SERVES 4

Tender potato dumplings, or gnocchi, get a special topping with this flavorful zucchini sauce.

2 large zucchini
2 large tomatoes
2 tablespoons olive oil
2 tablespoons minced garlic
1 cup marinara or tomato sauce
Juice of 1 lemon
Salt and freshly ground black pepper to taste
1 1-pound package potato gnocchi

1. Cut the zucchini into quarters lengthwise, slice quarters thinly widthwise and set aside. Dice the tomatoes, and set aside.

2. Heat the oil in a large skillet over medium heat, and add the garlic. Sauté for about 5 minutes, or until zucchini begins to brown. Increase heat to medium-high, and add tomatoes, marinara sauce, lemon juice, salt and pepper. Cook for about 8 minutes more, or until tomatoes soften. Remove from the heat.

3. Bring a large saucepan of lightly salted water to a boil over medium heat. Cook gnocchi according to package directions, or for 3 to 5 minutes. When done, gnocchi float to surface. Remove with a slotted spoon, and set aside.

4. To serve, spoon equal portions of the gnocchi onto individual plates, and top with the sauce.

PER SERVING: 300 CAL; 7G PROT; 15G FAT; 37G CARB; 20MG CHOL; 260MG SOD; 5G FIBER

WHITE BEAN SAUCE OVER TORTELLONI

This looks and tastes like an ultrarich cream-based sauce, but in reality, it's just a purée of white beans. If you have leftover sauce, refrigerate it for another use.

1 9-ounce package fresh tortelloni
1 bunch red chard, trimmed
1 19-ounce can cannelloni beans, drained and rinsed
½ cup Vegetable Stock (page 332)
1 tablespoon minced garlic
1 tablespoon fresh lemon juice
Salt and freshly ground black pepper to taste
Fresh basil for garnish
½ cup grated Parmesan cheese, garnish, optional

1. Heat a pot of lightly salted water over medium heat, and when it is boiling, cook the tortelloni according to package directions. Drain, rinsing the pasta under cold water.

2. Steam the chard in a large saucepan over medium heat with water on its leaves until it wilts. Remove from the pan with tongs, squeeze out excess moisture and set aside to drain.

3. Put the cannelloni beans, Vegetable Stock, garlic, lemon juice, salt and pepper into a food processor or blender, and purée until smooth. Heat in a large saucepan over medium heat until hot.

4. To serve, arrange the chard on individual plates as a bed for the tortelloni topped with the white bean sauce. Garnish each serving with basil and Parmesan cheese, if using.

PFR SERVING: 370 CAL; 20G PROT; 6G FAT; 62G CARB; 30MG CHOL; 810MG SOD; 10G FIBER

CHICKPEA STEW WITH FRIED POLENTA

This is a hearty peasant-style dish that calls for a strong red wine, loads of hot Italian bread and wedges of cheese. Fresh fruit makes the ideal dessert.

2 tablespoons vegetable oil
1 large onion, diced
1 tablespoon minced garlic
Salt and freshly ground black pepper to taste
2 15½-ounce cans chickpeas, drained
4 cups chunky stewed tomatoes with juice
1 1-pound tube prepared polenta, cut into 12 slices
½ cup chopped parsley
½ cup grated Parmesan cheese

1. Heat the oil in a large skillet over medium heat, and sauté the onion and garlic for 5 minutes, or until the onion starts to turn golden. Add the salt, pepper and 1 can of chickpeas, reduce the heat to medium-low and continue to cook.

2. Put the remaining 1 can of chickpeas and the tomatoes into a food processor or blender, and process until coarsely chopped. Pour into the skillet with the onion-chickpea mixture, and continue cooking.

3. Spray another skillet with nonstick cooking spray, and heat over medium heat. Pan-fry the polenta slices until they become soft and start to brown on both sides. Remove from the skillet using a spatula, cut into rough chunks and add to the stew.

4. To serve, spoon portions of stew onto individual plates, and garnish with parsley.

PER SERVING: 370 CAL; 15G PROT; 9G FAT; 60G CARB; 5MG CHOL; 1,110MG SOD; 10G FIBER

ORZO WITH "SAUSAGE"

Be creative with this dish, starting with orzo pasta but then trying another very small variety such as tiny shells. Add different peppers, perhaps a chopped onion, grated cheese or green peas. This is very adaptable to whatever suits your taste.

1 cup uncooked orzo

2 tablespoons vegetable oil

7 ounces soy breakfast "sausage"

1 bunch scallions, thinly sliced

1 red bell pepper, seeded and diced

1 green bell pepper, seeded and diced

Salt and freshly ground black pepper

1½ cups spaghetti sauce

1 teaspoon dried oregano

Pinch of sage

½ cup grated Parmesan cheese

1. Heat a pot of lightly salted water over medium heat, and when it is boiling, cook the orzo according to package directions. Drain, rinsing the pasta under cold water.

2. Heat the oil in a large skillet over medium heat. Crumble the "sausage" meat and sauté for 3 minutes, stirring often. Add the scallions, red and green bell pepper, salt and pepper, and sauté for 5 minutes, or until the peppers begin to wilt.

3. Add the spaghetti sauce, oregano, sage and orzo, and stir to combine well. Remove from the heat, and spoon onto individual plates. Sprinkle each serving with Parmesan cheese, if using.

PER SERVING: 340 CAL; 20G PROT; 7G FAT; 46G CARB; 10MG CHOL; 620MG SOD; 6G FIBER

ORZO-RICOTTA BAKE

This simple dish comes together quickly and, when served right out of the oven, provides a hearty cold-weather meal. Served at room temperature, this dish becomes a suitable spring or fall entrée. Best beverages for this would be hot mulled apple cider or a fragrant herbed tea.

1 cup uncooked orzo

1 tablespoon olive oil

8 ounces sliced mushrooms

1½ cups quartered artichoke hearts

1 tablespoon minced garlic

1½ cups shredded low-fat mozzarella cheese

1 cup low-fat ricotta cheese

1 cup Italian-seasoned breadcrumbs

1 cup chopped flat-leaf parsley

Salt and freshly ground black pepper to taste

1 teaspoon garlic powder

1. Preheat the oven to 425F. Spray a 2-quart baking dish with nonstick cooking spray.

2. Heat a pot of lightly salted water over medium heat, and when it is boiling, cook the orzo according to package directions. Drain, rinsing the pasta under cold water.

3. Heat the oil in a large skillet over medium heat. Sauté the mushrooms and artichoke hearts for 4 to 5 minutes. Add the garlic, and cook for 1 minute more. Remove from the heat, and place the vegetables in the baking dish. Stir the orzo into the mushroom mixture.

4. Meanwhile, stir together the mozzarella, ricotta, breadcrumbs and parsley. Season with salt, pepper and garlic powder. Spoon the cheese mixture over the vegetables, smoothing the top with the back of the spoon.

5. Bake about 15 minutes, or until the cheese melts and the top turns golden. Remove from the oven, and serve.

PER SERVING: 360 CAL; 21G PROT; 11G FAT; 45G CARB; 30MG CHOL; 760MG SOD; 5G FIBER

LINGUINE ONE-POT STRATA

If you cannot find fresh pasta, use dried instead, but adjust your cooking time.

9 ounces fresh linguine

2 tablespoons olive oil

1 leek, thinly sliced

6 ounces broccoli rabe, stems trimmed

2 cups quartered artichoke hearts

9 ounces vegetarian "meatballs"

2 cups pasta sauce

1 cup nonfat ricotta cheese

3 tablespoons grated Parmesan cheese

1. Preheat the oven to 450F. Spray a 2-quart baking dish with nonstick cooking spray, and set aside.

2. Heat a pot of lightly salted water over medium heat, and when it is boiling, cook the pasta according to package directions. Drain, rinsing the pasta under cold water.

3. Meanwhile, heat the oil in a large skillet over medium heat, and sauté the leek, broccoli rabe and artichoke hearts for about 4 minutes, or until softened. Remove from the heat, and set aside.

4. Line the bottom of the baking dish with half the linguine. Layer the "meatballs" on top, and spread 1 cup pasta sauce over the "meatballs." Layer the "meatballs" with sautéed vegetables.

5. Put the remaining linguine on the vegetables, and add the remaining pasta sauce. Spoon the ricotta cheese over the sauce, smoothing out to cover. Sprinkle with the Parmesan cheese.

6. Bake for 15 minutes, or until the top browns slightly. Remove from the oven, and serve.

PER SERVING: 350 CAL; 20G PROT; 8G FAT; 47G CARB; 40MG CHOL; 710MG SOD; 5G FIBER

BARLEY AND "MEATBALLS"

Quick-cooking barley is the key to success with this sturdy main course. Begin the meal with a light vegetable broth garnished with snipped chives, and serve lemon sorbet for dessert.

1 cup uncooked quick-cooking barley

2 to 3 tablespoons vegetable oil

1 13¾-ounce can roasted red peppers

9 ounces vegetarian "meatballs"

8 ounces sliced mushrooms

Salt and freshly ground black pepper to taste

½ cup snipped parsley for garnish

1. Cook the barley according to package directions.

2. Meanwhile, heat the oil in a large skillet over medium heat. Cut the peppers into long strips, and add to the skillet the "meatballs" and mushrooms. Sauté the mixture for 5 minutes, and season with the salt and pepper. Stir in the cooked barley, and sauté for 2 or 3 minutes more, adding 2 or 3 tablespoons water to prevent sticking, if needed.

3. To serve, remove from the heat, and spoon the mixture onto individual plates. Garnish each serving with parsley.

PER SERVING: 290 CAL; 16G PROT; 11G FAT; 33G CARB; 0MG CHOL; 570MG SOD; 7G FIBER

16

the young set

EVERY PARENT KNOWS THAT GETTING youngsters to eat well can be a struggle. But these tempting recipes will help solve the "what-do-we-eat" dilemma by offering children meals that are packed with flavor and color. And these dishes are not just for children alone: Parents, sit down and eat with your kids!

TROPICAL BANANA CHEESECAKES

Lure your children to the breakfast table with these tempting cupcake-sized cakes. You can serve the cakes solo or adorned with maple syrup or other fruit syrup.

8 ounces low-fat pineapple-flavored or plain cream cheese, at room temperature

1 large egg

½ cup low-fat ricotta cheese

2 tablespoons confectioners' sugar

1 teaspoon vanilla extract

½ cup graham cracker crumbs

2 bananas, quartered lengthwise and diced

1. Preheat the oven to 350F. Spray eight ½-cup sized muffin cups with nonstick cooking spray.

2. Put the cream cheese and egg into a mixing bowl and, using an electric beater, mix until well blended. Stir in the ricotta cheese, sugar and extract, and beat the mixture until smooth. Stir in the crumbs and diced bananas. Spoon the mixture into the muffin cups.

3. Bake for about 20 minutes, or until the cakes puff up and firm. Remove from the oven, and serve hot.

PER SERVING: 170 CAL; 4G PROT; 10G FAT; 17G CARB; 50MG CHOL; 140MG SOD; <1G FIBER

MOZZARELLA "MEATBALL" HEROES

Family members will enjoy these hefty heroes, ready in just minutes. Present the heroes open-faced, and eat as is or close them over to make a sandwich. To serve more than two, simply double the ingredients. If your child does not like "green things" in his food, just leave out the basil and parsley. Offer a tossed green salad, and end the meal with frozen yogurt.

2 5-ounce mini baguettes

2 teaspoons unsalted butter

1 cup shredded low-fat mozzarella cheese

10 mini vegetarian "meatballs"

1 cup spaghetti sauce

1 tablespoon minced garlic, or to taste

Salt and freshly ground black pepper

1 teaspoon dried basil

2 teaspoons minced parsley

1. Preheat the oven to broil.

2. Slice the baguettes in half lengthwise so that each opens up almost flat but is not completely separated. Hollow out the top rounded half of each roll. Butter top and bottom halves, sprinkle with ½ cup cheese each and set aside.

3. Meanwhile, spray a large skillet with nonstick cooking spray, and cook the "meatballs" over medium heat, stirring often, until they begin to brown, for 3 to 5 minutes. Add the spaghetti sauce, and reduce the heat to low.

4. Broil the mini baguettes until the cheese melts and browns, for about 3 minutes. Remove from the oven, and spoon 5 meatballs with sauce into the hollowed-out portion. Repeat with the second baguette. Sprinkle with basil and parsley, and serve.

PER SERVING: 770 CAL; 43G PROT; 21G FAT; 103G CARB; 30MG CHOL; 1,890MG SOD; 10G FIBER

BARLEY-MUSHROOM BURGERS

The batter for these "burgers" is very soft and runny, so turn the patties carefully, keeping the ingredients together. As the cheese cools, the patties firm up. Treat these luscious "burgers" to all the trimmings: coleslaw, pickles, sliced tomatoes and onions, and relish and ketchup. Add french fries and your kids will be in heaven.

½ cup uncooked quick-cooking barley

1 large egg, well beaten

1 cup low-fat ricotta cheese

1 cup shredded cheddar cheese

1 cup minced mushrooms

¼ cup minced parsley

Salt and freshly ground black pepper to taste

1. Cook the barley according to package directions, and when cooked, remove from the heat and set aside.

2. Meanwhile, combine the egg, ricotta cheese, cheddar cheese, mushrooms, parsley, breadcrumbs, salt and pepper. Stir the barley into the egg mixture.

3. Spray a large nonstick skillet or griddle with nonstick cooking spray. When it is hot, ladle about ½ cupful of mixture onto the hot skillet and cook until the bottom becomes golden. Using a spatula, turn the burger over carefully, and cook the second side until the mixture is firm and the cheese has melted. Remove from the skillet, and set aside. Repeat with the remaining mixture until it is used up.

PER SERVING: 180 CAL; 11G PROT; 9G FAT; 12G CARB; 100MG CHOL; 170MG SOD; 1G FIBER

LENTIL BURGERS

You can make these delicious, low-fat burgers from scratch in less than an hour, or enjoy them in almost no time from the freezer. Serve the burgers on buns with your favorite trimmings.

1 cup dry lentils

1 bay leaf

1 tablespoon vegetable oil

½ cup diced onion

½ cup diced celery

1 tablespoon chopped fresh tarragon

2 teaspoons chopped fresh marjoram

1 teaspoon ground cumin

½ teaspoon dark sesame oil

½ teaspoon fresh lemon juice

½ teaspoon salt

¼ teaspoon freshly ground black pepper

¾ cup rolled oats

¾ cup dry breadcrumbs

1. Cook the lentils and the bay leaf in 2½ cups water in a saucepan over medium heat until the lentil skins split easily, for about 45 minutes.

2. Meanwhile, heat the oil in a large skillet over medium heat, and sauté the onion and celery in the oil, stirring, until soft, for about 5 minutes. Remove from the heat, and stir in the remaining ingredients except the oats and breadcrumbs.

3. Preheat the oven to 400F. Spray a nonstick baking sheet with nonstick cooking spray, and set aside.

4. Process the oats in a blender or food processor until finely ground. Combine the oats and bread crumbs with the lentil mixture. Shape the mixture into 12 patties while it's still warm. You may freeze the patties at this point.

5. Bake the patties on a nonstick baking sheet until the patties are lightly browned on both sides. Remove from the oven, and serve or save for later use.

PER BURGER: 69 CAL; 3G PROT; 2G FAT; 10G CARB; 0MG CHOL; 166MG SOD; 4G FIBER

BARBECUED SEITAN BURGERS

Children can enjoy many different options on the "burger" theme, including these with hints of spicy seasonings.

12 ounces seitan

1 tablespoon olive oil

1 cup finely chopped onion

3 cloves garlic, minced

1/2 cup finely chopped green bell pepper

1/2 cup shiitake mushrooms, stemmed and finely chopped

1 teaspoon salt

1/4 teaspoon dried oregano

1/4 teaspoon dried thyme

1/4 teaspoon celery seed

1/4 teaspoon dry mustard

1/4 teaspoon ground ginger

1/8 teaspoon cayenne pepper

2 teaspoons canned chipotle chili in adobo sauce

1/2 cup whole wheat bread flour

1/4 cup yellow cornmeal

1 1/2 teaspoons medium-hot chili powder

1 teaspoon ground cumin

1/4 teaspoon freshly ground pepper

1/2 cup barbecue sauce

8 whole-grain buns, split

Avocado slices, tomato slices and mesclun for serving

1. Drain the seitan, squeeze to remove excess liquid and roughly chop for 2 cups. Put into a food processor, and pulse until broken into small pieces. Set aside.

2. Heat the oil over medium heat. Add the onion, and cook, stirring often, until softened, for about 4 minutes. Add the garlic, green pepper, mushrooms, 1/2 teaspoon salt, oregano, thyme, celery seed, mustard, ginger and cayenne. Increase the heat to medium-high, and cook, stirring often, for 5 minutes. Transfer the vegetables to a large bowl. Add the seitan pieces and chipotle, and mix well.

3. Light a charcoal fire, if using, about 30 minutes before serving. Otherwise, heat a gas grill to high at serving time.

4. Mix together the flour, cornmeal, chili powder, cumin, remaining 1/2 teaspoon salt and pepper. Gradually stir the flour mixture into the seitan mixture until well combined. Using 1/3 cup for each and packing firmly, form the mixture into 8 round patties.

5. Place the burgers on the grill, brush the tops with barbecue sauce and cook for 5 minutes. Turn the burgers, brush with more barbecue sauce and cook for about 4 minutes. Serve hot on buns with the remaining barbecue sauce, topped with avocado, tomato and mesclun.

PER BURGER: 215 CAL; 15G PROT; 4G FAT; 33G CARB; 0MG CHOL; 675MG SOD; 4G FIBER

CREAM CHEESE SANDWICHES

Combining ricotta cheese with cream cheese keeps the fat content in check in this kid-pleasing sandwich.

½ cup low-fat ricotta cheese

3 ounces light cream cheese

½ cup plain nonfat yogurt

1 clove garlic, crushed

1 tablespoon chopped fresh chives

1 tablespoon chopped fresh basil or
   1 teaspoon dried

1 tablespoon chopped fresh parsley

½ teaspoon salt

½ teaspoon fresh ground black
   pepper

8 slices whole-grain bread

Shredded lettuce

Sprouts

1 tomato, sliced

Mix together the cheese, yogurt, garlic, herbs, salt and pepper until smooth. Spread the mixture on 4 slices of bread. Top with the lettuce, sprouts, tomato and remaining bread slice.

PER SERVING: 256 CAL; 14G PROT; 8G FAT; 33G CARB; 22MG CHOL; 605MG SOD; 4G FIBER

VEGAN SUMMER SUB

Great picnic fare, this portable sandwich stuffed with veggies, soy meat and soy cheese slices makes a delectable lunch or dinner. Many supermarkets now offer already prepared hummus, so look for your favorite.

2 mini baguettes, about 5 ounces
   each

2 tablespoons soy mayonnaise

2 tablespoons Dijon mustard

2 tablespoons hummus

2 tablespoons relish

8 spinach leaves, or more as needed

4 vegetarian "turkey" slices

4 vegetarian "pastrami" slices

4 vegetarian Provolone-flavored
   cheese slices

4 thin slices red onion, cut in half

1 large tomato, thinly sliced and cut
   in half

1. Slice each baguette in half lengthwise, but do not cut entirely through the bread. Place the first baguette on foil or a dinner plate.

2. Spread one half of each baguette with mayonnaise and mustard. Spread the other half with hummus and relish. Starting with the spinach leaves, layer the ingredients in the baguette, folding the "turkey," "pastrami," and cheese slices in half. Tuck each folded slice side by side in layers. Finish with the onion and tomato slices.

3. Wrap in foil if using as picnic food, or serve immediately.

PER SERVING: 460 CAL; 23G PROT; 14G FAT; 65G CARB; 0MG CHOL; 1,390MG SOD; 7G FIBER

SLOPPY JANES

Everybody loves comfort food, and this vegetarian version of Sloppy Joes makes a casual dish suitable for lunch or dinner. Your kids will gobble these up.

4 Kaiser rolls

1 tablespoon vegetable oil, or more as needed

1 onion, diced

12 ounces soy "ground beef," crumbled

½ cup diced celery

½ cup sliced mushrooms

¾ cup barbecue sauce

¼ cup Vegetable Stock (page 332)

Dashes hot pepper sauce to taste, optional

4 ounces shredded low-fat cheddar cheese

1. Preheat the oven to 475F.

2. Slice the rolls in half, cutting off the upper third of the roll to leave the larger bottom section. Scoop out the inner portion of each bottom section, and set the tops and bottoms aside on a large baking sheet.

3. Heat the oil in a large skillet over medium heat. When hot, sauté the onion for about 5 minutes. Stir in the "ground beef," celery, mushrooms, barbecue sauce, stock and hot pepper sauce, if using. Cook over medium heat for 4 or 5 minutes, or until the mixture is heated through. Remove from the heat.

4. Spoon equal portions of the mixture into the bottom sections of the rolls. Sprinkle each filled roll with cheese, and spray the insides of the top sections of the rolls with nonstick cooking spray. Set the tops on the baking sheet, cut side up.

5. Bake the tops and bottoms for about 5 minutes, or until the tops brown and the cheese melts and spills down the sides of the rolls. Remove from the oven, and serve.

PER SERVING: 410 CAL; 32G PROT; 9G FAT; 59G CARB; 5MG CHOL; 1,240MG SOD; 7G FIBER

SOFT BLACK BEAN TACOS

Make this into a family meal with plenty of napkins and something chilled to drink, such as orange juice. Kids will enjoy making up their own tacos, and you may find they will ask for more. This makes enough for 2 tacos per person.

2 tablespoons vegetable oil

16 ounces Tex-Mex-flavored baked tofu, diced

2 cups refried vegetarian black beans

1 tablespoon taco seasoning, or to taste

½ cup green salsa

8 ounces crumbled goat cheese or 6 ounces shredded Monterrey Jack cheese

1 cup chopped cilantro leaves

1½ cups red salsa

2 cups guacamole

16 whole wheat tortillas or small soft corn tortillas

1. Heat a very large skillet, and add the oil. Sauté the tofu until browned. Remove from the heat, and put into a serving dish.

2. Put the black beans, taco seasoning and green salsa into the skillet, and heat over medium heat, stirring constantly, until heated through. Remove from the heat, and put the beans into a serving dish. Put the cheese, cilantro leaves, salsa and guacamole into separate serving containers.

3. Heat the tortillas over medium heat on a large skillet or griddle. Warm on both sides, but do not allow the tortillas to become crisp. Remove from the heat, and put onto a serving platter. Let each person make the tacos from the assorted ingredients at the table.

PER SERVING: 520 CAL; 23G PROT; 19G FAT; 61G CARB; 10MG CHOL; 1,080MG SOD; 9G FIBER

"BEEF" QUESADILLAS WITH BLACK BEANS

For snacks or a lunchbox treat, these tasty quesadillas go well with lemon yogurt, fresh fruit and lemonade.

1 tablespoon vegetable oil

6 ounces soy "steak" strips

1 teaspoon chili powder, or to taste

½ cup salsa

1 15.5-ounce can nonfat vegetarian
 refried black beans

6 whole wheat flour tortillas

1½ cup shredded cheddar cheese

Snips of cilantro

1. Heat the oil in a large skillet, and sauté the soy "beef" strips and chili powder for 2 to 3 minutes. Remove from the skillet, and set aside.

2. Heat the salsa and the refried beans in the skillet for about 5 minutes, and remove from the skillet. Rinse out the skillet, or heat a second skillet or griddle.

3. Place a tortilla on the work surface, and sprinkle ¼ cup of cheese on the surface. Top the cheese with "beef" strips, about ⅓ cup black beans, and a sprinkling of cilantro. Fold the tortilla over the filling, spray the skillet or griddle with nonstick cooking spray and cook the quesadilla until both sides are browned and the cheese had melted. Repeat with the remaining ingredients until all are used up. Serve the quesadillas warm or at room temperature.

PER SERVING: 240 CAL; 14G PROT; 8G FAT; 34G CARB; 15MG CHOL; 810MG SOD; 7G FIBER

BLACK BEAN FLAUTAS

Shaped like a flute, a flauta is a popular Mexican snack food that traditionally calls for corn tortillas. This version uses flour tortillas, but feel free to serve either corn or flour, and select a size that you prefer. For a variation, substitute about 4 cups canned vegetarian refried pinto beans for the mashed black beans. Spread on tortillas, and proceed with recipe.

About 4 cups canned black beans
 including bean liquid

2 teaspoons chili powder

½ teaspoon ground cumin

1 clove garlic, minced

1 bay leaf

12 6-inch flour tortillas

6 scallions, minced

2 tomatoes, chopped

1 cup shredded cheddar cheese or
 soy cheddar-flavored cheese

Salsa, sour cream or yogurt for
 dipping, optional

1. Combine the beans, bean liquid, chili powder, cumin, garlic and bay leaf in a saucepan. Cook over low heat for 10 minutes. Remove the bay leaf. Drain the bean mixture, reserving the liquid. Mash the beans, adding liquid as needed for desired consistency.

2. Preheat the oven to 400F.

3. Fill the tortillas with 1 or 2 heaping tablespoons of the bean mixture, and top with the scallions, tomatoes and cheese. Roll up each filled tortilla into a tube shape, and place them in a 9 x 13–inch baking pan, seam side down. Bake until lightly browned, for about 15 minutes. Use any leftover bean mix for dipping, or dip the flautas in salsa, sour cream or yogurt.

PER FLAUTA (WITHOUT SALSA, SOUR CREAM OR YOGURT): 83 CAL; 5G PROT; 3G FAT; 8G CARB; 10MG CHOL; 65MG SOD; 4G FIBER

BLACK BEAN QUESADILLAS

Depending on your choice of cheese and beans, you can really get creative with this Tex-Mex-inspired "sandwich." This version uses Monterey Jack cheese and black beans, but sharp cheddar with scarlet runner beans, and mozzarella with Anasazi beans are two more unusual favorites. Sprouted-wheat and whole wheat tortillas are available at natural food stores.

About 2 cups canned black beans, rinsed

1/4 cup chopped green or red tomatoes

3 tablespoons chopped cilantro leaves

12 black olives, pitted and thinly sliced

8 6-inch sprouted-wheat tortillas or whole wheat tortillas

4 ounces shredded jalapeño Monterrey Jack cheese or soy cheese

32 spinach leaves (about 10 ounces), stemmed and shredded finely

1/4 cup hot salsa, or to taste

1. Preheat the oven to 350F.

2. Mash the beans in a large bowl. Stir in the tomato, cilantro and olives. Spread the bean mixture evenly onto 4 tortillas. Sprinkle with the cheese, spinach and salsa. Top with the remaining tortillas.

3. Place the filled tortillas on an ungreased baking sheet, and bake until the cheese melts, for about 12 minutes. Alternatively, cook the tortillas on a cast-iron griddle over medium heat, turning once, until the cheese melts. Cut into wedges, and serve hot.

PER SERVING: 443 CAL; 21G PROT; 14G FAT; 56G CARB; 25MG CHOL; 646MG SOD; 8G FIBER

FAJITAS

Robust chili teams with seitan to make this 15-minute dish taste like it took an hour to prepare. Set out a platter of the savory mixture and bowls of garnishes such as guacamole, fresh tomato, grated cheese and salsa, and let diners fashion their own fajitas.

Whole wheat fajita wrappers, wrapped in foil

1 small red onion, chopped

2 medium-sized cloves garlic, minced

2 bell peppers, seeded and sliced into strips

1 pound seitan, cut into thin shreds

1 tablespoon chili powder

2 tablespoons low-sodium soy sauce, shoyu or tamari

Guacamole, optional

2 or 3 plum tomatoes, peeled and diced

Garnishes: low-fat grated cheddar cheese, salsa and low-fat sour cream

1. Heat the fajita wrappers in a 200F oven.

2. Spray a nonstick skillet with nonstick cooking spray, add the onion and cook, stirring, over medium-low heat until softened slightly. Add the minced garlic and bell peppers, and cook, stirring frequently, for 5 minutes more. Add the seitan, chili powder and soy sauce. Reduce the heat to low, and cook for 5 minutes.

3. To serve, put the fajita wrappers under a napkin to keep them warm, and arrange the fajita filling on a small platter. Spoon the guacamole, if using, tomatoes, cheese, salsa and sour cream into small dishes, and pass.

PER SERVING (WITHOUT GUACAMOLE): 203 CAL; 11G PROT; 5G FAT; 29G CARB; 0MG CHOL; 803MG SOD; 3G FIBER

The lush mango spread adds an exotic layer of flavor to these unusual fajitas.

Mango Spread

1 cup diced ripe mango

¾ cup silken tofu

2 tablespoons olive oil

1 tablespoon fresh lemon juice

1 tablespoon fresh lime juice

1 tablespoon honey

Dash of ground cumin

Dash of ground coriander

Not Quite BLT

2 teaspoons vegetable oil

8 slices Canadian-style veggie "bacon"

4 10-inch flour tortillas

1 small head Boston lettuce, separated into leaves

1 large tomato, diced

1 avocado, diced

¼ to ½ cup diced ripe mango, optional

1. To make the Mango Spread: Put all the ingredients into a blender or food processor, and purée until smooth. Adjust the seasonings to taste, adding salt and more lemon or lime juice as needed. Transfer to a small bowl, cover and refrigerate until serving time.

2. Heat the oil in a large nonstick skillet over medium heat. Add the "bacon" in batches, and cook according to the package directions, just until heated through. Transfer to a plate. Rinse, and dry the skillet.

3. Warm each tortilla in the same skillet over medium heat just until soft and pliable, for about 1 minute per side. Place 2 "bacon" slices down the center of each tortilla, overlapping slightly. Top with a row of lettuce leaves, then tomato, avocado and mango if desired, dividing equally. Season lightly with salt and pepper. Spoon some Mango Spread over the filling. Fold the bottom end of tortilla partially over the filling, then roll into a bundle and serve.

PER SERVING: 429 CAL; 8G PROT; 23G FAT; 51G CARB; 0MG CHOL; 381MG SOD; 6G FIBER

PASTA AND VEGGIE SALAD

To appeal to your children, vary the vegetables—peas, green beans and squash are all tasty—and use red or pink kidney beans or cannellini beans in place of the chickpeas.

1 pound pasta such as farfalle, rotini, twists, shells or large macaroni

¼ cup olive oil

2 large cloves garlic, minced or pressed

1 carrot, halved lengthwise and thinly sliced

1 cup corn kernels

½ green, red, or yellow bell pepper, seeded and diced

⅓ to ½ cup minced onion

1 tomato, chopped

1 15½-ounce can chickpeas, drained and rinsed

2 tablespoons fresh snipped chives

1 to 1½ tablespoons balsamic or herb vinegar

2 teaspoons dried basil leaves, crumbled or 2 to 3 tablespoons fresh basil, chopped

1 teaspoon salt

Freshly ground black pepper to taste

1. Heat a pot of lightly salted water over medium heat, and when it is boiling, cook the pasta according to package directions. Drain, toss with 1 tablespoon olive oil and 1 clove garlic, and set aside.

2. Combine the carrot, corn, pepper, onion, tomato, chickpeas and chives in a large mixing bowl, and toss well. Add the pasta, and toss to combine.

3. Mix the remaining olive oil, vinegar, 1½ tablespoons water, the remaining garlic, and the basil. Season with salt and pepper, and blend well. Drizzle the dressing over the salad, and toss well. Refrigerate for at least 30 minutes before serving.

4. To serve, toss again and taste the seasoning, adding extra if needed. Serve at cool room temperature.

PER SERVING: 230 CAL; 7G PROT; 7G FAT; 37G CARB; 0MG CHOL; 280MG SOD; 3G FIBER

CHEESY CONFETTI MACARONI

A colorful pasta dish should lure your children to the table. Serve this with a fruit salad and Cranberry Sparkler (page 81).

1½ cups uncooked elbow macaroni

½ cup grated carrot

½ cup grated yellow summer squash

1 tablespoon chopped fresh parsley

½ cup low-fat milk

½ cup grated low-fat cheddar cheese

1 teaspoon arrowroot

½ teaspoon mustard powder

½ teaspoon paprika

1. Heat a pot of lightly salted water over medium heat, and when it is boiling, cook the pasta according to package directions. Drain. Combine the macaroni with the carrot, squash and parsley in a bowl. Set aside.

2. Preheat the oven to 350F. Lightly oil a 1½-quart baking dish.

3. Whisk together the milk, cheese, arrowroot, mustard and paprika in a saucepan. Heat the mixture over medium-high heat, and cook, stirring, until the cheese melts and the mixture begins to thicken slightly. Pour over the macaroni, and mix well. Spoon the mixture into the prepared baking dish.

4. Bake until lightly browned and set, for about 40 minutes. Remove from the oven, and serve.

PER SERVING: 226 CAL; 10G PROT; 6G FAT; 34G CARB; 17MG CHOL; 109MG SOD; 2G FIBER

CREAMY SPINACH LASAGNA

Lasagna in any guise remains a constant family favorite. With this version, you sample two entirely different flavors of sauces for a unique main dish.

Tomato Sauce

½ tablespoon olive oil

1 small onion, minced

2 cloves garlic, minced

1 teaspoon dried oregano

½ teaspoon salt

¼ teaspoon freshly ground black pepper

2 28-ounce cans plum tomatoes

½ cup chopped fresh flat-leaf parsley

Béchamel Sauce

1 tablespoon margarine

1 tablespoon all-purpose white flour

1 cup skim milk

Salt and freshly ground black pepper to taste

Filling

12 ounces fresh spinach, trimmed

2 cups low-fat ricotta cheese

½ cup egg substitute or 2 large eggs, beaten

2 cloves garlic, minced

½ cup grated Parmesan cheese, optional

Salt and freshly ground black pepper to taste

1 pound lasagna noodles, cooked and drained

1 to 2 cups grated mozzarella cheese

1. Preheat the oven to 350F. Spray a 9 x 13–inch baking pan with nonstick cooking spray.

2. To make the Tomato Sauce: Heat the oil over medium heat in a large saucepan. Cook the onion and garlic, stirring, for 3 minutes. Add the oregano, salt, pepper and tomatoes. Cook over medium heat until mixture thickens, about 45 minutes. Using the back of a wooden spoon, mash the tomatoes as they cook. Add the parsley, and set aside.

3. To make the Béchamel Sauce: Melt the margarine in a small saucepan over medium heat. Whisk in the flour, and cook for 30 seconds. Slowly add the milk, whisking and cooking until thickened, for about 10 minutes. Add the salt and pepper. Set aside.

4. To make the Filling: Steam the spinach over medium heat in a steamer basket set into a large saucepan until wilted. Drain, squeeze out any excess water and chop coarsely. Transfer to a mixing bowl. Add the ricotta, egg substitute or eggs, garlic, Parmesan cheese, salt and pepper. Mix well, and set aside.

5. Spread half of the Béchamel Sauce over the bottom of the pan. Layer one-quarter of the noodles over the sauce, overlapping them slightly. Spread half of the tomato sauce over the noodles, and top with half of the mozzarella. Layer another one-quarter of the noodles, and spread with half of the spinach mixture. Continue with the noodles, Tomato Sauce, mozzarella, noodles and spinach mixture. Spread the remaining Béchamel Sauce over the top. Cover with foil.

6. Bake for 20 minutes. Remove the foil, and continue baking until bubbly, for about 15 minutes more. Remove from the oven, and serve.

PER SERVING: 437 CAL; 22G PROT; 12G FAT; 55G CARB; 38MG CHOL; 1,021MG SOD; 8G FIBER

MEXICANA CORN PASTA

Pinto beans and peppers in a spicy sauce top corn pasta to make an unusual and delicious dish.

1 cup canned tomato purée

1 medium-sized red onion, chopped

2 cloves garlic, minced

2 large roasted red bell peppers, chopped

1 roasted pasilla chile, chopped or 1 tablespoon chopped canned jalapeño chiles

2 teaspoons ground cumin

2 teaspoons ground oregano

2 teaspoons chili powder

Cayenne to taste

Juice of ½ lemon

1½ cups cooked pinto or kidney beans, rinsed

1 cup corn kernels, fresh or frozen

⅓ cup sour cream or plain yogurt

½ cup coarsely shredded cheddar cheese

14 ounces uncooked corn pasta

Cilantro leaves, minced

12 flour tortillas, optional

1. Heat the tomato purée in a large skillet over medium heat. Add the onion and garlic, and cook until the onion softens, for about 5 minutes. Stir in the red peppers and pasilla chiles, cumin, oregano, chili powder, cayenne and lemon juice. Add the beans and corn.

2. Spoon the sour cream into a mixing bowl, and stir in a heaping spoonful of the bean mixture, then stir the mixture back into the skillet. Add the grated cheese, and blend well.

3. Meanwhile, prepare the corn pasta according to the package directions, and drain. Put into a large serving dish, top the cooked pasta with the bean-cheese mixture and sprinkle with the cilantro. Serve at once, accompanied by the flour tortillas, if using.

PER SERVING: 408 CAL. 16G PROT; 6G FAT; 71G CARB. 15MG CHOL; 84MG SOD; 7G FIBER

PENNE, BROCCOLI AND MOZZARELLA PIE

SERVES 6

As always, pasta partners well with mozzarella cheese, especially when it's smoked.

5 tablespoons Italian-style dried breadcrumbs

3 teaspoons olive oil

1 medium-sized onion, chopped

1 10-ounce package frozen chopped broccoli (3 cups)

6 ounces dry penne pasta (1½ cups)

4 large eggs

¾ cup low-fat milk

½ to 1 teaspoon hot pepper sauce

1½ cups shredded smoked mozzarella cheese (5 ounces)

Salt and freshly ground black pepper to taste

1. Preheat the oven to 350F. Coat a 9-inch (1½-quart) deep-dish pie pan with cooking spray. Sprinkle with 2 tablespoons breadcrumbs, tilting the pan to coat evenly.

2. Heat a pot of lightly salted water over medium heat, and when it is boiling, cook the pasta according to package directions. Drain, and set aside.

3. Meanwhile, mix together the remaining 3 tablespoons bread crumbs and 1 teaspoon oil. Set aside. Heat the remaining 2 teaspoons oil in a nonstick skillet over medium heat. Add the onion, and cook, stirring often, until tender and light golden, for 4 to 5 minutes. Set aside.

4. Place the broccoli in a strainer, and rinse under cold running water to thaw. Drain well and set aside. Whisk the eggs, milk, hot sauce, salt and pepper together in a mixing bowl. Add the cheese, reserved onion, broccoli and pasta, and mix with a rubber spatula. Pour into the pan, spreading evenly. Sprinkle evenly with the reserved bread crumb mixture. (Pie can be prepared ahead to this point. Cover and refrigerate for up to 2 days. Bring to room temperature before baking.)

5. Bake the pie, uncovered, until the top is lightly golden and the filling is set, for about 45 minutes. (The tip of a knife inserted into the center should come out clean.) Transfer to a wire rack and cool slightly. Cut into wedges, and serve hot.

PER SERVING: 384 CAL; 27G PROT; 18G FAT; 28G CARB; 242MG CHOL; 435MG SOD; 4G FIBER

STRAW AND HAY PASTA

SERVES 4

Ribbons of green and yellow pasta—the "straw and hay"—are studded with chunks of tomato and dressed in garlicky olive oil. If you can't find flavorful fresh tomatoes, opt for canned ones.

1 cup coarsely chopped fresh tomatoes or 2 28-ounce cans stewed tomatoes, drained and coarsely chopped

1½ to 2 tablespoons olive oil

1 to 2 cloves garlic, pressed or minced

Dash cayenne

½ teaspoon salt

5 ounces fresh spinach fettuccine

5 ounces fresh plain fettuccine

¼ cup packed fresh basil leaves, slivered, or 1 tablespoon dried basil

1. Put the tomatoes in a large serving bowl. Warm the oil, garlic, cayenne and salt in a skillet over very low heat. When the garlic begins to sizzle, remove the skillet from the heat, and let sit for 10 minutes. Do not let the garlic brown or it will taste bitter. Pour the spice mixture over the tomatoes.

2. Heat a pot of lightly salted water over medium heat, and when it is boiling, cook the pasta according to package directions. Drain. Put into a serving bowl, and toss with the tomato mixture. Sprinkle with basil, toss again and serve.

PER SERVING: 250 CAL; 9G PROT; 7G FAT; 41G CARB; 0MG CHOL; 450MG SOD; 3G FIBER

RAVIOLI WITH MIXED GREENS

This dish is traditionally served with a light sauce of butter and fresh sage or other herbs. If you have a ravioli attachment for your pasta machine, or other ravioli maker, follow the manufacturer's directions. In place of broccoli rabe, use other types of greens. Just don't exceed a 1:2 ratio of bitter greens (such as collard or mustard greens) to nonbitter greens (such as spinach).

4 cups lightly packed spinach leaves

2 cups lightly packed broccoli rabe leaves

¼ teaspoon ground nutmeg

¼ cup grated Parmesan cheese, optional

¼ teaspoon salt, or to taste

1 recipe Fresh Pasta Dough (page 249)

1. Rinse the greens, but don't dry them. In a saucepan fitted with a steamer, steam the greens until wilted, for about 5 minutes. When the greens have cooled, squeeze out the water, and chop finely. Transfer the greens to a bowl. Mix with the nutmeg, Parmesan cheese and salt.

2. Roll an egg-sized ball of the fresh pasta dough using a pasta machine or rolling pin into a rectangle or circle as thinly as possible. Cut it into strips about 2 x 12 inches. Place 1 strip on a floured surface, and dot it with teaspoonfuls of the greens mixture about 1 inch apart from each other. Place a second strip of pasta on top. Press down around the portions of the filling, then cut the filled pasta into squares with a knife or pastry crimper.

3. Press the edges together a second time to be sure they stick. Transfer the ravioli to a floured plate. Repeat with the remaining dough and filling. Boil the ravioli in a pot of salted water for only 2 minutes. Drain and add the sauce of your choice.

PER SERVING (WITHOUT SAUCE): 268 CAL; 12G PROT; 4G FAT; 46G CARB; 110MG CHOL; 164MG SOD; 4G FIBER

SUPREME GREEN SPAGHETTI

This nutrient-packed vegetable sauce is a change from the usual tomato sauce served over spaghetti.

8 ounces uncooked spaghetti or other pasta

1 pound frozen chopped spinach or broccoli, thawed

½ cup skim milk

1 clove garlic, crushed

1 tablespoon unsalted butter, melted

Salt to taste

4 teaspoons grated Parmesan cheese, optional

1. Heat a pot of lightly salted water over medium heat, and when it is boiling, cook the pasta according to package directions. Drain.

2. Meanwhile, steam the spinach or broccoli until just cooked. Put into a blender, add the milk, garlic, butter and salt and purée. Pour the sauce over the hot pasta. Toss, sprinkle with Parmesan cheese and serve.

PER SERVING: 242 CAL; 9G PROT; 4G FAT; 44G CARB; 1MG CHOL; 184MG SOD; 7G FIBER

"TORT" AND CHEESE

An adaptation of the popular "mac-and-cheese" concept, this entrée becomes more than a pasta side dish or simple luncheon entrée with the addition of steamed broccoli rabe and sautéed Italian-seasoned soy "sausages." The recipe gives your children all the greens they'll need in a comfy pasta dish. As accompaniments, slice ripened tomatoes for a salad garnished with croutons, fresh basil leaves and perhaps slices of fresh mozzarella, and serve with wedges of toasted focaccia.

1 tablespoon vegetable oil

4 links Italian-flavored soy "sausage," thinly sliced on diagonal

1 bunch broccoli rabe, trimmed

3 tablespoons soy margarine or unsalted butter

3 tablespoons all-purpose flour

1 cup low-fat milk or soymilk

2 cups shredded low-fat or regular cheddar cheese

1 teaspoon minced garlic

1 teaspoon dried oregano

½ teaspoon crushed red pepper (optional)

Salt and freshly ground black pepper to taste

10 ounces fresh tricolored tortellini or other gourmet-flavored tortellini

1. Heat the oil in a large skillet over medium heat, and sauté the "sausage" until brown, for about 5 minutes.

2. Meanwhile, steam the broccoli rabe with the water on its leaves in a covered saucepan just until wilted, remove from the heat, and drain thoroughly, squeezing out excess water with tongs. Set aside, and keep warm.

3. To make the roux, heat the margarine over medium heat, and when melted, stir in the flour. Add the milk and cheese all at once, and whisk until the cheese melts and the sauce thickens. Stir in the garlic, oregano, crushed red pepper, if using, and salt and pepper to taste.

4. Cook the tortellini according to the package directions, for about 4 minutes, or until tender, and drain. To serve, arrange equal portions of broccoli rabe on each plate. Top with tortellini, cheese sauce and "sausage."

PER SERVING: 540 CAL; 36G PROT; 25G FAT; 46G CARB; 135MG CHOL; 810MG SOD; 4G FIBER

ASPARAGUS CHOWDER

This delicate and pretty soup is just the right weight for March's sweater weather. You can make the croutons up to 1 day in advance, and store them in an airtight container.

Parmesan Croutons (optional)

6 slices (½-inch thick) Italian country bread

2 tablespoons olive oil, preferably extra virgin

¼ cup grated Parmigiano-Reggiano cheese

Asparagus Stock

1 pound asparagus, tough ends trimmed

1 Vidalia onion, roughly chopped

1 small bay leaf

1 large carrot, trimmed, peeled and roughly chopped

1 large stalk celery with leaves, roughly chopped

6 stems fresh parsley

1 teaspoon salt

8 cups cold water

Soup

5 tablespoons olive oil

1 Vidalia onion, finely chopped

1 pound new potatoes, peeled and chopped into ½-inch pieces

¼ cup water

1 pound asparagus, tough ends trimmed and discarded

1 teaspoon salt

½ cup milk, heavy cream or half-and-half

Salt and freshly ground black pepper to taste

1. To make the Parmesan Croutons: Preheat the broiler. Adjust the rack to 8 inches below the broiler.

2. Brush both sides of the bread with the oil, and place the slices on a baking sheet. Broil for 3 to 10 minutes, turning as needed, until golden brown and crisp. Remove from the oven, and, when cool enough to handle, slice into cubes. Sprinkle with the Parmesan cheese, and broil for 1 to 2 minutes more, or until golden. Remove from the oven, and set aside.

3. To make the Asparagus Stock: Cut the tips off the asparagus, and set aside for garnish. Place asparagus spears in a soup pot with the remaining ingredients. Bring to a boil over medium heat, reduce the heat to low and cook, uncovered, for 20 minutes. Remove from the heat, and drain into a bowl, reserving the liquid. Discard the solids. Measure 6 cups stock—if you have less, add enough water to measure 6 cups.

4. To make the Soup: While the stock cooks, heat 2 tablespoons oil in a skillet over medium-low heat. Add half the onion, all the potatoes and water. Cover, and cook for 20 minutes, stirring several times, until vegetables are soft. Cut the tips off the asparagus, and set aside with the other tips for garnish. Cut the asparagus spears into 1-inch-long pieces.

5. Heat the remaining 3 tablespoons oil in a large pot over medium heat. Add the remaining onions and asparagus spear pieces, and cook, stirring frequently, for 3 to 5 minutes or until the onions have softened. Add the salt and strained Asparagus Stock, and bring to a slow boil. Cook over medium heat, uncovered, for 4 to 8 minutes, or until the asparagus are tender, the exact timing depending on the size and freshness of the asparagus. Using a slotted spoon, remove the asparagus from the pot, and put into a food processor. Process until smooth, adding stock as needed for processing. Transfer the purée to a very fine strainer, and press through to remove tough fibers. Return the purée to the soup pot. Add the potatoes and onions, and stir to mix. Add the milk, salt and pepper, and cook over medium-low heat.

6. Meanwhile, bring water to a boil. Add the asparagus tips, and cook until just tender. Remove from the heat, and strain.

7. To serve, ladle the soup into bowls, garnish each serving with asparagus tips, and pass the croutons, if using. Offer extra freshly ground black pepper.

PER SERVING: 170 CAL; 4G PROT; 9G FAT; 19G CARB; 0MG CHOL; 610MG SOD; 3G FIBER

BEANS AND FRANKS POT PIE

Here's one kids really love, and since the filling is made from convenience products, you can put it together in no time. This makes a great casual Friday night dinner.

Beans and Franks Filling

1 tablespoon vegetable oil

1 large onion, chopped

2 28-ounce cans vegetarian baked beans

6 tofu hot dogs, cut into ½-inch chunks

2 teaspoons mustard

Salt and freshly ground black pepper to taste

Cornmeal Biscuit Topping

1½ cups all-purpose flour

½ cup fine yellow cornmeal

1½ tablespoons granulated sugar

1½ teaspoons baking powder

½ teaspoon baking soda

4 tablespoons cold unsalted butter, cut into ¼-inch pieces

¾ cup buttermilk

1. To make the Beans and Franks Filling: Heat the oil in a 4-quart Dutch oven or flameproof casserole over medium heat. Add the onion, and cook, stirring often, until softened, for about 8 minutes. Stir in the beans, tofu dogs, mustard and salt and pepper to taste. Reduce the heat to low, and cook, stirring occasionally, while preparing the topping.

2. Preheat the oven to 400F.

3. To make the Cornmeal Biscuit Topping: Mix the flour, cornmeal, sugar, baking powder and baking soda in a mixing bowl. Cut in the butter with a pastry blender or 2 knives until the mixture resembles coarse crumbs. Make a well in the dry ingredients. Add the buttermilk all at once. Stir just until the mixture is blended, and the dough pulls together. Let the dough sit for 2 minutes.

4. Dust the dough with flour, and transfer to a floured work surface. Knead 4 or 5 times, then pat into a circle as large as the top of the Dutch oven. Using a sharp knife, cut the dough into 2-inch squares. Place the dough squares over the hot beans.

5. Bake until the topping is lightly golden, for about 20 minutes. Let cool for at least 10 minutes before serving.

PER SERVING: 360 CAL; 18G PROT; 8G FAT; 61G CARB; 13MG CHOL; 931MG SOD; 10G FIBER

TEX-MEX CORN PANCAKES

These hearty cakes can be heated up with chopped jalapeños, more chili powder and a sprinkle of hot pepper sauce, if your family likes things hot. You can even select a fiery salsa for a more assertive flavor. Whether with lunch or dinner, offer cut-up fresh fruit as an accompaniment.

1 cup creamed corn

½ cup fine cornmeal

¾ cup all-purpose flour

1 teaspoon baking powder

Salt to taste

½ cup chopped green chiles

1 large egg, well-beaten

2 teaspoons chili powder, or to taste

1½ cups salsa for garnish

1 cup shredded cheddar for garnish

1 cup cilantro leaves for garnish

1. Combine the corn, cornmeal, flour, baking powder and salt in a mixing bowl. Stir in the chiles, egg, and chili powder, mixing well.

2. Heat a large skillet over medium heat, and when hot, spray it with nonstick cooking spray. Spoon the batter by quarter or half cupfuls, and cook until the bottoms turn golden. Flip over, and cook the second side until golden. Remove from the heat, and keep warm until ready to serve. Continue cooking until all the batter is used up.

PER SERVING: 240 CAL; 7G PROT; 2.5G FAT; 49G CARB; 55MG CHOL; 670MG SOD; 3G FIBER

MASHED POTATO CAKES

Can't get your kids to eat their peas and carrots? Serve up the vegetables in these tempting cakes made from leftover mashed potatoes. Adults will enjoy these, too, as mashed potatoes are pure comfort food. You can even whip these up using the premade mashed potatoes available in some supermarkets. Panko breadcrumbs, a Japanese product, produce a uniquely crispy coating on fried foods. But you may use conventional breadcrumbs if you prefer, or omit breadcrumbs altogether. This recipe makes eight ½-cup cakes for children, or four larger 1-cup cakes for adults.

1 large egg, lightly beaten

Salt and freshly ground black pepper to taste

2 cups mashed potatoes

1 cup shredded cheddar cheese

1 cup fresh or frozen peas

1 cup shredded carrots

½ cup panko breadcrumbs, or more as needed

1. Combine the egg, salt and pepper in a mixing bowl. Stir in the mashed potatoes, cheese, peas and carrots. Put the breadcrumbs into a small bowl.

2. Spray a large skillet with nonstick cooking spray, and heat over medium heat. Scoop about 1 cup of the potato mixture from bowl, and sprinkle breadcrumbs on the top. Turn the potatoes out onto the hot skillet, fitting at least 2 cakes onto the skillet, and cook over medium heat until the bottoms start to brown and the cheese melts, about 5 minutes. Sprinkle breadcrumbs on the uncooked sides, spray the tops and turn the cakes over to brown the second side. Cook for 5 minutes more, turn the cakes a final time, and cook for about 3 minutes more. Remove from the skillet, and set aside.

3. Repeat with the remaining ingredients until all are used up. Serve immediately.

PER SERVING: 350 CAL; 14G PROT; 16G FAT; 37G CARB; 95MG CHOL; 570MG SOD; 5G FIBER

NEATLOAF

This loaf has a meaty flavor and is much lower in fat, cholesterol and sodium than the standard meatloaf. The next day, let your children and family enjoy "neatloaf" sandwiches with your favorite trimmings.

2 cups ground seitan

12 ounces firm tofu, drained and crumbled

1 slice bread, torn into crumbs

2 large eggs, slightly beaten, optional

¼ teaspoon ground cloves

⅛ teaspoon ground nutmeg

¾ teaspoon freshly ground black pepper

¾ teaspoon salt

1 tablespoon low-sodium soy sauce

1 tablespoon vegetarian Worcestershire sauce or additional soy sauce

2 tablespoons vegetable oil

½ cup minced celery

1 onion, diced

1 carrot, diced

¼ cup chopped fresh parsley

1. Preheat the oven to 350F. Oil a 9 x 5–inch loaf pan, and set aside.

2. Mash together the seitan, tofu, bread crumbs, eggs if using, and seasonings. Set aside.

3. Heat the oil in a large skillet over medium heat, and sauté the celery, onion and carrot, stirring, until soft, for about 7 minutes. Stir in the parsley, and remove from the heat. Add the vegetables to the tofu mixture, and mix well. Shape into a loaf, and place in the loaf pan.

4. Bake, uncovered, until well-browned, for about 1 hour. Remove from the oven, and serve.

PER SERVING: 140 CAL; 11G PROT; 8G FAT; 8G CARB; 0MG CHOL; 674MG SOD; 1G FIBER

OVEN-CRISP TOFU STICKS WITH KETCHUP SAUCE

SERVES 6

Most kids love this dish because it's a finger food with a ketchup sauce. For extra flavor, use herb-flavored tofu.

Ketchup Sauce

¼ cup tomato paste

2 tablespoons maple syrup

2 tablespoons fresh lemon juice

½ teaspoon puréed fresh ginger root

1 tablespoon minced fresh parsley

Cayenne pepper to taste

Salt to taste

Tofu Sticks

24 ounces firm or extra-firm water-packed tofu

⅓ cup fine cracker crumbs

2 tablespoons cornmeal

1½ tablespoons salt-free all-purpose seasoning

½ teaspoon ground chipotle chili or chili powder

¼ teaspoon salt

1. To make the Ketchup Sauce: Whisk together ¾ cup water, tomato paste, maple syrup, lemon juice and ginger in a small pan. Heat over medium heat until boiling, stirring constantly, and cook for 1 minute. Remove from the heat, and let cool. Add the parsley, and season with cayenne and salt.

2. Preheat the oven to 375F.

3. To make the Tofu Sticks: Drain the tofu, and wrap in paper towels for 10 to 15 minutes, pressing out any excess moisture. In a shallow bowl, mix together the cracker crumbs, cornmeal, seasoning, ground chipotle and salt. Set aside.

4. Spray a large wire cooling rack with olive oil or mesquite-flavored nonstick cooking spray. Cut each block of tofu into 12 sticks about 3 inches long and ¾-inch thick. Dredge each stick in the crumb mixture, and place the sticks on the wire rack. Spray them with the oil.

5. Bake the sticks until crisp and brown, for 35 to 45 minutes. Remove from the oven, and serve the tofu sticks warm. Drizzle the ketchup sauce on top, or serve it on the side.

PER SERVING: 253 CAL; 17G PROT; 11G FAT; 21G CARB; 0MG CHOL; 84MG SOD; 1G FIBER

SESAME-COATED TOFU

SERVES 4

The flavor of sesame seeds is mirrored in the sesame-based tahini paste.

2 tablespoons low-sodium tamari soy sauce

1 pound extra-firm tofu, cut into 8 triangle-shaped pieces, ½-inch thick

⅓ cup tahini

1 tablespoon fresh lemon juice

½ cup sesame seeds

2 tablespoons vegetable oil

1. Brush 1 tablespoon tamari over the tofu slices, and set aside.

2. Put the tahini, ⅓ cup water, lemon juice and the remaining 1 tablespoon tamari into a blender or food processor, and purée until smooth. Transfer the mixture to a shallow bowl.

3. Place the sesame seeds on a plate. Dip and coat the tofu slices in the tahini mixture, and then in the sesame seeds.

4. Heat the oil in a large skillet over medium heat. Add the coated tofu slices and cook until lightly browned, for about 2 to 3 minutes per side. Work in two batches if necessary. Serve hot.

PER TRIANGLE: 178 CAL; 6G PROT; 15G FAT; 5G CARB; 0MG CHOL; 225MG SOD; 2G FIBER

MEATLESS SPAGHETTI SAUCE

Sometimes it's easier to get vegetables into kids when the vegetables are disguised, as in the case of this spaghetti sauce. If you need to use that trick, chop the vegetables very finely so that they just make the sauce look and feel slightly textured. Otherwise, you can dice or cube the vegetables so they are recognizable. Either way, this is a full-flavored spaghetti sauce that will be enjoyed by the whole family. It may be used on pizzas or in lasagna or served over your favorite pasta. If you think so many vegetables make the sauce taste too sweet, add a little red wine vinegar. This amount of sauce will serve 8 adults.

¼ cup olive oil

2 cups diced onion

1 tablespoon minced garlic

1 cup diced mushrooms

1 cup diced zucchini

1 cup finely chopped carrot

1 cup diced green pepper

4 cups commercial marinara sauce, preferably organic

2 teaspoons dried basil

½ teaspoon dried oregano

1 teaspoon freshly ground black pepper

¼ cup Parmesan cheese or soy Parmesan cheese

Heat the olive oil over medium heat in a 4-quart saucepan. Add the onion and garlic, and sauté until soft, for about 5 minutes. Add the mushrooms, and sauté until browned, for about 5 minutes. Add the carrot and green pepper, and cook, stirring occasionally, for 10 minutes. Add the remaining ingredients, reduce the heat to medium-low and cook, uncovered, for 20 minutes. Taste, and adjust the seasoning to your taste.

PER SERVING: 70 CAL; 2G PROT; 4.5G FAT; 7G CARB; 0MG CHOL; 75MG SOD; 1G FIBER

GROSS GREEN SLIME

Nothing makes little boys (even little girls!) happier than something adults consider gross . . . and this fits that description. It will look best served in an old-fashioned sherbet glass garnished with an insect-shaped chewy candy. You may eliminate the banana if you prefer, and add more kiwis, but the banana changes the flavor to one that children are more likely to enjoy. It also thickens the mixture. Green slime looks even grosser with the addition of finely diced strawberries, mango or other colorful fruit.

8 kiwis, peeled and quartered

1 large banana peeled and sliced

6 gelatin-free gummi worms

Put the kiwis and banana into a blender, and purée until smooth. Taste, and if necessary, add some sugar or the sweetener of your choice because some bananas and kiwis are sweeter than others. Chill until serving time. Pour ⅓ cup into each dish, and garnish with a worm.

PER SERVING: 120 CAL; 2G PROT; 0.5G FAT; 28G CARB; 0MG CHOL; 0MG SOD; 3G FIBER

desserts

YOU DON'T NEED A SWEET TOOTH TO appreciate that desserts are often the crowning glory to a meal. That does not mean that these final touches need to be loaded with fat and calories. Even the freshest piece of fruit will do, but take a look at these healthful alternatives to the over-the-top pastry confections that so often tempt us.

FRESH PEACH TOFU ICE CREAM

This is a treat to be savored only when local peaches are completely ripe. That is when the flavor and texture are best for this frozen dessert. Lecithin granules are available at whole foods stores; they enrich and thicken the ice cream.

1½ cups whole or soymilk

½ cup almond oil or canola oil

⅓ cup rice syrup or other sweetener

¼ cup lecithin

1 cup drained silken soft tofu

2 teaspoons vanilla extract

2 tablespoons peach brandy, optional

3 large ripe peaches, peeled, pitted and chopped

1 large ripe peach, peeled, pitted and thinly sliced

1. Put all of the ingredients except the sliced peach into a blender or food processor, and purée until very smooth. Adjust the sweetness by adding more rice syrup or other sweetener, if desired. Stir in the sliced peach. Chill the mixture.

2. Pour the mixture into the ice cream machine, and freeze according to the manufacturer's directions. Or if you don't have an ice cream machine, pour the mixture into a glass baking dish, and freeze. When frozen, scrape into the work bowl of your processor or blender, and process until smooth. Refreeze. Process again, and freeze until serving time.

PER SERVING: 350 CAL; 6G PROT; 24G FAT; 30G CARB; 5MG CHOL; 80MG SOD; 0G FIBER

STRAWBERRY CASSIS TOFU ICE CREAM

Cassis is a liqueur made from black currants, and its flavor intensifies the taste of strawberries. If you don't want to use a liqueur, try to find cassis syrup at a fine foods store or a Middle Eastern market.

2 cups very ripe, sweet strawberries, hulled and cut in half (10 ounces)

1½ cups drained silken tofu (15 ounces)

½ cup almond oil or canola oil

1½ cups whole milk or soymilk

¼ cup rice syrup

¼ cup crème de cassis liqueur

⅓ cup lecithin granules

1 tablespoon vanilla extract

1 cup very ripe sweet strawberries, hulled and sliced

1. Put the 2 cups of strawberries, tofu, oil, milk, rice syrup, cassis, lecithin and vanilla in a food processor, and purée until smooth. Stir in the sliced berries. Chill the mixture.

2. Pour the mixture into the ice cream machine, and freeze according to the manufacturer's directions. Or if you don't have an ice cream machine, pour the mixture into a glass baking dish, and freeze. When frozen, scrape into the work bowl of your processor or blender, and process until smooth. Refreeze. Process again, and freeze until serving time.

PER SERVING: 270 CAL; 7G PROT; 24G FAT; 27G CARB; 5MG CHOL; 115MG SOD; 2G FIBER

BURGUNDY CHERRY MACADAMIA NUT
TOFU ICE CREAM

The macadamia nuts add a rich, creamy taste to this dessert. If you don't have them on hand, substitute pine nuts or cashews. Only these three nut varieties grind to a smooth consistency.

½ cup chopped macadamia nuts

1 cup drained silken tofu

½ cup rice syrup

½ cup almond oil or canola oil

¼ cup lecithin granules

1½ cups whole milk or soymilk

1 tablespoon fresh squeezed lemon juice

2 teaspoons almond extract, optional

2 teaspoons vanilla extract

3 cups pitted and chopped black cherries (divided)

1. Place the macadamias in a blender or food processor and process until smooth. Add the remaining ingredients saving out 1 cup of cherries. Process until smooth and chill.

2. Pour the mixture into the ice cream machine, and freeze according to the manufacturer's directions. Or if you don't have an ice cream machine, pour the mixture into a glass baking dish, and freeze. When frozen, scrape into the work bowl of your processor or blender, and process until smooth. Refreeze. Process again, add the remaining chopped cherries and freeze until serving time.

PER SERVING: 460 CAL; 7G PROT; 32G FAT; 41G CARB; 5MG CHOL; 115MG SOD; 3G FIBER

APRICOT ALMOND SORBET

Unless you have an apricot tree in the yard and can allow them to ripen naturally, you will never have full-flavored sweet apricots. That isn't a problem since dried apricots are so good. That's why this recipe calls for dried fruit instead of fresh.

3 cups apricot nectar

2 cups finely chopped dried apricots

2 cups almond milk

½ cup almond oil or canola

⅓ cup honey

1 tablespoon vanilla extract

1 teaspoon almond extract (optional)

1. Put the apricot nectar and apricots in a 2-quart saucepan, and bring to a boil. Cover, and set aside for 1 hour. Put the soaked apricots and the remaining ingredients in a food processor or blender, and purée until smooth. Taste and adjust the sweetness, if necessary.

2. Pour the mixture into the ice cream machine, and freeze according to the manufacturer's directions. Or if you don't have an ice cream machine, pour the mixture into a glass baking dish, and freeze. When frozen, scrape into the work bowl of your processor or blender and process until smooth. Refreeze. Process again, and freeze until serving time.

PER SERVING: 450 CAL; 3G PROT; 19G FAT; 69G CARB; 0MG CHOL; 55MG SOD; 4G FIBER

FROZEN BERRY-BANANA BARS

These fruit-filled frozen bars are cholesterol-free and very low in calories. If you have more mixture than molds, freeze the extra in another container until somewhat frozen, and eat it like ice cream before it freezes rock-solid.

1¼ cups fresh (or frozen, unsweetened) strawberries

1½ cups vanilla-flavored soymilk

1 small banana, cut into chunks

¼ teaspoon almond extract

1. Chill the strawberries, soymilk and banana thoroughly. Put the strawberries, soymilk, banana and almond extract in a food processor or blender, and purée until very smooth.

To freeze the bars, choose one of the following methods:

METHOD 1: Pour the blended mixture into a shallow nonreactive pan, and freeze until somewhat frozen but not rock hard. With an ice cream scoop or metal spoon, transfer chunks of the frozen mixture into a blender or food processor fitted with a metal blade; process until smooth. Spoon the mixture into the plastic molds or small paper cups at once, and proceed with step two.

METHOD 2: Pour the blended mixture into a small ice cream maker that holds about 5 cups. Freeze according to the manufacturer's directions until the mixture is somewhat frozen but still very soft. Then spoon the mixture into plastic molds (or small paper cups) and proceed with step two.

METHOD 3: When you're short on time—or for an icy, popsiclelike bar—pour the processed mixture from the food processor or blender directly into plastic molds (or small paper cups) Then proceed with step two.

2. When spooning the mixture into the molds, press down to remove air pockets and leave ⅛- to ¼-inch of head room. Place a wooden or plastic stick in the center of each one. Freeze for several hours. At serving time, run hot water over the mold to dislodge the bar.

PER BAR: 23 CAL; 0.5G PROT, 0.3G FAT; 4G CARB; 0MG CHOL; 2MG SOD; 0.5G FIBER

STRAWBERRY-BANANA GLACÉ

This cool, light dessert is the perfect finale to a hearty meal. Serve in goblets or wine glasses. To freeze bananas, peel them, wrap them in plastic and place in your freezer for at least 4 hours. Frozen raspberries, blueberries or mangoes can be substituted for the strawberries.

5 very ripe bananas, frozen

½ to 1 cup frozen strawberries

1 teaspoon vanilla extract

¼ to ½ cup soymilk or low-fat milk

Cut the bananas into ½-inch-thick slices. Break up the strawberries if they're clumped together. Put the strawberries, bananas, vanilla and about ¼ cup soymilk in a food processor or blender, and purée, adding more milk as necessary, until smooth and creamy. Do not overblend or the mixture will become runny. Spoon into serving glasses, and serve at once.

PER SERVING: 96 CAL; 1G PROT; 0.5G FAT; 21 CARB; 0MG CHOL; 2MG SOD; 2G FIBER

FROZEN STRAWBERRY BARS

These cool, creamy bars are particularly delicious in spring when strawberries are at their peak.

1¼ cups fresh or frozen, unsweetened strawberries

1½ cups vanilla-flavored soymilk

1 tablespoon fresh lemon juice

¼ teaspoon almond extract

¼ cup unsweetened apple juice concentrate

1. Chill the strawberries and soymilk thoroughly. Put the strawberries, soymilk, lemon juice, almond extract and apple juice concentrate in a food processor or blender and process until very smooth. To freeze the bars, choose one of the following methods:

METHOD 1: Pour the blended mixture into a shallow nonreactive pan, and freeze until somewhat frozen but not rock hard. With an ice cream scoop or metal spoon, transfer chunks of the frozen mixture into a blender or food processor fitted with a metal blade; process until smooth. Spoon the mixture into the plastic molds or small paper cups at once, and proceed with step two.

METHOD 2: Pour the blended mixture into a small ice cream maker that holds about 5 cups. Freeze according to the manufacturer's directions until the mixture is somewhat frozen but still very soft. Then spoon the mixture into plastic molds (or small paper cups) and proceed with step two.

METHOD 3: When you're short on time—or for an icy, popsiclelike bar—pour the processed mixture from the food processor or blender directly into plastic molds (or small paper cups) Then proceed with step two.

2. When spooning the mixture into the molds, press down to remove air pockets and leave ⅛- to ¼-inch of head room. Place a wooden or plastic stick in the center of each one. Freeze for several hours. At serving time, run hot water over the mold to dislodge the bar.

PER BAR: 23 CAL; 0.5G PROT; 0.3G FAT; 5G CARB; 0MG CHOL; 3MG SOD; 0.5G FIBER

HUCKLEBERRY ORANGE ICED MILK

Huckleberries are a close relative of blueberries. Wild Maine blueberries are a perfect substitute—cultivated blueberries will not have as much flavor.

2½ cups of granulated sugar or rice syrup

1 cup orange juice

Zest of 1 lemon

Zest of ½ orange

2 cups fresh or frozen huckleberries or wild blueberries (11 ounces)

3 cups whole milk

1. Heat the sugar and orange juice in a saucepan over medium heat until the mixture boils. Add the lemon and orange zests. Stir until the sugar is dissolved, remove from the heat and chill the mixture.

2. Combine the orange juice mixture, huckleberries and milk, pour into the ice cream machine and freeze according to the manufacturer's directions. Or if you don't have an ice cream machine, pour the mixture into a glass baking dish and freeze. When frozen, scrape into the work bowl of your processor or blender, and process until smooth. Refreeze. Process again, and freeze until serving time.

PER SERVING: 330 CAL; 4G PROT; 3G FAT; 76G CARB; 10MG CHOL; 40MG SOD; 1G FIBER

DAD'S FAVORITE CHOCOLATE ANGEL FOOD CAKE
SERVES 12

This cake is light as air, low in fat and simple to make. The trick is to prepare all the ingredients in advance. Be sure to let the egg whites come to room temperature so they reach their fullest volume when beaten. Serve it with strawberries and lightly sweetened whipped cream or hot chocolate fudge sauce and ice cream.

1¼ cups granulated sugar

1 cup all-purpose flour

½ teaspoon salt

12 egg whites at room temperature

1 tablespoon fresh lemon juice

3 teaspoons vanilla extract

1 tablespoon grated orange zest

3½ ounces dark chocolate-orange bars, grated

1. Preheat the oven to 350F.

2. Sift ¼ cup of the sugar with the flour and salt 3 times. Using an electric mixer at medium-high speed, beat the egg whites until frothy in a large grease-free bowl. Add the lemon juice and beat until soft peaks form. Evenly sprinkle the remaining 1 cup of sugar over the whites, ¼ cup at a time, and beat at medium speed for 1 to 2 minutes. Sift ¼ cup of the flour mixture over the egg whites and gently fold in using a rubber spatula. Add the vanilla and orange zest. Alternately, fold in the remaining flour mixture and grated chocolate until well blended. Scrape the batter into an ungreased 10-inch angel food or tube pan.

3. Bake until the cake is lightly browned and a knife inserted near the center comes out clean, for 40 to 45 minutes. Remove the pan from the oven and invert onto its feet or over the neck of a bottle. Let cool for 30 to 45 minutes. Run a knife around the edges of the pan and center of the tube to remove.

PER SERVING: 175 CAL; 5G PROT; 3G FAT; 34G CARB; 0MG CHOL; 56MG SOD; 1G FIBER

POACHED ORANGE CAKE
SERVES 8

This is a moist, dense cake made without flour. It has a rich taste that doesn't need any frosting.

1 large navel orange, unpeeled and seeded

1 cup ground almonds or almond flour

½ cup granulated sugar or honey

3 large eggs or 1½ cups egg substitute

1 teaspoon almond extract, optional

½ teaspoon baking powder

¼ cup sliced almonds

1. Preheat oven to 350F. Line an 8-inch springform pan with baking parchment (a circle in the bottom and a strip around the sides), and spray lightly with non-stick cooking spray.

2. Put the whole orange, including rind, in a 2-quart pan, and cover with water. Bring to a boil, and cook for 20 minutes. Drain, cool and cut the orange in quarters. Put the orange quarters in a food processor, and purée.

3. Put the almonds and sugar in a mixing bowl, and mix. Add eggs and almond extract, and whisk together.

4. Add the orange purée to almond mixture, and mix well. Sift the baking powder over top, and stir it in. Pour immediately into the pan. Sprinkle the sliced almonds evenly over top, and place in the oven.

5. Bake for 50 to 60 minutes, or until a skewer inserted in the center of the cake comes out clean.

PER SERVING: 180 CAL; 6G PROT; 10G FAT; 18G CARB; 80MG CHOL; 55MG SOD; 2G FIBER

TOTAL CHOCOLATE ECLIPSE CAKE

The rich flavor of chocolate eclipses the fact that no eggs, butter or refined sugars are used to make this dense, fudgy confection. Flaxseeds are available at natural food stores.

Cake

1½ cups unbleached all-purpose flour

¾ cup unsweetened cocoa powder

1 tablespoon baking powder

1 teaspoon baking soda

2 tablespoons flaxseeds

½ cup pitted dates, soaked in 1 cup hot water for 30 minutes

6 ounces silken extra-firm tofu

1 cup pure maple syrup

1 tablespoon corn oil

1½ teaspoons vanilla extract

Frosting

1 cup semisweet chocolate chips

½ cup raw cashews

6 ounces extra-firm silken tofu

¼ cup pure maple syrup

1 teaspoon vanilla extract

1. Preheat the oven to 350F. Grease two 9-inch-round cake pans, and dust with flour, tapping out the excess flour.

2. To make the Cake: Mix the flour, cocoa, baking powder and baking soda in a large bowl, and set aside. Grind the flaxseeds to a fine powder in a food processor or blender. Add ½ cup water, and process until thick and frothy, for about 30 seconds. Add the dates and their soaking liquid, the tofu, maple syrup, oil and vanilla, and process until smooth. Transfer to a large bowl.

3. Stir the dry ingredients into the wet ingredients, blending until smooth, Divide the batter evenly between the prepared pans.

4. Bake until the cakes spring back when lightly pressed, 20 to 25 minutes. Cool the cakes in the pans on a wire rack for 10 minutes. Invert onto wire racks, remove the pans and cool completely.

5. To make the Frosting: Melt the chocolate, stirring until smooth, in the top of a double boiler set over simmering (not boiling) water. Remove from the water, and set aside.

6. Put the cashews into a food processor or blender, and pulverize. Add ⅓ cup water, and blend until smooth. Add the tofu, maple syrup and vanilla, and process until smooth. Add the melted chocolate, and process until smooth. Transfer to a medium bowl, and refrigerate until chilled.

7. To frost the cake, spread about ⅔ cup of the frosting over the top of 1 layer. Cover with the second layer, and spread the top and sides with the remaining frosting. Cut into wedges, and serve.

PER SERVING: 319 CAL; 7G PROT; 10G FAT; 55G CARB; 0MG CHOL; 229MG SOD; 4G FIBER

HONEY-YOGURT CAKE WITH SYRUP

This rich treat is based on a classic Greek dessert. Farina is a wheat flour or meal that is the basis for cooked cereals.

Cake

3 cups uncooked farina

½ cup unbleached white flour

2 teaspoons baking powder

1 teaspoon baking soda

1½ cups honey

2 cups plain yogurt

½ cup coarsely chopped blanched almonds

2 tablespoons frozen orange juice concentrate

Syrup

3 cups honey

1 thin slice orange

1. Preheat the oven to 350F. Grease a 9 x 13 inch baking pan, and set aside.

2. To make the Cake: Sift together the farina, flour, baking powder and baking soda into a bowl. Make a well in the center, and add the honey, yogurt, almonds and orange juice concentrate. Stir until just combined. Do not overmix. Pour the batter into the prepared pan.

3. Bake until the top is golden brown, for about 45 minutes. Remove from the oven.

4. Meanwhile, to make the Syrup: Combine the honey, orange slice and 2½ cups water in a saucepan. Bring to a boil, reduce the heat to low, and cook for 5 minutes. Remove, and discard the froth and orange slice.

5. Pour the syrup over the cake. Gently poke the cake surface with a toothpick. Let cool, and allow all of the syrup to be absorbed.

PER SERVING: 501 CAL; 4G PROT; 4G FAT; 120G CARB; 5MG CHOL; 148MG SOD; 1G FIBER

ULTIMATE CHOCOLATE "CHEESECAKE"

This creamy "cheesecake," made with tofu, is lighter than conventional versions but just as satisfying. It keeps up to three days, loosely covered with foil. For a great variation, try it with a cherry topping.

1 cup chocolate graham cracker crumbs

¼ cup ground blanched almonds

3 tablespoons granulated sugar

2 tablespoons soft spread or softened margarine

19 ounces silken tofu (2⅓ cups)

1 8-ounce tub tofu "cream cheese"

½ cup fat-free chocolate topping or chocolate syrup

¾ cup granulated sugar

2 tablespoons unsweetened cocoa powder

1 teaspoon vanilla extract

1 teaspoon fresh lemon juice

1. Preheat the oven to 350F. Spray an 8½-inch springform pan with nonstick cooking spray. Cover a baking sheet with foil.

2. Combine the graham cracker crumbs, almonds and sugar in a medium bowl. With a fork, work in the soft spread, finishing by using your fingertips. Press the mixture evenly over the bottom and part way up the sides of the springform pan. Refrigerate for 30 minutes.

3. Put the tofu into a food processor, and purée. Add the "cream cheese," and purée until smooth. Add the fudge sauce, sugar, cocoa, vanilla and lemon juice, and process until blended. Pour the filling into the crust. Tap the pan on the counter several times to release any air bubbles. Place the pan on the prepared baking sheet, and place in the center of the oven.

4. Bake 1 hour (center will still be wobbly). Turn off the oven, and leave in the oven with the door closed for 1 hour. Transfer the pan to a wire rack, and cool completely, for 3 to 4 hours. Refrigerate for at least 8 hours, covering with plastic wrap after 4 hours. If the top of the cake looks wet just before serving, blot it gently with a paper towel. Place on a serving plate, carefully remove the side of the pan, and serve.

PER SERVING: 238 CAL; 6G PROT; 7G FAT; 42G CARB; 0MG CHOL; 129MG SOD; 2G FIBER

QUIXOTIC CHEESECAKE

The combination of chocolate, eggplant and cream cheese sounds unusual, but the finished product is ultra-delicious—and wins everyone's applause.

Nut Crust

5 tablespoons softened unsalted butter
½ teaspoon salt
½ cup granulated sugar
2 cups untoasted walnuts

Cheesecake Filling

1 large eggplant
4 large eggs
¾ teaspoon salt
1 cup granulated sugar
1 cup semisweet chocolate chips
1 8-ounce package cream cheese
2 teaspoons vanilla extract

Sauce

Juice of 3 oranges and 2 lemons
½ cup granulated sugar
2 tablespoons unsalted butter
¾ teaspoon salt
¼ teaspoon ground cloves
3 pieces chopped crystallized ginger
½ cup coarsely chopped walnuts

1. To make the Nut Crust: Put the butter, salt and sugar into a food processor, and process until creamy. Add the walnuts, and process until the ingredients are smooth. Place the nut mixture in a 10-inch deep-dish pie plate. Using a spatula, build up the sides, and smooth out the bottom to form a crust. Set aside.

2. Preheat the oven to 325F.

3. To make the Cheesecake Filling: Slice off the stem end of the eggplant. Cut off about 2 inches more, and peel. Cut into 1-inch cubes, and put into a food processor. Process the eggplant, yielding about ½ cup eggplant purée. Add the eggs, and process. Add the salt, sugar and chocolate chips, and process on high speed for 1 minute. Add the cream cheese and vanilla, and process. Let the chocolate bits stay in the mixture, as these sink to form the bottom cheesecake layer. Pour the mixture into the nut crust. Slice the remainder of the eggplant, skin on, into ⅛-inch-thick rounds. Wrap in plastic, and set aside.

4. Bake 55 minutes, or until the center is firm. Remove from the oven, and cool at least 30 minutes.

5. Meanwhile, to make the Sauce: Combine the orange and lemon juices, sugar, butter, salt, cloves and chopped ginger in a large saucepan. Heat over medium heat, stirring often, until boiling. Reduce the heat to low, stirring occasionally. Place the eggplant slices in the saucepan, and cook 25 minutes.

6. Toast the walnuts until golden. Remove the eggplant slices from the sauce, and arrange the eggplant attractively on the cheesecake, overlapping slices if necessary. Add the nuts to the sauce.

7. Spoon 6 tablespoons of sauce, including nuts, over the eggplant slices. Cover the cheesecake in plastic or foil, and refrigerate for at least 2 hours. Refrigerate the remaining sauce.

8. To serve, heat the sauce over low heat. Using a sharp knife, cut the cheesecake into 12 portions, and place on plates. Spoon the sauce over each serving, and pass.

PER SERVING: 520 CAL; 9G PROT; 33G FAT; 53G CARB; 110MG CHOL; 540MG SOD; 4G FIBER

FIVE-FLAVOR POUND CAKE

The Caramel Drizzle makes an intense icing, and a decorative sugar adds glamour to this festive cake.

Five-Flavor Pound Cake

3 cups all-purpose flour

1 teaspoon salt

1 teaspoon baking soda

1 cup (2 sticks) unsalted butter

2½ cups granulated sugar

6 large eggs

1 cup low-fat sour cream

1 teaspoon vanilla extract

1 teaspoon rum extract

1 teaspoon coconut flavoring

1 teaspoon lemon extract

1 almond extract

Caramel Drizzle

1 cup firmly packed brown sugar

½ cup low-fat milk or vanilla soymilk

2 tablespoons unsalted butter or margarine

¼ teaspoon salt

1 teaspoon vanilla extract

1½ cups confectioners' sugar

1. Preheat the oven to 350F. Spray a decorative or regular 10-inch tube pan or Bundt pan with nonstick cooking spray.

2. To make the Five-Flavor Pound Cake: Sift and measure the flour in a mixing bowl. Add the salt and baking soda, sift again and set aside. Cream the butter and sugar with an electric mixer. Add the eggs, one at a time, incorporating each well. Add the flour alternately with the sour cream, beginning and ending with the flour. Mix for at least 2 minutes on medium speed. Add the extracts, one at a time, incorporating each before the next addition. Continue mixing the batter until it is shiny, for 3 to 5 minutes. Pour the batter into the cake pan, and place the pan in the center of the oven.

3. Bake for 1 hour, or until the cake is golden and a toothpick inserted in the center comes out clean. Remove from the oven, and cool the cake slightly on a wire rack before turning it out onto a serving plate. Cool the cake completely before drizzling with the Caramel Drizzle.

4. To make the Caramel Drizzle: Combine the brown sugar, milk, butter and salt in a saucepan. Bring to a boil over medium-high heat, stirring constantly. Reduce the heat to low, and cook until slightly thick, for about 5 minutes, stirring occasionally. Remove from the heat, stir in the vanilla and gradually beat in the confectioners' sugar. Stir until smooth and creamy. Let the icing cool slightly, then pour over the cake. The icing hardens as it cools.

PER SERVING: 630 CAL; 7G PROT; 23G FAT; 100G CARB; 160MG CHOL; 770MG SOD; 1G FIBER

CAROB CAKE WITH KIWI TOPPING

The mildly sweet kiwi fruit makes an unusual topping for this luscious cake. The cake is sweetened with brown rice syrup, which has the consistency and golden color of honey but is less pronounced in flavor.

Carob Cake

½ cup plus 2 tablespoons whole wheat pastry flour

½ cup unbleached flour

¼ cup carob powder or unsweetened cocoa powder

½ teaspoon baking soda

⅛ teaspoon salt

¼ cup granulated sugarcane juice

¼ cup vegetable oil

½ cup plus 2 tablespoons honey or maple syrup

½ tablespoon cider vinegar

1 teaspoon vanilla extract

Topping

2 pounds firm tofu

¾ cup brown rice syrup

½ cup honey

¾ cup fresh lime juice (preferably key lime juice)

2 tablespoons vegetable oil

1 tablespoon arrowroot

Glaze and Garnish

¾ teaspoons agar-agar flakes

6 tablespoons brown rice syrup

1 to 2 drops peppermint extract

2 to 3 kiwi fruit, peeled and sliced or 1 cup sliced strawberries

1. Preheat the oven to 350F. Lightly oil and flour an 8- or 10-inch round springform pan, and set aside.

2. To make the Cake: Sift together the whole wheat flour, unbleached flour, cocoa, baking soda and salt into a medium bowl.

3. Combine the sugarcane juice, oil, honey or maple syrup, vinegar, vanilla and 6 tablespoons water in a separate bowl, and mix until blended. Add the liquid ingredients to the dry ingredients, and stir until just blended. Pour the batter into the prepared pan.

4. Bake in the center of the oven for 25 to 35 minutes, or until a toothpick inserted in the center comes out clean.

5. Meanwhile, to make the Topping: Put the tofu, syrup, honey, lime juice, vegetable oil and arrowroot into a food processor or blender, and purée until smooth. Pour into the top part of a double boiler set over simmering water. Heat until the mixture thickens to the consistency of heavy cream. Let cool.

6. Pour the cooled topping onto the cake, and spread it evenly with a spatula. Refrigerate until the topping sets completely, for about 2 hours.

7. Meanwhile, to make the Glaze: In a small saucepan, dissolve the agar-agar in 6 tablespoons water. Add the syrup and peppermint extract. Bring to a simmer, then remove from heat. Let cool slightly.

8. To serve, remove the chilled cake from the refrigerator. Arrange the fruit on top. While the glaze is still warm, drizzle it over the fruit. Refrigerate the cake for 10 to 15 minutes before cutting.

PER SERVING: 511 CAL; 9G PROT; 13G FAT; 95G CARB; 0MG CHOL; 88MG SOD; 0G FIBER

FUDGE-GLAZED PUMPKIN CAKE

An eggless pumpkin cake, infused with warm spices, is topped with a thin chocolate glaze.

Cake

½ cup rolled oats
2 cups whole wheat pastry flour
½ cup yellow cornmeal
1 teaspoon baking soda
1 teaspoon baking powder
½ teaspoon sea salt
1½ teaspoons ground cinnamon
¼ teaspoon ground nutmeg
¾ teaspoon ground ginger
⅛ teaspoon ground cloves
1 12⅓-ounce package lite silken
    extra-firm tofu

Prune Purée

2 cups pitted prunes
1½ tablespoons vanilla extract
½ cup canned pumpkin purée
2 cups evaporated cane juice
1½ teaspoons vanilla extract

Fudge Glaze

3 tablespoons arrowroot
¼ cup unsweetened cocoa powder
⅓ cup brown rice syrup
1 teaspoon vanilla extract
¼ teaspoon almond extract

1. Preheat the oven to 350F. Spray a tube pan with nonstick cooking spray.

2. To make the Cake: Put the rolled oats in a food processor or blender, and pulse until powdered. Put the oats in a large bowl, and combine with the flour, cornmeal, baking soda, baking powder, salt, cinnamon, nutmeg, ginger and cloves. Set aside.

3. To make the Prune Purée: Put the prunes and vanilla in a food processor, and process for 30 seconds. Add ¾ cup water in a steady stream through the feed tube with the motor running. Blend until smooth. Store the prune purée in a covered container in the refrigerator; it will keep for at least 3 weeks.

4. Drain the tofu, put in a food processor and purée until smooth. Add ½ cup of the prune and the pumpkin purées, and blend. Add the sugar and vanilla. Blend until smooth. Fold the tofu mixture into the dry ingredients, and scrape the batter into the prepared pan.

5. Bake for 50 minutes, or until a tester inserted in the cake comes out clean. Set aside on a rack to cool.

6. Meanwhile, to make the Fudge Glaze: Combine the arrowroot and cocoa in a medium bowl. Heat the rice syrup in a small pan on the stove for 30 seconds. Using a wire whisk or fork, add the syrup to the cocoa mixture. Add the vanilla and almond extracts, and blend thoroughly. Drizzle immediately over the cooled cake.

PER SERVING: 107 CAL; 1G PROT; 0G FAT; 27G CARB; 0MG CHOL; 2MG SOD; 3G FIBER

MANGO-ALMOND CRUMB CAKE

Using a food processor to whip up the cake batter makes this an easy-to-assemble confection with slivered or sliced almonds and almond essence underscoring its flavor. This cake stars as a tropical dessert when topped with mango sorbet.

Cake

¼ pound unsalted butter, at room temperature

1 teaspoon almond extract

1 teaspoon coconut extract

1 cup granulated sugar

½ cup all-purpose flour

½ cup cake flour

2 extra-large eggs

Pinch salt

⅓ cup slivered dried mangoes, optional

1 mango, peeled and cubed

¾ cup slivered or sliced almonds

Streusel Topping

½ cup all-purpose flour

¼ cup superfine sugar

¼ cup brown sugar

3 tablespoons shredded coconut

⅓ cup firm unsalted butter

1 teaspoon almond extract

Pinch ground cardamom, optional

1. Preheat the oven to 375F. Lightly spray a 9-inch round or square cake pan with nonstick cooking spray. Set aside.

2. To make the Cake: Put the butter, almond and coconut extracts and sugar in a food processor, and purée until smooth. Add the flours, eggs and salt, and pulse until mixture is well combined. Scoop batter into prepared pan. Scatter candied mangoes, if using, mango cubes and almonds over cake batter.

3. Bake for 15 minutes.

4. Meanwhile, to prepare the Streusel Topping: Place the flour, sugars and shredded coconut in mixing bowl, and stir. Cut in butter and, using fingers, work mixture together until it forms small clumps. Sprinkle on almond extract, and work into mixture. Sprinkle Streusel Topping over cake.

5. Bake for 30 to 35 minutes more, or until a toothpick inserted in center comes out clean and the Streusel Topping has browned. Remove from oven, and cool before slicing.

PER SERVING: 530 CAL; 7G PROT; 28G FAT; 63G CARB; 115MG CHOL; 170MG SOD; 2G FIBER

Serve this treat with whipped cream, peach ice cream or a warmed fruit syrup.

4 tablespoons unsalted butter plus 4 tablespoons softened unsalted butter

½ cup firmly packed brown sugar

1 cup granulated sugar

3 large eggs

1 teaspoon almond extract

1 teaspoon lemon extract

Grated zest of 1 lemon

1 teaspoon salt

1 teaspoon baking powder

½ teaspoon baking soda

1½ cups all-purpose flour

½ cup buttermilk

3 large peaches, peeled and sliced

1 cup blueberries, rinsed

½ cup slivered almonds

1. Preheat the oven to 350F.

2. Melt 4 tablespoons of butter in a large ovenproof skillet over medium heat. Add the brown sugar, and reduce the heat to low. Let the sugar and butter cook for about 10 minutes, or until slightly caramelized.

3. Meanwhile, combine the remaining 4 tablespoons of butter and the granulated sugar in a mixing bowl, and beat until creamy. Add the eggs, one at a time, beating after each addition. Add the almond extract, lemon extract and lemon zest. Beat in the salt, baking powder, baking soda and flour, and stir in the buttermilk.

4. Remove the skillet from the heat, and place the peach slices, blueberries and almonds on the caramelized sugar. Pour the batter over the top, and place in the oven.

5. Bake for 45 to 50 minutes, or until the top is puffy and golden. Remove from the oven, invert and slice, or slice in the skillet, and serve.

PER SERVING: 450 CAL; 7G PROT; 17G FAT; 68G CARB; 110MG CHOL; 480MG SOD; 3G FIBER

On Selecting Sweeteners

In these days of counting calories and carbs, vegetarians and vegans keep an eye on sugar intake for reasons other than weight. Most cane sugars are filtered through cow bone char (although beet sugar is not). But consumers generally have no way of knowing what is their sugar's source, unless they buy unprocessed, unrefined, certified organic and natural sugars, or purchase products from companies that sell beet sugar only. If you're saying no to sugar, consider these sweet alternatives: agave nectar (from a succulent plant); barley malt syrup (from fermented barley); blackstrap molasses (from the final stage of sugar making); brown rice syrup (from sprouted brown rice); evaporated cane juice (from dehydrating leftover crystals from fresh cane juice); maple syrup and sugar (from maple tree sap); muscovado sugar (from the juice of the sugar cane); stevia (from the leaves of a shrub native to some South American countries); Sucanat® (from the evaporated syrup of crushed sugar cane); and turbinado sugar (from unrefined sugar that has been steamed clean).

Most people love the combination of chocolate and coffee, which here gets a real flavor boost from the potent espresso.

Cake

7 ounces soft tofu

½ cup mild honey

1 teaspoon vanilla extract

½ cup brewed espresso or very
   strong coffee

½ cup unsweetened cocoa powder

1¼ cups unbleached flour or whole
   wheat pastry flour

1 tablespoon baking powder

1 teaspoon baking soda

Sauce

10 ounces soft tofu

½ cup honey

1 teaspoon vanilla extract

¾ cup brewed espresso or very
   strong coffee

1 to 2 tablespoons brandy or cognac

Optional Garnishes

Fresh or frozen berries of choice

Mint sprigs

Confectioners' sugar

1. Preheat the oven to 350F. Lightly oil an 8½-inch Bundt pan and set aside.

2. To make the Cake: Put the tofu, the honey and vanilla in a food processor or blender, and purée until smooth. Add the espresso or coffee and cocoa, and process to blend.

3. Sift the flour with the baking powder and baking soda into a bowl. If using a food processor, add the flour mixture to the tofu mixture, and process until smooth. If using a blender, transfer the tofu mixture to a bowl, add the flour mixture and beat well. Pour the mixture into the prepared pan

4. Bake until firm to the touch and a toothpick comes out clean, for about 25 minutes. Remove from the oven and cool the cake for 10 to 15 minutes in the pan, then remove from the pan and continue to cool on a baking rack.

5. Meanwhile, to make the Sauce: Combine the tofu, honey, vanilla, coffee and brandy or cognac in a food processor or blender and process until creamy. Transfer to a bowl, cover and refrigerate at least 1 hour before using. (The sauce will thicken as it cools; dilute with more espresso if necessary.)

6. To serve, slice the cake into 8 to 10 slices, and place on individual dessert plates. Spoon ¼ to ⅓ cup sauce over each serving, and garnish with berries, mint and confectioners' sugar, if using.

PER SERVING WITH SAUCE: 196 CAL; 6G PROT; 2G FAT; 17G CARB; 0MG CHOL; 268MG SOD; 3G FIBER

Use any combination of fresh berries, about one cup per person. Serve these with whipped cream or ice cream if you like.

1 ¼ cups all-purpose flour

1 ½ cups granulated sugar

⅓ cup unsweetened cocoa powder

½ teaspoon baking soda

¼ teaspoon salt

⅔ cup buttermilk

¼ cup vegetable oil

4 tablespoons unsalted butter, melted and cooled

1 large egg, beaten

1 teaspoon vanilla extract

4 cups hulled and sliced strawberries

2 cups blackberries

2 cups blueberries

2 cups frozen sweetened raspberries

1. Preheat the oven to 375F. Grease 8 to 10 muffin cups, or line the muffin tin cups with paper or foil liners, and set aside.

2. Whisk together the flour, ¾ cup of the sugar, the cocoa powder, baking soda and salt. In a separate bowl, whisk together the buttermilk, oil, melted butter, egg and vanilla. Make well in center of dry ingredients, add the buttermilk mixture, and stir just to combine. Overmixing will make the cake tough.

3. Spoon the batter into the prepared muffin cups, filling each about two-thirds full. Sprinkle the tops with ¼ cup of the sugar.

4. Bake for 20 to 25 minutes, or until a toothpick inserted into the center comes out clean. Remove from the oven, and cool in the muffin tin.

5. Mix the cleaned berries gently. Put thawed raspberries in a blender or food processor, and purée until smooth. Add the remaining ½ cup sugar, and process until dissolved. Strain to remove the seeds, if desired. Pour over the berries. Mix and chill.

6. To serve, break each cake in half horizontally, and place the bottom in a bowl. Spoon about 1 cup of berries over the bottom of the cake, and cover with the cake top.

PER SERVING: 380 CAL; 4G PROT; 12G FAT; 68G CARB; 35MG CHOL; 190MG SOD; 7G FIBER

CHOCOLATE CUPCAKES

Kids gobble up these delicious cupcakes, which have neither eggs nor dairy products. You'll love them, too.

Cupcakes

2½ cups unbleached flour

⅔ cups unsweetened cocoa powder, sifted

2 cups granulated sugar

2 teaspoons baking soda

½ teaspoon salt

6 tablespoons vegetable oil

1 teaspoon vanilla extract

2 tablespoons cider vinegar, white vinegar or rice vinegar

Icing

1⅓ cups unsweetened cocoa powder, sifted

1½ cups granulated sugar

⅔ cup cornstarch

2 cups plain lite soymilk or skim milk

½ teaspoon vanilla extract

Optional Decorations

12 small cookies such as animal crackers or amaretti

Finely shredded unsweetened coconut

Colored sprinkles

1. Preheat the oven to 375F. Line a 12-cup muffin tin with paper or foil liners, and set aside.

2. To make the Cupcakes: Combine the flour, cocoa, sugar, baking powder and salt in a bowl, and mix to blend.

3. Mix the vegetable oil, vanilla and vinegar in a small bowl. Add 2¼ cups plus 2 tablespoons water and blend to mix. Add the liquid ingredients to the dry ingredients, and mix just until blended. Do not overmix. Fill the muffin cups with the batter. Bake until a toothpick inserted in the cupcakes comes out clean, for 20 to 25 minutes. Remove the cupcakes, and place on a rack to cool.

4. To make Icing: Whisk together the cocoa and the sugar in a medium saucepan. Combine the cornstarch and milk in a separate bowl until no lumps remain. Whisk the cornstarch mixture into the cocoa-sugar mixture. Cook over medium heat, stirring constantly and scraping the bottom and sides of the pan with a heatproof rubber spatula, until the mixture is glossy, about 7 minutes. Remove from the heat and stir in the vanilla. Beat to remove any lumps (strain through a fine sieve if necessary). Cool completely, stirring occasionally.

5. Ice the cooled cupcakes. While the icing is still sticky, decorate the cupcakes by placing a cookie in the center and sprinkling with coconut or colored sprinkles, if using.

PER CUPCAKE: 406 CAL; 7G PROT; 4G FAT; 86G CARB; 0MG CHOL; 240MG SOD; 7G FIBER

NO-ROLL PIECRUST

This crust becomes its flaky best if allowed to chill at least 20 minutes before filling.

¾ cup unbleached white flour

1 tablespoon sesame seeds

3 tablespoons unsalted butter or margarine

1 tablespoon white vinegar

½ to 1 tablespoon ice water as needed

1. Spray a 9-inch pie pan with nonstick cooking spray, and set aside.

2. Put the flour, sesame seeds, and butter or margarine in a food processor, and process until the mixture resembles a coarse meal.

3. Add the vinegar slowly with the machine running, and add tiny drops of ice water, stopping the machine as soon as the dough leaves the sides of the bowl. Put the dough into the pie pan, and press it with your fingertips to cover the bottom and sides evenly. Chill for 20 to 30 minutes. Use as the recipe directs.

PER SERVING: 81 CAL; 1G PROT; 5G FAT; 8 CARB; 11MG CHOL; 44MG SOD; 0G FIBER

APPLE-CINNAMON STRUDEL

Delicious and *less than a gram of fat per serving? You better believe it!*

Strudel

8 medium-sized Granny Smith apples, peeled, cored and sliced

½ cup raisins

2 tablespoons honey or brown sugar

Ground cinnamon to taste

Ground nutmeg to taste

6 sheets frozen phyllo, partially thawed and covered with a damp tea towel

Cinnamon Sauce

2 cups apple cider

4 teaspoons cornstarch or arrowroot

Ground cinnamon to taste

Ground nutmeg to taste

1. Preheat the oven to 400F. Lightly spray a cookie sheet with nonstick cooking spray or a mist of water. Set aside.

2. To make the Strudel: Mix the apples and raisins in a bowl with the honey or brown sugar. Sprinkle with the cinnamon and nutmeg.

3. Lay 1 sheet of phyllo on the prepared cookie sheet. Lay another sheet of phyllo on top of the first one, spray with nonstick cooking spray or water and place a third sheet on top.

4. Spoon half of the apple mixture on the phyllo, and roll up lengthwise, turning in the ends to enclose the filling. Cut ¾ of the way through the roll to make 7 servings. Repeat the procedure with the other 3 sheets of phyllo and the remaining apple mixture.

5. Bake until lightly browned, for 15 to 20 minutes. Remove from the oven.

6. Meanwhile, to make the Cinnamon Sauce: Combine the cider, cornstarch or arrowroot, cinnamon and nutmeg in a small saucepan, and whisk thoroughly until smooth. Heat to a boil, stirring constantly. Remove from the heat.

7. Use a sharp knife to separate slices of the strudel. Serve warm, topped with the warm sauce.

PER SERVING WITH 2 TABLESPOONS SAUCE: 105 CAL; 1G PROT; 0.2G FAT; 24G CARB; 0MG CHOL; 38MG SOD; 3G FIBER

APRICOT CREAM TART

Phyllo, a paper-thin flaky pastry, replaces the usual pie crust in this light sweet-tart dessert.

8 sheets frozen phyllo

1 cup dried apricots

½ cup honey

½ teaspoon agar-agar powder or 1 tablespoon agar-agar flakes, dissolved in 2 tablespoons water

8 ounces soft tofu

½ teaspoon vanilla extract

2 to 3 teaspoons fresh lemon juice

1 16-ounce can apricot halves

¼ to ⅓ cup fruit-sweetened apricot jam

1 ounce melted chocolate for decorating, optional

1. Preheat the oven to 350F. Spray a 9-inch pie pan with nonstick cooking spray.

2. Place a sheet of phyllo in the pan, and spray the phyllo with nonstick cooking spray. Fold the edges inward so they do not extend beyond the rim of the pan. Put down another phyllo layer, spray and fold. Repeat this procedure with the remaining phyllo until the pan is covered. Bake until crispy and golden brown, for 15 to 20 minutes.

3. Meanwhile, combine the apricots, honey and 2 cups water in a saucepan, and cook over medium-low heat until the apricots are very soft and the liquid has reduced to a heavy syrup. Add the dissolved agar-agar, and cook for several minutes more minutes.

4. Put the mixture into a food processor or blender. Add the tofu, vanilla and lemon juice, and purée until smooth. Pour into the crust. Drain the apricot halves, and arrange them on the tart.

5. Melt the apricot jam in a small saucepan over low heat, and brush it on top. Drizzle the chocolate on top in a zigzag fashion. Chill at least 1 hour before serving.

PER SERVING: 330 CAL; 8G PROT; 3G FAT; 67G CARB; 0MG CHOL; 119MG SOD; 5G FIBER

UPSIDE-DOWN PEACH PIE

It's hard to believe that a slice of this delicious pie—with its crunchy-sweet topping—has only 52 calories and almost no fat.

Filling

4 cups sliced, fresh peeled and pitted peaches

3 tablespoons whole wheat flour

1/3 cup unsweetened apricot preserves

2 teaspoons fresh lemon juice

1/8 teaspoon grated nutmeg

Topping

1 tablespoon maple syrup

1/2 teaspoon vanilla extract

1/4 cup quick-cooking rolled oats

1 tablespoon cornmeal

1. Preheat the oven to 375F.

2. To make Filling: Gently mix the peaches with the flour in a bowl, and transfer to a 9-inch pie plate. Mix together the preserves, lemon juice and nutmeg in a small bowl, and spoon the mixture over the peaches.

3. Bake for 30 minutes. Remove from the oven, and set aside. Reduce the oven temperature to 350F.

4. Meanwhile, to make the Topping: Combine the maple syrup and vanilla in a bowl. Add the oats and cornmeal, and mix well. Crumble the topping mixture over the cooked peach filling, and return the pie to the oven for 15 minutes more. Serve warm or cold.

PER SERVING: 52 CAL; 1G PROT; 0.2G FAT; 13G CARB; 0MG CHOL; 1MG SOD; 3G FIBER

LOUISIANA SWEET POTATO PIE

This treat conjures up Deep South sweets, often highly caloric. But this one comes to the table without loads of fat and calories.

1/2 cup evaporated skim milk

1 teaspoon apple cider vinegar

1 teaspoon baking soda

2 cups cooked, mashed sweet potatoes

1 tablespoon unsalted butter or margarine, melted

1/3 cup honey, or to taste

1 teaspoon baking powder

1/2 teaspoon ground cinnamon

1/2 teaspoon ground nutmeg

1/4 teaspoon salt

3/4 cup egg substitute or 3 large eggs, beaten

1 9-inch pie crust, chilled (see No-Roll Pie Piecrust on page 402)

Ground cinnamon for garnish, optional

1. Preheat the oven to 400F.

2. Combine the evaporated milk, vinegar and baking soda in a small bowl, and mix to blend. Set aside.

3. Combine the sweet potatoes, honey, baking powder, cinnamon, nutmeg, salt and egg substitute or eggs in a food processor or blender and process to blend. Add the milk mixture, and process until smooth. Pour into the piecrust.

4. Bake for 10 minutes. Reduce the heat to 300F, and bake for 45 to 50 minutes more or until set. Remove from the oven, and cool completely. Slice and serve at room temperature or lightly chilled. Sprinkle with cinnamon, if desired.

PER SERVING: 234 CAL; 4G PROT; 6G FAT; 29G CARB; 15MG CHOL; 323MG SOD; 3G FIBER

DATE AND PECAN BREAD PUDDING

Although this bread pudding is made with dates and pecans, you may use a whole range of dried fruits and nuts. Think about cranberries and almonds, orange peel and walnuts, raisins and walnuts, cashew and figs or dried pineapple and cashews. Plan to make this cake one day ahead because it needs to be refrigerated overnight.

3 large eggs or ¾ cup egg substitute

2½ cups vanilla soymilk

½ cup brown sugar

2 teaspoons vanilla extract

2 teaspoons ground cinnamon

4 cups bread cubes, preferably whole wheat

1 cup chopped dates, raisins or prunes

½ cup chopped pecans

1. Beat together the eggs, milk, sugar, cinnamon and vanilla in a large mixing bowl. Put the bread cubes, date and pecans in a separate large bowl. Pour the egg mixture over the bread, stirring to combine and moisten the bread. Cover the bowl, and refrigerate overnight—the dates should soften overnight.

2. Preheat the oven to 350F. Butter a 3-quart baking dish. Pour the mixture into the dish.

3. Bake the pudding for 50 minutes, or until the top browns and mixture firms. Remove from the oven, and cool slightly before serving.

PER SERVING: 350 CAL; 9G PROT; 12G FAT; 52G CARB; 105MG CHOL; 230MG SOD; 4G FIBER

COCONUT TROPICAL PUDDING

This lush, creamy, soft pudding—infused with coconut, vanilla and almond flavors and sparked by a topping of colorful strawberries—beckons after a meal of grilled vegetables and tofu, or after any Asian-inspired or Pacific Rim–based main dish. The strawberries add a festive splash of color against the white pudding. Do not whisk the cornstarch, as it will break down, and that prevents it from thickening properly. Instead, stir gently and slowly with a wooden spoon.

3 tablespoons cornstarch

2 egg yolks

Pinch salt

½ cup granulated sugar, or to taste

2 cups light coconut milk

1 teaspoon vanilla extract

1 teaspoon almond extract

½ cup shredded coconut

6 coconut macaroons, crumbled

1 quart strawberries, rinsed, stemmed and sliced, for garnish

1. Combine the cornstarch, egg yolks, salt and sugar in a mixing bowl. Stir in ¼ cup of the coconut milk to make a paste.

2. Pour the remaining coconut milk into a large saucepan, and, stirring gently with a wooden spoon, add the cornstarch mixture to the pan. Heat over medium heat, and bring to a boil, stirring slowly and gently. Immediately reduce the heat to medium-low, add the vanilla and almond extracts and continue stirring occasionally, carefully scraping the sides of the pan.

3. Remove the pan from the heat when the pudding is thickened but not stiff, and pour the pudding into a serving bowl. Stir in the shredded coconut, and sprinkle the top with crumbled coconut macaroons. Serve the warm pudding with strawberries.

PER SERVING: 510 CAL; 6G PROT; 24G FAT; 69G CARB; 105MG CHOL; 160MG SOD; 5G FIBER

DOUBLE CHOCOLATE BREAD PUDDING

SERVES 12

This bread pudding can be served as is or with raspberry sauce or warm fudge sauce poured over the top. To make the recipe ahead, cool completely in pan on a wire rack, then cover with foil and refrigerate up to 3 days. Wrap slices in foil and warm in the oven. You might want to top this with some of the Chocolate Sauce (page 416).

⅓ cup dried cranberries

¼ cup apple juice

2 large eggs

3 large egg whites

1 cup lightly packed light brown sugar

2 tablespoons unsweetened cocoa powder

3 cups chocolate soymilk

1 teaspoon vanilla extract

1-pound loaf challah egg bread, torn into 1-inch pieces

½ cup pitted prunes, chopped

1. In a small bowl, soak cranberries in apple juice until they're plump, about 20 minutes.

2. Preheat the oven to 350F. Coat a 9 ½-inch tube pan with nonstick cooking spray.

3. Whisk together the eggs, egg whites, brown sugar and cocoa in a large mixing bowl. Whisk in the soymilk and vanilla until well blended. Add the bread pieces. Drain the cranberries, and add to the bread mixture along with the prunes. Stir with a fork until the bread is thoroughly moistened. Let stand for 10 minutes.

4. Pack the mixture into the prepared pan. Place the pan on a baking sheet, and bake until the bread pudding is puffed and lightly browned and a knife inserted near the center comes out clean, for about 50 minutes. Transfer the pan to a wire rack, and cool for 20 minutes. Unmold onto a serving plate. Serve warm.

PER SERVING: 230 CAL; 7G PROT; 3G FAT; 43G CARB; 31MG CHOL; 294MG SOD; 2G FIBER

INDIAN PUDDING

SERVES 6

A New England dish from Colonial days, this cornmeal-based pudding is traditionally made with molasses. This updated version is sweetened with maple syrup and sparked with ginger.

4 cups low-fat milk

1 cup maple syrup

¼ cup unsalted butter

⅔ cup yellow cornmeal

½ teaspoon dried ginger

¼ teaspoon ground allspice

1 cup dried cranberries or cherries

1. Preheat the oven to 300F. Butter a 2-quart baking dish.

2. Combine 3 cups milk and the maple syrup in a medium saucepan, and cook over medium heat until just boiling. Add the butter.

3. Combine the cornmeal, ginger and allspice in a bowl. Gradually stir the cornmeal mixture into the hot milk. Reduce the heat to low, and cook until thickened and the mixture coats the back of a spoon, for about 5 minutes. Fold in the cranberries or cherries.

4. Spoon the mixture into baking dish, and pour the remaining milk over the top of the pudding. Do not stir. Bake until the milk has been absorbed and the top is golden brown, for 1½ to 2 hours. Serve warm.

PER SERVING: 343 CAL; 7G PROT; 10G FAT; 58G CARB; 28MG CHOL; 170MG SOD; 6G FIBER

SPICED CARROT PUDDING

Use a fancy charlotte mold or other decorative shape to dress up this pudding.

1 to 3 teaspoons unsalted butter or margarine, for the mold

1 to 3 teaspoons granulated sugar, for the mold

2 cups raisins

1 cup grated, unpeeled Granny Smith apples or other tart green apples

1 cup chopped, toasted pecans or walnuts (page 47)

1 cup grated, unpeeled carrots

1 cup grated, peeled potatoes

¾ cup all-purpose flour

1 teaspoon baking soda

½ teaspoon ground cinnamon

½ teaspoon ground nutmeg

½ teaspoon ground allspice

Pinch ground cloves

½ cup unsalted butter or margarine

1 cup granulated sugar

1. Grease an 8-cup mold with the 3 teaspoons butter, and dust lightly with the sugar. Set aside.

2. Combine the fruit, nuts, carrots and potatoes in a bowl and set aside. Combine the flour, baking soda, cinnamon, nutmeg, allspice and cloves in a separate bowl. Using an electric mixer, beat the butter and sugar together in a mixing bowl until light and fluffy. Stir in the carrot mixture with a wooden spoon. Add the flour mixture, and blend until just combined.

3. Spoon the batter into the prepared mold. The mold should not be more than two-thirds full. Run a knife through the batter to release any air pockets. Cover the mold with its lid or with a double-thickness of foil pressed tightly to the sides and tied with string.

4. Pour 1 inch of water into the bottom of a large saucepan or other pot that is a little larger than the mold. Set a trivet, an inverted heatproof bowl or custard cups in the bottom of the pot to create a platform. Bring the water to a boil. Set the mold on the platform, cover the pot and steam until the center springs back slightly when touched, for about 2½ hours. Remove the mold from the pot, and uncover. Let the pudding sit 10 minutes before unmolding. To unmold, place a platter or plate over the mold then invert. Slice and serve warm or room temperature.

PER SERVING: 222 CAL; 2G PROT; 7G FAT; 34G CARB; 0MG CHOL; 97MG SOD; 2G FIBER

RICE PUDDING WITH DATES

In this Middle Eastern recipe, dates—not sugar—are the primary sweetener. The pudding is delicious warm or cold.

2 cups cooked white rice

15 pitted dates, finely chopped

2 cups low-fat milk

3 tablespoons granulated sugar

1. Put the rice in a food processor or blender, and process until coarsely crumbled. Transfer the rice to a large saucepan. Add the dates, milk and sugar.

2. Cook, covered, over low heat, until the dates are tender, for 15 to 20 minutes. Remove from the heat, and serve warm or chilled.

PER SERVING: 188 CAL; 5G PROT; 1G FAT; 42G CARB; 3MG CHOL; 42MG SOD; 1G FIBER

PEANUT BUTTER PUDDING

Serve as is or layer the pudding in parfait glasses with crushed gingersnaps or chocolate graham crackers. You could also pour the pudding into a prebaked, cooled graham cracker crust and freeze overnight for a scrumptious no-fuss pie.

1 12.3-ounce package extra-firm tofu, well drained

¼ cup plus 2 tablespoons creamy peanut butter

⅓ cup brown sugar

2 to 3 teaspoons vanilla extract

1. Put all the ingredients into a food processor or blender, and purée until smooth and creamy.

2. Divide the mixture among dessert dishes, cover with plastic wrap and refrigerate for at least 3 hours before serving.

PER SERVING: 240 CAL; 11G PROT; 15G FAT; 17G CARB; 0MG CHOL; 40MG SOD; 1G FIBER

SUMMER PUDDING

Summer pudding is an old-time English dessert that makes use of stale white bread and fresh summer berries, lightly cooked to release their juices. It's lovely served on its own or with whipped cream. Use blueberries, strawberries and raspberries. Plan to make this one day ahead of serving because the pudding must be refrigerated overnight.

8 cups berries, hulled, rinsed and dried

⅔ cup granulated sugar

14 to 16 ½-inch-thick slices firm Italian bread, crusts removed

1. Combine the berries and sugar in a large, nonaluminum saucepan. Cook over medium heat until the sugar is dissolved and the berries release their juice but still retain some shape, for about 10 minutes.

2. Place the berries in a large sieve over a bowl to catch the juices. Swirl some of the berry juice in the bottom and up the sides of a flat-bottom, glass or ceramic mold or bowl with a 3-quart capacity.

3. Cover the bottom and sides up to 1½ inches from the top of the mold with the bread slices, cutting pieces to fit any holes. Pour a little more reserved juice over the bread on the sides.

4. Add half of the fruit. Top with a layer of bread, piecing to fit. Cover with remaining fruit, then with a layer of bread, piecing to fit. Pour in all but ½ cup of the remaining juice, brushing with a pastry brush to cover the bread.

5. Cover the top bread layer with plastic wrap. Place a flat plate or pot or smaller mold on top. Weight with four 15-ounce cans (pumpkin, beans, tomatoes). Set on a plate to catch any drips. Refrigerate overnight.

6. To serve, remove the weights and plastic wrap. Loosen the edges of the pudding carefully with a spatula. Invert onto a serving plate. Brush any white bread spots with the reserved juice. Slice into wedges with a serrated knife.

PER SERVING: 203 CAL; 4G PROT; 1G FAT; 47G CARB; 0MG CHOL; 209MG SOD; 5G FIBER

FRUIT AND CRÊPE PUDDING

This pudding is as beautiful as it is delicious—and it has only 6 grams of fat per serving.

2 cups soymilk

½ cup honey

2 teaspoons powdered agar-agar or ¼ cup flaked agar-agar, dissolved in 2 tablespoons water

¼ cup cornstarch dissolved in 3 tablespoons water

2 teaspoons vanilla extract

10 ounces soft tofu

2 tablespoons orange liqueur

12 No-Cholesterol Dessert Crêpes (page 413)

4 cups chopped or sliced fruit in season such as strawberries, bananas, kiwi, pears, papayas, mangoes, oranges

Fruit syrup, optional

1. Combine the soymilk and honey in a medium saucepan, and cook over low heat until hot. Add the dissolved agar-agar, and stir until the mixture boils for several minutes. Add the dissolved cornstarch, and cook until thickened. Add the vanilla, whisk to blend and set aside.

2. Put the tofu and orange liqueur into a food processor or blender, and purée until smooth. Add the soymilk, and blend to mix. Pour into a bowl, cover and chill in the refrigerator until set and custardlike, for about 2 hours.

3. To assemble, place a crêpe on the bottom of a 2-quart glass bowl. Place 3 or 4 crêpes around the side of the bowl so that the bowl is completely covered. Spread about ½ cup custard on the bottom and place a layer of fruit on top. Place a crêpe on top and spread more custard over it. Top with another layer of fruit. Continue layering, ending with a crêpe. (If the edges of some crepes are jutting out on the side of the bowl, fold them over.) Place a plate on top of the pudding to hold it down. Refrigerate at least 2 hours.

4. To serve, remove the plastic wrap from the pudding, and place a platter over the top. Invert to unmold. Garnish with more fruit, or drizzle with fruit syrup, if using. Cut the pudding into wedges.

PER SERVING WITHOUT SAUCE: 310 CAL; 8G PROT, 6G FAT; 56G CARB; 0MG CHOL; 167MG SOD; 5G FIBER

MANGO-PINEAPPLE CREAM PUDDING

Exotic and creamy, this instant-ready pudding will please the whole family.

1 pound silken soft tofu

1 6-ounce container pineapple yogurt

1 cup crushed pineapple

2 ripe mangoes, peeled

½ cup confectioners' sugar

2 cups graham cracker crumbs

Put tofu, yogurt, pineapple, mangoes and confectioners' sugar into the container of a food processor or blender, and purée until smooth. Pour half the pudding mixture into a decorative 3-quart dessert bowl, spread the pudding with 1 cup graham cracker crumbs, add the remaining pudding and top with the remaining crumbs. Refrigerate until ready to use.

PER SERVING: 260 CAL; 7G PROT; 5G FAT; 47G CARB; 0MG CHOL; 190MG SOD; 2G FIBER

ALMOST TRADITIONAL CHOCOLATE MOUSSE

SERVES 6

This sinfully rich dessert is a chocoholic's dream! It's easy to make, too.

¾ cup low-fat milk

6 ounces semisweet chocolate chips

½ cup egg substitute

2 tablespoons unsalted butter or margarine, at room temperature

1 tablespoon grated orange zest

¼ cup strong brewed coffee

2 tablespoons orange liqueur

Nondairy topping or whipped cream, for garnish, optional

1. Heat the milk in a medium saucepan until almost boiling.

2. Combine the chocolate chips, egg substitute, butter, orange zest, coffee and orange liqueur in a food processor or blender. Add the hot milk and process at high speed until smooth and creamy, about 2 minutes.

3. Pour into a medium bowl or individual custard cups, cover and chill for at least 2 hours before serving. Garnish with a rosette of nondairy topping or whipped cream, if using, before serving.

PER SERVING: 230 CAL; 5G PROT; 12G FAT; 8G CARB; 12MG CHOL; 84MG SOD; 2G FIBER

POACHED PLUMS

SERVES 6

The number of plums in each serving is your choice; however, larger plums should be used if you are serving fewer of them. Be careful that you don't buy "prune" plums, which are very tart. And do warn guests that the pits are still hiding in the plums.

18 small, very ripe plums (about 4 pound)

½ cup honey

½ teaspoon cloves

2 tablespoons vanilla extract

3 cups red wine

Mint sprigs or almond slices for garnish, if desired

1. Wash the plums, and put them in a 4-quart glass or stainless saucepan. Add the honey, cloves, vanilla, wine and enough water to cover. Bring to a boil over medium heat. Cover, and cook for 15 minutes. Use a slotted spoon to carefully transfer the cooked plums to a bowl.

2. Return the pan to the heat, and cook until the liquid reduces to about 3 cups. Taste, and add more honey if necessary.

3. To serve, place 3 plums in each of 6 bowls, and spoon the cooking liquid over them. Garnish with mint sprigs or a few almond slices.

PER SERVING: 450 CAL; 3G PROT; 19G FAT; 69G CARB; 0MG CHOL; 55MG SOD; 4G FIBER

PEAR COBBLER

Serve this dessert with scoops of ice cream, or for an indulgent breakfast, try it with a dollop of yogurt. You can substitute apples, plums, peaches, nectarines, cherries or blueberries for the pears, if you prefer.

4 peeled, sliced pears
¼ cup raisins or currants
4 teaspoons brown sugar
¼ teaspoon ground cinnamon
¼ teaspoon vanilla extract
1 cup rolled oats
3 tablespoons whole wheat pastry flour
4 teaspoons margarine

1. Preheat the oven to 325F.

2. Combine the pears, raisins or currants, 3 teaspoons brown sugar, cinnamon and vanilla in a medium bowl, and stir to mix. Transfer the mixture to an 8-inch-square baking pan.

3. Mix the oats, remaining 1 teaspoon brown sugar, flour and margarine in a small bowl with a fork until the margarine is evenly distributed and the mixture is crumbly. Spoon it on top of the pear mixture.

4. Bake until browned, for about 45 minutes. Remove from the oven, and let cool slightly before serving. Serve warm or chilled.

PER SERVING: 245 CAL; 5G PROT; 4G FAT; 41G CARB; 0MG CHOL; 27MG SOD; 7G FIBER

MAPLE RUM RICE CUSTARD WITH CHOCOLATE SAUCE

If you enjoy creamy desserts like pudding and flan, try this treat, which has only 3 grams of fat per serving. Serve it in bowls or goblets layered with chocolate sauce.

Maple Rum Rice Custard
1 cup white medium- or short-grain rice
2 cups soymilk or rice milk
½ cup maple syrup
1 teaspoon vanilla extract
2 tablespoons light or dark rum

Chocolate Sauce
½ cup unsweetened cocoa powder
½ to ¾ cup light honey
1 teaspoon vanilla extract

1. To make the Maple Rum Rice Custard: Combine the rice, soymilk or rice milk, maple syrup and 2½ cups water in a large saucepan, and bring to a boil. Reduce the heat to low, cover and cook until the rice is very soft and most of the liquid has been absorbed, for about 1¼ hours

2. Put the cooked rice mixture into a blender or food processor, and purée until very smooth. Transfer to a bowl, cover tightly and chill for several hours.

3. To make the Chocolate Sauce: Combine the cocoa, 1 cup water, honey, and vanilla extract in a medium saucepan and whisk to mix. Bring to a boil, lower the heat and simmer gently, stirring often, until the sauce has thickened and is reduced to 1 cup, about 15 to 20 minutes. Let cool.

4. To serve, spoon the maple-flavored rice into small bowls or goblets, and drizzle with the Chocolate Sauce.

PER SERVING: 336 CAL; 6G PROT; 3G FAT; 69G CARB; 0MG CHOL; 18MG SOD; 5G FIBER

TOFU CLAFOUTI

Clafouti is a home-style French dessert of whole, sweet cherries baked in custard. When you don't have cherries, you can substitute blueberries, raspberries, blackberries or diced peaches. Without the fruit, this is an excellent baked custard recipe. Make half the recipe (without the cherries), and stir in 8 ounces of melted chocolate chips for an eggless French Pots de Crème.

1 cup fructose or sweetener of your choice

3 10.5-ounce packages extra-firm silken tofu, drained if necessary

2 tablespoons almond oil or canola oil

2 tablespoons lemon juice

1 teaspoon ground cinnamon

1 tablespoon vanilla extract

2 cups pitted black cherries

1. Preheat the oven to 350F. Butter a 9-inch square cake pan, and set aside.

2. Put all the ingredients except the cherries in a blender, and purée until smooth. Pour into the pan, and add the cherries.

3. Bake for 60 minutes, or until a thin knife blade inserted into the center comes out clean. Serve warm.

PER SERVING: 340 CAL; 9G PROT; 10G FAT; 54G CARB; 0MG CHOL; 45MG SOD; 2G FIBER

BAKED HAWAII

With a blending of coconut, pineapple and macadamia nuts, this pie takes its cues from the tropics. Be sure to squeeze out any excess juice from the pineapple shreds, or it may dilute the filling. A quick freezing of the filling mix firms it up fast.

1 package instant coconut-flavored pudding mix

1¾ cups nonfat milk

1 teaspoon vanilla extract

1 prepared crumb pie shell

1¾ cups canned shredded pineapple

¼ cup brown sugar

¼ cup crushed macadamia nuts as garnish

¼ cup shredded coconut as garnish

2 tablespoons diced crystallized ginger, or more as desired, for garnish

1. Preheat the oven to 450F.

2. Mix the instant pudding with the milk and vanilla extract, and pour into the prepared pie shell. Put in the freezer immediately.

3. Drain the pineapple, and reserve juice for another use. Squeeze the excess juice from the shreds, and put the shreds in a baking dish. Sprinkle with the brown sugar, and bake for 15 minutes, or until the sugar bubbles. Remove from the oven.

4. Take the firmed pudding mixture from the freezer just before serving, spoon the pineapple mixture over the top and garnish with the macadamia nuts, coconut shreds and crystallized ginger.

PER SERVING: 310 CAL; 4G PROT; 11G FAT; 51G CARB; 0MG CHOL; 450MG SOD; 2G FIBER

NO-CHOLESTEROL DESSERT CRÊPES

These sweetened crêpes are just right for desserts. They're so good, it's hard to believe that they have neither dairy products nor eggs. Chickpea flour, or besan, *is available at natural food stores and Indian markets.*

¼ cup granulated sugarcane juice or sugar

2 tablespoons egg substitute or ½ beaten egg

½ cup whole wheat pastry flour

½ cup unbleached flour

⅓ cup chickpea flour

½ teaspoon salt

Vegetable oil for the crêpe pan

1. Whisk together the sugarcane juice or sugar, egg substitute and 1½ cups plus 2 tablespoons water in a large bowl. Stir in the whole wheat flour, unbleached flour, chickpea flour and salt, and whisk until blended; do not overmix. Or, process all the ingredients in a blender or food processor.

2. Place a crêpe pan or a nonstick 8-inch skillet over low heat. Brush it lightly with oil, and let the pan heat for a few minutes.

3. Remove from the heat, and pour in 3 to 4 tablespoons of the batter and tilt the pan so that the batter coats the bottom of the pan evenly. Cook for a few minutes over medium-low heat. The crêpe will become lightly browned. Flip the crêpe with a spatula, and cook on the other side for 30 seconds. Slide it onto a plate. Repeat with the remaining batter, stacking the crêpes on the plate. Use them at once, or wrap them in plastic and refrigerate for up to one week.

PER CRÊPE: 74 CAL; 2G PROT; 0.2G FAT; 16G CARB; 0MG CHOL; 107MG SOD; 2G FIBER

CHOCOLATE FONDUE

You will need either a special chocolate fondue pot or a heat defuser to place under a ceramic fondue pot. Or simply heat your chocolate on the stove before serving and reheat as needed.

Chocolate Fondue

½ cup heavy cream

1 pound chocolate chips or chopped semisweet chocolate

2 tablespoons Grand Marnier or other fruit liqueur or orange juice

Accompaniments

1 pint ripe strawberries

2 large navel oranges

4 regular bananas or 8 baby bananas

1 medium-sized fresh pineapple, peeled, cored and cubed

2 cups dried apricots

4 ounces dried papaya (optional)

4 ounces dried mango (optional)

3 cups cubed cake, either angel food or pound cake

1 pound assorted finger cookies

1. Wash and hull the strawberries, and let air dry. Peel the oranges, using your hands to keep skin on sections unbroken. Break apart the sections, and place on a rack to dry for 1 hour. Cut regular bananas into 1-inch lengths.

2. Heat the cream in a saucepan over medium heat, and bring to a boil. Remove from the heat, and add the chocolate, softening for 3 minutes. If not totally melted, place the pan over lowest heat, and stir constantly until melted. Stir in the Grand Marnier, and remove from the heat.

3. Transfer the chocolate to a fondue pot or ceramic pot, and serve with accompaniments. Do not continue to heat at the table.

PER SERVING: 220 CAL; 2G PROT; 15G FAT; 24G CARB; 15MG CHOL; 10MG SOD; 2G FIBER

MIXED DRIED FRUIT TURNOVERS

Choose your favorite dried fruit for this recipe. Try a combination of apples, raisins and pears or perhaps a mixture of peaches, apricots and banana.

1 cup coarsely chopped mixed dried fruit

½ cup apple juice

¼ cup chopped walnuts

1¼ teaspoons ground cinnamon

⅛ teaspoon black walnut extract or vanilla extract, optional

¼ cup granulated sugar

3 tablespoons vegetable oil

8 sheets frozen phyllo, thawed

1. Combine the dried fruit, apple juice and ¼ cup water in a small saucepan, and let soak for 1 hour.

2. Preheat the oven to 400F.

3. Bring the dried fruit mixture to a boil over medium heat, and cook, partially covered, until the liquid is absorbed and the fruit is soft, for about 10 minutes. Add the walnuts, ¼ teaspoon of the cinnamon and the walnut extract, if using. Set aside.

4. Combine the sugar and the remaining 1 teaspoon cinnamon in a small bowl. Pour the vegetable oil into another small bowl.

5. Cut a sheet of phyllo lengthwise into 4 strips. (Keep the remaining sheets covered with a damp tea towel to prevent them from drying out.) Brush the strips lightly with oil, and sprinkle with the cinnamon-sugar mixture. Lay another strip on top of the first, and brush with the oil again and sprinkle with the cinnamon-sugar mixture. Spoon 1 tablespoon of the fruit-nut mixture at one end of strip. Fold the short edge at a diagonal over the filling (like folding a flag) so that it meets the long edge and forms a triangle. Brush the triangle lightly with the oil, and sprinkle with the cinnamon-sugar mixture. Continue folding the strip back and forth like a flag, brushing with the oil and sprinkling with the cinnamon-sugar, until you reach the end. Place the turnover on a cookie sheet. Repeat the process with the remaining phyllo, oil, cinnamon-sugar mixture and filling. Place on an ungreased baking sheet.

6. Bake, turning once, until lightly browned, for about 10 minutes. Remove from the oven, and serve warm or room temperature.

PER TURNOVER: 101 CAL; 2G PROT; 4G FAT; 17G CARB; 0MG CHOL; 41MG SOD; 1G FIBER

RASPBERRY CHILL

This snappy, user-friendly recipe comes together in just minutes, providing a cooling bite for a heated main course. To gild the lily, garnish this sweet with fresh raspberries. Offer this with a fruity herbed tea and vanilla cookies.

2 cups frozen raspberries

1 pound package lite silken soft tofu

¼ cup vanilla soymilk

¼ cup brown rice syrup

1 pint fresh raspberries for garnish

½ cup crushed pecans for garnish

1. Put the frozen raspberries, tofu, soymilk and brown rice syrup in a blender, and process until smooth.

2. Pour or spoon into a serving dish or individual compotes, and garnish with the fresh raspberries and pecans before serving.

PER SERVING: 180 CAL; 7G PROT; 7G FAT; 26G CARB; 0MG CHOL; 95MG SOD; 5G FIBER

ANGEL BERRY PARFAIT

Head to your grocer's to stock up on the few basics needed to whip this quick dessert into shape: a premade angel food cake, soft tofu, frozen berries and confectioners' sugar. If you have one, use a pretty glass bowl so you can show off the various layers of this parfait. Make this shortly before you plan to use it, as the cake tends to disintegrate from the moisture.

1 14-ounce premade angel food cake

½ cup apple juice

1 pound silken soft tofu

1 pound frozen blackberries or mixed berries

⅔ cup confectioners' sugar or to taste

1. Cube cake, and arrange half the pieces around the bottom of a decorative 3-quart bowl. Set aside.

2. Put apple juice and tofu into a blender or food processor, and process until smooth. Add berries, a cup at a time, and process after each addition. Add sugar, and process until smooth.

3. Spoon berry mixture over cake cubes, smoothing out mixture to cover cubes evenly. Cube remaining cake, and layer them over berry mixture, pressing down firmly. Eat immediately, or refrigerate parfait until ready to use.

PER SERVING: 320 CAL; 8G PROT; 2.5G FAT; 69G CARB; 0MG CHOL; 250MG SOD; 4G FIBER

CHOCOLATE RICOTTA CREAM

This chocolate dessert is light, luscious and barely sweet. Serve with dried or fresh fruit, perhaps grapes, pineapple, oranges or kiwi.

1 15-ounce container part-skim ricotta cheese

2 tablespoons sifted unsweetened cocoa powder

5 tablespoons fructose or honey

¼ teaspoon ground cinnamon

½ teaspoon vanilla extract

1 tablespoon toasted sliced almonds for garnish (page 47)

Put the ricotta cheese into a food processor or blender, and process for 1 minute. Add the cocoa, fructose or honey, cinnamon and vanilla, and process until creamy smooth. Add more fructose or honey to taste, if desired. Spoon into martini glasses, goblets or onto dessert plates. Garnish with almonds, and serve at once.

PER SERVING: 144 CAL; 9G PROT; 5G FAT; 5G CARB; 22MG CHOL; 89MG SOD; 1G FIBER

RASPBERRY SAUCE

This sauce is a snap to make.

1 cup frozen raspberries

2 tablespoons fresh lemon juice

¼ to ⅓ cup honey

Purée the frozen raspberries and lemon juice in a blender. Sweeten with the honey, and purée until smooth.

PER SERVING (2 TABLESPOONS): 65 CAL; 0.3G PROT; 0G FAT; 17G CARB; 0MG CHOL; 1MG SOD; 1G FIBER

CHOCOLATE SAUCE

Low-fat yet rich-tasting, this sauce is a winner.

1½ cups skim milk or low-fat vanilla soymilk

4 tablespoons unsweetened cocoa powder

1 large egg or equivalent egg substitute

5 tablespoons honey or brown sugar

1 teaspoon vanilla extract

Put all the ingredients into a blender, and purée until smooth. Transfer to a small saucepan. Heat, stirring constantly, until thickened and beginning to boil. Remove from the heat. Chill before serving.

PER SERVING (2 TABLESPOONS): 43 CAL; 2G PROT; 1G FAT; 7G CARB; 18MG CHOL; 6MG SOD; 0G FIBER

entertaining and holidays

LET FOOD BE THE MAGNET THAT DRAWS friends and family together around your table. But throwing a party or toasting special holidays does not mean hours in the kitchen. This selection of recipes spans the globe in a way that touches us all, and unites us under one roof—yet they are generally easy to assemble. Some have many ingredients, others only a few, but each dish will make your meal a celebratory occasion.

company's coming

SOY CHEESE FONDUE

You may use any soy cheese for this fondue, but different brands melt differently and some may not melt completely. Soy cheeses also come in varying flavors, so feel free to choose your favorite.

Soy Cheese Fondue

2 tablespoons canola oil

1 pound flavored tempeh, cubed

1 pound baked tofu, cubed

3 tablespoons cornstarch

3 cups white wine or rice milk

2 teaspoons crushed garlic

1 teaspoon salt

½ teaspoon cayenne, or to taste

½ teaspoon freshly ground black pepper

2 tablespoons fresh lemon juice

1½ pounds soy cheese, shredded

Accompaniments

1 loaf rye bread, cubed

1 loaf seven-grain bread, cubed

3- to 4-quart combination raw and cooked vegetables for dipping, such as carrot sticks, bell peppers, celery, radishes, baby carrots, broccoli pieces and sugar snap peas, cut into serving size pieces

1. Heat the oil in a skillet, and sauté the tempeh until crisp and brown. Remove from the heat, and set aside. Repeat with the baked tofu. Keep warm until serving time, or reheat in the oven.

2. Mix the cornstarch in ¼ cup of the wine or rice milk. Place the remaining liquid in the saucepan, whisk in the cornstarch mixture, and heat over medium heat. Bring to a boil, and add the garlic, salt, cayenne, pepper and lemon juice. Return to a boil, and cook for 2 minutes, stirring constantly.

3. Add the cheese, a generous handful at a time, and stir into the wine until the cheese melts, about 6 minutes. Repeat until the cheese is used up.

4. Transfer the cheese mixture to a fondue pot or slow cooker. Keep the fondue warm over an alcohol burner or in a slow cooker on the lowest setting. Serve with bread and vegetables for dipping.

PER SERVING (WITHOUT ACCOMPANIMENTS): 130 CAL; 4G PROT; 1G FAT; 8G CARB; 0MG CHOL; 390MG SOD; 0G FIBER

CHEDDAR AND CHILI PARTY CHEESECAKE

SERVES 40

This makes a conversation-stopper for a congenial gathering. Be sure to pass this with a small cheese knife and crackers, or your guests may end up eating this like an entrée dish. This needs a day to chill thoroughly, so plan to make this in advance of the party.

¼ cup finely ground tortilla chips

¼ cup grated Parmesan cheese

1½ pounds regular cream cheese at room temperature

¾ pound grated sharp cheddar cheese

1 cup low-fat ricotta cheese

¾ cup chopped scallions

4 large eggs or 1 cup egg substitute

¼ finely chopped jalapeño chiles

1 tablespoon red chili powder

1 tablespoon minced garlic

2 tablespoons whole milk

1. Preheat the oven to 325F. Generously butter a 9-inch springform pan, and set aside.

2. Mix together the tortilla chips and Parmesan cheese. Coat the inside of the pan, and refrigerate until ready to use.

3. Put all the remaining ingredients into the bowl of a heavy-duty mixer, and beat until smooth. Pour into the chilled pan.

4. Bake for about 1 hour and 15 minutes. Turn off the oven, open the oven door and cool the cheesecake. When cool, refrigerate overnight. Serve with crackers.

PER SERVING: 110 CAL; 5G PROT; 10G FAT; 2G CARB; 50MG CHOL; 130MG SOD; 0G FIBER

SAMOSAS

SERVES 24

Anyone who is at all familiar with Indian food will know about samosas, filled pastries eaten as snacks or appetizers, and great for parties. Unlike the traditional recipe, this version uses thawed puff pastry instead of homemade dough to hold the filling. Offer the samosas with a vibrant sweet-hot chutney, such as the Cilantro Chutney, page 176.

2 tablespoons vegetable oil

1 large onion, peeled and chopped

6 ounces soy ground "beef"

1 large tomato, diced

1 teaspoon ground cayenne

1 teaspoon ground cumin

1 teaspoon curry powder

1 teaspoon minced garlic

1 tablespoon grated fresh ginger

½ cup chopped cilantro

Salt to taste

1 17.3-ounce package puff pastry sheets, thawed

1. Preheat the oven to 375F. Line 2 baking sheets with foil to prevent sticking.

2. Heat the oil in a large skillet over medium heat. Sauté the onion for 5 minutes, or until turning brown. Add the ground "beef," tomato, cayenne, cumin, curry powder, garlic and ginger, and continuing sautéing until fragrant, about 5 minutes more. Stir in the cilantro and salt to taste, and remove from heat.

3. Flour a flat work surface lightly, and roll out 1 sheet of dough until it is about 10 x 14 inches in diameter. Cut the first sheet into 3 long strips along its fold lines, then cut 4 equal-sized triangles from each strip. Spoon about ¾ tablespoon "meat" filling into the center of triangle, and fold the dough over the filling so the triangle corners meet on the long edge. Make sure the filling is covered, and crimp the edges shut all around, forming a smaller triangle. Place the samosa on the baking sheet. Repeat the procedure until the dough and the filling mixtures are used up.

4. Bake until puffy and golden, for 12 to 15 minutes. Remove from the oven, and set aside until ready to eat.

PER SERVING: 140 CAL; 3G PROT; 9G FAT; 11G CARB; 0MG CHOL; 80MG SOD; <1G FIBER

MY HERO

Call your friends over to watch a big game and serve them this big sandwich. Be sure to select a wide loaf, such as a bâtarde, that is about 1 foot long. A bâtarde is simply a wider and heftier version of the French baguette. The following ingredients are only suggestions, but their combination provides a delicious filling for a sizable sandwich, ideal for entertaining friends or feeding a hungry family. Feel free to make your own choices, and try building the hero even taller.

1 1-pound *bâtarde* loaf

2 tablespoons low-fat mayonnaise, or more as needed

2 ounces mixed sprouts

1 tablespoon Dijon mustard

1 tablespoon sweet relish

1 large hard-boiled egg, mashed

4 romaine or leaf lettuce leaves

½ cucumber, very thinly sliced

6 paper-thin slices red onion

1 4-ounce package soy "pepperoni" slices

1 8-ounce package soy cheddar-flavored cheese slices

6 ounces coleslaw

1. Slice the loaf in half lengthwise, but not all the way through. Open the two sides out flat.

2. Mix the mayonnaise, sprouts, mustard, relish and egg together, and spread the mixture the length of one half of the bread. Start layering the other ingredients along the length of the loaf, beginning with the lettuce leaves and ending with the coleslaw. Close the loaf, slice into sections and serve.

PER SERVING: 360 CAL; 22G PROT; 8G FAT; 53G CARB; 40MG CHOL; 1,240MG SOD; 3G FIBER

WHITE AND GREEN CHILI

A bowl of chili can come in many guises and this version, made with white or pale ingredients, gets texture from the pumpkin seeds and tortilla chips

1 tablespoon vegetable oil

3 baby white or Yukon gold potatoes, diced

1 onion, diced

1 cup green salsa

6 tomatillos, diced

About 6 cups navy beans, drained and rinsed

½ to 1 cup Vegetable Stock (page 332)

Salt and freshly ground black pepper to taste

1½ cups toasted pumpkin seeds for garnish

1½ cups crumbled tortilla chips, preferably guacamole-flavored, for garnish

¾ cup grated low-fat cheddar cheese

2 teaspoons chili powder, or to taste

1. Heat the oil in a large saucepan over medium heat. Sauté the potatoes and onion until golden, for about 10 minutes. Add the salsa, tomatillos, navy beans and Vegetable Stock. Reduce the heat to medium-low, and cook, stirring often for about 20 minutes.

2. Remove from the heat. Serve the chili in a large bowl, or spoon it into individual serving dishes, and garnish with the pumpkin seeds, tortilla chips, cheese and sprinkles of chili powder.

PER SERVING: 830 CAL; 43G PROT; 36G FAT; 91G CARB; 5MG CHOL; 840MG SOD; 18G FIBER

MEGA-VEGGIE LASAGNA

This foolproof dish is perfect when entertaining a casual crowd. The lasagna can be assembled quickly without having to first cook the pasta, as the recipe calls for the oven-ready pasta that cooks in the pan during baking.

1 9-ounce package oven-ready sheets of lasagna

3 tablespoons olive oil

1 onion, diced

12 ounces unflavored soy ground "meat"

1 green bell pepper, diced

1 pound eggplant, skin on and cubed

1 large tomato, chopped

1½ cups firmly packed artichoke hearts, drained

1 tablespoon garlic powder

4 cups marinara sauce

1 tablespoon dried oregano

Salt and freshly ground black pepper to taste

4 cups low-fat ricotta cheese

4 cups low-fat shredded mozzarella

1. Preheat the oven to 400F. Spray a nonstick 9 x 13 lasagna baking pan with nonstick cooking spray.

2. Smooth 1 cup tomato sauce over bottom of the pan. Place 8 sheets of lasagna over the bottom of the pan, overlapping the sheets as needed to fill all gaps.

3. Heat 2 tablespoons oil in a large skillet over medium heat, and brown the onions for about 1 minute. Add the soy ground "meat," and sauté for 2 to 3 minutes. Add the bell pepper, eggplant, tomato, artichoke hearts, and 2 cups marinara sauce, and cook for about 5 minutes, stirring occasionally. Stir in the oregano, salt and pepper.

4. Spoon half the soy "meat"–eggplant mixture over the lasagna sheets, and top with the ricotta cheese. Place the remaining lasagna sheets on top of the ricotta, and spoon and smooth on the remaining marinara sauce. Spoon on and smooth out the remaining soy "meat"–eggplant mixture, and sprinkle with mozzarella. Cover the baking pan tightly with foil.

5. Bake for about 45 minutes, or until the top layer of cheese melts and is bubbly. Remove from the oven, and serve hot or cool and refrigerate for later use. If refrigerated, you will need to reheat the lasagna in a preheated oven until warmed through.

PER SERVING: 350 CAL; 27G PROT; 13G FAT; 28G CARB; 35MG CHOL; 680MG SOD; 6G FIBER

GREEN CHILE RICE AND BEANS

Firm baked tofu adds its unique texture to this party dish. Serve with plenty of warm tortillas.

2 6- to 8-ounce packages Tex-Mex flavored baked tofu, cubed

2 tablespoons vegetable oil

3 cloves garlic, minced

2 medium-sized onions, diced

1 cup chopped green chiles

1 tablespoon red chile powder

1 teaspoon ground cumin

½ teaspoon freshly ground black pepper

1 teaspoon salt

1½ cups uncooked long-grain rice

2 cups cooked pinto beans

3 cups Vegetable Stock (page 332) or water

1. Heat the oil in a large skillet, and sauté the tofu until brown, for 5 to 7 minutes. Add the garlic and onion to the skillet, and sauté for 3 minutes. Add the green chiles, chili powder, cumin, pepper and salt, and cook for 5 minutes.

2. Add the rice, beans and Vegetable Stock, cover, reduce the heat to low and cook for 25 to 30 minutes, or until all the liquid is absorbed. Remove from the heat, and serve.

PER SERVING: 490 CAL; 24G PROT; 12G FAT; 73G CARB; 0MG CHOL; 970MG SOD; 9G FIBER

RUSSIAN PIROGI

Pirogi are savory turnovers that may contain such fillings as mushrooms or cheese. These are suitable for serving as an entrée for a party meal starting with Chilled Ginger Borscht with Mushrooms (page 311).

Dough

¾ cup unbleached white flour

¾ cup whole-wheat flour

⅛ teaspoon cream of tartar

Dash salt

½ cup plus 1 tablespoon lukewarm water

1 tablespoon vegetable oil

1 large potato, steamed, peeled and mashed

Filling

1 teaspoon virgin olive oil

1 large onion, chopped

1 cup finely chopped white button mushrooms

Salt and freshly ground black pepper to taste

Topping

1 teaspoon vegetable oil

1 or 2 onions, chopped

½ cup yogurt or nondairy sour cream

2 tablespoons soy "bacon" bits

1. To make the Dough: In a large bowl, combine the flours, cream of tartar and salt. In a separate bowl, combine the water, oil and ¼ cup mashed potato. Reserve the remaining potato for the filling. Stir the wet mixture into the flour mixture. Knead for 5 to 10 minutes on a floured surface until smooth. Cover the dough, and let rest for 30 minutes.

2. To make the Filling: Meanwhile, heat the oil in a skillet over medium heat, and cook the onion and mushrooms, stirring for about 5 minutes, until lightly browned. Transfer to a bowl and combine with the reserved potato. Season with salt and pepper.

3. To assemble the pirogi, divide the dough in half. Roll out each half to ⅛-inch thick on the floured board. Cut out 3-inch circles with a cookie cutter or a glass dipped in flour. Place a generous teaspoonful of the filling in the center of each circle. Fold in half, and pinch the edges together to seal. Keep the filled pirogi between two towels to prevent drying.

4. To make the Topping: Heat the oil in a skillet over medium heat, and sauté the onions until golden. Stir together the yogurt and soy "bacon" bits, and stir in the onions.

5. Bring a large pot of water to the boil, and add several pirogi to the water, taking care not to overcrowd them. Using a slotted spoon, remove the pirogi when they float to the surface, in about 3 minutes. Transfer to a serving dish, garnish with the Topping and serve.

PER SERVING: 49 CAL; 2G PROT; 2G FAT; 7G CARB; 1MG CHOL; 17MG SOD; 0.8G FIBER

JAMAICAN COOK-UP RICE

The term "cook-up" is a Caribbean expression that refers to a dish that incorporates the ingredients you have on hand in the kitchen. In this version, you combine rice, beans and vegetables with a little coconut milk and curry powder for a zesty tropical flavor. This will double or triple easily if you expand your party.

1 tablespoon canola oil

1 medium-sized yellow onion, diced

1 medium-sized red bell pepper, seeded and diced

2 or 3 cloves garlic, minced

½ Scotch bonnet chile, seeded and minced (optional)

2 cups uncooked long-grain white rice

1 15-ounce can red kidney beans, drained and rinsed

½ cup canned coconut milk

2 teaspoons curry powder

½ teaspoon dried thyme

½ teaspoon freshly ground black pepper

½ teaspoon salt

1. Heat the oil in a large saucepan over medium heat. Add the onion, bell pepper, garlic and the chile, and cook, stirring often, until the vegetables begin to soften, about 5 minutes.

2. Stir in 3½ cups of water, the rice, beans, coconut milk and seasonings, and bring to a simmer. Reduce the heat, cover, and cook until the rice is tender and the liquid is absorbed, for 15 to 20 minutes. Fluff the rice with a fork, and let stand, covered, for 5 to 10 minutes. Spoon the rice onto plates, and serve hot.

PER SERVING: 323 CAL; 9G PROT; 3G FAT; 64G CARB; 0MG CHOL; 441MG SOD; 6G FIBER

MUSHROOM EXTRAVAGANZA

For a dress-up meal, plan to mix mushroom varieties, including some of the more exotic ones, such as chanterelles, cremini, morels and porcini. Do not use a very dry sherry or white wine, because the mushrooms need a sweeter background accent.

1½ cups quinoa shell pasta or regular shell pasta

2 tablespoons vegetable oil

1 pound mushrooms, mixed varieties

4 ounces goat cheese

½ cup sherry

1 cup mushroom broth

2 tablespoons all-purpose flour

Salt and freshly ground black pepper to taste

½ cup minced parsley

1. Cook the quinoa pasta according to package directions, drain and set aside. Slice mushrooms from the cap through the stem in large pieces.

2. Meanwhile, heat the oil in a large skillet, and sauté the mushrooms, stirring often, until the mushrooms begin to soften. Mix the goat cheese, sherry, broth and flour together in a bowl, and pour over the mushrooms, stirring well. Season with salt and pepper.

3. Continue cooking until the liquid thickens and reduces slightly. Spoon the pasta onto individual serving plates. Remove the mushrooms from the heat, and spoon equal portions over the pasta. Sprinkle with parsley, and serve.

PER SERVING: 370 CAL; 14G PROT; 17G FAT; 36G CARB; 20MG CHOL; 300MG SOD; 4G FIBER

TEX-MEX TAMALE PIE

Got a big crowd coming over for a casual evening? Offer this flavor-packed dish—fancier than the version on page 297—with plenty of chilled beer or fruit juice, and a stack of warmed tortillas.

Crust

¾ cup cornmeal

½ teaspoon salt

1 tablespoon vegetable oil

Filling

2 tablespoons vegetable oil

1 12-ounce package taco-flavored ground soy "beef"

1 cup chopped onion

1 cup raisins

1 tablespoon minced garlic

1 tablespoon chipotles in adobo sauce

1 15.5-ounce can hominy

1 15.5-ounce can corn kernels

1 tablespoon chili powder

1½ cups pitted black olives

2 cups salsa

Salt to taste

1½ cups shredded cheddar or Monterey Jack cheese

1. To make the Crust: Combine the cornmeal, salt and chili powder with 2 cups of water in a saucepan, and bring to a boil over medium heat. Reduce the heat to low, cover the pan, and cook until the water is absorbed. Remove from the heat, and spoon the mixture into a 3-quart ovenproof baking dish

2. Preheat the oven to 375F.

3. To make the Filling: Heat the oil in a large skillet, and sauté the onions and ground "beef" until golden. Add the raisins, garlic, chipotles in adobo, hominy, corn kernels and chili powder, stirring to mix well, and reduce the heat to low. Cook for 5 minutes, or until heated through. Stir in the olives, salsa and salt and cook for 3 to 4 minutes more. Spoon the mixture into the baking dish, and top with the cheese.

4. Bake for about 45 minutes, or until the cheese is bubbly and the filling is heated through. Remove from the oven, and serve hot or at room temperature.

PER SERVING: 330 CAL; 14G PROT; 12G FAT; 44G CARB; 20MG CHOL; 960MG SOD; 7G FIBER

CAULIFLOWER AND POTATO CURRY

SERVES 4

Reminiscent of India's glorious vegetable curries, this fulsome dish calls for hot pita or Indian-style bread as an accompaniment, as well as a dish of chilled yogurt and hot Indian chai tea on the side.

2 tablespoons vegetable oil

1 onion, diced

8 baby Yukon gold potatoes, quartered

2 tablespoons minced fresh ginger

1 tablespoon minced garlic

2 teaspoons ground cumin

2 teaspoons curry powder

1 teaspoon ground turmeric

½ head cauliflower, cut into florets

2 cups chickpeas

1 cup Vegetable Stock (page 332)

½ cup nonfat or low-fat plain yogurt

2 green chiles, thinly sliced

½ cup chopped cilantro leaves as garnish

1. Heat the oil in a large wok or skillet over medium-high heat, and sauté the onion until golden, for about 5 minutes. Stir in the potatoes, and continue cooking and stirring until the potatoes begin to brown, for about 10 minutes more.

2. Stir in the ginger, garlic, cumin, curry powder, turmeric, florets and Vegetable Stock, and reduce the heat to medium, stirring often. Cook until the cauliflower becomes tender, for 12 to 15 minutes. Remove from the heat, stir in the yogurt and chiles and serve. Garnish servings with cilantro leaves.

PER SERVING: 480 CAL; 16G PROT; 9G FAT; 88G CARB; 0MG CHOL; 250MG SOD; 12G FIBER

BRUNSWICK STEW

Thick and rich in flavor, this updated Southern classic is perfect for feeding a crowd.

1 tablespoon canola oil

⅓ cup low-sodium soy sauce

2 cloves garlic, minced

1 small piece fresh ginger, peeled and minced

1 tablespoon granulated sugar

1 pound extra-firm tofu

8 ounces tempeh, diced

8 ounces seitan, diced

2 stalks celery with leaves, chopped

1 large onion, chopped finely

2 quarts water or Vegetable Stock (page 332)

1 10-ounce package frozen baby lima beans

1 10-ounce package frozen green peas

1 16-ounce can whole-kernel corn

1 28-ounce can chopped tomatoes with juices

2 large potatoes, peeled and diced

3 tablespoons low-sodium soy sauce

1 tablespoon liquid smoke, or to taste, optional

1 teaspoon ground allspice

½ teaspoon hot pepper sauce, or to taste

1 teaspoon freshly ground black pepper

1 tablespoon prepared yellow mustard

3 tablespoons vegetarian Worcestershire sauce

1. Combine the oil, soy sauce, 2 tablespoons water, garlic, ginger and sugar in a stockpot, and heat over medium heat. Crumble the tofu into the mixture, and increase the heat to medium-high. Cook, stirring, until the liquid has evaporated and the tofu is browned. Add the tempeh and seitan. Cook, stirring, until these have browned, for about 5 minutes.

2. Add the remaining ingredients to the tofu mixture. Bring to a boil, and reduce the heat to low. Cook, uncovered, until the stew is thick, for about 45 minutes. If the stew looks dry, add ½ to 1 cup water and soak for 10 minutes more.

PER SERVING: 176 CAL; 11G PROT; 4G FAT; 21G CARB; 0MG CHOL; 568MG SOD; 5G FIBER

PEPPER POT PIE

This dish is filled with plenty of cheese, so it is very satisfying, and very dressy too. Serve this as a summer celebration with friends, when the best of the produce is at your farmers' market.

1 sheet puff pastry, thawed

2 tablespoons vegetable oil

2 red bell peppers, cut into thin strips

1 green bell pepper, cut into thin strips

1 cup diced eggplant

1 sweet onion, diced

4 ounces crumbled feta cheese

4 ounces pitted oil-cured olives

2 tablespoons chopped oil-packed sun-dried tomatoes

2 cups shredded mozzarella cheese

1. Preheat the oven to 375F.

2. Flour a work surface, and roll out the sheet of puff pastry dough to about 11 x 11 inches. Place it into a 3-quart baking dish, pressing the dough into the dish and pulling the corners over the container rim.

3. Heat the oil in a large skillet over medium heat, and sauté the peppers, eggplant and onion for about 10 minutes. Remove from the heat, and stir in the feta cheese, olives and sun-dried tomatoes. Spoon the mixture into the baking dish, and top with the mozzarella cheese.

4. Bake for 35 to 40 minutes, or until the cheese melts completely and the filling is heated through. Remove from the oven, and serve.

PER SERVING: 740 CAL; 24G PROT; 54G FAT; 42G CARB; 60MG CHOL; 1,210MG SOD; 3G FIBER

MEDITERRANEAN DEEP-DISH VEGETABLE STRATA

This is a showy dish, ideal for a dressy meal. With all the varied flavors of the sunny Mediterranean, you could fill several deep-dish casseroles with assorted veggie combinations, so let this recipe just be a guide. The important thing to remember is to layer the vegetables so that when you slice into the pie, you will be able to portion out a cross section of all the ingredients. If you decide to use artichoke hearts, look for the frozen ones.

1 sheet puff pastry, thawed

1 tablespoon olive oil

1 cup diced eggplant

2 large eggs

8 ounces nonfat cream cheese at room temperature

1 teaspoon Dijon mustard, or to taste

Salt and freshly ground black pepper to taste

9 ounces low-fat Swiss cheese, grated

2 leeks, well rinsed and thinly sliced

2 red bell peppers, seeded and diced

2 zucchini, diced

2 cups artichoke hearts, preferably frozen and thawed

1 cup French fried onion rings

¾ cup grated Parmesan cheese

1. Preheat the oven to 375F.

2. Flour a work surface, and roll out the sheet of puff pastry dough to about 11 x 11 inches. Place it into a 3-quart baking dish, pressing the dough into the dish and pulling the corners over the container rim.

3. Heat the oil in a large skillet over medium heat, and sauté the eggplant for about 8 minutes.

4. Meanwhile, using an electric beater, beat the eggs until foamy. Blend in the cream cheese, mustard, salt and pepper, and continue beating until the mixture is smooth. Fold in about 7 ounces of the cheese.

5. Layer the vegetables, beginning with the leeks. Add the red pepper and eggplant, and spoon in half the sauce over the vegetables. Continue layering, adding the zucchini and the artichoke hearts. Top with the onion rings, the remaining sauce and the remaining Swiss cheese. Sprinkle the Parmesan cheese over the top.

6. Bake for about 50 minutes, or until the pastry turns golden, and the cheese has melted throughout. Remove from the oven, and serve while hot.

PER SERVING: 430 CAL; 24G PROT; 24G FAT; 29G CARB; 75MG CHOL; 700MG SOD; 2G FIBER

COULIBIAC

Russians love to eat, and this is an adaptation of a traditional dish served at family gatherings. Different ingredients including hard-cooked eggs and rice often form the filling, all encased in a crisp golden crust. Here, fragrant brown mushrooms and green cabbage flavored with garlic and juniper berries join with the rice to create the layers of this impressive celebratory entrée. Look for juniper berries in specialty food stores, or order them from mail order sources or online.

Filling

1 teaspoon dried juniper berries

2 cloves garlic, peeled

¼ teaspoon salt

2 tablespoons plus 2 teaspoons vegetable oil

½ small head green cabbage, finely shredded

20 ounces cremini mushrooms, chopped

1 tablespoon chopped fresh sage leaves or 1 teaspoon dried sage

Salt and freshly ground black pepper to taste

2 cups peeled, sliced parsnips

1 tablespoon chopped fresh thyme or 1 teaspoon dried thyme

2 cups cooked brown rice

1 17¼-ounce package frozen puff pastry, thawed

1 beaten egg, mixed with 1 teaspoon water, or milk

1. To make the Filling: Crush the juniper berries, garlic and salt into a paste using a mortar and pestle. Heat 1 tablespoon of the oil in a large skillet over medium heat. Add the garlic paste, and stir-fry for 1 minute. Add the cabbage, and cook, stirring until coated with the oil and paste mixture. Cover, and cook for 2 minutes until wilted and bright green. Transfer to a bowl, and set aside.

2. Heat 1 tablespoon of the remaining oil in the skillet, and add the mushrooms, sage, salt and pepper. Cook, stirring occasionally, until the mushrooms soften, about 8 minutes. Remove from the heat, and set aside.

3. Wipe out the skillet, and heat the remaining 2 teaspoons of oil over medium heat. Add the parsnips and thyme, and cook, stirring often, until they begin to soften, for about 5 minutes.

4. Preheat the oven to 375F.

5. Unfold 1 puff pastry sheet, and place on a lightly floured surface. Roll out into a 14-inch square, then cut the dough into a 14-inch circle. Transfer the circle to an ungreased 8½-inch springform pan, and press gently to fit into the bottom and sides. There will be some overhang.

6. Spoon half the rice over the pastry. Using a slotted spoon, layer the mushrooms over the rice, then cover with the cabbage, remaining rice and parsnips. Carefully fold the pastry overhang over the filling. Brush the edges with the beaten egg or milk. Unfold the second puff pastry sheet on a lightly floured surface. Roll out slightly, and cut out into an 8½-inch circle. Place the circle of dough over the top, and press the edges to seal. Brush the top with the egg wash, and, using a small sharp knife or razor blade, slash the top in a cross-hatch pattern.

7. Bake for 35 to 40 minutes. When well browned, loosely cover the top with foil. Reduce the heat to 350F. Remove the sides of the pan, and brush the sides with the egg wash. Bake until the sides are golden, for about 40 minutes. Remove from the oven, and let cool slightly before serving. Cut into wedges, and serve.

PER SERVING: 340 CAL; 6G PROT; 20G FAT; 35G CARB; 20MG CHOL; 170MG SOD; 4G FIBER

ROSEMARY-SCENTED VEGETABLE PHYLLO TART

Elegant and sophisticated, this tart makes a showy centerpiece on your buffet.

2 10-ounce packages chopped frozen spinach, thawed and squeezed dry

¼ cup fresh rosemary (or 2 tablespoons dried)

1 medium-sized onion, minced plus 2 medium-sized onions, sliced and separated into rings

3 cloves garlic, pressed or minced

½ to 1 cup crumbled feta cheese

½ cup skim milk

1 teaspoon salt, or more to taste

1 teaspoon freshly ground black pepper

1 teaspoon olive oil

½ cup white wine

4 medium-sized zucchini, sliced on the diagonal

1 pound white button mushrooms, sliced

1 1-pound package phyllo

8 roasted red bell peppers, patted dry and cut into long, thick strips

1 14-ounce jar marinated artichoke hearts, drained and chopped

6 ounces sun-dried tomatoes, reconstituted in hot water and cut into slivers

¼ cup lightly packed fresh basil leaves, slivered

½ cup pine nuts, toasted (see page 47)

Sprigs of fresh rosemary, for garnish, optional

1. Preheat the oven to 375F. In a food processor, purée the spinach, rosemary, onion, garlic, feta, milk, salt and pepper until smooth. If the mixture is too dry to purée, add a bit more milk for desired consistency. Set aside.

2. In a large nonstick skillet, coat the bottom with the oil. Add the wine and heat to a simmer. Cook the zucchini, stirring, for 5 minutes; remove and drain on paper towels. Cook the onions, stirring, for 5 minutes; remove and drain on paper towels. Cook the mushrooms, stirring for 5 minutes; remove and drain on paper towels.

3. Line a jelly-roll pan or large deep-dish pizza pan with foil, leaving the ends of the foil sticking up beyond the edge of the pan. Spray the foil with the olive oil cooking spray or brush with oil.

4. To form the tart crust, lay down 1 sheet of phyllo and brush lightly or spray with olive oil. Keep the rest of the phyllo covered to prevent drying. Crinkle down the edges of phyllo that extend beyond the pan. Lay down the remaining sheets of phyllo, spraying or brushing each with oil and crinkling down the edges.

5. Smooth the spinach purée mixture over the phyllo crust. Arrange the zucchini, onions, mushrooms, roasted peppers, artichoke hearts and sun-dried tomatoes over the spinach mixture. Bake for 15 minutes. If the edges of the crust are browning too quickly, lower the oven temperature to 325F and bake for 5 minutes more. If the crust is just beginning to turn golden, keep the oven temperature at 375F and bake until the phyllo is golden and crisp and the vegetables are warmed, for about 5 minutes more.

6. Sprinkle the tart with fresh basil and toasted pine nuts. Tuck rosemary sprigs into the crinkled edges of the crust to garnish. Serve at once.

PER SERVING: 281 CAL; 11G PROT; 9G FAT; 37G CARB; 27MG CHOL; 652MG SOD; 6G FIBER

ELEGANT POLENTA WITH ROASTED VEGETABLES

Italians usually serve polenta unadorned by cheese or oils, but this recipe takes polenta to new levels with liberal amounts of cheese and a few drizzles of olive oil. You can vary the type of cheese you select, but keep it Italian. The roasted vegetables to serve alongside or over top of the polenta can be chosen according to taste and the season, but use sturdy vegetables, as leafy ones overcook. The amount of vegetables you select depends entirely on you as well—the recipe below is a guideline only.

Vegetables for roasting, such as sliced red and green sweet peppers, sliced eggplants, quartered potatoes, sliced sweet potatoes, Brussels sprouts, sliced carrots and rutabagas, and sliced leeks and onions

Olive oil and balsamic vinegar for marinating vegetables

½ pound polenta

2½ teaspoons salt

2 tablespoons olive oil

1 tablespoon minced garlic

6 ounces grated fontina cheese

6 ounces grated provolone cheese

Freshly ground black pepper for garnish

1. Preheat the oven to 375F.

2. Prepare the vegetables, placing cut-up pieces into a large mixing bowl. Combine enough olive oil and balsamic vinegar to coat the vegetables when tossed. Arrange the vegetables in a large baking pan, pouring any marinade over top. Roast, stirring occasionally, for 45 minutes to 1 hour, or until all vegetables are crisp-tender.

3. Meanwhile, heat 6 cups of water over medium heat in a large saucepan. When it is boiling, slowly pour in the polenta, stirring continuously. When all the polenta has been added, stir in the salt, oil and garlic, and reduce the heat to medium-low.

4. Continue stirring while sprinkling in the cheeses, and continue cooking and stirring until all the cheese is incorporated and the polenta thickens to a consistency like mashed potatoes, or for about 20 minutes. Remove from the heat, and spread out on a serving platter or spoon onto individual plates. Serve with the roasted vegetables.

PER SERVING (WITHOUT MARINADE OR VEGETABLES): 210 CAL; 10G PROT; 13G FAT; 15G CARB; 30MG CHOL; 870MG SOD; 2G FIBER

MUSHROOM STROGANOFF WITH TEMPEH AND TOFU

SERVES 6

This dish demands your undivided attention—if you overheat it, the sauce will separate irreparably. If you don't mind a few extra calories, splurge on real sour cream; it has a distinctly wonderful flavor. If you can't find meaty mushrooms, substitute white button mushrooms.

1 pound pasta of your choice

2 tablespoons unsalted butter or canola oil

1 large white onion, thinly sliced

1 clove garlic, crushed

2⅓ cups sliced mushrooms, such as shiitake or oyster mushrooms

2⅓ cups sliced white button mushrooms

8 ounces tempeh, sliced into ½-inch-thick strips

2 cups low-fat sour cream or soy substitute

1 cup silken silken tofu

2 tablespoons low-sodium soy sauce

1 tablespoon dry sherry

1 teaspoon dry mustard

2 teaspoons dried dillweed, crumbled

Dash paprika

1. Heat a pot of lightly salted water over medium heat, and when it is boiling, cook the pasta according to package directions. Drain, rinse, drain again and set aside.

2. Heat the butter or oil in a large skillet over medium heat. Sauté the onion and garlic until soft and translucent, for about 5 minutes. Add the mushrooms and tempeh, and continue to cook, stirring, until the mushrooms are completely soft. Remove from the heat, and set aside.

3. Put the sour cream or soy substitute, tofu, soy sauce, sherry and mustard into a food processor or blender, and purée until smooth. Transfer the mixture to the top of a double boiler. Stir in the mushroom mixture, and heat until warmed. Do not overheat. Stir in the dillweed and paprika. Pour the stroganoff over the pasta. Serve at once.

PER SERVING: 520 CAL; 23G PROT; 17G FAT; 69G CARB; 35MG CHOL; 200MG SOD; 5G FIBER

BRAZILIAN BLACK BEAN STEW

SERVES 6

Here's a quick vegetarian version of the Brazilian national dish known as feijoada. *This stew entices the eye with the colorful contrast of black beans and sweet potatoes and pleases the palate with nourishing ingredients.*

1 tablespoon vegetable oil

1 large onion, chopped

2 medium-sized cloves garlic, minced

2 medium-sized sweet potatoes, diced

1 large red bell pepper, diced

1 14.5-ounce can diced tomatoes with liquid

1 small hot green chile pepper, minced, or more to taste

2 16-ounce cans black beans, drained and rinsed

1 ripe mango, pitted, peeled and diced

¼ cup chopped fresh cilantro

¼ teaspoon salt

1. Heat the oil in a large pot over medium heat. Add the onion, and cook, stirring often, until softened, for about 5 minutes. Stir in the garlic, and cook, stirring, until the onion is golden, for about 3 minutes. Stir in the sweet potatoes, bell pepper, tomatoes (with liquid), chile and 1½ cups water. Bring to a boil. Reduce the heat to low, cover, and simmer until the potatoes are tender but still firm, for 10 to 15 minutes.

2. Stir in the beans, and cook, uncovered, until heated through, for about 5 minutes. Stir in the mango, and cook until heated through, for about 1 minute. Stir in the cilantro and salt. Serve hot.

PER SERVING: 326 CAL; 16G PROT; 4G FAT; 61G CARB; 0MG CHOL; 211MG SOD; 17G FIBER

WINTER PEAR SALAD IN RASPBERRY VINAIGRETTE

This crunchy salad contains a wonderful mélange of flavors. Serve it on individual salad plates or arrange it on a large, round tray at your buffet table.

Salad

8 cups torn radicchio, rinsed and dried

10 Bosc pears, cored and sliced thinly

1 cup Gorgonzola cheese, crumbled feta or grated Parmesan cheese

2 cups chopped, toasted walnuts (see page 47)

½ cup chopped Italian flat-leaf parsley

1 cup fresh raspberries, optional

Vinaigrette

½ cup raspberry vinegar

½ cup olive oil

1 teaspoon salt

1 teaspoon freshly ground black pepper

1. To make the Salad: Make an attractive bed of radicchio on salad plates or a large platter. Arrange pear slices on the radicchio in fan shapes. Scatter the cheese over the pears. Sprinkle the walnuts, parsley and raspberries, if using, over the salad.

2. To make the Vinaigrette: Put all the ingredients in a jar, seal tightly and shake to combine. Just before serving, drizzle the vinaigrette over the salad.

PER SERVING: 279 CAL; 5G PROT; 19G FAT; 20G CARB; 13MG CHOL; 328MG SOD; 4G FIBER

VEGETARIAN CASSOULET

Cassoulet is a hearty French dish that is, except for the beans, a vegetarian's nightmare with its layers of duck, goose, veal, smoked sausage and loads of saturated fat. This revised recipe highlights many of the great smoked soy products on the market.

1 cup low-sodium vegetable broth, Vegetable Stock (page 332) or water

1 tablespoon olive oil

6 cloves garlic, minced

1 medium-sized onion, diced

2 medium-sized stalks celery, chopped

2 small carrots, chopped

1 cup chopped mushrooms

1 pinch plus 1 teaspoon coarsely ground pepper

1 teaspoon salt

1 15-ounce can navy beans

1½ cups diced seitan

1⅓ cups diced smoked tempeh

1½ cups diced smoked tofu

1 tablespoon chopped fresh thyme or 1 teaspoon dried thyme

⅓ cup breadcrumbs

Olive oil cooking spray

1. Preheat the oven to 400F.

2. Bring the stock or water to a simmer in a small saucepan, cover and keep warm. Heat the oil in a 5-quart Dutch oven over medium-high heat. Add the garlic, onion, celery, carrots, mushrooms, pinch of pepper and ½ teaspoon of the salt, and cook, stirring often, for about 3 minutes. Stir in the beans and hot stock. Season with the remaining ½ teaspoon salt and 1 teaspoon pepper. Add the seitan, tempeh, tofu and thyme. Mix gently. Bring the mixture to a slow simmer, and cook for 1 minute. Sprinkle evenly with breadcrumbs, lightly coat the top with olive oil cooking spray and transfer to the oven.

3. Bake, uncovered, for 15 minutes, or until the top is browned. Remove the cassoulet from the oven, and let stand for 5 to 10 minutes before serving.

PER SERVING: 324 CAL; 24G PROT; 7G FAT; 41G CARB; 0MG CHOL; 589MG SOD; 9G FIBER

VEGETABLE TAGINE

Tagines are flavorful Moroccan stews loaded with cooked vegetables and signature spices like cumin, coriander and ginger. This version is a wonderful opportunity for vegetarians to experience international fare at its best. Serve over couscous for a true Moroccan meal. The type of tomatoes used will determine the amount of stock or water needed to cook the vegetables. Crushed tomatoes will require about 1 cup of water. Diced tomatoes may not require as much water. Stovetop cooking may require slightly more water. The finished stew should be somewhat dry, not soupy, and the vegetables should be tender and shapely, not soggy.

2 tablespoons olive oil

4 shallots, chopped

2 cloves garlic, minced

1-inch piece peeled fresh ginger, minced

1 stalk celery, chopped

3-inch cinnamon stick

1½ teaspoons ground coriander

1½ teaspoons ground cumin

1½ teaspoons paprika

1 teaspoon salt

1 teaspoon freshly ground black pepper

⅛ teaspoon cayenne, or to taste

1 32-ounce can crushed or diced tomatoes

1 large carrot, peeled and cut into chunks

5 ounces green beans, ends trimmed

1 small butternut squash or sweet potato, peeled and cut into chunks

½ head cauliflower, cut into florets

½ fennel bulb, trimmed and cut into chunks

Vegetable Stock (page 332) or water as needed

¼ teaspoon crushed saffron

1 cup cooked or canned and rinsed chickpeas

½ cup pitted kalamata olives

½ cup halved pitted prunes

3 tablespoons chopped fresh parsley

1. Preheat the oven to 350F.

2. Heat the oil in a large Dutch oven over medium heat. Add the shallots, garlic, ginger, celery and cinnamon stick, and cook, stirring often, until the shallots and celery begin to soften, for about 5 minutes. Add the coriander, cumin, paprika, salt, pepper and cayenne. Cook, stirring constantly, until the spices are fragrant, for about 1 minute. Stir in the tomatoes, carrot, green beans, squash or sweet potato, cauliflower and fennel. Add enough vegetable stock or water to cover the vegetables. Stir in the saffron.

3. Cover and bake until the vegetables are tender, for 40 to 45 minutes. About 5 minutes before the stew is done, stir in the chickpeas, olives and prunes. Stir in the parsley just before serving.

PER SERVING: 260 CAL; 8G PROT; 9G FAT; 43G CARB; 0MG CHOL; 790MG SOD; 10G FIBER

RATATOUILLE TERRINE

Ideal for a casual fall dinner party, the terrine may be made up to three days ahead. Cover it tightly in the pan and refrigerate. Unmold and bring to room temperature before serving. The sauce can be made up to three days ahead and refrigerated. Simply bring to room temperature before using. Select a tapenade variety that does not include anchovies. Feel free to roast your peppers in your own oven, or to save time, buy preroasted red peppers available in cans or jars. To round out the meal, start with a spinach salad, offer hot pita bread or sweet potato biscuits, and end with an apple dessert.

Eggplant Terrine

2 medium-sized eggplants (2½ pounds), cut lengthwise into ½-inch-thick slices

⅓ cup olive oil

¼ cup jarred tapenade black olive paste

3 medium-sized red bell peppers

7 ounces soft, mild goat cheese, thinly sliced

Fresh Herb Sauce

¼ cup chopped fresh basil

¼ cup chopped fresh flat-leaf parsley

1 small clove garlic, sliced

4 teaspoon balsamic vinegar

6 tablespoons olive oil

Salt and freshly ground black pepper to taste

1. Preheat the broiler.

2. To make the Eggplant Terrine: Arrange the eggplant slices in a single layer on a baking sheets. Brush both sides of the eggplants with oil, and sprinkle with salt to taste. Broil the eggplants in batches until golden and tender, for 4 to 5 minutes per side. Transfer the eggplants to paper towels to drain.

3. Roast the peppers by broiling them, turning every 5 minutes until the skins blister and char, for 10 to 15 minutes. Transfer the peppers to a paper bag, close and let them steam until cool enough to handle. Use a small sharp knife to peel off the charred skin, and discard the seeds and ribs. Cut the peppers lengthwise into 3 sections

4. Line an 8½ x 4½-inch loaf pan with plastic wrap, leaving a 3-inch overhang. Layer the eggplants, olive paste, bell peppers and cheese in the pan, beginning and ending with the eggplants. Cover with a plastic overhang, and place 3- to 4-pound weight on top. Chill for 24 hours.

5. To make the Fresh Herb Sauce: Put the basil, parsley, garlic, vinegar, oil, 2 tablespoons water, salt and pepper in a food processor or blender, and purée until smooth.

6. To serve, remove the weight, invert the terrine onto a cutting board and discard the plastic wrap. Cut the terrine into ¾-inch-thick slices. Pour the Fresh Herb Sauce onto serving plates, tilting to spread the sauce. Arrange the terrine slices on the sauce.

PER SERVING: 339 CAL; 8G PROT; 28G FAT; 15G CARB; 15MG CHOL; 170MG SOD; 6G FIBER

TURKISH-STYLE VEGETABLE STEW

This easy stew is good served with a grain, such as rice or barley, as well as with pita bread. In summer, try replacing parsley with a tablespoon of chopped fresh mint or dill. Finish each serving with a sprinkling of crumbled feta cheese.

2 teaspoons vegetable oil

1 medium-sized onion, halved and sliced

2 medium-sized cloves garlic, peeled and crushed

6 ounces green beans, trimmed, halved lengthwise then crosswise

6 ounces okra, trimmed and cut into ½-inch-thick slices

1 28-ounce can whole peeled Italian-style tomatoes, drained, ½ cup juice reserved

½ cup canned vegetable broth or Vegetable Stock (page 332)

½ teaspoon ground cumin

2 medium-sized zucchini, quartered lengthwise and cut into ½-inch chunks

¼ cup chopped fresh parsley

¾ teaspoon coarse salt

½ teaspoon freshly ground pepper

1. Heat the oil in a large saucepan over medium-low heat. Add the onion and garlic, and cook until the onion is softened, for about 5 minutes. Stir in the green beans, okra, tomatoes, reserved tomato juice, broth and cumin. Bring to a boil, breaking up the tomatoes with a wooden spoon. Reduce the heat to low, partially cover, and cook, stirring occasionally, for 15 minutes.

2. Increase the heat to medium-low. Stir in the zucchini, parsley, salt and pepper, cover and cook until the zucchini is just tender, for about 8 minutes. Serve hot.

PER SERVING: 140 CAL; 6G PROT; 3G FAT; 24G CARB; 0MG CHOL; 758MG SOD; 7G FIBER

COCONUT CURRY AND NOODLES

Pungent and fiery, this silken curry accents a bowl of noodles garnished with tofu and assorted greens. This makes such an unusual dish that you may want to double or triple the recipe, and serve it to a table full of friends. Be sure to buy Thai red curry paste made without fish sauce or shrimp paste. You may have leftover curry sauce; if so, refrigerate for up to 2 days.

1 12-ounce package somen noodles

3 tablespoons vegetable oil plus extra for frying

1 onion, diced

2 tablespoons minced garlic

2 tablespoon minced ginger

1 teaspoon ground turmeric

3 to 3½ cups low-fat coconut milk

¼ cup brown sugar

1 tablespoon red curry paste, or to taste

2 green chiles, seeded and thinly sliced

2 tablespoons fresh lime juice, or more to taste

Salt to taste

6 large hard-boiled eggs, quartered, for garnish

About 1 pound extra-firm tofu, cubed, for garnish

2 cucumbers, peeled and shredded, for garnish

1 bunch watercress, trimmed and blanched, for garnish

1. Cook the noodles according to the package directions, drain and set aside.

2. Heat the oil in a large wok or skillet over medium heat, and sauté the onion, garlic, ginger and turmeric for 3 minutes. Reduce the heat to medium-low, and continue cooking until the mixture becomes very aromatic.

3. Stir in 1¾ cups coconut milk, the brown sugar, red curry paste, chiles, lime juice and salt. Continue cooking and stirring for about 15 minutes, or until the mixture reduces and thickens. Add the remaining coconut milk, stir to combine well and cook until heated through. Remove from the heat.

4. To serve, put a serving of noodles into a large soup bowl, and pour about ¼ cup coconut curry over the noodles. Garnish the noodles with the egg, tofu and a portion of cucumbers and watercress. Repeat until the noodles are used up, and add more coconut curry if desired.

PER SERVING: 670 CAL; 24G PROT; 26G FAT; 82G CARB; 210MG CHOL; 550MG SOD; 6G FIBER

celebrate the holidays

HOPPIN' JOHN

This Southern dish is traditionally served over rice on New Year's Day to bring good luck during the new year.

1¼ cups dry black-eyed peas
4 cups fresh water
1½ cups chopped onion
1 clove garlic, minced
1 bay leaf
½ teaspoon freshly ground black
   pepper
¼ teaspoon cayenne
8 ounces tempeh
1 tablespoon low-sodium soy sauce
Salt to taste

1. Soak the peas overnight in a large pot of water, or boil them for 2 minutes, cover and let stand for 1 hour. Drain, then cover with 4 cups fresh water and bring to a boil. Add the onion, garlic, bay leaf, black pepper and cayenne. Bring to a boil, cover, reduce the heat to low and cook for 1 hour, stirring occasionally.

2. Brush the tempeh on both sides with soy sauce, and set aside for 5 minutes. Chop the tempeh coarsely, and add to the peas. Cook for another hour, stirring frequently. Remove, and discard the bay leaf. Mash the peas slightly to make a sauce. Stir in salt, and serve.

PER SERVING: 165 CAL; 12G PROT; 3G FAT; 22G CARB; 0MG CHOL; 193MG SOD; 5G FIBER

THREE KINGS' BREAD

Here's the perfect bread to serve at the Epiphany—January 6th—celebrating the time when the Wise Men found Jesus in the manger.

Basic Sweetened Bread Dough
   (page 132)
¾ cup raisins
¾ cup chopped nuts
⅓ cup chopped or dried cherries
1½ tablespoons grated orange peel
Golden Glaze (page 93) or glaze of
   your choice
Whole nuts and candied or dried
   fruit for decoration, optional

1. Make the Basic Sweetened Bread Dough, adding the raisins, nuts, cherries and orange peel with the final 3 cups flour.

2. Divide the risen dough into thirds. Roll each third into a 20-inch-long roll. Join the ends of each roll to form 3 separate rings. Place the rings on greased cookie sheets. Cover with a dishcloth and let rise until doubled in bulk, for 1 to 2 hours.

3. Preheat the oven to 350F.

4. Bake until the crusts are golden brown, for about 30 minutes. Cool on racks, and glaze with Golden Glaze. Decorate with nuts and fruit to resemble the "crowns" of the Three Kings.

PER SERVING (WITHOUT GLAZE): 281 CAL; 6G PROT; 7G FAT; 50G CARB; 0MG CHOL; 269MG SOD; 2G FIBER

BLACK-EYED PEA CROQUETTES

A tradition in the African-American community is that black-eyed peas should be eaten on New Year's Day for good luck. The traditional dish is called Hoppin' John (page 437), which is a mix of black-eyed peas, rice and pork sausage. There are several theories on how this dish got its name—such as children used to hop around the dining room table before the dish was served—but here is a new twist on this old favorite. The mix may be made a day ahead, but add the breadcrumbs when you make the patties.

6 cups water

2 cups uncooked black-eyed peas

1 teaspoon salt

1 tablespoon canola oil

1 small onion, diced

1 tablespoon minced garlic

1½ cups canned fire-roasted tomatoes, diced

¼ teaspoon chili paste, or more to taste

1 tablespoon balsamic vinegar

Salt and freshly ground black pepper to taste

3 scallions, thinly sliced

2 large eggs, lightly beaten

4 cups fresh breadcrumbs

Flour for dusting

1. Bring 6 cups of water to a boil over high heat, and add the peas and 1 teaspoon salt. Cook the peas for 1 hour or until tender. Remove from the heat, and set aside to cool.

2. Meanwhile, heat the oil over medium heat, and sauté the onion until translucent, for about 7 minutes. Add the garlic and tomatoes, bring to a boil and reduce the heat to low. Add the chili paste, balsamic vinegar, salt and pepper, and cook for 20 minutes. Remove from the heat, and set aside to cool.

3. Combine the peas and tomato mixture. Put half of the pea mixture in a food processor and purée, or mash half with the back of a wooden spoon in a bowl. Add the mashed mixture to the remaining beans, and add the scallions, eggs and breadcrumbs. The mixture should be thick but moist. If it is too moist, add more breadcrumbs. Form the mixture into 1½-inch round patties, about ½-inch thick.

4. Heat the oil in a large skillet over medium-high heat. Dust each patty with flour, and gently place in the skillet. Cook for about 2 minutes on each side, and repeat the process until all of the mixture is used, adding more oil if needed. Remove from the heat, drain on paper towels and serve hot.

PER SERVING: 90 CAL; 2G PROT; 6G FAT; 6G CARB; 20MG CHOL; 110MG SOD; 1G FIBER

ST. PATRICK'S DAY STEW

To get into the spirit of St. Paddy's Day, serve this stew with new potatoes, boiled cabbage and soda bread. And you don't have to be Irish to enjoy it!

1 large onion, sliced

½ small cabbage, sliced thinly

3 cups cubed winter squash

2 parsnips, peeled and sliced

½ cup rolled oats

6 cups water or Vegetable Stock (page 332)

½ cup dulse (seaweed)

Salt to taste, optional

Freshly ground black pepper to taste, optional

Chopped fresh chives, for garnish

1. Heat ¼ cup water in a stockpot, and cook the onion and cabbage, stirring, for 3 minutes. Add the squash, and cook for 2 minutes more. Add the parsnips, and sprinkle the oats over the vegetables. Add the water, cover and cook over medium heat until the squash is tender, for about 20 minutes.

2. Rinse the dulse in a fine strainer, and add to the stew. Season with salt and pepper, if desired. Garnish with chives, and serve hot.

PER SERVING: 219 CAL; 9G PROT; 1G FAT; 45G CARB; 0MG CHOL; 287MG SOD; 6G FIBER

SU CAI JIAO (VEGETABLE DUMPLINGS)

The most common—and possibly most popular—food in Beijing during Chinese New Year are the dumplings. Since the New Year falls in winter, only bok choy is in season, so local cooks mix it with dry mushrooms and bamboo shoots, and serve the dumplings with black vinegar and fresh garlic. Traditionally, the cook will slip a bright, new coin into the center of selected dumplings so the lucky eater will find some good fortune. The correct way to eat is to poke a small hole in the center of the dumpling with chopsticks so that the dipping sauce can seep inside. Look for preserved cabbage and squares of fried tofu at your Asian market.

4 ounces dried Chinese mushrooms
2 ounces bamboo shoots
2 ounces peeled jícama
10 ounces bok choy
1 ounce preserved cabbage
1 ounce fried tofu, diced
½ teaspoon salt
Pinch white pepper
1½ teaspoons granulated sugar
2 teaspoons dark sesame oil
2 teaspoons vegetable oil
30 wonton wrappers
1 large egg, lightly beaten
1 tablespoon minced garlic
6 tablespoons black vinegar

1. Soak the dried mushrooms in water for about 30 minutes, or until they soften. Squeeze out the water, and dice.

2. Cut all the vegetables into small dice, and press under weights for several hours to squeeze out all liquid—the vegetables must be dry when mixed with the tofu and seasoning ingredients. Mix the dry vegetables with the tofu, salt, pepper, sugar and oils.

3. To make the dumplings, place each wrapper on a flat surface. Spoon about 1 teaspoon of filling into the center, and fold the dough over in half. Moisten the edges of each wrapper, and pinch shut to seal in the filling. Repeat with the remaining wrappers and filling.

4. Steam the dumplings over boiling water for about 5 minutes. Remove from the heat, and set aside.

5. To serve, arrange the dumplings in a serving dish. Combine the garlic and black vinegar and pass as dipping sauce.

PER SERVING: 240 CAL; 12G PROT; 5G FAT; 38G CARB; 5MG CHOL; 900MG SOD; 5G FIBER

Chalupas are the most popular street snack in Puebla, Mexico—and a wonderful way to celebrate Cinco de Mayo. If very small tortillas are not available, trim store-bought corn tortillas to size with a cookie cutter. Queso fresco is a nonmelting Mexican cheese. In the mountains of northern Puebla, tiny, thick-skinned tomatoes with intense flavor are prized for this salsa.

Chalupas

½ cup vegetable oil

12 3-inch corn tortillas

Salsa de Jitomate

3 dried guajillo chiles, stemmed, seeded and cut open flat

3 dried arbol chiles or other small, spicy dried chiles, stemmed and unseeded

1 pound ripe red tomatoes

6 cloves garlic, unpeeled

1 teaspoon dried Mexican oregano

1 teaspoon kosher or sea salt

½ cup crumbled Mexican queso fresco or feta or goat cheese

1. To make the Chalupas: Heat the oil in a large skillet over medium-high heat. Carefully place several tortillas in the oil. Cook, turning, until thoroughly heated but still pliable with a chewy texture but not brittle. Remove from the heat, drain on paper towels, and continue until all the tortillas are used up.

2. To make the Salsa: Heat a heavy, ungreased skillet over medium-high heat. Flattening the guajillo chiles with a spatula, toast the chiles for 2 minutes per side until the chiles change color and release aromas. Remove to a bowl of hot water. Toast the arbol chiles for 30 seconds, and add to the water. Soak the chiles for at least 30 minutes or up to several hours until soft.

3. Roast the tomatoes and unpeeled garlic cloves until each is covered with black spots. Remove from the heat, cut out the tomato stem ends and transfer the tomatoes to a blender. Trim the hard ends from the garlic, peel and scoop into the blender. Add the chiles and enough water to facilitate blending, and purée until well blended. Pour the salsa into a bowl, and stir in the oregano and salt. Let sit for at least 30 minutes for the flavors to meld.

4. To serve, top the mini corn tortillas with the salsa and a sprinkle of cheese. At a buffet, serve the salsa in a decorative bowl, and allow guests to serve themselves.

PER SERVING: 80 CAL; 2G PROT; 6G FAT; 5G CARB; 5MG CHOL; 180MG SOD; 1G FIBER

MEDITERRANEAN RAGOUT

Similar to ribollita *(the "reboiled" Italian soup of vegetables and bread), this recipe is a perfect vehicle for putting a wide variety of farm-fresh vegetables to good use—try it on the Fourth of July! Day-old bread, which functions as a thickener, gives the stew a comforting finish. Use a good quality olive oil—it tastes great drizzled over the completed stew.*

3 tablespoons olive oil

2 large leeks, sliced

2 medium-sized stalks celery, sliced

2 medium-sized carrots, sliced

6 medium-sized cloves garlic, minced

1 tablespoon chopped fresh rosemary

⅛ teaspoon crushed red pepper

2 cups low-sodium vegetable broth

8 ounces fresh cranberry beans, shelled, or 1 cup frozen baby lima beans

4 ounces green beans, trimmed and cut into 2-inch pieces

3 ripe medium-sized tomatoes, seeded and coarsely chopped

6 cups Swiss chard leaves, cut into ½-inch-wide ribbons

1 cup sliced zucchini

2½-inch-thick slices day-old country bread, cubed

1 cup Parmesan shavings, optional

1. Heat 1 tablespoon of the oil in a Dutch oven or deep sauté pan over medium heat. Add the leeks, and cook, stirring often, until softened but not browned, for 1½ to 2 minutes. Add the celery, carrots, garlic, rosemary and red pepper, and cook, stirring, for 1 minute. Add the broth and cranberry beans, and bring to a simmer. Reduce the heat to medium-low, cover, and cook for 15 minutes. Add the green beans, cover, and cook for 5 minutes. Stir in the tomatoes, chard and zucchini, and return to a simmer. Cover, and cook until the vegetables are tender, for 6 to 10 minutes. Remove from the heat, and season with salt and freshly ground pepper to taste.

2. Add the bread, and stir to moisten. Cover the Dutch oven, and let stand until the bread has softened and the stew has thickened, for about 5 minutes. Spoon the stew into shallow soup bowls, and drizzle some of the remaining oil over each serving. Garnish with Parmesan shavings, if desired, and serve immediately.

PER SERVING: 236 CAL; 8G PROT; 8G FAT; 30G CARB; 0MG CHOL; 234MG SOD; 8G FIBER

TZIMMES WITH POTATO DUMPLINGS

Tzimmes is a sweetened dish of stewed vegetables and dried fruit. Here it's simmered with hearty potato dumplings. The dish traditionally is served as part of the last meal before the Yom Kippur fast, but it's also eaten at festive meals throughout the year.

Dumplings

3 large potatoes, peeled and grated finely

1 medium-sized potato, peeled, cooked and mashed

1 tablespoon melted unsalted butter or margarine

⅓ cup matzoh meal, or as needed

2 large eggs, beaten (or ½ cup egg substitute)

½ teaspoon salt

¼ teaspoon ground cinnamon

Freshly ground pepper to taste

Tzimmes

1 pound carrots, peeled and chopped

2 large sweet potatoes, peeled and chopped

8 to 10 pitted prunes, optional

2 tablespoons brown sugar or maple syrup

1 tablespoon minced onion

¼ teaspoon ground ginger

Pinch of salt

1½ tablespoons cornstarch or arrowroot dissolved in 1½ tablespoons water

1. To make the Dumplings: To remove excess starch, place the grated potatoes in the center of a dishcloth. Twist it closed, and dip in cold water. Tightly twist the cloth to squeeze out as much liquid as possible.

2. Transfer the potatoes to a large mixing bowl, and stir in the remaining dumpling ingredients. If the mixture isn't firm enough to shape, add a little more matzoh meal. Shape into 2 dumplings.

3. To make the Tzimmes: Place half of the carrots and potatoes, prunes, brown sugar or maple syrup, onion, ginger and salt in a large saucepan. Add the dumplings and top with the remaining vegetables. Add cold water to barely cover. Bring to a boil, lower the heat, cover and barely simmer until the dumplings are cooked and the vegetables are fork-tender, about 1 hour.

4. Uncover, increase the heat to high and cook until the liquid is reduced by half. Remove from the heat. Transfer the dumplings to a plate. Add the dissolved cornstarch or arrowroot to the saucepan, and stir until the liquid is thick and clear, for about 1 minute. Slice each dumpling into thirds, and serve topped with the *tzimmes*.

PER SERVING: 240 CAL; 5G PROT; 4G FAT; 46G CARB; 76MG CHOL; 301MG SOD; 5G FIBER

SPICY CRANBERRY-ZINFANDEL RELISH

What a bright addition to a Thanksgiving or Christmas holiday table! This relish can be made several days in advance of use, and it keeps in the refrigerator for two weeks.

1 cup dried cranberries

¾ cup red zinfandel

¼ teaspoon mustard seeds

½ teaspoon vegetable oil

½ small onion, finely diced

1 clove garlic, finely chopped

2 teaspoons fresh ginger, grated

¼ teaspoon cayenne or ½ orange habanero pepper, cut into very thin strips

1 tablespoon granulated sugar or 2 tablespoons brown rice syrup

¼ teaspoon salt

¼ cup vinegar, rice or white wine

1. Soak the cranberries in the wine. Meanwhile, heat a nonstick skillet over medium high heat. When the skillet is hot, add the mustard seeds and toast until the seeds begin to pop. Remove the pan from the heat briefly and add the oil, onions, ginger and hot pepper.

2. Return the pan to the heat, and sauté the mixture until the onions are translucent. Add the sugar, salt and cranberries with their soaking liquid. Cook the mixture until it just boils. Add the vinegar, and cool completely.

PER SERVING: 80 CAL; 0G PROT; 0G FAT; 14G CARB; 0MG CHOL; 75MG SOD; 1G FIBER

PUMPKIN-AND-BROWN RICE PANCAKES

Try these golden pancakes when you're in the mood for an out-of-the-ordinary autumnal breakfast—like on Thanksgiving morning.

½ cup cooked brown rice

1 cup buttermilk

1 large egg

2 egg whites

1 teaspoon canola oil

2 tablespoons honey

½ cup fresh, cooked pumpkin or canned pumpkin

⅓ cup apple juice

¾ cup whole wheat pastry flour or unbleached white flour

1 teaspoon baking powder

½ teaspoon ground cinnamon

¼ teaspoon ground nutmeg

1. Combine the rice, buttermilk, egg and egg whites, oil, honey, pumpkin and apple juice in a mixing bowl. Sift the remaining ingredients into a second bowl. Combine the contents of the 2 bowls, stirring until just blended.

2. Preheat a nonstick griddle over medium heat. Drop the batter by the spoonful onto the griddle. Cook until bubbles appear, and flip the pancakes over to cook the other side until lightly browned. Remove from the heat, and serve hot.

PER PANCAKE: 74 CAL; 3G PROT; 1G FAT; 13G CARB; 19MG CHOL; 72MG SOD; 1G FIBER

PUMPKIN CHEESECAKE TORTE

Having a Halloween party? Treat your guests to this pumpkin-rich cheesecake. You may want to also add this confection to your Thanksgiving table for a celebratory conclusion to the meal.

Crust

1⅓ cups graham cracker crumbs

4 tablespoons soft canola margarine or unsalted butter

Cheesecake

1 pound soft silken tofu, drained

1 15-ounce can solid-pack pumpkin

4 ounces soy "cream cheese," at room temperature

1 cup granulated sugar

1 teaspoon vanilla extract

¾ teaspoon ground cinnamon plus additional for dusting

½ teaspoon ground nutmeg

½ teaspoon ground allspice

¼ teaspoon ground cloves

1. Position the rack in the center of the oven. Preheat the oven to 350F. Spray an 8½-inch springform pan with nonstick cooking spray.

2. To make the Crust: Put the graham cracker crumbs and margarine into a food processor, and process until evenly moistened. Firmly press the crumb mixture into the bottom and about ½-inch up the sides of the pan. Bake until set, for about 10 minutes. Transfer to a wire rack, and cool completely.

3. To make the Cheesecake: Put the tofu into a food processor, and purée until smooth. Add the pumpkin, and process until blended. Add the soy "cream cheese," sugar, vanilla, cinnamon, nutmeg, allspice and cloves, and process until smooth and well combined. Pour the mixture into the cooled crust.

4. Bake on the center rack of the oven for 45 minutes. Turn the oven off. Let the cheesecake cool in the oven for 1 hour without opening the door. Transfer to a wire rack and cool completely. Cover loosely with plastic wrap and refrigerate for at least 8 hours or overnight.

5. To serve, run a long, thin knife around the inside edge of the pan to loosen the cake. Remove the sides of the pan. Lightly dust the top of the cheesecake with cinnamon, and serve at room temperature.

PER SERVING: 201 CAL; 4G PROT; 7G FAT; 31G CARB; 0MG CHOL; 100MG SOD; 2G FIBER

SPICED PUMPKIN CUSTARD

This low-fat pumpkin custard is just right for Thanksgiving and other harvest feasts.

¾ cup pumpkin purée

1 tablespoon molasses

1 tablespoon honey

⅔ cup maple syrup

3 tablespoons ground cinnamon

1 teaspoon ground ginger

½ teaspoon ground cloves

1 teaspoon ground nutmeg

2¾ cups skim milk

2 tablespoons arrowroot powder or cornstarch

4 large eggs, beaten or 2 tablespoons egg substitute mixed in ½ cup water

1 cup nonfat vanilla yogurt

1. Preheat the oven to 350F. Lightly oil eight 1-cup soufflé or custard dishes, and place them on a baking sheet.

2. Combine the pumpkin, molasses, honey, maple syrup, cinnamon, ginger, cloves and nutmeg in a large saucepan.

3. Mix ¼ cup milk in a small bowl with the arrowroot or cornstarch until smooth. Add the remaining 2½ cups milk, and pour the milk-arrowroot mixture into the pumpkin mixture in the saucepan. Stir well.

4. Bring to a boil over medium heat, whisking frequently, and cook until thickened to the consistency of heavy cream. Remove from the heat. Stir in the beaten eggs or egg substitute and water. Pour into the baking dishes.

5. Bake until firm, for about 30 minutes. Remove from the oven, and let cool slightly. Serve with a dollop of nonfat yogurt.

PER SERVING: 180 CAL; 8G PROT; 3G FAT; 31G CARB; 108MG CHOL; 109MG SOD; 0.2G FIBER

RUTABAGA PIE

Pumpkin meets its match in this custardy dessert, which is less dense than traditional pumpkin pie. If you want a change of dessert selections this Thanksgiving or Christmas, consider this option.

Filling

1¼ pounds rutabaga, peeled and cut into ½-inch cubes

½ cup firmly packed light brown sugar

¼ cup dark corn syrup

1 teaspoon vanilla extract

1 teaspoon ground cinnamon

½ teaspoon ground ginger

¼ teaspoon salt

3 large eggs, lightly beaten

1 cup heavy cream

Crust

1½ cups all-purpose flour

½ teaspoon salt

½ cup shortening

4 to 5 tablespoons ice water

1. To make the Filling: Bring a generous amount of water to a boil in a large saucepan over medium heat. Add the rutabaga, and cook until very tender, for about 30 minutes. Drain well.

2. Meanwhile, to make the Crust: Mix the flour and salt together in a mixing bowl. Cut in the shortening until the mixture resembles coarse meal. Stir in just enough ice water to hold the dough together. Do not overmix. Roll out the dough on a floured surface, and fit into a 9-inch ovenproof glass or other pie plate.

3. Put the cooked rutabagas into a food processor or food mill, and purée until smooth. Measure 2 packed cups of rutabaga purée, and place in large bowl.

4. Preheat the oven to 400F.

5. Stir the brown sugar, corn syrup and spices into the rutabaga purée, mixing well. Fold in the eggs, and stir in the heavy cream until well blended. Pour the mixture into the pie crust.

6. Bake for 45 minutes, or until set. Cool before serving.

PER SERVING: 350 CAL; 5G PROT; 20G FAT; 36G CARB; 95MG CHOL; 230MG SOD; 2G FIBER

MOROCCAN SHEPHERDS' PIE

This dish takes its flavors from traditional Mediterranean vegetable tagines but seals them in a festive crust fashioned from mashed white and sweet potatoes squeezed through a chef's piping bag or spooned on artistically in alternating rows. Consider serving this as the centerpiece for a holiday or other celebratory meal.

Sweet Potatoes

3 large sweet potatoes

¼ cup orange juice

¼ teaspoon ground cumin

⅛ teaspoon ground cinnamon

¼ cup olive oil, optional

Sea salt and freshly ground black pepper to taste

Vegetable Filling

2 tablespoons olive oil

2 onions, diced

3 cloves garlic, minced

2 large carrots, diced

1 pound soy burger "meat" or 4 vegan burgers, crumbled

1 teaspoon ground cumin

1 teaspoon ground coriander

½ teaspoon ground cinnamon

1 teaspoon freshly ground black pepper

Strands saffron, optional

4 tomatoes, peeled, seeded and diced or 3¼ cups diced canned tomatoes

1 cup Vegetable Stock (page 332)

1 head cauliflower

1 large or 2 small zucchini or other squash, cut into 1-inch cubes

1 head broccoli, cut into bite-size florets

⅛ cup raisins, optional

¼ cup slivered almonds

White Potatoes

3 pounds potatoes, peeled and cut into 1- to 2-inch chunks

2 teaspoons salt

¼ cup olive oil

Sea salt and freshly ground black pepper to taste

1. Preheat the oven to 350F. Lightly oil a 10 x 15–inch baking dish.

2. To make the Sweet Potatoes: Bake the sweet potatoes until soft, for about 1 hour. Remove from the oven, and set aside to cool. When cool enough to handle, peel and mash with the orange juice, spices and olive oil, if using. Season with salt and pepper.

3. To make the Vegetable Filling: Heat the oil in a large skillet over medium-high heat. When hot, add the onions, garlic, carrots, soy "meat" and spices. Cook the mixture for about 7 minutes, or until the soy "meat" is browned and crusty but not burnt.

4. Reduce the heat to medium, and add the tomatoes, stock and cauliflower. When the mixture is warmed through, add the zucchini, broccoli, raisins and almonds. If needed, heat the mixture in 2 batches. Transfer the mixture to a baking dish. Cover loosely with foil, and bake for 30 to 45 minutes.

5. To make the White Potatoes: Combine the potatoes and salt in a large pot with water to cover by 3 inches. Bring to a boil over high heat. Reduce the heat to medium, and cook the potatoes for 10 minutes more, or until tender. Remove from the heat, and drain the potatoes, reserving 2 cups of the cooking liquid. Mash the potatoes with the olive oil, then slowly add 1 cup of the cooking liquid, or enough to give the potatoes a moist, fluffy consistency. Season with salt and pepper.

6. Fill 2 large pastry bags, one with mashed white potatoes and one with mashed sweet potatoes. Remove the baking dish from the oven. Pipe a decorative design on top of the pie, alternating colors for drama.

7. Return the casserole to the oven for 15 minutes, or until the potatoes are heated through. Just before serving, place under the broiler, and cook until the crust is lightly browned.

PER SERVING: 290 CAL; 10G PROT; 9G FAT; 48G CARB; 0MG CHOL; 600MG SOD; 9G FIBER

NOODLE-CURRANT LATKES

Serving a slightly sweet noodle pudding called lukshen kugel *is traditional in many Jewish homes for Chanukah. This recipe borrows the cooking technique traditionally used for potato pancakes (latkes) to turn this kugel into a crispy noodle pancake. Top it with applesauce and sour cream.*

1 8-ounce package thin egg noodles

2 large eggs, beaten or ½ cup egg substitute

½ cup currants

1 tablespoon all-purpose flour

1 teaspoon ground cinnamon

2 tablespoons brown sugar

¼ teaspoon salt

1. Cook the noodles according to the package directions until *al dente*, and drain. In a large mixing bowl, mix together the noodles, eggs, currants, flour, cinnamon, brown sugar and salt, and set aside.

2. Spray a large nonstick skillet with nonstick cooking spray. Place over high heat for 30 seconds. Reduce the heat to medium, and drop the noodle mixture by heaping tablespoons into the skillet, flattening each mound into a pancake with the back of the spoon. Fry the latkes until browned and crisp, for about 4 minutes on each side. Remove from the heat, and keep warm until serving.

PER SERVING: 153 CAL; 5G PROT; 2G FAT; 27G CARB; 80MG CHOL; 133MG SOD; 1G FIBER

NOODLE KUGEL

Kugel is a type of baked noodle or vegetable pudding, usually served for holidays and major celebratory meals as an accompaniment. What makes this version so different and so spectacular is the use of very thin, very short noodles instead of the more common broader ones. This dish freezes well.

1 cup granulated sugar

1 cup whole milk

1 pound low-fat or regular cottage cheese

2 cups low-fat or regular sour cream at room temperature

2 sticks butter or margarine at room temperature

5 large eggs, beaten

8 ounces low-fat or regular cream cheese at room temperature

8 ounces thin soup noodles

Ground cinnamon to taste

1. Preheat oven to 450F. Grease 9 x 13–inch baking dish, and set aside.

2. Cook noodles for 5 minutes in lightly salted boiling water. Drain well, and set aside to cool. Combine sugar, butter, cottage cheese, sour cream, cream cheese and milk in large bowl, and mix well. Stir in noodles and eggs, and sprinkle top with cinnamon. Place in baking dish.

3. Bake for 5 minutes, reduce heat to 350F and continue baking 45 to 50 minutes longer, or until lightly browned on top.

PER SERVING: 440 CAL; 14 G PROT; 28 G TOTAL FAT (16 SAT FAT); 34 G CARB; 175 MG CHOL; 420 MG SOD; 1 G FIBER

VEGAN MAPLE CHEESE PIE

Smooth as custard and accented with maple syrup, this luscious pie deserves star billing because it has the flavor and texture of a rich and creamy cheesecake, minus the calories—a perfect ending to a holiday meal, and it's particularly nice at Thanksgiving. For an extra-fancy touch, garnish the pie with pecan halves just before serving.

1 premade 10-inch deep-dish graham cracker crust

1½ pounds vegan cream cheese

6 ounces nonfat vanilla or plain soy yogurt

¾ cup brown or maple sugar or light brown Muscovado sugar

¼ cup egg replacer

6 tablespoons maple syrup

2 teaspoons vanilla extract

Pinch salt

1. Preheat the oven to 350F.

2. Combine the cream cheese, yogurt, maple sugar, egg replacer, 3 tablespoons maple syrup and vanilla extract, and beat with an electric mixer until smooth and well blended. Spoon into the prepared crust, and drizzle the top with the remaining 3 tablespoons of maple syrup.

3. Bake for about 40 minutes, or until it is firm in the center. Remove from the oven, and cool on a wire rack. Refrigerate for up to 4 hours before slicing and serving.

PER SERVING: 420 CAL; 4G PROT; 26G FAT; 40G CARB; 0MG CHOL; 520MG SOD; <1G FIBER

EASY HOLIDAY FRUITCAKE

If you're tired of commercially produced candied fruitcakes, you'll enjoy this easy, flavorful, moist version.

1 cup all-purpose flour

1 cup granulated sugar

1 teaspoon salt

½ teaspoon baking powder

½ cup plus 2 teaspoons thawed orange juice concentrate

2 large eggs, slightly beaten, plus 2 egg whites (or equivalent egg substitute)

1 cup chopped pecans

1 cup chopped walnuts

1 10-ounce jar maraschino cherries, drained and patted dry

1 cup chopped pitted dates

1 cup chopped dried figs or raisins

½ cup confectioners' sugar

1. Preheat the oven to 300F. Grease a 9 x 5-inch loaf pan, and set aside.

2. Mix the flour, sugar, salt, baking powder, ½ cup orange juice concentrate, and eggs or egg substitute together. Blend in the nuts, cherries, dates, and figs or raisins. Mix well. Spoon the batter into the pan.

3. Bake for 2 hours. Cover the cake with foil, and bake until a toothpick inserted in the center comes out clean, for about 15 minutes more. Remove from the oven, and let sit for 15 minutes before removing the cake from the pan.

4. Meanwhile, in a small bowl, stir together the confectioners' sugar, 1 teaspoon water and remaining 2 teaspoons orange juice concentrate. Drizzle over the cake while it's still hot. Cool the cake completely. To store, wrap it in plastic wrap, then in foil and refrigerate.

PER SERVING: 364 CAL; 5G PROT; 14G FAT; 64G CARB; 22MG CHOL; 185MG SOD; 4G FIBER

WINTER JEWEL FRUITCAKE WITH WHITE ICING

Try to find fruits dried without added sugar when making this holiday fruitcake. The cake slices more easily if made two or three days in advance. Decorate the cake as fancifully as you like.

Fruitcake

3 cups bread flour or 2 cups all-purpose flour and 1 cup soy flour

1 tablespoon baking powder

1½ teaspoons baking soda

⅛ teaspoon salt

2 teaspoons Jamaican baking spice mix or ½ teaspoon each ground cinnamon, cloves, allspice and mace

½ cup chopped crystallized ginger

1 cup golden raisins

2½ cups dried cranberries

2 cups diced, dried apricots

2 cups sliced almonds

1½ cups applesauce

⅔ cup vegetable oil

1 cup barley malt or molasses

⅛ cup vinegar

Icing

⅓ cup confectioners' sugar

Cold water

Fresh lemon juice

Apricots, orange peel or almonds, for garnish (optional)

1. Preheat the oven to 300F. Grease and flour a 10-cup Bundt pan.

2. To make the Fruitcake: Mix the flour, baking powder, soda, salt and spices in a large mixing bowl until well combined. Add all the fruits and nuts to the flour mixture, and toss until well coated.

3. Blend together the applesauce, oil, barley malt and vinegar. Working quickly, mix the wet ingredients into the dry, stirring only until mixed thoroughly. Pour the batter into the pan, and place in the center of the oven.

4. Bake for 1½ hours, or until done. Cool the cake completely on a rack.

5. Meanwhile, to make the Icing: Put the confectioners' sugar in a bowl, and whisk in enough cold water to form a thick paste. Add 2 to 3 drops of lemon juice. Drizzle the icing over the cake in swirls or an attractive pattern, add garnish, if desired, and serve.

PER SERVING: 450 CAL; 7G PROT; 17G FAT; 69G CARB; 0MG CHOL; 210MG SOD; 5G FIBER

menus

MOST OF US ARE FACED WITH THE DAILY CHALLENGE of preparing from one to three meals for ourselves and our families, and sometimes for a gathering of friends. The following menus offer a game plan, whether for a celebratory occasion demanding spectacular food, a weekend brunch for friends with casual fare or a simple family breakfast that will keep everyone energized until lunchtime. Whatever your skill level in the kitchen, you can follow these meal plans or assemble complementary dishes on your own. Get creative and have fun!

DINNERS FOR ENTERTAINING

Almost-Classic French Onion Soup (page 301)
Deep-Dish Sun-Dried Tomato Quiche (page 285)
Sugar Snap Peas with Mushrooms (page 183)
Apricot Almond Sorbet (page 388)
Better than Champagne (page 70)

Athenian Mushrooms (page 67)
Gingered Green Soup (page 302)
Avocado Salad with Citrus Vinaigrette (page 142)
Risotto with Zucchini Petals and Basil (page 265)
Quixotic Cheescake (page 394)

Tomato and Herb Bruschetta (page 68)
Olive-Tomato Crostini (page 63)
New Potatoes with Leeks and Fennel (page 148)
Eggplant with Caramelized Onions, Tomatoes and Mint (page 225)
Burgundy Cherry Macadamia Nut Tofu Ice Cream (page 388)

EVERYDAY MEALS

Four-Bean Bake (page 357)
Steamed Broccoli with Garlic (page 187)
Strawberry-Banana Glacé (page 389)

Red, Red Salad (page 342)
Robust Tortilla Soup (page 341)
Fresh Peach Tofu Ice Cream (page 387)

Pasta Shells with Black-Eyed Peas and Artichokes (page 248)
Shredded Carrot Gratin (page 180)
Honey-Yogurt Cake with Syrup (page 393)

Creamy Vegetable Soup (page 318)
Mounded Portobello Mushrooms (page 347)
Raspberry Chill (page 414)

Almost-Classic French Onion Soup (page 301)
Sesame-Coated Tofu (page 384)
Baked Hawaii (page 412)

"Beef" Stroganoff (page 350)
Autumn Red Cabbage with Pears (page 180)
Frozen Strawberry Bars (page 390)

Parmesan "Chicken" on English Muffins (page 341)
Aïoli Potato Salad (page 150)
Angel Berry Parfait (page 415)

UNDER THIRTY MINUTES

Fava Bean Salad with Feta (page 337)
Cajun-Style Rice (page 349)

Portobello Pizzas (page 338)
Peppers Galore (page 358)

Texas Tofu (page 360)
Kasha and Parsley Big Bowl (page 342)

SEASONAL

SPRING

Barbecued Tempeh with Bell Peppers (page 294)
Baked Beans with Mustard and Tomatoes (page 202)
Upside-Down Peach Pie (page 404)

Primavera Salad (page 157)
Cashew, Tempeh and Carrot Curry (page 210)
One-Rise Breadsticks (page 131)

SUMMER

Pita Crisps with Spinach, Red Pepper and Feta (page 65)
Corn Four Ways (page 360)
Summer Pudding (page 408)

Sloppy Janes (page 371)
Summer Garden Pasta Salad (page 162)
Cran-Raspberry Crisp (page 133)

AUTUMN

Braised Seitan with Fragrant Tomato Gravy (page 229)
Golden Vegetables (page 179)
Peanut Butter Pudding (page 408)

Autumn Vegetables (page 181)
Basic Polenta (page 200)
Spiced Carrot Pudding (page 407)

WINTER

Pressure Cooker Winter Vegetable Soup with Black Barley
   (page 321)
Easy Manicotti alla Romana (page 245)
Pear Cobbler (page 411)

Winter Pear Salad in Raspberry Vinaigrette (page 431)
Crisp Black Sesame Tofu (page 289)
Almost Traditional Chocolate Mousse (page 410)

TABLE FOR ONE

Avocado Salad with Citrus Vinaigrette (page 142)
Spaghetti Pie (page 245)
Poached Orange Cake (page 391)

Black Bean and Vegetable Hash (page 121)
Dandelion Greens with Spicy Vinaigrette (page 141)
Poached Plums (page 410)

MAIN-DISH SALADS

Spinach Salad with Crisped Tempeh (page 150)
Bread
Honey-Yogurt Cake with Syrup (page 393)

Quinoa and Black Bean Salad (page 170)
Fruit and Crêpe Pudding (page 409)

ETHNIC

HISPANIC

Chipotle Black Bean Soup (page 317)
Southwestern Pinwheels (page 70)
Sweet-and-Spicy Layered Fruit Salad (page 155)

Navy Beans in Gypsy Sauce (page 276)
Flame-Toasted Whole Wheat Tortilla (page 137)
Mixed Dried Fruit Turnovers (page 414)

INDIAN

Samosas (page 419)
Cilantro Chutney (page 176)
Cashew Stew (page 327)
Raita (page 144)
Indian-Spiced Yellow Split Peas with Brussels Sprouts
   (page 206)

Easy Chapatis (Indian Flatbread) (page 138)
Rice Pudding with Dates (page 407)

ITALIAN

Focaccia with Coarse Salt and Fennel (page 139)
Mediterranean Ragout (page 441)
Capellini-Tomato Pie (page 253)
Italian Ice

Penne with Asparagus and Spring Herbs (page 251)
Tuscan Bread Salad (page 154)
Ultimate Chocolate "Cheesecake" (page 393)

JAPANESE

Grilled Tofu with Wasabi-Honey Glaze (page 279)
Brown rice
Curried Beans and Greens (page 212)
Green tea ice cream

EASTERN EUROPEAN

Cucumber, Walnut and Yogurt Salad (page 152)
Basmati Rice-Stuffed Cabbage (page 266)
Baked Potato and Apples "Anna" (page 192)
Poached Plums (page 410)

GREEK

Braised Artichokes and New Potatoes with Lemon-Dill
    Sauce (page 228)
Greek-Style Rice Pilaf (page 361)
Fresh fruit
Honey-Yogurt Cake with Syrup (page 399)

MIDDLE EASTERN

Babaghanza Fondue (page 284)
Herb-Stuffed Grape Leaves with Minty Yogurt Sauce
    (page 62)
Artichokes with Light Lemon Dipping Sauce (page 184)
Rice Pudding with Dates (page 407)

FRENCH

Provençal Soup with Pistou (page 307)
Barley Croquettes (page 197)

Low-Fat Cheese Sauce (page 174)
Mushroom-Chard Crêpes (page 354)
Orange-Scented Asparagus with Sweet Red Pepper and
    Kiwi (page 186)
Apricot Cream Tart (page 403)

DOWN HOME DIXIE

Memphis-Style Sweet Potato Pudding (page 194)
Grilled Tofu Kabobs Chipotle with Corn on the Cob and
    Asparagus (page 288)
Hoppin' John (page 437)
Feather-Bed Biscuits (page 131)
Five-Flavor Pound Cake (page 395)

BARBECUE

Tropical Fruit Salad (page 153)
Barbecued Tofu (page 287)
Grilled Portobello Mushrooms (page 179)
Peach Glow Smoothie (page 89)

Macaroni and Cheese (page 250)
Sautéed Peppers and Squash with Capers and Cayenne
    (page 187)
Grilled Vegetables with Greens and Croutons (page 160)
Brownies

Barbecued Tofu and Apples (page 281)
Hot Corn Sticks (page 129)
Pineapple-Mango Chutney (page 176)
Fresh Peach Tofu Ice Cream (page 387)

BREAKFAST

Good Grains Pancakes (page 92)
Berry Pancake Topping (page 93)
Sun Juice (page 85)

Overnight Whole-Grain Cereal (page 101)
Low-Fat Apricot-Pecan Muffins (page 125)
Coconut-Banana Smoothie (page 88)

Italian Omelet (page 106)
Cheese Muffins (page 127)
Spiced Tomato Sunset (page 83)

SUNDAY BRUNCH

Raisin-Cheese Blintzes (page 96)
Slow-Scrambled Eggs Over Asparagus (page 99)
Blueberry Buttermilk Coffeecake (page 130)
B-Vitamin Juice (page 87)
Exotic Ice Tea (page 79)

Apple-Chard Quiche (page 104)
Best Burritos (page 118)
Swedish Pancakes (page 91)
Pomegranate Spritzer (page 81)
Earl Grey Tea Punch (page 78)

LUNCH

Tofu Salad Sandwich (page 120)
Baked chips
Carrot sticks
Icy Sherried Lemonade (page 82)

Brain Power Pita Pockets (page 116)
Celery sticks
Cookies
Wild Orange Shake (page 89)

Vegan Summer Sub (page 370)
Lavender Lemonade (page 78)
Brownies

SPECIAL OCCASIONS

NEW YEAR'S DAY BRUNCH

Better than Champagne (page 82)
Spiced Tomato Sunset (page 83)
Black-Eyed Peas with Tomatoes and Herbs (page 199)
Toast
Spanish Tortilla (page 106)
"Chicken" and Creamy Grits (page 344)
Savory Eggplant-Dill Muffins (page 125)
Avacado Salad with Citrus Vinaigrette (page 142)

SUPER BOWL PARTY

Caribbean Spice Popcorn (page 67)
Four-Bean Bake (page 357)
Sloppy Falafel Sandwiches (page 113)

Veggies and dip
Apple-Cinnamon Strudel (page 403)

VALENTINE'S DAY

Artichokes with Quinoa Filling and Sweet Red Pepper
    Coulis (page 73)
Seashells with Butternut Squash (page 247)
Dandelion Greens with Spicy Vinaigrette (page 141)
Chocolate-Espresso Cake with Espresso Sauce (page 400)

ST. PATRICK'S DAY

St. Patrick's Day Stew (page 438)
Broiled Potato "Croquettes" with Orange and Nutmeg
    (page 192)
Colcannon (page 204)
Scones
Carob Cake with Kiwi Topping (page 396)

EASTER

Sweet Pea Soup with Quinoa (page 305)
Bean Couscous with Pomegranates (page 257)
Asparagus Risotto with Mushrooms and Sun-Dried
    Tomatoes (page 265)
Black-Eyed Peas with Tomatoes and Herbs (page 199)
Strawberry Cassis Tofu Ice Cream (page 387)

PASSOVER

Noodle Kugel (page 446)
Root Vegetable Soup (page 320)
Broccoli Rabe with White Beans and Potatoes (page 229)
Polenta Torta with Roasted Squash (page 221)
Fresh fruit

MOTHER'S DAY

Curried Mango Omelet (page 104)
Apple-Pecan Tea Loaf (page 129)
Angel Berry Parfait (page 415)
Peach Glow Smoothie (page 89)

PICNIC

Pita with Hummus, Tomato, Red Onion, Cucumber and
    Black Olives (page 114)
Falafel Updated (page 115)

Springtime Layered Egg and Asparagus Salad (page 158)
Cheese Muffins (page 127)
Chocolate Cupcakes (page 402)

FOURTH OF JULY

Baked Beans (page 355)
Bald Eagle Valley Tomato Salad (page 142)
Hot Potato Salad (page 148)
Mushroom "Burgers" (page 118)
Very Berry Good Treats (page 133)

ROSH HASHANAH

Noodle-Currant Latkes (page 446)
Tzimmes with Potato Dumplings (page 442)
Shredded Carrot Gratin (page 180)
Savory Eggplant-Dill Muffins (page 125)
Date and Pecan Bread Pudding (page 405)
Fresh fruit

THANKSGIVING

Veggies and dip
Walnut-Stuffed Baby Red Potatoes (page 58)
Mushroom Bourguignon in a Whole Pumpkin (page 208)
New Potatoes with Leeks and Fennel (page 148)
Sweet-Tart Cranberry Muffins (page 126)
Fudge-Glazed Pumpkin Cake (page 397)

CHRISTMAS BUFFET

Autumn Pear Salad (page 143)
Potato-Pumpkin Soup (page 318)
Pasta with Portobello Mushrooms in Mustard Sauce
    (page 250)
Gratin of Yams and Pineapple (page 194)
Vegetable Tagine (page 433)
Three Kings' Bread (page 437)
Winter Jewel Fruitcake with White Icing (page 448)
Mango-Citrus Cocktail (page 85)

KWANZAA FEAST

Grilled Plantains (page 185)
Grilled Vegetables with Greens and Croutons (page 160)
Butternut Squash-Peanut Soup (page 300)
Jambalaya (page 292)

Banana Condiment (page 177)
Sweet Potato Stir-Fry (page 196)
Braised Greens with Vinegar and Sesame Seeds (page 184)
Cornbread
Double Chocolate Bread Pudding (page 406)

HORS D'OEUVRES PARTY

Baked Stuffed Tomatoes (page 71)
Asian "Chicken" Rolls (page 69)
Spicy Potatoes (page 72)
Gougères (page 60)
Athenian Mushrooms (page 67)
Grilled Asparagus Bruschetta with Chèvre and Tapenade
    (page 58)
Walnut-Stuffed Baby Red Potatoes (page 58)

KID'S BIRTHDAY PARTY

Grilled Vegetable Pizza (page 235)
Fajitas (page 373)
Fresh fruit
Pasta and Veggie Salad (page 375)
Tropical Banana Cheesecakes (page 367)
Chocolate Cupcakes (page 402)
Fruity Spritzer (page 81)

WEDDING

Herb-Stuffed Grape Leaves with Minty Yogurt Sauce
    (page 62)
Focaccia with Coarse Salt and Fennel (page 139)
Wild Mushroom Ragu with Golden Polenta (page 218)
Artichokes with Green Herb Sauce (page 183)
Eggplant Steak with Chickpeas, Roasted Red Peppers, Feta
    Cheese and Black Olives (page 224)
Apricot Cream Tart (page 403)
Wedding cake

mail-order sources

The Bean Bag
VEGAN, ORGANIC
P.O. Box 567
Clarksburg, CA 95612
800.845.BEAN (2326)
Fax: 916.744.1870
www.beanbag.net
beans4you@beanbag.net

Bob's Red Mill
GLUTEN-FREE, ORGANIC
5209 S.E. International Way
Milwaukie, OR 97222
800.349.2173
Fax: 503.653.1339
www.bobsredmill.com

Enjoy Life Foods
GLUTEN-FREE
1601 N. Natchez
Chicago, IL 60707
888.50.ENJOY (36569)
Fax: 773.889.5090
www.enjoylifefoods.com
NOTE: Enjoy Life Foods also carries many vegan products.

Frontier Natural Products Co-Op
ORGANIC
P.O. Box 299
Norway, IA 52318
800.669.3275
Fax: 800.717.4372
www.frontiercoop.com
customercare@frontiercoop.com

Garden Spot Distributors
GLUTEN-FREE, ORGANIC
438 White Oak Road
New Holland, PA 17557
800.829.5100
Fax: 877.829.5100
www.gardenspotdist.com
info@gardenspotdist.com

The Gluten-Free Pantry
GLUTEN-FREE
P.O. Box 840
Glastonbury, CT 06033
860.633.3826 (Inquiries and Customer Service)
800.291.8386 (Orders only)
Fax: 860.633.6853
www.glutenfree.com
pantry@glutenfree.com

Gold Mine Natural Food Co.
ORGANIC, ETHNIC
7805 Arjons Drive
San Diego, CA 92126-4368
800.475.FOOD (3663)
Fax: 858.695.0811
www.goldminenaturalfood.com
sales@goldminenaturalfood.com
NOTE: Gold Mine Natural Food Co. also carries macrobiotic products.

Melissa's
ORGANIC
Melissa's/World Variety Produce, Inc.
P.O. Box 21127
Los Angeles, CA 90021
800.588.0151
www.melissas.com
hotline@melissas.com

The Oriental Pantry
ETHNIC
423 Great Road (Route 2A)
Acton, MA 01720
978.264.4576
Fax: 781.275.4506
www.orientalpantry.com

Pangea Vegan Products
VEGAN
2381 Lewis Avenue
Rockville, MD 20851
800.340.1200
Fax: 301.816.8955
www.veganstore.com
info@veganstore.com

Road's End Organics, Inc.
VEGAN, GLUTEN-FREE, ORGANIC
120 Pleasant Street, E-1
Morrisville, VT 05661
877.247.3373
Fax: 270.638.2265
www.chreese.com

SATAY
ETHNIC
Texas Food Research, Inc.
3202 W. Anderson Lane, Suite 203
Austin, TX 78757
512.467.9008
800.678.8374
Fax: 512.467.0347
www.satayusa.com
tfri@satayusa.com

Simply Natural Foods
ETHNIC, ORGANIC
Discount Natural Foods, Inc.
146 Londonderry Turnpike #10
Hooksett, NH 03106
888.392.9237
www.qualitynaturalfoods.com
sales@discountnaturalfoods.com
NOTE: Simply Natural Foods also
carries macrobiotic items.

Tamale Molly
ETHNIC, GLUTEN-FREE, VEGAN
901 West San Mateo, Suite N-1
Santa Fe, NM 87505
877.509.1800
www.tamalemolly.com
info@tamalemolly.com

glossary

NEW TO VEGETARIAN COOKING? OR NEED SOME refreshers about marketplace standbys? This glossary focuses on foods that are the cornerstones of vegetarian cooking, but it also defines a range of other ingredients that make up a well-stocked kitchen. For an ingredient that may be specific to certain recipes in this book, check the index for help finding the definition. Otherwise, use this glossary as a general learning tool to broaden your understanding of the vegetarian kitchen.

Acorn squash—This oval-shaped winter squash has ribbed dark-green skin. A common way to prepare this vegetable is to slice it in half crosswise and to remove the seeds before baking. Look for those with a yellowish orange tinge, an indication that they are ripe and sweet. A large acorn squash is better than a small one, and heavy is better than light. The lighter the squash, the more likely it is to be dehydrated and fibrous. You can eat the orange flesh of acorn squash right out of the shell.

Adzuki beans; azuki beans [ah-ZOO-kee; AH-zoo-kee]— These small, reddish Japanese treasures aren't well known, unless you are familiar with macrobiotic diets. They are believed to be the most easily digested bean and have a flavor similar to red beans. You may substitute adzuki beans for pinto or red beans in Hispanic dishes, or add them to soups. Look for them whole or powdered in Asian markets and some supermarkets.

Agar-agar [AH-gahr; AY-gahr]—This flavorless, freeze-dried sea vegetable works like gelatin, helping to set food. Agar-agar has stronger setting properties than gelatin, so you won't need as much of it. Also, unlike gelatin, agar-agar will set at room temperature. You can find it in natural food

stores and Asian markets. It is sold in blocks and in powdered, flake or stick form.

Amaranth [AM-ah-ranth]—High in protein and full of flavor, these greens are used in salads or in cooked foods. You may also be familiar with amaranth in seed form, which is often used in cereals, or in flour form (ground seeds). Look for amaranth in natural food stores.

Amaretto [am-ah-REHT-toh]—Known for its almond flavor, this liqueur is often made from the pits of apricots.

Anaheim chile [AN-uh-hime]—One of the most commonly available chiles, this mild pepper was named after the California city of Anaheim. The chiles have just a hint of spiciness and are known for their sweet taste. Anaheims are usually medium green in color, with a slender, elongated shape. A red variety is often called the *chile Colorado*. Purchase Anaheims fresh or canned. They are commonly used in salsas or are stuffed and eaten. Use the dried red variety to make a decorative string or wreath of chiles, known as a *ristra*.

Ancho chile [AHN-choh]—This dried chile has a deep reddish-brown color and a flavor that can be mild or strong—the ancho is sweet and tastes slightly fruity. It has a broad shape and is about 3 to 4 inches long. When it is fresh and green, the *ancho* is called a *poblano* chile.

Anise [AN-ihss]—Anise is a small annual plant that is a member of the parsley family. Both the leaves and seeds of this plant are edible and have a licorice flavor. Anise seeds are greenish-brown and oval-shaped, and they have been used throughout history as a digestive aid. Use them to add flavor to cakes, cookies and breads. Also try them toasted in tomato sauces and stews. Anise can be bought whole, ground or as dried seeds.

Aquavit [AHK-wuh-veet]—This clear liquor from Scandinavia is flavored with caraway seeds. Distilled from grain or potatoes, aquavit is served icy cold in a shot glass.

Arrowroot—Derived from the root of a tropical American plant, this thickener makes shiny, transparent sauces. Mix arrowroot with cold water before adding it to your recipe, then bring it to a boil. You can replace arrowroot with cornstarch measure for measure. Arrowroot is tasteless, so unlike cornstarch, it will not have a chalky aftertaste if undercooked. Use arrowroot in puddings, sauces and other cooked foods.

Arugula [ah-ROO-guh-lah]—This bitter, scented salad green has smooth, dark-green leaves and a strong peppery taste. Arugula is sold in small bunches with roots attached. Look for bright green, fresh leaves. Arugula is very perishable and should be refrigerated for no more than 2 days, wrapped in a plastic bag. It's an excellent source of iron as well as vitamins A and C. Arugula is a tasty addition to salads, soups and sautéed vegetable dishes. It mixes well with milder lettuces such as Bibb. Look for it in specialty produce markets and some supermarkets.

Bamboo shoots—These shoots come from a certain species of bamboo plant and are ivory in color. They are cut when the plant is still young, so they are tender, yet crisp. While fresh shoots are occasionally available at Asian markets, whole and sliced canned shoots are more common and readily available.

Barley—The seed of barley grass, barley has been used for centuries in various dishes and baked goods. Whole-grain barley is more nutritious than other varieties, as only the outer husk has been removed. Scotch barley has the husk removed and is then ground. More common is pearl barley, which has been husked, steamed and polished. Pearl barley lends itself to lighter dishes and is often used in soups. If you plan to use barley flour or barley meal in bread-baking, keep in mind that it must be mixed with a flour containing gluten. Quick-cooking barley makes this chewy grain even easier to use—it can be ready in 10 to 15 minutes.

Barley malt syrup—Sometimes called *malted barley syrup*, this dark, thick sweetener (maltose being its main sugar) is well tolerated by people with diabetes. It is prepared from sprouted, dried barley. It can replace honey or molasses in most baked goods.

Belgian endive—See **Endive**

Black beans—These small, oval-shaped beans have black skins and a cream-colored flesh. Black beans make a great addition to soups and chilis, and they are integral to the Cuban classic dish, black beans and rice. Also known as *black turtle beans*, they have a robust flavor that works well with strong herbs and spices.

Black-eyed peas—Popular in Southern and soul food cookery, these legumes are creamy white with a black spot or "eye." They have a fresh flavor that makes them great partners in salads made of strong-flavored greens. Also try Hoppin' John (page 437), a black-eyed pea favorite. Black-eyed peas can be bought fresh or dried.

Bok choy [bahk CHOY]—This leafy green Chinese vegetable is a member of the cabbage family. It has a mild cabbage taste, crisp white stalks and tender green leaves. Bok choy goes by many names: *pak choi, Chinese white cabbage, white-mustard cabbage, celery mustard,* etc. Although it is often mislabeled as such, don't confuse it with Chinese cabbage or napa cabbage. Use it raw in salads, cooked in a stir-fry or as a vegetable side dish. It will keep for about 4 days in a plastic bag in the refrigerator.

Bouquet garni [boo-KAY gahr-NEE]—This refers to a grouping of herbs (traditionally parsley, thyme and bay leaf) that are placed in a cheesecloth bag or tied tightly together. Use bouquet garni to flavor soups and broths. Remove the bag or tied bunch before serving.

Broccolini—Also called *baby broccoli*, Broccolini is the trademarked name for a hybrid of broccoli and kale. Broccolini has long, slender stalks topped with tiny florets, making it look like a little broccoli head. It has a crisp texture and a sweet flavor with a subtle, peppery touch.

Broccoli rabe (raab or rapini)—This vegetable is related to both the turnip and cabbage families and has 6- to 9-inch stalks and clusters of tiny florets. Its leafy greens have a strong, bitter flavor and can be cooked many ways including steaming and frying. Also try it in salads or soups. Look for broccoli rabe from fall to spring in specialty produce markets and in many well-stocked supermarkets.

Brown rice syrup—This natural sweetener is mild-tasting and expensive. It's made by adding sprouted, dried barley or barley enzymes to cooked rice and allowing the mixture to ferment until it breaks down into sugars.

Brown sugar—See **Sugar**

Buckwheat—Buckwheat groats (or *kasha*) is an Eastern European favorite. In Russia, the term kasha encompasses all cooked cereal grains. In America, kasha refers to buckwheat groats, which have a toasty, nutty flavor. Kasha's strong flavor can be cut with other grains, such as cooked brown rice. Kasha is great to have on hand because it cooks quickly—a pot of it is ready in 30 minutes. It makes a terrific pilaf and is especially good with onions and mushrooms. Kasha is gluten-free and high in calcium, vitamin E and the B complex vitamins.

Buckwheat flour—The seeds of the buckwheat plant are used to make this strongly-flavored flour. Even ¼ or ⅓ cup creates a strong loaf. It's a flavor you'll either love or detest. Buckwheat flour is also used for pancakes and as an addition to some baked goods.

Bulgur wheat [BUHL-guhr]—Bulgur wheat is composed of steamed and ground wheat kernels. Bulgur has a nutty flavor and tender, chewy texture, and comes in a variety of grinds. It works well in *tabbouleh* (a Middle Eastern salad with parsley and mint), pilafs and as a base for thick sauces and stews.

Burdock—This slender root vegetable has brown skin and grayish-white colored flesh. Burdock has an earthy-sweet flavor and a texture that is both tender and crisp. Choose firm, young burdock that are about 16 inches long and no more than 1 inch in diameter. Do not wash until you're ready to use it. Although you should scrub it before cooking, you don't need to peel burdock. It can be sliced or shredded and used in soups or with other vegetables.

Butterhead lettuce (Boston and Bibb lettuce)—These lettuces have small, round heads of light green leaves with a sweet flavor. The leaves are tender, so use care when washing them.

Butternut squash—This large squash is 8 to 12 inches long, 3 to 5 inches at its widest point and weighs from 2 to 3 pounds. The smooth shell is yellow to tan in color. Butternut squash has a lovely buttery, nutty taste and can be baked, steamed or simmered. It peels easily and has flesh tender enough to dice or slice.

Cacao nibs [kah-KAY-oh; kah-KAH-oh]—Roasted cocoa beans that have been separated from their husks, cacao nibs contain no sugar or vanilla. Use them wherever you would use chocolate chips or nuts. Ground into a paste with a little sugar added, nibs make lovely bittersweet chocolate.

Cajun seasoning—This spice blend usually includes a combination of chili powder, garlic, ginger, coriander, cumin, cardamom, fennel, thyme, allspice and oregano. Ready-made mixes make it easy to create tasty dishes. Try it with tofu and grilled or roasted vegetables, or add it to dips. It can be quite spicy, so adjust the amount used to your personal taste.

Cannellini beans [kan-eh-LEE-nee]—These white Italian beans are sometimes called *white kidney beans*. Sold either dried or cooked and canned, these beans have a very smooth texture and an elusive nutty flavor. Try them in stews, minestrone soups and salads.

Caraway seeds [KEHR-uh-way]—These aromatic seeds come from an herb in the parsley family and have a nutty, licorice flavor. Caraway seeds are commonly used in German, Austrian and Hungarian cooking. Use them to flavor breads, cakes, stews and vegetables.

Cardamom [KAR-duh-muhm]—This fragrant spice is a member of the ginger family native to India, and it grows in many tropical areas. Cardamom seeds are encased in small pods about the size of a small berry. Each pod holds 17 to 20 tiny seeds. Cardamom is commonly used in Scandinavian and East Indian cooking and has a warm, cinnamon-like flavor. It is a key ingredient in *garam masala,* and its sweet flavor enhances curries, stews and vegetables. Cardamom can be bought either in the pod or ground. Keep in mind that ground cardamom seeds begin to lose their essential oils as soon as they are ground, so ground cardamom is not as full-flavored as pods. If using pods, lightly crush the pod, and add both the pod and seeds to the mixture. The shell falls apart during cooking. Also, be careful when using cardamom—a little goes a long way.

Cardoon [kahr-DOON]—This vegetable is popular in Europe and tastes like a cross between celery, artichoke and salsify (a root vegetable with a taste resembling an oyster). The cardoon looks like a bunch of wide, flat celery and can be found from late winter through spring. Choose firm stalks with a silvery gray-green color. To prepare, first remove the tough outer parts. Cut the rest to the size you need, and soak them in water with a little vinegar or lemon juice to prevent browning. Try them boiled, baked or braised. With most recipes, you should precook cardoons for about 30 minutes in boiling water. Cardoons are a good source of potassium, calcium and iron, but they can be high in sodium.

Carob [KAHR-uhb]—An acceptable replacement for chocolate, carob comes from the dried, roasted and ground pods of a Mediterranean evergreen known as the locust tree. If combined with sugar and other refined ingredients, carob is no more healthful than chocolate, save for the fact that it's caffeine-free.

Chambord [sham-BORD]—This French liqueur has a deep red color and a strong black raspberry taste.

Chard—Also called *Swiss chard*, this member of the beet family has crisp green leaves and celery-like stalks. A variety sometimes called *rhubarb chard* has darker leaves and reddish stalks, along with a stronger flavor. *Ruby chard* is bright red and its leaves have a hint of green. You can find it fresh year-round, but it is tastiest during the summer months. Look for tender leaves and firm stalks. Prepare the greens like spinach and the stalks like asparagus. Chard is a good source of iron and vitamins A and C.

Chervil [CHER-vuhl]—This aromatic herb is a member of the parsley family and has feathery dark green leaves. The root of this plant is also edible. Chervil is available dried but tastes best when fresh. You can find it fresh or dried in most supermarkets. Popular in French cooking, chervil has a mild flavor with a hint of licorice. Its delicate leaves make a nice addition to salads, vegetable dishes and creamy sauces. Like dill, chervil grows well in cool places, so if you live somewhere that's not too warm, try growing your own.

Chickpeas—Also called *garbanzo beans*, these round, tan legumes are a little bigger than peas. They are firm and have a mild, nutty flavor. Chickpeas are used in many ethnic dishes such as couscous and hummus. They also work well in stews, minestrone soups and various Mexican dishes. Chickpeas are available canned, dry and sometimes fresh. Though they take some quite some time to cook anyway, if dry chickpeas are older than a year, they will practically never soften, no matter how long they are cooked. It is best to buy them from a Middle Eastern or Latin market or natural food stores.

Chili pastes and sauces, Asian—Chili pastes, which are sometimes labeled sauces, are made primarily from ground or crushed fresh chilies, salt, oil, garlic, and sometimes vinegar. Chili sauces are made from similar ingredients, plus other ingredients to achieve the desired end result.

Chiles—These immature pods of various peppers add heat and color to recipes. Of the most popular peppers in the United States, the Anaheim is the mildest and the habañero is the hottest. Well-known peppers like jalapeño and serrano are acceptably hot to a lot of people—just keep some milk, yogurt, rice or bread nearby in case your tongue feels like fire. Small, pointy chiles tend to be hottest, while larger, rounded ones are milder. The seeds are the hottest part and can be removed to reduce the heat of most chiles. When choosing chiles, look for a glossy, deep color. The peppers should be firm and have thick walls with no soft spots. It's wise to handle peppers with gloves because they can burn your skin.

Chipotles [chih-POHT-lays]—These hot chiles have a wrinkled, dark brown skin and are really dried, smoked jalapeños. They have a smoky flavor with a hint of a chocolate taste. Look for them dried, ground or packed in adobo sauce.

Chutney [CHUHT-nee]—This condiment is made from a mixture of fruit, spices, vinegar, lemon and sugar. It ranges in texture from chunky to smooth and can be tangy or sweet and hot. Try chutney with curried dishes or sweeter chutneys as a spread. It is available in jars or you can make your own.

Cilantro [sih-LAHN-troh]—Also known as *Chinese parsley*, the dark green, lacy leaves of the coriander plant have a pungent flavor and refreshing taste. Cilantro is great with rice and beans and is a popular addition to Mexican, South American and Asian dishes. Add fresh leaves at the last minute to salads, salsas and vegetables. To keep cilantro fresh, keep the leaves dry and sealed in their bags. To store loose leaves, shake off any moisture and wrap them in paper towels. Roll up the towels and seal them carefully in a plastic bag with as little air as possible. Cilantro should keep for several days.

Coriander [KOR-ee-an-der]—This relative of the parsley family is known for both its seeds (its dried fruit) and its leaves (cilantro) and is native to the Mediterranean and to

Asia. The seeds have a light fragrance and a flavor like a combination of lemon, caraway and sage. The whole seeds are tasty when lightly toasted and are often used in Indian and Asian dishes. Use them as a seasoning and garnish.

Corn—Many people believe corn is a vegetable, but it's a grain. Coarsely ground whole dry kernels produce corn grits, which can be turned into a tasty cereal.

Corn flour—Made from finely ground cornmeal, this flour can be yellow or white. Corn flour is milled from the whole kernel and is used for breading and in baked goods.

Cornmeal—Cornmeal is dried corn kernels that have been ground to be fine-, medium- or coarse-textured. Cornmeal is either yellow, white or blue, depending on the type of corn used. If the word *degerminated* is on the package, then the germ (which contains protein and minerals) has been removed. Manufacturers often enrich cornmeal, adding vitamins and minerals. Cornmeal is used to make cereal, polenta, bread, muffins and other baked goods. Look for cornmeal that has a soft texture.

Corn pasta—Are you allergic to wheat or simply looking for a flavor change? Pasta made from corn is a wise choice. Take care in cooking it—if cooked too long, corn pasta becomes pasty.

Couscous [KOOS-koos]—It's a pasta, technically speaking, but couscous is very much like a grain. The granular semolina is a staple of North African cuisine. It soaks up water like other grains and becomes light and fluffy when cooked. Both whole-grain and refined versions cook up quickly.

Cranberry beans—Also called *shell beans* or *shellouts* and known as *borlotti beans* in Italy, these beans have large, irregularly shaped tan pods spotted with red. The beans themselves have a tasty nutty flavor. Cranberry beans are available fresh in the summer and dried year-round.

Crème fraîche [krehm FRESH]—This aged, thickened cream has a smooth, rich texture and is generally as thick as sour cream. Crème fraîche has a nutlike flavor with a slight tang. Although crème fraîche is available in some US markets with a hefty price tag, it's easy to make your own version at home. Combine 1 cup heavy cream with 2 tablespoons of buttermilk in a nonreactive container, cover and let stand at room temperature overnight, or until it thickens. Stir well before covering, and refrigerate for up to 10 days.

Crookneck squash—This term refers to several varieties of summer squash that have long, curved necks that are slightly thinner than the base. Crooknecks have a light to dark yellow skin that can range in texture from almost smooth when young to bumpy as the squash grows. Their flesh is creamy and mild-flavored. They average from 8 to 10 inches long, but taste best when they're younger and slightly smaller.

Cumin [KYOO-mihn]—Similar in shape to a caraway seed, cumin is the dried fruit of a plant in the parsley family. It has aromatic, nutty-tasting seeds. Used whole or ground, cumin adds spark to salads, curries and rice dishes.

Curly endive—See **Endive**

Currant [KUR-uhnt]—The word currant refers either to a small, dried Zante grape or to the relative of the gooseberry. Currants can be black, red or white. The black ones are most commonly used in syrups, preserves and liqueurs. The red and white berries are good for eating plain. Also try them in jams, jellies and sauces. Look for fresh currants during their peak season of June through August.

Daikon radishes [DI-kuhn; DI-kon]—Meaning "large root" in Japanese, these Asian radishes have a crisp texture and sweet flavor. Look for firm, smooth daikon, ranging in length from 5 to 15 inches. Try them in salads or cooked in a variety of ways.

Dandelion greens [DAN-dl-i-uhn]—This weed has green jagged-edge leaves with a slightly bitter, tangy flavor. While some people call them weeds, the greens make a zesty addition to salads and are delicious cooked like spinach. Even the roots can be eaten as vegetables. Dandelion greens are a great source of vitamin A, iron and calcium. The best and the most tender greens are found in early spring. Choose those with bright green, crisp leaves; avoid those that are yellowing or limp.

Delicata squash [dehl-ih-KAH-tah]—Also called *sweet potato squash*, the delicata has an oblong shape and can range from 6 to 9 inches in length and 2 to 3 inches in diameter. Its skin is light yellow with green stripes. Pick squash that are firm and heavy for their size. Like other winter squash, the delicata is delicious baked or steamed.

Dill—This annual herb has been around for thousands of years and grows to be about 3 feet tall. Dill has delicate leaves (called *dillweed*) with a light tangy taste and small, pungent tan seeds. Use dillweed in salads, soups and sauces. Dill seed is used for the brine in which dill pickles are cured.

Dulse [duhlss]—Dulse is a coarse-textured purplish sea-weed that is most often used in soups and condiments, but the thin sheets make an unusual, salty snack food. When dried, dulse is rubbery and chewy.

Edamame [eh-dah-MAH-meh]—Also known as green soy-beans, edamame are fresh soybean pods. Although they can be found fresh seasonally in Japanese grocery stores and some supermarkets, they can also be bought frozen, in which case they have already been steamed. Put them in boiling water for a few minutes, then refresh them in ice water and serve lightly salted. You can also find shelled edamame that are ready to use in soups and salads, or in other dishes, as you wish.

Egg Replacer—This product is a combination of starches and leavening agents that bind and leaven cooked and baked foods. Egg Replacer is a boon for vegans or for people who want to reduce dietary cholesterol.

Egg substitute—Sold in cartons as a liquid, egg substi-tutes are usually a mixture of egg whites, tofu, corn oil, food starch, skim-milk powder, artificial color and additives. Egg substitutes are cholesterol-free but have a sodium content that is comparable to that of real eggs. Try them scrambled and also in most recipes calling for whole eggs.

Endive [EN-dyv; AHN-deev; ahn-DEEV]—Endive is avail-able in three main kinds: Belgian endive, curly endive and escarole. *Belgian endive* is a small, oblong-shaped head of whiteish, firmly-packed leaves. Serve cold as part of a salad or cook it by braising or baking. *Curly endive* grows in looser heads of delicate green leaves that have curly, somewhat prickly edges. The cream colored center leaves form a com-pact heart. *Escarole* has broad, crisp, light green leaves and a pale yellowish heart. It has the mildest flavor of the three. Escarole and curly endive can be found year-round. Try them in salads, as a vegetable or in soups.

Escarole—See **Endive**

Evaporated cane juice—Evaporated cane juice is an unbleached alternative sweetener that is light in color and finely granulated. It can be substituted on a one-for-one basis for refined white sugar. This type of natural cane sugar is available at natural food stores and some supermarkets.

Fava beans [FAH-vuh]—These beige, flat beans look like oversized lima beans. They come in large, inedible pods. Because of their texture and earthy flavor, fava beans are popular and used in countless way, including in soups and salads, and puréed for a yummy dip. They are sold dried, canned, and occasionally fresh. If using fresh favas, you will need to remove the tough outer skins by blanching them. *Habas* are dried favas that have had their skins removed.

Fennel [FEHN-uhl]—This fragrant plant has stems similar to celery with delicate green fronds. *Florence fennel*—also known as *finocchio*—has a rounded, broad base that can be used like a vegetable in salads, cooked, or in soups. Use the feathery leaves as a garnish or to add flavor to almost-cooked foods. *Common fennel* is the source of fennel seeds, a popular licorice-like seasoning in baked goods and savory foods.

Fines herbes [FEEN erb; FEENZ ehrb]—This French mix-ture of herbs includes parsley, chives, chervil and tarragon. A classic *fines herbes* mixture consists of 1 part tarragon, 2 parts chervil, 8 parts parsley and 1 part chives. Many recipes call for *fines herbes* to be chopped. In that case, chop the first three together, then snip the chives separately (to keep from mashing them) and combine all four.

Flageolet [fla-zhoh-LAY]—These small French kidney beans range in color from creamy to light green. They are rarely available fresh but can be purchased dried, canned and sometimes frozen. Because of their tasty tender flavor, they don't need any fancy preparation.

Fructose [FRUHK-tohs; FROOK-tohs]—This sweetener is a boon to diabetics because fructose does not produce the highs and lows in blood-sugar levels that table sugar (sucrose) does. However—and this may come as a surprise—commercial fruc-tose is more refined than table sugar. Though fructose is found naturally in fruit, commercial fructose is made from sucrose (which already has gone through a number of washings, filter-ing—sometimes with the use of animal bones—and bleach ings) by using enzymes to isolate the fructose. It also is very sweet, almost twice as sweet as table sugar, although it contains half the calories. Look for it in granulated and syrup forms. When fructose is heated, it loses some of its sweetening power.

Garam masala [gah-RAHM mah-SAH-lah]—This Indian blend of ground spices is sweet and pungent. Mixes are usu-ally a cook's secret, and some mixes may contain up to 12 spices and include black peppercorns, cardamom, cinnamon, cloves, coriander, cumin, fennel, mace, nutmeg and other spices. It's easy to make your own garam masala, but pre-pare it in small batches so it will stay fresh. You can find it in Indian markets and at most supermarkets. Be sure to store garam masala in a tightly covered jar.

Garbanzo beans—see **Chickpeas**

Ginger, fresh—With its knobby shape, fresh ginger has a thin, grayish skin and a vibrant and pungent aroma and taste. Readily available in the produce section of most supermarkets, fresh ginger should have a smooth, pale beige skin without blemishes. At home, store well-wrapped fresh ginger in your freezer for up to 6 months or in the refrigerator for up to 3 weeks. To use it, simply grate or slice it. Fresh ginger has nearly a dozen antiviral compounds and adds zip to recipes. Do not substitute dried ginger for fresh—the flavor is not the same.

Gluten flour [GLOO-tihn]—This refined wheat flour is treated to remove most of the starch (leaving a higher gluten content). The low starch content makes for better rising. It's used mainly in combination with low-gluten flour (such as rye flour) and to make low-calorie "gluten" breads. Gluten flour is high in protein.

Gnocchi [NYOH-kee; NOH-kee]—Made from potatoes or flour, gnocchi means "dumplings" in Italian. If you are making them at home, you can also add eggs, cheese and spinach to the dough, then shape it. Gnocchi, however, are readily available fresh or vacuum-packed at most markets.

Granulated sugarcane juice—This sugar is made from sugarcane juice that is dehydrated and then milled into a powder. Only the water is removed, leaving intact the sugarcane's natural vitamins and minerals. Its nutrients are minimal.

Grapeseed oil—The oil is extracted from grape seeds and has a very delicate grape flavor and aroma. Use it in salad dressings and for sautéing. Look for it in specialty food stores and well-stocked supermarkets.

Great Northern beans—These white beans look like lima beans and have a distinct flavor and firm texture. Available dried, they require soaking before cooking. Great Northern beans are delicious in stews, sandwich spreads and dips. They can be mashed and used to thicken soups. They are versatile and can be seasoned subtly or boldly.

Groats—Groats are defined as any hulled, crushed grains, such as barley or buckwheat. They are available in coarse, medium and fine grinds. Try them in cereals, as a side dish with vegetables and in soups.

Habañero chile—Although it is small, the tiny habañero packs a mighty punch, making it one of the hottest chiles around. As it ripens, it turns a bright orange. Try it fresh or dried in a spicy sauce.

Hearts of palm—This refers to the inner part of the stem of the cabbage palm tree, which grows in tropical climates. Hearts of palm are thin, cream-colored and pricey. They look similar to white asparagus and taste somewhat like artichokes. They are only available fresh in Florida. Look for canned hearts of palm at well-stocked supermarkets. Once opened, store them in an airtight, nonreactive container in their own liquid and refrigerate them for up to one week. Try them in salads or as a cooked vegetable.

Herbes de Provence [EHRB duh proh-VAWNS]—This mixture of dried herbs is similar to those most commonly used in the Provence region of southern France. *Herbes de Provence* commonly contains basil, rosemary, sage, fennel seed, thyme, marjoram, summer savory and lavender. Look for it in the spice section of large supermarkets.

Hijiki [hee-JEE-kee]—With its salty marine flavor and black color, this sea vegetable tastes and looks best cooked with sweet vegetables like carrots and squash. It can also be used in soups.

Hoisin [HOY-sihn; hoy-SIHN]—A thick Chinese seasoning sauce, hoisin is spicy yet sweet and is also used as a table condiment. Hoisin is a mixture of soybeans, chilies, garlic and a variety of other spices. Look for it in Asian markets and large supermarkets.

Hominy—Hominy is dried white or yellow kernels of corn with the hull and germ removed. Look for it canned, ready-to-eat or dried. Hominy makes a delicious addition to soups or stews, and is equally good as a side dish.

Honey—The oldest known sweetener, honey is a product of busy bees that have collected the nectar of flowers and turned it into a golden syrup. You can buy various flavors, depending on the source of the nectar. In baking, use a lightly flavored honey, such as clover, so the honey doesn't overwhelm the flavor of the recipe's other ingredients. Honey contains few nutrients. Store tightly sealed liquid honey in a cool, dry place for up to a year.

Jalapeño chile [hah-lah-PEH-nyoh]—These smooth, dark green peppers can be very hot, with a taste that is peppery. Jalapeños turn bright red when they are fully ripe. They are about 2 inches long and 1 inch in diameter and have rounded tips. Jalapeños are often quite hot, but they are easily seeded, making them less hot. Look for them fresh and canned and try them in a variety of sauces and dishes. Dried jalapeños are called *chipotles*.

Jícama [HEE-kah-mah]—This large root vegetable comes from Mexico and South America. It has brown skin and a crispy white flesh. It has a nutty, slightly sweet flavor and is tasty raw, steamed, baked or fried. Jícama ranges in size from about 5 ounces up to 6 pounds. The size has nothing to do with taste, so buy only the size you need. Look for jicama with smooth, thin skin. Thick skin usually indicates that the jicama is starchy, instead of sweet and juicy. Jícama contains a decent amount of vitamin C and potassium.

Kabocha squash [kah-BOH-chah]—These attractive winter squash offer a firm, dense and rich-tasting orange flesh that is slightly sweet. Kabocha squash are sold at Asian markets and many well-stocked supermarkets. Pick squash that weigh about 2 to 3 pounds, are heavy for their size and have no soft spots. If kabocha squash are unavailable, substitute another winter squash, but the flavor won't be the same.

Kalamata olives [kahl-uh-MAH-tuh]—These oblong Greek olives are dark purple and have a rich, almost fruity taste. They usually have small cuts so they will soak up more of the olive oil or vinegar that they are marinated in. Kalamatas are usually ½ to 1 inch long.

Kamut [kah-MOOT]—Kamut is a wheat that is very high in protein and has never been hybridized. One of the oldest grains, its kernels are larger than those of most wheat. Kamut has a tasty nutlike flavor and is one of the most nutritious grains. Look for it as a whole grain and as flour in natural food stores and some supermarkets. Commercially, it is used for cereal, pastas and crackers.

Kasha [KAH-shuh]—see **Buckwheat**

Kelp—Kelp is a generic name for edible seaweeds.

Kidney beans—These are related to red beans, which are smaller and rounder than kidney beans. Kidney beans are firm and medium in size with deep red skin and cream-colored flesh. They have a full-bodied flavor that lends itself well to a variety of dishes—salads, chilis and Mexican dishes such as red beans and rice. Unfortunately, kidney beans tend to be gas producing.

Kimbap [kihm-BAP]—Also called *seaweed rolls*, kimbap resembles Japanese sushi. This traditional Korean snack contains steamed rice and various vegetables rolled in seaweed sheets and is served in bite-size pieces.

Kimchi [KIHM-chee]—Also spelled *kimchee, kim chee* or *kimch'i*, this condiment contains spicy Korean pickled vegetables. Although there are hundreds of recipes for kimchi, the most typical one includes fermented cabbage. Kimchi keeps indefinitely when refrigerated.

Kirsch [KEERSH]—Meaning "cherry" in German, Kirsch is a clear brandy made from the juice and pits of cherries.

Knish [kuh-NISH]—This Jewish pastry is made with a piece of dough wrapped around a filling of cheese, mashed potatoes and buckwheat groats. Enjoy knishes as an appetizer or side dish.

Kombu [KOHM-boo]—A member of the kelp family, kombu can add rich flavor to soup stock and even be cooked with legumes to prevent flatulence. It has a white powder covering that delivers most of its flavor, so when preparing kombu, gently wipe the surface; do not wash it.

Kosher salt—This salt is coarser than table salt and has no additives. It is commonly used in Jewish cooking, and some people prefer its flavor and unique texture to that of table salt.

Latkes [LAHT-kuhz-]—Latkes are pancakes made from grated potatoes mixed with eggs, matzo meal, onions and seasonings. Latkes are traditionally served on Jewish holidays as a side dish.

Laver [LAY-vuhr]—This dried seaweed has a fresh, pungent taste. Deep purple in color, it comes in square, tissue-thin sheets. To prepare it, soak laver in cold water for about an hour before using; it will double in size. Serve it fried as an appetizer or cooked in soups.

Lecithin [LEHS-uh-thihn]—This oily matter is obtained from legumes and egg yolks and is used to preserve and add moisture to food. Use lecithin-based oil sprays instead of other fatty oils for greasing pans and sautéing vegetables. You can find these sprays at any supermarket.

Lemongrass—A crucial flavoring in Thai, Malaysian, Burmese and Vietnamese cooking, this herb looks like a long woody stalk and has thin leaves. Lemongrass has a pleasant citrus taste and aroma. The grass actually comes as clumps of tall stalks that look like leeks but are tough and need a sharp knife for cutting. Look for it fresh or dried in specialty markets and some supermarkets. Select healthy green stalks and white roots. To use it, pound the firm white bulb part, and slice it according to recipe directions. Use it in soups, stir-fries, Asian curries and Western salad dressings.

Lentils—These small, disc-shaped legumes have an earthy flavor and come in different varieties: brown, green, yellow and red. Brown lentils are the lentils most often consumed in the West. Green, yellow and red lentils, with the exception of the French lentils, can be classified as Indian lentils, since it is in India that they are eaten the most. Lentils are extremely high in protein, do not need to be presoaked and cook quickly. Perhaps that's why they make a popular soup. But you can also use lentils in pilafs or mash them into burgers, seasoned as you like. Regular brown lentils are commonly found in supermarkets, while green, yellow and red lentils often have to be purchased in Middle Eastern or East Indian markets.

Lima beans [LY-muh]—You can find these favorites of the American South fresh, frozen, canned and dried. There are two varieties of lima—the baby lima, which tastes somewhat sweet, and the Fordhook, which tastes more beany. Canned, dried and frozen lima beans are available year-round and are labeled according to variety.

Liquid aminos—Derived from soybeans, this liquid flavoring tastes like soy sauce. Look for bottles of it in natural food stores.

Mâche [MAHSH]—Also called *corn salad*, mâche actually has nothing to do with corn. Its small, deep-green leaves are delicate and have an almost fruity, nutty taste. Also try mâche steamed as a vegetable. Mâche is considered a gourmet green and can often be hard to find—and pricey. Check specialty produce markets.

Maple syrup—It is made by boiling the sap from maple trees to about one-fortieth of its original volume. It has only a tiny amount of nutrients, but it is pure, unlike pancake syrup, which is mostly colored corn syrup. Refrigerate maple syrup after opening.

Mascarpone [mahs-kahr-POH-nay]—Originally from Italy, mascarpone is a very rich double- or triple-cream cheese that may be eaten on its own with perhaps a sprinkling of sugar, used in baked goods such as the popular Italian dessert tiramisù, or used in place of cream cheese in cheesecakes.

Matzo; matzoh [MAHT-suh]—Traditionally eaten during the Jewish Passover holiday, this thin, unleavened bread is made with only flour and water. Some more modern versions may include other flavorings. Matzo can be found in Jewish markets and at most supermarkets.

Mesclun [MEHS-kluhn]—This mixture of small salad greens is readily available in the produce section of most supermarkets. Mesclun may include greens such as arugula, chervil, dandelion, frisée, mizuna, oak leaf, mâche, radicchio and sorrel. Look for mesclun with crisp, healthy leaves.

Millet [MIHL-leht]—Millet has a mild flavor that is delicious with a variety of seasonings. It cooks up quickly and makes for tasty pilafs and stuffings. Ground millet is used as a flour. Look for it in natural food stores.

Mirin [MIHR-ihn]—This sweet Japanese rice wine adds flavor to stir-fries and sauces. Look for it in Asian markets and the ethnic section of some supermarkets. Most commercial mirin contains corn syrup, which masks its true flavor, so check the label.

Miso [MEE-soh]—This salty paste is made from cooked, aged soybeans and sometimes from grains as well. It's thick yet spreadable, and is used for flavoring in much of Japanese cooking. It may be spread thinly on bread for a savory snack or used for flavoring in various dishes and as a soup base. Miso comes in many varieties, including low-salt. As a rule, the darker varieties are saltier and more strongly flavored than the lighter ones. Look for it in Asian markets, well-stocked supermarkets and natural food stores. Miso should be stored in an airtight container in the refrigerator.

Mizuna [mih-ZOO-nuh]—This fragile salad green is from Japan and can be found in produce markets and farmers' markets during warm months. Look for mizuna with crisp, feathery leaves.

Molasses [muh-LAS-sihz]—This dark, thick liquid remains after sucrose has been extracted from sugarcane or sugar beet juice. Unlike most other sugars, molasses can have a fair share of nutrients. Just three ounces of molasses sugar contains 90 percent of the recommended dietary allowance (RDA) of iron and 44 percent of the RDA for calcium. A rule of thumb: The darker the molasses, the greater the nutritional value.

Mung beans—These beans are usually found in their sprouted form, but small, dark green mung beans are tasty cooked up in a pot like any other bean. They are widely used in Asian cooking. They need no presoaking and when cooked have a tender-crisp texture and a flavor similar to that of green split peas. Flour made from dried mung beans can be used to make noodles. Mung beans combine well with garlic, tomatoes, ginger and chiles.

Muscovado [muhs-koh-VAH-doh]—This is an unrefined cane sugar available in both a light and a dark form, and it contains about 13 percent molasses. It has a soft, fine-grained texture and is available at supermarkets and many natural food stores.

Mushrooms:

Black trumpet—This mushroom ranges from 2 to 5 inches tall and, as the name suggests, resembles a trumpet in shape. Its flesh is delicate and can range in color from grayish-brown to nearly black. Black trumpets have an outstanding buttery flavor. Look for fresh mushrooms summer through fall in specialty produce markets. They can also be purchased dried, then reconstituted.

Button—These commercial mushrooms are available fresh all year. Some find their taste to be bland, but mixing them with other "wild" mushrooms produces a wonderful flavor.

Chanterelles [shan-tuh-REHLS]—These mushrooms resemble a trumpet or vase and have a color that ranges from orange to yellow. They are occasionally available fresh in markets during the summer and winter. Chanterelles can be eaten alone or as with other foods. Fresh chanterelles take longer to cook than most other mushrooms and tend to toughen if overcooked. They're relatively expensive, so save them for special dishes. Choose those that are plump and spongy. Also, they are very delicate, so clean them carefully with a damp paper towel.

Cremini [kray-MEE-nee]—Also called *common brown mushrooms*, these mushrooms are dark brown in color and firmer than regular white mushrooms. Cremini have an earthy taste and caps that range in size from ½ to 2 inches in diameter.

Enoki [en-oh-kee]—Also called *enokitake or enokidake*, these long-stemmed mushrooms have tiny white button tops. They have an almost crisp texture and mild taste. In some parts of the country, enoki are available fresh year-round in Asian markets and some supermarkets. Common to Japanese cuisine, these mushrooms appear as garnishes for soups or other dishes. If you are using them in a cooked dish, add them toward the end of the cooking time.

Morels [muh-REHLS]—These wild mushrooms are relatives of the truffle, and have a smoky, nutty taste. Usually, the darker the mushroom cap, the stronger the flavor. Morels grow wild and are available fresh in the early spring. Pick those that are spongy and heavy for their size. They require a thorough cleaning under running water, since they have many areas where dirt and insects can hide.

Oyster—These fan-shaped mushrooms grow both wild and cultivated in close clusters, often on rotting tree trunks. The flavor of raw oyster mushrooms is fairly strong and slightly peppery, but becomes mild and buttery when cooked. They also have a silky-smooth texture. Look for them at well-stocked supermarkets throughout much of the year.

Porcini [pohr-CHEE-nee]—An Italian favorite, porcini mushrooms are tan in color and vary widely in size. These mushrooms can weigh from 1 ounce up to 1 pound each and their caps can be 1 to 10 inches in diameter. Their meaty texture and strong flavor make them a gourmet treat. Choose fresh mushrooms that have firm, large caps and light-colored undersides. They can be found dried in most supermarkets but need to be reconstituted by soaking in hot water for about 20 minutes before use. They can be substituted for other mushrooms in most recipes.

Portobello [por-toh-BEHL-loh]—The mature form of the cremini mushrooms, portobellos are sometimes called "the steak of vegetarians." Portobellos have flat caps that can measure 7 inches round. Look for them in most supermarkets. Remove their thick stems; discard them or save them for soup stocks and sauces. Delicately scrape away the black gills from the underside, as these tend to darken whatever the mushrooms are cooked with. You can use portobellos chopped, but they're more impressive and interesting if cooked whole. Roast, broil or grill them whole or sliced for use in sandwiches, salads, and appetizers, or as part of an entrée.

Shiitake [shee-TAH-kay]—A regular in Japanese cuisine, shiitake mushrooms are dark brown and impart a complex and flavorful dimension to the dishes in which they appear. The caps have a delicious meaty flavor, but the stems are extremely tough and are usually removed for use in soups and sauces. Shiitakes are easiest to find in spring and fall. When purchasing fresh shiitakes, look for plump, whole mushrooms with edges that curl under. Also available are dried shiitakes that can be reconstituted by soaking in hot water for about 20 minutes before use.

Napa cabbage—The most common variety of asian cabbage, known also as *Chinese cabbage,* is football-shaped with a tightly packed head and crisp, veined leaves that are cream-colored with green tips. Use napa cabbage raw or steam, stir-fry or bake it. If wrapped in plastic, sturdy napa cabbage keeps in the refrigerator for as long as three weeks.

Navy beans—This white legume, also known as the *Yankee bean* and a staple of the US Navy for many years, looks like a miniature version of the Great Northern bean. An excellent addition to soups, pilafs and salads, it is widely available canned.

Noodles, Asian:

Bean thread—Known as *cellophane*, *glass*, or *transparent* (in Japanese, *harusame*) *noodles*, these thin, clear strands are made from mung bean flour and water. The noodles are brittle and tough. To soften them, soak them in hot water for 15 minutes. Softened noodles will be translucent and gelatinous. Unless they are going into a liquid dish, drain them briefly before use. Look for bean threads in Asian grocery stores and in the ethnic section of large supermarkets.

Ramen [RAH-mehn]—You may have tried ramen, those squiggly noodles that come in packages on supermarket shelves (usually in the soup aisle). Some brands that come with a flavor packet, such as mushroom or chicken, are fried before packaging and are high in fat. Other brands have been baked, not fried, so their fat content is significantly lower. Check out natural food stores for the widest selections.

Rice noodles—The term *rice sticks* refers to rice-flour noodles that are about 1/4-inch wide. You have probably noticed these noodles in the supermarket—they are the nearly transparent white noodles packaged in cellophane. Also look for them at Asian markets.

Rice vermicelli—Made from rice paste and water, these dried white noodles, also known as *meehoon* and *beehoon* (or *bihon*) noodles, are extremely popular in many Asian countries. They can easily be softened by soaking in hot water for about 5 minutes before cooking. Rice vermicelli are sold dried in bundles and packages and are available at most Asian markets.

Soba [SOH-buh]—Most soba are a combination of buckwheat and wheat flours, though these long, thin, flat noodles are sometimes called *buckwheat noodles*. These Japanese noodles have a dark brownish-gray color, are virtually fat-free and are relatively high in protein and other nutrients. *Chasoba* is a variation of the noodle that is made with green tea.

Somen [SOH-mehn]—Somen is a thin, almost angel-hair Japanese pasta made from whole-wheat flour or a mixture of whole wheat and unbleached white flours (or sometimes refined white flour). A yellow version made with egg yolks is called *tamago somen*. Try somen in soups or even served cold as a warm-weather dish.

Udon [oo-DOHN]—Here's another Asian noodle, the sister of *somen*. Both are made from whole wheat flour or a mixture of whole wheat and unbleached white flours (or sometimes refined white flour), but udon is thick and tubular. It can be round or square and can also be made from corn flour. Fresh and dried udon are available in Asian markets and some supermarkets.

Nori [NOH-ree]—A dark green seaweed available in very thin sheets, nori is popular in Asian cooking and is commonly used to wrap sushi and rice balls. It is also useful for adding a hint of seafood flavoring to vegetarian dishes. You can eat it as is, but many people prefer to toast it before adding it to recipes, especially soups; a light toasting intensifies its flavor. Look for nori at Asian markets and many supermarkets.

Nutritional yeast—Unlike baker's yeast, which is fairly tasteless and used in baking, nutritional yeast is a good source of protein, iron and several B vitamins. It has an unusual flavor—a cross between meaty, cheesy and nutty—though it's made of yeast only. Some people like to sprinkle it on casseroles, soups, dips and even popcorn. It has been known to cause flatulence, so start out easy, just ¼ teaspoon or so a day. It is also sometimes called brewer's yeast.

Okra [OH-kruh]—Brought to America by African slaves, the okra plant is still a favorite food in the South. Its pods are green and have uneven skin and an oblong shape. When cooked, okra thickens the liquid in which it is cooked. Add okra to soups, stews and sauces to thicken and add flavor. Okra can be found fresh year-round in the South and from spring through fall in the rest of the country. Choose firm, brightly colored pods with a velvety feel and no blemishes. Okra is also available canned and frozen.

Olive oil, extra virgin—Extra-virgin olive oil is cold pressed, a process that uses no chemicals and leaves the olive oil very low in acid. This type of olive oil is a bit more expensive than more acidic types, but the result is worth it. Extra-virgin olive oil ranges in color from very pale yellow to deep green. The darker the color of the olive oil, the stronger the flavor will be. Extra-virgin olive oil is an excellent choice for sautéing, but not for frying, as the oil won't hold up under high heat.

Orange blossom water—Also know as *orange-flower water*, this liquid is a popular flavor booster in many Mediterranean dishes as well as Western baked goods, sweets and various drinks.

Orzo [OHR-zoh]—This very small, rice-shaped pasta is often used in soups and salads.

Panko [PAHN-koh]—Popular in Japanese cooking, these coarse breadcrumbs give a crisp, crunchy coating when used to crust fried foods. Look for panko in Asian markets and most supermarkets.

Pearl tapioca [tap-ee-OH-kuh]—Made from a starchy substance from the root of the cassava plant, pearl tapioca is available in regular or quick-cooking varieties. Some brands need soaking or lengthy cooking to soften the pearls before further use. Look for pearl tapioca in most supermarkets or Asian markets.

Pepitas [puh-PEE-tahs]—Pepitas are edible pumpkin seeds that are dark green when their white shell is taken away. Popular in Mexican cooking, pepitas have a pleasantly light flavor that becomes stronger when the seeds are roasted and salted. You can buy pepitas salted, roasted and raw, whole or shelled.

Pepper sauce, hot—This spicy condiment comes in several varieties, most of which include chiles, spices, vinegar and vegetables such as tomatoes, onions and green peppers. You can make your own hot pepper sauce or try one of the many varieties available at supermarkets and specialty stores.

Peppercorns—One of the most popular spices, freshly ground pepper has much more flavor than preground pepper. Peppercorn berries come as green, black and white. Green peppercorns are unripened and taste milder than black or white peppercorns. Black peppercorns have the strongest flavor with a taste that is sweet, fruity and warm. White peppercorns are fully ripened and milder tasting, and have had their skins removed.

Pesto [PEH-stoh]—Originating in Genoa, Italy, this classic is an uncooked sauce made with fresh basil, pine nuts, garlic, Parmesan or pecorino cheese and olive oil. You can make your own by finely chopping the ingredients in a food processor or crushing them with a mortar and pestle. Premade pestos are widely available, as are varieties of pestos made with other herbs.

Phyllo [FEE-loh]—Phyllo are paper-thin sheets of pastry dough used in Greek and Middle Eastern food preparation, as in spanakopita or baklava. Look for fresh phyllo dough in Greek markets and frozen phyllo dough in supermarkets. If unopened, phyllo can be refrigerated for up to 1 month. Follow package directions for use and storage.

Pimentos; pimientos [pih-MEN-tohs; pih-MYEHN-tohs]—These large, red peppers are sweeter and more fragrant than red bell peppers. Canned and bottled pimentos are available year-round, and fresh pimentos may be found from late summer to early fall in produce markets and some supermarkets. You may have eaten them as the stuffing in green olives, but the majority of the crop is used to make paprika.

Piñon [PIHN-yuhn]—The Spanish word for pine nut, or the Italian for *pignolia*, piñon grow inside pine cones, and come as either the Chinese pine nut or the milder-tasting Italian pine nut. The more readily available, the Italian pine nut is oblong in shape and sold in most supermarkets. Store in an airtight container in the refrigerator for up to 3 months, or freeze it for up to 9 months.

Pinto beans—These are small, tasty pale pink beans with reddish streaks. They are popular throughout the United States and in Spanish and Mexican cooking, turning up in refried beans and chili. They cook to a creamy texture, making them a perfect base for strong spices like chiles, garlic and other seasonings. Pinto beans are available canned and dried.

Plantains [PLAN-tayns]—Plantains, also called *cooking bananas*, look like larger, greener bananas. Unlike their sweeter relatives, plantains may be cooked and eaten as a vegetable. Fully ripe, black-skinned plantains are best for mashing. Refrigeration will stop plantains from ripening, and they will keep for about 1 week.

Poblano chile [poh-BLAH-noh] This very dark green, tapered chile has a deep flavor that ranges from mild to strong. The darker the chile, the stronger the flavor. Look for them fresh during their peak season, summer and early fall, or purchase them canned. Poblanos are a key ingredient for *chiles rellenos*.

Polenta [poh-LEHN-tah]—A rustic dish served daily in Northern Italy, polenta is both the term for the grain and for the cooked cornmeal. When prepared, it looks like cooked grits. The texture of polenta varies, depending on how and where the corn has been milled; some varieties will absorb more liquid than others. Medium-coarse polenta retains a nice texture when cooked. The finer the polenta, the smoother texture it has. Although it takes 25 minutes to cook regular polenta, quick-cooking versions are now available. They're simple and can be ready in as little as 10 minutes. Because of its mild taste, it serves as a perfect backdrop for ingredients with more stronger flavors. When cool, polenta becomes firm and is easily sliced.

Posole [poh-SOH-leh]—This thick Mexican or Native American soup or stew is traditionally served in winter, especially on New Year's Eve or New Year's Day for good luck. Posole is often accompanied by lettuce, radishes, onions, cheese and cilantro, which can be added to the soup according to personal taste.

Potato starch—Also called *potato flour*, this flour is made from potatoes that have been cooked, dried and ground. It is often used as a thickener and in some baked goods because it produces a moist crumb.

Prune purée—This sweetener, substituted for butter or other fats in baked goods, can trim away calories and cholesterol. Prune purée adds moisture and a flavor that may be mild or strong, depending on other ingredients used.

Quinoa [KEEN-wah]—Containing more protein than any other grain, this ancient grain hailing from the Andes has been called the "supergrain of the future." Because it contains all eight essential amino acids, it is considered a complete protein. Quinoa is also higher in unsaturated fats and lower in carbohydrates than most grains, and provides a balanced source of vital nutrients. Bead-shaped and about the size of mustard seeds, the white quinoa cooks like rice (taking about half the cooking time of regular rice) and expands to four times its original volume. Its flavor is delicate and has been compared to that of couscous. It's available packaged as a grain, ground into flour and in several forms of pasta. Quinoa can be found in natural food stores and many supermarkets. Some brands require rinsing before use to rid the grain of any bitterness; check package directions.

Red beans—See **Kidney beans**

Rice:

Arborio [ar-BOH-ree-oh]—This Italian-bred grain has starchy kernels that are short and fat. Arborio is used to make risottos because it is slightly chewy and extra flavorful when paired with the various additions to the basic risotto recipe.

Basmati brown—This rice is similar to regular basmati rice, only with a fuller flavor. Some people say that once you have basmati brown rice, you won't want "that white stuff" again! Look for quick-cooking varieties that can be ready in 20 minutes.

Basmati white [bahs-MAH-tee]—This fragrant rice has a nutty flavor and aroma due to the fact that the grain has been aged to lower its moisture content. This long-grained rice is delicious as a side dish, especially with Indian and Middle Eastern meals. Basmati can be found in Indian and Middle Eastern markets as well as many supermarkets.

Black—A grain with a delicate, nutty taste and soft texture, this rice is popular in Southeast Asia for use in desserts. Elsewhere it is popular with or in savory dishes. The rice gets dark purple when cooked.

Brown—This is the whole, unpolished grain with the outer husk intact, making it much chewier than white rice. Brown rice also takes twice as long to cook, because each kernel is enclosed in a thin layer of high-fiber bran. However, there is a *quick brown rice* (which has been partially cooked, then dehydrated) that only takes about 15 minutes to cook, and an *instant brown rice* that takes only 10 minutes. The bran adds a nutty flavor to brown rice, is high in fiber and contains many vitamins and minerals. Brown rice is delicious with curried vegetables and makes an excellent pilaf, side dish, soup or salad. Because of the bran, brown rice can become rancid, so it will stay good for only about 6 months.

Jasmine—The taste and aroma of this long-grain rice from Thailand is similar to that of basmati rice, but it is less expensive.

Long-grain—There are both white and brown varieties of this rice. This rice is four to five times longer than it is wide. When cooked, long-grain rice produces easily separated, light and fluffy grains.

Short-grain—This rice has nearly round grains with a high starch content. This variety is also called *pearl rice*. When it is cooked, short-grain rice tends to become moist, causing the grains to stick together. For this reason it is preferred in Asian cuisine, because it is easy to eat with chopsticks.

Rice paper—Made from ground rice and water, this "paper" is used to wrap up ingredients and may be eaten as is or fried. Look for rice paper wrappers in Asian markets and some supermarkets.

Romesco [roh-MEHS-koh]—This finely ground mixture of tomatoes, red bell peppers, garlic, onion, almonds and olive oil is a classic Spanish sauce. This sauce is gaining in popularity; try it on grilled or roasted vegetables, such as onions, eggplant, asparagus, zucchini, artichokes or potatoes.

Rutabaga [ROO-tuh-bay-guh]—Round like a turnip, this root vegetable is a member of the cabbage family and has a creamy colored skin and mild flavor. Select those that are heavy for their size and have smooth, firm skin. They will keep in a cool dry place for about 1 month. Rutabagas may be mashed and served alone or added to mashed potatoes for a rich, turniplike flavor. They make a great side dish for holiday meals.

Rye flour—Rye flour contains less gluten than whole wheat or all-purpose flour. Therefore, without being combined with a higher gluten flour, rye flour will not produce an evenly-risen loaf of bread. Also, rye flour is heavier than most flours. Replace about ½ cup of whole wheat flour with rye flour, and follow the bread recipe as usual. If desired, add some caraway seeds for an authentic taste and appearance.

Saffron [SAF-ruhn]—This very expensive spice used to flavor and tint food comes from the dried stigmas of a small crocus. It can be found in both threads or powdered form. Threads have a more pronounced flavor, so these are preferable in cooking. Select those with a deep orange color, and crush them just before using. Saffron adds rich flavor to risotto and paella dishes and is a French and Spanish favorite. Luckily, a little saffron goes a long way.

Salsa [SAHL-sah]—Thanks to today's inventive cooks, salsa ranges in spiciness from mild to intensely spicy and often contain fruits or loads of chiles for added zest. The word refers to both cooked or fresh sauces. Look for fresh salsas in a market's refrigerated section or experiment with making your own. Unopened cooked salsas can be stored at room temperature for 6 months; once opened, they will keep in a refrigerator for up to 1 month.

Savory [SAY-vuh-ree]—This herb is a relative of the mint family and comes in two varieties, summer and winter. Savory has a fragrance and taste similar to a cross between thyme and mint. Summer savory is milder than the winter variety, but both have a fairly robust flavor and should be used sparingly. Look for fresh savory in specialty produce markets; dried savory is available year-round.

Savoy cabbage—Unlike regular cabbage, savoy cabbage does not have a compact head, but rather loose, veined leaves that range in color from pale to dark green. It has a mild flavor and is excellent for cooking. Pick a head that is heavy for its size, with crisp leaves.

Scallions [SKAL-yuhns]—Scallions have a white stem end and long, tapered green leaves, all of which are edible. Scallions are best used raw for flavoring and garnishes and can be cooked whole as a vegetable. Scallions are available year-round but are at their best during spring and summer.

Sea salt—Sea salt is the mineral extracted by evaporating seawater. Use granular sea salt in a salt mill.

Seitan [SAY-tan]—Derived from wheat, this versatile food is popular for its healthfulness and its versatility, and it is a good backdrop for a variety of spices and herbs with which it's cooked. Seitan is high in protein and has a firm texture that is chewy and meatlike. For the best texture and flavor, add seitan to dishes toward the end of cooking. Look for it in the refrigerator section of natural food stores, Asian markets and some supermarkets.

Semolina [seh-muh-LEE-nuh]—This flour is made from durum wheat that is coarsely ground and is used in many gourmet pastas. It is also used to make gnocchi, puddings and soups. Cream of Wheat is a good substitute if semolina is not available.

Serrano chile [seh-RRAH-noh]—This small, slightly pointed chile is even hotter than the jalapeño, and more flavorful. You can buy fresh serranos in Mexican markets and some supermarkets. Also look for them canned, pickled or packed in oil. Use them fresh or cooked in various dishes.

Sesame oil—Sesame oil comes in two main varieties. The lighter-colored sesame oil has a mild nutlike flavor and is easy to cook with or use in dressings. Dark, or toasted sesame oil, like other dark oils, has a deeper flavor and aroma and adds great flavor to Asian dishes, but is generally not used alone for stir-frying.

Shallots [SHAL-uhts; shuh-LOTS]—Although shallots are members of the onion family, they look like garlic and have a thin, papery skin. Their skin color can vary from beige to pink, and their flesh is ivory colored. Their mild taste is something like a mix of onion, garlic and leeks, and they can be used in the same way as onions.

Shichimi togarashi [shee-CHEE-mee toh-gah-RAH-shee]—This peppery Japanese condiment is a mix of seasoning including red chili flakes (*togarashi*), white sesame seeds, white poppy seeds, nori flakes and black hemp seeds. Look for shichimi togarashi in different degrees of spiciness at Asian markets.

Sofrito [soh-FREE-toh]—This richly flavored sauce is a mix of sautéed onions, garlic, oregano, cumin, bell peppers and tomatoes. The ingredients in sofrito vary between Latin regions such as Mexico and Cuba. Try it in soups, stews, tamales and paella, and as a marinade.

Sorrel [SOR-uhl]—This perennial herb has several varieties, all with some degree of sourness because it contains oxalic acid. Similar in appearance to spinach, sorrel leaves come in many shades of green. Choose fresh sorrel for its brightly colored, crisp leaves. Younger sorrel is milder and works well in salads or cooked as a vegetable. The more acidic sorrels are used to flavor more savory foods.

Soybeans—These medium-sized yellowish beans taste bland, but soybeans are champs in nutrition. They are a rich source of protein, iron and vitamin E and are low in carbohydrates. Combine them with other beans and spice them as you like, and soybeans can taste as delicious as any other bean. You can buy them in bulk from natural food stores or through mail order (page 454). Or try one of the soybean spin-off products, such as tofu or soymilk (see pages 473 and 471). These are easier to digest than the whole bean.

Soybean oil—Soybean oil is the natural oil extracted from whole soybeans. It is the most widely used oil in the United States, accounting for more than 75 percent of our total vegetable fats and oils intake. Oil sold under the generic name "vegetable oil" is usually 100 percent soybean oil or a blend of soybean oil and other oils. Check the label to be certain. Soybean oil is cholesterol free and high in polyunsaturated fat. It is also used to make margarine and shortening.

Soy cheese—For people who pass up dairy foods, soy cheese is a big plus with a similar but not identical flavor to cows' milk cheese. Made from tofu or soymilk and a number of other ingredients, soy cheese is cholesterol free but high in fat. Fortunately, it comes in full-, low- and nonfat versions and in a variety of types including cheddar, mozzarella and Parmesan. (A word to the wise: Some soy cheese makers add casein to their products to make them melt when heated. Casein is a milk protein, and milk is the only place you'll find it naturally. There is no plant source for casein.) Some dairy-free soy cheeses are very soft, however, and are a fair imitation of dairy cheese. Soy cheeses can be found in natural food stores and most supermarkets.

Soy cream cheese—Soy cream cheese has a significantly lower fat content than its dairy counterpart and is sold in plain and seasoned versions. (Again, some soy cream cheeses contain casein, so read labels carefully.) Soy cream cheese is best enjoyed chilled or at room temperature (many separate when heated) and can be found in natural food stores and most supermarkets.

Soy flour—This finely ground flour is made from roasted soybeans and has twice the protein of wheat flour. It is also low in carbohydrates. Because it is gluten free, it is often mixed with other flours rather than used alone. It is also useful to thicken sauces. There are three types of soy flour available: natural or full fat, which contains the natural oils found in soybeans; defatted, which has had the oils removed; and lecithinated, which has had lecithin added. Soy flour is sold in natural food stores and in some supermarkets.

Soy mayonnaise—This eggless version of mayonnaise also has no saturated fat. Look for it in natural food stores and some supermarkets.

Soymilk—Made primarily from soybeans and water, soymilk is a delicious and healthy alternative to cows' milk. Some brands taste more beany than others, so check out a few of them and select your favorite. And now with "lite" versions available, you may drink soymilk with little concern about fat. The original version of soymilk has 4 to 6 grams of fat per cup. It gives a protein boost, with 10 grams of this macronutrient per cup, and is a good source of B vitamins. Soymilk is also cholesterol free and low in sodium and calcium, although it is usually fortified with calcium. Soymilk can be substituted for regular milk in most recipes; because soymilk has a slightly different taste from dairy milk, you may need to experiment. Pasteurized soymilk should last up to 10 days, but check the labeling on the package. Soymilk is also sold in aseptic packages and can last unopened up to 6 months. Once it is opened, refrigerate the product and use it within 7 to 10 days.

Soynut butter—This spread made from roasted soybeans is similar in texture to peanut butter. Soynut butter generally is lower in fat than peanut butter.

Soy sauce—Used widely in Chinese and Japanese cooking, this sauce is made from water, soybeans, wheat and salt. It provides great flavoring for soups, sauces and marinades. Look for it in lite and low-sodium versions.

Soy sour cream—This lactose-free product is made from soymilk treated with a souring agent. Soy sour cream is very similar to dairy sour cream and can be substituted in equal amounts for it. It can be found in natural food stores as well as some supermarkets.

Soy yogurt—Cultured from soymilk and available in many flavors, soy yogurt is lactose- and cholesterol-free. It's available plain or fruit flavored and can be found in natural food stores and some supermarkets. Use it in any way that you would use dairy yogurt.

Spaghetti squash—This cylinder-shaped winter squash is pale yellow with flesh that, when cooked, can be scraped out by the tines of a fork into spaghetti-like strands. Weighing from 4 to 8 pounds, spaghetti squash are usually available year-round and are best from early fall through winter. Look for squash that are evenly colored, with hard, smooth skins. Avoid unripe squash, which have a green color. Try spaghetti squash as a side dish or in a casserole.

Spelt—This ancient cereal grain has a mild nutlike flavor and is easy to digest. It has slightly more protein than wheat and can be acceptable to those with wheat allergies. Spelt flour is available in natural food stores and is a good alternative for wheat flour in baked goods.

Split peas—A smart introduction for people new to legumes, split peas make a tasty soup. (Feel free to make additions such as barley or rice.) They can also be added to stews, but because they become mushy, they don't work as well in dishes such as chilis as do other legumes. Split peas are available in supermarkets and in bulk at natural food stores. They do not require presoaking before cooking.

Star anise—Native to China, star anise is a star-shaped brown pod that contains a small seed in each of its eight sec-

tions. It comes from an evergreen tree and has a more bitter flavor than that of anise seed. Star anise is a commonly used spice in Asian cooking and is also used in baked goods. Look for it whole in Asian markets and some supermarkets.

Sugar; brown sugar—Table sugar (*sucrose*) has been blamed for a host of diseases, but the only proven ailment it causes is tooth decay. However, there have been questions regarding sugar's role in suppressing the immune system, which works to keep the body healthy. Brown sugar is simply white sugar that has a small amount of molasses added to it. In either case, sugar amounts to empty calories. It's smarter to skip the sugar—at least as much as possible and reasonable—and fill up on whole foods.

Sumac [SOO-mak]—Don't worry, this spice is not related to the poisonous sumac found in the United States. This dark red, slightly acidic seasoning is made from berries that grow on wild sumac bushes throughout the Middle East and parts of Asia and Italy. Sumac has a light fruity taste that goes well with vegetables. Look for it in Middle Eastern markets.

Summer squash—This type of squash has an edible skin and tender seeds. The flesh of summer squash is juicer than winter squash and has a milder flavor. As the name suggests, it is best from early through late summer, although some types of summer squash are available year-round in certain areas. Choose smaller squash with bright-colored skin that is blemish free. They do not take long to cook, and are high in vitamins A and C as well as niacin.

Tahini [tah-HEE-nee]—Popular in Middle Eastern cooking, tahini is a paste made from ground raw or toasted sesame seeds. It's used to flavor various dishes such as hummus and baba ghanoush. Try it as a sandwich spread too.

Tamari; shoyu [tuh-MAH-ree, SHOH-yoo]—Tamari is similar to a naturally brewed soy sauce. It has a mellow flavor and is used as a table condiment, as a dipping sauce or for basting. By definition, it ought to be wheat-free, but some brands contain wheat. Shoyu is made of soybeans and wheat that go through an age-old Japanese fermentation process resulting in a rich soy sauce. Regular soy sauce may replace tamari or shoyu in recipes.

Tapenade [TA-puh-nahd; ta-pen-AHD]—This thick paste hails from the Provence region of France and is made from capers, olives, olive oil, lemon juice and seasonings. Use it as a condiment or sandwich spread. Read labels before buying it, as some brands are made with anchovies.

Tapioca starch [tap-ee-OH-kuh]   This flour is made from the starchy substance extracted from the root of the cassava plant. It is used much like cornstarch as a thickening agent.

Tarragon [TEHR-uh-gon]—This perennial aromatic herb has long, thin, dark green leaves and a licorice flavor. Used widely in French cooking, tarragon works well in many dishes and sauces and is also an important ingredient in herbal mixtures such as *fines herbes*. Look for it fresh in the summer and early fall or in dried and powdered forms. Because of its assertive flavor, use it sparingly.

Tempeh [TEHM-pay]—Tempeh is a cultured food made from soybeans and sometimes grains. The grayish blocks are held together by a mold, but don't be shy to try this soy-food. Tempeh has a yeasty, nutty flavor and tastes similar to fresh mushrooms. It readily absorbs flavors and holds its shape when cooked. It can be served many ways—on skewers, as burgers with all the trimmings, over grains, even crumbled and added to sauces and casseroles. Tempeh is sold fresh and frozen; store it in your refrigerator for up to two weeks or in your freezer for up to 3 months. There should be no sign of tempeh's culture at the time of purchase. As tempeh ages, it will get white spots, which will turn black. It's okay to eat tempeh that has a few black spots. The older tempeh gets, the stronger its flavor. So, for starters, eat fresh tempeh, which tastes mild. Then try experimenting with older, more pungent tempeh. Find tempeh cakes fresh and frozen in natural food stores and some supermarkets.

Textured Vegetable Protein (TVP)—The name of this meat substitute is quite a mouthful, which is why almost everyone refers to it as "TVP," a registered trademark of the American soy king, Archer Daniels Midland Company. It is also called *Textured Soy Protein*, or "TSP." It is basically a dehydrated soy product made from the flakes that remain after oil is extracted from soybeans. TVP is sold plain and flavored, and in mince, flakes and chunks. Reconstituted with water and added to casseroles, soups or stews, it lends a meaty texture. Meat replacers, many of which are fashioned from TVP, can taste so meatlike that some vegetarians won't touch them. Others—and especially new vegetarians who might have a craving for meaty chili or sloppy joes—welcome meat replacers onto their dinner plates.

Meat replacers (or analogs, as they are known among manufacturers) contain soy protein or tofu and other ingredients, and come in many forms: burgers, sausages, hot dogs, chicken nuggets and fish fillets, to name a few. Although they are excellent sources of protein, iron and B vitamins, they can be rather high in fat and sodium, so be sure to read labels carefully. Generally, many meat taste-alikes are lower in fat than their meat counterparts. But when you (or your children) crave the taste of meat (or want to be one of the gang), meat replacers may do the trick. Consider the following soy-based products: **Ground "meat":** Plain and taco seasoned; works well in sauces, chilis and as a filling for tacos, burritos or crêpes. **"Sausage":** Crumbles or links are lean and may need extra oil for pan-frying. **"Pepperoni":** Good in sandwiches and on pizzas. **"Chicken"** and **"steak" strips:** Good in stews and stir-fries. **"Meatballs":** Use on subs or pizzas, in stews and over spaghetti.

Thai chile [TI]—These small chiles, about 1 inch long and ¼ inch in diameter, have a fiery hot flavor. Thai chilies range in color from green to red when fully ripe and are popular in many Asian dishes. In its dried form, it is called the *bird chili*.

Tofu [TOH-foo]—Tofu, which also goes by the descriptive yet funny-sounding name *soybean curd*, has become a household word, though perhaps not a regularly eaten food in most homes. Maybe the wiggly, white rectangular blocks of tofu scare some people, but they needn't. Dozens of cookbooks have been devoted to tofu, attesting to this Asian food's respectability and versatility. It doesn't have much flavor on its own—just a very mild cheeselike taste—but we've known a number of people to eat it straight from the carton.

Tofu picks up the flavors of the foods and seasonings in which it's cooked. Tofu cooked in chili tastes like chili, and tofu cubes added to a stir-fry flavored by ginger, soy sauce and mirin have a zippy, salty and sweet taste. It can also be cubed and sautéed, then dipped into a variety of sauces. We could go on and on.

But most importantly, tofu is worth trying in a few different dishes. Though tofu is rich in protein, with about 10 grams in 4 ounces of the medium-firm variety, it's high in fat, too—about 50 percent of its total calories come from fat. But there's no need to remove it from your foods-to-eat list. Tofu now comes in fat-reduced versions. One brand boasts that a 3-ounce slice of its extra-firm "lite" tofu has only 1 gram of fat and 35 calories.

Another variation in tofu is firmness. You can buy it in three types: soft, firm and extra firm. In general, select soft tofu when making sauces, pie fillings, dips and puddings. Buy firm or extra-firm tofu for cubing, skewering or any preparation method in which you want the soyfood to hold its shape. Flavored tofu also is on the market. Try one when you're in the mood for a flavor change.

When you bring tofu home, handle it one of two ways. If it's water packed, store it in your refrigerator and change the water daily after opening the package. If it's vacuum (aseptically) packaged, you can store it in your pantry until you're ready to use it. Once opened, keep the package covered with water and refrigerated. In any case, buy tofu as far ahead of its expiration date as possible. If it becomes slimy, sour or otherwise unappetizing, throw it out.

Silken tofu comes in soft, regular and firm varieties and is named for its silky-smooth custardlike texture. Silken tofu results from coagulating the soymilk in the packaging and not removing any whey. Japanese-type silken tofu may be aseptically packaged, which allows it to be stored for up to nine months without refrigeration. Once opened, use it within five to seven days. Use the creamy soft tofu in blended desserts such as shakes and cream pies, or substitute puréed silken soft tofu for part of the mayonnaise, sour cream, cream cheese or ricotta cheese in a recipe. In Japan, silken tofu is enjoyed "as is," with a little soy sauce and chopped scallions as a topping.

Tofu-based desserts—If you've got a hankering for something cold and creamy, and do not want to eat dairy products, a tofu-based dessert may be the answer. But be advised that some tofu-based desserts are no more nutritious than many super-rich ice creams. Be sure to read the labels.

Tomatillo [tohm-ah-TEE-oh]—This firm fruit (also called *Mexican green tomato*) belongs to the same family as the tomato. It looks like a small tomato except that it is green and has a thin papery covering. While tomatillos turn yellow as they ripen, they are most often used while still green. Their flavor is more acidic than that of tomatoes and has hints of fruits and herbs. They are available sporadically in specialty produce markets and some supermarkets. Tomatillos are popular in Mexican and Southwest cooking and in guacamole. Try them raw in salads and salsas. Tomatillos are rich in vitamin A and contain a fair amount of vitamin C.

Triticale flour [triht-ih-KAY-lee]—This simple grain hybrid of rye and wheat is very nutritious and contains more protein and less gluten than wheat. It has a sweet yet hearty nut flavor. It can be found in several forms including whole, flakes and flour, and it can be purchased in natural food stores and some supermarkets. Replace half of the whole wheat flour in your bread recipe with triticale flour for a protein boost.

Turbinado sugar [tur-bih-NAH-doh]—This is sugar that has been steam cleaned, but not bleached. Its coarse crystals are tan in color and have a light molasses flavor. It has no more nutrients than table sugar. It can be used as a sweetener for bananas and grapefruit, as well as a topping for cereals. Some prefer it to brown sugar in cobblers and crisps.

Turmeric, ground [TER-muh-rihk]—This bright yellow-orange spice has an intense bitter flavor. Turmeric is popular in Indian cuisine, especially in curry preparations, and is used to add both flavor and color to foods. It's also an important ingredient in mustard. Turmeric is available in most supermarkets.

Unbleached all-purpose white flour—Because some of the wheat bran is retained during milling and refining, unbleached flour is often thought to be more nutritious. It is also slightly heavier than bleached flour. But this flour loses the nutritional showdown against whole wheat flour, with about half the calcium and one-fourth the iron, phosphorus, potassium and B vitamins. For people accustomed to white bread, mixing together unbleached white flour and whole wheat flour while getting used to the stronger flavor of whole wheat is a gentle way to go. Use it for piecrusts, coffee cakes, muffins and cookies.

Vegetable shortening—Vegetable shortening is a solid fat made from vegetable oils that have been hydrogenated. This process creates trans fatty acids and transforms the mixture into a saturated fat, eliminating any benefits from polyunsaturated fats. Vegetable shortening is flavorless and used in place of other fats in cooking and baking. Store it at room temperature for up to a year.

Vinegars [VIHN-ih-gers]—A splash of vinegar can add that special something to a dish. But which one to choose? There's balsamic, the queen of vinegars; red wine vinegar; herbed vinegar; and run-of-the-mill white vinegar, among others. Here's a rundown:

> **Balsamic**—Sold in supermarkets, it has a mellow sweet-sour flavor. Integral to Italian cooking, it is aged for years in wooden barrels.

> **Rice**—Common in Chinese and Japanese cooking, rice vinegar is subtle, sweet and less acidic than other vinegars you might have on your shelf. Japanese rice vinegar

is pale to golden yellow and also comes seasoned with sugar.

Herb and **fruit**—Taste like their chosen flavorings, but with a kick. Use them in dishes in which you want extra flavor.

Umeboshi—Made from the pickled, slightly sour umeboshi plum. Look for it in well-stocked supermarkets or Asian markets.

Wine—Taste great on salads. Use white with light-colored foods, because red wine vinegar may turn them pinkish.

White, cider and **malt**—Pungent and make good choices for pickling.

Wakame [wah-KAH-meh]—This mild-flavored sea vegetable is green, making it seem very much like leafy land vegetables. It's used like a vegetable in soups as well as in salads. Brown varieties have a stronger flavor. Look for wakame both fresh and dried in Asian markets.

Wasabi [WAH-sah-bee]—Also called *Japanese horseradish*, wasabi has a potent, sinus-clearing punch and is used as a flavor accent. It is available dried or as a paste; look for wasabi at Asian markets and at well-stocked supermarkets in the ethnic foods section.

Whole wheat flour—This full-flavored flour contains the wheat germ, which means that it also has a higher fiber, nutritional and fat content than white flour. If you're baking bread, select "bread flour" made from hard red spring wheat (which makes the highest loaves) or red winter wheat. Bread flours are high in gluten, which helps make light, airy loaves. Choose stone-ground flour or very finely ground flour. The latter will be lighter, but you might prefer the more robust flavor of stone ground. Any type of wheat flour will suffice if it is not being used for baked goods, such as thickening a gravy.

Whole wheat pastry flour—Milled from lower-protein flour (and therefore not a good choice for bread baking), whole wheat pastry flour makes tender muffins, quick breads and pancakes. Other than protein content, this flour does not differ significantly from regular whole wheat flour.

Wild rice—Guess what? It isn't even rice. It's the seed of a tall, aquatic grass native to North America. Wild rice is known for its rich nutlike flavor and chewy texture. The price of it remains high, but consider cooking it with brown rice to make an elegant pilaf. Be sure to clean wild rice thoroughly before you cook it. Place the rice in a bowl and fill it with cold water. Stir it several times and let it sit for a few minutes. Any undesirable parts will float to the top, where they can be skimmed or poured off. Wild rice takes about 40 minutes to cook, but is available precooked for quicker preparation.

Winter squash—This type of squash has a thick skin and hard seeds. Its flesh is deep yellow to orange and is firmer and more flavorful than that of summer squash. Winter squash is best from early fall through the winter, with most varieties available year-round. Select squash that are heavy for their size, with deep-colored, blemish-free skins. Winter squash takes longer to cook than summer squash; remove the seeds and bake, steam or simmer it. They are a good source of iron, riboflavin and vitamins A and C.

Worcestershire sauce [WOOS-tuhr-shuhr; WOOS-tuhr-sheer]—A popular seasoning sauce, it commonly contains anchovies, but you can find vegetarian versions in most markets. With as much zippy flavor as the original, vegetarian Worcestershire sauce seasons soups and works as a table condiment.

Zahtar [ZAH-tahr]—This popular Middle Eastern spice mixture is a blend of toasted sesame seeds, dried marjoram, oregano, thyme and sumac. It can be combined with olive oil to make a pungent bread dip. Look for it at Middle Eastern groceries.

Zest—Zest is the scrapings from the outermost skin of citrus fruits. Use a citrus zester, paring knife or vegetable peeler. The fragrant oils in zest add a lot of flavor to foods. Choose organic fruits, which have not been treated with dyes and pesticides, if possible. Use zest to flavor almost any dish.

index